ORAN'S DICTIONARY OF THE LAW

3rd Edition

Daniel Oran, J.D.

Mark Tosti, J.D.
Contributing Author

WEST

TM

THOMSON LEARNING

Africa • Australia • Canada • Denmark • Japan • Mexico • New Zealand • Philippines
Puerto Rico • Singapore • Spain • United Kingdom • United States

NOTICE TO THE READER

Publisher does not warrant or guarantee any of the products described herein or perform any independent analysis in connection with any of the product information contained herein. Publisher does not assume, and expressly disclaims, any obligation to obtain and include information other than that provided to it by the manufacturer.

The reader is expressly warned to consider and adopt all safety precautions that might be indicated by the activities herein and to avoid all potential hazards. By following the instructions contained herein, the reader willingly assumes all risks in connection with such instructions.

The Publisher makes no representation or warranties of any kind, including but not limited to, the warranties of fitness for particular purpose or merchantability, nor are any such representations implied with respect to the material set forth herein, and the publisher takes no responsibility with respect to such material. The publisher shall not be liable for any special, consequential, or exemplary damages resulting, in whole or part, from the readers' use of, or reliance upon, this material.

West Legal Studies Staff:
Business Unit Director: Susan Simpfenderfer
Executive Acquisitions Editor: Marlene McHugh Pratt
Acquisitions Editor: Joan Gill
Editorial Assistant: Lisa Flatley
Executive Marketing Manager: Donna Lewis
Channel Manager: Nigar Hale
Executive Production Manager: Wendy Troeger
Production Editor: Betty L. Dickson
Cover Design: Lauri Baram

Printed in Canada
5 6 7 8 9 10 XXX 05 04 03 02

For more information, contact Delmar, 3 Columbia Circle, PO Box 15015, Albany, NY 12212-0515; or find us on the World Wide Web at http://www.westlegalstudies.com

Library of Congress Cataloging-in-Publication Data
Oran, Daniel.
    Oran's Dictionary of the Law / Daniel Oran.—3rd ed.
        p. cm.
    Rev. ed. of: Oran's dictionary of the Law. 2nd ed. ©1991.
    ISBN 0-7668-1742-3
        1. Law—United States—Dictionaries. I. Title
KF156.069 1999
349.73'03—dc21   99-047650

About the Authors

Daniel Oran is a graduate of Hamilton College and Yale Law School. He has practiced law in Connecticut and the District of Columbia. In addition, he has been Assistant Director of the National Paralegal Institute, Professor of Law at Antioch Law School, staff counsel to a member of Congress and the House Appropriations Committee, and president of Foresight, Incorporated. He has written an internationally reprinted novel and business text as well as professional and popular articles on paralegal education, psychiatry and law, poverty law, and individual rights.

Mark Tosti, contributing author, is a graduate of Princeton University, Columbia College, and the Washington College of Law of The American University. He practices general business, entertainment, and intellectual property law, and was Professorial Lecturer of Law at The American University. In addition, he has been the producer, director, and editor of several feature films.

Contents

Introduction

This is a guidebook to a foreign language. The language of Law uses mostly English words, but they rarely mean what they seem. Many look like everyday English, but have technical definitions totally different from their ordinary uses. Some mean several different things, depending on the area of law or business they come from. The language of Law also contains more "leftovers" than most languages. Hundreds of Latin, Old French, Old English, and obsolete words are still used in their original forms.

When I wrote my first law dictionary in 1975, I hoped that most of these old words would be long buried by the first decade of the twenty-first century, but like Chucky, Freddy, and assorted vampires and aliens, they just won't die. "Plain language" court rules and federal commissions can't kill them. Things are even worse now. A flood of new technologies has created many legal sub-specialties and . . . surprise . . . an explosion of confusing new legal words.

The dictionary has two main purposes. Like any specialized dictionary, it helps the reader to understand and use a technical vocabulary. It also tries to help the reader to recognize and discard the many vague words that sound precise and that lawyers often use as if they were precise.

The book was written with the needs of many different readers in mind: lawyers, law and pre-law students, paralegals, legal secretaries, consumers, businesspersons, and persons in law-related fields such as criminal justice, journalism, social work, and government. Because the dictionary covers so many different fields, I need suggestions for additional words and definitions. If you have any ideas for the next edition, please send them to the e-mail address listed at the end of the book.

I have tried to make this guidebook as complete, clear and easy to use as possible. Using it, you will be able to understand most contracts, court decisions, laws, and lawyers.

Acknowledgments

By this third edition, I've accumulated huge debts to people who were willing to invest their time correcting ignorance. Some, like Tom Emerson, taught me how to "think like a lawyer." Others, like Fred Rodell, taught me how to stop writing like one. Bill Statsky gave me several excellent ideas for the first edition and has contributed to each succeeding one. Sally Determan corrected large portions of the first edition and my wife, Elaine, read the whole thing without mentioning "divorce" out of context. Mark Tosti contributed hundreds of hours of hard work and intellectual rigor to the second edition.

An alphabetical listing of names cannot begin to thank all those who have helped me. I hope that everyone has been properly listed, but no one has been properly thanked: Silvia Arrom, Sandy Augliere, Edwin Barrett, Max Baucus, Henry Black, Tom Blackwell, David Boris, Elizabeth Boris, Jay Boris, Katrina Boris, Linda Boris, Maria Boris, Paul Boris, Stephanie Boris, Fred Brandow, Margery Braunstein, Jonah Brown, Beau Brown, Edgar Cahn, Jean Cahn, Karen Clark, Dean Determan, Charles Docter, Henry Docter, Marcie Docter, Ashley Doherty, Marcie Evans, Stanley Field, Joseph Fortenberry, Leslie Foster, Robert Foster, Robert Fracasso, William Fry, Royce Givens, Ronald Greene, Sunny Greene, Lonn Hoklin, Carolyn Hunter, Richard Jackson, Nick Kalis, Barbara Lampe, Martin Lampe, Liz Loeb, Sam Mansfield, Barbara Martin, Rick Martin, Edward Mattison, Steve Merlan, Rachel Mosher, Kirsten Mueller, Edward Oberhofer, Christina Oran, Daniel D. Oran, David Oran, Max Oran, Minerva Oran, Karen Pierce, Flavia Ploog, Victoria Powell, Connie Rappaport, Steve Rappaport, Bonnie Rathjen, Charles Reich, Karen Reivich, David Robinson, Ruth Robinson, Sandra Robinson, Susan Sands, Peter Schulman, Martin Selegman, Gary Selers, Jay Shafritz, Allan Smith, Carl Smith, Helene Smith, Joel Smith, Josh Smith, Rose Smith, John Stein, Doris Surick, Herman Surick, Stuart Surick, Stuart R. Surick, Charles Todd, Cindy M. Tosti, Marian Tosti, Thomas Weck, Dorothy Weitzman, and Thomas Willging.

Many thanks also go to the publishing team who produced this edition: Joan Gill, Betty Dickson, Lisa Flatley, Mary Jo Graham, Dana Wilson, Denise Sadler, and Lori Kueter.

Not on the list are the anonymous reviewers who told it straight and the many people who wrote to suggest additions and corrections to prior editions. This third edition would not have been the same without their help.

Reading the Definitions

Finding the Word

Skim the area near where the word should be. The word you want may be printed in the definition of a nearby word. Also, look up both halves of a compound word or two-word phrase. The word you want may be in either place.

Boldface

If a word in a definition is in **boldface,** it is defined in the dictionary. You can look it up if you need it. If you are also directed to "see that word," you must understand the boldface word in order to understand the definition.

Italics

Italics are used to emphasize a word or to illustrate its use.

Ordinary English

Everyday English definitions of legal words are omitted unless needed to avoid confusion.

Pronunciation

Most Words

Most words in this dictionary are easy to pronounce. No pronunciations are given for these words. The same is true for most Latin words, which may be pronounced almost any way they are read because they have at least three acceptable pronunciations: "classical," "church," and "English" Latin.

Accent Marks

Some words need accent marks for the strong syllable. This is done by underlining the emphasized part of the word. For example, "Testimony" means that the "Tes" syllable is spoken stronger than the rest of the word.

Problem Words

Legal words that are hard to pronounce have the pronunciations in square brackets after the definitions. For example, after the definition for "indictment," you will find "[pronounce: in-dite-ment]." This dictionary uses English sounds, not technical pronunciation marks.

The Basic 50

These fifty words are used frequently in definitions. They are among the most basic words in the law. If you are using this dictionary as a learning tool, rather than as an occasional reference, look up those words you do not know and those for which you know only an ordinary English meaning:

Action	Duty	Opinion
Agency	Estate	Party
Appeal	Evidence	Plaintiff
Bill	Executive	Pleading
Case	Federal	Property
Civil	Grounds	Regulate
Complaint	Judgment	Right
Constitutional	Judicial	Security
Contract	Jury	Sentence
Conviction	Law	Statute
Corporation	Legislate	Testimony
Court	Liability	Title
Creditor	Mortgage	Tort
Criminal	Motion	Trust
Debtor	Negligence	Verdict
Deed	Negotiable	Will
Defendant	instrument	Witness

A *1.* (Latin) From, for, with (and when translated into smooth English can also mean: because, by, in, of, on, and other related words). *2.* Atlantic Reporter (see **National Reporter System**).

A.A.A. *1.* Agriculture Adjustment Act (7 U.S.C. 601). *2.* American Academy of **Actuaries**. *3.* American **Accounting** Association. *4.* **American Arbitration Association.**

A.A.f.P.E. **American Association for Paralegal Education.**

A.A.L.S. Association of American Law Schools.

A.A.P. **Affirmative action** plan (or program).

A.B.A. **American Bar Association.**

A.B.A.J. American Bar Association Journal.

A.B.C. **test** The rule that an employee need not be covered by unemployment insurance if the employee is an independent worker who performs jobs free of the employer's control and away from the employer's place of business.

A.C.L.U. American Civil Liberties Union. A group that supports basic **constitutional** freedoms by going to court, by supporting and fighting **legislation,** and by public education.

A.D.A. **Americans with Disabilities Act.**

A.D.E.A. Age Discrimination in Employment Act (29 U.S.C. 621). A federal law that prohibits age-based **discrimination** against persons over forty years old.

A.D.R. *1.* **Alternative dispute resolution.** *2.* **American Depository Receipt.** *3.* **Asset Depreciation Range.** *4.* Automatic **dividend** reinvestment. *5.* Administrative dispute resolution.

A.F.I.S. Automated fingerprint identification system.

A.F.L.-C.I.O. American Federation of Labor–Congress of Industrial Organizations. The largest organization of **labor unions** in the United States.

A.G. **Attorney general.**

A.G.I. **Adjusted gross income.**

A.I.C.P.A. American Institute of Certified Public Accountants.

A.J. *1.* Associate Judge (or Justice). All judges but the Chief Judge (or Justice). *2.* Administrative Judge. See **administrative law judge.**

A.k.a. Also known as.

A.L.A. Association of Legal Administrators (people who manage law offices).

A.L.I. **American Law Institute.**

A.L.I. test See *Model Penal Code* under **insanity.**

A.L.J. **Administrative law judge.**

A.L.R. **American Law Reports.**

A.L.S. **Automated litigation support.**

A.L.T.A. American Land Title Association.

A.M.T. **Alternative minimum tax.**

A.P.A. **Administrative Procedure Act.**

A.P.R. **Annual percentage rate.**

A.R. (Latin) Anno Regni. "In the year of the reign of." An abbreviation used to date famous cases and laws by year within the rule of a particular English king or queen.

A.R.M. Adjustable rate **mortgage.** A mortgage with interest rates that change during the course of the mortgage.

A.T.F. Bureau of Alcohol, Tobacco, and Firearms of the U.S. **Treasury** Department.

A.T.L.A. American Trial Lawyers Association.

A.W.O.L. Absent without leave; a military offense similar to but less serious than **desertion.**

A coelo usque ad centrum (Latin) From the heavens to the center of the earth. The theoretical limit of a landowner's property rights. These rights may be limited by other conflicting rights, such as the right of planes to pass (**air rights**) or the right of others to drill for oil (**mineral rights**).

A contrario sensu (Latin) On the other hand; in a contrary sense.

A force (Latin) Of necessity.

A fortiori (Latin) With stronger reason; by force of logic. For example, if it is true that a twenty-one-year-old person is an adult, then, *a fortiori,* a twenty-five-year-old person is an adult. [pronounce: ah for-she-o-ri]

A gratia (Latin) By **grace** (see that word).

A large (Latin) Free or **at large.**

A latere (Latin) **Collateral;** from the side.

A mensa et thoro (Latin) "From bed and board" (literally, "from bed and table"). A phrase that describes a type of legal **separation** or limited **divorce** (see that word).

A posteriori (Latin) From the effect to the cause. A method of reasoning that starts with experiments or observations and attempts to discover general principles from them.

A prendre See **profits a prendre.**

A priori From the cause to the effect. A method of reasoning that starts with general principles and attempts to discover what specific facts or real-life observations will follow from them. [pronounce: ah pri-o-ri]

A quo (Latin) From which. For example, a *court a quo* is a court from which a case has been removed, and a *court ad quem* is the court to which it is transferred.

A rendre See **profits a rendre.**

A rubro ad nigrum (Latin) "From red to black." Describes the interpretation of a **statute** by its title.

A vinculo matrimonii (Latin) "From the marriage bonds." *1.* A complete **divorce.** *2.* An **annulment.**

Ab (Latin) *1.* Same as **A** (see that word) but used before a vowel. *2.* Abridgment.

Ab actis (Latin) A court **clerk** or a **registrar.**

Ab ante (Latin) In advance; before.

Ab antiquo (Latin) Since ancient times.

Ab inconvenienti (Latin) "From inconvenience." A weak argument, offered only because you are forced to put up some sort of argument.

Ab initio (Latin) From the very beginning; entirely and completely since the start. [pronounce: ab in-ish-ee-o]

Abaction Forcibly carrying something away.

Abandon Give up something completely and finally (see **abandonment**).

Abandonee A person to whom a property right is relinquished or abandoned.

Abandonment *1.* Complete and final giving up of property or rights with no intention of reclaiming them and to no particular person. For example, throwing away a book is *abandonment,* but selling or giving it away is not. *2.* A lawsuit may be thrown out of court if it is *abandoned* by failure to take any action on it for too long a time. *3.* Children are *abandoned* if they are either deserted or no longer cared for or looked after. *4.* A husband or wife is *abandoned* if the other leaves without consent, without just cause, and with the intent to stay away permanently. In some states, failure to perform an important duty of the marriage is also *abandonment*. *5. Abandonment of service* occurs if a public utility permanently cuts off a customer.

Abatable nuisance   A **nuisance** (see that word) that is easily stopped or made harmless.

Abate   *1.* Destroy or completely end. *2.* Greatly lessen or reduce.

Abatement   *1.* Reduction or decrease. *2.* Proportional reduction. For example, if a pot of money does not have enough to pay everyone it owes, each person may have to be satisfied with an *abatement* of his or her share. *3.* Complete elimination. For example, see **abatable nuisance.** *4.* An ending or delaying of a lawsuit for technical reasons such as failure to include all necessary persons. This ending is now usually called a **dismissal** (see that word). *5.* The order of reduction or elimination. For example, if a person leaves "five hundred dollars to John and five hundred dollars to my heirs," John gets five hundred dollars and the heirs' share may *abate* to zero if there is only five hundred dollars.

Abator   *1.* A person who takes possession of land illegally when the owner dies. *2.* A person who stops a **nuisance.**

Abbroachment (or abbrochment)   Buying up goods at wholesale to control the supply and then resell at much higher resale prices.

Abdication   *1.* The act of giving up the throne (by a king or other monarch). *2.* Giving up a public office by ceasing to perform its functions rather than by formally resigning.

Abduction   *1.* The criminal offense or **tort** of taking away a person who is in the care of another. *2.* **Kidnapping.** *3.* Tricking or persuading a wife or husband to leave the other.

Abet   Encourage, request, order, or help another person to commit a crime.

Abettor   A person who **abets** (see that word) a crime.

Abeyance   *1.* In suspension, waiting, or held off for a while. *2.* Waiting for, or being without, an owner.

Abide   *1.* Accept the consequences (usually of a court's **judgment**). *2.* Be satisfied with. *3.* Wait for. *4.* Obey; for example, most persons *abide* by the law. *5.* An *abiding conviction* is a juror's belief in a defendant's guilt **beyond a reasonable doubt.**

Ability to pay   A measure that juries are rarely permitted to use in deciding how much money a **defendant** must pay a **plaintiff** (one exception is some types of **punitive damage** awards). An **arbitrator,**

however, may consider *ability to pay* in deciding a wage or benefit increase dispute between an employer and a union.

Abjudication   A judge's decision that takes something away from a person. (*Not* **adjudication.**)

Abjuration   Taking an oath to give up property, rights, or personal convictions and opinions. For example, when you become a citizen of the U.S. as an immigrant, you *abjure* (promise to give up) allegiance to all foreign governments.

Abnegation   Denial or renunciation.

Abnormally dangerous activity   **Ultrahazardous activity.**

Abode   Home or dwelling place.

Abolish   Completely do away with. Often refers to eliminating something previously thought to be permanent.

Aboriginal   Referring to ancient inhabitants. In the U.S., **Native American.**

Abortion   The destruction of a fetus in the womb.

About   Near in time, distance, quantity, or quality; approximately. *About* is an imprecise word, but not so imprecise as to legally undo a deal based on a phrase like "about a million widgets" or "about May first."

Above   *1.* Higher. Usually refers to a higher or **appellate** court. *2.* Before. *Above cited* or *above mentioned* may mean "appears earlier on this page," "earlier in this chapter," "earlier in this book," etc.

Abr.   Abridgment.

Abridge   *1.* Shorten. An *abridgment* of a book is a condensation of its ideas into a shorter work. *2.* Infringe upon. To *abridge* a right is to make the right less useful or complete.

Abrogation   The destruction, repealing, or **annulling** of a former law.

Abscond   Hide or sneak away to avoid arrest, a lawsuit, or creditors.

Absentee landlord   A **landlord** who does not live on the premises, especially one who cannot be contacted easily by the tenants.

Absentee voting   Voting by mail or other means if the voter has an approved reason to miss going to the polls on election day.

Absolute   Complete, final, and without restrictions. For example, an *absolute* **deed** is a transfer of land without a **mortgage** or other **lien;** *absolute* law is natural, as opposed to human-made; *absolute* **liability** is responsibility for harm to another whether or not you are at fault; and *absolute* **privilege** is freedom from all claims of **defamation.**

Absolute nuisance   A **nuisance** (see that word) that is not caused by **negligent** conduct.

Absolution   Freedom or release from an obligation or a debt.

Absolutism   Government power unchecked by legal restraints or safeguards. Control by a king, dictator, or ruling group with nearly complete power over the people.

Absorption   The process by which a thing (a right, a company, etc.) continues its life by becoming a part of another thing. For example, when one business **merges** with another, the continued right of seniority for employees is called *absorption*.

Absque   (Latin) Without; but for. For example, *absque hoc,* "but for this," was a technical phrase used by a **defendant** to introduce new facts that hurt the **plaintiff's** case even if the plaintiff's facts were correct. [pronounce: ab-skway]

Abstain   Refrain, hold off, keep hands off.

Abstention doctrine   The principle that a court should refrain from using its **jurisdiction** to take a case when there is a good reason to have the matter handled by a state court (or an agency) that also has jurisdiction. The doctrine is usually applied by a federal court to allow a state court to rule on a matter of state law or because a related matter is already being handled by a state court. See **Burford, Pullman,** and **Younger doctrines** for *types* of abstentions.

Abstract   *1.* A summary. For example, an *abstract* of **title** is a condensed history of the ownership of a piece of land that includes information on transfers of ownership and on anyone who has (or might have had) rights (such as **liens**) in the land; an *abstract of record* is a summary of a **trial** record for an **appeals** court; and an *abstract of judgment* is a summary (or copy) of a court decision that, when filed with the proper records office, creates a *judgment* **lien** against property of the person who lost the case. *2.* See **abstraction.**

Abstraction   Taking something (usually money) with the intent to commit **fraud.**

Abuse   *1.* Misuse. *2.* Insult forcefully. *3.* Inflict regular, serious, physical or psychological harm such as child abuse. *4. Abuse of discretion* is the failure to use sound, reasonable judgment when a person (such as a judge) is under a legal duty to do so. *5. Abuse of process* is using the legal system unfairly; for example, prosecuting a person for writing a "bad check" simply to put on pressure to pay.

Abut   *1.* Border on (or physically touch with nothing in between). Compare **adjacent.** *2.* For *"abutter's right,"* see **ancient lights.**

Academic freedom   The right of teachers and students to teach and learn without being harassed for their political, religious, or other beliefs. This is _not_ a **constitutional** right, like many other freedoms, but it is protected primarily by those freedoms (such as freedom of speech) plus long-standing traditions and institutions such as **tenure.**

Accede _1._ Come into a job or public office. _2._ Agree, consent, or give in.

Accelerated depreciation See **depreciation.**

Acceleration _1._ Shortening of the time before a future event will happen. _2._ An _acceleration clause_ is a section of a **note** or contract that makes an entire debt come due immediately because of a failure to pay on time or because of some other failure.

Accept Receive with approval, satisfaction, or the intention to keep (see **acceptance**).

Acceptance _1._ Agreeing to an **offer** and thus forming a **contract.** _2._ Taking something offered by another person with the intention of keeping it. For example, the **Uniform Commercial Code** explains several ways a buyer can _accept_ goods from a seller: by telling the seller that the goods received are right; by saying that the goods will be taken despite problems; by failing to reject the goods in reasonable time; or by doing something that makes it seem like the buyer now owns the goods. _3._ In **negotiable instruments** law, a person's _acceptance_ of a check may be by signing and depositing it, and a bank can _accept_ the check by cashing it. There are technical rules of acceptance for more complicated negotiable instruments. _4._ A _banker's acceptance_ is a trade device in which a bank promises to pay a certain amount at a future date (a negotiable time **draft** or a guaranteed **bill of exchange**). A _trade acceptance_ is the same thing promised by a company instead of a bank. These are both called _"acceptance credit,"_ are often used to finance international trade, and are bought and sold as investments.

Access _1._ Opportunity to approach. For example, most city lots have _access_ to the street. _2._ Right to approach. For example, _access_ to public records includes both their practical availability and the right to see them. _3._ In **paternity suits,** claiming that the mother had several lovers is called the **defense** of _multiple access._

Accession _1._ The right to own things that become a part of something already owned. For example, if land builds up on a riverbank by **accretion,** the bank's owner will also own the new land by _accession._ _2._ The right to things, such as crops, produced on owned property. _3._ See **accede.**

Accessory _1._ A person who helps commit a crime without being present. An _accessory before the fact_ is a person who, without being present, encourages, orders, or helps another to commit a crime. An *accessory after the fact* is a person who finds out that a crime has been committed and helps to conceal the crime or the criminal. *2.* Something connected to something more important.

Accident   An unexpected event, especially one with harmful effects. The word has no precise legal meaning. It can include events that are predictable or unpredictable, somebody's fault or nobody's fault.

Accommodation   A favor done for another person, usually involving a **cosigner** who helps another person get a loan or credit.

Accommodation line   Business that is accepted not on its own merits but to get other business or as part of a "package."

Accommodation paper   A **bill** or **note** that is signed by one person as a favor to help another person get a loan. The person signing promises to pay if the person getting the loan fails to pay.

Accommodation party   A person who signs an **accommodation paper** (see that word) as a favor to another person.

Accommodation personnel   **Dummy** (see that word) incorporators.

Accomplice   A person who knowingly and voluntarily helps another person commit or conceal a crime. This includes persons who **aid, abet,** or act as **accessory.** The *accomplice rule* is the principle that a criminal defendant is entitled to have the jury told that a prosecution witness is also facing criminal charges, since a witness who faces such charges might testify falsely in hopes of leniency.

Accord   *1.* Any agreement, treaty, or contract. *2.* An agreement to pay (on one side) and to accept (on the other side) late payment or less than all a debt or obligation is worth as full payment for that obligation. For example, there is an *accord* if a person agrees to take one hundred dollars as payment in full for one hundred and fifty dollars worth of damage to an auto, and the person who did the damage agrees to pay the one hundred dollars. *3.* An *accord and satisfaction* is an *accord* that has been completed by payment and a full **release.**

Account   *1.* A list of money paid and owed by one person or business to another. *2.* An *account payable* is a debt not yet paid. *3.* An *account receivable* is a debt not yet collected. *4.* An *account rendered* is an *account receivable* that has been presented to the debtor for examination and payment.

Account stated   An exact figure for money owed, calculated by the person to whom the money is owed, and accepted as accurate by the person who owes the money.

Accountable   Responsible or **liable.**

Accountant A person who specializes in preparing and analyzing financial records. Accountants set up financial record keeping systems, fill them in, and check up on them. Accountants' duties include **auditing**, **bookkeeping**, and preparing financial **statements**. Normally, persons who do just bookkeeping do not have accounting skills. Some accountants become _certified public accountants_ by satisfying state professional requirements. The _accountant-client privilege_ is the requirement in some states that accountants keep most client communications confidential. See also **kovel accountant**.

Accounting _1._ A system of setting up financial record books, especially for tax purposes. Two of the most common methods for recording money in and out are the _accrual method_ (recording debts owed to and by a company when the debt becomes a legal obligation, which may be before the money is actually paid) and the _cash method_ (recording debts when paid). _2._ Giving a full financial explanation of a transaction or of an entire business. _3._ Making good on money owed. For example, a court may order one partner to pay another. This is called an _accounting for profits._

Accounting changes See **statement**.

Accounting identity A statement that two numerical things are equal by accepted definition; for example, "**assets** equal **liabilities** plus stockholder's **equity**."

Accounting period See **fiscal**.

Accounts payable Money owed to suppliers.

Accounts receivable Money owed by customers.

Accredit Give official status or recognition. For example, an _accredited_ law school has been approved by a state, by the Association of American Law Schools (see **A.A.L.S.**), or by the **American Bar Association**.

Accredited investor **Sophisticated investor**.

Accretion _1._ The gradual adding on of land by natural causes such as the deposit of dirt by a river on its bank. Compare with **avulsion**. _2._ Any gradual accumulation.

Accroachment Taking over or exercising power with no authority to do so.

Accrual basis A method of **accounting** that shows expenses **incurred** and income earned in a given time period, whether or not cash payments have actually changed hands during that period.

Accruals Regular, short-term business obligations, such as employees' wages.

Accrue *1.* Become due and payable. For example, in tax law, income *accrues* to a taxpayer when the taxpayer has an unconditional right to it and a likelihood of being able to receive it. *2.* An accrued **dividend** is a share of a company's earnings that has been formally declared as payable to the stockholders, but not yet paid. *3.* Become **vested,** reach **maturity,** or become legally complete. *4.* For *accrual bond,* see **Z bond.**

Accumulated earnings tax A federal tax on certain unused income of a corporation that piles up profits without either distributing them to stockholders in the form of **dividends** or plowing the money back into the business.

Accumulated retained earnings See **retained earnings.**

Accumulation trust A **trust** that keeps its income during the trust period rather than paying it out regularly to a **beneficiary.**

Accumulative sentence (or judgment) A **cumulative sentence.**

Accusation A formal charge, made to a court, that a person is guilty of a crime.

Accusatory body A group such as a **grand jury** that decides whether enough evidence exists to formally accuse someone of a crime.

Accusatory instrument A document that charges a person with a crime; for example, an **indictment,** an **information,** a **presentment,** or a criminal **complaint** (see those words).

Accusatory stage The time when a criminal suspect has a right to counsel because the investigation has started to focus on the suspect, the suspect is in custody, and questioning has started.

Accused The person against whom an **accusation** is made; the criminal **defendant.**

Acid test See *quick ratio* under **quick assets.**

Acknowledgment *1.* An admission or declaration that something is genuine or has happened. For example, a father's statements that a child is his is an *acknowledgment* of paternity. *2.* Signing a formal paper and swearing to it as your act before an official such as a **notary public;** also, the notary public's formal statement (often a *certificate of acknowledgment*) that the signer is who the signer claims to be and did in fact sign. [pronounce: ak-<u>nol</u>-ledg-ment]

Acquest (or acquet or acquets) Something bought or received as a gift, rather than received by inheritance.

Acquiescence Silent agreement; knowing about an action or occurrence and remaining quietly satisfied about it or, by silence, appearing to be satisfied.

Acquisition charge　A charge for paying off a loan before it comes due. Also called a *"prepayment penalty."*

Acquit　Set free from an obligation; formally clear of an accusation. See **acquittal.**

Acquittal　*1.* A formal legal determination that a person who has been charged with a crime is innocent. *2.* A **release** from an obligation.

Acquittance　A written **discharge** of an obligation. A **receipt** can be an *acquittance* of an obligation to pay money owed.

Act　*1.* A law passed by one or both **houses** of a **legislature.** *2.* Something done voluntarily that triggers legal consequences.

Act in pais　Something done out of court and without being a part of the court's official proceedings. [pronounce: act in pay]

Act of bankruptcy　Any one of several actions (such as hiding property from creditors) that used to make a person **liable** to be proceeded against as a **bankrupt** by **creditors. Bankruptcy** law now provides for this sort of *involuntary bankruptcy* only when a person cannot pay debts as they come due.

Act of God　An event caused entirely by nature alone, especially a cataclysmic event. Also called **force majeure.** In contract law, however, *force majeure* is often defined as an unavoidable natural *or man-made* event.

Act of State doctrine　The rule, principle, or convention that a court should not question the legality of acts in a foreign country by that country's government.

Acting　Holding a temporary rank or position. Filling in for someone else.

Actio　(Latin) *1.* A **right** and also the legal proceedings taken to enforce the right; an "**action**" or lawsuit; for example, in Roman law, an "*actio damni injuria*" was a lawsuit for **damages.** *2.* Action, doing something; for example, *actio non* means "someone did not do something." It may refer to **nonfeasance,** non-**performance,** etc.

Action　*1.* A civil lawsuit or criminal prosecution. Actions are categorized in many ways. See, for example, **civil action** and **common law action.** *2.* An act or related series of acts; conduct or behavior. See **actus.**

Action on the case　See **trespass** *(on the case)* or see **case.**

Actionable　An act or occurrence is actionable if it provides legal reasons for a lawsuit. For example, "*actionable words*" are statements by one person that are serious enough to support a lawsuit (or "*action*") for **libel** or **slander** by another person.

Active trust　A **trust** for which the **trustee** has a duty to act with prudence. Compare with **passive trust.**

Acts and Resolves   See **statutes at large.**

Actual   Real, substantial, and presently existing as opposed to possible or theoretical.

Actual authority   In the law of **agency** (see that word), the right and power to act that a **principal** (often an employer) intentionally gives to an **agent** (often an employee) or at least allows the agent to believe has been given. This includes both **express** and **implied** *authority* (see those words).

Actual cash value   The fair, usual, or reasonable cash price that something will bring on the open market; the same as **market value.**

Actuarial method   A system of accounting for finances in a record book. For example, the *actuarial method* mentioned in the Uniform Consumer Credit Code is a company's method of applying payments made by a consumer first to **interest** and finance charges, then to paying off **principal** (the basic debt).

Actuary   A person who specializes in the mathematics of **insurance;** for example, the possibility of a person dying by a certain age, the money that should be paid for a certain type of insurance, etc.

Actus   (Latin) An **act.** For example, an *"actus reus"* is a "wrongful deed" (such as killing a person) which, if done with **mens rea,** a "guilty mind" (such as *"malice aforethought"*), is a crime (such as *first degree* **murder**).

Ad   (Latin) To, for (and when translated into smooth English can also mean: about, by, because, until, near, and other related words).

Ad damnum   (Latin) "To the **damages.**" An ad damnum clause is that part of a **plaintiff's** original court papers that sets out the amount of money the plaintiff is seeking.

Ad hoc   (Latin) "For this"; for this special purpose; for this one time; for example, an *ad hoc committee* is a temporary one set up to do a specific job.

Ad hominem   (Latin) "To the person." Arguments or statements made against an opponent personally, rather than against the opponent's argument or position.

Ad idem   (Latin) To the same point; proving the same thing; in agreement.

Ad infinitum   (Latin) Forever; limitless.

Ad interim   (Latin) Meanwhile; for now; in the meantime.

Ad litem   (Latin) "For the suit"; for the purposes of this lawsuit. For example, a *guardian ad litem* is a person who is appointed to represent a child (or other person lacking legal **capacity**) in a lawsuit.

Ad quem   (Latin) To which (see **a quo** for an example of its use).

Ad sectam   (Latin) At the suit of. "Ad sectam Jones" means that Jones is the **plaintiff.**

Ad valorem   (Latin) According to value. For example, an _ad valorem tax_ is a tax on the value of an item, rather than a fixed tax on the type of item. An ad valorem tax might tax a ten-dollar hat fifty cents and a twenty-dollar hat one dollar, while a specific hat tax might tax all hats seventy-five cents regardless of price or value.

Ad vitam   (Latin) For life.

Adaptation right   The right to produce a **derivative work** (see that word).

Addict   A person who regularly uses something (especially a drug) to the extent that he or she no longer has control over the use.

Addition to tax   A tax penalty, such as for late payment.

Additur   _1._ The power of a trial court to increase the amount of money awarded by a **jury** to a **plaintiff.** _2._ The power of an **appeals** court to deny a new trial to the **plaintiff** if the **defendant** agrees to pay the plaintiff a certain amount of extra money. _3._ Compare with **remittitur.**

Add-on   More goods bought before old goods are paid for; often, the contract for the original goods is rewritten to include the new things. An _add-on clause_ is a provision in an **installment** _contract_ that combines payment obligations for previously bought and newly bought things so that nothing is owned "free and clear" until everything has been paid for.

Adduce   Present or bring forward **evidence** in a **trial.**

Adeem   "Take away" (see **ademption**).

Ademption   _1._ Disposing of something left in a **will** before death, with the effect that the person it was left to does not get it. _2._ The gift, before death, of something left in a will to a person who was left it. For example, Ed leaves a chair to Joan in his will, but gives her the chair before he dies. _3._ Compare with **advancement.**

Adequate   A general word for "enough." It has no precise legal meaning.

Adhesion   "Stick to." For example, a "_contract of adhesion_" is one in which all the bargaining power (and the contract terms) favor one side. This often occurs when buyers have no choice among sellers of a particular item, and when the seller uses a pre-printed form contract to unfair advantage.

Adjacent   Near or close by. Perhaps touching, but not necessarily so.

Adjective law   Procedural law. Compare with **substantive law.**

Adjoining owners   Persons whose land touches a particular piece of land and who may have special rights against it under local **zoning** laws and under general laws of property.

Adjourn   Postpone or suspend business (see **adjournment**). [pronounce: a-jurn]

Adjournment   Putting off business or a session to another time or place. The decision of a court, legislature, or other meeting to stop meeting either temporarily or permanently. See also **recess.**

Adjudge   Old word for performing a judge's duties (pass **judgment,** make a decision, etc.).

Adjudicate   To judge (see **adjudication**).

Adjudicated form   A **form** may be called "*adjudicated*" if a court has called it legally binding or has interpreted it in a way that makes it useful for later users.

Adjudication   The formal giving, pronouncing, or recording of a **judgment** (see that word) for one side or the other in a lawsuit.

Adjudicative facts   Facts about the persons who have a dispute before an **administrative agency.** These are the "who, what, where, when, and how" facts that are similar to the facts that would go to a jury in a court trial. They are different from **legislative facts** (see that word).

Adjunction   Strong, permanent attachment; for example, a patch sewn onto a coat.

Adjuration   Swearing to something under **oath.**

Adjust   Settle or arrange; bring persons to agreement, especially as to amount of money owed. The process is called "*adjustment.*"

Adjusted basis   The "cost" of property for tax purposes, reduced by the total **depreciation** (see that word) deductions taken on the property and increased by the cost of **capital** improvements made to the property. Improvements are different from **repairs.** See **basis.**

Adjusted gross estate   A dead person's **estate** minus deductions for the cost of handling the estate, funeral expenses, debts, etc.

Adjusted gross income   A technical federal income tax word that means, in general, a person's or family's **income** minus certain investment and business deductions, some employee moving and travel expenses, alimony paid, and other specified subtractions.

Adjuster   A person who either determines or settles the amount of a claim or debt. For example, an *insurance adjuster* acts for an insurance company to determine and settle claims.

Adjustment board   An agency that hears **appeals** from **zoning** decisions.

Adjustment securities   Stocks, etc., that are issued during a **corporate reorganization.** The "adjustments" are usually changes that make the new stock worth less than the stock it replaced.

Admeasure   Divide and give out by shares.

Administer   *1.* Manage; take charge of business. *2.* Settle and distribute the **estate** (property, money, etc.) of a dead person. *3.* Give; for example, *administer* an **oath.**

Administration   *1.* Managing or running a business, organization, or part of a government. *2.* Supervision of the estate of a dead person. This usually includes collecting the property, paying debts and taxes, and giving out what remains to the **heirs.** *3.* The persons currently running the **executive** branch of the government.

Administrative agency   A sub-branch of the government set up to carry out the laws. For example, the police department is a local *administrative agency* and the **I.R.S.** is a national one.

Administrative board   A broad term that sometimes means **administrative agency** (see that word) and sometimes means a courtlike body set up by an agency to hold **hearings.**

Administrative Conference of the U.S.   A federal organization set up to improve the legal procedures by which federal **agencies** operate.

Administrative discretion   A public official's right to perform acts and duties that are not precisely "covered" by a law or rules and that require the use of professional judgment and common sense within the bounds set by the law.

Administrative law   *1.* Laws about the duties and proper running of an **administrative agency** (see that word) that are imposed on agencies by **legislatures** and courts. *2.* **Rules** and **regulations** written by administrative agencies.

Administrative law judge   An official who conducts **hearings** for an **administrative agency.** Also called "*hearing officer*" or "*examiner.*"

Administrative Procedure Act (5 U.S.C. 500)   A law that describes how U.S. agencies must do business (hearings, procedures, etc.) and how disputes go from these federal agencies into court. Some states also have administrative procedure acts.

Administrative remedy   A means of enforcing a right by going to an **administrative agency** (see that word) either for help or for a decision. Persons are often required to "exhaust administrative remedies," which means to fully submit their problems to the proper agency for decision before taking them to court.

Administrative search (or inspection) See **search.**

Administrator A person appointed by the court to supervise the **estate** (property) of a dead person. If the supervising person is named in the dead person's **will,** the proper name is **executor.** For administrators **cum testamento annexo** *(CTA)* and **de bonis non** *(DBN),* see those words.

Admiralty *1.* A court that handles most maritime (seagoing) matters, such as collisions between ships and shipping claims. This is usually a federal **district court.** *2.* Maritime law.

Admissible Proper to be used in reaching a decision; describes **evidence** that should be "let in" or introduced in court, or evidence that the **jury** may use.

Admission *1.* An *"admission"* is a voluntary statement that a fact or a state of events is true (see **admissions**). *2. "Admission to the bar"* is the formal procedure in which a lawyer is permitted to practice law. *3. "Admission to bail"* is the court's decision to allow a person accused of a crime to be released if bail money is put up. *4. "Admission of evidence"* is a decision by a judge to allow evidence to be used by the jury (or, if no jury, by the judge).

Admissions Confessions, concessions, or voluntary acknowledgments. Statements made by a **party** to a lawsuit (or the party's representative) that a fact exists which helps the other side or that a point the other side is making is correct. For *admissions of party opponent,* see **party admission.**

Admit See **admission.**

Admonition *1.* Oral advice by a judge to a jury. *2.* A reprimand given by a judge to a lawyer. *3.* A reprimand given by a judge in place of a jail **sentence** or other serious punishment.

Admonitory tort An *intentional* **tort** (see that word) of the type for which punishing the wrongdoer is more important than compensating the person hurt.

Adopt *1.* Accept, choose, or take as your own property, acts, or ideas. *2.* Pass a law and put it into effect. *3.* Formally accept a child of another as your own, with all of the rights and duties there would have been if it had been your own. (In some states, it is possible to adopt an adult in order to make that person your **heir.**)

Adopt by reference See **incorporate by reference.**

Adoption The formal, voluntary process by which an adult is legally declared the parent of a child not the adult's own.

Adoptive admission Approval of another's statements by approval, by silence, by actions, or by failure to deny them.

Ads. Short for **ad sectam.**

Adult A person over the legal age a state has set for full rights and responsibilities to begin.

Adult offender An **adult** who commits a crime, a juvenile who commits a crime and is tried as if an adult, or a juvenile who commits a crime and is tried after becoming an adult.

Adulteration Mixing inferior, cheaper, or harmful things in with better ones (to increase volume, lower costs, etc.).

Adultery Voluntary intercourse between a married person and a person who is not the husband or wife. *Adultery* may be defined more narrowly by state laws.

Advance *1.* Pay money before it is due; loan money; supply something before it is paid for. *2.* An increase in price. *3.* A *motion to advance* is a request for an immediate trial.

Advance directive A document such as a **durable power of attorney, healthcare proxy,** or **living will** that specifies your healthcare decisions and who will make decisions for you if you cannot make your own. *Advance directives* often specify a **DNR** (do not resuscitate) order.

Advance sheets "Hot off the press" unbound copies of case **decisions** that will later be printed with other cases in bound form.

Advancement Money or property given by a parent to a child (or to another **heir**) that the parent intends to be deducted from the child's eventual share in the parent's **estate** when the parent dies. Compare with **ademption.**

Adventure *1.* A risky commercial venture; any commercial venture. *2.* A shipment of goods by sea; any shipment of goods.

Adversarial memorandum See **external memorandum.**

Adversary proceeding *1.* A **hearing** (see that word) with both sides represented. *2.* A special **bankruptcy** lawsuit, with special rules, brought by the debtor or **trustee,** often to recover money or property held by a creditor.

Adversary system The system of law in the U.S. The judge acts as the decision maker between opposite sides (between two individuals, between the state and an individual, etc.) rather than acting as the person who also makes the state's case or independently seeks out **evidence.** This latter method is called the "**inquisitorial system.**"

Adverse Opposed; having opposing interests; against. For example, "*adverse actions*" by employers towards employees include firing, demoting, etc., and an "*adverse land use*" is a use, such as a factory in a neighborhood of single-family homes, that harms the local properties.

Adverse inference (or interest) rule *1.* An **administrative agency's** inference that, when relevant information is withheld from the agency with no good excuse, the information is **adverse** to the person or organization keeping it back. *2.* If a judge thinks a **party** has failed to produce a **witness** who should be produced, the judge may tell the jury to assume that the witness's **testimony** would have been unfavorable to that party.

Adverse interest Having opposing needs and desires from those of a person with whom you are associated.

Adverse party A **party** (see that word) on the other side of a lawsuit. From the perspective of an appeals court, a party who, when a case is **appealed,** might be hurt by a successful appeal. **Notice** of the appeal must be given to all *adverse parties* even if they were originally on the side that is now appealing.

Adverse possession A method of gaining legal **title** to land by openly and conspicuously occupying the land continuously for a number of years (as set by state law) while claiming ownership of the land.

Advice *1.* View or opinion. *2.* The **counsel** given to clients by their lawyers. Doing something *"on advice of counsel"* is a **defense** to certain lawsuits and criminal charges if the person told the truth to the lawyer and acted in **good faith** on the lawyer's good faith advice. *3.* This is *not* "*advise*" (give advice).

Advice and consent The **constitutional** right of the U.S. **Senate** to advise the president on **treaties** and major presidential appointments and to give its consent to these actions (by a two-thirds vote for treaties and a majority vote for appointments).

Advise *1.* Give advice. *2.* Give formal notice.

Advisement Consideration. A case "under advisement" means that the judge has heard the **evidence** or **arguments** and will delay a **decision** in the case until it has been thought over for a while.

Advisory jury A jury that a federal judge can call to help decide **questions** *of fact* even though the judge has the right to decide them alone.

Advisory opinion A formal opinion by a judge or judges about a question of law submitted by the **legislature** or by an **executive** (administrative) officer, but not actually presented to the court in a concrete lawsuit.

Advocacy Forceful persuasion; arguing a cause, right, or position.

Advocate *1.* A person who speaks for another person, for a "cause," or for an organization in order to persuade others. *2.* A lawyer. *3.* To speak, write, etc., in favor of something. *4.* The *advocate witness rule* is the principle that a lawyer should not represent a client in a case in which the lawyer might have to testify.

Aequitas (Latin) **Equity.** [pronounce: ek-we-tas]

Affair A **lawsuit,** or an action or event that could turn into a lawsuit.

Affect To change; to act upon or influence. *Affect* and *effect* are often confused in legal writing. Proper use of the words is illustrated by these sentences: When you effect (cause) a change, you affect (change) something. When you affect (change) something, you produce an effect (the change itself).

Affected class *1.* See **class action.** *2.* A defined group of persons discriminated against for the same illegal reason, such as race.

Affecting commerce *1.* An activity that generally concerns business or commerce. *2.* An activity that is likely to lead to a **labor dispute** that could obstruct the free flow of commerce.

Affects doctrine The principle that the **commerce clause** of the Constitution allows the federal government to **regulate** commerce within a state if it greatly *affects* interstate commerce.

Affiant A person who "swears to" a written statement; a person who makes an **affidavit** (see that word). [pronounce: a-fi-ant]

Affidavit A written statement sworn to before a person officially permitted by law to administer an **oath.** For example, an *affidavit of service* is a sworn statement that a legal paper has been "served" (mailed, handed to, etc.) upon another person in a lawsuit.

Affiliate A person or company with an inside business connection to another company. Under **bankruptcy, securities,** and other laws, if one company owns more than a certain amount of another company's voting **stock,** or if the companies are under common control, they are *affiliates.*

Affiliation proceeding Same as **paternity suit.**

Affinity Relationship by marriage. For example, a wife is related by affinity to her husband's brother.

Affirm *1.* Make firm; repeat agreement; confirm. *2.* When a higher court declares that a lower court's action was valid and right, it "*affirms*" the decision. *3.* Reaccept and make solid a **contract** that is breakable. *4.* State positively. *5.* See **affirmation.**

Affirmance See **affirm.**

Affirmation *1.* A solemn and formal declaration in place of an **oath** for those persons whose principles or religious beliefs forbid oath taking. *2.* The *Affirmation of Professional Responsibility* is a set of ethical guidelines provided by the **National Federation of Paralegal Associations.**

Affirmative action *1.* Steps to remedy past **discrimination** in hiring, promotion, etc.; for example, by recruiting more minorities and women. *2.* Any administrative action taken to right a wrong, rather than to punish anyone for causing it.

Affirmative charge A **charge** that removes an issue from the jury's consideration, usually by the judge's instructions on a particular **count.** Compare with **formula instruction.**

Affirmative defense That part of a **defendant's answer** to a **complaint** (see those words) that goes beyond denying the facts and arguments of the complaint. It sets out new facts and arguments that might win for the defendant even if everything in the complaint is true. The **burden of proof** for an *affirmative defense* is on the defendant. For example, an *affirmative defense* to a lawsuit for injuries caused by an auto accident might be the **contributory negligence** of the person who was hurt. Some other affirmative defenses in **civil** cases are **accord** and *satisfaction,* **assumption of risk,** and **estoppel.** Affirmative defenses in **criminal** cases include **insanity** and **self-defense.**

Affirmative order A judge's or **administrative agency's** order that a person (or organization) not only stop doing something but that the person take positive steps to undo the damage.

Affirmative relief Money (**damages**) or other benefit (for example, **specific performance**) awarded to a **defendant** in a lawsuit. To get affirmative relief, the defendant must either make a **counterclaim** against the **plaintiff** or a **cross-claim** against another defendant.

Affix Attach physically (as a tree to the ground or a gutter to a house) or place upon (as a signature on a document). To affix something usually means to put it in place permanently. See **fixture.**

Afforce Make something larger or stronger.

Affreightment A shipping contract.

Aforesaid Previously identified; already mentioned. This word is often used unnecessarily or imprecisely.

Aforethought Planned in advance; done with **premeditation.** See **malice aforethought.**

After-acquired property Property received after a certain event, such as the date a person **mortgages** other property. Some mortgages have an "*after-acquired property clause*" which means that anything added to the mortgaged property is subject to the mortgage just as if it were mortgaged directly. And in **bankruptcy** law, most property acquired after the bankruptcy petition is filed is protected from creditors.

After-acquired title rule   The legal principle that if a person transfers ownership to land for which he or she has no good **title** (right of ownership) and then gets good title to it, the title automatically goes to the person to whom the property was transferred.

After-born child rule   The legal principle that if a child is born after a **will** is made, the child should still inherit whatever children inherit (under the will or by state law) unless the will specifically excludes later-born children.

After-discovered evidence   See **newly discovered evidence.**

Aftermarket   *1.* **Secondary market.** *2.* Something added to a product by someone other than the manufacturer.

Against interest   See **declaration** *against interest.*

Against the evidence   Not consistent with the bulk of the **evidence.** A **trial** judge may order a new trial if the **jury** has clearly given its **verdict** by mistake or due to an improper motive or bias. Compare with **directed verdict** and **non obstante veredicto.**

Age discrimination   See **discrimination.**

Age of consent   The age at which persons may marry without parents' approval or the age at which a person is legally capable of agreeing to sexual intercourse. If a man engages in sex with a woman below that age (usually sixteen), most states call the crime **statutory rape.**

Age of majority (or capacity)   Age at which a child gains full right to enter into binding **contracts,** make a **will,** vote, etc. This age varies from state to state (though often eighteen) and from purpose to purpose.

Age of reason   Age at which a child may be capable of acting responsibly. This is often the age of seven. Below that age, a child's actions are never a crime, and the child's **testimony** is often considered to be unreliable.

Aged accounts receivable   See **aging schedule.**

Agency   *1.* A relationship in which one person acts for or represents another by the latter's authority. This usually creates a **fiduciary** relationship. See **agent.** *2.* Short for **administrative agency.** And an *agency practitioner* is a person (whether or not a lawyer) who is authorized to practice (represent people) before an administrative agency.

Agency shop   A business in which workers are not required to join a union but are required to pay the equivalent of union dues and fees. *Agency shops* are not permitted under certain state **right to work laws.** Compare with **union shop** and **closed shop.**

Agent   A person authorized (requested or permitted) by another person to act for him or her; a person entrusted with another's business. Some of the many types of agent include: **bargaining agent;** *independent agent* (an **independent contractor**); and *managing agent* (a company employee who runs a part of the company's business and acts with independent judgment much of the time). A person need not be called an agent to be one for legal purposes.

Aggravated assault   A criminal **assault** (see that word) that is more serious than a *simple assault.* Defined differently in different states, *aggravated assault* often means "assault with a **deadly weapon**" or "assault with the intent to kill, rob, or rape."

Aggravation   Actions or occurrences that increase the seriousness of a crime, but are not part of the legal definition of that crime; for example, see **aggravated assault.**

Aggregate method   Projecting costs for a whole pension or insurance plan rather than for each individual in it.

Aggregation   *1.* In **patent** law, a collection of several separate ideas, mechanisms, etc., that is not patentable because the components do not interact to produce a new, useful result. Compare with **combination.** *2.* In civil procedure, the *aggregation doctrine* is the principle that separate money claims cannot be combined to reach the minimum monetary amount required to bring a lawsuit in federal court.

Aggressive collection   Various judicial means of collecting a debt, such as **attachment, execution, garnishment,** etc. (see those words).

Aggrieved party   A person whose personal or property rights have been violated by another person or whose interests are directly harmed by a court's **judgment.**

Aging schedule   A list showing how long **accounts receivable** have been owed and are overdue. See also **collection ratio.**

Agio   Extra money paid to convert from one currency to another. The *interest agio* is the difference between the interest rates of two countries. [pronounce: aj-ee-o]

Agistment   A type of **bailment** (see that word) in which a person uses his or her own land for the care and pasturing of another's animals.

Agostini v. Felton (521 U.S. 203) A 1997 U.S. Supreme Court decision that permitted the use of public school remedial education teachers in parochial schools.

Agrarian reform Laws that break up large landholdings and give the land to small farmer-owners.

Agreed case A lawsuit in which all the important facts are stipulated (agreed upon) between the sides, so that the judge needs to answer only the legal questions in dispute.

Agreement _1._ A **contract.** _2._ Complete understanding between persons, often called a "meeting of minds." _3._ An intention of two or more persons to enter into a contract with one another combined with an attempt to form a valid contract. An _agreement_ may include the language used plus background facts and circumstances.

Agricultural Marketing Agreement Act (7 U.S.C. 671) A federal law that regulates the sale of farm products and gives price protection to farmers. See **parity.**

Aid and abet Intentionally help or encourage another person to commit a crime.

Aid and comfort _1._ Help or encourage. _2._ To "_aid and comfort the enemy_" is one way of committing **treason,** according to the U.S. **Constitution.**

Aider The legal conclusion that once a jury gives a **verdict,** those facts that the jury logically needed to reach the verdict are assumed to be properly **alleged** and proved.

Air rights _1._ The ownership rights, belonging to a landowner, to the air space directly above the land. _2._ The right to use part of the air space above another's land; for example, airplanes usually have _air rights_ over property, but they may have to compensate the landowner for the owner's air rights if they regularly fly too low. See **a coelo usque ad centrum.**

Airbill A **bill of lading** (see that word) for shipment by air.

Alcometer See **evidential breath test.**

Alden v. Maine (119 S.Ct. 2240) The 1999 U.S. Supreme Court decision that individuals may not sue states to enforce federal rights except when Constitutionally protected civil rights are at issue.

Alderperson (man, woman) _1._ A person elected to a city council or other local governing body. _2._ A local judge.

Aleatory contract A **contract** with effects and results that depend on an uncertain event; for example, **insurance** agreements are _aleatory._ [pronounce: a-lee-a-to-ree]

Alford plea   A *guilty* **plea** in federal court that does not admit personal participation in the alleged criminal acts, but that agrees to imposition of a sentence. It is similar to a plea of **nolo contendere** and comes from the case *Alford v. U.S.*, 400 U.S. 25 (1970).

Alia   (Latin) *1.* Other things. *2.* Other persons.

Alias   (Latin) *1.* Short for "alias dictus" or "otherwise called"; a fictitious name used in place of a person's real name. *2.* An *alias* **writ** or **summons** (see those words) is a second (or third, etc.) one put out through the court if the first one did not work.

Alibi   (Latin) "Elsewhere"; the claim that at the time a crime was committed a person was somewhere else. [pronounce: al-eh-bi]

Alien   *1.* Any person who is not a U.S. **citizen,** whether or not that person lives in the U.S. permanently. *2.* A foreigner. [pronounce: a-lee-en]

Alien and Sedition Acts   Federal laws of 1798 that made it a crime to criticize the government in certain ways, gave the president the right to deport undesirable foreigners, lengthened residency requirements for citizenship, etc. Most of the Acts' provisions are no longer in effect.

Alienable   Legally able to be sold or transferred; subject to removal, taking away, transfer, or denial.

Alienate   Transfer, convey, or otherwise dispose of property to another person. The process is called "*alienation*" when land is transferred.

Alienation clause   A part of an **insurance** policy that **voids** (ends) the policy if the property being insured is sold or otherwise transferred.

Alienation of affection   Taking away the love, companionship, or help of another person's husband or wife. This is the basis for a lawsuit in a few states.

Alienee   A person to whom property is transferred.

Alieni juris   (Latin) Under another person's legal control.

Alienor   A person who transfers property to another person.

Alimony   Payments by a divorced husband to his ex-wife (or by wife to ex-husband) for ongoing personal support. Unlike child **support,** periodic alimony is considered to be income of the recipient, who must pay taxes on it. The person who pays the alimony may deduct it. Also see **lump-sum settlement.**

Aliquot   (Latin) A part; a fractional or proportional part. [pronounce: al-ee-quo]

Aliunde   (Latin) *1.* From another place; from outside this document. Sometimes a document may be explained by information *aliunde* (other papers, **testimony** by the person who drew up the document, etc.) and sometimes not. *2.* The *aliunde rule* is that a **jury's** verdict may not be called into question by a **juror** unless new **evidence** (from some separate, independent source) is first used to establish the probable truth and importance of the juror's statements. [pronounce: al-ee-<u>und</u>]

Alive A word with no definite legal meaning. A child may be alive for purposes of **inheritance** once the child is conceived; alive for other purposes once it is capable of independent life if artificially removed from the mother's body; alive if actually breathing or giving other more technical signs of life, no matter how briefly; etc. For the similar problem of when life legally ends, see **death.**

All events test The principle that when taxes are paid on an **accrual basis,** income is considered to belong to the taxpayer once all events have occurred that give the taxpayer a legal right to the income and once the amount can be closely figured.

All faults "With all faults" is the same as "**as is.**"

All fours See **on all fours.**

Allegation A statement in a **pleading** that sets out a fact that the side filing the pleading expects to prove.

Allege State; assert; charge; make an **allegation;** for example, "*alleged*" often means "*merely* stated" or "*only* charged."

Allegiance Loyalty and obedience to the government of which a person is a citizen. *Local allegiance* is the temporary obedience (but not personal loyalty) that a person owes to the country he or she is living in temporarily.

Allen charge A judge's instruction to a **jury** sometimes used when the jury in a criminal case is having difficulty reaching a decision. The judge tells the **jurors** to listen more favorably to each other's opinions. This charge (from the 1896 case *Allen v. U.S.,* 164 U.S. 492) has also been called the *dynamite instruction, shotgun charge,* etc., and is prohibited or limited in some states.

Allision A boat hitting a stationary object such as a docked boat.

Allocation *1.* Putting something in one place rather than in another. For example, crediting all of a payment to one **account** when there are several possible accounts to credit. *Allocation of income* refers to the process in **trust** accounting by which income is put into one pot to continue the trust or into another pot to be paid out. *Allocation of income* also refers to the **I.R.S.'s determination** (see those words) that income belongs to one of two companies controlled by the same persons, rather than to the other company. *2.* Proportional distribution (of money, of blame, etc.).

Allocution   The procedure in which a judge asks a prisoner whether he or she has any way to show that **judgment** should not be **pronounced** against him or her or has any last words to say before a sentence is given out. This is sometimes known as *"calling the prisoner."*

Allodial   An old word describing land that was owned freely and completely.

Allograph   A document written or signed by one person for another person.

Allonge   A piece of paper attached to a **negotiable instrument** (see that word) to provide space for **endorsements** (signatures).

Allotment   A share or portion; sometimes, the dividing-up process itself. For example, an *"allotment certificate"* is a document that tells prospective buyers of **shares** in a company how many shares they may buy and the **schedule** of payments for the shares; and a *"land allotment"* is a dividing-up of a piece of land for sale as building lots.

Allowance   *1.* A **deduction.** *2.* A regular payment. For example, a *temporary allowance* in a divorce may be **alimony** plus child **support** (see those words). *3.* See **cost of living allowance.** *4.* A *family (or spousal) allowance* is a state-set percentage of an **estate** that is given to the immediate family (or the spouse) even if the **will** gives them less.

Alluvion (or alluvium)   See **accretion.**

Alter ego   (Latin) Second self. If persons use a **corporation** as a mere front for doing their own private business, a court may disallow some of the protections that the law gives to the corporation's owners. Under the *"alter ego rule"* the court may hold the persons individually **liable** for their actions taken through the corporation. See also **corporate veil** and **instrumentality.**

Alteration   *1.* Making a thing different from what it was before without destroying its identity; a change or modification. *2.* Writing or erasing on a document that changes its language or meaning.

Alternate valuation date   Under federal tax rules, the **administrator** of a dead person's property may set a value for the property based on the date of death or on the *"alternate valuation date,"* the day the property is sold or given out. If six months go by before the property is disposed of, the choice is between the value as of the day of death and six months after, so long as the later value is less than the earlier.

Alternative contract   A **contract** that gives one or both of the persons making the agreement the choice of more than one way to fulfill the contract's terms.

Alternative dispute resolution   Ways to resolve legal problems without a court decision; for example, **arbitration, mediation, minitrial, rent-a-judge, summary jury trial,** etc.

Alternative minimum tax   The income tax paid by persons who would otherwise escape most taxes because they have large **exemptions, deductions,** and **credits.**

Alternative pleading   Asserting facts that are mutually exclusive (that cannot logically all be true) in the same **pleading** (see that word). This is now permitted in federal court and most state courts as long as each alternative fact or statement could stand on its own without the others.

Alternative relief   Asking the court, in a **pleading,** for help in ways that might contradict one another; for example, asking for either the return of a borrowed book or for payment of its value. Most courts allow this type of request.

Alternative writ   See **show cause order.**

Am. Jur.   **American Jurisprudence.**

Amalgamation   A complete joining or blending together of two or more things into one; for example, a **consolidation** or **merger** of two or more corporations to create a single company.

Ambassador   A high-ranking diplomatic representative; usually the top representative of one country to another.

Ambiguity   Uncertainness. The possibility that something (often the text of a document) can be interpreted in more than one way.

Ambit   Boundary line; limit; border.

Ambulance chaser   (Slang) _1._ A lawyer or a person working for a lawyer who follows up on street accidents to try to get the legal business involved. _2._ A lawyer who improperly solicits business or tries to get others to bring lawsuits.

Ambulatory   Movable; capable of being changed or revoked; able to walk.

Amend   Improve; correct; change; formally alter a document or law.

Amendment   _1._ A change made to a **bill** during its passage through a **legislature** or to a law already passed. _2._ One of the provisions of the U.S. **Constitution** enacted since the original Constitution became law. _3._ A change made to a **pleading** that is already before a court.

Amercement   A fine, especially one imposed by a judge or imposed on an official for misconduct.

American Arbitration Association   An organization that publishes **arbitration** rules and supplies **arbitrators** to help settle labor and other disputes.

American Association for Paralegal Education   A group of schools and teachers that promotes research, technical information, standards, and a certification process for **paralegal** education programs.

American Bar Association   The largest voluntary organization of lawyers in the country. Its branches and committees are involved in almost every area of legal practice and government activity.

American clause   A provision in some marine **insurance** policies that makes the insurance company **liable** for the full amount of certain claims even if other insurance covers the same claims.

American Depository Receipt   A substitute for direct ownership of foreign stock. ADRs are issued by American banks and traded on American stock exchanges.

American Digest System   A giant collection of summaries of every **reported** case (written **opinion**) in the U.S. since the sixteen hundreds. The years up to 1896 are in a *Century Digest,* each ten-year period after that is in a *Decennial Digest,* and the latest few years are in a *General Digest.* Each *Digest* has many volumes. The cases are organized by subjects according to the *Key Number System* (see **key numbers**).

American Jurisprudence   A multivolume legal encyclopedia. It is cross-referenced with **American Law Reports** (see that word).

American Law Institute   An organization that writes and proposes "model" or "uniform" laws and conducts a variety of legal education programs. Among its projects are the **Restatement of Law** and the **Uniform acts,** which are often adopted by many states.

American Law Reports   A large series of books that selects important cases, prints them in full, and gives an **annotation** (a commentary) that is often long and that discusses a whole area of the law.

American rule   The principle that the winner of a lawsuit may not collect costs or attorney's fees from the loser. This "rule" has many exceptions. For example, if the opponent has brought the lawsuit in **bad faith,** a court may award attorney's fees to the winner.

Americans with Disabilities Act   (42 U.S.C. 1201) The 1990 federal law that prohibits **discrimination** based on physical or mental **disability** in employment, public services, or places of public accommodation such as restaurants.

Amicable action   A lawsuit (involving a real, not a made-up problem) that is started by agreement of the two sides.

Amicus curiae   (Latin) "Friend of the court." A person allowed to give argument or appear in a lawsuit (usually to file a **brief,** but sometimes to take an active part) who is not a **party** to the lawsuit. [pronounce: a-_me_-kus _cure_-ee-i]

Amnesty   A wiping out, by the government, of guilt for persons guilty of a crime; a general governmental forgiving; a general pardon.

Amortization   _1._ Paying off a debt in installments, usually by making regular and equal payments. To determine how to _amortize_ an ordinary loan, calculate the total interest for the whole time until the loan is paid off, add that total to the amount of the loan, and divide the total by the number of payments. _2._ Apportioning the value and costs of an intangible asset (such as money owed, a **copyright,** or a **patent**) year-by-year over the estimated useful life of the asset. See **useful.** _3._ Any dividing up of benefits or costs by time periods, especially for tax purposes. It is called _amortization_ for **intangibles** such as money owed, **depreciation** (see that word) for durable physical objects used in a business, and **depletion** (see that word) for natural resources such as oil.

Amotion   Putting or taking out; for example, evicting a tenant from a house, removing a person from a public or corporate office, taking someone's personal property, etc.

Amount in controversy   See _amount_ under **jurisdictional.**

Anaconda clause   See **dragnet clause.**

Analogy   Similarity; resemblance; likeness; correspondence. Lawyers often reason or argue "by analogy." For example, when there is no previous case exactly deciding an issue (a "**precedent**"), lawyers will argue from other cases that have similar facts or are decided by the same general principles.

Analytical jurisprudence   A method of studying legal systems by analyzing and comparing legal principles in the abstract without considering their ethical backgrounds or practical applications.

Anarchist   _1._ A person who advocates the abolishment of all governments. _2._ A person who believes that an absence of government is the best government and that people will cooperate voluntarily if left alone.

Anarchy   Absence of government; absence of law.

Anathema   A religious punishment in which all members of a church are forbidden to have anything to do with the person being punished.

Ancient   A word meaning "old," without having a precise legal definition. For example, an *ancient watercourse* is a stream that has existed "beyond memory"; an *ancient deed* is at least thirty (in some states twenty) years old, especially one kept in proper custody; and *ancient streets* having nothing to do with time, but with the fact that a landowner is presumed to have given a street to the surrounding lot owners or to the public use if the lots were sold by the landowner.

Ancient lights   The doctrine, no longer accepted in the U.S., that windows that have had outside light for over a certain length of time cannot be blocked off from light by an adjacent landowner.

Ancient writings   Documents over a certain age (usually thirty years) that are presumed to be genuine, usually because they have been in continuously proper **custody** (keeping).

Ancillary   Supplementary; additional; subsidiary; "on the side."

Ancillary administration   A proceeding in a state where a dead person had property, but which is different from the state where that person lived and has his or her main **estate administered** (see those words).

Ancillary jurisdiction   The power of a court (especially a federal court) to handle matters related to the main case even if the court would not independently have the power to consider these matters. Federal courts, for example, have *ancillary jurisdiction* over *compulsory* **counterclaims.**

And/or   Either one or both. A vague term, best replaced by words that say exactly what you mean. For example, "I like ham and/or eggs" could be "I like ham; I like eggs; and I like them served together."

Animal rights   A popular term for the legal obligation to obey animal treatment laws and environmental laws or for the assumed legal and moral rights of animals themselves.

Animo   (Latin) With intention; for example, *animo furandi* (with intention to steal), *animo testandi* (with intention to make a will), or *revertendi* (return); *donadi* (make a gift); *manendi* (remain, make the place a **domicile** or permanent **residence**); or *revocandi* (revoke).

Animus   (Latin) Mind or intention (see **animo**).

Animus et factum   (Latin) "Intention plus fact"; the intention to do something plus the act itself.

Ann. (or An.)   *1.* Annual. *2.* Annotated.

Annex   Attach (usually something small to something large); for example, attaching a small piece of land to a large one or a small school district to large one. *Annex* can also refer to attaching a side document to the main one or putting a permanent light fixture on a wall.

Annotated statutes A set of books containing the laws plus commentary (history, explanations, cases discussing each law, etc.); for example, Connecticut General Statutes Annotated.

Annotation _1._ A note or commentary intended to explain the meaning of a passage in a book or document. _2._ A legal _annotation_ is usually an explanation of a **case,** including a comparison to other similar cases. It usually follows the text of the **decision** in a collection of cases.

Annual exclusion The amount of money a person can give away each year without paying a **gift tax** and without using up any of the **unified transfer tax** credit each person has.

Annual percentage rate The true cost of borrowing money, expressed in a standardized, yearly way to make it easier to understand **credit** terms and to "shop" for credit.

Annual report (or statement) _1._ A report most public **corporations** are required to provide each year to stockholders and to the government. Many companies also make it available to the public. The report usually contains a **balance sheet, statements** (see that word) of income, spending, **retained earnings,** and other financial data, plus a summary of ownership of the company's **stocks** and **bonds,** an explanation of **accounting** practices used, an **auditor's** report, comments about the year's business and future prospects, etc. (Parts of the report may have different names from those given here.) _2._ Any yearly report of an organization.

Annuity _1._ A fixed sum of money, usually paid to a person at fixed times for a fixed time period or for life. If for life, or for some other uncertain period of time, it is called a **contingent** _annuity._ _2._ A _retirement annuity_ is a right to receive payments starting at some future date, usually retirement, but sometimes a fixed date. There are many ways a retirement annuity can be paid. For example, _life_ (equal monthly payments for the retiree's life); _lump sum_ (one payment); _certain and continuous_ (like _life,_ but if the person dies within a set time period, benefits continue for the rest of that period); and _joint and survivor_ (benefits continue for the life of either the retiree or the spouse). _3._ An account with an investment or insurance company that is tax-free until retirement and works like the examples in no. 1 and no. 2.

Annul Make void; wipe out. See **annulment.**

Annulment _1._ The act of making something **void** or wiping it out completely. _2._ The _annulment_ of a marriage "wipes the marriage off the books," as opposed to a **divorce,** which only ends the marriage. A marriage will not usually be _annulled_ by a court unless it was **invalid** in some way from the beginning.

Anomalous Unusual; abnormal.

Anon Anonymous (author unknown).

Answer *1.* The first **pleading** by the **defendant** in a lawsuit. This pleading responds to the charges and demands of the **plaintiff's complaint.** The defendant may deny the plaintiff's charges, may present new facts to defeat them, or may show why the plaintiff's facts are legally invalid. *2.* Take on the **liability** of another person, as in to "answer for someone's debt."

Ante (Latin) Before.

Ante litem motam (Latin) Before the lawsuit was started; before anyone would have a reason to lie.

Ante natus (Latin) Before birth; born prior. The "status" of a person born before another person or before a major political event such as a revolution. *Antenatal* means "concerning pregnancy or a fetus."

Antecedent debt A debt that predates another transaction. In **contract** law, the prior debt may sometimes make a fresh promise to pay enforceable even if the debt itself is too old to collect. And in **bankruptcy** law, an *antecedent debt* is one owed for a long enough time before the **filing** of bankruptcy that it is considered a valid debt rather than an attempt to give money to one person in preference to other **creditors.**

Antedate Predate; "backdate." Date a document earlier than the date it was actually signed. This may be a crime.

Antenuptial Before a marriage. An *antenuptial* or *prenuptial agreement* is a contract between persons about to marry. It usually concerns the way property will be handled during the marriage, the way it will be divided in case of **divorce,** and the limits on spousal support obligations.

Anticipation *1.* The act of doing a thing before its proper time or simply doing it "before" something else. *2.* Paying off a **mortgage** before it comes due, especially when there is no "prepayment penalty." *3.* The right under some **contracts** to deduct some money (usually based on the current interest rate) when paying early. *4.* In **patent** law, an invention is *anticipated* if someone else has already patented substantially the same thing. *5.* Expectation or prior knowledge.

Anticipatory breach Breaking a contract by refusing to go through with it once it is entered into, but before it is time to fully perform (do your side or share).

Anticipatory search warrant A **search warrant** permitting a future search at a specific place because specific evidence of a crime will probably arrive there.

Anti-discrimination act *1.* **Civil Rights** *Acts. 2.* **Robinson-Patman Act.**

Antidumping act (or duty) See **dump.**

Anti-injunction act *1.* A federal law (28 U.S.C. 2283) that prohibits federal courts from stopping state court proceedings unless an injunction is specifically authorized by law, is needed to prevent relitigation of a federal court **judgment,** or meets other specific criteria. *2.* Various laws limiting the rights of employers to get an injunction against a legal strike.

Anti-john law A law that makes it a criminal offense to be a prostitute's customer or to solicit the services of a prostitute.

Antilapse statutes Laws passed in most states to allow the **heirs** of someone who will inherit under a will to inherit themselves if the person who was supposed to inherit dies before the person making the will dies. Otherwise, that part of the property in the will would **lapse** (go to others).

Antinomy An inconsistency, conflict, or contradiction between apparently valid ideas, authorities, laws, or provisions in a law.

Anti-Racketeering Act See **R.I.C.O .** (Also refers to an earlier federal law, the *Hobbs Act* (18 U.S.C. 1951) prohibiting **extortion** and other interference with interstate commerce.)

Antitrust acts Federal and state laws to protect trade from **monopoly** control and from **price fixing** and other **restraints of trade** (see those words). The main federal antitrust laws are the **Sherman, Clayton,** Federal Trade Commission, and **Robinson-Patman** Acts.

Apex rule In mining law, a miner may follow and exploit a mineral vein on public land from the top (usually the discovery point) to any underground point on public land to which the vein leads, even if it goes outside the surface boundary of the miner's claim or passes under another claim. Also called "*extralateral right rule.*"

Apostille (or appostille) A **certificate of authority.** [pronounce: ah-pos-til]

App. Ct. Appellate court (see **appellate**).

Apparent Easily seen; superficially true. For example, *apparent authority* is the **authority** an **agent** seems to have, judged by the words or actions of the person who gave the authority or by the agent's own words or actions. You may be **liable** for the actions of a person who has *apparent authority* to act for you.

Appeal *1.* Ask a higher court to review the actions of a lower court in order to correct mistakes or injustice. *2.* The process in no. 1 is called "*an appeal.*" An appeal may also be taken from a lower level of an **administrative agency** to a higher level or from an agency to a court.

Appeal bond Money put up by someone appealing a court's decision. This money is to pay the other side's costs in case the person appealing fails to go forward with an honest **appeal.**

Appealable order An action by a judge that is sufficiently final so that an appeal from the **order** will not disrupt the way the judge is handling the case. See **interlocutory** for examples of when an order is "final enough" to be *appealable.*

Appeals council The place to **appeal** when dissatisfied with the ruling of an **administrative law judge** in a Social Security case.

Appearance *1.* The coming into court as a **party (plaintiff** or **defendant)** to a lawsuit. A person who does this *"appears."* *2.* The formal coming into court as a lawyer in a specific lawsuit; often also called "entering" the case.

Appellant The person who **appeals** a case to a higher court. Compare with **appellee.**

Appellate Refers to a higher court that can hear **appeals** from a lower court or refers to an appeal.

Appellate jurisdiction The power and authority of a higher court to take up cases that have already been in a lower court and the power to make decisions about these cases. The process is called *appellate review.* Also, a trial court may have *appellate jurisdiction* over cases from an **administrative agency.**

Appellee The person against whom an **appeal** is taken (usually, but not always, the winner in the lower court). Compare with **appellant.**

Append Add or attach. Something *appendant* has been added or attached to another thing.

Appoint *1.* Give a person a job or duty; for example, to *appoint* a person to serve on a committee. Nonelected government jobs, especially high-level ones, are called *appointments.* *2.* Give a **power of appointment** (see that word).

Appointive asset An **estate** asset that will be given out by **power of appointment.**

Apportionment Dividing up; dividing fairly and proportionately; dividing by shares; dividing up land for the purpose of creating voting districts.

Appose Examine the keeper of written records about those records. Compare with **depose.**

Appraisal (or appraisement) *1.* Estimating the value of property. Usually, the appraisal is done by an impartial expert. This is not the same as **assessment**. *2*. Fixing the fair value of **stock** as of a particular time or for a particular purpose. For example, a court may *appraise* the value of stock when stockholders in a **corporation** quarrel and some must be bought out. *Appraisal remedies (or rights)* in most states give **minority stockholders** the right to be bought out at the price the stock was before the corporation took an unusual or extraordinary action, such as a **merger** or sale of major **assets.**

Appraiser   An impartial expert chosen to set a value on a piece of property.

Appreciable   *1*. Measurable; able to be estimated, weighed, or perceived by the senses. *2*. Existing, or significant, but *not* necessarily substantial or great in size, quantity, or value. *3*. Capable of increasing in value. See **appreciate**. [pronounce: a-<u>preesh</u>-a-ble]

Appreciate   *1*. Increase in value. *2*. Estimate the value of something. *3*. Understand or realize.

Appreciation   *1*. The increase in value of property excluding increases due to improvements. *2*. Any increase in value.

Apprehension   *1*. The capture or arrest of a person on a criminal charge. *2*. Fear. *3*. Understanding; knowledge of something.

Appropriation   *1*. A **legislature's** setting aside for a specific purpose a portion of the money raised by the government; for example, a "*highway appropriation*." "*Appropriations*" is the name of each congressional committee that makes spending decisions. *2*. A governmental taking of land or property for public use. *3*. Taking something wrongfully; for example, using a person's picture and name in an advertisement without permission. *4*. In private business, setting aside money for a major purchase or long-term project. *5*. Any setting aside or application of money or property for a particular purpose.

Approval   Short for "*on approval.*" A type of sale in which the buyer may return the goods if they are unsatisfactory even if they are all the seller claims they are.

Approximation   Close, but not exact. When provisions of a **charitable trust** cannot be carried out as written, a court may, in order to save the trust from failing, under the **doctrine** *of approximation,* carry out the general purposes of the trust. See also **cy-pres.**

Appurtenance   Something that belongs to or is attached to something else. For example, both a **right of way** and a barn may be an *appurtenance* to land.

Appurtenant   Belonging to or added onto (see **appurtenance**).

Arbiter   A person, such as a judge or **arbitrator,** who is chosen to decide a disagreement.

Arbitrage   Simultaneously buying and selling similar financial items (such as two stocks, commodity contracts, currencies, etc.) to profit from price differences between them. If the items are identical and traded in different places, it is called *arbitrage* or *space arbitrage.* If one item is or will become exchangeable for the other, it is *kind* or *convertible arbitrage.* If the items are stock in companies that may merge or become involved in a takeover, it is *risk arbitrage.* And if the items are contracts for the immediate and future delivery of a commodity, it is *time arbitrage.* [pronounce: ar-bi-trazh]

Arbitrament   The power to decide something, the decision in an **arbitration,** or the **award** in that arbitration.

Arbitrary   *1.* Describes action taken according to a person's own desires; without supervision, general principles, or rules to decide by. *2.* Describes action taken capriciously, in bad faith, or without good reason.

Arbitration   Resolution of a dispute by a person (other than a judge) whose decision is binding. This person is called an *arbitrator.* Submission of the dispute for decision is often the result of an agreement (an *"arbitration clause"*) in a contract. If arbitration is required by law, it is called *"compulsory."*

Arbitration acts   Laws that help (and sometimes require) the submission of certain types of disputes (often **labor** disputes) to an **arbitrator.**

Arbitration of exchange   The **arbitrage** of **bills** *of exchange* (see those words) in order to take advantage of the different values of national currencies in different international money markets.

Arbitrator   A person who conducts an **arbitration** (see that word). This person is usually not a public official, is often chosen by the persons having the dispute, and is often an impartial expert in the field or one trained in the law.

Architect's lien   See **lien.**

Area variance   A **variance** permitting deviation from certain structural zoning requirements (such as building placement) but not from *use* requirements.

Area-wide agreement   One **union** making the same **labor contract** with many companies in one geographical area. The process of achieving an *area-wide agreement* is called *"area bargaining."*

Arguendo   (Latin) Hypothetically and for the purpose of discussion. For example, assume something is true (whether true or false) for the sake of argument.

Argument *1.* Persuasion by laying out facts, law, and the reasoning that connects them. *2.* The oral, in-court presentation of no. 1.

Argumentative *1.* Stating not only facts, but conclusions. *2.* Disputatious and controversial.

Arise Originate or come into being. For example, a lawsuit *arises* at the time when the principal events leading to the lawsuit occur. This is before the lawsuit *commences,* or when the first papers are filed in court. Also, a case *arises* under the **Constitution** when a constitutional right is claimed or when the case cannot be decided without referring to the Constitution.

Aristocracy Government by a nobility based on birth, wealth, or social position.

Armed robbery Taking property directly from a person by using or threatening violence and while carrying a dangerous weapon. In many states, *armed robbery* is an aggravated (see **aggravation**) form of the crime of **robbery.** The robber need not use or reveal the existence of the weapon for there to be an armed robbery.

Armistice A complete suspension of fighting between nations with the hope that the suspension will become permanent. An *armistice* is more than a truce (which can be for a limited time or place) and less than a peace treaty (which is permanent or long-lasting).

Arm's length Not on close terms; describes a contract that is not done by a person especially responsible to another, such as by a lawyer responsible to a client or a **trustee** responsible to a trust. If an agreement is not clearly "*at arm's length*" its validity is often tested by its result: was the price paid a fair one; was it a price that would have been reached on the open market?

Arms, right to The right given by the **Second Amendment** to the U.S. **Constitution** for the people to "keep and bear arms" in order to guarantee "a well-regulated militia." This right does not allow a person to carry a gun in violation of state or federal laws.

Arraign To bring a **defendant** before a judge to hear the charges and to enter a **plea** (guilty, not guilty, etc.). [pronounce: ah-<u>rayn</u>]

Arraignment See **arraign.**

Arrangement with creditors A plan under the Federal **Bankruptcy** Act that allows a financially weak person or company to settle debts for less than full value, to gain additional time to pay, or to otherwise keep from going under completely. See **Chapter Eleven** for **corporations** and **Chapter Thirteen** for persons and small businesses.

Array *1.* The entire group of people from which a **jury** can be selected. A *"challenge to the array"* is an objection to the procedures by which the group was chosen. *2.* The group of jurors (and, sometimes, alternates) who will participate in a case. *3.* To *impanel* (choose) the jury or to call them one by one as they are chosen.

Arrears (or arrearages) Unperformed, overdue obligations, including money owed. Being *"in arrears"* often means being behind in paying a debt.

Arrest The official taking of a person to answer criminal charges. This involves at least temporarily depriving the person of liberty and may involve the use of force. An arrest is usually made by a police officer with a **warrant** or for a crime committed in the officer's presence.

Arrest of judgment A judge's temporary stopping of the enforcement of a **judgment** because of some apparent defect in the proceedings.

Arrest record *1.* The official form filled out by the police when a person is arrested. *2.* A list of times a person has been arrested, with convictions and sentences also noted.

Arrogation *1.* Claiming something or taking something without having any right to it. *2.* The **adoption** of an adult.

Arson The **malicious** and unlawful burning of a building.

Art *1.* Special knowledge or skill. *2.* A process or method. *3. Words (or terms) of art* are technical or scientific words, or ordinary words used in a special way in a particular area of law, business, or science. *4.* "Art." is short for **article.**

Artful pleading doctrine The principle that a **plaintiff** cannot defeat **removal** of a case from state court to federal court by phrasing a federal **cause of action** as solely a state one. (In general, a **defendant** can have a case removed only if the plaintiff's **complaint** shows a reason to do so.) Compare with **well-pleaded complaint doctrine.**

Article A separate and distinct part of a document.

Article I and III Courts *Article I Courts,* such as the U.S. tax court, are created by **statute** under Article I of the U.S. Constitution. Judges of these courts may be removed and have their salaries reduced. Judges of Article III courts, such as the U.S. district courts, have lifetime positions and guaranteed salaries.

Articled clerk A lawyer's apprentice in England. Few states in the U.S. still allow entry into the legal profession by apprenticeship (known as *reading for the law*) and examination rather than by graduation from law school and examination.

Articles *1.* The separate main parts of a document, book, set of rules, etc. *2.* A law with several parts. *3.* A system of rules; for example, "*articles of the navy.*" *4.* Certain types of contracts; for example, "*articles of partnership,*" which set up a partnership, or "*articles of association,*" which set up non-**stock** (often nonprofit) organizations.

Articles of Confederation The document that held together the thirteen original American colonies before the adoption of the **Constitution.**

Articles of incorporation The document used to set up a **corporation.** *Articles of incorporation* contain the most basic rules of the corporation and control other corporate rules such as the **bylaws.**

Articulable suspicion The requirement that a peace officer be able to justify a brief investigatory stop or a "pat down" for weapons. This is less than **probable cause** to conduct a full search or to make an arrest.

Articulated pleading Using separate paragraphs, separately numbered, for each important fact in a court paper such as a **complaint** or **answer.**

Articulo mortis (Latin) Death throes; at the point of death.

Artifice **Fraud** or deceit.

Artificial person An entity or "thing," especially a **corporation,** that the law gives some of the legal rights and duties of a person.

Artisan's lien A **mechanic's lien.**

As is A condition of sale that disclaims **warranty.** A thing sold *"as is"* is sold in a possibly defective condition, and the buyer must take it with no promises other than it is as seen and described. An as is *house* sale, however, may require the disclosure of **latent** *defects.*

As per "In accordance with"; "with reference to."

Ascendants Parents, grandparents, etc. *Ascendants* can **inherit** property in the same way descendants (children, etc.) can, and *"ascent"* is the word that describes this type of inheritance.

Ascent See **ascendants.**

Asportation An old word for the theft and removal of personal property.

Assault An intentional threat, show of force, or movement that could reasonably make a person feel in danger of physical attack or harmful physical contact. It can be a **crime** or **tort.** Compare with **battery.**

Assay *1.* Examine something to discover its size, weight, number, value, or quality. *2.* The chemical testing of a metal's purity.

Assemblage *1.* An **assembly.** *2.* Combining many things (such as small lots of land) into one.

Assembly *1.* A large meeting. *2.* The lower **house** of many state **legislatures.** *3.* The *right of assembly* in the **First Amendment** to the U.S. **Constitution** guarantees the right of the people to meet for political purposes, especially to protest government actions. *4. Unlawful assembly* is the gathering of people in a disruptive way, such as obstructing traffic on a busy street.

Assent Approval; demonstrated agreement.

Asservation An **asseveration.**

Assess *1.* Set the value of something. *2.* Set the value of property for the purpose of taxing it. *3.* Charge part of the cost of a public improvement (such as a sidewalk) to each person or property directly benefiting from it.

Assessable *1.* Liable to pay extra. For example, *assessable stock* is **stock** with ownership that may require payment of more than the original investment to keep a share in the company; and an *assessable insurance* **policy** may require the person **insured** to start paying higher **premiums** if a loss is too expensive. *2.* Liable to be put on the tax rolls and taxed.

Assessed valuation The value placed on real estate for property tax purposes by the government. It is usually less than the property's **market value.**

Assessment *1.* Deciding on the amount to be paid by each of several persons into a common fund. *2.* The process of listing and evaluating the worth of property for taxing it. This is not **appraisal** (see that word). *3.* A payment beyond what is normally required of members of a group. *4.* Periodic payments by persons who have **subscribed** to buy **stock** from a **corporation.** *5.* Deciding the amount of **damages** that the loser of a lawsuit must pay. *6.* An extra payment.

Assessment ratio The **assessed valuation** of property divided by the property's **market value.**

Assessment work Mining or improvements on a mining **claim** on public land in order to avoid losing your right to the claim.

Assessor *1.* A person who evaluates the worth of things; especially a government official who evaluates land and buildings for tax purposes. *2.* A person who advises a judge on scientific or technical matters during a lawsuit.

Asset acquisition Buying a company by purchasing all its **assets** rather than by buying its stock.

Asset allocation Spreading and shifting money among various *types* of investments in an attempt to get the highest profit and least risk.

Asset depreciation range   The choice of "lifetimes" the **I.R.S.** will let you use when you claim **depreciation** on a particular **asset** (property). See **M.A.C.R.S.**

Assets   Money, property, and money-related rights (such as money owed) owned by a person or an organization. In a business, "_capital assets_" or "_fixed assets_" are those assets that cannot be turned into cash easily (such as buildings); "_current assets_" or "_liquid assets_" are those things that can be turned into cash easily (such as easily marketable **securities** or goods for sale); and "_frozen assets_" are those assets that are legally tied up, often because of a lawsuit. For other types of assets, such as **quick assets,** see those words.

Asseveration   A solemn **oath** or **declaration.**

Assign   _1._ To appoint or select for a particular purpose or duty. _2._ To formally transfer; for example, to **deed** over land to another person. _3._ To point out, set forth, or specify. For example, to "_assign errors_" is to specify them in a legal document, and an "_assignable error_" is an error that can be used as the basis for an **appeal.** _4._ See **assignment.**

Assigned account   A debt owed to a company that the company uses as **security** for its own debt to a bank. Also called _pledged_ **accounts receivable.**

Assigned counsel   A lawyer appointed by the court to represent someone, usually in a criminal case, who is too poor to hire a lawyer.

Assigned risk   A type of **insurance** (such as automobile insurance for a person who has had many accidents) that insurance companies handle because state law requires it. These persons pay extra for insurance and are often assigned to each insurance company by the state, often at random.

Assignee   Person to whom something is given or transferred. The _assignee clause_ in federal law prohibits lawsuits in federal courts that got there only because one person transferred rights to another person in another state in order to get the necessary _diversity_ **jurisdiction** to bring the lawsuit (see **diversity of citizenship**).

Assignment   _1._ See **assign.** _2._ The transfer of property, rights in property, or money to another person. For example, an _assignment of wages_ involves an employer paying part of an employee's salary directly to someone to whom the employee owes money. Most states limit this. An _assignment of income_ involves an attempt to have income taxed to someone else by turning over either the income or the income-producing property to that person. Tax laws make this hard to do.

Assignor Person who sells, gives, or otherwise transfers ownership of something to another person.

Assigns Persons to whom property is or will be transferred.

Assise (or assize) Old word with various meanings including: certain English courts, laws, and **writs.**

Assistance of counsel Representation by a lawyer. The **Sixth Amendment** to the U.S. **Constitution** gives every person the right to a lawyer ("effective assistance of counsel") in a criminal prosecution. See **assigned counsel.**

Assistance, writ of A judge's command that the **sheriff** help a person take possession of land (once the court has decided that the person has a right to take possession).

Associate company A company owned or controlled by a **holding company.**

Associate justice The title of each judge (other than the chief justice) on an **appeals** court.

Association *1.* Any group of persons joined together for a particular purpose. *2.* An entity (such as a **limited partnership** or **trust**), other than a **corporation,** which is taxed by the **I.R.S.** as if it were a corporation because it acts like, or has several important characteristics of, a corporation.

Assume *1.* To take up or take responsibility for; to receive; to undertake. See **assumption.** *2.* To pretend. *3.* To accept without proof.

Assumpsit "He promised"; an old word meaning a promise to do or pay something. Certain types of lawsuits had this name. For example, "*indebitatis assumpsit*" was "he promised to pay the debt," but it was based not on an actual promise but on the fact that money was owed, whether or not there was an actual promise to pay.

Assumption Formally transforming someone else's debt into your own debt. Compare with **guaranty.** The assumption of a **mortgage** usually involves taking over the seller's "mortgage debt" when buying a property (often a house).

Assumption of risk Knowingly and willingly exposing yourself (or your property) to the possibility of harm. In most states, a person who assumes a risk of harm cannot win a **negligence** lawsuit against the person responsible for the harm because *assumption of risk* is a valid **affirmative defense.** See also **comparative negligence rule** and **no fault** *insurance.*

Assurance *1.* **Insurance** (see that word); and *assured* means insured. *2.* A **pledge** or **guaranty.** *3.* An old word for the document that transfers real property and for the transfer itself.

Assured **Insured** person.

Asylum Protection given by one country to a fugitive from criminal prosecution by another country. The availability of _asylum_ may be limited by a **treaty** of **extradition.**

At bar Currently being handled in court; "before this court."

At issue In dispute. A legal point is "_at issue_" in a lawsuit when one side clearly asserts it and the other side clearly denies it. The lawsuit itself is "at issue" when all major legal points are clearly asserted and denied.

At large _1._ Unlimited; fully; in detail; everywhere. _2._ Free, unrestrained, uncontrolled. _3._ See **statutes at large.** _4._ An _at large election_ is one in which each person chooses from among all the candidates, rather than just candidates from one geographic subarea.

At-risk The amount of money a person could actually lose if an investment goes bad. _At-risk rules_ are tax rules limiting income tax **deductions** to those investments for which you are _at risk_ personally.

At will See **will.**

Ats. Short for **ad sectam;** "at the suit of."

Attaché (French) An official attached to an embassy, to an ambassador's staff, or to some other diplomatic mission, especially for a particular reason, such as a naval _attaché._ [pronounce: at-ah-shay]

Attachment _1._ Formally seizing property (or a person) in order to bring it under the control of the court. This is usually done by getting a court **order** to have a law enforcement officer take control of the property. See also **garnishment** and **levy.** _2._ A document added onto another document. _3._ A **security** interest, such as a **mortgage,** _attaches_ if it is valid and can be enforced by the person who has it against the person who holds the attached property.

Attachment bond Money put up to free property that has been attached. The bond substitutes for the property and guarantees that if the person who attached it wins in court, there will be money to pay the claim. See **attachment.**

Attainder The wiping out of **civil rights** that may occur when a person is found guilty of a **felony** or receives a death **sentence.** It usually includes the government's taking of all the person's property. This is no longer done in the United States. A _bill of attainder_ was a **legislative** act pronouncing a person guilty (usually of **treason**) without a trial and sentencing the person to death and _attainder._ This is now prohibited by the U.S. **Constitution.**

Attaint _1._ An old English process, no longer done, of conducting an investigation into whether a **jury** had given a deliberately false **verdict.**

If so, the person wronged was given back everything lost and the jurors were sent to prison and stripped of all they owned. *2.* What happens in **attainder** (see that word).

Attempt *1.* An act that goes beyond preparation, but which is not completed. *2.* An effort to commit a crime that goes beyond preparation and that proceeds far enough to make the person who did it guilty of an *"attempt crime."* For example, if a person fires a shot at another in a failed effort at murder, the person is guilty of *attempted murder.*

Attendant circumstances The factual background of an event; sometimes, the facts that add up to an **element** of a crime or a lawsuit.

Attenuation The weakening of a connection. For example, if many things happen between two events, the connection between these two events becomes *"attenuated."* The *attenuation doctrine* is the principle that the connection may become so weak between illegal police action (in search, investigation, arrest, or interrogation) and the evidence gained as a result of that illegal action, that the evidence may be used. This is an exception to the **fruit of the poisonous tree doctrine.**

Attest Swear to; act as a witness to; certify formally, usually in writing.

Attestation The act of witnessing the signing of a document and signing that you have witnessed it.

Attorn *1.* Turn over money or goods to another person. *2.* See **attachment.**

Attorney *1.* Lawyer (*"attorney at law"*). *2.* Any person who acts formally for another person (*"attorney in fact"*). [pronounce: a-tur-ney]

Attorney general The chief law officer of a state or of the U.S. (The U.S. attorney general is also the head of the Department of Justice and a **cabinet** member.)

Attorney of record The lawyer listed in court papers as representing a person and who is responsible to the person and the court for all work done (and not done) in the lawsuit. The *attorney of record* is empowered to receive all legal papers from the court and from the other side in the case.

Attorney-client privilege The right of a client, and the duty of that client's lawyer, to keep confidential the contents of almost all communication between them. Exceptions may include discussion of possible future crimes and discussions held in the presence of the client's friends.

Attorney's lien The right of lawyers, in some circumstances, to hold a client's money (or property, such as legal papers) already in the lawyer's hands, or to get at a client's money in the court's hands, to pay for attorney's fees.

Attornment   Agreeing to pay rent to, and be a tenant of, a new landlord who buys the land you rent.

Attractive nuisance   A legal principle, used in some states, that if a person keeps dangerous property in a way that children might be attracted to it and be able to get at it, then that person is responsible even if the children are trespassing or at fault when they get hurt.

Attribution   Saying (or deciding) that something belongs to (or was said by) a particular person.

Atty (or att'y)   Short for **attorney.**

Audit   An official examination of an **account** or of a person's or an organization's financial situation. The two most common audits are the annual outside examination of a company's total finances by "auditors" and the inspection by the **I.R.S.** of a person's tax records. This I.R.S. examination can be a *field audit* (at the taxpayer's home or place of business), a *correspondence audit* (conducted by mail), or an *office audit* (at the I.R.S. office).

Audit trail   A cross-reference from a bookkeeping record to its source to properly explain the record, document it, or check its accuracy.

Auditor   An official who examines **accounts** and decides whether they are accurate.

Augmented estate   The property left by a dead person after subtracting for various claims and expenses and adding in the value of property held by the husband or wife and of certain other property disposed of to "insiders," disposed of shortly before death, or in which the dead person retained some rights.

Authentication   *1.* A formal act certifying that a public document (a law, a record of **deeds,** etc.) is official and correct, often so that it may be admitted as **evidence.** *2.* Any **evidence** that proves that a document actually is what it seems to be. *3.* An *"authentic act"* may be something sworn to before a **notary public.**

Author   A broad word for the creator of a written, musical, or visual work. An author, who need not be a person and need not have created any original material, has specific rights under **copyright** (see that word) laws.

Authoritarianism   **Absolutism** (see that word), whether or not there is a formal legal system in place that makes it look like government power is *not* **absolute.**

Authorities   **Citations** to references taken from laws, decisions, texts, etc., in support of a legal position argued by an advocate, a decision maker, or a scholar.

Authority *1.* Permission to act. *2.* Power to act. *3.* Legal right to act. *4.* See **authorities.** *5.* For **apparent, binding, express, implied,** and **persuasive** *authority,* see those words.

Authorization card A form signed by a worker giving a **union** the right to represent him or her. If a union gets a majority of employees to sign cards, the company must usually deal with that union in **collective bargaining.** Another way a union can get these rights is through an *authorization election.*

Authorize Give the right to act. "*Authorized*" means officially permitted. For example, a corporation's *authorized issue* is the maximum number of stock shares it is permitted to **issue** under its **articles of incorporation.** And a nonlawyer may be *authorized* to perform some of the services normally considered the **practice** *of law* (see **unauthorized practice of law**).

Autocracy A form of government in which one person has total power over a country.

Automated litigation support The creation, management, and use of computerized databases to support such activities as the preservation, search, and retrieval of hard copy documents, **deposition** annotation, trial presentation and analysis, etc.

Autopsy Examination of a dead body to find out the cause of death.

Autoptic evidence Demonstrative evidence.

Autre (or auter) (French) Another. For example, "*autre vie*" means "during another person's lifetime," and "*autre droit*" means "in another's right" or for another person. [pronounce: <u>oh</u>-tr vee; oh-tr <u>dwa</u>]

Autrefois acquit (or convict) (French) Previously **acquitted** (or **convicted**). A person cannot be tried for a crime for which he or she has already been acquitted or convicted. See **double jeopardy.**

Auxiliary Aiding, **subsidiary, ancillary.**

Avails Profits or **proceeds.**

Aver Declare, assert, **allege,** set out clearly and formally.

Average *1.* A general mathematical term that can mean the *mean,* the *median,* or the *mode* (see those words in a good general dictionary). When used in a contract without further definition, the meaning of *average* may be obvious from the context of the contract or from the general use of the word in the trade, or it may be so vague as to make the contract fail. *2.* For **general** and **particular average loss,** terms in marine **insurance,** see those words.

Averment Statement of facts.

Avigational easement   **Air rights.**

Avoidable consequences doctrine   See the *doctrine of* **mitigation of damages.**

Avoidance   *1.* Escaping or evading. Compare **evasion** for an important tax difference. *2.* In **pleading,** admitting facts in the other side's pleadings while showing why these facts should not have the legal effect intended. Also called *confession and avoidance. 3.* **Annulling** or canceling.

Avowal   An offer of **proof** (made out of the **jury's** hearing) in order to have it just in case an **appeals** court says that the witness should have been allowed to **testify** before the jury.

Avulsion   The sudden loss or gain of land, such as when a storm tears away part of a riverbank and deposits land on the other side. Compare with **accretion.**

Award   *1.* To give or grant by formal process. For example, a jury *awards* **damages** and a company *awards* a **contract** to a bidder. *2.* The decision of an **arbitrator** or other nonjudge in a dispute submitted to him or her.

Axiom   A basic truth or principle from which others are deduced.

B.A.C.   Blood alcohol concentration.

B.B.B.   **Better Business Bureau.**

B.F.   Old abbreviation for the Latin "bona fides" (good faith); also for "bonum factum" (a good act). This meant "approved."

B.F.O.Q. (or B.F.Q.)   "Bona fide occupational qualification." An employer's legitimate need to discriminate in hiring based on race, sex, age, etc. There are very few B.F.O.Q.'s permitted.

B.F.P.   **Bona fide** purchaser.

B.I.A.   Bureau of Indian Affairs. The branch of the U.S. **Interior** Department that acts as **trustee** for Indian lands and handles most programs for Native Americans not handled by the *Administration for Native Americans* of **H.H.S.**

B.J.   Bar Journal.

B.L.M.   Bureau of Land Management. An agency of the U.S Department of the Interior that manages huge amounts of (mostly Western) U.S. public lands and its mineral rights.

B.N.A.   Bureau of National Affairs. A publisher of **looseleaf services** in specialty areas of the law.

Baby act   "*Pleading the baby act*" means using a persons **minority** (underage) as a **defense** against a lawsuit based on a contract made by the minor.

Baby Doe   The young child equivalent of Jane or **John Doe** (see that word).

Bachelor of Laws   See **L.L.B.**

Back   *1.* To **indorse,** sign, or assume financial responsibility for something; for example, cosigning a loan **note.** *2.* To supply money for a business venture.

Backbond   A bond given by a person to the **surety** (see that word) who backs the person's debt. For example, when John promises to pay Mary's debt to Sue if Mary fails to pay it, Mary may give a *backbond* to John, promising to repay any losses.

Backdoor spending   Government spending, and entering into obligations for future spending, that is not a direct part of an **appropriation** and, thus, is not directly controllable each year by the **legislature.**

Back-end load Charging a large part of the commissions and selling costs at the *end* of a deal to buy insurance, to invest in a mutual fund, to lease property, etc.

Backwardation (or backadation) Paying money to postpone the delivery of (and full payment for) purchased stock.

Bad debt A debt that has become uncollectable. There are different rules for tax **deductions** based on business, investment, and personal bad debts. A typical business bad debt might be an unsecured bank loan with no monthly payments made for several months despite collection efforts.

Bad faith Dishonesty or other failure to deal fairly with another person. *Bad faith* need not involve **fraud**. See **good faith**.

Bad law A judicial decision or administrative ruling that fails to follow **precedent** (see that word) or fails to comply with a statute or regulation.

Bad person test The idea that the best way to know what a law means is to see how a bad person "interprets" it through behavior: carefully figuring out what the law allows and pushing its limits.

Bad tendency A test for whether free speech should be limited because it might lead to action that is illegal and dangerous. This test has been replaced by the **clear and present danger test.**

Badge of fraud A strong suspicion of fraud. The phrase is usually used when examining a transfer of property to see if it is a fake used to keep the property away from **creditors.** In this case a *badge of fraud* might be a hurried sale of property made to a relative to avoid a creditor's claims on the property.

Bail *1.* A person who puts up money or property to allow the release of a person from jail. *2.* The money or property put up by the person in no. 1. This money, often in the form of a **bail bond,** may be lost if the person released does not appear in court. *3.* The process of releasing the person for whom a bail bond was supplied.

Bail bond A written statement of debt that is put up by an arrested person and others who back it up. It promises that the arrested person will show up in court or risk losing the amount of the bond.

Bail jumping See **jump bail.**

Bailee A person to whom property is loaned or otherwise entrusted. See **bailment.**

Bailiff *1.* A sheriff's deputy or a court official who keeps the peace in court. *2.* Any of several low-level officials. *3.* A superintendent or steward.

Bailment   A temporary delivery of property by the owner into another person's custody (keeping). Examples of *bailments* include: the loan of a book to a friend, the storage of property in a commercial warehouse, the repair of an automobile in a repair shop, etc. A *bailment for term* is a delivery of property for a set length of time.

Bailor   A person who entrusts property to another. See **bailment**.

Bail-out   *1.* Any situation in which one person saves another from financial loss. *2.* A conversion of **ordinary** *income* to capital gains (see **capital** *gains tax*), or any other attempt by the owner of a business to get better tax treatment of profits.

Bait and switch   Advertising one item to get people to come into a store and then persuading them to buy a different item. This may be illegal if the original item was never really available or if it was not really as advertised.

Bajakajian v. U.S.   (524 U.S. 321) The 1998 U.S. Supreme Court decision that forfeiture of an amount of money grossly disproportionate to the seriousness of the crime for which the person was convicted violates the excess fines clause of the **Eighth Amendment**.

Baker v. Carr   (369 U.S. 186) A 1962 Supreme Court decision that started a series of cases requiring "one person, one vote" standards for the **reapportionment** of all state and federal election **districts**.

Balance   *1.* An amount left over. For example, the difference between a debt and the payments already made on the debt is called a *balance due.* In bookkeeping a *balance* is the difference between the amounts in the **debit** and **credit** columns. If the debit total is larger, the account has a *debit balance.* *2.* Equality of the *credit* and *debit* columns in an account. If the two columns add up to the same amount, the account is said to be "*in balance*" or "*balanced.*"

Balance of payments   **Balance of trade** plus certain other financial transactions such as international loans.

Balance of trade   The value of exports to a country minus the imports from it.

Balance sheet   A complete summary of the financial worth of a company, broken down by **assets** and **liabilities** (see those words) which balance each other. A corporation's annual balance sheet will show what it owns and owes as of a given day and will include **stockholder's equity** as a separate item. Also called *statement of financial condition (or position).* Also see **statement**.

Balanced portfolio   Investments that are spread among stocks, bonds, and other investments to have some with the potential for higher gains and others with lower risks. A *balanced fund* is a **mutual** fund that does the same thing.

Balancing test *1.* A **doctrine** in **constitutional law** that says a court should balance constitutional rights such as *free speech* against the right of the government to control conduct it calls harmful. The court should decide for the side with more important needs in each individual situation. The doctrine says that no rights are **absolute.** *2.* Any judicial decision-making principle that "balances" rights or responsibilities.

Balloon loan A loan in which the last payment, known as the *balloon payment,* is much larger than any of the regular payments. The loan structure may make the borrower think that low payments will pay off the debt, but the installment payments often pay only interest, leaving a large balloon payment of **principal** that may need to be **refinanced.** The federal Truth-in-Lending law requires the clear disclosure of a balloon payment, and many state laws prohibit them to consumers.

Ballot *1.* Pieces of paper or other objects or recording methods used to cast a (usually secret) vote in an election. *2.* The total vote in an election. *3.* A list of candidates running for office.

Ban *1.* An old word for a public notice or proclamation of an intended marriage, a law, a public command, a fine, etc. *2.* Now, a prohibition.

Banc (French) Bench; place where the court normally does business. An **appellate** court sits "*en banc*" (or "*in banc*") when all the judges of the court participate in the court's decision.

Banishment See **deportation.**

Bank *1.* A commercial business that the laws allow to receive deposits, make loans, and perform other money-related functions. *2.* See **banc.** *3.* For *bank book,* see **passbook.** A *bank bill* or *bank note* is a document that promises to pay a certain sum of money to the **bearer** on *demand. Bank credit* is a written promise by a bank that a person may borrow up to a certain amount from the bank. A *bank draft* is a check or similar document made out by a bank officer to take out funds from the bank or from another bank where the bank has funds. *Bank paper* is a commercial document (such as a bank note or *bill of* **exchange**) good enough to be bought by a bank or used as **collateral** for a bank loan.

Bank Holding Company Act (12 U.S.C. 1841) A federal law that places restrictions on companies that have partial control of more than one bank.

Bank Secrecy Act (12 U.S.C. 1951) A federal law that requires banks to report all large cash transfers, requires persons to report all carrying or sending of large amounts of money in or out of the country, and to report on any foreign bank accounts.

Banker's lien   A bank's right to take for its own the money or property left in its care by a customer if the customer owes an overdue debt to the bank and if the money, to the bank's knowledge, belongs fully to the customer.

Bankrupt   A person going through a **bankruptcy** proceeding.

Bankruptcy   The procedure, under the Federal Bankruptcy Act (11 U.S.C. 101), by which a person is relieved of all debts (except for **secured** debts, **fraudulent** debts, and certain other debts) once the person has placed all property and money under the court's supervision, or the procedure by which an organization in financial trouble is either restructured by the court or ended and turned into cash to pay **creditors** and owners. *Bankruptcy* is a legal word and, while triggered by **insolvency** (see that word), the two words do not mean the same thing. A bankruptcy can be *voluntary* (started by the person in financial trouble) or *involuntary* (started by the person's creditors). Bankruptcies are handled by the **federal courts.** A typical bankruptcy involves a **trustee** appointed by the court who takes charge of the **bankrupt's** property, gets a list from the bankrupt of all debts owed, and distributes the property proportionally among those creditors who **file** and prove their claims. When this is done, the court allows the bankrupt to keep some personal property and grants a **discharge** which frees the bankrupt from listed debts that qualify. This is done under **Chapter Seven** of the Bankruptcy Act. See also **Chapter Nine** for local government debt adjustment, **Chapter Eleven** for business reorganizations short of full bankruptcy, **Chapter Twelve** for family farmer debt adjustment, and **Chapter Thirteen** for personal and small business "partial" bankruptcies with special plans.

Bar   *1.* The entire group of lawyers permitted to practice law before a particular court or in a particular **jurisdiction.** *2.* The part of some courtrooms where prisoners stand. *3.* The court itself or the judge at work in court. See **at bar.** *4.* A barrier or prohibition.

Bar act   A state law that sets up what a lawyer may and may not do.

Bar association   A voluntary group of lawyers, as opposed to a group of lawyers who are required to be members of a court's **integrated bar** (see that word). There are bar associations on the national, state, and local levels, and bar associations of specialists in particular legal fields.

Bar examination   A written test that a lawyer must pass in order to practice law. Some states use the "multi-state" exam and some rely on their own tests or a combination of the two.

Bar treaty   An agreement between lawyers and other occupations about activities that will not be considered **unauthorized practice of law.**

Bare   With very limited legal rights, duties, effect, or protection. See also **naked** and **nude.**

Bareboat charter   Rental or lease of a boat without a crew and, usually, assuming full responsibility for the boat.

Bargain   A mutual understanding, **contract,** or agreement.

Bargain and sale   *1.* An old two-step method of transferring land ownership, which is now an ordinary sale with full transfer of **title.** *2.* A sale **deed** with no title **warranties.** See **quitclaim deed.**

Bargaining agent   A **union** that has the exclusive right to represent all the employees of a certain type at a company.

Bargaining unit   Those employees in a company who are best suited to be treated as one group for purposes of being represented by a union. The workers must have a "mutuality of interest."

Barometer   A business index (such as the unemployment rate) that shows general economic trends; or a stock that tends to go up (or down) in price when the general stock market goes up (or down).

Barratry   *1.* The offense of stirring up quarrels or lawsuits (usually applied to a lawyer's trying to stir up a lawsuit from which the lawyer can profit). *2.* A **fraudulent** or illegal act done by a captain or crew of a ship that harms the ship's owner or the owners of the ship's cargo.

Barrister   *1.* An English lawyer who argues in actual court trials. Compare with **solicitor.** *2.* A lawyer.

Barter   An exchange of things (or services) for other things, as opposed to a sale of things for money.

Base   *1.* Inferior or subordinate; mixed or impure. *2.* Basic or underlying; that upon which something is added or calculated. For example, a *base period* is a minimum time something must happen before something else can legally happen, or it is a standard time period used for financial comparisons and calculations.

Basement court   (Slang) Traffic, small claims, or other low-level court.

Basic form (or policy)   A standard **home owners' policy** that covers the most common insurable risks to a home.

Basic patent   An entirely new and unpredicted process or product. A **patent** that may open up a whole new field of discovery. A pioneer patent.

Basis   In tax law, a property's cost for tax purposes. To see how this cost may not be the same as the purchase price, and to see how *basis* may change during ownership or upon transfer, see **adjusted basis, carryover basis, step-up basis,** and **substituted basis.**

Basis point 1 percent of 1 percent (.0001)

Basket buy One purchase of several different things for one price.

Bastardy action Same as **paternity suit.**

Bath (Slang). A big loss. "*Taking a bath*" is losing big in a **stock** or business deal, and a "*big bath*" is a company's abandoning of an unprofitable line of business and taking a **writeoff** for taxes.

Batson challenge A defendant's claim (from the 1986 case *Batson v. Kentucky,* 476 U.S. 79) that the prosecutor has used a **peremptory** *challenge* to exclude a juror based on race. This type of challenge has since been extended to **civil** cases.

Battered (or abused) child syndrome A pattern of continuing injuries that could not be accidental, so they, and the physical and psychological harm they cause, are presumed to be caused by a person close to the child.

Battered (or abused) woman (or wife) syndrome Continuing **abuse** of a woman by a spouse or lover, and the resulting physical or psychological harm.

Battery An intentional, unconsented to, physical contact by one person (or an object controlled by that person) with another person. It can be a **crime** or a **tort.** Compare with **assault.**

Battle of the forms The attempts by a buyer and a seller to indirectly make the sales contract favor their side by the "fine print" on the forms they alternately exchange to make the deal.

Bear arms See **arms, right to.**

Bear market A large, long-term drop in stock or other security prices. A "*bear*" is someone who thinks the market will fall. Compare with **bull market.**

Bear raiding An illegal attempt by a group of investors to drive down the price of a stock by a rapid series of sales.

Bearer A person in possession of a **negotiable instrument** (for example, a check) that is made out "payable to bearer," that is indorsed in **blank** (signed, but no name filled in on the "payable to" line), or that is made out to "cash" or other indication that no one specific person is meant to cash it.

Bearer instrument (or paper) A check or other financial document as described in **bearer** (see that word).

Before and after rule   A way of measuring the value of real estate when part of the land is taken for public use. You subtract the **market value** of the property remaining from the market value of the whole property before the taking.

Behoof   Old word meaning "use" or "benefit."

Belief   A sense of firmness about the truth of an idea that lies somewhere between "suspicion" and "knowledge."

Belief-action rule   The principle that a person may believe anything without restriction, but when belief turns into action, that action is only sometimes protected by the **Constitution.** See **symbolic speech.**

Belligerent   *1.* A country at war with another country, as opposed to a neutral country that takes no part. *2.* Rebels who have organized a government while they fight, so that their war is considered lawful by international standards.

Below   Lower; usually refers to a lower court.

Bench   *1.* The place where judges sit in court. *2.* Judges collectively are "the bench."

Bench conference   A private meeting at the judge's **bench** among the judge, lawyers for both sides of a case, and sometimes the **parties.** It is often called to discuss something out of the jury's hearing, and it may or may not be made part of the **record** of the case.

Bench memo   Either a short **brief** on an issue raised during a trial or a legal memorandum prepared for a judge by the judge's clerk.

Bench warrant   A paper (sometimes called **capias**) issued directly by a judge to the police or other **peace officers** ordering the arrest of a person.

Beneficial   Giving a profit or advantage. [pronounce: ben-eh-<u>fish</u>-al]

Beneficial association (or company, corporation, or society)   See **nonprofit organization.**

Beneficial interest (or use)   The right to profits resulting from a **trust,** contract, **estate,** or property rather than the legal ownership of these things.

Beneficiary   *1.* A person (or organization, etc.) for whose benefit a **trust** is created. *2.* A person to whom an **insurance** policy is payable. *3.* A person who inherits under a **will.** *4.* Anyone who benefits from something or who is treated as the real owner of something for tax or other purposes. See, for example, **creditor beneficiary.** [pronounce: ben-eh-<u>fish</u>-ee-ary]

Benefit   *1.* Any advantage, profit, or privilege. *2.* Money paid by an insurance company, by a retirement plan, by an employer (other than wages), etc.

Benefit (or be<u>nev</u>olent) association (or company, corporation, or society) See **nonprofit organization.**

Benefit of bargain rule The principle that in some lawsuits where the value of an item was _promised_ to be a certain amount, the buyer can get the difference between the promised value and the real value. In normal lawsuits based on **fraud** in the sale of something for more than it is worth, the buyer can get only the difference between what was paid and what the item is really worth.

Benefit of cession The right that some **debtors** had in old England to avoid imprisonment for debts if the debtor turned over all property to the **creditors.** [pronounce: session]

Benefit of clergy _1._ The right that clergymen had in old England to avoid trial by all nonchurch courts. _2._ "_With benefit of clergy_" means formally married.

Benefit-security ratio The money a pension plan must pay out compared to what it has set aside to make the payments.

Bequeath _1._ Give **personal** property or money (as opposed to real estate) by **will.** _2._ Give anything by will. Compare with **devise.**

Bequest _1._ A gift by will of personal property. _2._ Any gift by will.

Berne Convention An international treaty that protects the copyrighted works of citizens of one signatory country in all the other countries that sign.

Best efforts More than **good faith** efforts, but less than a promise, to do a thing. "_Best efforts_" of an **underwriter** do not include the usual underwriter's obligation to buy any unsold **securities.**

Best evidence rule A rule of **evidence** law that often requires that the most reliable available proof of a fact must be produced. For example, if a painting (best _primary evidence_) is available as evidence, a photograph of the painting _(secondary evidence)_ may not do.

Best use **Highest and best use.**

Bestiality Sexual intercourse between a human and an animal, a crime in most states.

Bestow Give or **grant** something.

Beta A measure of how closely the value of a **stock** (and the money it pays its owners) parallels that of the stock market generally. _Beta_ figures are often used to describe the variability of an entire **portfolio** of stocks. [pronounce: bay-ta]

Better Business Bureau A local business-supported organization that handles complaints about business practices, provides consumer information, and generally promotes ethical business dealings. National standards and support for these local bureaus are provided by the Council of Better Business Bureaus.

Betterment *1.* An **improvement** rather than a **repair.** *2.* A *betterment (or occupying claimant) act* is a law that permits a tenant (or other **good faith** occupant of a building or land) to recover from the landlord (or owner) the cost of necessary permanent improvements made to the property (once the occupant has moved out). *Betterment theory* is the principle that these costs may be recovered without a law specifically permitting it.

Beyond a reasonable doubt The level of proof required to **convict** a person of a crime. For a **jury** to be convinced "*beyond a reasonable doubt,*" it must be fully satisfied that the person is guilty. This is the highest level of proof required in any type of trial. It does not mean "convinced 100 percent," but it comes close to that meaning.

Beyond (legal) memory Ancient (see that word).

Biannual Either twice a year (as a synonym for semiannual) or once every other year (as a synonym for one meaning of **biennial**). Scholars have fistfights over this, so define the word if you use it. [pronounce: bi-<u>an</u>-you-ell]

Bias *1.* A preconceived opinion that makes it difficult to be impartial. *2.* A preconceived opinion by the judge about one or more of the persons involved in a lawsuit, as opposed to an opinion about the subject matter.

Bias crime **Hate** *crime.*

Bicameral Having two chambers. A two-part **legislature,** such as the U.S. Congress, is *bicameral:* composed of the Senate (the "*upper house*" or "*upper chamber*") and the House of Representatives (the "*lower house*" or "*lower chamber*").

Bid *1.* An offer to pay a specific price at an auction. *Bidding up* or *by-bidding* is artificially raising the price at an auction by an insider who has no real intention of actually buying. *2.* An offer to perform work or supply goods at a given price. An *open bid* reserves the right to reduce the price to meet the competition. *3.* An application for a new job with your current employer.

Bid and asked The range of prices quoted in an **over-the-counter** exchange of **stock.** *Bid* is the selling price and *asked* is the purchase price. The difference is dealer profit. Another way of looking at it is that *asked* is the average price requested by those persons recently willing to sell and *bid* is the average price offered by those persons recently willing to buy.

Bid in   An owner's bid at an auction to prevent a sale at too low a price, or an owner's purchase at a **foreclosure** sale.

Bid shopping   Disclosing low bids on **contract** work in order to get lower bids from others.

Biennial   Either once every two years (compare **biannual**) or lasting for two years (a "biennium"). [pronounce: bi-<u>enny</u>-al]

Biennium   A two-year period. A spending period for a state with a **legislature** that meets only once every two years.

Bifurcated trial   Separate hearings for different issues in the same case; for example, for guilt and sanity or guilt and punishment in a criminal trial, or for **liability** and **damages** in a complicated auto injury trial.

Big board   A popular term for the display that lists **stock** prices at the New York Stock Exchange.

Big Six   The six largest U.S. accounting firms.

Bigamy   The crime of being married to two or more husbands or wives at the same time.

Bilateral contract   A deal that involves promises, **rights,** and **duties** on both sides. For example, a contract to sell a car is _bilateral_ because one person promises to transfer ownership of the car and the other person promises to pay for it. See **contract** for the difference between bilateral and **unilateral** contracts.

Bilateral mistake   **Mutual mistake.**

Bill   _1._ A formal written statement sent to a higher court, either to inform it of certain facts or to request certain actions. For example, a _bill of exceptions_ is a list of objections to the rulings and actions of the trial judge by one side. _2._ A **draft** of a law proposed to a **legislature** or working its way through the legislature. _3._ A law passed by a legislature when it proceeds like a court; for example, a _bill of_ **impeachment.** _4._ An unusually important declaration; for example, the **Bill of Rights** (see that word). _5._ A list of debts, contract terms, or items; for example, a _bill of lading_ (list of goods shipped). _6._ A type of **negotiable instrument** (see that word), promising the payment of money; for example, a _bill of exchange_ (a written **order** from A to B, telling B to pay C a certain sum of money). _7._ A statement of details in court; for example, a _bill of particulars_ (a breakdown of one side's demands against the other in a lawsuit) or a _bill of indictment_ (the formal accusation of a crime presented to a grand jury). _8._ The old word for the first court paper in an **equity** trial. The modern word for the first **pleading** is often "**complaint.**"

Bill of at<u>tain</u>der   See **attainder.**

Bill of lading   A document given by a railroad, shipping company, or other **carrier** that lists the goods accepted for transport and sometimes lists the terms of the shipping agreement. Some of the laws concerning bills of lading are found in Article 7 of the **Uniform Commercial Code,** the Federal Bills of Lading Acts, and the **Interstate Commerce Act.**

Bill of pains and penalties   Similar to a *bill of* **attainder** (see that word), but with lesser punishment. It is prohibited by the Constitution.

Bill of particulars   A detailed, formal, written statement of charges or claims by a **plaintiff** or the **prosecutor** (given upon the **defendant's** formal request to the court for more detailed information). See also **motion** *for more definite statement.*

Bill of review   A request that a court **set aside** a prior **decree.** It is a new **suit,** not a reopening of the old one.

Bill of Rights   The first ten **amendments** (changes or additions) to the U.S. **Constitution:** *First,* **freedom of speech,** religion, press, assembly, and to petition the government; *Second,* the right to keep weapons; *Third,* freedom from being forced to give room or board to soldiers; *Fourth,* freedom from unreasonable searches and seizures and the requirement that **warrants** be supported by **probable cause;** *Fifth,* the requirement that crimes be **indicted,** the prohibition against **double jeopardy,** the freedom from being a witness against yourself in a criminal trial, and the requirement that no rights or property be taken away without **due process of law** and just compensation; *Sixth,* the rights to a speedy criminal trial, an impartial jury, knowledge of the charges, **confrontation** of adverse witnesses, **compulsory process** of witnesses, and the help of a lawyer; *Seventh,* the right to a jury trial in most civil cases; *Eighth,* the prohibitions against excessive **bail,** excessive fines, and cruel and unusual punishment; *Ninth,* the fact that some rights are spelled out in the Constitution does not mean that these are all the rights the people have; *Tenth,* any powers not kept solely for the U.S. belong to the states and to the people.

Billable hour   A unit of time that can be charged to clients. Law firms often divide the hour into fifteen-, ten-, or six-minute pieces and charge a client for the whole piece if most of it is used for the client's work.

Billing cycle   The regular time interval (often one month) between dates when bills are sent out to customers.

Bind   *1.* Hold by legal obligation. *2.* See **binding over.** [pronounce "bi" as "by"]

Binder *1.* A temporary, preliminary **insurance** contract. *2.* The agreement made when a deposit is paid on a home purchase.

Binding authority Sources of law that *must* be taken into account by a judge in deciding a case; for example, **statutes** from the same state or decisions by a higher court of the same state.

Binding instructions A judge's formal, written instructions to the jury, usually given after the prosecution and defense have both "rested their cases," explaining the boundaries within which the jury must make its **findings.** Many instructions state that the jury must decide the *case* or an *issue* a certain way if it decides that certain *facts* are true.

Binding over *1.* An act by which the court requires a **bond** or **bail** money. *2.* An act by which a court transfers a criminal defendant to another court in the same system. *3.* Ordering that a criminal defendant be placed in jail pending the outcome of a hearing or trial.

Bipartisan *1.* Describes something agreed to by either large numbers of Democratic and Republican politicians or by their leadership. *2.* Describes a government board or commission that by law must be composed of equal numbers of Republicans and Democrats.

Bkpt. Abbreviation for **bankrupt.**

B/L **Bill** *of lading.*

Black Acre A fictional piece of real estate used in teaching law; often used together with "White Acre."

Black code The pre–Civil War laws of southern states that controlled the conduct of slaves and regulated slavery.

Black letter law Important basic legal principles, rules, or laws that are accepted by most judges in most states or that are well accepted in a particular state.

Black Lung Act A federal law providing for payments and treatment for coal miners with black lung disease.

Black market The sale of goods that are stolen, prohibited, or under government control and taxation without submitting to that control.

Blacklist A list of persons to be avoided, such as a list circulated by merchants of persons who cannot be counted on to pay their bills.

Blackmail Illegal pressure or **extortion** of money by threatening to expose a person's illegal or embarrassing act. Some states require the threat to be in writing for it to be the crime of *blackmail* and not just **extortion.**

Blackstonian doctrine The principle that courts do not create the law but merely discover and announce it.

Blank *1.* A space left in a written or printed document, especially a space that is to be filled in. *2.* A printed document (a "form") with spaces to be filled in.

Blank check offering See **shell company.**

Blank indorsement Signing a **negotiable instrument,** such as a check, without specifying to whom it is being signed over (leaving a blank in that space) and thus not limiting who can cash it.

Blanket Covering most (or many) things. For example, a *blanket search warrant* is either a **search warrant** to search several places or an **unconstitutional** search warrant that permits taking everything found without specifying the things that may be seized.

Blasphemy Cursing or ridiculing God or the majority religion. Antiblasphemy laws violate the *establishment of religion clause* of the **First Amendment** to the U.S. **Constitution.**

Blind trust An arrangement in which a person turns over management of his or her investments to another and ceases to know the specific investment choices. Government officials often do this to avoid **conflict of interest.**

Block positioning A **broker's** buying a part of a large block of **stock** from a client (because all of it cannot be sold immediately) and then selling it off piece by piece.

Blockage rule A tax rule that sometimes allows the valuation of a large block of **stock** at less than the sum of the values of the individual **shares** of stock, because it is often hard to sell large blocks all at once without driving down the value of the stock.

Blockbusting Convincing owners to sell their homes because another ethnic group is rumored to be moving into the area. This may be illegal if done by real estate agents.

Blocked *1.* Money is "*blocked*" when there are government restrictions on taking it out of the country or exchanging it for foreign currency. *2.* "*Blocked*" also refers to bank accounts, checks, and other financial things that are temporarily kept from payment for any reason.

Blotter *1.* The police record form for **booking** (see that word) a **defendant.** Also, the cumulative record of arrests and other events kept by the police. *2.* See **waste-book.**

Blue Book *1.* A book or pamphlet showing the proper form of legal **citation,** usually the *Uniform System of Citation.* *2.* The **A.L.R.** *Bluebook of Supplemental Decisions* that updates A.L.R. **annotations.** *3.* Many other books and pamphlets, such as a list of the organizations and employees of a state government or a book of estimated prices for used cars.

Blue chip   Describes a large company with a history of stability and profits; also, the stock of such a company.

Blue flu   Coordinated calling in sick by police officers. This is done in place of a strike because, in most places, police officers are not allowed to strike. Other city employees have similar names for similar **job actions.**

Blue law   A state or local law that forbids selling or other activities on Sunday; originally, any law based on religious restrictions.

Blue list   Daily listing of **municipal** bond offerings.

Blue pencil doctrine   The principle that a court can "scratch out" an illegal or unreasonable part of a contract and enforce the rest. This principle is of very limited applicability.

Blue ribbon jury   A **jury** specially chosen to try important or complex cases. This practice is rarely permitted.

Blue sky bargaining   Making obviously unreasonable demands at the start of a negotiating session, often to impress those you represent, to delay real "nuts and bolts" discussions, or to set a far-out basis for later compromise.

Blue sky law   Any state law **regulating** sales of **stock** or other investment activities to protect the public from fly-by-night or **fraudulent** stock deals, or to ensure that an investor gets enough information to make a reasoned purchase of stock or other **security.**

Board   *1.* A publicly appointed or elected group of persons chosen to oversee a public function. For example, a *board of alderpersons* is the governing body of some local governments; a *board of supervisors* runs some county governments; a *board of elections* runs many elections; the *Board of Patent Appeals* reviews decisions in **patent** application cases; and a state professional *licensing board* examines the qualifications of various specialists. *2.* A private governing body or other more "loosely knit" governing organization. For example, a *board of directors* is the group that, along with the **officers,** runs a corporation, and a *board of trade* is an association of merchants with common interests.

Board certified   Formally qualified as a specialist. Lawyers can be certified in particular areas of legal practice, usually by having proven experience in the field and passing a test given by the "specialization board" of a state bar association.

Board lot   **Round lot.**

Boarder A person who pays for regular meals (or meals plus a room) in a house.

Body *1.* A person or an organization, such as a "*body corporate*" (a **corporation**). *2.* The main or most important part of a document. *3.* A collection of laws.

Body execution Legal authority to deprive a person of freedom and to jail the person.

Body heirs Children, grandchildren, etc. (but not adopted ones).

Body of the crime See **corpus delicti.**

Body politic (or corporate) The government; the citizens of a government as a group; a city, state, county, or even a school district.

Bogus False and intended to deceive. For example, a "*bogus check*" is a check given by a person who has no active account at the bank named on the check.

Boiler room sales High-pressure sales of **stock,** often of doubtful value, usually by telephone.

Boilerplate Standardized, recurring language found in a document or a form for a document, such as those sold in formbooks. The word implies standardization or lack of tailoring to the individual legal problem.

Bolstering Using **evidence** or **testimony** to add credibility to prior evidence or testimony that has not been disputed. This is usually not permitted.

Bona (Latin) *1.* Goods, property, or possessions, as in *bona vacantia* (unclaimed abandoned goods). *2.* Good. As in **bona fide.**

Bona fide (Latin) Good faith; honest; real. For example, a *bona fide purchaser* in commercial law is a person who buys something honestly, pays good value, and knows of no other person's claim to the thing bought. For *bona fide occupational qualification,* see **B.F.O.Q.**

Bona immobilia (Latin) Immovable property or land.

Bond *1.* A document that states a debt owed by a company or a government. The company, government, or government agency promises to pay the owner of the bond a specific amount of interest for a set period of time and to repay the debt on a certain date. A bond, unlike a **stock,** gives the holder no ownership rights in the company. Examples of this type of bond include: *adjustment bond* (**issued** when a corporation is reorganized); *convertible bond* (can be turned into stock); *coupon bond* (with coupons that are clipped and presented for payment of interest); *debenture bond* (backed by the general credit of a company or government, rather than by specific property); *guaran-*

teed bond (backed by a company other than the one that put it out); *industrial development bond* (put out by a local government to build business facilities that are then leased to pay off the bond); *municipal bond* (put out by state, county, or local governments to finance government projects); *registered bond* (the bond owner's name is on file with the company); *serial bond* (any of several bonds issued at the same time with different payback times); *series bond* (any of several bonds of the same exact type, but put out at intervals); *term bond* (all of which come due at the same time); and *U.S. savings bond. 2.* A document that promises to pay money if a particular future event happens, or a sum of money that is put up and will be lost if that event happens. Examples of this type of bond include: *appeal bond* (to cover the costs of the other side if the judge orders it when an **appeal** is filed); *attachment bond* (used to get back property that has been attached [see **attachment**] and to guarantee that the person who attached it will be paid if you lose the lawsuit concerning the property); *completion bond* (to make sure that a person finishes a job properly and within a time limit); *fidelity bond* (used to protect a business against an employee's stealing); **peace bond** (see that word); and *submission bond* (to ensure that a dispute will be submitted to binding **arbitration**). *3.* Other words frequently used when discussing bonds are: *bond conversion* (exchanging bonds for stock); *bond discount* (the amount a bond sells for that is cheaper than its **face** price); *bond issue* (all the bonds put out at one time); *bond premium* (the amount a bond sells for that is more expensive than its face price); and *bond rating* (the appraisal of soundness and value given to bonds by one of several rating companies such as Standard and Poor's or Moody's. Rating systems differ, but the highest rating given by Moody's is AAA and their lowest rating of an "investment quality" bond is Baa.

Bonded warehouse   A special storage place for goods that are held until a federal tax is paid for the right to sell the goods. Bonded warehouses are used for alcoholic beverages and for imported goods stored for possible exportation.

Bondsman (or bondswoman)   Any person who "puts up" or "posts" a bond, especially a **bail bond** for another person, usually for a fee.

Bonification   A **waiving** of taxes, especially on export goods.

Book entry   *1.* Ownership of **securities** recorded "on the books" of a brokerage firm, with the customer getting transaction confirmations and monthly statements, but not ownership **certificates**. See also **street name**.   *2.* Anything written in an **accounting** record.

Book value *1.* Net worth; clearly proven **assets** minus **liabilities.** *2.* The worth of something as recorded on a company's **financial statement.** *3.* Cost minus **depreciation.**

Booking The writing down, by the police, of facts about a person's arrest and charges along with identification and background information. This is recorded on the police **blotter** in the police station. Sometimes "*booking*" includes questioning the person and setting bail.

Bookkeeping Writing down the financial transactions of a business in a systematic way.

Boolean search A database search that includes or excludes words by specifying AND, OR, NOT, etc.

Boot Something extra thrown into a bargain. In tax law, the taxable part of an otherwise nontaxable deal such as a **like-kind exchange.**

Bootstrap sale Using the **assets** of a newly bought company to pay part of the cost of buying the company.

Borough A division of land within a state ranging from very big to very small, depending on the state. It may be equivalent to a **county,** a **town,** or other things. [pronounce: burr-oh]

Borrowed servant rule The principle that if one employer "loans" an employee to another, the "borrowing" employer is **liable** for that employee's actions. Some states apply the rule only if the "loaning" employer gives up all control over the employee.

Bottomry A loan using a boat as **security,** often to repair or equip the boat.

Bought and sold notes A **broker's** notifications to a buyer and a seller that a transaction has taken place.

Boulevard rule The principle that a driver entering a main road from a side road must yield right-of-way to main road traffic.

Bowers v. Hardwick (478 U.S. 186) The 1986 U.S. Supreme Court decision that permitted states to regulate some private sexual relations between consenting adults.

Boycott The refusal to do business with and the attempt to stop others from doing business with a company. In labor law, a *primary boycott* involves a union and an employer while a *secondary boycott* involves companies that do business with (usually by buying from) the union's employer.

Bracket See **tax bracket.**

Brady material Information, known to the prosecutor, that is favorable to a criminal defendant's case. *Brady material* must be disclosed to the defense.

Brain death rule According to this rule a person is dead if the brain has totally and irreversibly stopped functioning, even if other bodily processes still go on without outside help. For a person to be brain dead there must be no response to external stimuli; no spontaneous movements, breathing, or reflexes; and a flat reading for a full day on a machine that measures the brain's electrical activity.

Brandeis brief A **brief** (see that word) in a lawsuit, usually on **appeal,** that includes information about economic and sociological studies in addition to the usual legal material.

Breach Breaking a law or failing to perform a duty. [pronounce: breech]

Breach of close See **quare.**

Breach of contract Failure, without legal excuse, to live up to a significant promise made in a **contract.** Breach also includes refusing to perform your part of the bargain or making it hard for the other person to perform his or her part of the bargain.

Breach of promise Short for "breach of promise to marry." See **heartbalm acts** for its legal effect.

Breach of the peace A vague term for any illegal public disturbance; sometimes refers to the offense known as "disorderly conduct." It is defined and treated differently in different states.

Breach of trust The failure of a **trustee** to do something that is required by the **trust.** This includes conducting trust business illegally, **negligently,** or even forgetfully.

Breaking Using force or some kind of destruction of property (including things that do not permanently destroy, such as picking a lock), usually to illegally get into a building by *breaking and entering.*

Breaking a case *1.* Solving a crime. *2.* An informal agreement among appeals court judges as to which judges, at least temporarily, favor the **appellant** and which favor the **appellee.** This helps decide who will write the **opinions** and what will be in them.

Breaking a close See **quare.**

Breaking bulk (or bail) The crime of opening a container entrusted to your care and stealing *part* of the contents.

Breathalyzer A brand of **evidential breath test.**

Brethren "Brothers" or male colleagues on a court. "Colleagues" is now more usual.

Breve (Latin; plural is *brevia)* Old word for a **writ** (see that word). *Brevia de cursu* are writs issued automatically or "as a matter of course."

Bribery The offering, giving, receiving, or soliciting of anything of value in order to influence the actions of a public official.

Bridge loan Temporary financing to "bridge" a short time period between a purchase and the start of long-term financing.

Brief *1.* A written summary or condensed statement of a series of ideas or of a document. *2.* A written statement prepared by one side in a lawsuit to explain its case to the judge. It usually contains a fact summary, a law summary, and an argument about how the law applies to the facts. Most such "briefs" are *not* brief. *3.* A summary of a published **opinion** in a case. Preparing the summary helps in understanding the opinion and simplifies later review. *4.* A document prepared by a lawyer to use at a trial. It usually contains lists of **witnesses, evidence,** and **citations** as well as arguments to be presented.

Bright line rule *1.* A rule or principle that is simple and straightforward; a rule that avoids or ignores ambiguity. *2.* The principle that once a suspect has requested **counsel,** the suspect may no longer be questioned without counsel (unless the suspect starts, and willingly cooperates with, further discussion).

Bring suit (or bring an action) Start a lawsuit, usually by filing the first papers.

Broad form (or policy) A type of **home owners' policy** that insures against more **risks** than does the **basic form.**

Broad interpretation (or construction) Giving a law or **constitutional** provision a meaning that expands its application. See **liberal construction.**

Brocage Brokerage. See **broker.** [pronounce: bro-caj]

Brocard A famous, and probably ancient, legal saying or principle.

Broker An **agent** who is employed by many different persons to buy, sell, make bargains, or enter into **contracts.** For example, an *insurance broker* sells insurance for more than one company; a *real estate broker* acts for the seller or buyer of land and buildings; and a *securities broker* buys and sells stocks, bonds, etc., for others.

Broker-dealer A person or company required by state or federal **securities** laws to be registered in order to buy and sell securities as a business. A company that sells its own stock is usually exempt from registration as a *broker-dealer.*

Brother Old expression for "fellow lawyer."

Brown decision *Brown v. Board of Education* (347 U.S. 483). A 1954 U.S. Supreme Court decision that racial segregation in public schools violates the *equal protection clause* (**equal protection of**

laws) in the **Fourteenth Amendment** to the U.S. **Constitution.** Prior to the *Brown decision,* it was lawful to maintain "separate but equal" segregated facilities.

Bruton error The admission as **evidence** of a **co-defendant's** confession that implicates the defendant when the co-defendant does not testify and the defendant claims innocence. (From *Bruton v. U.S.,* 391 U.S. 123.)

Brutum fulmen (Latin) An empty threat; a **judgment** that is unenforceable due to an imperfection.

Bubble A gigantic business project, plan, or scheme based on exaggerated hopes or unsound claims.

Bucket shop An illegal business where persons accept orders to buy and sell stock, commodities, and other securities without actually placing the orders.

Budget *1.* Money allowed for a particular purpose. *2.* An estimate of money that will be taken in and spent in a particular time period.

Budget authority An **appropriation** or other law permitting the government to spend certain money.

Budget Reform Act A federal law that set up budget committees, required annual budget **resolutions** with spending targets, moved the **fiscal** year to begin October 1, and made other changes designed to gain greater congressional control of the federal budget.

Buggery **Sodomy** or **bestiality** (see those words).

Building code Rules and standards for the construction or use of buildings. Some codes are part of local law and others are statewide or national.

Building line An imaginary line that is a certain distance inside (and usually parallel to) the border of a lot, outside of which no new structure may usually be built.

Bulk *1.* Unpackaged goods or cargo such as a truckload of grain. But see no. 2. *2.* Unbroken packages. See **breaking bulk.** *3.* The largest part. See **bulk transfer.**

Bulk transfer According to the **Uniform Commercial Code,** a *"bulk transfer"* is "not in the ordinary course of business" and of "a major part of materials, supplies, or other inventories." Rules against "bulk sales," "bulk mortgages," or "bulk transfers" are to protect a merchant's **creditors** from being cheated.

Bull market A long-term upward price trend in **stock** or other **security** prices. A *"bull"* is someone who thinks the **market** will rise. Compare with **bear market.**

Bulletin   Name for many different types of legal publications, such as **law journals** or pamphlets with **agency** rules.

Bumping   *1.* An employee taking the job of another employee with weaker "job rights" (fewer years of service, lower rank, etc.). This usually happens during layoffs. *2.* An airline's refusing a place to a ticketed customer because more airplane seats were sold than are available. The bumped customer may have special financial and legal rights.

Bundle of rights   All the rights of **fee simple** ownership of land (such as the rights to occupy, to use, to sell, to lease, to mortgage, etc.).

Bundled   Grouped into one, such as an hourly billing rate that does not break out specific costs or **overhead** into separate items.

Burden of going forward (or burden of proceeding or burden of production)   *1.* The requirement that one side in a lawsuit produce evidence on a particular issue or risk losing on that issue. *2.* The requirement that the **plaintiff** produce enough evidence to avoid a **directed verdict, dismissal,** or **nonsuit.**

Burden of proof (or burden of persuasion)   *1.* The requirement that to win a point or have an issue decided in your favor in a lawsuit you must show that the weight of evidence is on your side, rather than "in the balance" on that question. Compare with **standard of proof.** *2.* Sometimes also includes the **burden of going forward.**

Bureaucracy   An organization, such as an **administrative agency** or the army, with the following general traits: a chain of command with fewer people at the top than at the bottom; well-defined positions and responsibilities; fairly inflexible rules and procedures; "red tape" (many forms to be filled out and difficult procedures to go through); and **delegation** of authority downward from level to level. [pronounce: bue-<u>rock</u>-ra-see]

Burford doctrine   The principle that federal courts should usually **abstain** from deciding cases that involve complex state regulations when federal court involvement might hurt the state's ability to maintain coherent state policy in important state matters. Compare with **Pullman doctrine** and **Younger doctrine.**

<u>**Burglary**</u>   Breaking and entering the house of another person at night with the intention of committing a **felony** (usually theft). Some states do not require a "**breaking,**" or that the building be a house, or that it be at night for it to be *burglary.*

Bursar   A **treasurer** or person who dispenses money.

Bursting bubble theory   The principle that when credible evidence contradicts the facts that support a **presumption,** the presumption ceases to exist.

Business agent   *1.* A nonemployee that represents a company commercially; sometimes, any sales **agent.** *2.* A **labor union** employee who handles worker complaints and other union business, usually by traveling from one union workplace to another.

Business entry rule   See **business records exception.**

Business expense   In tax law any normal expense necessary for producing income, not only those expenses that are a part of a trade or business. The **I.R.S.** has complex rules for deciding whether or not these expenses may be deducted from taxable income.

Business judgment rule   The principle that if persons running a **corporation** make honest, careful decisions within their corporate powers, no court will interfere with these decisions even if the results are bad.

Business organization   Any venture, structure, group, or company set up to make a profit. Common types of business organizations include: **association, corporation, joint adventure, partnership, sole** *proprietorship,* and **trust** (see those words). In addition, an association, partnership, or corporation may be **limited, limited liability,** and **professional** (see those words). Dozens of different words with overlapping, conflicting, and changing meanings are used to define business organizations in each state, in the many **Model Acts** and **Uniform Acts** used selectively by most states, and in federal agencies such as the **I.R.S.** Contrast **nonprofit organization.**

Business records exception   An exception to the "*hearsay exclusion rule.*" The exception allows original, routine records (sometimes whether or not part of a "business") to be used as **evidence** in a trial even though they are **hearsay** (see that word).

Business trust   A company set up in the form of a **trust** (see that word) that is similar to a **corporation** (see that word) in most, but not all, ways.

"But for" rule   *1.* In **tort** law, the principle that **negligence** alone will not make a person responsible for damage unless "*but for*" that negligence the damage would not have happened. For example, a failure to signal a turn may be negligent, but if the other driver was looking the other way, the failure to give a turn signal was not the cause of the accident. *2.* In both tort and **criminal** law, the general principle that responsibility exists only where causation exists even if the defendant did something wrong.

Buy American acts Various state and national laws that require government agencies to give a preference to U.S.-made goods when making purchases.

Buy and sell agreement An agreement among partners or owners of a company that if one dies or withdraws from the business, his or her share will be bought by the others or disposed of according to a prearranged plan.

Buy down Pay extra **points** to get a lower mortgage interest rate.

Buy in (or buying in) See **bid in.**

Buyer 60 contract A purchase of **stock** at higher than the going price with the right to pay for the stock sixty days later.

By-bidding See **bid.**

Bylaws **Rules** or **regulations** adopted by an organization such as a **corporation,** club, or town.

Bypass trust A **trust** in which the **beneficiary** (such as the **grantor's** spouse) is given an **interest** (such as an income for life) that does not make the trust property part of the beneficiary's **estate.** This allows the trust property to go later to others (such as the grantor's children).

Byrnes Act (18 U.S.C. 1231) A federal law that prohibits bringing in strikebreakers from out of state.

C. *1.* An old abbreviation for the Latin "cum" (with). *2. Circa* (Latin) About. Approximately a certain date, as in c. 1917. *3.* © is the symbol for **copyright.**

C.A. **Court of appeals.**

C.A.F. Cost and freight.

C.A.L.R. Computer-assisted legal research.

C.B.(O.)T. (and C.B.O.E.) Chicago Board of Trade (a major **futures** exchange) and Chicago Board **Options** Exchange.

C.C. **Circuit,** city, **civil,** or county court; civil, **criminal, crown,** or **chancery** case; civil or criminal code; chief **commissioner;** etc.

C.C.A. Circuit **court of appeals.**

C.C.C. **Commodity Credit Corporation.**

C.C.H. Commerce Clearing House. A publisher of **looseleaf services.**

C.D. **Certificate** of deposit.

C.E.A. Council of Economic Advisors (to the U.S. president).

C.E.B. *Continuing education of the bar.* See **C.L.E.**

C.E.O. Chief Executive Officer.

C.E.R.C.L.A. See **superfund.**

C.F. & I. (or C.I.F.) The price includes cost, freight, and insurance (all paid by seller).

C.F.R. **Code of Federal Regulations.**

C.F.T.C. **Commodity Futures Trading Commission.**

C.I.A. Central Intelligence Agency. The U.S. international spying department.

C.I.O. See **A.F.L.-C.I.O.**

C.J. *1.* Chief judge; chief justice; circuit judge. *2.* **Corpus Juris.**

C.J.E. Continuing judicial education.

C.J.S. **Corpus Juris** Secundum.

C.L. Civil law.

C.L.A./C.L.A.S. A *Certified Legal Assistant,* professionally **certified** by the **National Association of Legal Assistants.** A *Certified Legal Assistant Specialist,* certified at an advanced level.

C.L.E. *Continuing legal education* courses required of practicing lawyers in many states.

C.L.S. Critical Legal Studies.

C.M.O. Collateralized mortgage obligation.

C.N. *Code Napoleon.* See **Code Civil.**

C.O. *1.* **Conscientious objector.** *2.* Commanding or **corrections** officer.

C.O.B. Close of business.

C.O.B.R.A. *Consolidated Omnibus Budget Reconciliation Act of 1985.* The federal law that guarantees a time period of continued health insurance coverage to terminated employees who continue to pay premiums.

C.O.D. Collect on delivery. The price of goods or the delivery charges are paid to the person who delivers the goods.

C.O.G.S.A. Carriage of Goods by Sea Act.

C.O.L.A. *1.* **Cost of living adjustment.** *2.* **Cost of living allowance.**

C.P. Common pleas court.

C.P.A. Certified public **accountant.**

C.P.I. Consumer Price Index.

C.P.S.C. Consumer Product Safety Commission.

C.R.S. Congressional Research Service.

C.R.T. Critical race theory.

C.S.C. Civil Service Commission. It used to **regulate** federal employment (job classification, merit-system examinations, etc.), but now that this task has been split among other federal agencies, the name is used by only a few *state* employment regulatory boards.

C.T.A. Cum testamento annexo.

C & F Costs and freight.

C corporation A regular private **corporation** that pays income taxes and distributes taxable **dividends** to shareholders because it has not chosen to be an **S corporation** (see that word).

Ca. Alternate abbreviation for **C** no. 2.

Ca. sa. Abbreviation for **Capias** *ad satisfaciendum.*

Cabinet The advisory board of the head of a government. For example, the *cabinet* serving under the U.S. president is composed of the heads of the major government departments such as State, Defense, Treasury, etc., plus a few other high government officials such as the vice president; about fifteen persons in all.

Cachet See **lettres de cachet.**

Caducary **Forfeit.**

Caete_rorum **(Latin)** "As to the rest." When an **administrator** has not been given enough authority to handle all of a dead person's property, a court may give additional power *caeterorum.*

Cafeteria plan A **benefit** plan that allows employees to choose benefits from a list up to a certain dollar value. Also called *smorgasbord plan.*

Calendar The day-by-day schedule of trials in a given court; a **docket** (see that word). A *calendar call* is the announcing in court of a list of active cases to find out the status of each, primarily whether or not they are ready for trial, and sometimes to assign trial times or dates.

Call *1.* Public announcement (usually of a list). *2.* A formal demand for payment or other action according to the terms of a contract; for example, the formal request to purchase stock under a **contract** or **option** that allows its owner to buy a certain number of **shares** at a certain price on or by a certain day. Also, the demand by a company that persons who promised to buy stock now actually come up with the money is a *call. 3.* See **calling.** *4.* See **locative call.**

Call numbers A way of identifying authors and books by a combination of letters and numbers. In most systems, the first letter is the first letter of the author's last name. No two authors or books share the same numbers. See **Dewey decimal system** and **Library of Congress system** for *subject* identification systems.

Call premium The amount over the **par** or **face** value of a **bond** or other **security** that a company must pay when the company calls it in for repurchase.

Callable Subject to being gathered in and paid for. *Callable bonds* may be paid off before **maturity** (coming due) by the company that put them out. This is often done when interest rates go down.

Call-in pay Pay certain employees are entitled to if called to work, but no work becomes available.

Calling *1.* "*Calling the docket*" is a **calendar** *call. 2.* "*Calling the jury*" is the selection of a **jury list** (see that word for the different meanings). *3.* "*Calling the plaintiff*" is the final in-court call for an absent **plaintiff** before awarding **judgment** to the **defendant.** *4.* "*Calling a prisoner*" is **allocution.** *5.* See **call.**

Calumny An old word for **defamation, slander, libel,** or false accusations.

Calvo doctrine The idea that a country should not normally be held responsible to outsiders for harm done by disturbances or fighting within the country, and that no other country has a right to intervene in a disturbance to protect its citizens' property or claims.

Cambism **Foreign exchange.**

Camera (Latin) Room; chamber. See **in camera.**

Campbell's Act See **Lord Campbell's Act.**

Cancel *1.* Wipe out, cross out, or destroy the effect of a document by defacing it (by drawing lines across it, stamping it "canceled," etc.). *2.* Destroy, **annul,** set aside, or end. The process is called "*cancellation.*" Under the **Uniform Commercial Code,** "*cancellation*" means ending a **contract** because the other side has **breached** (broken) the agreement.

Candidate for office A person may be a candidate for office under various laws if he or she takes formal steps to run for office, raises or spends money on it, etc. A person may also be a candidate if he or she is put forward as a **nominee** of a group or receives any votes, whether or not that person agrees to run.

Canon A law, rule, or principle, especially a religious law or an ethical rule of conduct.

Canon law Christian religious law.

Canonical disability A problem, such as impotence or the existence of a blood relationship, that can permit the **annulment** of a marriage under **canon law.**

Canons of construction Principles to guide the **interpretation** or **construction** of written documents to decide their legal effect.

Canons of ethics A prior version of the **Rules of Professional Conduct.**

Canvass *1.* Examine and count votes in an election to determine the authenticity of each vote and the accuracy of the totals. *2.* Solicit sales orders, votes, opinions, etc., by going door-to-door or phoning.

Cap rate **Capitalization** rate. See **discounting.**

Capacity *1.* Ability to do something, such as the mental ability to make a rational decision. *2.* Legal right to do something. *3.* Legal ability to do something. For example, a child of four lacks the *capacity* to commit a crime or make a contract.

Capacity costs Those fixed business costs (see **fixed charges**) that directly relate to producing or selling goods or services (as opposed to those fixed business costs, such as for research and development, known as **programmed costs**).

Capias (Latin) "That you take." A **writ** from a judge to the **sheriff** or the police commanding them to take a **defendant** into **custody.** A *capias ad respondendum* is a writ to bring a person to court to answer a claim or defend a charge, and a *capias ad satisfaciendum* is a writ to bring a person to court to pay a **judgment.**

Capital   _1._ Head, chief, or major. For example, _capital crimes_ are those punishable by death, and _capital punishment_ is the death penalty. _2._ **Assets** or worth. _3._ This is _not "capitol"_ (a building). _4._ Relating to wealth, especially to wealth or assets held for a long time. For example, _capital assets_ (almost all property owned other than consumables and things held for sale; _personal capital assets_ include personally owned **stocks,** land, trademarks, jewelry, etc., and _business capital assets_ are described under **assets**); _capital budget_ (a list of planned spending on large, long-term projects); _capital charges_ (money needed to pay off an investment's **interest** plus **amortization**); _capital cost_ (an improvement to property that can be depreciated by taking tax **deductions** little by little during the life of the improvement); _capital gains tax_ (a tax on the profit made on the increase in value of a _capital asset_ when it is sold); _capital goods_ (things used to produce other things, rather than for final sale); _capital market_ (the way long-term **securities** such as **bonds** are bought and sold); _capital rationing_ (a company's choice among long-term projects because of a shortage of funds or the inability to borrow at good interest rates); _capital return_ (payments received that are not taxed as income because they are merely the return of money paid out); _capital stock_ (all stock put out by a corporation in exchange for money invested in the company; a _capital stock tax_ is a tax on the **face** or **par** value of the stock); _capital surplus_ (money paid into a corporation by shareholders over the par value of the stock); and _capital structure_ (the amount of a company's assets compared to its long-term debt and to its short-term debt). For _types_ of capital, such as **fixed capital** or **venture capital,** see those words.

Capitalism   Private ownership of most means of production and trade combined with a generally unrestricted marketplace of goods and services.

Capitalization   _1._ See **capitalize.** _2._ A company's long-term financing, such as stocks, bonds, and **retained earnings.** _3._ For _thin capitalization,_ see **thin corporation,** and for **undercapitalization,** see that word.

Capitalization rate   See **discounting.**

Capitalization ratio   The proportion of **bonds** and of each type of **stock** put out by a company compared to its total financing. A _bond ratio,_ for example, might show that 20 percent of the company's finances comes from (and is tied up in) bonds.

Capitalize   _1._ Treat the cost of something (a purchase, an improvement, etc.) as a **capital** _asset_ by breaking the cost into annual parts and taking an annual tax **deduction** for each part. *2.* Issue **stocks** or **bonds** to cover an investment. *3.* Figure out the **net** *worth* or **principal** on which an investment is based. For example, figure out what the sale price should be for a **mortgage** that brings in a hundred dollars a month for ten years. (This figure will be *much* less than one hundred dollars times twelve months times ten years.)

Capitation tax   A tax on a person at a fixed rate, regardless of income, assets, etc.; a "head tax."

Capitulary   A collection of laws. A **code** (see that word).

Capricious   Not based on fact, law, or reason.

Caption   *1.* The heading or introductory section of a legal paper. The *caption* of a court paper usually contains the names of the **parties,** the court, and the case number. *2.* Taking or seizing something or someone. This may be legal (arresting a person) or illegal (stealing a boat).

Care   *1.* Safekeeping or **custody.** *2.* Attention, heed, or caution. There are various types and levels of *care* (often named and defined differently in different courts) that apply to different situations. For example, in a normal driving situation, a person must act with *"reasonable care."* One definition of reasonable care is "ordinary or due care; what may be expected from a normal person under the circumstances."

Career criminal (or offender) Habitual   *criminal.*

Carnal knowledge   Sexual intercourse.

Carrier   A person or organization that transports persons, property, or information. A *common carrier* does this for the general public.

Carrier's lien   The right of a shipping company or other mover of property to hold the things shipped until the shipping costs have been paid.

Carrol doctrine   The rule in **F.C.C.** cases that a broadcast **license** holder can challenge the grant of a competitive license. It is from *Carroll Broadcasting v. F.C.C.* (258 F.2d. 440).

Carryback (and carryover) rules   Tax rules that allow a person or company to use losses to reduce taxes in the years prior to (or the years following) the loss.

Carrying charges   *1.* The costs of owning property, such as land taxes, mortgage payments, etc. *2.* **Interest.**

Carryover basis   The cost for tax purposes of a property when it is transferred by gift or certain other ways and the old owner's **basis** becomes the new owner's *carryover* basis.

Cartel   A close (often formal) association of companies carrying on the same or similar businesses. The companies in a *cartel* often act to limit competition among themselves and drive out competition by others.

Carve out   *1.* Separate an investment from its income; for example, sell the rights to a bond's interest for a set number of years. *2.* Make an exception to a rule.

Case   *1.* Lawsuit; a dispute that goes to court. *2.* The judge's **opinion** in a lawsuit. *3.* The **evidence** and arguments presented by each side in a lawsuit. *4.* Short for *trespass on the case,* an old form of lawsuit seeking recovery for indirect injury. *5.* A criminal investigation, proceeding, suspect, defendant, or convict.

Case in chief   The main **evidence** offered by one side in a lawsuit. This does not include evidence offered to oppose the other side's case.

Case in point   A prior decision of the same court, or of a higher court, that decides a similar legal question.

Case method (or case system)   The way most law schools teach law: by studying **cases** (judicial **opinions**) in each subject of the law to learn legal analysis and to draw general legal principles from the cases.

Case of first impression   See **first impression.**

Case reserved (or made)   An agreed-to set of facts that have been proved in a trial for the use of an **appellate** court.

Case stated (or agreed)   An agreed-to set of facts that allows a judge to decide a case without a trial.

Casebook   A bound, organized collection of edited, written court **opinions** (usually **appellate** court opinions) together with supporting text, often used to teach a single law school subject.

Caselaw   All reported judicial decisions; the law derived from judges' **opinions** in lawsuits (as opposed to, for example, the laws passed by a **legislature**).

Cases and controversies   Real (not hypothetical or faked) disputes that turn into lawsuits. The U.S. Constitution gives the federal courts the power to decide certain "cases and controversies."

Cash basis   A method of accounting that reflects income and expenses only when actually received or paid. Compare with **accrual basis.**

Cash cycle   The time between a company's payment for raw materials (or wholesale goods) and its collection of payment for the finished product (or for the goods' resale).

Cash dividend   An ordinary **dividend** (see that word) as opposed to a **stock dividend.** A cash dividend is paid by check, not in cash.

Cash flow *1.* What is taken in minus what is paid out in a given time period. *2.* A company's **net** profits plus **depreciation.**

Cash out Sell completely.

Cash price The price at which a merchant sells (or would sell) goods or services to consumers when no **credit** is given. If the merchant charges a higher price than his or her normal *cash price,* federal law may call the difference interest charged for credit given.

Cash surrender value The amount of money an insurance policy will bring if cashed in with the company. Compare with **cash value.**

Cash value The same as **market value;** the price something would bring if it sold for cash on the open market. Compare with **cash surrender value.**

Cashier's check A **certified** *check* (see that word) made out in the bank's own name and signed by a bank official.

Castle doctrine The principle (now greatly restricted) that you can use any force necessary to protect your own home or its inhabitants from attack. Also called "*dwelling defense doctrine.*"

Casual Accidental, by chance, unexpected, unintentional.

Casual ejector See **ejectment.**

Casualty *1.* Any accident; an unexpected accident; an inevitable accident. *2.* An injured or killed person.

Casualty loss A sudden loss of, or damage to, property due to fire, storm, accident, or similar occurrence. It is **deductible** for tax purposes if certain tax rules are followed.

Casus (Latin) An occurrence, chance event, or accident that causes something. For example, *casus belli* is an event that causes (or is used to justify) a war; and *casus fortuitus* is a chance event or unavoidable accident.

Catch 22 An unwritten rule, or an unreasonable combination of otherwise reasonable rules, that keeps you from getting what you want.

Catch time charter A boat rental with payment for only the time it is in actual use.

Catching **Unconscionable** (see that word). A *catching bargain* was originally a high interest loan to someone who would eventually inherit money or property.

Categorical *1.* Absolute; leaving no doubt. A *categorical question* is a **leading question** (see that word). *2.* Fitting into one category. For example, *categorical assistance programs* (such as "Aid to the Blind") have qualification requirements in addition to financial need.

Caucus *1.* A meeting of voters to choose **delegates** to a convention or to choose **candidates** for public office. *2.* An informal subgroup of a larger group such as a **legislature** or a convention.

Causa (Latin) Cause, reason, or motive. [pronounce: cow-sa]

Causa causans (Latin) See **proximate cause.**

Causa mortis (Latin) "Because of impending death." A *gift causa mortis* is a gift made by a person who thinks he or she is dying. If the person recovers, the gift becomes **void.** Occasionally, a *gift causa mortis* is found to be an attempt to avoid a tax on property given by **will** if the gift comes too close to death.

Causa proxima (Latin) See **proximate cause.**

Cause *1.* That which produces an effect. *2.* Motive or reason. *3.* Lawsuit or legal action. *4.* Short for "*just cause*" in the removal of a person from office or dismissal of a person from a job. *5.* Many "cause" words, such as **proximate cause,** are listed under their own headings.

Cause of action *1.* Facts sufficient to support a valid lawsuit. For example, a *cause of action* for **battery** (see that word) must include facts to prove an intentional, unconsented-to physical contact. *2.* The legal theory upon which a lawsuit ("**action**") is based.

Caution A formal warning.

Cautionary instructions *1.* Part of a judge's **charge** to a **jury** that tells the jury it may use a particular piece of evidence only to answer certain specific questions and not to form any more general impressions from it. *2.* Part of a judge's charge that cautions the jury against talking with outsiders about the case and against being influenced by anything outside the trial itself.

Cautionary lien (or judgment) *1.* A **lien** (see that word) put on a **defendant's** property to make sure that if the defendant loses the case there will be something available to pay the lien. *2.* A lien put on a property primarily to warn others that **title** to the property is not **clear.** This may be **recorded** in the land records or in a **judgment book.**

Caveat (Latin) "Beware"; warning. *Caveat emptor* means "let the buyer beware." While this is still an important warning, laws and court decisions provide many safeguards to the buyer. [pronounce: kav-ee-at]

Caveator A person who makes a formal **objection,** or who files a paper asking that a court proceeding be stopped for reasons not yet before the court. [pronounce: kav-ee-ator]

Cease and desist order An **administrative agency's** command that a person or organization stop doing something. It is similar to a court's **injunction.**

Cede   *1.* **Assign, grant,** or give up. *2.* Transfer land from one government to another. [pronounce: seed]

Cedent   A person who **cedes** something. (*Not* the person who gets it.)

Ceiling   A highest limit.

Celebration   Formal ceremony.

Censorship   *1.* The denial of **freedom of speech** or **freedom of the press.** *2.* The review of books, movies, etc., to prohibit publication and distribution, usually for reasons of morality or state security.

Censure   A formal reprimand.

Census Bureau   The federal agency that counts the population every ten years and maintains records of its characteristics.

Center of gravity doctrine   The rule that a court should use the law of the state which has the most important contact with the events, persons, and issues involved in the lawsuit.

Century Digest   (Abbreviated Cent. Dig.) See **American Digest System.**

Ceremonial marriage   A marriage performed by a legally approved person, based on a legally valid license, and complying with all state laws as to blood tests, etc.

Certificate   A written assurance that something has been done or some formal requirement has been met. For example, a *certificate of convenience and necessity* is an operating license for a public utility such as a bus or gas company; a *certificate of deposit* is either a written receipt for a bank deposit or a bank deposit for a certain number of months or years that pays a higher rate of interest than an ordinary **demand** savings account; a *certificate of incorporation* is a document showing a state's formal recognition of a company as a **corporation** established under that state's laws; and a *certificate of occupancy* permits a building or apartment to be used because it meets building, **zoning,** or health requirements.

Certificate of acknowledgment   See **acknowledgment.** Compare **certificate of authority.**

Certificate of authority (or authentication, capacity, magistracy, official character, prothonotary, verification, etc.)   A document that accompanies a notarized document out of state to prove that the **notary public** has a valid license. Compare *certificate of acknowledgment* under **acknowledgment.**

Certification   *1.* See **certificate** and **certified.** *2.* The process by which a federal court refers a question concerning state law to the state's highest court and holds off from deciding a case until that question is decided. Also, the process by which a trial court refers an **interlocu-tory** decision to an **appellate** court if the **question** *of law* involved should be resolved before the trial continues.

Certification mark   A mark or label placed on goods by an organization (other than the manufacturer or seller of the goods) to show that the goods meet the organization's quality standards, come from a partic-ular region, or were made by certain unions, etc. *Certification marks* can qualify for federal **trademark** protection.

Certification proceeding   A procedure taken by the National Labor Re-lations Board (see **N.L.R.B.**) to find out if the employees of a com-pany want a particular **union** to represent them.

Certified   Officially passed, "checked out," or approved. For example, a *certified check* is a check that a bank has marked as "guaranteed cashable" for its customer. A *Certified Legal Assistant (C.L.A.)* is a **paralegal** who has met several requirements including passing the **N.A.L.A.** exam, and a *Certified Professional Legal Secretary (P.L.S.)* is a legal secretary who has met several requirements including pass-ing the **N.A.L.S.** exam.

Certiorari   (Latin) "To make sure." A request for *certiorari* (or "cert." for short) is like an **appeal,** but one which the higher court is not required to take for decision. It is literally a **writ** from the higher court asking the lower court for the **record** of the case. [pronounce: sir-sho-rare-ee]

Cession   A giving up of something; see **cede.**

Cessionary bankrupt   A person who gives up everything he or she owns to be divided among **creditors.**

Cestui que   (French) "He or she who." For example, a *cestui que trust* is a person who has a right to the property, money, and **proceeds** being managed by another. The modern phrase is "**beneficiary** of a **trust.**" [pronounce: set-i kuh]

Cf.   (Latin abbreviation) "Compare." For example, "*cf. Hamlet*" means "look at *Hamlet* for a comparison with, or an explanation of, what is being discussed."

Ch.   Short for chapter; **chancellor; chancery;** chief; etc.

Chain discount   A further discount calculated on an already discounted price, so that the total discount is not as much as the sum of the dis-count percentages.

Chain of custody   The chronological list of those in continuous pos-session of a specific physical object. A person who presents physi-cal **evidence** (such as a gun used in a crime) at a trial must account for its possession from time of receipt to time of trial in order for the evidence to be "admitted" by the judge. It must thus be shown that the *chain of custody* was unbroken.

Chain of title   A list of the consecutive passing of the ownership of a piece of land.

Chain picketing   *1.* A tightly grouped, moving picket line to prevent anyone from crossing. *2.* Picketing several retail outlets of one company.

Chain referral   See **pyramid sales scheme.**

Challenge   *1.* A direct, expressed objection or contrary claim. *2.* A formal objection to the qualifications of a prospective juror or jurors. See **peremptory.**

Chamber of commerce   A local association of businesses that promotes the area's trade. Also called *board of trade.*

Chamber of Congress (or legislature)   See **bicameral.**

Chambers   A judge's private office. Business that takes place there is "in chambers."

Champerty   Taking over or taking part in a lawsuit being brought by another person, by, for example, buying the other person's claim or by sharing any "winnings" of the suit. Champerty is restricted by law in many states.

Chancellor   *1.* Once the king or queen's **minister** who handed out royal justice, now the judge of a court of **equity** or **chancery.** *2.* The head of a university system, especially a state system. *3.* The head of state, or other high-ranking official, of certain countries.

Chance-medley   An old word for a sudden (usually free-for-all) fight during which a person kills in self-defense.

Chancery   An old court that handled **equitable** *actions.* The **equity** power is now part of regular courts in most states.

Change in financial position   See **statement.**

Change of venue   Transfer of a case from one court to another.

Chapter Eleven   A reorganization of an **insolvent** (broke) **corporation** under the federal **bankruptcy** laws, supervised by a federal bankruptcy court, in which ownership is transferred to a new corporation made up of old owners and **creditors.** In some cases the business can continue to operate during the process.

Chapter Nine   The adjustment of a local government's debts under the **bankruptcy** laws.

Chapter Seven   See **bankruptcy.**

Chapter Thirteen   A procedure under the federal **bankruptcy** laws for an individual or small business in financial trouble to pay off only a proportion of its debts (called a "*composition*"), get extra time to pay them (called an "*extension*"), or both. This process used to be called a "*wage earner's plan*," but is now called a "*rehabilitation*" because the person's **credit** and finances are made good again. Payments may be made from a regular source of income or from a combination of income and the sale of property.

Chapter Twelve   A debt payment and relief plan for family farmers under the **bankruptcy** laws.

Character evidence   **Testimony** about a person's personal traits and habits that is drawn from the opinions of close associates, from the person's reputation in the community, or from the person's past actions.

Characteristic line   See **beta.**

Characterization   Classification or **interpretation.**

Charge   *1.* A **claim, obligation,** burden, or **liability.** *2.* The judge's final summary of a case and instructions to the jury. *3.* A formal accusation of a crime, such as an **accusatory instrument** or one **count** of that accusation. *4.* Purchase using an established credit account.

Charge d'affairs   Usually an **ambassador's** chief assistant. A diplomatic representative of high, but not highest, rank who often is responsible for taking care of a country's business in another country when the ambassador cannot. [pronounce: <u>shar</u>-jeh da-fair]

Charge-off   Lowering the value of something in a company's records. For example, when a debt becomes too difficult to collect, it may be charged off (also called *writeoff*).

Charging instrument   See **accusatory instrument.**

Charitable   A gift or organization is *charitable* for **tax** purposes if it meets several tests. A gift must be made to a government-qualified nonprofit organization to benefit humankind in general, the community in general, or some specific type of people (so long as the individuals are not specified). Also, the organization's and the gift's purpose must be for the relief of poverty; protection of health or safety; prevention of cruelty; government; or advancement of education, religion, literature, science, etc. A qualified organization must use its money and staff to advance these purposes, rather than to benefit specific individuals. With few exceptions, it may not lobby or otherwise try to influence **legislation.** If the gift and the organization meet these standards, the giver may **deduct** the gift from income and the organization is exempt from paying taxes. For gifts generally, see **gift,** and for charitable organizations generally, see **nonprofit organization.**

Charitable remainder trust   A **trust** that gets money (or property) for **charitable** purposes after others get use of the money first.

Charitable trust   A **trust** set up for a public purpose such as to support a school, church, charity, etc.

Charta   An old English word for **charter, deed,** or other formal document. More loosely, any written document.

Charter   *1.* An organization's basic starting document (for example, a corporation's **articles of incorporation**). *2.* Rent a ship or other large means of transportation.

Chartered accountant   The British name for a Certified Public **Accountant.**

Chattel   Item of personal property. Any property other than **land.**

Chattel mortgage   A **mortgage** on personal property.

Chattel paper   A document that shows both a debt and the fact that the debt is **secured** (see that word) by specific personal property.

Check   *1.* A document in which a person tells his or her bank to pay a certain amount of money to another person. It is a type of **negotiable instrument** (see that word). *2.* A restraint. For example, each of the three major branches of the U.S. federal government "*checks and balances*" the others so that no one branch can control the country.

Check-off   A system in which **union** dues are collected directly from a worker's pay for the union by the company.

Chicago v. Morales   (119 S.Ct. 1849) The 1999 U.S. Supreme Court decision that struck down as vague an anti-loitering law that gave police discretion to arrest anyone who refused to move on and remained "in one place with no apparent purpose" in the presence of a suspected gang member.

Chicanery   **Fraud.**

Child Abuse   Physical, emotional, or sexual injury inflicted on a child, whether done intentionally or through neglect. *Child abuse reporting acts* require *designated (or mandated) reporters* such as doctors, nurses, and teachers to report suspected child abuse. For *child abuse syndrome,* see **battered (or abused) child syndrome.**

Child pornography   **Pornography** (see that word) showing children engaged in sexual activity.

Chilling   *1.* Holding down the sales price of an item to get it cheaply (usually at an auction and usually by telling lies about the property's value). *2.* A law or practice has a "*chilling effect*" if it discourages a person from taking advantage of a **constitutional right,** especially the right of free speech or other **First Amendment** right.

Chinese wall   Administrative safeguards (and physical separation) that keep individuals (or entire parts of an organization) separate for various reasons, such as to protect client confidences or to avoid legal problems such as **conflict of interest.** A *"contaminated"* or *"tainted"* employee who is walled off from any contact with a particular client or case is *"quarantined."*

Chirograph   An old word for a document protected against fraud by a means involving handwriting; for example, a document signed by **witnesses.**

Chit   *1.* A **promissory note.** *2.* A meal or drink **voucher.**

Choate   Complete; valid against all later claims. Compare with **inchoate.** For example, a *choate* **lien** is one that needs nothing more to be done to make it enforceable. [pronounce: ko-ate]

Choice of law   Deciding which **jurisdiction's** laws apply to a lawsuit, to a document, etc. See **conflict of laws.**

Chose   (French) A thing; a piece of personal property. [pronounce: shows]

Chose in action   A right to recover a debt or to get **damages** that can be enforced in court. These words also apply to the thing itself that is being sued on; for example, an accident, a contract, stocks, etc.

Chronic persistent vegetative state   A deep, long-term, irreversible coma that is not brain death (see **brain death rule**), but still may justify stopping life support in some U.S. states.

Churning   The act of a **broker** who makes more trades (for example, of stock) than are beneficial to a customer's **account** in order to increase the broker's own **commissions.**

Cir. Ct.   **Circuit court.**

Circuit   The entire geographical area served by a single **circuit court.** [pronounce: sir-kit]

Circuit court   The name given to different types and levels of courts in different states and to a **United States Court** *of appeals,* originally because judges "rode circuit" (held court for a while in each place) to serve outlying areas.

Circuit court of appeals   See **United States court** *of appeals.*

Circular note   A **letter of credit.**

Circumstantial evidence   Facts that *indirectly* prove a main fact in question. For example, **testimony** that a person was seen walking in the rain is **direct evidence** that the person walked in the rain, but testimony that the person was seen indoors with wet clothing is *circumstantial evidence* that the person walked in the rain.

Citation *1.* A notice to appear in court. *2.* A reference to a legal authority and where it is found. For example, "17 U.DI.L.R. 247" is a *citation* to an article that begins on page 247 of volume 17 of the University of Dull Law Review. See also **pinpoint citation.** *3.* A notice of a violation of law; for example, a *health board citation.*

Citator A set of books or a database that lists relevant legal events subsequent to a given **case, statute,** or other **authority.** It will tell, for example, if a case has been **overruled, distinguished,** or **followed** (see those words). This is done by looking up the case by its **citation** (see that word) and checking whether there are citations to other cases listed under it. If there are, it means that the case was mentioned in these later cases. Two leading citators are *Shepard's* and *KeyCite.*

Cite *1.* Summon a person to court. *2.* Refer to specific legal references or **authorities.** *3.* Short for "**citation.**" *4. Cite checking* is looking at all the citations in a document to verify accuracy and proper form.

Citizen *1.* A person born in the U.S., a person who goes through the formal process of **naturalization,** or most children born abroad to a U.S. citizen. *2.* A person is a citizen of the state where he or she has permanent residence, and a corporation is a citizen of the state where it was legally created.

Citizen's arrest An arrest by a private person, rather than by a police or other law enforcement officer. A person usually may arrest another for any crime committed in his or her presence or for a **felony** committed elsewhere.

Civil *1.* Not **criminal.** (See **civil action, civil commitment, civil procedure,** etc.) *2.* Having to do with the government. See **civil law, civil rights, civil service,** etc.

Civil action Every lawsuit other than a **criminal** proceeding. A lawsuit that is brought to enforce a right or to redress a wrong, rather than a court action involving the government trying to prosecute a criminal; in general, a lawsuit brought by one person against another.

Civil code **Code Civil.**

Civil commitment *1.* Confinement by a non**criminal** process in a mental hospital or other treatment facility for insanity or for alcohol or drug addiction. The usual justification for confining a person who has not committed a crime is that he or she "is a danger to self or others." See **insanity.** *2.* Jailing a person for **nonsupport,** civil **contempt,** or to secure a **capias** (see that word).

Civil conspiracy See **conspiracy.**

Civil damage acts **Dram shop acts.**

Civil death   The loss of all rights, such as the right to make contracts or to sue, that occurs in some states to persons who are **convicted** of serious crimes (usually those persons **sentenced** to life imprisonment).

Civil disabilities   The loss of some rights that occurs when a person has been **convicted** of a crime. These may include the loss of the right to vote, to hold public office, to hold certain state-**licensed** jobs, etc.

Civil disobedience   Breaking a law to demonstrate its unfairness or to focus attention on a problem. It may imply a willingness to pay a penalty, serve a **sentence**, etc., as part of the demonstration.

Civil law   *1.* Law handed down from the Romans. *2.* Law that is based on one elaborate document or "**code**," rather than a combination of many laws and judicial **opinions**. See **Code Civil**. *3.* Government by civilians as opposed to government by the military. *4.* "Non**criminal** law." See **civil action**. *5.* The law of an organized government as opposed to **natural law** or **anarchy**. *6.* In land law, the *civil law rule* is the principle that a downhill adjoining landowner must accept natural drainage from the uphill owner but must be protected from an artificial drainage increase. Compare with **common enemy doctrine**.

Civil liberties   See **civil rights**.

Civil procedure   The laws and rules that govern how non**criminal** lawsuits are handled by the individuals involved and by the court.

Civil rights   *1.* The rights of all citizens that are guaranteed by the Constitution or by other laws. Civil rights include **freedom of speech, freedom of association**, and **freedom of religion**. *2.* The *Civil Rights Amendments* are the **Thirteenth, Fourteenth**, and **Fifteenth Amendments** to the U.S. **Constitution** that deal with slavery, **discrimination**, and the right to vote. *3.* The *Civil Rights Acts* are federal laws passed after the Civil War (1866–1875) and since 1957 that prohibit discrimination based on *race, color, age, sex, religion, disability, or national origin*. The Acts originally dealt with giving full civil rights (such as the rights to sue and to vote) to former slaves, then with equal access to public accommodations and equal employment and housing rights, and, more recently, with discrimination based on age or disability and with workplace *harassment*. The Acts survive, in changed form, in Title 42 of the U.S. Code.

Civil service   All nonmilitary government employees chosen by a standardized, supervised method rather than by political appointment or election.

Civil suit   See **civil action**.

Civilian   *1.* Not a member of the armed forces. *2.* Not a member of the police department.

Cl.   **Clause.**

Clafin trust   A **trust** (see that word) ending on a precise date that cannot be changed by the **beneficiary** or by others. It is from the case *Clafin v. Clafin* (20 N.E. 454), and is also called an "indestructible trust."

Claim   *1.* Demand as your own; assert; urge; insist. *2.* One side's case in a lawsuit. *3.* The part of a **patent** application that describes what the applicant thinks is new about the invention and defines the limits of what the patent seeks to protect.

Claim and delivery   An old form of lawsuit to get back property wrongfully withheld plus **damages.**

Claim for relief   The core of a modern **complaint** (first **pleading** in a lawsuit). It may be a short, clear statement of the claim being made that shows that if the facts **alleged** can be proved, the **plaintiff** should get help from the court in enforcing the claim against the **defendant.**

Claim jumping   Staking out or filing a mining claim on land that has been claimed by another.

Claim of right doctrine   A rule in tax law that if a person receives money under a *claim of right* (the assertion or honest impression that it belongs to or was owed to the person), he or she must pay taxes on the money that year even if there is a good chance that it must be returned later. See also **constructive receipt of income.**

Claim preclusion   See **res judicata.**

Claimant   *1.* A person who claims property or a right. *2.* A **plaintiff.**

Claims Court   *1.* See court of *Federal Claims* under **United States Courts.** *2.* **Small claims court.**

Claims made policy   An insurance policy that pays claims made within a specified time period even if the acts or loss on which the claim is based occurred outside that time period. Contrast **occurrence policy.**

Class action   A lawsuit brought for yourself and other persons in the same situation. To bring a *class action* you must convince the court that there are too many persons in the class (group) to make them all individually a part of the lawsuit and that your interests are the same as theirs, so that you can adequately represent their needs.

Class directors   Corporate **directors** whose terms of office are staggered. This helps assure continuity of leadership and may make takeover attempts more difficult.

Class gift   A gift, usually in a **will,** to a group of persons (such as "my grandchildren") whose shares will depend on the number of such persons in the "class" at the time the persons actually receive the gift.

Classified   *1.* Secret. *2.* Put into a special category or "class."

Clause   A single paragraph, sentence, or phrase. [pronounce: claws]

Clayton Act   (15 U.S.C. 12) A 1914 federal law that extended the **Sherman Act's** prohibition against **monopolies** and price discrimination.

Clean bill   *1.* A **bill** (see that word) that has been substantially rewritten by a legislative committee. *2.* Any bill (such as a **bill of lading**) that is clear and in final form with no marginal notation or other qualifying words.

Clean hands   The status of having acted fairly and honestly in all matters connected with a lawsuit you are bringing. The *clean hands doctrine* requires a person to have clean hands if the person uses an **equitable** (see that word) *defense* or seeks *equitable* **relief.**

Clean-up clause   A part of an ongoing loan agreement that requires all loans to be paid off by a certain time, after which no new loans will be given for a short time, the *"clean-up period."*

Clear   *1.* Final payment on a check by the bank on which it was drawn *clears* the check. The process of sending a check to that bank and making payment is called *clearing,* and it takes place in an association (or at a place) called a **clearinghouse.** *2.* Free from doubt or restrictions. *3.* Free of taxes; free of **liens** or other **encumbrances;** free of any claims at all.

Clear and convincing evidence   Stronger **evidence** than a *preponderance of the evidence* (evidence that something is more likely to be true than false) but not as strong as **beyond a reasonable doubt.** *Clear and convincing evidence* is required for a few **civil** lawsuits, such as those involving the **reformation** of a contract.

Clear and present danger test   A test of whether or not speech may be restricted or punished. It may be if it will probably lead to violence soon or if it threatens a serious, immediate weakening of national safety and security. The test was first stated in *Schenck v. U.S.* (249 U.S. 47 (1919)), applied in *Dennis v. U.S.* (341 U.S. 494 (1951)) to punish advocacy of the forcible overthrow of the U.S. government, and revised in *Yates v. U.S.* (354 U.S. 298 (1957)) to permit such advocacy in the abstract, but not coupled with action.

Clear title   Legal ownership that may pass freely to another person.

Clear view doctrine   See **plain view doctrine.**

Clearance card   *1.* A document given to a ship by **customs** authorities allowing it to leave port. *2.* A document given to a worker leaving a job that states the worker was a good worker (or at least in good standing) when employment ended.

Clearing   *1.* See **clear**. *2.* The departure of a boat from a port after receiving a **clearance card**. *3.* The actions or legal proceedings needed to get a **clear title** to something.

Clearinghouse   A transfer facility, such as the one that transfers checks and other items between depository banks and paying banks and that settles balances due between such banks.

Clemency   *1.* Lenient sentencing of a convicted criminal by a judge. *2.* Reducing the punishment of a criminal, especially by action of the president of the U.S. or a governor of a state.

Clergy's (or cleric's) privilege   The right and duty of a person's spiritual advisor to keep confidential most communications involving religious advice, solace, and related religious functions.

Clerical error   A mistake made while copying something or writing it down, as opposed to a mistake in judgment or decision-making.

Clerk   A court official who keeps court records, official files, etc.

Clerkship   The employment of a law student, prospective lawyer, or lawyer in a temporary position as legal assistant to a judge or to a lawyer.

Client   A person who employs a lawyer. For some purposes, a person who merely discusses a possible attorney-client relationship with a lawyer is a *client.* [pronounce: kli-ent]

Client security fund   See **I.O.L.T.A.**

Clifford trust   A **trust** (see that word) that you set up to give the income to someone else and eventually return the **principal** (original money put in) to yourself.

Clinton v. Jones   (520 U.S. 681) The 1996 U.S. Supreme Court decision that a civil lawsuit may proceed against a sitting U.S. president.

Clinton v. New York   (524 U.S. 417) The 1998 U.S. Supreme Court decision that a president's *line-item* **veto** (see that word) of a specific part of a congressional **appropriations** act violates the presentment clause (Article I, Section 7, Clause 2) of the U.S. Constitution.

Close   *1.* Old word for an enclosed or well-marked piece of land. *2.* See **closing.**

Closed corporation (or close corporation)   A **corporation** with total ownership in a few hands.

Closed mortgage   A **mortgage** that cannot be paid off in advance (before **maturity**) without the mortgage-holder's agreement. See also **open-end mortgage** and **closed-end mortgage.**

Closed shop   A company where only members of a particular **union** may work in certain jobs. This is now prohibited in most cases.

Closed-end investment company   An investment company with a fixed number of shares sold to investors and sometimes traded on an exchange.

Closed-end mortgage   A **mortgage** that allows no additional borrowing under the same agreement. See also **closed mortgage** and **open-end mortgage.**

Closed-end question   **Directed question.**

Closely held   Refers to stock or a company that is owned by a family or by another company.

Closing   _1._ The final meeting for the sale of land at which all payments are made, the property is formally transferred, and the **mortgage** is fully set up by filling out all necessary papers for the mortgage lender. _Closing costs_ are all charges for finishing the deal, such as transfer taxes, mortgage fees, credit reports, etc. These costs are all set down on a _closing statement_ also known as a **settlement** _sheet_ or _closing agreement._ _2._ In **I.R.S.** procedure, a _closing agreement_ is an agreement with a taxpayer that settles an issue of tax liability.

Cloture   A formal process of ending debate in a meeting.

Cloud on title   An apparent **claim** against or **encumbrance** to property that, if valid, would lower the property's value or weaken its legal ownership.

Cluster zoning   See **zoning.**

Co   _1._ A prefix meaning with, together, equally, or unitedly. For example, a _co-defendant_ is a person who is a full **defendant** along with another person in a trial. _2._ Abbreviation for county or company.

Coaching   A lawyer telling a **witness** how to **testify.** This may be improper, or even illegal, if the lawyer tells the witness to lie or "coaches" while the witness is actually testifying.

Cobuyer   Persons with an ownership right in a thing being purchased, persons who merely put up some of the money, **cosigners,** etc.

Coconspirators rule   The principle that statements by a member of a proven **conspiracy** may be used as **evidence** against any of the members of the conspiracy.

Code   *1.* A collection of laws. *2.* A complete, interrelated, and exclusive set of laws.

Code Civil (or Code Napoleon)   The law of France as first established in 1804 and used with revisions since. Much of Louisiana law is based on this.

Code of Ethics and Professional Responsibility   Ethical guidelines of the **National Association of Legal Assistants.**

Code of Federal Regulations   The compilation of all the **rules** and **regulations** put out by federal **agencies.** It is updated each year and divided into subject areas.

Code of Hammurabi   The first full-scale set of laws, written four thousand years ago in Babylon. It was "modern" in many of its provisions.

Code of Judicial Conduct   Rules regulating judges' conduct adopted by the **American Bar Association** and in use in many states.

Code of Military Justice   The laws and rules governing all of **military law.** The Code sets up a system of military courts, judges, and lawyers; a system of punishments for crimes; and all the rules for trial and appeal.

Code of Professional Responsibility   A prior version of the **Rules of Professional Conduct** of the **American Bar Association.**

Code pleading   The system of **pleading** that replaced **common law** and **equity** pleading with a standardized system. See **pleading** for descriptions.

Co-defendant   A person who is a **defendant** along with another person in a trial.

Codex   (Latin) A **code** or collection of laws; any book.

Codicil   A supplement or addition to a **will** that adds to it or changes it. [pronounce: cod-i-sill]

Codification   Collecting and arranging a government's **statutes** and **caselaw** on a particular subject into one complete system, approved in one piece by the **legislature.** Compare **consolidation** no. 4.

Coemption   Buying up all of a particular thing.

Coercion   Compulsion or force; making a person act against free will. *Criminal coercion* includes such things as trying to change a person's actions by threatening to commit a crime against the person, threatening to accuse the person of a crime, or threatening to expose a secret that would destroy the person's reputation. [pronounce: co-er-shun]

Cognation   *1.* Relationship by blood, rather than by marriage. *2.* A **lineal,** rather than **collateral,** relationship. *3.* Any family ties.

Cognizance   **Judicial** power to decide a matter; the judicial decision to "take notice" of a matter and accept it for decision.

Cognovit note   A written statement that a **debtor** owes money and "*confesses judgment*," or allows the **creditor** to get a **judgment** in court for the money whenever the creditor wants to or whenever a particular event takes place (such as a failure to make a payment).

Cohabitation   *1.* Living together. *2.* Living together as if husband and wife. *3.* Living together and having sexual intercourse. *4.* Having sexual intercourse.

Cohan rule   The principle of tax law that, while a taxpayer must keep adequate records of **deductions,** if a deduction is proved but the amount is uncertain, a reasonable amount may be allowed. The rule is the product of several different tax cases.

Coif   A headpiece once worn by judges and lawyers to cover a wig. [pronounce: koyf]

Coinsurance   *1.* A division of **risk** between an insurance company and its customer on all losses less than 100 percent if the amount of insurance is less than the value of the property. For example, if a watch worth 100 dollars is insured for 50 dollars and suffers 50 dollars worth of damage, the company will pay only 25 dollars. *2.* Any sharing of an insurance risk between insurance company and customer or a sharing of a risk between insurance companies.

Cold blood   **Premeditation.**

Collapsible corporation   A company set up to earn money by building up its **assets,** then going out of business and distributing its profits back to the owners. The **I.R.S.** has rules that limit the tax benefits of this sort of arrangement.

Collateral   *1.* "On the side." For example, "*collateral ancestors*" include uncles, aunts, and all persons similarly related, but not direct ancestors such as grandparents. *2.* Money or property put up to back a person's word when taking out a loan.

Collateral attack   An attempt to avoid the *effect* of a court's action or decision by taking action in a different court proceeding. The opposite of a **direct attack** (see that word).

Collateral estoppel   Being stopped from making a claim in one court proceeding that has already been disproved by the facts raised in a prior, different proceeding. (In most states, *collateral estoppel* occurs only if the facts were important for the judge's decision in the prior case. In some states, the lawsuit must be between the same persons.) *Collateral estoppel* applies to claims and issues, while **res judicata** applies to entire lawsuits.

Collateral inheritance tax   A tax on money and property inherited by *collateral relatives* (relatives other than spouses, parents, grandparents, children, etc.).

Collateral order rule   The principle that a court's **order** may be **appealed,** even if it is not a final order in a case, if it is final as to important rights or claims that are totally separate from the main issues in the case.

Collateral source rule   The principle that if a person gets payments for an injury from a source other than the person who caused it (such as the injured person's own insurance company), the person who caused the injury must still pay for it.

Collateral warranty   *1.* A guarantee about land or buildings that was made by an ancestor. *2.* A **warranty** of **title** to land made by someone other than the person selling it. Such a promise can be enforced only by the buyer, not by others who later buy the land.

Collateralized mortgage obligation   A bond, paying fixed, regular interest, backed by a pool of mortgages that has had its payments separated into short-term through long-term parts.

Collation   *1.* Comparing a copy to the original to assure correctness. *2.* **Hotchpot.** *3.* The process of putting sheets of paper into proper order, especially sorting multiple copies of printed book pages.

Collection ratio   A comparison of **accounts receivable** and sales that shows a business's debt-collecting efficiency. See also **aging schedule.**

Collective bargaining   Negotiations between a union and an employer of union members, usually concerning wages, hours, and working conditions. Federal law often requires an employer to collectively bargain with a union.

Collective bargaining agreement   A contract between a **union** and an employer of union members.

Collective bargaining unit   All the employees of one type or all the employees of one department in a company.

Collective mark   A distinctive design or logo used to indicate membership in an organization, such as a union. A group's **trademark.**

Collective work   Under **copyright** law, a collection of individual works such as an issue of a magazine or an encyclopedia. The individual works are themselves copyrightable. All *collective works* are **compilations.**

Collectivism   See **communism** and **socialism.**

Collector   A temporary **executor** or **administrator** of an **estate.**

Colloquium   A **plaintiff's** explanation of a **defendant's** possibly harmless words in such a way that they become offensive and so connected to the plaintiff that they are **defamation** (**libel** or **slander**).

Colloquy   A discussion, often in private, among lawyers or among lawyers and the judge, during a trial, deposition, or other proceeding.

Collusion   *1.* Secret action taken by two or more persons together to cheat another or to commit **fraud.** For example, it is *collusion* if two persons agree that one should sue the other because the second person is **covered** by insurance. *2.* An agreement between husband and wife that one of them will commit (or appear to commit) an act that will allow the other one to get a **divorce.**

Color   Appearance or semblance; looking real or true on the surface, but actually false. For example, acting *"under color of law"* is taking an action that looks official or appears to be backed by law, but which is not. In most cases ("color of authority," "color of office," etc.) "color" implies deliberate falseness, but in other cases ("color of right," "color of title," etc.) "color" does not imply *deliberate* falseness.

Color of title   Apparent, but not actual, ownership, based on a document such as a **deed** or a court **decree.**

Colorable   *1.* False; counterfeit; having the appearance, but not the reality. *2.* **Prima facie.**

Comaker   A second (or third or more) person who signs a **negotiable instrument,** such as a check, and by doing so promises to pay on it in full.

Combination   *1.* A group of persons working together, especially for an unlawful purpose. *2.* A putting together of inventions, each of which might be already **patented,** but which by working together produce a new, useful result. A *combination* may qualify for a separate patent.

Comfort letter   A letter from an **accounting** firm saying that, upon informal review, a company's financial records seem to be in order although full, official approval requires an **audit.**

Comity   Courtesy and respect. A willingness to do something official, not as a matter of right, but out of goodwill and tradition. For example, nations often give effect to the laws of other nations out of *comity,* and state and federal courts depend on comity to help keep their decisions consistent with each other. Also, *union comity* is a courtesy extended by one union to another, usually by treating the other union's member as if one of its own for some purposes.

Comment period   A time period after an **administrative agency** publishes a **regulation** during which the agency must accept public comment and may not begin to act on the regulation.

Comment upon evidence doctrine   A rule that a **trial** judge may not give the jury his or her opinion about whether **evidence** offered is true or false.

Commerce   *1.* The buying, selling, transporting, or exchanging of goods or services. *2.* Short for the Department of Commerce, the **cabinet** department that promotes U.S. trade, economic development, and technology. It includes the **patent** office and many scientific and business-development branches.

Commerce clause   The provision of the U.S. **Constitution** (Article I, Section 8) that gives Congress the power to control trade with foreign countries and from state to state. This is called the *commerce power.* Congress can regulate anything that "affects interstate commerce" or uses the "instrumentalities of interstate commerce" (and can keep the states from regulating interstate commerce because the federal government has this power under the **supremacy clause**).

Commercial code   See **Uniform Commercial Code.**

Commercial insurance   *1.* Insurance against a business loss due to another company's failure to perform a **contract.** *2.* Insurance against general business losses beyond the company's control.

Commercial paper   A **negotiable instrument** (see that word) related to business; for example, a **bill** *of exchange.* Sometimes, the word is restricted to a company's short-term **notes.**

Commercial speech   Expression, such as newspaper ads, related solely to the economic interest of the "speaker" and its audience. *Commercial speech* is entitled to **First Amendment** protection but not to the extent that personal or political expression is protected.

Commercial unit   An item or group of items that would lose value or commercial viability if subdivided into separate parts.

Commingling   Mixing together; for example, putting two different persons' money into one bank account in a way that makes separate accounting difficult or risks the loss of money entrusted to the person controlling the account. See also **confusion.**

Commission   *1.* A written grant of authority to do a particular thing, given by the government to one of its branches or to an individual or organization. *2.* An organization like one mentioned in no. 1. *3.* Payment (to a salesperson or other **agent**) based on the amount of sales, on a percentage of the profit, etc. *4.* Doing a criminal act.

Commission merchant   A **factor.**

Commission on Civil Rights   A federal fact-finding group that monitors enforcement of the **Civil Rights** _Acts._

Commission on Uniform State Laws   An organization that, along with the **American Law Institute,** proposes various **Model Acts** and **Uniform Acts** for adoption by the states.

Commissioner   _1._ The name for the heads of various government **boards** and **agencies.** _2._ A person appointed by a court to handle special matters, such as to conduct a court-ordered sale or to take **testimony** in complicated, specialized cases.

Commitment   The formal process of putting a person into the official care of another person such as the warden of a prison or the head of a psychiatric hospital. See **civil commitment.**

Commitment fee   A payment to a lender for making a loan or opening an ongoing **line of credit.**

Committee   _1._ A subgroup that a larger group appoints to do specialized work; for example, the Agriculture Committee of the House of Representatives. _2._ A person or group of persons appointed by a court to take care of the money and property of a person who is legally _incompetent_ (see **incompetency**). A type of **trustee.**

Committee of the whole   A procedure in which a **legislature** works as if it were a **committee** in order to get business done more quickly and informally. Decisions of the "_committee of the whole_" are then voted on by the legislature acting as a "real" legislature.

Commodity   _1._ Anything produced, bought, or sold. _2._ A raw or partially processed material. _3._ A farm product such as corn.

Commodity Credit Corporation   A federal agency that stabilizes the price and supply of crops by making loans and **price support** payments, controlling acreage under production, etc.

Commodity Futures Trading Commission   The federal agency that regulates contracts to buy and sell future supplies of raw products such as corn, silver, etc. See **futures.**

Common   _1._ A piece of land used by many persons. _2._ Usual; ordinary; regular; applying to many persons or things.

Common carrier   See **carrier.**

Common council   A local (town or city) **legislature.**

Common count   See **count.**

Common disaster   When two people die in the same accident with no way to tell who died first (for **insurance** or **inheritance** purposes). A *common disaster clause* in a **will** spells out what the person making the will wants to happen to his or her property if the person to whom the property is left dies at the same time. See also **simultaneous death act.**

Common enemy doctrine   The right of a landowner to keep out river or other surface water even if the water is diverted to another person's property. Compare with **civil law** *rule.*

Common fund rule   If a person goes to court to get a particular fund of money and if others benefit from the lawsuit, the person receives all lawsuit costs and lawyers' fees from the fund before the others take their shares.

Common law   *1.* Either all **caselaw** (see that word) or the caselaw that is made by judges in the absence of relevant **statutes.** *2.* The legal system that originated in England and is composed of caselaw and statutes that grow and change, influenced by ever-changing custom and tradition.

Common law action   *1.* A **civil** (as opposed to **criminal**) lawsuit that is between private individuals or organizations and contains a request for **damages.** *2.* A lawsuit, such as those in no. 1, that is not based on a written law or **statute.**

Common law marriage   A legally binding marriage that occurs without license or ceremony under the laws of many states when a man and woman hold themselves out as married (or live together as if married) for a specified time period.

Common law pleading   See **pleading** no. 3, then the rest of the entry.

Common law trust   **Business trust.**

Common pleas court   The name for several different types of **civil** trial courts.

Common scheme (or plan or design)   *1.* Two or more different crimes planned together. *2.* Two or more persons planning the same crime. *3.* Dividing a piece of land into lots with identical restrictions on land use.

Common situs picketing   **Picketing** an entire construction site by a union having a dispute with one of the **contractors** doing work. This is generally illegal.

Common stock   **Shares** in a **corporation** that depend for their value on the value of the company. These shares usually have voting rights (which other types of company stock may lack). Usually, they earn a **dividend** (profit) only after all other types of the company's obligations and stocks have been paid.

Commonwealth _1._ A state or country, especially a democratic one. _2._ The **people** (see that word) of a state or country. Also, the people as a group are called "_the commonalty_" and the public good or welfare is called "_the commonweal._"

Communication intelligence Information obtained by intercepting others' messages by wiretapping, radio surveillance, and other means.

Communism A system in which most property is owned by the state and most economic and social decisions are made by the government in a theoretically classless society run by "the masses."

Community _1._ Neighborhood, locality, etc. A vague term that can include very large or very small areas. _2._ A group with common interests. _3._ Shared. See **community property.**

Community property Property owned _in common_ (both persons owning it all) by a husband and wife. "_Community property states_" are those states that call most property acquired during the marriage the property of both partners no matter whose name it is in.

Community trust An organization set up to administer a **charitable** or public **trust.**

Commutation Changing a criminal punishment to one less severe. Compare with **pardon** and **reprieve.**

Commutative contract A **contract** with **mutual** rights and duties.

Commuted value **Present worth.**

Comp. _1._ Compiled. _2._ Compensation. _3._ **Comparables.**

Compact An agreement or contract (usually between governments).

Compact clause The provision of the U.S. **Constitution** (Article I, Section 10, Clause 3) that prohibits states from making agreements with other states or foreign countries without congressional approval.

Company Any organization set up to do business. For various types of company, such as **holding** or **trust,** see those words.

Comparable worth The idea, as expressed in the federal _Equal Pay Act,_ that men and women should receive equal pay for jobs with equal duties or that require equal skills.

Comparables Similar, nearby properties used to estimate a property's **market value.**

Comparative negligence rule A legal rule, used in many states, by which the amount of "fault" on each side of an accident is measured and the side with less fault is given **damages** (money) according to the difference between the magnitude of each side's fault. (A different rule is that any **negligence** at all stops that side from getting any damages in most situations. See **contributory negligence.**)

Comparative rectitude rule   A legal rule by which a divorce is given to the person in a marriage who the judge decides has behaved better. It is also called a *least fault divorce.*

Compelling state interest   A strong enough reason for a state law to make the law **constitutional** even though the law classifies persons on the basis of race, sex, etc. or uses the state's police powers to limit an individual's constitutional rights.

Compensating balance   A minimum amount of money that a person or company must keep in a no-interest checking account to compensate a bank for loans or other services.

Compensation   *1.* Payment for loss, injury, or damage. *2.* Payment of any sort for work or services performed.

Compensatory damages   **Damages** awarded for the actual loss suffered by a **plaintiff.** Compare with **punitive damages.**

Competency proceeding   A **hearing** to determine a person's mental capacity. It may be for a **civil commitment** (see that word) or to determine whether a person is competent to stand trial in a **criminal** case. Competency to stand trial depends on the ability to understand what is happening and why and to assist in the **defense** of the case. *Competency* may be different from *sanity* (see **insanity**).

Competent   *1.* Properly qualified, adequate, having the right natural or legal qualifications. For example, a person may be *competent* to make a **will** if he or she understands what making a will is, knows that he or she is making a will, and knows generally how making the will affects persons named in the will and affects relatives. *2.* See **competency proceeding.**

Competent evidence   **Evidence** that is both relevant to the point in question and the proper type of evidence to prove the point; evidence that cannot be kept out by any **exclusionary rule** (see that word).

Compilation   Under **copyright** law, a work formed by assembling pre-existing data or other shorter works. Compare with **collective work.**

Compiled statutes   See **code.**

Complainant   *1.* A person who makes an official complaint. *2.* A person who starts a lawsuit (see **plaintiff**).

Complaint   *1.* The first main paper filed in a **civil** lawsuit. It includes, among other things, a statement of the wrong or harm done to the **plaintiff** by the **defendant,** a request for specific help from the court, and an explanation why the court has the power to do what the plaintiff wants. _2._ Any official "complaint" in the ordinary sense; for example, a complaint to the police about a noisy party. _3._ A _criminal complaint_ is a formal document that charges a person with a crime.

Complete voluntary trust A **trust** that has been set up in all its details (**trustee, beneficiary,** limits, methods, etc.).

Complex trust Any **trust** other than a **simple** trust, especially one in which **trustees** have wide **discretion** to pay out or accumulate income.

Compliance Acting in a way that does not violate a law or the terms of an agreement. For example, when a state gets federal money for a state project, the project must be in _compliance_ with the federal law that allows the money and, sometimes, with the **regulations** of the federal agency that gives it out.

Complicity _1._ Participation in a wrong. _2._ Participation in a crime as an **accomplice.** [pronounce: com-pliss-ity]

Compos mentis (Latin) Of sound mind; sane and **competent.**

Composition A formal agreement, involving a **debtor** and several creditors, that each **creditor** will take less than the whole amount owed as full payment. For a "_composition in bankruptcy,_" see **Chapter Thirteen.**

Compound _1._ Combine parts or ingredients into a whole. _2._ Compromise. Rid yourself of a debt by convincing the **creditors** to accept a smaller amount. _3._ See **compound interest.** _4._ See **compounding a felony.**

Compound interest Interest on interest. Adding interest to the **principal** (the main debt) at regular intervals and then computing the interest on the newly increased principal plus interest.

Compounding a felony Accepting money or other gain in exchange for not prosecuting or not testifying about a major crime.

Comprises Made up of; includes.

Compromise verdict A jury's agreement reached by **jurors** giving up strongly held opinions in exchange for other jurors giving up different strongly held opinions, rather than by jurors changing opinions due to reasoned persuasion. This type of **verdict** (for example, a **quotient verdict**) is not usually permitted.

Comptroller The financial officer of a company or a government agency. For example, the comptroller general of the U.S. heads the General Accounting Office, which **audits** government agencies and investigates their problems. [pronounce: con-troll-er]

Compulsion _1._ **Duress.** _2._ An overpowering impulse.

Compulsory counterclaim See **counterclaim.**

Compulsory process Official action to force a person to appear in court or to appear before a **legislature** as a witness. This is usually by **subpoena,** but sometimes by **arrest.** A **party** in a **civil** case may often compel a witness to come to court and a **criminal** defendant always has that right under the **Sixth Amendment.**

Compurgator See **wager of law.**

Con *1.* Short for "contra"; against; on the other hand. *2.* A prefix meaning "with" or "together." *3.* Short for *"constitutional." 4.* Short for convict (or former convict, as in "ex-con"). *5.* Short for "confidence," as in a "con" man who takes advantage of a person's confidence to "con" (cheat) the person.

Concentration banking See **lockbox system.**

Conception In **patent** law, an inventor's completely formed idea for an invention. The *date of conception* is the day this idea, and not merely its general principles, is put down on paper. See also **reduction** *to practice.*

Concert of action rule The rule that, unless a **statute** specifies otherwise, it is not a **conspiracy** (see that word) for two persons to agree to commit a crime if the definition of the crime itself requires the participation of two or more persons. Also called *Wharton Rule* and *concerted action rule.*

Concerted activities *1.* In labor law, activities protected by the National Labor Relations Act. These include the rights to strike, picket peacefully, boycott (in ways not prohibited), etc. *2.* See **concert of action rule.**

Conciliation The process of bringing together two sides to agree to a voluntary compromise.

Conclusion of fact *1.* A **finding** *of fact* needed to reach a **conclusion of law** (see bold words). *2.* A factual inference drawn from other facts.

Conclusion of law *1.* An argument or answer arrived at by not only drawing a conclusion from facts, but also applying law to the facts. For example, it is only a conclusion of fact to say that a person hit another person with a car, but it is a *conclusion of law* to say that the accident was the driver's fault. *2.* A judge's application of legal principles to facts that can support those principles. *3.* See also **legal conclusion.**

Conclusive Beyond dispute; ending inquiry or debate; clear. For example, a *"conclusive presumption"* is a legal conclusion that cannot be changed by any facts. *Not* **conclusory.**

Conclusory Describes an assertion that is not supported by facts. *Not* **conclusive.**

Concordat A formal agreement between two countries; a **compact.**

Concur Agree. A *"concurring opinion,"* or *"concurrence,"* is one in which a judge agrees with the result reached in an **opinion** by another judge in the same case but not necessarily with the reasoning that the other judge used to reach the conclusion.

Concurrent "Running together"; having the same authority; at the same time. For example, courts have *concurrent jurisdiction* when each one has the power to deal with the same case; *concurrent sentences* are prison terms that run at the same time; and federal and state governments have *concurrent power* to govern in many areas.

Concurrent resolution See **resolution.**

Concurrent sentence doctrine The principle that an appeals court need not review the validity of the convictions based upon each **count** in a criminal trial if the defendant was given **concurrent** *sentences* for the counts and if the appeals court upholds the validity of one of the counts.

Condemn (or condemnation) *1.* Find guilty of a criminal charge. *2.* A governmental taking of private property with payment, but not necessarily with consent. *3.* A court's decision that the government may seize a ship owned privately or by a foreign government. *4.* An official ruling that a building is unfit for use.

Condition *1.* A future, uncertain event that creates or destroys rights and obligations. For example, a **contract** may have a *condition* in it that if one person should die, the contract is ended. Conditions may be **express** or **implied** (see those words). Also, they may be **precedent** (if a certain future event happens, a right or obligation is created) or *subsequent* (if a certain future event happens, a right or obligation ends). *2.* A requirement. For example, a *condition of employment* is a requirement for keeping a job, such as the requirement that a police officer live in the city of employment.

Conditional Depending on a **condition** (see that word); unsure; depending on a future event. For example, a *conditional sale* is a sale in which the buyer gets **title** (full legal ownership) only after full payment. And, in landlord-tenant law, a *conditional limitation* is a lease clause that gives the landlord the right to end the lease before its regular expiration if, for example, the tenant fails to pay the rent.

Conditional use See **special use permit.**

Condominium Several persons owning individual pieces of a building (usually an apartment house) and managing it together. Compare with **cooperative.**

Condonation Willing forgiveness by a wife or husband of the other's actions that is enough to stop those actions from being **grounds** for a **divorce.** Condonation can occur by the behavior of the parties. For example, a resumption of marital relations after learning of adultery may be condonation.

Conduit A channel or passage. An organization (such as a corporation) is considered a *conduit* for tax purposes if certain tax benefits or consequences merely *pass through* on their way to the actual owners of the organization.

Confederacy *1.* A general word for persons who band together to do an illegal act. A more usual word for this is "**conspiracy**" (see that word). *2.* A loose union of independent governments. A more usual word for this is "*confederation.*" *3.* The shorthand name for the *Confederate States of America,* the eleven states that seceded from the United States during the Civil War.

Conference committee A committee composed of representatives of both **houses** of a **legislature** to work out differences between versions of a **bill** passed by each house. Agreements are then usually voted on by each house. The members are *conferees* or *managers.* Compare **joint committee.**

Confession *1.* A voluntary statement by a person that he or she is guilty of a crime. *2.* Any admission of wrongdoing.

Confession and avoidance See **avoidance.**

Confession of judgment A process in which a person who borrows money or buys on credit signs in advance to allow the lawyer for the lender to get a court judgment without even telling the borrower. See **judgment** and **cognovit.**

Confidential relation Any relationship where one person has a right to expect a higher than usual level of care and faithfulness from another person; for example, client and attorney, child and parent, employee and employer. Another name for these relationships, if a strong duty exists, is a **fiduciary** *relationship.*

Confidentiality *1.* The requirement that a lawyer, or anyone working for a lawyer, not disclose information received from a client. There are exceptions to this requirement; for example, if the lawyer is told that the client is planning to commit a crime. *2.* The requirement that certain other persons (such as clergy, physicians, husbands, wives, etc.) not disclose information that is considered to be *privileged communication.*

Confirmation *1.* Formal approval, especially formal written approval. *2.* A notice that something has been received, sent, ordered, etc.

3. Agreeing that something is correct. For example, a document in which a company's supplier or customer verifies financial figures or item counts for a review of the company's finances by an **auditor.** *4.* The transfer of legal **title** to land to a person who has possession of the land. *5.* A **contract** that reaffirms a prior agreement that might have been otherwise difficult to prove or enforce. *6.* The approval of a presidential appointment by Congress.

Confiscation   The government's taking of private property without payment. The government may lawfully confiscate property that is illegal to possess (**contraband**) or property that is the "fruit" of certain illegal activity (such as a car bought with money from a drug deal). Government action may also have the *effect* of confiscation if, for example, it taxes a product's sale at 100 percent of the product's value.

Conflict of interest   Being in a position where your own needs and desires could possibly lead you to violate your duty to a person who has a right to depend on you, or being in a position where you try to serve two competing **masters** or clients. A conflict need not even be intentional. For example, a judge who holds XYZ stock may be unconsciously influenced in a case concerning the XYZ Company.

Conflict of laws   The situation that exists when the laws of more than one state or country may apply to a **case** and a judge must choose among them. *Conflict of laws* is also the name for the legal subject concerned with the rules used to make such choices.

Conformed copy   An exact copy of a document with written explanations of things that could not be copied. For example, the handwritten signature and date might be replaced on the copy by the notation "signed by Jonah Brown on July 27, 1977." Compare with **examined copy.**

Conforming   *1.* See **nonconforming lot** and **nonconforming use.** *2.* The *Uniform Commercial Code's* term describing **goods** that meet all contract requirements.

Conformity hearing   After a judge decides in favor of one side in a lawsuit, the judge may tell the lawyer for the winner to draw up a **judgment** or **decree** to carry out the judge's decision. A *conformity hearing* may then be held to decide whether the judgment or decree properly reflects the judge's decision.

Confrontation   The **constitutional** right, under the *confrontation clause* of the **Sixth Amendment,** of a criminal **defendant** to see and cross-examine all **witnesses** against him or her.

Confusion *1.* Mixing or blending together. For example, *confusion of goods* is a mixing together of the property of two or more persons with the effect that it is not possible to tell which goods belong to which person. See also **commingling.** *2.* **Merger.** When a **creditor** and a **debtor,** a landlord and a tenant, etc., become the same person, usually because of an **inheritance,** and separate legal rights and duties become one, often ending the duty.

Conglomerate A company composed of other companies, or that owns other companies, especially a powerful company with holdings in many different industries.

Congress *1.* The **legislature** of the United States (the House of Representatives plus the Senate); often abbreviated "Cong." *2.* A meeting of officials (often of different countries).

Congressional Record A daily printed record of proceedings in the U.S. **Congress.** It tells how each **bill** was voted upon, which bills were sent to and from each **committee,** etc.

Conjoint **Joint.** Together as one.

Conjugal Having to do with marriage. For example, *conjugal rights* are a husband and wife's legal interest in the other's companionship, love, and sexual relationship.

Conjunctive Containing several interconnected parts, rights, duties, etc. Compare with **disjunctive.**

Connecting up A thing may be admitted into **evidence** subject to *connecting up* with later evidence showing that its **admission** was correct.

Connivance The consent (or help) of a husband or wife to the other's acts in order to obtain a **divorce** based on those acts.

Connubial Concerning marriage.

Consanguinity Having a blood relationship; kinship.

Conscience of the court A court's **equity** power.

Conscientious objector A person who has religious objections to participating in a war. To avoid serving in the armed forces, a person need not necessarily belong to an organized religion.

Conscious parallelism A business's independent decision to take the same actions (usually to set the same product prices) as another business. This is probably not a violation of **antitrust** laws.

Consecutive sentence A **cumulative sentence.**

Consensual crime **Victimless crime.**

Consensus ad item (or ad idem) (Latin) **Meeting of minds.**

Consent Voluntary and active agreement.

Consent decree *1.* A **divorce** that is granted against a person who is in court or represented by a lawyer in court and who does not oppose the divorce. *2.* A settlement of a lawsuit or prosecution in which a person or company agrees to take certain actions without admitting fault or guilt for the situation causing the lawsuit. Also a *consent order* or *consent judgment.*

Consequential damages Court-ordered compensation for *indirect* losses or other indirect harm. Also, in contract law, sometimes called *special damages.*

Conservator A guardian or preserver of another person's property appointed by a court because the other person cannot legally manage it.

Consideration The reason or main cause for a person to make a **contract;** something of value received or promised to induce (convince) a person to make a deal. For example, if Ann and Sue make a deal for Ann to buy a car from Sue, Ann's promise to pay a thousand dollars is *consideration* for Sue's promise to hand over the car and vice versa. Without consideration a contract is not valid. The concept of *consideration* has two parts: *valuable* (can be valued in money) and *good* (legally sufficient). Ann and Sue's deal is an example of both parts of the concept. *Consideration* for a valid contract between close relatives, however, can be *good* even if not *valuable* because their "*love and affection*" may be legally sufficient even if it cannot be valued in money.

Consignment Handing over things for transportation or for sale, but keeping ownership.

Consol *1.* A **bond** that keeps on paying interest forever and never gets paid off. *2.* An abbreviation for *consolidated. 3. Not **consul, counsel,*** or **council.**

Consolidated statements *1.* Financial statements of legally separate companies combined as if they were one company. *2.* See **statement** *of income.*

Consolidation *1.* Combining the trials of different lawsuits that are on the same general subject and between the same persons. They are treated as only one lawsuit. A *consolidated appeal* is two **appellants** becoming one if their interests are the same. *2.* Generally, bringing together separate things and making them into one thing; often abbreviated *consol. 3.* Two **corporations** joining together to form a third, new one. Compare with **merger.** *4.* Collecting a government's **statutes** on a particular topic and making minor changes. Compare **codification.** *5.* A *consolidation loan* is a loan that repays other loans, usually to improve the interest rate or extend the payment time.

Consonant statement rule   If a witness's believability has been damaged, the witness's prior out-of-court statements that back up his or her current **testimony** may be used to prove that the witness is believable. These "consonant statements" may be used even though out-of-court statements are **hearsay** and are not normally permitted as **evidence,** but because they are hearsay, they may *not* be used to directly prove what the witness claims.

Consortium   *1.* The right of a husband or wife to the other's love and services. **Damages** are sometimes given to one spouse to compensate for the *loss of consortium* that occurs when the other spouse is wrongly killed or injured. *2.* A group of companies that band together for a large project. [pronounce: con-<u>sore</u>-shum]

Conspiracy   *1.* A crime that may be committed when two or more persons agree to do something unlawful (or to do something lawful by unlawful means). The agreement can be inferred from the persons' actions. A person can be guilty of both conspiracy to commit a crime and the crime itself (without violation of the right against **double jeopardy**), but certain crimes that require more than one person (such as **bribery**) are not usually also conspiracy. In some states, a conspiracy requires an *overt act* by one of the persons. Under the *Pinkerton rule* (*Pinkerton v. U.S.,* 328 U.S. 640 (1946)), a conspirator may be charged with acts done by coconspirators. *2. Civil conspiracy* is the name for a lawsuit for damages based on a *criminal conspiracy.*

Constable   A local peace officer who does court-related work.

Constant dollars   Current costs or prices as measured in preinflated (or predeflated) dollars of a set prior year.

Constant payment mortgage   The usual type of home owner's **mortgage,** in which equal monthly payments are made, with the proportion of each payment going to **principal** increasing and **interest** decreasing until the mortgage is paid off. Compare with **direct reduction mortgage.**

Constitute   Make up or put together. For example, *duly constituted* means properly put together and formally valid and correct.

Constitution   *1.* A document that sets out the basic principles and most general laws of a country, state, or organization. *2.* The U.S. Constitution is the basic law of the country, on which most other laws are based, and to which all other laws must yield. Often abbreviated "Const." or "Con."

Constitutional   1. Consistent with the **constitution;** not in conflict with the fundamental law contained in a state or federal constitution.

2. Depending on a constitution. For example, a *constitutional court* is one empowered by the U.S. Constitution.

Constitutional convention   Representatives of the people of a country who meet to write or change a **constitution.** Article V of the U.S. Constitution (which was written and adopted in the Philadelphia Constitutional Convention of 1787) allows a convention if two-thirds of the state **legislatures** call for one.

Constitutional fact doctrine   The principle that a federal court can ignore an administrative agency's decision that it has not violated a person's constitutional rights.

Constitutional law   The study of the law that applies to the organization, structure, and functions of the government, the basic principles of government, and the validity (or *constitutionality*) of laws and actions when tested against the requirements of the **Constitution.**

Constitutional right   A right or freedom guaranteed to the people by the **Constitution** (and, thus, safe from **legislative** or other governmental attempts to limit or end the right).

Construct validation   See **validation.**

Construction   A decision (usually by a judge) about the meaning and legal effect of ambiguous or doubtful words that considers not only the words themselves but also surrounding circumstances, relevant laws and writings, etc. (Looking at just the words is called "**interpretation,**" although *interpretation* is sometimes used to mean *construction* also.) See also **strict** *construction* and **liberal construction.**

Construction draw   A type of **mortgage** or other agreement in which a builder gets money as it is needed for building.

Constructive   True legally even if not factually; "just as if"; established by legal interpretation; inferred; implied. For example, a *constructive eviction* might occur when a landlord fails to provide heat in winter. This means that the tenant might be able to treat the legal relationship between landlord and tenant *as if* the landlord had thrown the tenant out without good reason. This might give the tenant the right to stop paying the rent.

Constructive contract   See **quasi contract.**

Constructive delivery   See **symbolic delivery.**

Constructive desertion   Forcing a husband or wife to leave. For example, when Mary is forced to leave because conditions at home are so bad that it amounts to John's forcing her out of the house, John has *constructively deserted* Mary, and Mary may get a divorce based on this in some states.

Constructive knowledge (or notice)   Knowledge that a person in a particular situation should have; that the person would have if he or she used reasonable care to keep informed; that is open for all to see; for example, knowledge of a properly recorded mortgage on a house you plan to buy.

Constructive receipt of income   A person who gains actual control of income will be taxed on it whether he or she actually takes the cash. For example, taxes must be paid in the year that savings account interest is earned, not in the later year it might actually be collected. See also **claim of right doctrine.**

Constructive trust   A situation in which a person holds legal **title** to property, but the property should, in fairness, actually belong to another person (because the title was gained by **fraud,** by a clerical error, etc.). In this case, the property may be treated by a court *as if* the legal owner holds it in **trust** for the "real" owner.

Construe   Decide the meaning of a document. See **construction.**

Consuetudo   (Latin) A custom or common practice. For *consuetudo mercatorum,* see **law merchant.**

Consul   A country's foreign representative, below the rank of **ambassador,** who usually can handle the country's and its citizens' business and private matters, but not usually political matters. *Consuls* usually work in *consulates* in foreign cities where there are no embassies. (*Not* **council, counsel,** or **consol.**)

Consular court   A court held by the **consuls** (representatives) of one country inside another country.

Consumer   A person who buys (or rents, travels on, or uses) something for personal, rather than business use.

Consumer credit   Money, property, or services offered to a person for personal, family, or household purposes "on time." It is *"consumer credit"* if there is a finance charge or if there are more than four **installment** payments.

Consumer Credit Protection Act   (15 U.S.C. 1601) A federal law requiring the clear **disclosure** of **consumer credit** (see that word) information by companies making loans or selling on credit. The act requires that **finance charges** (see that word) be expressed as a standard **annual percentage rate (APR),** gives consumers the right to back out of certain deals, **regulates** credit cards, restricts wage **garnishments,** etc. It is also called the *Truth-in-Lending Act.* Many states have adopted legislation similar to the federal act.

Consumer Price Index A federal Labor Department statistic that traces prices for goods and services bought by an "average consumer."

Consumer Product Safety Commission A federal agency that sets product safety standards, bans hazardous consumer products, etc.

Consummate Finish; complete what was started or intended.

Consummation *1.* Completion of a thing; carrying out an agreement. *2.* "Completing" a marriage by having sexual intercourse.

Contemner A person who commits **contempt.**

Contemplation of death An action taken in *contemplation of death* is one caused by or influenced strongly by thinking about your own probable imminent death. See **causa mortis.**

Contemporaneous objection rule The principle that an objection to the introduction of **evidence** must be made at the time the evidence is offered or the right to **appeal** its introduction is **waived.**

Contempt *1.* An act that obstructs a court's work or lessens the dignity of the court. This is usually *criminal contempt. 2.* A willful disobeying of a judge's command or official court order. Contempt can be *direct* (within the judge's notice) or *indirect* (outside the court and punishable only after proved to the judge). It can also be *civil contempt* (disobeying a court order in favor of an opponent) or *criminal contempt.* (See no. 1.) *3.* It is also possible to be in *contempt* of a **legislature** or an **administrative agency.**

Content validation See **validation.**

Contest *1.* Oppose or defend against a lawsuit or other action. *2.* Oppose the validity of a **will.**

Context *1.* Surrounding words. *2.* The whole document.

Continental Congress See **Declaration of Independence.**

Contingent Possible, but not assured; depending on some future events or actions *(contingencies)* that may or may not happen. For example, a *contingent estate* is a right to own or use property that depends on an uncertain future event for the right to take effect; and a *contingency reserve* is a fund of money set aside by a business to cover possible unknown future expenses (such as a **liability** that results from a lost lawsuit).

Contingent fee Payment to a lawyer of a percentage of the "winnings," if any, from a lawsuit rather than payment of a flat amount of money or payment according to the number of hours worked. A *defense (or negative or reverse) contingent fee* is payment based on the money the lawyer saves a client compared to the potential losses the client thinks are likely.

Contingent remainder   See **remainder.**

Continuance   The postponement of court proceedings to a later day or session of court.

Continuing appropriation   *1.* An **appropriation** of money by a government that continues automatically until it is revoked, used up, or the authorization is revoked. *2.* An appropriation passed by a **continuing resolution** (see that word).

Continuing jurisdiction   The power of a court to continue to control a matter even after the court has decided the case. Continuing jurisdiction allows the court to modify its own previous **orders,** especially in child **custody** or **support** cases.

Continuing offense   A single crime, such as a **conspiracy,** that can contain many individual acts over time. Even if the earlier acts might be too old to prosecute individually (because of a *statute of* limitations), the continuing nature of the crime allows these acts to be included in the crime prosecuted.

Continuing resolution   An act of a **legislature** that allows a government agency to continue spending at past levels when its **appropriation** has run out. Compare with **continuing appropriation.**

Contra (Latin)   *1.* Against; on the other hand; opposing. For example, *contra bonos mores* means "against good morals" or "offending the public conscience," and *contra pacem* means "against the peace" or "offending public order." *2.* In **accounting,** *contra accounts* are set up to show subtractions from other **accounts,** and *contra balances* are account **balances** that are the opposite (positive or negative) of what usually appears.

Contraband   Things that are illegal to import, export, transport, or possess.

Contract   An agreement that affects or creates legal relationships between two or more persons. To be a *contract,* an agreement must involve: at least one promise, **consideration** (something of value promised or given), persons legally capable of making binding agreements, and a reasonable certainty about the meaning of the terms. A contract is called **bilateral** if both sides make promises (such as the promise to deliver a book on one side and a promise to pay for it on the other) or **unilateral** if the promises are on one side only. According to the **Uniform Commercial Code,** a contract is the "total legal obligation which results from the parties' agreement," and according to the Restatement of the Law of Contracts, it is "a promise or set of promises for the breach of which the law in some way recognizes a duty." For the many different types of contracts, such as **output, requirements,** etc., see those words.

Contract Clause The provision in Article I of the U.S. **Constitution** that no state may pass a law abolishing contracts or denying them legal effect.

Contract for deed A **land sales contract.**

Contract sale See **conditional** *sale.*

Contract under seal An old form of **contract** that required a **seal** (see that word), but no **consideration** (see that word).

Contractor *1.* A person who takes on building or related work on a project basis as an **independent contractor.** A *"prime contractor"* or *"general contractor"* is in charge of the whole project and makes *"subcontracts"* with others (*subcontractors*) for parts of the job. *2.* An **independent contractor.**

Contravention Violation of law, rule, or custom; the act of failing to uphold a law or principle.

Contribution *1.* The sharing of payment for a debt (or **judgment**) among persons who are all **liable** for the debt. *2.* The right of a person who has paid an entire debt (or judgment) to get back a fair share of the payment from another person who is also responsible for the debt. For example, most **insurance** policies require that if another insurance company also **covers** a loss, each must share payment for ("contribute to") the loss in proportion to the maximum amount each covers.

Contributory A person who must pay up in full the price of **stock** owned in a company because the company is going out of business and owes money.

Contributory negligence Negligent (careless) conduct by a person who was harmed by another person's **negligence;** a **plaintiff**'s failure to be careful that is a part of the cause of his or her injury when the **defendant**'s failure to be careful is also part of the cause. *Contributory negligence* is an **affirmative defense** to negligence in some states. Compare with **comparative negligence.**

Controlled substances acts Federal and state laws to control or ban the manufacture, sale, and use of dangerous drugs (such as certain narcotics, stimulants, depressants, and hallucinogens that may cause addiction or abuse).

Controller **Comptroller.**

Controlling decision **Precedent** (see that word).

Controlling interest Enough shares of **stock** to decide a stockholder vote. This is either more than half the shares or enough shares for practical control because many small stockholders do not vote.

Controversy Any **civil** lawsuit that involves real legal rights at stake, rather than a hypothetical or potential invasion of rights. See **cases and controversies.**

Controvert Dispute, deny, or oppose.

Contumacy *1.* The refusal to appear in court when required to by the law. *2.* The refusal to obey a court order. See **contempt.**

Contumely Rudeness; scornful treatment.

Convenience and necessity See **certificate.**

Convention *1.* A meeting of representatives for a special purpose, such as to draw up a **constitution** or to nominate a **candidate** for an election. *2.* An agreement between countries on nonpolitical and nonfinancial matters such as fishing rights.

Conventional *1.* Usual or ordinary. *2.* Caused by an agreement between persons rather than by the effect of a law. For example, a *conventional mortgage* is one that involves just a person lending and a person borrowing money on a house as opposed to a mortgage that also involves a government subsidy or guarantee, and a *conventional lien* is one created by an agreement, rather than by a law or a lawsuit.

Conversion *1.* Any act that deprives an owner of property without that owner's permission and without just cause. For example, it is *conversion* to refuse to return a borrowed book. *2.* The exchange of one type of property for another; for example, turning in one type of **stock** to a company and getting another in return. The *conversion ratio* would be the number of shares you get for each share turned in and the *conversion price* the value of each new share (which is called a *conversion security*).

Convertible (noun) A **bond** or *preferred* **stock** that can be exchanged for **common stock** (see those words).

Conveyance *1.* A transfer of **title** to **land.** *2.* Any sale.

Conveyancer A person who prepares deeds and mortgages, examines titles, and otherwise helps transfer real estate.

Convict *1.* Find a person guilty of a crime. *2.* A person in prison.

Conviction *1.* The result of a criminal trial in which a person is found **guilty.** *2.* Firm belief.

Cooley doctrine The principle (from *Cooley v. Board of Wardens,* 53 U.S. 299) that a state may not **regulate** matters that are purely national and that require national regulation. See also **pre-emption.**

Cooling off period *1.* A period of time in which no action of a particular sort may be taken by either side in a dispute; for example, a *cool-*

ing off period of a month may be required after a union or a company files a *grievance* under a **grievance procedure** against the other. During this period the union may not strike and the company may not engage in a **lockout** against the employees. *2.* A period of time in which a buyer may cancel a purchase. Many states require a three-day cancellation period for door-to-door sales. *3.* An automatic delay in some states, in addition to ordinary court delays, between the filing of **divorce** papers and the divorce **hearing**.

Cooperative An organization set up to help the persons who form it and who use it. The word covers many different types of organizations set up for many different purposes. *Cooperatives* include: *apartment co-ops* (an apartment building owned by an organization of residents who **lease** the individual apartments, unlike a **condominium**); *consumer co-ops* (stores, utilities, health facilities, etc.); *marketing co-ops* (for example, one set up by milk producers in a certain area); *financial co-ops* (like **credit unions**); etc. Organizations like **labor unions** and **trade** associations are sometimes referred to as *cooperatives.*

Coordinate jurisdiction **Concurrent** (see that word) jurisdiction.

Cop a plea (slang) Agree as a **defendant** to a **plea bargain,** which typically involves pleading guilty to fewer or to lesser criminal charges.

Coparcenary An old word for a situation where several persons **inherit** property to share as if they were one person. These persons were called parceners.

Copartnership A **partnership.**

Copyhold An old form of holding land at the **will** of the lord of an area, but recorded in the record books in keeping with local custom.

Copyright The right to control the copying, distributing, performing, displaying, and adapting of *works* (including paintings, music, books, and movies). The right belongs to the creator, or to persons employing the creator, or to persons who buy the right from the creator. The right is created, regulated, and limited by the federal *Copyright Act of 1976* and by the Constitution. The symbol for copyright is ©. The legal life (*duration*) of a copyright is the author's life plus fifty years, or seventy-five years from publication date, or one hundred years from creation, depending on the circumstances.

Coram (Latin) Before; in the presence of. For example, *"coram nobis"* (before us) is the name for a request that a court change its **judgment** due to the excusable failure of a **defendant** to raise facts that would have won the case. *"Coram vobis"* is a request for a higher court to order a lower one to correct the same sort of problem as raised by a *coram nobis*. These requests are no longer used in most places. "*Coram non judice*" means "before a non-judge." It describes a finding or judgment by a court with no **jurisdiction,** which means that the judgment is **void.**

Core proceeding   Any non-**bankruptcy** court case or administrative proceeding that can legitimately be taken under the control of the bankruptcy court in one of its cases. The bankruptcy laws define several types of procedures that are so closely related to bankruptcy that they are *core,* but other types of proceedings may also become core if they directly affect the bankruptcy court's work in a particular case.

Co-respondent (or corespondent)   The "other man" or "other woman" in a divorce suit based on **adultery.** See also **correspondent.**

Corner   *1.* Owning enough of some **stock** or **commodity** to have control over the selling price in the general marketplace. *2.* Owning **contracts** for more future delivery of a commodity than is produced of that commodity. When the persons who have promised to deliver cannot do it, the price shoots sky high and the person with the *corner* greatly profits.

Corollary   A secondary or "side" deduction or inference in logic or argument.

Coroner   A doctor or other public official who conducts inquiries into the cause of any violent or suspicious death. If the case is serious, there is a *coroner's inquest* or hearing. Many places have replaced coroners with **medical examiners** (see that word).

Corporal punishment   Physical punishment (beating, etc.).

Corporate   Concerning or belonging to a **corporation.** For example, the *corporate opportunity doctrine* is the principle that company officers and directors should be prevented from personally exploiting a business opportunity properly belonging to the company.

Corporate reorganization   See **reorganization.**

Corporate veil   The legal assumption that actions taken by a **corporation** are not the actions of its owners, and that these owners cannot usually be held responsible for corporate actions. When the owners are held responsible, the *corporate veil* is said to be *pierced.*

Corporation   An organization that is formed under state or federal law and exists, for legal purposes, as a separate being or an "*artificial person.*" It may be public (set up by the government) or private (set up by individuals), and it may be set up to carry on a business or to perform almost any function. Large business corporations owned by _stockholders_ are governed by publicly filed _articles of incorporation_ and more detailed private _bylaws,_ and managed by a _board of directors_ who delegate authority to _officers._ The stockholders have no **liability** for corporate debts beyond the value of their stock. See also **close(d) corporation, C corporation,** and **S corporation.** See **business organization** for other organizations set up to make a profit. Abbreviated "_Corp._"

Corporation counsel   The lawyer who represents a city or town in **civil** matters.

Corporeal   Having body or substance; visible and tangible. [pronounce: cor-_por_-ee-al]

Corpus   (Latin) "Body"; main body of a thing as opposed to attachments. For example, _"corpus juris"_ means "a body of law" or a major collection of laws, and a **trust corpus** is the money or property put into the trust, as opposed to interest or profits.

Corpus delicti   (Latin) "The body of the crime." _1._ The material substance upon which a crime has been committed; for example, a dead body (in the crime of murder) or a house burned down (in the crime of arson). _2._ The fact that proves that a crime has been committed. _3._ The _corpus delicti rule_ is the principle that the prosecutor must produce evidence that a crime has been committed even if the defendant has confessed to the crime before the trial.

Corpus Juris   A legal encyclopedia that is cross-referenced with the **American Digest System.**   _Corpus Juris Secundum_ is its most recent update.

Corpus juris civilis   (Latin) "The body of the civil law"; the main writings of Roman law.

Corrections   _1._ The government agency that supervises prisons, parole programs, etc. _2._ The word stockbrokers use for everything from tiny stock market dips to the Great Depression.

Correlative   Describes ideas that have a mutual relationship and depend on one another for their meaning. For example, "parent" and "child" are _correlative_ terms, as are "right" and "duty."

Correspondent   _1._ A person who collects **mortgage** loan payments for the lender. _2._ A bank or other financial institution that performs regular services for another. _3._ See also **co-respondent.**

Corroborate   Add to the likely truth or importance of a fact; give additional facts or evidence to strengthen a fact or an assertion; back up what someone else says.

Corrupt practices act   *1.* A state law that **regulates** political campaign methods and spending. *2.* A federal law (18 U.S.C. 602) that regulates international corporate financial activities.

Corruption of blood   An old punishment for a crime by which a person was deprived of the right to take property, hold it, or pass it on to **heirs** at death.

Cosigner   A general term for a person who signs a document along with another person. Depending on the situation and on the state, a cosigner may have *primary* responsibility (for example, to pay a debt if the person who made the cosigned loan comes first to the cosigner for the money) or only a *secondary* responsibility (to pay a debt only after the person who took out the loan doesn't pay).

Cost and freight   The price quoted includes cost and freight, but not insurance or any other charge.

Cost effective   *1.* Benefits exceed (or will exceed) costs; profits exceed (or will exceed) losses. *2.* The alternative course of action with the highest benefits-divided-by-costs ratio is called "*cost effective.*"

Cost of living adjustment   A wage increase automatically tied to the inflation rate.

Cost of living allowance   Extra pay or expenses for working in a high-cost living area.

Cost of living clause   A provision in a **contract,** such as a labor agreement or a retirement plan, that gives an automatic wage or benefit increase tied to inflation as measured by a standard indicator, such as the **Consumer Price Index.**

Cost-plus contract   A **contract** that pays a **contractor** for the cost of labor and materials plus a fixed percentage of cost as profit.

Costs   Expenses of one side in a lawsuit that the judge orders the other side to pay or reimburse. "*Costs to abide the event*" are given by an **appeals** court and include the cost of the appeal and sometimes the cost of a retrial.

Cotenancy   Property ownership by two or more persons with each having an **undivided right** to the whole property, such as *joint tenancy, tenancy in common,* and *tenancy by the entirety.* See **tenant.**

Council   A local or city **legislature,** sometimes called "*common council.*" (*Not* **consul, counsel,** or **consol.**) [pronounce: <u>kown</u>-sel]

Counsel   *1.* A lawyer for a client. *2.* Advice (usually professional advice). *3.* See **of counsel.** *4. Not* **consul, council,** or **consol.**

Counsel, right to   The **constitutional** right of a **defendant** to have a lawyer at every important stage of a **criminal** proceeding from formal

charge through all **hearings, sentencing,** and **appeal.** This **Sixth Amendment** right applies in all crimes that might be punished by a jail term and applies also to juvenile delinquency proceedings.

Counsellor   Lawyer.

Count   *1.* Each separate part of a **complaint** or an **indictment** (see those words). Each *count* must be able to stand alone as a separate and independent **claim** or **charge.** *2.* The *"common counts"* were once the various **forms of action** (for example, **assumpsit**) for money owed.

Counter   Opposing or contradicting. For example, a counter-**affidavit** disputes the claims of another person's affidavit.

Counterclaim   A claim made by a **defendant** in a **civil** lawsuit that, in effect, "sues" the **plaintiff.** It can be based on entirely different things from the plaintiff's **complaint** (a *permissive counterclaim*) and may even be for more money than the plaintiff is asking. A counterclaim often must be made if it is based on the same subject or transaction as the original claim (a *compulsory counterclaim*); otherwise, the person with the counterclaim may not be permitted to sue for it later.

Counterfeit   *1.* Forge, copy, or imitate without authority or right, with the purpose of passing off the copy as the original. *2.* The copy in no. 1. [pronounce: <u>kown</u>-ter-fit]

Countermand   Take back or greatly change orders or instructions.

Counteroffer   *1.* A rejection of an **offer** and a new offer made back. A *counteroffer* sometimes looks like an **acceptance** with new terms or conditions attached, but if these terms or conditions have any substance at all, it is really a rejection, and no contract is made until the counteroffer is accepted. But see no. 2. *2.* Under the **Uniform Commercial Code,** a *counteroffer* for the sale of goods may be an acceptance plus new proposed **contract** terms.

Counterpart   *1.* A copy or duplicate of a document. *2.* An unsigned copy of a signed original document. *3.* A copy of a document that is signed by one person in a deal and given to the other person, who has signed the original in exchange. *4.* A *counterpart* **writ** is a copy that is issued to **defendants** in a county other than the one in which a lawsuit is heard, but one in which the court does have **jurisdiction.**

Countersign   Sign a document in addition to the primary or original signature in order to approve the validity of the document. A bank may ask a person to *countersign* his or her own check made out to "cash," and a company may require a supervisor to countersign all orders written by lower-ranking employees.

Countervailing   Opposing; equal to; balancing out.

County The largest geographical and political division of a state. A *county court* is usually a low-level state court.

County commissioners Elected county officials with various duties. These duties may include running the county government or managing its financial affairs, its police, its low-level judicial work, etc. Also called *county supervisors.*

Coupon A **certificate** of interest or a **dividend** due on a certain date. The coupons are detached one by one from the primary document (**bond,** loan agreement, etc.) and presented for payment when due.

Course of business What is normally done by an individual company. This is different from "*custom*" or "*usage,*" which is what is normally done by a particular *type* of company.

Course of dealing The history of business between two persons *before* the current business deal. Compare **course of performance.**

Course of employment Directly related to employment, during work hours, or in the place of work.

Course of performance The way each side carries out an ongoing business deal. Compare **course of dealing.**

Court *1.* The place where judges work. *2.* A judge at work. For example, a judge might say, "the court (meaning 'I') will consider this matter." *3.* All the judges in a particular area.

Court hand An old system of Latin shorthand once used in England for legal documents.

Court martial A military court for trying members of the armed services according to the **Code of Military Justice.** There are three types of *courts martial.* A "*summary court martial*" is for the least serious military crimes, allows only sentences under two months or lesser penalties, and gives very few procedural protections to the person accused. For example, there need be no lawyer present, and the officer who acts as a judge is the fact-finder as well as decider. A "*special court martial*" is an intermediate military court. It has most of the protections of a regular criminal trial and may hand out punishments ranging from a "bad conduct" discharge to several months in prison. A "*general court martial*" can try the most serious military cases and can hand out sentences up to the death penalty. It has all the procedural protections of a regular criminal trial and usually includes a panel of officers, a trained judge, and trained military lawyers. See also **military law.**

Court of _____ A few courts are defined here, but most are listed by their individual names or subject matters (such as a **probate** court), or under **United States courts.**

Court of appeals (or error)   A court that decides **appeals** from a **trial** court. In most states it is a middle-level court (similar to a **United States Court** *of Appeals*), but in some states it is the highest court.

Court of inquiry   A military court that conducts investigations to determine the need for **adjudication** in another military court.

Court packing   A government executive's appointing as judges only those persons who conform to the executive's own philosophy. Court packing may include adding additional judgeships or otherwise restructuring the court.

Covenant   A formal promise, agreement, or restriction, usually in a **deed** or **contract** (or the contract itself). For example, a *covenant for quiet enjoyment* is a promise that the seller of land will protect the buyer against a defective **title** to the land and against anyone who claims the land; a *covenant running with the land* is any agreement in a deed that is binding for or against all future buyers of the land; and a *covenant not to compete* is a part of an employee contract, partnership agreement, or agreement to sell a business in which a person promises not to engage in the same business for a certain amount of time after the relationship ends. *2.* A **treaty.** *3.* To promise or agree formally.

Cover   *1.* Make good. *2.* Protect (for example, insurance **coverage**). *3.* Protect yourself from the effects of a business deal that falls through or isn't made good on; for example, buy what you need from a new company when the original one can't make good on a sale.

Coverage   *1.* The amount and type of **insurance** on a person, an object, a business venture, etc. *2.* The *ratio* of a company's income that is available to pay **interest** on its **bonds** (or to pay **dividends** on its *preferred* **stock**) to the interest itself (or to the dividends).

Coverture   The status that married women used to have; the special rights and legal limitations of a married woman.

Craft union   A **labor union** whose members all do the same kind of work (plumbing, carpentry, etc.) for different types of industries and employers.

Created   See **fixed work.**

Creative financing   Any financing (usually home-purchase) outside the normal pattern. It is used to complete a deal that would have failed otherwise. It may be risky.

Credentials   The right to represent a country, a group of voters, or an organization (or the document that proves that right). A "*credentials committee*" is a group that sorts out who has the right to represent subgroups at a political convention.

Credibility The believability of a **witness** and of the **testimony** that the witness gives.

Credit *1.* The right to delay payment for things bought or used. *2.* Money loaned. *3.* See **credits.** *4.* A deduction from what is owed. For example, a *tax credit* is a direct subtraction from tax owed (for other taxes paid, for certain special purposes such as a part of child care expenses, etc.). See also **deduction, exemption,** and **exclusion.** *5.* Believe something is true.

Credit bureau A place that keeps records on the **credit** used by persons and on their financial reliability.

Credit line See **line of credit.**

Credit rating An evaluation of the ability of a person or business to pay debts. Usually, a **credit bureau** makes an evaluation based on past payments and current finances, then sells the information in credit reports to businesses that are considering making a loan or offering other **credit.**

Credit union A financial organization that uses money deposited by a closed group of persons and lends it out again to persons in the same group.

Creditor A person to whom a debt is owed.

Creditor beneficiary When Alan and Betty have a contract in which Alan promises to do something that financially benefits Charles, Charles is a *creditor beneficiary.*

Creditor's bill (or suit) A request that a court help a **judgment creditor** find, get an accounting for, or get delivery of property owed by a debtor when the property cannot be seized and sold.

Creditor's committee (or meeting) A committee or meeting of persons to whom a **bankrupt** person owes money or who hold **security** interests in a bankrupt's property.

Creditor's position The part of a property's sale price that is put up by the **mortgage** lender.

Credits Records in an account book of money owed to you or money you have paid out. (The opposite of **debits.**)

Crim. Con. **Criminal conversation.**

Crime Any violation of the government's **penal** laws. An illegal act.

Crime against humanity See **war crime.**

Crime against nature See **sodomy.**

Crimen (Latin) Crime. For example, a *crimen falsi* is a "crime of fraud or falsehood" and includes **fraud, perjury, embezzlement,** and any other crime that involves lying or **deceit** and that might affect a person's believability as a **witness.**

Criminal _1._ Having to do with the law of crimes and illegal conduct. _2._ Illegal. _3._ A person who has committed a crime.

Criminal action The procedure by which a person accused of a crime is brought to trial and given punishment.

Criminal conversation Causing a married man or woman to commit **adultery.** Most states now prohibit lawsuits against the seducer. _Criminal conversation_ is a **tort,** not a **crime.**

Criminal forfeiture The loss of property to the government because it was involved in a crime; for example, the seizure of an automobile used to smuggle narcotics.

Criminal mischief The crime (or **tort**) of deliberately damaging another's property; usually applied to acts of vandalism such as slashing tires or painting graffiti.

Criminal syndicalism See **syndicalism.**

Criminology The study of the cause, prevention, and punishment of crime.

Criterion validation See **validation.**

Critical Legal Studies The study of law based on the idea that the hidden purpose behind the law's seemingly neutral language is to reinforce the control of dominant groups, so that the law itself discriminates against the disadvantaged.

Critical race theory The application of **Critical Legal Studies** to the idea that the law itself discriminates against racial minorities and perpetuates racism.

Critical stage That point in a **criminal** investigation or proceeding at which a person's rights might be violated. The **Sixth Amendment** to the **Constitution** requires that a person must have the opportunity to get a lawyer (or, if poor, have one provided) at this point. It may be as early as the first questioning by the police, but never later than the first **hearing.**

Cross-action (or cross-bill, complaint, or demand) _1._ A **counterclaim** or a **cross-claim** (see those words). _2._ A separate lawsuit against someone suing you.

Cross-claim A claim brought by one **defendant** against another, or by one **plaintiff** against another, that is based on the same subject matter as the plaintiff's lawsuit.

Cross-collateral   **Collateral** given to **secure** an unsecured debt in exchange for a new loan.

Cross-examination   The questioning of an opposing **witness** during a trial or **hearing**. See **examination**.

Crossing   A **broker's** buying a **stock** or other **security** from one client and selling it to another without going through an **exchange.**

Cross-license   License a **patent** to another company in exchange for that company's license of a similar patent. Doing this on a large scale is **patent pooling.**

Cross-picketing   **Picketing** by two or more **unions** that claim to represent the same workers.

Cross-remainder   Property that is inherited by several persons as a group. As each person dies, the others share that person's interest.

Cross-rules   An old word for **show cause** (see that word) orders that are given to both sides in a lawsuit.

Crown cases   In English law, **criminal** cases brought by the crown (government).

Cruel and unusual punishment   Punishment, by the government, that is prohibited by the **Eighth Amendment** to the Constitution. Recently, the courts have decided that many types of punishment should be discontinued as *"cruel and unusual"* because they shock the moral sense of the community.

Cruelty   In the law of **divorce,** harsh treatment by a husband or wife that gives the other **grounds** for a divorce. Its definition is different in each state, and may vary widely from the common meaning. The formal definition has no strong connection to what it actually takes to get a divorce nominally based on that definition. Some states' words for *cruelty* are: *"extreme cruelty," "intolerable cruelty," "willful cruelty,"* and *"intolerable severity."*

Ct. App.   **Court of Appeals.**

Culpable   Blamable; at fault. A person who has done a wrongful act (whether **criminal** or **civil**) is described as *"culpable."*

Culprit   A person who has committed a crime but has not yet been tried. This is not a technical legal word.

Cultural defense   A **defense** to a crime, based on the argument that immigrants to the U.S. should not be held responsible for crimes that would not have been crimes in their home countries. Also called *traditional behavior defense.* It is not widely accepted by U.S. courts.

Cum   (Latin) With.

Cum onere   (Latin) "Burdened with an **encumbrance**" (see that word).

Cum rights   With rights. A **stock** *cum rights* is a stock that gives its owner the right to buy more stock at a specified price.

Cum testamento annexo   (Latin) "With the **will** attached." Describes an **administrator** who is appointed by a court to supervise handing out the property of a dead person whose will does not name **executors** (persons to hand out property) or whose named executors cannot or will not serve.

Cumulative evidence   **Evidence** that is offered to prove what has already been proved by other evidence.

Cumulative legacy   Similar gifts (usually different amounts of money) to the same person in different parts of a **will**. There may be a **presumption** that the later gift was meant to replace the earlier one rather than to be added to the earlier one.

Cumulative sentence   An additional prison term given to a person who is already **convicted** of a crime, the additional term to be served after the previous one is finished.

Cumulative voting   The type of voting in which each person (or each share of **stock**, in the case of a **corporation**) has as many votes as there are positions to be filled. Votes can be either concentrated on one or on a few candidates or spread around.

Curative admissibility doctrine   The principle that if one side in a trial introduces normally **inadmissible** evidence, the other side may introduce the same type of evidence.

Curator   A person appointed by a court to take care of a person (and that person's property) who cannot take care of himself or herself (such as a child or someone mentally **incompetent**), or to take care of the property only (for example, for a **spendthrift**).

Cure   *1.* Remove a legal defect. For example, it is a *cure* when a seller delivers goods, the buyer rejects them because of some defect, and the seller then delivers the proper goods within the proper time. *2.* Correct a legal error. For example, an error in the course of a trial is *cured* if the **judgment** or **verdict** is in favor of the side complaining about the error. Compare with **aider.**

Curia   (Latin) Old European word for court.

Current   *1. Current* has many meanings; for example: immediate, within the same **accounting** period, within a year, within a few months, easily converted to cash, etc. *2. Current assets* are a company's cash plus those things such as short-term **securities, accounts receivable,** and **inventory** (see those words) that can probably be turned into cash within a few months. *3. Current liabilities* are a company's debts, such as **accounts payable** (see that word), wages, short-term borrowing, and taxes that must be paid within a few months. *4.* The *current ratio* is a company's *current assets* divided by its *current liabilities.* It is a measure of a company's short-term financial strength. See also **working capital** and **quick assets.**

Curtesy   A husband's right to part of his dead wife's property. This right is **regulated** by **statute** and varies from state to state. Compare with **dower.**

Curtilage   An area of household use immediately surrounding a home.

Cusip number   A number given by the Committee on Uniform Securities Identification Procedures of the American Bankers Association to identify each **issue** of **securities.**

Custodial interrogation   Questioning by police after a person has been deprived of freedom in any way. To use statements made during a *custodial interrogation* against the maker in court, a **Miranda warning** must have been properly given by the police. [pronounce: kus-<u>to</u>-dee-al]

Custody   Rightful possession without ownership; a general term meaning care and keeping. Parents normally have *custody* of their children, a warden has *custody* of prisoners, and a person has *custody* of a book loaned by another.

Custom   Regular behavior of persons in a geographical area or in a particular type of business that gradually takes on legal importance so that it will strongly influence a court's decision.

Custom house   The office where goods going into or out of a country are inspected and registered, and where taxes are paid.

Customs   *1.* Taxes payable on goods brought into or sent out of a country. (Also called "**duty.**") *2.* Short for the *U.S. Customs Service,* which oversees and taxes goods brought in and out of the United States.

Cut throat pricing   See **predatory intent.**

Cy-pres   (French) "As near as possible." When a dead person's **will** can no longer legally or practically be carried out, a court may (but is not obligated to) order that the dead person's **estate** be used in a way that most nearly does what the person would have wanted. The doctrine of *cy-pres* is now usually applied only to **charitable trusts.** [pronounce: see-pray]

D **Defendant; dictum; digest; district;** and many other law-related words.

D.A. **District Attorney.**

D.b.a. Doing business as.

D.B.E. **De bene esse.**

D.b.n. **De bonis non.**

D.C. District court; District of Columbia.

D.E.A. Drug Enforcement Administration. The branch of the U.S. Department of **Justice** that enforces narcotic and drug laws.

D.I.S.C. **Domestic International Sales Corporation.**

D.J. District judge.

D.N.A. fingerprinting (or I.D.) Comparing body tissue samples (such as blood, skin, hair, or semen) to see if the genetic materials match. It is used to identify criminals by comparing their DNA with that found at a crime scene and used to identify a child's parent. Most states allow its use as **evidence.**

D.N.R. Do not resuscitate. An order on a terminally ill patient's chart that the patient should not be revived if the heart or breathing stops. DNR orders require an **advance directive** and, even with one, are not always automatically carried out.

D.O. Department of _____. For the U.S. **cabinet** departments of **commerce, defense, energy, interior, justice, labor, transportation,** etc., see those words.

D.T.C. Depository Trust Corporation. A **clearinghouse** for stock and other securities transactions.

D.U.I. Driving under the influence (of alcohol or drugs). Replaces **D.W.I.** in many states.

D.W.A.I. Driving while ability impaired. Either the same as **D.U.I.** and **D.W.I.** or a lesser offense involving a lower concentration of blood alcohol.

D.W.B. Driving while black (or brown). Slang for selective police traffic stops of minority drivers.

D.W.I. *1.* Driving while intoxicated. See **D.U.I.** *2.* Died without issue; dying without issue. "Issue" means "children." In some states, this means dying without ever having had any children; in others, dying leaving no living children. *3.* Descriptive Word Index. An index to West **digests.**

Dactylography   The study of fingerprint identification.

Damage   The loss or harm that occurs when a person's legal rights suffer an **injury** (see that word for a comparison of *damage, damages,* and *injury*).

Damages   *1.* Money that a court orders paid to a person who has suffered **damage** (a loss or harm) by the person who caused the **injury** (the violation of the person's rights). See **injury** for a more complete comparison of *damage, damages,* and *injury. 2.* A **plaintiff's** claim in a legal **pleading** for the money defined in definition no. 1. *Damages* may be **actual** and **compensatory** (directly related to the amount of the loss) or they may be, in addition, *exemplary* and **punitive** (extra money given to punish the **defendant** and to help keep a particularly bad act from happening again). Also, merely **nominal** *damages* may be given (a tiny sum when the loss suffered is either very small or of unproved amount). *3.* For other types of damages (such as **consequential, future, incidental, liquidated, speculative** or **treble**), see the individual words.

Damnum   (Latin) A loss, harm, or damage. For *damnum absque injuria,* see **injuria.**

Dangerous instrumentality   Things that are potentially harmful in and of themselves, such as electricity, or are designed to be harmful, such as guns.

Dartmouth College Case   See **Trustees of Dartmouth College v. Woodward.**

Database   A computer program that organizes separate files for access by standardized search commands.

Date of issue   The day a document is formally put out or takes effect. The day that shows on the document itself; *not necessarily* the day it actually appears. For example, the *date of issue* of an **insurance** policy is the first day the policy says it will take effect, *not* the day the insurance is agreed to or the day the document is delivered.

Davis v. Monroe County   (119 S.Ct. 1661) The 1999 U.S. Supreme Court decision that federally-funded schools may be liable under Title IX of the **civil rights** *acts* if school officials ignore severe, pervasive **sexual harassment** of one student by another.

Davis-Bacon Act   (40 U.S.C. 276) A federal law regulating wages on **public works** and building projects.

Day book   A book or ledger in which a merchant records each day's business as it happens.

Day certain   A specific future date.

Day in court   A vague term referring to the right to be notified of a court proceeding involving your interests, and the right to be heard when the case comes up in court.

Day order   See **order.**

De   (Latin) Of, by, from, affecting, as, or concerning. Often the first word of the name of an old English **statute** or **writ.**

De bene esse   (Latin) "As well done (as possible)." Provisional, temporary, subject to later challenge or change. For example, a **deposition** _de bene esse_ involves pretrial **testimony** that may be used only if the witness is not available for the trial. [pronounce: de ben-e es-se]

De bonis non   (Latin) "Of the goods not (already taken care of)." Refers to an **administrator** appointed to hand out the property of a dead person whose **executor** (person chosen to hand it out) has died.

De bonis propriis   (Latin) "From his or her own goods." When a person managing another's property, **trust,** or **estate** has committed **waste** (see those words), repayment _de bonis propriis_ (from the manager's own funds) may be required.

De facto   (Latin) In fact; actual; a situation that exists in fact whether or not it is lawful. For example, a _de facto corporation_ is a company that has failed to follow some of the technical legal requirements to become a legal **corporation,** but carries on business as one in good faith, and a _de facto government_ is one that has at least temporarily overthrown the rightful, legal one. See **de jure** _segregation_ for another illustration.

De jure   (Latin) Of right; legitimate; lawful, whether or not true in actual fact. For example, a president may still be the _de jure_ head of a government even if the army takes actual power by force. _De jure segregation_ is a separation of races that is the result of government action while **de facto** (see that word) _segregation_ is caused by social, geographic, or economic conditions only. [pronounce: de joo-re]

De minimis   (Latin) Small, unimportant. Also, short for "_de minimis non curat lex_" (the law does not bother with trifles).

De novo   (Latin) New. For example, a _trial de novo_ is a new trial ordered by a judge when a previous trial is so flawed that it will be made **void.** In some states, some types of _trial de novo_ are a matter of right.

De son tort   (French) "Of his own wrong." A person who takes on a duty, such as being **executor** of a **will,** without any right to take on the duty, will be held responsible for all actions he or she takes as executor. In the case of a will, the person would be called an *executor de son tort.*

Dead   Worthless, unused, without life, or obsolete.

Dead freight   Money paid by a shipper for that part of a ship's or vehicle's capacity that is not filled.

Dead man's acts   Laws, now mostly abolished, that prevented a person from **testifying** in a civil lawsuit, against a dead person's representative, about things that the dead person might have testified to. The laws were meant to prevent fraud.

Deadly weapon   Any instrument likely to cause serious bodily harm under the circumstances of its actual use. Such things as a fan belt used to choke a man and a fire used to burn an occupied house have been called *deadly weapons* by courts.

Dealer   *1.* A person who buys and sells things as a business. *2.* Under **S.E.C.** law, a *dealer* is a person who buys and sells **securities** for him or herself, rather than for customers (a **broker**).

Death   The end of life. The medical definition of the exact moment of death is not agreed upon, but see **brain death rule.** *Presumptive death* is "legal death" resulting from an unexplained absence for a length of time set by state law, often seven years. See also **civil death** and see **life.**

Death knell exception   An exception, based on the probability of **irreparable injury,** to the rule that an **intermediate order** (see that word) cannot be appealed. [pronounce knell: nell]

Death statute   A law that permits **wrongful death actions.**

Deathbed declaration   See **dying declaration.**

Debar   Exclude a person from doing something; for example, from doing government contract work. *Not* **disbar.**

Debauchery   Wrongful or illegal sexual intercourse, but not necessarily **rape.**

Debenture   A corporation's obligation to pay money (usually in the form of a **note** or **bond**) often un**secured** (not backed up) by any specific property. Usually refers only to long-term bonds. [pronounce: de-ben-chur]

Debit card   A plastic card that allows a person to make a purchase that is paid for by a direct subtraction from the person's bank account. It looks like a credit card but works like a check.

Debits   Records in an **account** book of money you owe or of money paid to you. (The opposite of **credits.**)

Debt *1.* A sum of money owed because of an agreement (such as a sale or loan). *2.* Any money owed.

Debt financing (or debt capital) A company's raising money by issuing **bonds** or **notes** rather than by issuing **stock.** Raising money by issuing stock is called **equity financing.**

Debt poolers (or debt adjusters or debt consolidators) Persons or organizations who take a person's money and pay it out to **creditors** by getting the creditors to accept lower monthly payments, less money, etc. Unless these services are nonprofit credit counseling organizations, the chances are that the debtor will wind up paying much more than by making the arrangements him or herself.

Debt ratio Total debts divided by total **assets.** *Debt-equity ratio* is *long-term* debt divided by **equity** (assets minus debts).

Debt service Regular payments of **principal,** interest, and possibly other costs made to pay off a loan.

Debtor A person who owes money.

Debtor in possession A **bankrupt** company or family farm that continues operations, and is temporarily free from debt repayment, with its managers or owners taking on some of the duties of a bankruptcy **trustee.**

Debtor's position The part of a property's sale price that is put up by the person buying the property, rather than by the **mortgage** lender. Compare with **creditor's position.**

Decedent A dead person. [pronounce: de-<u>seed</u>-ent]

Deceit Intentionally misleading another by making false statements that cause that person harm.

Decennial Digest Abbreviated "Dec. Dig." See **American Digest System.**

Decision Any formal deciding of a dispute, such as a judge's resolution of a lawsuit.

Decision on the merits A final decision that fully and properly decides the subject matter of a case, with the effect that other lawsuits may not be brought by the same person on the same subject against the same opponent.

Decisional law **Caselaw.**

Declarant A person who makes a statement or **declaration,** whether formal or informal.

Declaration *1.* An unsworn statement made out of court. For example, a *dying declaration* made by a person who is about to die may sometimes be admitted as **evidence,** as may a *declaration against interest* (a statement that when made is so contrary to the speaker's interests that it would not likely have been made unless true). *2.* A formal statement. A *declaration of intention* is a statement made by a person who wants to become a U.S. **citizen.** *3.* A public proclamation; for example, the **Declaration of Independence.** *4.* An old word for the first paper filed in a lawsuit. It was a **common law** (see that word) **pleading** and corresponds to the current word "**complaint.**" *5.* An announcement of a set-aside of money. For example, a *declaration of dividends* is a corporation's setting aside part of its profits to pay stockholders; and a *declaration of estimated tax* is a statement and set-aside of money required by the **I.R.S.** of persons who have income from which taxes have not been withheld. *6.* For *declaration of condominium,* see **master** *deed.*

Declaration of Independence   The July 4, 1776 announcement by the Continental Congress (representatives of the thirteen colonies) that because of specified grievances the colonies were no longer subject to British rule, but were free states. The Declaration is not a part of U.S. law, but its principles are reflected in the **Constitution.**

Declaration of Paris   An 1856 agreement among the major naval powers that abolished **privateering** and provided other protections of merchant shipping during time of war.

Declaration of trust   A written statement by a person owning property that it is held for another person. This is one way of setting up a **trust.**

Declaratory judgment   A **judicial** opinion that states the rights of the **parties** or answers a legal question without awarding any **damages** or ordering that anything be done. A person may ask a court for a *declaratory judgment* only if there is a real, not theoretical, problem that involves real legal consequences.

Declaratory statute   A law that is passed to clarify prior law. It may be to explain the meaning of a prior **statute** or to clear up uncertainty in judge-made law.

Deconstruction   Examining the premises behind a legal rule to show that they could lead to a conflicting rule.

Decree   *1.* A **judgment** (see that word) of a court that announces the legal consequences of the facts found in a case and orders that the court's decision be carried out. Specialized types of decrees include **consent decree,** *divorce decree,* and *decree nisi* (one that takes effect only after a certain time and only if no person shows the court a good reason why it should not take effect). *2.* A proclamation or **order** put out by a person or group with **absolute** authority to give orders.

Decrement   An amount of decrease, especially of a property's value.

Decretal Relating to a **decree.**

Decriminalization An official act (usually passing a law) that makes what was once a crime no longer a crime.

Dedi et concessi (Latin) "I give and grant." Old formal words used to transfer land or other property.

Dedication *1.* The gift or other transfer of land or rights in land to the government for a specific public use, such as a park, and its acceptance for that use by the government. *2.* Voluntarily or involuntarily giving your **copyright** (or other right) to the public. It was once true that if you published a work without a copyright notice the work was considered to be *dedicated* to the public.

Deductible *1.* That which may be taken away or subtracted. Something that may be subtracted from income for tax purposes. *2.* That part of a loss that must be borne by a person with **insurance** before the insurance company will pay the rest. For example, a **policy** with a "$100 deductible" **clause** will pay nothing on a $100 loss, and pay $200 on a $300 loss.

Deduction *1.* A conclusion drawn from principles or facts already proved. *2.* Any subtraction of money owed. *3.* Subtractions from income for tax purposes. *Itemized deductions* are those nonbusiness expenses that may be subtracted from **adjusted gross income** (see that word). These include certain medical payments; taxes; interest payments, such as home mortgages; charitable contributions; professional expenses; etc. There are detailed tax rules governing all such deductions. The *standard deduction* is a specific dollar amount that can be deducted from income by those taxpayers who do not itemize their deductions. See also **credit, exclusion,** and **exemption.**

Deed A document by which one person transfers the legal ownership of **land** to another person. For various types of deeds, such as **quitclaim** or **special warranty,** see those words.

Deed of trust A document, similar to a **mortgage,** by which a person transfers the legal ownership of land to independent **trustees** to be held until a debt on the land is paid off. Compare with **declaration of trust.**

Deem *1.* Treat as if. For example, if a fact is *"deemed true,"* it will be treated as true unless proven otherwise. *2.* Hold to be; determine to be. For example, if a **statute** says that a certain act is "deemed to be a crime," it is a crime.

Deep pockets Capacity to pay a lot of money. The one person (or organization), among many possible **defendants,** best able to pay a **judgment** has the *deepest pockets.* This is the one a **plaintiff** is most likely to sue.

Deep Rock doctrine   The principle that even if an **insider** has a better formal claim to the property of a company that is going out of business, a court may give the property to **creditors** if that is fairer. The principle is stated in *Taylor v. Standard Gas* (306 U.S. 307).

Deface   *1.* Make illegible or unreadable by erasing, scrawling over, or other means. *2.* Deliberately destroy or mar a building, monument, public display, or public symbol such as a flag.

Defalcation   *1.* Failure to return or properly pay out money trusted to your care. There is the assumption that the money was misused. *2.* Setting off one claim against another; deducting a smaller debt due to you from a larger one you owe to someone.

Defamation   Transmission to others of false statements that harm the reputation, business, or property rights of a person. Spoken defamation is **slander** and written defamation is **libel.**

Default   *1.* A failure to perform a legal duty, observe a promise, or fulfill an obligation. For example, the word is often used for the failure to make a payment on a debt once it is due. *2.* Failure to take a required step in a lawsuit; for example, to file a paper on time. Such *default* can sometimes lead to a "*default* **judgment**" against the side failing to file the paper.

Defeasance clause   The part of a **mortgage** document that says that the mortgage is ended once all payments have been made or once certain other things happen.

Defeasible   Subject to being defeated, ended, or undone by a future event or action.

Defect   *1.* An error in the design (*design defect*) or production (*manufacturing defect*) of a product. *2.* The absence of something required to make a thing legally sufficient or binding. For example, a *defective title* to land means that someone not named on the title documents has an ownership claim to all or part of the land. *3.* Switch allegiance.

Defendant   The person against whom a legal action is brought. This legal action may be **civil** or **criminal.**

Defendant in error   An **appellee.**

Defense   *1.* The sum of the facts, law, and arguments presented by the side against whom legal action is brought. *2.* Any counter-argument or counter-force. *3.* In **negotiable instrument** law, a *real defense* is good against any holder, and a *personal defense* is good against anyone except a **holder in due course** (see that word). *4.* The U.S. Department of Defense. The **cabinet** department that runs the army, navy, etc. Also called "The Pentagon." *5.* A property divider.

Deferred charges A company's current spending for long-term needs such as research. This spending can be deducted from taxes over several years, not all at once.

Deferred compensation (or income) _1._ Any payment for work done that is withheld until, or payable at, some future date (or the occurrence of some future event). But see no. 3. _2._ Payments to employees, such as those made under a **pension plan** (see that word) that satisfies **I.R.S.** rules, that will not be taxed until the employee actually gets the money. I.R.S. _qualified plans_ also allow the employer to take a tax **deduction** when the money is paid into the plan, while _nonqualified plans_ make the employer wait for the deduction until the employee is taxed. _3._ Payments received before the work is done to earn them. **Accrual basis** taxpayers may pay taxes on this income in the later year the work is done. In this sense, the word really refers to the delay of taxation, not delay of receipt.

Deficiency A lack or shortage. For example, a _deficiency_ in a legal paper means that it lacks something to make it proper or able to take legal effect. Also, the difference between a tax owed and the amount paid is a _tax deficiency._ [pronounce: de-fish-en-see]

Deficiency judgment (or decree) A court's decision that a person must pay more money to a **creditor** than the amount brought by the sale of property used to **secure** a debt. For example, when an auto dealer repossesses (takes back) a car for failure to make payments and then sells the car for eight hundred dollars, if the debt owed is one thousand dollars, some states will allow the car dealer to obtain a two hundred dollar _deficiency judgment._ The same thing can happen in a mortgage **foreclosure.**

Deficit Something missing or lacking; less than what should be; a "minus" **balance.** For example, if a city takes in less money than it must pay out in the same time period, it is called "_deficit financing_" or "_deficit spending._"

Defined benefit (or contribution) plan See **pension plan.**

Definite sentence See **determinate sentence.**

Definitive Capable of finally and completely settling a legal question or a lawsuit.

Deflator A numerical figure used to change current cost figures to past **constant dollars** by removing increases due to inflation.

Deforcement Old word for using force to keep a person from possessing his or her own land.

Defraud *1.* To cheat someone out of something of value by making false statements. *2.* Sometimes used more broadly to mean any type of cheating.

Degree *1.* A step, grade, or division; for example, a "step removed" between two relatives (brothers are related in the *first degree,* grandparent and grandchild in the *second*). Also, a *degree* describes the division of a crime or group of crimes into different levels of severity (*first degree* murder carries a more severe maximum punishment than *second degree* murder). *2.* A general measure of importance, such as a **standard.** (See that word for *degree of care* and *degree of proof.*)

Dehors Outside of; beyond the scope of. [pronounce: de-<u>hor</u>]

Del credere (Italian) An **agent** who sells goods for a person and also **guarantees** to that person that the buyer will pay in full for the goods. [pronounce: del <u>cred</u>-er-e]

Delectus personae (Latin) "Choice of person." The right of a **partner** to choose additional partners. A person's right to veto the admission of a new member.

Delegate *1.* A person who is chosen to represent another person or group of persons. *2.* To choose a person to represent you or to do a job for you.

Delegation *1.* The giving of authority by one person to another. For example, a boss often *delegates* responsibility to employees. But see no. 2. *2.* The giving of a task to another *without* giving up responsibility for its accomplishment. *3.* An entire group of **delegates** or representatives. *4.* An old word for a person taking over the debt of another person with the agreement of the person owed the debt. *5. Delegation of powers* is the **constitutional** division of authority between branches of government and also the handing down of authority from the president to **administrative agencies.**

Deliberate *1.* To carefully consider, discuss, and work towards forming an opinion or making a decision. *2.* Well advised; carefully considered; thoroughly planned. *3.* Planned in advance; premeditated; intentional. *4. Deliberate indifference* is a seemingly contradictory phrase describing the failure to provide adequate or timely medical care to prisoners. It includes acts or omissions that so seriously harm a prisoner's health or safety that the prison officials' knowledge of the risk to the prisoner's health or safety is inferred.

Deliberative process privilege The government's right to keep some internal policy-making documents private if they were written before adoption of the policy they discuss and if disclosure of candid or personal comments would stifle communication within the agency. See **privilege** no. 6.

Delictum   (Latin) A crime, **tort,** or wrong. Also shortened to _delict._

Delinquency   Failure, omission, or violation of duty; misconduct. For example, an overdue debt is called a _delinquency._

Delinquent   _1._ Overdue and unpaid. _2._ Willfully and intentionally failing to carry out an obligation. _3._ Short for "_juvenile delinquent_," a **minor** who has done an illegal act or who seriously misbehaves.

Delist   Remove a **stock** (or other **security**) from a stock (or other) **exchange.** This is more than a temporary suspension of trading in that stock.

Delivery   _1._ The transfer of property other than **land** from one person to another. (Usually the transfer of goods that have been sold.) _2._ An act other than physically handing over an object that has the legal effect of a physical transfer.

Demand   _1._ A forceful claim that presupposes that there is no doubt as to its winning. _2._ The assertion of a legal right; a legal obligation asserted in the courts. _3. On demand_ is a phrase put on some **promissory notes** or other **negotiable instruments** indicating that a specified amount of money must be paid immediately when the **holder** of the note requests payment. A _demand deposit_ is money given to a bank that may be taken out at any time; for example, a checking account. _4._ The strength of buyer desire for and willingness and ability to pay for a product.

Demeanor   Physical appearance and behavior. The demeanor of a witness is not what the witness says, but how the witness says it, including, for example, tone of voice, hesitations, gestures, and apparent sincerity.

Demense   An old word for **domain.** [pronounce: de-_mens_]

Demise   _1._ A **lease.** _2._ Any transfer of property (especially **land**). _Not_ **devise.** _3._ Death.

Democracy   Government by the people, either directly or indirectly through representatives; ideally, as a basis for a system highly protective of individual liberties.

Demonstrative evidence   All **evidence** other than **testimony.**

Demonstrative legacy (or bequest)   A gift of a specific sum of money in a **will** that is to be paid out of a particular fund where, if the fund has no money, the gift becomes a _general legacy_ on an equal footing with other general legacies.

Demur   To make a **demurrer** (see that word).

Demurrage   The extra money paid to the owner of a ship or railroad car by a person who uses it longer than the agreed period.

Demurrer   A legal **pleading** that says, in effect, "even if, for the sake of argument, the facts presented by the other side are correct, those facts do not give the other side a legal argument that can possibly stand up in court." The *demurrer* has been replaced in many courts by a **motion** *to dismiss.*

Denaturalization   The involuntary loss or revocation of citizenship previously acquired through **naturalization.** Compare with **expatriation.**

Denial   1. Any part of a **pleading** that contradicts claims made in an opponent's previous pleading. *2.* A refusal or rejection; for example, a *denial* of **welfare** benefits to a family that makes too much money to qualify. *3.* A deprivation or withholding; for example, a *denial* of a **constitutional** right.

Dennis decision   See **clear and present danger test.**

Dep.   *1.* Short for **"deputy."** *2.* Short for "department" ("dept." is more common). *3.* Short for **deposition** ("depo" is more common).

Department of _____   For U.S. departments (such as the Department of Justice) see the named word (**justice**).

Departure   See **variance.**

Depecage   Apply the laws of different states to different issues in the same lawsuit. [pronounce: day-pe-saj]

Dependent   *1.* A person supported primarily by another person. *2.* Conditional. For example, a *dependent contract* is one in which one side does not have to do something in the contract until the other side does something it is required to do.

Dependent relative revocation   The legal principle in some states that if a person **revokes** (takes back or cancels) a **will** with the intention of making a new one, and that new one is either never made or fails to become effective because of a **defect,** there is a **rebuttable** *presumption* (an assumption) that he or she would have preferred the old will to no will at all. If the presumption is not rebutted, the old will is given effect.

Depletion   Using up a finite natural resource (such as coal or oil). See **depletion allowance.**

Depletion allowance   The amount allowable, under tax rules, as a **deduction,** corresponding theoretically to the loss in value of property due to the removal of oil, gas, or minerals.

Deponent   Person who gives sworn **testimony** out of court. See **deposition.**

Deportation   Expelling a foreigner from a country and sending that person to another country.

Depose   *1.* Give sworn **testimony** out of court. See **deposition.** *2.* Ask the questions that are answered in a **deposition.** For example, a lawyer might say "I *deposed* Mr. Smith today." *3.* Take away a person's public office against his or her will. This usually applies to a head of state's forcible removal.

Deposit   *1.* Place property in another's hands for safekeeping. *2.* Give someone money as part payment, **earnest money** (see that word), or **security** for a purchase. *3.* Money placed in a bank or similar financial institution. *Demand deposits* may be taken out at any time and *time deposits* must be left in for a certain length of time.

Deposit in court   Place money or other property in the temporary custody of a court, pending the outcome of a court decision. For example, a person who admits a debt or **liability,** but does not know exactly to whom it is owed, may *deposit* money with a court to be held for the person whom the court finally decides is owed the money. Money may also be deposited in court when the amount owed or the question of owing is in doubt.

Depositary   A person or organization (especially a bank) that receives a **deposit** (see that word). Compare with **depository.**

Deposition   *1.* The process of taking a witness's sworn out-of-court **testimony.** The questioning is usually done by a lawyer, with the lawyer from the other side given a chance to attend and participate. *2.* The written record of no. 1.

Depository   The place (such as a bank) where a **deposit** (see that word) is kept. Compare with **depositary.**

Depreciable life   The time period over which an asset's tax **depreciation deductions** are taken.

Depreciation   A fall in value or reduction in worth, especially a reduction due to deterioration. [pronounce: de-pree-shee-a-shun]

Depreciation deduction   In tax law, the amount, allowable as a **deduction** (see that word), theoretically corresponding to the loss in value of investment or business property (such as an office building or computer) due to the assumed physical deterioration of the property. If an equal amount of depreciation is deducted in each year of a property's useful life, it is called *straight line depreciation.* If more of the depreciation is taken early, it is called *accelerated depreciation.* There are many complicated methods of calculating value and deciding how to *depreciate* it.

Deputy An official authorized to act for another person; often the second-in-command of an organization who may act in place of the head; an assistant to a sheriff.

Deraign Prove; vindicate; disprove things said against you. [pronounce: de-<u>rain</u>]

Derelict *1.* Property that is thrown away or **abandoned** intentionally. *2.* An abandoned boat, whether or not abandoned intentionally.

Dereliction *1.* The permanent (or at least long-term) receding of water from a shore or bank, and the "creation" of new land due to a lower water level. *2.* **Abandonment** of property. *3.* A refusal or failure to perform a public office or duty.

Derivative Based on something else. In finance, a *derivative* is a document, such as an **option,** with a value that depends on the value of something else (such as a stock). Many *derivatives* are highly complex, and strange new ones appear regularly.

Derivative action A lawsuit by a stockholder of a **corporation** against another person (usually an officer of the company) to enforce claims the stockholder thinks the corporation has against that person.

Derivative evidence **Evidence** that is collected by following up on evidence gathered illegally. See **exclusionary rule** and **fruit of the poisonous tree doctrine.**

Derivative tort *1.* A **tort** lawsuit based on harm done by a person committing a crime. *2.* A tort lawsuit against a **principal** for action by the principal's **agent** (see those words).

Derivative work In **copyright** law, a work (such as a translation, musical arrangement, art reproduction, abridgment, or condensation) separable from, but based on, one or more *preexisting works.* The owner of the copyright in the preexisting work usually has the *adaptation right* to prevent others from creating *derivative works.* An authorized derivative work is separately "copyrightable."

Derogation Partial **repeal** or partial abolishing of a law by a later law.

Derogation (or derogatory) clause A phrase inserted in a **will** with instructions that no later will lacking this phrase should be treated as valid. It is an attempt to protect against later wills being faked or extracted by pressure, but courts will usually treat such a clause as **evidence** only and not automatically enforce it.

Descent *1.* Inheritance from parents or other ancestors. *2.* Getting property by inheritance of any type, rather than by purchase or gift. *Descent and distribution* usually refers to **intestate succession** (see that word).

Descriptive word index   A large set of books in dictionary form that allows you to find which cases have discussed a topic by tracing down exact words or catchphrases. For example, if you are interested in cases involving tires that blow out during a skid, you might look up "tires," "blowouts," or "skidding." This function is increasingly performed by **database** searching.

Desecrate   **Deface** or otherwise damage a public building, church, graveyard, etc.

Desertion   _1._ Abandoning a military post and duty without permission, either to escape danger or with no intention of returning. _2._ Abandoning wife, husband, or child with no intention of either returning or of reassuming the financial and other duties of marriage or parenthood. _3._ Any abandonment of a job or duty.

Design   In law, a purpose plus a plan to carry it out. In **tort** law, a _design defect_ is a fault in the design of a product, especially one that results in injury to a user even though the product is properly manufactured. And in **patent** law, a _design patent_ is granted for a new way something looks, as opposed to a regular patent for the way a new thing works.

Designated reporter   See **child abuse.**

Designer drug   A synthetic drug that is altered from an illegal drug to mimic its effects without being illegal, or a new synthetic psychoactive drug generally.

Desire   When used in a **will,** the word _desire_ can mean anything from a small preference to a total command. For example, "I leave all my jewelry to Tom and desire that Joe get my gold ring" could mean that either Tom or Joe gets the ring.

Desk audit   _1._ A review of a job or jobs in the **civil service** (see that word) to see if the duties fit the pay and rank and to see if the person filling the job has the right qualifications. _2._ The review of a federal tax return by an I.R.S. employee who needs no additional information from the taxpayer.

Desk jobbing   **Wholesaling** by **drop shipment** (see those words).

Despoil   Take something away from a person illegally, usually by force or threats.

Destination contract   An agreement for the sale of goods in which the risk of loss of, or damage to, the goods passes from seller to buyer when the goods are delivered to a specific destination.

Destroy   _1._ With regard to wills, contracts, or other legal documents, "_destruction_" does not necessarily mean total physical destruction. You can _destroy_ a document's _legal effect_ by less extreme methods, such as tearing it in half or writing over it. *2. Destruction* may mean many different things. For example, in an **insurance** contract, "destruction" may mean a total wreck or merely harm that makes something useless for its intended purpose.

Desuetude   Disuse. Refers to an obsolete law, custom, or practice that is no longer used or in effect. An obsolete law is *"in desuetude."*

Detainer   *1.* **Unlawful detainer.** *2.* Holding a person against his or her will. *3.* A **warrant** or court **order** to keep a person in **custody** when that person might otherwise be released. This is often used to make sure a person will serve a **sentence** or attend a trial in one state at the end of a prison term in another state or in a federal prison.

Detention   Holding a person against his or her will. *Detention for questioning* is the holding of a person, by a policeman or similar public official, without making a formal **arrest.**

Determinable   *1.* Possibly ended; subject to being ended if a certain thing happens. *2.* Can be found out or decided upon.

Determinate sentence   See **sentence** no. 2.

Determination   *1.* A final decision (usually of a court or other formal decision-maker such as a **hearing examiner**). *2.* Any formal decision. For example, the **I.R.S.** puts out *determination letters* to explain whether or not an organization has been given **tax exempt** status. *3.* The ending of a right or interest in property. When this happens, the right *determines.*

Determine   *1.* Decide. *2.* End.

Detinue   A legal action to get back property held unlawfully by another person, plus **damages** due to the wrongful withholding. [pronounce: <u>det</u>-i-new]

Detournement   An old word for taking money or financial documents entrusted to your care and cashing them or using them for your own purposes. Similar to **embezzlement.**

Detraction   Removing inherited property from a state and transferring that property's **title** to a new state.

Detriment   *1.* Any loss or harm. *2.* Giving up something of value (such as a right, benefit, or property). *3.* An obligation taken on, or a right given up, as part of making a **contract.**

Detrimental reliance   See **promissory estoppel.**

Devaluation   Reducing the value of a country's money relative to other countries' money.

Devastavit (Latin) "He has wasted." An old word for mismanagement of property by the **administrator** of a dead person's **estate.** The administrator could be held personally **liable** for any loss. See also **de bonis propriis** and **waste.**

Development *1.* A piece of land subdivided into building lots and sold, or built upon and then sold. *2.* Preparation of a mining site to make the minerals accessible by stripping, blasting, tunneling, etc.

Devest See **divest.**

Deviance Noticeable differing from average or normal behavior. The word is usually applied to things society in general does not condone, such as illegal drug use.

Deviation *1.* A departure from usual conduct, such as an employee's use of work time for personal business. *2.* A change from original terms or plans, such as a **contractor's** substituting one type of wood for another specified in building plans. *3.* Allowing the specific terms of a **will** or **trust** to be ignored in order to accomplish its general purposes. See also **cy-pres.**

Devise *1.* The gift of **land** by **will.** *2.* Any gift by will. Compare with **bequest.** *Not* "**demise.**" [pronounce: de-viz]

Devisee Person to whom land is given by **will.**

Devisor Person who makes a **will** containing a gift of land.

Devolution *1.* The transfer or transition by process of law from one person to another of a right, **liability, title,** property, or office (often by death). *2.* The decentralization of government or the transfer of functions "downward" from national to state government.

Devolve To go by **devolution** (see that word).

Dewey decimal system A library reference system that classifies all subjects by number. For example, the numbers in the 340's are for law, 343 is for criminal law, and 343.2 is for a special subject under criminal law. Each new number after the decimal point subdivides the previous number (and its subject) further. Compare with **Library of Congress system.**

Dicta Views of a judge that are not a central part of the judge's decision, even if the judge argues them strongly and even if they look like conclusions. One way to decide whether a particular part of a judge's **opinion** is *dicta* is to examine whether it was necessary to reach the result. If it could be removed without changing the legal result, it is probably dicta. If it is dicta, it is not binding **precedent** (see that word) on later court decisions, but it is probably still worth quoting if it helps your case.

Dictum (Latin) *1.* Singular of **dicta** (see that word). *2.* Short for "*obiter dictum*" (a remark by the way, as in "by the way, did I tell you . . ."); a digression; a discussion of side points or unrelated points.

Dictum page See **pinpoint citation.**

Dies (Latin) *1.* A day; days; court day. *2. Dies gratiae* are **grace** days. [pronounce: dee-es]

Diet A word used in various countries meaning **legislature.**

Digest A collection of parts of many books, usually giving not only summaries, but also excerpts and condensations. For example, the **American Digest System** covers the decisions of the highest court of each state and of the Supreme Court. It is divided into volumes by time periods. It collects **headnotes** (summaries given at the top of each case) and is arranged by subject categories.

Digesting *1.* Creating a **digest.** *2.* Summarizing **discovery** documents such as **depositions.**

Dilatory Tending or intending to cause delay or gain time.

Diligence Carefulness, prudence, or doing your duty.

Dilution *1.* The use of a **trademark** by a product so unlike the original that, while it will cause no confusion, it may still lower the trademark's value. *2. Dilution* of **stock** occurs when the stock is watered (see **watered stock**) or when more stock is sold than the value of the company can support. *3.* Lowering a group's voting power through **reapportionment.** This may be a violation of **equal protection of laws.**

Diminished responsibility doctrine The principle that having a certain recognized form of *diminished mental capacity* while committing a crime should lead to the imposition of a lesser punishment or to lower the **degree** of the crime. The states use a variety of terms, such as "*partial insanity*," for these concepts and define them in many ways. Conditions involved may include mental retardation, alcohol or drug impairment, trauma, disease, etc.

Diminution *1.* Reduction. For example, *diminution* in value is one way to calculate **damages** for property or rights that have been injured or taken. *2.* Incompleteness.

Diplomatic immunity A diplomat's freedom from **prosecution** under most of the host country's criminal laws.

Diplomatic relations Ongoing, formal country-to-country communications and the permanent exchange of **ambassadors** and other officials.

Direct Immediate or straight. This word, in different settings, may be the opposite of indirect (not direct), collateral (on the side), or cross (opposing).

Direct action *1.* A lawsuit by a person against his or her own **insurance** company instead of against the person who did the harm or against that person's insurance company. *2.* A lawsuit by a stockholder to enforce his or her own rights against a **corporation** or its officers rather than to enforce the corporation's rights in a **derivative action** (see that word).

Direct attack An attempt to have a judge's decision overturned (**annulled, reversed, vacated, enjoined,** etc.) by a proceeding started for that specific purpose (an **appeal,** an **injunction** hearing, etc.). Compare with **collateral attack.**

Direct cause See **proximate cause.**

Direct evidence Proof of a fact without the need for other facts leading up to it. For example, *direct evidence* that dodos are not extinct would be a live dodo. For the difference between direct and **circumstantial evidence,** see that word.

Direct examination The first questioning in a trial of a **witness** by the side that called that witness.

Direct line Grandparents, parents, children, grandchildren, etc., rather than brothers, uncles, nieces, etc.

Direct placement Sale by a company of its own **securities** (such as **stock**) directly to buyers (especially to large institutional investors) rather than through offers to the general public.

Direct reduction mortgage A type of mortgage in which the payment size decreases with each payment because **interest** is paid on only the principal still owed. Compare with **constant payment mortgage.**

Direct selling A manufacturer selling directly to a customer rather than through a wholesaler or retailer.

Direct tax *1.* A tax that is paid directly to the government by the person taxed. For example, income tax is direct, but a manufacturing tax is not because it is passed on to the buyer in the form of higher prices. *2.* An **ad valorem** *tax* (see that word). *3.* The opposite of an **indirect tax** (see that word).

Direct trust A **trust** stated in words rather than one created by law or by implication.

Direct writer An insurance **agent** who generally represents only one insurance company.

Directed question A question that is tightly phrased to be answered in one or two words, such as "yes."

Directed verdict A **verdict** (see that word) in which the judge takes the decision out of the jury's hands. The judge does this by telling them what they must decide or by actually making the decision. The judge might do this when the person suing has presented facts which, even if believed by a jury, cannot add up to a successful case.

Director *1.* Head of an organization, group, or project. *2.* A person elected by the shareholders (owners) of a **corporation** to serve on its *board of directors* which decides basic **corporate** policy and hires the **officers** (president, etc.) to run the company's day-to-day operations. *3.* Directors as a group are a *board of directors.* Those who are also major stockholders, officers, or employees of the company are called *inside directors,* and those with no such interests are *outside directors.*

Directory *1.* Not mandatory. Merely advisory, instructing, or procedural. For example, *directory language* in a **statute** merely instructs an official and may not invalidate (overturn) actions of an official who fails to follow instructions. But see no. 2. *2. Mandatory.* For example, a *directory trust* has specific instructions and leaves no **discretion** to the **trustee.** But see no. 1. You cannot tell what *directory* means unless you already know exactly how it has come to be used in a particular area of the law.

Disability *1.* A *legal disability* is the lack of legal capacity to do an act. For example, a married person is disabled from remarrying until the marriage ends in an **annulment,** in **divorce,** or by the spouse's death. *2.* A *physical* or *mental disability* is the absence of adequate physical or mental powers or the lowering of earning ability due to this absence. Under the **Americans with Disabilities Act,** the impairment "substantially limits one or more of life's activities." *Disability* is defined in different ways under **workers' compensation laws** (see that word) and Social Security laws, but it always includes the inability to perform the person's usual job.

Disaffirm Repudiate; take back consent once given; refuse to honor former promises or stick by former acts (usually used in situations where the person has a legal right to do so).

Disallow Refuse, deny, or reject.

Disaster loss A loss (such as a building damaged in a flood) that takes place in a *disaster area* designated by the president of the United States. The persons who suffer these losses are given special loan benefits.

Disbar Take away a lawyer's right to practice law. *Not* **debar.**

Disburse Pay out of a fund of money.

Discharge *1.* Release; remove; free; dismiss. For example, to *discharge* a **contract** is to end the obligation by agreement or by carrying it out;

to *discharge* a prisoner is to release him or her; to *discharge* a court **order** is to cancel or revoke it; to *discharge* a person in **bankruptcy** is to release him or her from all or most debts; to *discharge* a person from the army is to release him or her from service; and to *discharge a bill* is to move it from a **committee** to the full **house** of a **legislature**. *2.* The documents showing that no. 1 has taken place; for example, *discharge papers* from the army. *3.* Do or perform a duty.

Disciplinary rules   State rules listing and explaining what lawyers are prohibited from doing and what they should probably not do. Serious violations can lead to **disbarment**. The whole subject, or sometimes just the "gray areas," is called *legal ethics.* See also **Rules of Professional Conduct.**

Disclaimer   *1.* The refusal, rejection, or renunciation of a claim, a power, or property. *2.* The refusal to accept certain types of responsibility. For example, a *disclaimer clause* in a written sales contract might say "we give you, the purchaser, promises A, B, and C, but *disclaim* all other promises or responsibilities."

Disclosure   Revealing something that is secret or not well understood. For example, the *disclosure* in a **patent** application is the statement of what the invention is, what it does, and how it works. In **consumer** law, *disclosure* refers to what information must be made available in a loan or other **credit** deal and how that information must be presented to make it clear. And lawyers have many disclosure requirements, such as to disclose a **conflict of interest.**

Discontinuance   Another word for either **nonsuit** or **dismissal** (see those words).

Discount   *1.* A deduction or lowering of an amount of money; for example, the amount by which a price is lowered. *2.* Pay interest in advance. *3.* See **discounting.**

Discount rate   *1.* The percentage of the **face** value of a commercial **note, bill, mortgage,** etc., that is deducted from the payment by a buyer such as a bank. See also **rediscount rate.** *2.* The rate set by the Federal Reserve Board for the charge made by Federal Reserve Banks to certain other banks borrowing money from them. *3.* See **discounting.**

Discounting   Calculating the present value of money to be paid or collected in a future payment or a series of future payments (sometimes called "*discounted cash flow*"). The process involves answering the question: "How much money would I need to invest today at a certain interest rate to equal what is changing hands in the future?" The calculation is the reverse of compounding interest, and the interest rate used is called the "**discount rate**" (see that word) or the "*capitalization rate.*"

Discoverable   Must be turned over if requested in **discovery**.

Discovered peril doctrine   See **last clear chance doctrine**.

Discovery   *1.* The formal and informal exchange of information between sides in a lawsuit. Two types of *discovery* are **interrogatories** and **depositions.** *2.* Finding out something previously unknown. For example, in **patent** law, a *discovery* is finding out something new rather than inventing a device or process. Also, the *discovery* of a **fraud** or of medical **malpractice** occurs when the person harmed finds out the problem (or should have found out if careful).

Discredit   Damage a person's believability or refute a claim that a document is genuine.

Discretion   *1.* Intelligent, prudent conduct; the capacity to act intelligently and prudently. *2.* The power to act within general guidelines, rules, or laws, but without either specific rules to follow or the need to completely explain or justify each decision or action. For example, a *discretionary account* occurs when a customer gives a stockbroker great leeway in deciding what stocks to buy and sell, when to buy, etc. Compare with **ministerial.** *3.* The ability to understand right from wrong, so you are responsible for your actions.

Discretionary review   See **certiorari**.

Discretionary trust   A **trust** (see that word) that allows some leeway in carrying out its terms.

Discrimination   *1.* The failure to treat individuals equally. The setting up of sham or irrelevant categories to justify treating individuals unfairly. *2.* Illegally unequal treatment based on race, color, religion, sex, age, handicap, or national origin. This is often called *invidious* discrimination.

Disfranchise (or disenfranchise)   Formally take away certain rights, such as the right to vote, from a **citizen.**

Disgorge   Give up something upon legal demand.

Dishonor   Refuse to accept or pay a **negotiable instrument** (see that word) when it comes due.

Disinterested   Impartial; not biased or prejudiced; not affected personally or financially by the outcome. (The word, however, does *not* mean "uninterested" and does *not* mean "lacking an opinion.")

Disintermediation   The process that occurs when large numbers of people take their money out of bank savings and similar accounts and put the money directly into investments that pay higher rates of interest (and that the banks might have invested in with the same money).

Disjunctive *1.* An "or" statement which, if one part is true, the other part is false; for example, "John was in New York yesterday at noon or he was in Boston yesterday at noon." *2.* Referring to things that need not be interrelated; for example, a list of requirements of which only one must be satisfied. Compare with **conjunctive.**

Dismissal A court **order** or **judgment** that ends a lawsuit. It may be "with **prejudice**" (no further lawsuit may be brought by the same persons on the same subject) or "without prejudice."

Disorderly conduct A vague term for actions that disturb the peace or shock public morality. The prohibited conduct must be precisely defined by state criminal laws, and the conduct must not be protected by the Constitution, or the laws are unconstitutional under the **due process** clause of the fourteenth amendment.

Disorderly house A building with occupants who behave in a way that creates a neighborhood **nuisance.** These often include places for gambling or prostitution.

Disparagement The discrediting, belittling, or "talking down" of something or someone. Under some circumstances, you can be sued for doing it; for example, *disparagement* of **title** and *disparagement of* **property.** Also, a seller's disparagement of an advertised item may be part of prohibited **bait and switch** (see that word) sales tactics.

Disparate impact **Discrimination** based on race, color, religion, sex, national origin, age, or disability that results from a practice that does not seem to be discriminatory and was not intended to be so.

Disparate treatment Intentional **discrimination** based on a person's race, color, religion, sex, national origin, age, or disability.

Dispatch A speedy sending off or completion.

Dispensation An exemption from a law or permission to do something usually forbidden.

Disposable earnings **Gross** or "total" pay minus payments (such as taxes and Social Security) required by law. This is not exactly the same as take home pay, since voluntary payments (such as health insurance) may further reduce "take home."

Dispose *1.* Sell, give, or otherwise transfer ownership of something. *2.* See **disposition.**

Disposition *1.* Final settlement or result. A court's *disposition* of a case may be to give a **judgment,** dismiss the case, pass sentence on a criminal, etc. *2.* Giving something up or giving it away. *3.* A **bequest** or **devise**. Giving any form of property by will. *4. Not* **dispossession.**

Dispositive facts   Facts that clearly settle a legal issue or dispute.

Dispossession   *1.* **Ouster.** Wrongfully putting a person off his or her property by force, trick, or misuse of the law. *2.* A legal proceeding by a **landlord** to evict a **tenant.** *3. Not* **disposition.**

Dispute   A disagreement between persons about their rights or their legal obligations to one another.

Disqualify   Make ineligible. For example, a judge may be *disqualified* from deciding a case involving a company if the judge owns **stock** in that company.

Disseisin   An old word for **dispossession** or for wrongfully putting another person off land owned by that person.

Dissent   A judge's formal disagreement with the decision of the majority of the judges in a lawsuit. If the judge puts it in writing, it is called a *dissenting opinion.*

Dissolution   Ending or breaking up. For example, *dissolution* of a **contract** is a **mutual** agreement to end it, *dissolution* of a **corporation** is ending its existence, and *dissolution* of a marriage is any formal, legal ending of a marriage other than by **annulment.**

Distinguish   Point out basic differences. To *distinguish* a **case** is to show why it is irrelevant (or not very relevant) to the lawsuit being decided.

Distrain   To take another person's personal **property** either lawfully or unlawfully. For example, a landlord might *distrain* a tenant's property to make sure that back rent will be paid.

Distress   *1.* The process of **distraining** (see that word) property. *2.* Forced. A *distress sale* of goods might be a "going out of business" sale in which prices are low, and a distress sale of land might be due to a mortgage **foreclosure.**

Distributee   **Heir;** person who inherits.

Distribution   Division by shares; for example, giving out what is left of a dead person's **estate** after taxes and debts are paid.

Distributive finding   A **finding** (see that word) in which a jury decides part of a case in favor of one side and part in favor of the other side.

Distributor   Wholesaler; a person or company that buys things for resale to other than the end user.

District   A subdivision of any of several different types of geographical areas (such as countries, states, or counties) for judicial, political, or administrative purposes. "*Districting*" is the process of drawing a district's boundary lines for purposes of **apportionment** (see that word).

District attorney   The top **criminal** prosecuting lawyer of each federal **district** (called the "U.S. attorney") and of each state district. At the substate level, this person may also be called the "*state's attorney.*"

District court   *1.* **Trial** courts of the **United States Courts** system. *2.* In some states, low-level state courts (or even **appeals** courts).

Disturbing the peace   A vague term, defined in different ways in different places, for interrupting the peace, quiet, or good order of a neighborhood.

Divers   *1.* Many; several. *2.* Different; many different. [pronounce: dive-ers]

Diversification   *1.* A company's adding new product lines or going into an entirely new business. *2.* An investor's buying new types of **stock** or other **securities,** usually to reduce the risk of one stock's sudden fall in price.

Diversion   *1.* A turning aside; for example, the unauthorized changing of the course of a river or the unauthorized use of a company's funds or of **trust** funds. *2.* *Pretrial diversion* (or *intervention*) is a turning aside of persons from the regular course of criminal prosecution into special programs that avoid the stigma of a criminal conviction if they are successfully completed.

Diversity of citizenship   The situation that occurs when persons on one side of a case in **federal** court come from a different state than persons on the other side. *Complete diversity* (all the **plaintiffs** are from a different state than all the **defendants**) allows the court to accept and decide the case based on the court's *diversity* **jurisdiction,** provided that certain other criteria are met. Only *minimal diversity* (at least one plaintiff comes from a different state than at least one defendant) is needed for **interpleader** between states. *Manufactured diversity* (improperly creating diversity for the sake of obtaining federal jurisdiction) is prohibited. *Diversity of citizenship* also applies to suits between citizens and foreign nationals.

Divest   *1.* Deprive, take away, or withdraw. *2.* Sell or otherwise dispose of legal title. For example, you can *divest* yourself of a car by selling it.

Divestiture   A court **order** to a company that it sell or get rid of something (another company, **stock,** property, etc.) because of **antitrust acts.** The company's carrying out of the court order is also called *divestiture* (or *divestment*).

Divided court   An **appellate** court whose decision is not unanimous.

Divided custody   A child living with each divorced parent part of the time. *Legal* **custody** remains either *joint* (both parents have decision-making power) or *sole* (only one has the power).

Dividend   A share of profits or property; usually a payment per **share** of a **corporation's stock** (see those words). A few of the many different types of dividends include: *asset* (or *property*) dividend (paid in the form of property instead of cash or stock; for example, a blivit manufacturer might give each owner a blivit); *consent dividend* (declared to avoid a personal **holding company** or **accumulated earnings tax,** but never actually paid; this dividend, however, is taxed to the owners as if paid and increases their tax **basis**); *constructive dividend* (unreasonable compensation paid to an owner that will be taxed like a dividend, often consisting of unusually high wages, bargain purchases of company property, etc.); *cumulative dividend* (if not paid regularly, usually on preferred **stock,** it accumulates and must be paid before any **common stock** dividends are paid); *deficiency dividend* (paid to make up for a missed one; often to avoid paying a personal holding company tax); *scrip dividend* (paid in **scrip,** in **certificates** of ownership of stock not yet issued, or in short-term loan **notes;** done to divide profits but delay paying them out); and *stock dividend* (a dividend paid in the form of stock, which often involves dividing up of the increased worth of a company by **issuing** more stock).

Divisible   Can be divided into completely separate parts that do not depend on each other. For example, a *divisible contract* has parts that will be enforced by a court even if other parts are not legally valid; a *divorce decree* is considered *divisible* because the divorce itself may be final while alimony, support, and custody decisions may be ongoing; and a *divisible offense* is a crime that includes other lesser crimes (**murder** includes **assault, battery,** etc.). See also **severable.**

Divorce   The ending of a marriage by court order. It is different from an **annulment** (which legally determines that a marriage never existed) and from a *limited divorce* (which provides for a "legal separation" and is a step toward a divorce but does not end the marriage).

Do, lego   (Latin) "I give and **bequeath.**" Old words introducing a gift in a **will.**

Dock   A name sometimes used for the place in the courtroom where the prisoner stays during a trial.

Docket   *1.* A list of cases, usually with file numbers, scheduled for trial in a court. A *docket call* is a court session in which lawyers for cases on the docket announce readiness for trial, announce settlements, and handle other procedural matters. *2.* A list of specific actions taken in a court. For example, an _appearance docket_ lists all lawyers appearing in cases and may list the formal steps taken; and a _judgment docket_ is a list of all final actions taken by a court (often used to give notice to the public of new **liens** on property). _3._ Any book of short entries or summaries.

Doctor-patient privilege   The right of a patient in some states to keep out of some legal proceedings some information communicated in a doctor-patient relationship. Also known as _physician-patient privilege._

Doctrine   A legal principle or rule. A _doctrine_ may be accepted in one **jurisdiction,** rejected in another, and modified in a third.

Document   Something with a message on it; for example, a **contract,** a map, a photograph of a message on wood, etc. An _ancient document_ is an old document, produced from proper **custody** (safekeeping), that is presumed to be genuine if it is over a certain age. A _public document_ is a document that is, or should be, open for public inspection.

Document of title   A piece of paper that is normally accepted in business as proof of a right to hold goods; for example, a **bill of lading** or a **warehouse receipt.** A _document of title_ can be _negotiable_ (you have no right to the goods without the document) or _nonnegotiable_ (you can use the document to prove your right to the accompanying goods).

Documentary evidence   Evidence supplied by writings and all other **documents** (see that word).

Documentary originals rule   See **best evidence rule.**

Documentary stamp   A stamp that must be purchased and put on a **document** before it can be **recorded** in the public records of some cities or states.

Doing business   A general, flexible term meaning carrying on enough business for profit within a state so that another person can sue the company in that state. _Doing business_ also means that the state itself can tax the company or otherwise claim **jurisdiction** (see that word) over it.

Doli capax   (Latin) "Capable of crime"; old enough to know right from wrong and not insane.

Dollar averaging   Buying a fixed dollar amount of a **stock** (or other **security**) at regular intervals (usually getting a different number of **shares** each time).

Dolus   (Latin) **Fraud, deceit,** or crime.

Domain   Ownership and control (usually by the public). For example, national forests are in the _public domain_ (owned and controlled by the

U.S. for the benefit of the public). Some writings, inventions, and other works are in the *public domain* (available for use by anyone). Also see **eminent domain.**

Dombrowski doctrine The rule (from *Dombrowski v. Pfister,* 380 U.S. 479 (1965)) that a federal court will stop state officials from **prosecuting** a person under a state law that is so broad or vague that it affects rights guaranteed by the **First Amendment** to the U.S. **Constitution.**

Dome See **doom.**

Domestic *1.* Relating to the home. For example, *domestic relations* is the branch of law that deals with **divorce, custody, support, adoption,** etc. *2.* Relating to the state. For example, a *domestic corporation* is a corporation created under the laws of the state in question. *3.* Relating to internal matters of a particular country.

Domestic International Sales Corporation A type of U.S. company whose income comes primarily from foreign sales. A *D.I.S.C.* may get special tax breaks.

Domicile A person's permanent home, legal home, or main residence. The words "abode," "citizenship," "habitancy," and "residence" sometimes mean the same as *domicile* and sometimes not. A *corporate domicile* is the **corporation's** legal home (usually where its headquarters is located); an *elected domicile* is the place the persons who make a **contract** specify as their legal homes in the contract. [pronounce: <u>dom</u>-i-cile]

Domiciliary Relating to a person's permanent home. For example, a *domiciliary administration* is the handling of a dead person's **estate** (property) in the state of the person's legal **domicile.** [pronounce: dom-i-<u>sill</u>-ee-ary]

Dominant Possessing rights against another thing. For example, a *dominant estate* has rights (such as an **easement**) in another piece of land.

Dominant cause See **proximate cause.**

Dominion Legal ownership plus full actual control over something.

Donated stock (or surplus) **Stock** given back to a **corporation** by its shareholders, often for resale.

Donatio (Latin) A gift. For *donatio mortis causa,* see **causa mortis** *gift.*

Donative As a gift; related to a gift. For example, a *donative trust* is a **trust** set up as a gift for another person.

Donee A person to whom a gift is made or to whom a **power** is given.

Donee beneficiary   If David and Paul have a contract that benefits Jonah, Jonah is the *donee beneficiary.*

Donor   A person making a gift to another or giving another person power to do something.

Doom   Old word for a law or for a judge's decision.

Dormant   "Sleeping," inactive, silent or concealed. For example, a *dormant partner* is a partner who has a financial interest, but takes no control over the business and is usually unknown to the public; and a *dormant judgment* is a **judgment** that can no longer be enforced because too much time has gone by, because the person who originally got it died, etc. Some dormant judgments can be "**revived**" by taking the proper legal steps. See also **lapse.**

Dormant commerce clause   The principle that the **commerce clause** prevents state regulation of interstate commerce even if the specific regulated activity is not covered by federal laws.

Double entry   A system of **bookkeeping** that shows every transaction as both a **debit** and a **credit** (see those words) and by using both horizontal rows and vertical columns of numbers. If the total of the horizontal rows and the vertical columns is not the same, it is easier to find out where mistakes are than if the records were kept with only one "entry" for each item.

Double hearsay   **Hearsay** that itself contains hearsay. For example, it would be *double hearsay* if John testified in court that he heard Mary say something that Mary heard from someone else.

Double indemnity   Insurance coverage that results in a double payoff if something happens in a certain way; for example, a ten thousand dollar life insurance payment for a person's death and twenty thousand for that person's accidental death would be a *double indemnity* against accidental death.

Double insurance   Insurance from more than one company on the same **interest** in the same thing. It is usually not possible to collect more than a thing is worth.

Double jeopardy   A second prosecution by the same government against the same person for the same crime (or for a **lesser included offense**) once the first prosecution is totally finished and decided. This is prohibited by the U.S. **Constitution.**

Double taxation   *1.* Two taxes imposed on the same property by the same government during the same time period for the same purpose. This is not legal. But see no. 2. *2.* Any time the same money is taxed twice. A legal form of *double taxation* is taxing a **corporation** on its profits, then taxing its stockholders on their **dividends** from the corporation.

Double will See **reciprocal** *will.*

Doubt Uncertainty of mind about proof in a trial. For example, *"beyond a reasonable doubt"* is the **standard** *of proof* to convict a person of a crime. It is the highest standard of proof required in any type of trial, but does not mean "beyond *all* doubt."

Doubtful title The opposite of **marketable** *title.*

Dow Jones Industrial Average The changing price of a group of 30 selected stocks of the largest U.S. industrial **corporations.**

Dower A wife's right to part of her dead husband's property. This right is now **regulated** by **statute** and varies from state to state. (This is *not "dowry,"* a nonlegal word for property a bride brings into a marriage.) Compare with **curtesy.**

Down payment The cash that must be paid at the time that something is bought using credit.

Draconian law A law that is especially harsh or severe.

Draft A **bill** *of exchange* or any other **negotiable instrument** (see those words) for the payment of money *drawn* by one person on another. To use an ordinary personal **check** as an example: one person (the **drawer**) writes the check directing payment by a bank (the **drawee**) to another person (the **payee**). An *overdraft* is writing a check for more money than there is in the account; a *sight draft* is payable on demand; and a *time draft* is payable after a certain number of days.

Drafter (or draftsman or draftswoman) A person who writes a legal document (especially the person who creates an original document) such as a **contract** or a legislative **bill.**

Dragnet clause A provision in a **mortgage** or similar document in which **security** is given not only for the present debt, but for past and future debts.

Drago doctrine The principle that one country should not intervene militarily in another country to force or secure payment of debts owed by the second country to citizens of the first.

Dram shop acts Laws that make bars and stores **liable** for some acts done by persons who got drunk or bought liquor there.

Draw *1.* Prepare a legal document. *2.* Write out and sign a **bill** *of exchange* or make a **note** (see those words). *3.* Take money out of a bank account. *4.* Money advanced to a salesperson. This money is later subtracted from the salesperson's sales **commissions.** The fund that a draw comes from is called a *drawing account. 5.* Choose a **jury.**

Drawee　*1.* A person to whom a **bill** *of exchange* (see that word) is addressed, and who is requested to pay the amount of the bill. *2.* A bank that has a **deposit** withdrawn from it.

Drawer　The person drawing a **bill** *of exchange* (see that word) or writing a check to pay another person.

Dred Scott case　*Scott v. Sanford* (60 U.S. 393). The 1867 U.S. Supreme Court decision that slaves and former slaves were not citizens even if they lived in non-slave states. This decision was overturned by the Thirteenth and Fourteenth Amendments.

Dress　See **trade dress.**

Droit　(French) *1.* Right or justice. *2.* A law or the law. For example, *droit international* is **international law.** [pronounce: drwah]

Drop shipment　The delivery of goods directly from manufacturer to retailer or to **consumer** for which a **wholesaler** earns a profit for placing the order.

Drug-free zone　An area, such as that surrounding and including a school, within which the penalties for drug sales or "possession with intent to distribute" are increased.

Drunkometer (or Drunk-o-meter)　A brand of **evidential breath test.**

Dry　*1.* **Passive;** inactive; **formal** or **nominal** only. For example, a *dry* **trust** is one in which the **trustee** is legal owner of property, but has no duties to perform other than the passive act of having the property in his or her name, and gains no profits from the trust. *2.* Describes a state, country, or city where alcoholic beverages cannot be sold (or served).

Dual capacity doctrine　The principle that an employer is liable for an employee's injury even if that injury is covered by workers' compensation, if the employer's conduct contributed to the injury and the injury did not occur as a part of the employer-employee relationship. Compare with **dual purpose doctrine.**

Dual citizenship　Simultaneously holding citizenship in two countries. This can occur because a person was born in one country to parents who are citizens of another or because a country of which a person is a citizen still recognizes that citizenship after the person becomes a citizen of another country.

Dual contract　Two contracts for the same deal that are used in two different places, or one is kept secret, usually to inflate the value of real estate to a lender or to reduce it to tax authorities.

Dual court system　The federal and state courts in the United States.

Dual purpose doctrine   The rule that in most cases if an employee is on a business trip, he or she is acting within the normal **course of employment** (see that word) even if doing something personal. Compare with **dual capacity doctrine.**

Dual sovereignty doctrine   The principle that both a state and the U.S. may have legitimate interests in the same matter. This means that successive state and federal prosecutions for the same conduct do not necessarily violate the constitutional prohibition against **double jeopardy.**

Dubitante   With doubts.

Duces tecum   (Latin) "Bring with you." A **subpoena** (see that word) *duces tecum* commands a person to come to court with documents or other pieces of **evidence.** [pronounce: <u>due</u>-kiss <u>tay</u>-kum]

Due   *1.* Owing; payable. *2.* Just, proper, regular, lawful, sufficient, or reasonable. For example, *due care* means proper or reasonable care for the situation. (See also **due diligence.**)

Due-bill   An "**I.O.U.**," especially a company's I.O.U., that can be sold by the person to whom money is owed to another person, and then cashed in for goods or services.

Due date   Day a tax or debt must be paid.

Due diligence   Enough care, enough timeliness, or enough investigation to meet legal requirements, to fulfill a duty, or to evaluate the risks of a course of action. *Due diligence* often refers to a professional investigation of the financial risks of a **merger** or a **securities** purchase, or to the legal *obligation* to do the investigation. *Due diligence* is also used as a synonym for **due** *care.*

Due notice   Reasonable notice (as determined by each individual situation).

Due process of law   The *due process clauses* of the Fifth and Fourteenth Amendments to the U.S. Constitution require that no person be deprived of life, liberty, or property without *due process of law.* What constitutes due process of law varies from situation to situation, but the core of the idea is that a person should always have **notice** and a real chance to present his or her side in a legal dispute ("*procedural due process*"; see **procedural law**) and that no law or government procedure should be **arbitrary** or unfair ("*substantive due process*"; see **substantive law**). Some of the specifics of *due process* include the right to a **transcript** of court proceedings, the right to question adverse witnesses, etc.

Dummy   Sham; make believe; set up as a "front." For example, *dummy incorporators* are persons who initially set up a corporation to meet the formal requirements of a state's corporation laws and then drop out. Dummy incorporation is permitted in most cases.

Dump   *1.* Sell something in other countries for less than it is sold at home. Federal law prohibits some sales of this sort by foreign companies, and international trade agreements prohibit others. *2.* Unload large quantities of goods regardless of price.

Dun   Demand payment on an overdue debt.

Dun and Bradstreet   A major supplier of business credit ratings.

Duplicate   *1.* A copy. *2.* A new document made to take the place of an original.

Duplicity   *1.* Joining two or more separate reasons for a lawsuit in one paragraph, two or more subjects in one **act** passed by a legislature, etc. This is now usually permitted. Charging two or more unrelated crimes in one **indictment,** however, is usually not permitted. *2.* Deception or "double dealing."

Durable power of attorney   A **power of attorney** that lasts as long as a person remains incapable of making decisions, usually about healthcare. It is a form of **advance directive.**

Duress   *1.* Unlawful pressure on a person to do what he or she would not otherwise have done. It includes force, threats of violence, physical restraint, etc. *2.* *Duress of goods* is the **tort** of taking someone's property, holding it with no right to do so, and improperly demanding something for its return.

Durham rule   The principle, used in *Durham v. U.S.* (214 F.2d. 862 (1954)), that a **defendant** is not guilty of a crime because of **insanity** (see that word) if he or she was "suffering from a disease or defective mental condition at the time of the act and there was a causal connection between the condition and the act." The rule is no longer used in full in any state, but some parts survive in the *Model Penal Code.*

Duty   *1.* An obligation to obey a law. *2.* A legal obligation to another person, who has a corresponding **right.** *3.* Any obligation, whether legal, moral, or ethical. *4.* A tax on imports or exports.

Duty of tonnage   Governmental port charges or port taxes on a boat.

Dwelling defense   See **castle doctrine.**

Dyer Act   A 1919 law making it a federal crime to take a stolen motor vehicle across a state line.

Dying declaration   See **declaration.**

Dynamite instruction   An **Allen charge.**

E.A.P. Employee assistance program. A referral program for employees with problems such as drug dependency that require medical treatment or counseling.

E.B.I.T. Earnings before interest and taxes.

E.B.T. *1. Examination before trial* of a **party** to a lawsuit. It is a part of the **discovery** process. *2.* **Evidential breath test.**

E.D. Eastern **district.**

E.E.O.C. **Equal Employment Opportunity Commission.**

E.F.T.S. Electronic fund transfer system.

E.g. Abbreviation for the Latin "exempli gratia" (for the sake of example). It is used in most law books to take the place of "for example."

E.I.S. **Environmental Impact Statement.**

E.O. **Executive order.**

E.P.A. Environmental Protection Agency. A U.S. **agency** that enforces pollution control, does environmental research, etc.

E.P.S. Earnings per **share.**

E.R.I.S.A. **Employee Retirement Income Security Act.**

E.S.A. *1.* Endangered Species Act. *2.* Employment Standards Administration.

E.S.O.P. Employee stock ownership plan.

E.S.O.T. Employee stock ownership trust. A **trust fund** set up to fund an employee stock ownership plan, giving tax benefits to employer and employee.

E & O **Errors and omissions** insurance.

Earmarked Set aside for a particular purpose; describes money or property that is easily identified so that it can be separated from similar things. For example, if a lender *earmarks* a loan to pay one specific **creditor** of the borrower, and the borrower then goes **bankrupt,** the bankruptcy **trustee** cannot claim the money paid as part of the debtor's **assets.** See **preference.**

Earned income *1.* Money or other compensation received for work. It does not include, for example, the profits gained from renting property. *2.* The *earned income credit* is a *tax* **credit** given to some low-income workers.

Earned premium   The part of a paid **premium** that an insurance company may keep if the policy is canceled, because it has "earned" that part by providing **coverage** that has been used, or will be used, before the cancellation date.

Earned surplus   Retained earnings.

Earnest money   A **deposit** paid by a buyer to hold a seller to a deal and to show the buyer's **good faith.** It is usually, but not always, kept by the seller if the buyer fails to complete the deal. Compare **option.**

Earnings multiple   The number by which an annual stock **dividend** must be multiplied to equal the stock's selling price.

Earnings per share   A company's profits available to pay **dividends** on its **common stock** divided by the number of **shares** of such stock. *"Primary" earnings per share* and *"fully diluted" earnings per share* divide the available profits by not only the shares of common stock, but by everything that can be turned into common stock (**convertible** stock and bonds, **options, warrants,** etc.).

Earnings report   See **statement** *of income.*

Earnout   The sale of a business in which the final purchase price depends on future profits.

Easement   The right of a specific nonowner of a piece of land (such as a next-door neighbor, the government, or a public utility) to use part of the land in a particular way. This right usually stays with the land when it is sold. Typical *easements* include the right of the owner of a piece of land with no streetfront to use a specific strip of another person's land to reach the street, or the right of a city to run a sewer line across a specific strip of an owner's land. The land that gives up an easement is the **servient** *estate* and, if there is one particular property that benefits from the easement, it is called the **dominant** *estate.* (Easements involving two properties are *easements appurtenant* and easements involving only one are *easements in gross.*) Easements may be *affirmative* (where the landowner must permit something) or *negative* (where the landowner is prohibited from doing something). A *reciprocal negative easement* may be created when a landowner sells part of a property and places a negative easement on it. That easement may then also restrict the part kept by the owner.

Ecclesiastical courts   Religious courts, once powerful in England, that affected the development of the law. Religious law was called **canon law.**

Economic realities test   *1.* The principle that a court should consider the totality of a commercial situation, rather than look at only its documents, when deciding a case. *2.* The principle that a key factor in deciding whether a person is an employee is whether the "employer" has the practical ability to control the person.

Economic rent   **Ground rent.**

Economic strike   A refusal to work because of a dispute over wages, hours, working conditions, etc. It is different from an **unfair labor practice** (see that word) strike and may result in loss of job.

Edict   A major law made by a king or other head of state.

Editorial privilege   **Journalist's privilege.**

Educational expenses   Employee spending to gain skills for a current job or to meet an employer's educational requirements. Some *educational expenses* are tax **deductible,** but expenses to gain skills for a *new* job or to meet *minimum* educational requirements are not deductible. "*Educational expenses*" sometimes refer to only the deductible ones.

Effect   *1.* To do, produce, accomplish, or force. *2.* A result. *3.* This is *not* "**affect.**" See that word for how to remember the difference.

Effective counsel   A lawyer who is honest, knowledgeable, and competent, not necessarily one who commits few errors or who uses excellent judgment. For a criminal defendant to challenge a conviction based on *ineffective counsel,* the conviction must have been affected by the lawyer's conduct.

Effective rate   See **tax rate.**

Effects   *1. Personal* **property.** *2.* Personal property of a person making a will or of a dead person. *3.* For *effects doctrine,* see **affects doctrine.**

Efficient breach theory   The **law and economics** principle that if it is economically efficient to **breach** a contract and pay **damages,** you should be allowed to do it.

Efficient cause   See **proximate cause.**

Efficient market   A **stock, commodity,** etc., trading place or method that immediately gets and uses all available information, so that prices reflect full and current information. See also **fraud on the market theory.**

Eighteenth Amendment   The 1919 **constitutional** amendment that prohibited the manufacture, sale, and transportation of alcoholic beverages until the amendment's **repeal** in 1933 by the **Twenty-first Amendment.**

Eighth Amendment   The U.S. **constitutional** amendment prohibiting excessive **bail** or **fines** and **cruel and unusual punishment.**

Eight-hour laws   The federal laws that established the eight-hour workday and required payment for overtime.

Eire   See **Eyre.**

Ejectione firmae   (Latin) A **writ** of **ejectment** for a tenant who was wrongfully thrown out.

Ejectment   The name for an old type of lawsuit to get back land taken away wrongfully. It was used primarily to establish **title** to land and was brought against a fictitious **defendant** called the "*casual ejector.*"

Ejusdem generis   (Latin) Of the same kind or type. Under the *ejusdem generis rule,* when a list in a document is followed by general words, those words should apply only to things of the same kind as the things on the list. [pronounce: ee-use-dem]

Election   *1.* Any act of choosing. *2.* Choosing from among legal rights. For example, a husband or wife may have to *elect* (choose) between what was left in a **will** by the other one and what state law reserves as a minimum share of a husband's or wife's **estate.** (A husband might leave a wife "the house and ten thousand dollars" and state law may allow the wife to take one-third of the husband's total estate. The wife can have one but not both of these.) In the same sense, *election of remedies* is the choice of legally contradictory courses of action to protect a right. *3.* The choosing of an official by voting. A *general election* is one held regularly to choose public officials; a *primary election* is to choose the **candidates** of political parties; and a *special election* is to fill a vacancy at other times than those of a general election.

Election contest   A challenge to the accuracy or validity of **election** results. **Ballots** are usually recounted and their validity is examined.

Elective   Chosen, allowing a choice, or available as a choice. See **election** for these and other uses.

Elector   *1.* A voter. *2.* Member of the **electoral college** (see that word).

Electoral college   A name for the persons chosen by voters to elect the president and vice president of the United States. The *electoral college* is now almost a formality, and the vote of the general public in each state directly controls the election. Theoretically, however, some *electors* might decide to vote differently from their instructions, a choice that could change the result of a close election.

Electronic citation   An online **public domain** *citation* (see that word).

Eleemosynary   Charitable. For charitable organizations generally, see **nonprofit organization.** [pronounce: el-e-mos-e-nary]

Eleganter   Correctly, formally, and accurately.

Element   A basic part. For example, some of the *elements* of a **cause of action** for **battery** are an intentional, unwanted physical contact. Each of these things ("intentional," "unwanted," etc.) is one "*element*."

Eleventh Amendment   The U.S. **constitutional** amendment that prohibits the federal courts from handling a lawsuit against one of the states that is brought by a noncitizen of that state.

Eligibility   Being legally qualified. For example, *eligibility* for Social Security benefits means meeting all the legal requirements to get the benefits.

Elisor   A person appointed by a court to act as a **sheriff** or **coroner** if the sheriff or coroner cannot do the job needed.

Eloignment   An old word for removing or concealing something from the reach of a court.

Emancipation   Setting free. For example, a child is *emancipated* when the child is old enough so that the parents have no further right to control or obligation to support him or her.

Embargo   *1.* A government's refusal to allow the transportation of certain things into or out of the country. *2.* A government's stopping the ships or planes of another country from coming in or going out.

Embedded   Not broken out as a separate item. Part of a larger statistic.

Embezzlement   The **fraudulent** and secret taking of money or property by a person who has been trusted with it. This usually applies to an employee's taking money and covering it up by faking business records or **account** books.

Emblements   Crops grown by a tenant farmer, especially crops planted and harvested during the tenancy. In some cases, the tenant has the right to the *emblements* even if the harvest is subsequent to the tenancy.

Embracery   An old word for attempting to bribe a jury.

Emergency doctrine   *1.* The rule that a person (such as a driver) is not required to take the same action in an emergency that would be required at other times, as long as the person used proper care before the emergency and did nothing reckless during the emergency. *2.* The rule that if no proper person is available to give consent for emergency medical treatment for an unconscious adult or for a child, absolutely necessary treatment may be given anyway. *3.* See also **Good Samaritan doctrine** and **rescue** *doctrine*. *4.* The rule that a **search warrant** may not be needed if a law officer thinks that a life may be in danger. (Also called *emergency exception*.)

Eminent domain   The government's right and power to take private land for public use by paying for it.

Emit   Put out, **issue,** put into circulation.

Emolument   Any financial or other gain from employment.

Emotional distress   **Mental anguish.**

Empanel   See **impanel.**

Emphyteutic lease   A **lease** on land that is long term and can be passed on to another person as long as the rent is paid.

Empirical   Based on observation or experiment.

Employee Retirement Income Security Act   (29 U.S.C. 1001) A federal law that established a program to protect employees' pension plans. The law set up a fund to pay pensions when plans go broke and regulates pension plans as to *vesting* (when a person's pension rights become permanent), nondiversion of benefits to anyone other than those entitled, nondiscrimination against lower-paid employees, etc. See **pension plan, vested,** and **annuity.**

Employers' liability acts   Federal and state laws defining the circumstances under which an employer must pay for an employee's injuries and illnesses. These laws commonly deny an employer the benefit of the **fellow servant rule** and the defense of **contributory negligence.** Many of these laws are now called **workers' compensation laws** (see that word), especially when they set up a fund for payments.

Empty chair   *1.* For *empty chair rule,* see **adverse inference rule.** *2.* The *empty chair defense* is an attempt to put all the blame on a **defendant** who has already settled and is out of the case.

En   (French) In. For example, *en ventre sa mere* means "in its mother's womb." [pronounce: ahn vahn-tre sa mare]

En banc   (French) All the judges of a court participating in a case all together, rather than individually or in panels of a few.

En gros   (French) In **gross;** total; **wholesale.** [pronounce: ahn grow]

Enabling clause   The part of a **statute** that gives officials the power to put it into effect and enforce it. Compare with *enacting clause* under **enact.**

Enabling power   **Power of appointment.**

Enabling statute (or act)   A law that grants new powers to do something, usually to a public official, a county, or a city.

Enact   Put a **statute** into effect; pass a statute through a **legislature;** establish by law. An *enacting clause* is an introduction to a **statute** (such as "Be it enacted that . . .") that authorizes the statute as law. Compare with **enabling clause.**

Encroachment An unlawful burden placed on another's land or another's rights in land, especially the placement of a structure (such as a fence or a building) on another's land.

Encumber Make property subject to a **charge** or **liability**. See **encumbrance.**

Encumbrance A **claim, charge,** or **liability** on property, such as a **lien** or **mortgage,** that lowers its value.

End balance method Charging a full month's **interest** on all bills unpaid at the end of each monthly billing period. (If a purchase is made on the last day of the month and payment made one day later, "1 percent interest" could turn into a true **annual percentage rate** (see that word) of over 300 percent by this method.)

End position The legal and financial status that a person who signs a **contract** will have at the end of the contract; for example, the choices available to someone who has **leased** equipment (renew the contract, return the equipment, pay for damages, etc.).

Endorsement _1._ **Indorsement.** _2._ A change added to an insurance policy.

Endowment _1._ Setting up a fund, usually for a public institution such as a school. _2._ The fund in definition no. 1. _3._ An **insurance** policy that pays a set amount at a set time or, if the person insured dies, pays the money to a **beneficiary.**

Energy The U.S. Department of Energy. The **cabinet** department that handles energy regulation and development, including nuclear waste cleanup and nuclear weapons development.

Enfeoffment **Feoffment.**

Enforcement _1._ Carrying out the commands of a law. For example, the _enforcement_ powers of several U.S. **constitutional** amendments give Congress the power to **enact** laws to carry out the amendments' purposes. _2._ Putting something into effect. For example, the _Enforcement of Foreign Judgments Act,_ adopted by many states, gives persons who hold money **judgments** in other states the same right to collect on them (by **levy** and **execution**) that a citizen of the state would have to collect on a judgment in the state. _3._ Short for _law enforcement_ or police.

Enfranchise _1._ Make free. _2._ Give the right to vote.

Engage Take part in or do. To "_engage_" in a particular activity is to do it more than once, and probably regularly.

Engagement **Contract** or obligation.

Engel v. Vitale   (370 U.S. 421) The 1962 Supreme Court decision that prohibited prayer in public schools as a violation of the constitutional separation of church and state.

English rule   The principle that the winner of a lawsuit can collect costs and attorney's fees from the loser. Compare **American rule.**

Engrossment (or engrossing)   *1.* Making a final or "good" copy of a document, often just prior to using it for some formal purpose, such as voting on a **bill** or executing a **deed.** *2.* **Cornering** a market.

Enhancement   Increasing or making larger. For example, a criminal penalty may be *enhanced* (made longer or worse), even though "enhancement" is usually thought of as being good, as increasing value or attractiveness, etc.

Enjoin   Require or command. A court's issuing of an **injunction** (see that word) directing someone to do or, more likely, to refrain from doing certain acts.

Enjoyment   The exercise of a right; the ability to use a right. See **quiet** for *covenant for quiet enjoyment.*

Enlarge   *1.* Make larger. *2.* Extend a time limit. *3.* Release a person from **custody.**

Enoch Arden laws   State laws concerning the time period and necessary conditions for a spouse to be presumed dead after a long absence with no knowledge by the remaining spouse of the person's fate.

Enroll   *1.* **Register** or **record** a formal document in the proper office or file. *2.* See **engrossment.**

Enrolled agent   A person authorized to represent taxpayers in all **I.R.S.** proceedings.

Enrolled bill   *1.* A **bill** that has gone through the steps necessary to make it a law. *2.* The *enrolled bill rule* is that once a law has been fully formalized, its wording may not be challenged by referring to previous versions.

Ensue   Follow later, especially follow later as a logical result.

Entail   Restrict an **inheritance** in **land** so that it can be passed on only to children, then children's children, etc. Create a **fee tail.**

Enter   *1.* Go into; for example, go into a building unlawfully to commit a crime. See **breaking.** *2.* Go onto land in order to take possession. *3.* Become a part of. *4.* Place formally on the **record;** write down formally in the proper place. (The thing written down in an *entry.*) For example, to *enter an appearance* is to submit a piece of paper to a court saying that you are now formally a part of a case, either as a **party** or as a lawyer.

Entering judgment (or entry of judgment)   The formal act of recording a court's **judgment** in the court's judgment **docket** after the judgment has been given or announced.

Enterprise   *1.* A business organization or activity. For example, *enterprise liability* is either the potential liability taken on by a business (such as workers' compensation) or that taken on by an entire industry (such as one that produces a defective product and the individual manufacturers cannot be identified). And an *enterprise zone* is an area identified for special business tax and development benefits. *2.* Under **R.I.C.O.**, a group or organization with a shared purpose and personnel, with a structure that exists apart from the racketeering activity itself.

Enticement   *1.* An old form of lawsuit brought because of the seduction or taking away of a wife. *2.* Trying to persuade a child to come to a secluded place with the intent to commit an unlawful sexual act.

Entirety   As a whole; not divided into parts. See **tenant.**

Entitlement   **Absolute** (complete) right to something (such as Social Security) once you show that you meet the legal requirements to get it.

Entrapment   The act of government officials (usually police) or agents of inducing a person to commit a crime that the person would not have committed without the inducement. This is done for the purposes of prosecuting the person. It is not lawful in most cases, and a criminal charge based on *entrapment* should fail, especially if the person has never before engaged in similar activity or indicated a desire or *predisposition* to do so. *Entrapment* is an **affirmative defense** (see that word).

Entry   *1.*   The act of entering. See **enter.** *2.* Something recorded in the proper record book.

Enumerated   Mentioned specifically; listed one by one.

Enumeratio unius   (Latin) **Expressio unius.**

Enure   See **inure.**

Environmental Impact Statement   Documents required by federal and state laws to accompany proposals for projects or programs that might harm the environment.

Envoy   An **ambassador** or special government **minister.**

Eo   (Latin) *"That,"* as in the phrases *eo die* (on that day); *eo instanti* (at that instant); *eo intuitu* (with that intent); and *eo nomine* (by that name).

Equal Credit Opportunity Act   (15 U.S.C. 1691) A federal law prohibiting discrimination based on race, religion, disability, color, sex, age, or national origin, in any **credit** transaction.

Equal degrees   An equal number of steps or **degrees** (see that word) away from a common ancestor.

Equal Employment Opportunity Commission   A federal agency that works toward ending discrimination based on race, religion, disability, color, sex, age, or national origin in all work-related activities such as hiring, promotion, etc. And an *equal opportunity employer* is one that pledges to do the same.

Equal protection of laws   The **constitutional** requirement that a state government not treat equals unequally, set up illegal categories to justify treating persons unfairly, or give unfair or unequal treatment to a person based on that person's race, religion, disability, color, sex, age, or national origin. This is based on the *equal protection clause* of the **Fourteenth Amendment.** See also **compelling state interest, strict scrutiny test,** and **suspect classification.**

Equal Rights Amendment   A failed U.S. constitutional amendment forbidding discrimination based on sex.

Equal Time Act   (47 U.S.C. 315) A federal law that may require radio and television stations that give (or sell) time to a qualified candidate for public office to also give (or sell) time to all other qualified candidates under the same terms and conditions.

Equalization   The process of adjusting **assessments** and taxes on real estate in order to make sure that properties are properly valued and are taxed fairly according to value.

Equipment trust   The method of financing business equipment in which **title** to the property is held by **trustees** until paid for.

Equitable   *1.* Just, fair, and right for a particular situation. For example, an *equitable distribution* of money or property is a *fair* division, but not necessarily an *equal* one. And *equitable election* is choosing between two things when it is not fair to have both. The *doctrine of equitable election* is the rule that a person cannot accept something given in a **will** and also challenge the validity of the will for other purposes. Also, whenever something *should* exist but does *not* exist under a strict interpretation of the law, a court may decide in fairness that it *does* exist. Thus, there can be such things as *equitable* **adoptions, mortgages, liens,** etc. An *equitable adoption* is a court's allowing a person to **inherit** property from someone who promised to **adopt** him or her and who acted as if the adoption really took place. An *equitable* _mortgage_ is a court's deciding that a **deed** transferring property was really given to **secure** a debt, so that a **mortgage,** not a complete transfer of property, exists. In each case, "_equitable_" can be read as "not strictly according to law, but we'll enforce it because of fairness." _2._ An "_equitable action_" is a lawsuit based on a court's **equity** (see that word) powers, often to enforce rights like those in definition no. 1. _3._ An _equitable_ **defense** is one based on the court's equity powers. _4._ For _equitable estoppel,_ see **estoppel.** _5._ For _equitable servitude,_ see **restrictive covenant.** [pronounce: e̲k̲-wit-a-bl]

Equitable abstention doctrine   See **abstention doctrine.**

Equitable restraint doctrine   The principle that a federal court should not interfere in a state criminal prosecution except to prevent **irreparable injury** to the defendant or if there has been **bad faith** in prosecuting the defendant.

Equitable tolling   The principle that lawsuits for certain types of **torts** are not barred by the _statute of_ **limitations** unless the plaintiff has failed to use **due** _care_ to discover the harm done. See **discovery** and **toll.**

Equity   _1._ Fairness in a particular situation. _2._ The name for a system of courts that originated in England to take care of legal problems when the existing laws did not cover some situations in which a person's rights were violated by another person. _3._ A court's power to "do justice" where specific laws do not cover the situation. _4._ The value of property after all charges against it are paid. This is also called _net worth_ or _net value._ _5._ **Stock.** Sometimes **common stock** only.

Equity financing (or capital)   A corporation raising money by selling **stock** (ownership shares) rather than by _debt financing_ (selling **bonds** or borrowing). Stocks, and other **securities** similar to stocks, are called _equity securities_ or _equity shares._

Equity investor   A person who buys equipment that is then **leased** to another in a deal with special tax advantages.

Equity of a statute   The principle that **statutes** not only permit and forbid conduct but also state general policy for situations similar to, but not expressly covered by, the statute. See **liberal construction.**

Equity of redemption   The right of a person to stop a mortgage **foreclosure** by paying all money owed, interest, and costs within a state-specified time period.

Equivalents   Two devices or processes that do basically the same thing, in basically the same way, to get basically the same result. If two devices or processes are _equivalents,_ and one is merely the result of one company's minor changes to another company's patented product, the production, sale, or use of the changed device or process may be a patent **infringement.**

Erasure of record   The procedure by which a person's **criminal record** (see those words) or juvenile delinquency record may be destroyed, or at least sealed and made unavailable for public access.

Ergo   (Latin) Therefore.

Erie v. Tompkins   (304 U.S. 64) The 1938 Supreme Court decision that, except for situations involving the Constitution or **federal** laws, the law used to decide a case in federal court should be *state* law. This case ended the idea that **federal common law** (see that word) applied to all state cases.

Erratum   (Latin) Mistake in printed or written material.

Error   A mistake made by a judge in the procedures used at trial, or in making legal **rulings** during the trial. Some errors must be objected to at the time in order to ask a higher court to review the case. If the error could have affected the outcome, it is called *reversible error, plain error,* or *fatal error* by the higher court. If it is trivial, it is called *harmless error.*

Errors and omissions   Insurance that covers professional mistakes, but not intentional wrongdoing. It is often a part of a lawyer's **malpractice** policy.

Escalator clause   *1.* A provision in a **contract** that allows a price to rise if costs rise. Or, in the case of a maximum payment **regulated** by the government (such as rent controls), for the price to rise if the maximum is raised or eliminated. *2.* See **cost of living clause.**

Escape clause   A **contract** provision that allows a person to avoid doing something or to avoid **liability** if certain things happen.

Escheat   The state's getting property because no owner can be found. For example, if a person dies and no person can be found who can legally inherit that person's property, the government gets it by *escheat.* [pronounce: es-<u>cheet</u>]

Escobedo rule   When a suspect in police **custody** has asked for and been denied a lawyer, nothing the suspect says after that can be used in a criminal trial. The rule is from *Escobedo v. Illinois* (378 U.S. 478). See also **Miranda warning.**

Escrow   Money, property, or documents belonging to person A and held by person B until person A takes care of an obligation to person C. For example, a mortgage company may require a homeowner with a **mortgage** to make monthly payments into an *escrow* account to take care of the yearly tax bill when it comes due.

Esq.   Short for "Esquire"; a title given to lawyers.

Essence   Indispensable basis or core. See **"time is of the essence."**

Essoin   An old English word for an excuse for being absent from court, presented by a person called an _essoiner_ sent for the purpose. [pronounce: es-<u>soyn</u>]

Establish   _1._ Settle or prove a point. _2._ Set up, create, or found.

Establishment clause   That part of the **First Amendment** to the U.S. **Constitution** that states "Congress shall make no law respecting an _establishment_ of religion." See **freedom of religion.**

Estate   _1._ The **interest** a person has in property; a person's right or **title** to property. For example, a "_future estate_" is a property interest that will come about only in the future if an uncertain event takes place. _2._ The property itself in which a person has an interest; for example, _real estate_ (land and buildings) or a _decedent's estate_ (things left by a dead person). _3._ For types of _estates,_ such as **absolute, conditional, executed, executory, contingent, dominant, servient, vested,** at **will,** in **common,** in **expectancy,** in **fee simple,** in **fee tail,** etc., see those words.

Estate planning   Carrying out a person's wishes for property to be passed on at his or her death and gaining maximum legal benefit from that property by using the laws of **wills, trusts, insurance, property,** and **taxes.**

Estate tax   A tax paid on the property left by a dead person. It is paid on the property as a whole before it is divided up and handed out. This is different from an **inheritance** tax, which is based on the money each individual inherits and is paid by each **heir** separately (unless the will says otherwise).

Estate trust   A **trust** (see that word), used to qualify property for the **marital** deduction from **estate** taxes, that puts property into a trust for a surviving spouse with the remaining trust property going into that spouse's estate at death for federal tax purposes.

Estimated tax   Some persons with income other than salaries must estimate, "report," and pay income tax four times a year.

Estoppel   _1._ Being stopped by your own prior acts from claiming a right against another person who has legitimately relied on those acts. For example, if a person signs a **deed,** that person may be _estopped_ from later going to court claiming that the deed is wrong. _2._ Being stopped from proving something (even if true) in court because of something you said before that shows the opposite (even if false).

Estoppel by judgment   The inability to raise an issue against a person in court because a judge has already decided that precise issue between the persons.

Estoppel certificate   A **certificate** given by a mortgage lender, such as a bank, to a prospective real estate purchaser. It details the status of a mortgage on the property, including the amount due as of that date, and acts as an **estoppel** against the lender claiming otherwise later.

Estover   *1.* An allowance for basics such as food, shelter, and clothing. *2.* A tenant's right to cut and use timber for basic property maintenance (and sometimes for fuel).

Et al.   (Latin) Abbreviation for *et alii* ("and others"). For example, "*Smith et al.*" means "Smith plus certain other persons."

Et non   (Latin) "And not"; has the same use as **absque** *hoc.*

Et seq.   (Latin) Abbreviation for *et sequentes* ("and the following"). For example, "*page 27 et seq.*" means "page twenty-seven and the following pages."

Et ux.   Abbreviation for *et uxor* ("and wife") seen in old legal documents. For example, "This deed made by John Smith *et ux.*"

Et vir. (or et con.)   (Latin) "And husband." See **et ux.**

Ethics   *1.* Professional standards of conduct for lawyers and judges. See **Rules of Professional Conduct.** *2.* Standards of fair and honest conduct in general.

Euclidian zoning   See **zoning.**

Eurodollar   A U.S. dollar deposited with a bank in Europe (or anywhere outside the U.S., especially if used in European money markets).

Euthanasia   **Mercy killing.**

Evaluation agreement   A contract in which a person who accepts an idea for evaluation promises to pay for its use or to neither use it nor disclose it to others.

Evasion   Eluding or dodging. *Tax evasion* is the illegal nonpayment or underpayment of taxes due. *(Tax avoidance* is the legal reduction or nonpayment of taxes by using **deductions, exemptions, exclusions,** etc.)

Evasive   Elusive or shifty. If a **pleading** is *evasive,* the other side in the lawsuit may demand a *more definite statement.* If an answer to a question asked in **discovery** is *evasive,* the other side may get a court **order** compelling a proper answer.

Evergreen contract   An agreement that automatically renews itself each year unless one side gives advance notice to the other side that it will end.

Eviction   A landlord putting a tenant out of property, either by taking direct action (a "_self-help_" _eviction,_ often illegal) or, more often, by going to court.

Evidence   _1._ All types of information (observations, recollections, documents, concrete objects, etc.) presented at a trial or other hearing. Statements made by the judge and lawyers, however, are not _evidence._ 2. Any information that might be used for a future trial. _3._ For types of evidence, such as **circumstantial, demonstrative, direct, hearsay, parol, probative, real, state's,** etc., see those words.

Evidence law   The rules and principles about whether evidence can be admitted (accepted for proof) in a trial and how to evaluate its importance.

Evidential breath test   A device that is accepted by courts as an accurate measure of alcohol in the blood because it accurately measures the percentage of alcohol in the driver's breath.

Evidentiary fact   A fact that is learned directly from **testimony** or other **evidence.** Important factual conclusions inferred from _evidentiary facts_ are called "_ultimate facts._"

Evidentiary harpoon   Inadmissible **evidence** deliberately placed before a jury to prejudice it against a criminal defendant.

Ex   (Latin) A prefix meaning many things including: out of, no longer, from, because of, by, and with.

Ex aequo et bono   (Latin) By **equity** and **good faith;** in justice and fairness.

Ex arbitrio judicis   (Latin) By the judge's **discretion.**

Ex assensu curiae   (Latin) By leave of the court; with the judge's consent.

Ex cathedra   (Latin) "From the chair"; authoritative.

Ex contractu   (Latin) "From a **contract.**" A lawsuit based on a contract, rather than on a **tort.**

Ex curia   (Latin) Out of court.

Ex debito justitiae   (Latin) "From a debt of justice." Something that may be done as of right, without asking permission or court approval. [pronounce: deb-ee-tow jus-tish-ee-i]

Ex defectu sanguinis   (Latin) "From a defect of blood"; because there are no children.

Ex delicto   (Latin) "From wrongdoing." A lawsuit based on a **tort** (or on a **crime**) rather than on a **contract.**

Ex dividend   Describes a **stock** sold without the right to collect a **dividend** that has been declared but not yet paid.

Ex facie   (Latin) _1._ "From the **face**" of a document. _2._ Apparently. [pronounce: ex fay-she-iy]

Ex facto   (Latin) As a matter of fact; happening because of a fact, a person's actions, or an occurrence.

Ex gratia   (Latin) From **grace** or as a favor and not as a right.

Ex integro   (Latin) New.

Ex lege   (Latin) As a matter of law; as a result of a law.

Ex mero motu   (Latin) "On his own **motion** or motive"; voluntarily.

Ex necessitate legis   (Latin) "From legal necessity"; **implied** by law.

Ex necessitate rei   (Latin) "From the necessity of the case or matter"; **implied** from the facts.

Ex officio   1. By the power of the office (official position) alone. 2. Acting as a private citizen, not as an official. (This is a popular, not legal, meaning.) [pronounce: ex o-fish-ee-o]

Ex parte   (Latin) With only one side present. For example, an *ex parte order* is one made on the request of one side in a lawsuit when (or because) the other side does not show up in court (because the other side failed to show up, because the other side did not need to be present for the order to **issue,** or because there *is* no other side). [pronounce: ex par-tee]

Ex post facto   (Latin) After the fact. An *ex post facto law* is one that retroactively attempts to make an action a crime that was not a crime at the time it was done, or a law that attempts to reduce a person's rights based on a past act that was not subject to the law when it was done. *Ex post facto* laws are prohibited by the U.S. **Constitution** (Article1, Section 9).

Ex rel.   Short for the Latin *ex relatione,* "on relation," or "from the information given by." When a case is titled "*State ex rel. Doe v. Roe*" it means that the state is bringing a lawsuit for Doe against Roe.

Ex rights   Describes a **stock** sold without its special right to buy additional shares.

Ex tempore   (Latin) 1. Without preparation. 2. Because of the passage of time.

Ex vi termini   (Latin) "From the force of the word (or phrase)"; explained by itself with no need to refer to other words.

Exaction   An official wrongfully demanding payment of a fee for official services when no payment is due.

Examination   1. An investigation; for example, the search through **title** records for any problems before buying property or the inquiry by the **patent** office into the novelty and usefulness of an invention. 2. A questioning; for example, the questioning of a witness under **oath** or the questioning in a hearing of a **bankrupt** about his or her financial situation. *3.* The order of questioning a witness is usually *"direct examination"* (by the side that called the witness), *"cross examination"* (by the other side), *"redirect," "recross,"* etc.

Examined copy   A copy of a public record that has been compared with the original and found to be both accurate and genuine. Compare with **conformed copy.**

Examiner   *1.* The name for a type of **hearing examiner** or **administrative law judge.** *2.* A person authorized to conduct an official examination; for example, a *bank examiner* (who looks into a bank's dealings); a *bar examiner* (who evaluates tests taken by those who apply for **bar** admission); etc.

Exceptio   (Latin) An **exception** or **objection.**

Exception   *1.* Leaving something or someone out intentionally; an **exclusion.** *2.* A formal disagreement with a judge's refusal of a request or overruling (see **overrule**)of an **objection.** It is a statement that the lawyer does not agree with the judge's decision, and expresses this disagreement to note it for possible later **appeal;** however, it is not necessary to *take exception* to appeal the decision in most courts.

Excess   Too much. For example, *"excess of jurisdiction"* refers to a judge's actions that go beyond the proper actions he or she can take under the court's powers.

Excess policy   **Insurance** that pays for only losses greater than those covered by another policy.

Excess profits tax   A tax on those business profits in excess of what is considered reasonable (calculated by return on investment or past yearly averages). The tax is usually imposed only in time of war. Compare with **accumulated earnings tax.**

Excessive bail or fine   **Bail** or a **fine** that is disproportionate to the offense committed. These are forbidden by the **Eighth Amendment** to the U.S. **Constitution.**

Exchange   *1.* A swap or **barter;** a transaction that involves no money and in which no price or value is set for any item involved. *2.* An organization set up to buy and sell **securities** such as **stocks.** *3.* The payment of debts in different places by a transfer of **credits** such as by **bill** *of exchange. 4.* See **like-kind exchange.**

Exchequer   The English treasury department. [pronounce: e̲x-check-er]

Excise   A tax on the manufacture, sale, or use of goods or on the carrying on of an occupation or activity. Compare with **sales tax.**

Excited utterance   A statement made about an event, during or just after the event, by a person who is still emotional as a result of the event. In-court testimony about another's *excited utterance* is often admissible as **evidence** as an exception to the **hearsay** *rule.*

Exclusion   *1.* Keeping (or leaving) someone or something out. For example, *exclusions* in an insurance policy are the persons, property, or types of losses that will not be covered. *2.* Not counting something as income for income tax purposes. For example, while a gift of money from father to son is within the general definition of "income," most such gifts are, by law, *excluded* from (not counted as) the son's income, so that no income tax is payable on the gift. Compare with **deduction, exemption,** and **credit.**

Exclusionary clause   A part of a **contract** that tries to restrict the legal remedies (see **remedy**) available to one side if the contract is broken.

Exclusionary rule   *1.* A reason why even **relevant** (see that word) **evidence** will be kept out of a trial. *2.* *"The exclusionary rule"* often means the rule that illegally gathered evidence may not be used in a **criminal** trial. The rule has several exceptions, such as when the evidence is used to impeach (see **impeachment**) a defendant's testimony and when the evidence was gathered in a **good faith** belief that the process was legal. *3.* An *exclusionary hearing* is a pretrial proceeding in which a judge decides whether evidence claimed to be illegally gathered may be used in the trial.

Exclusive   *1.* Shutting out all others; sole; one only. For example, if a court has *exclusive jurisdiction* over a subject, no other court in the area can decide a lawsuit on that subject, and if a **union** has *exclusive recognition* or *exclusive bargaining rights,* the employer may not even consult with another union. *2.* For *exclusive agency listing* and *exclusive listing,* see **listing.** *3.* One type of *exclusive contract* is an **output contract.**

Exculpate   Provide an **excuse** or **justification;** show that someone has not committed a crime or a wrongful act.

Exculpatory clause   A provision in a **trust** arrangement by which the **trustee** is relieved of all responsibility for things that go wrong or for losses if the trustee acts in good faith.

Exculpatory "no" doctrine   The principle, accepted in most federal courts, that a defendant who falsely denies guilt cannot be charged with the additional crime of making a false statement because the statement is covered by the **Fifth Amendment** protection against self-incrimination.

Excusable neglect A procedural failure (such as failure to file a court paper on time) that results from circumstances (such as an illness) beyond a person's control. A judge may accept these circumstances as a reason to grant the person's request (such as to permit a late filing).

Excuse A reason that will stand up in court for an unintentional action. For example, if you killed someone by accident and it was not your fault, it is *excusable homicide.* Compare with **justification.**

Execute Complete, make, perform, do, or carry out. For example, to *execute a* **contract** is to sign it and make it valid and to *execute an obligation* created by the contract is to carry it out or perform it. *Executed* means completed, signed, done, etc. Compare with **executory.**

Execution *1.* Carrying out or completion (see **execute**). *2.* Signing and finalizing (and handing over, if needed) a document such as a **deed.** *3.* The government's putting a person to death. *4.* An official carrying out of a court's **order** or **judgment.** For example, a *body execution* is a court order to a **sheriff** or other official to bring a person to court; and a **writ** *of execution* orders a court official to take a **debtor's** property to pay a court-decided debt, usually by then holding an *execution sale.*

Execution-proof **Judgment-proof.**

Executive *1.* The branch of government that carries out the laws (as opposed to the **judicial** and **legislative** branches). The administrative branch. *2.* A high official in a branch of government, a company, or other organization.

Executive agreement A document, similar to a **treaty,** that is signed by the president of the United States but does not require the approval of the **Senate** (as a treaty does).

Executive Office of the President The organizations that give the president of the United States most of the direct staff help on national issues. These organizations include the *Office of Management and Budget, National Security Council, Council on Environmental Quality,* etc.

Executive officer One of several top officials of a company or one particular official.

Executive order A law put out by the president or a governor that does not need to be passed by the **legislature.**

Executive privilege The right of the president of the United States and subordinates to keep some information (primarily documents) from public disclosure. The privilege is used most often for military and diplomatic secrets. See also **Freedom of Information Act.**

Executive session A closed meeting of a **committee,** a **board,** etc.

Executor   A person selected by a person making a will to **administer** the will and to hand out the property after the person making the will dies. Compare with **administrator.**

Executory   Still to be carried out; incomplete; depending on a future act or event. Compare with *executed* under **execute.**

Exemplars   **Evidence** of physical identification of a person such as fingerprints, voiceprints, blood samples, handwriting samples, **lineup** identifications, etc.

Exemplary damages   **Punitive damages.**

Exemplification   An official copy of a public document used as **evidence.**

Exempt property   See **exemption** no. 3.

Exemption   *1.* Freedom from a general burden, duty, service, or tax. *2.* The subtraction from income for tax purposes of a certain amount of money for yourself, your spouse, and each dependent (such as a child living at home). Each *exemption* lowers the income on which a person must pay taxes. See also **credit, deduction,** and **exclusion.** *3.* Property that may be kept by a **debtor** when property is taken away from the debtor by a court order such as in a **judgment** debt or **bankruptcy.**

Exequatur   Having a U.S. lawsuit *"clothed with an exequatur"* means having it validated by the local court in order to have it recognized and enforced overseas.

Exercise   Make use of. For example, to *"exercise a purchase option"* is to make use of a right to buy something by buying it.

Exercise price   See **striking price.**

Exhaustion of remedies   A person must usually take all reasonable steps to get satisfaction from an **administrative agency** before taking a problem with that agency to court (and to get satisfaction from a state government before going into federal court). This is called *exhaustion of administrative (or state) remedies.*

Exhibit   *1.* Any object or document offered and marked as **evidence** (in a **trial, hearing, deposition, audit,** etc.). *2.* Any document attached to a **pleading, affidavit,** or other formal paper.

Exigence (or exigency)   A sudden event that requires immediate attention; an urgent state of affairs. *Exigent circumstances* may permit law officers to conduct a search or arrest a person without a **warrant.**

Eximbank   The U.S. Export-Import Bank that finances some purchases of U.S. goods in foreign countries.

Exlex   A made-up word for "outside the law" or "without legal authority."

Exoneration   *1.* Clearing of a crime or other wrongdoing; exculpation. *2.* Removal of a burden or a **duty.** *3.* The right of a person who pays a debt for another person to be reimbursed by that person. *4.* The right to be paid off on a **negotiable instrument.**

Exordium   The introductory clause of a **will,** stating that it is a valid will, etc.

Expatriation   The voluntary giving up of a person's citizenship (see **citizen**). This includes doing a voluntary act, such as joining another country's army, that the person may not consider as "voluntarily" giving up citizenship, but that the country stripping the citizenship does.

Expectancy   Something hoped for. For example, an **inheritance** under a **will** is an *expectancy* because the person making the will might change his or her mind. A right is *expectant* if a change in circumstances can end it. For *expectancy damages,* see **expectation damages.**

Expectation damages   Money awarded in some **breach** *of contract* lawsuits to replace the profits that probably would have been made from a deal that fell through.

Expectation of privacy   The belief that you (or your possessions) are in a place, or engaged in an activity, where you have a right to expect privacy. This belief is required to challenge the **Fourth Amendment** *reasonableness,* and thus the validity, of a search or seizure. See also **zone of privacy.**

Expensing   Taking an expense **deduction** from taxable income for the full purchase price of something used in business, rather than taking a series of **depreciation** deductions on the business **asset.**

Experience rating   An insurance company's calculation of the likely claim rate and cost for each type of *risk* (such as collisions by a particular type of car) that it insures.

Experience tables   **Mortality tables.**

Expert witness   A person possessing special knowledge or experience who is allowed to **testify** at a trial not only about facts (like an ordinary witness) but also about the professional conclusions he or she draws from these facts.

Exploit   *1.* Make use of; use a natural resource; take advantage of an opportunity. *2.* Take unfair advantage; use illegally.

Exports clause   See **import-export clause.**

Expository statute   A law that is **enacted** to explain the meaning of a previously enacted law.

Express   Clear, definite, direct, or actual (as opposed to **implied**); known by explicit words.

Express contract   A **contract** with terms stated in oral or written words. Compare with **implied-in-fact contract.**

Expressio unius   (Latin) Short for "expressio unius est exclusio alterius" (the mention of one thing rules out other things not mentioned). The phrase expresses a rule of thumb sometimes used for interpreting documents.

Expropriation   The taking of private property for public use; a taking by **eminent domain** (see that word); a governmental seizure (*nationalization*) of foreign holdings in the country.

Expulsion   Casting out; remove from membership. Most **houses** of **legislatures** have the power to vote to *expel* a member for engaging in prohibited conduct.

Expunge   Blot out, obliterate, or strike out. For example, to *expunge* an **arrest record** is to wipe it completely and physically "off the books."

Extension   *1.* A lengthening of time; for example, in the **term** of a **lease** or in the time a person may pay a debt. *2.* "*Extending a case*" means a judge's applying the rule that decided a case to another case that is only somewhat similar. *3.* "*Extension of remarks*" is the inclusion of speeches and materials in the **Congressional Record** that were not actually presented orally in a **House** or **Senate** session.

Extenuating circumstances   Surrounding facts that make a crime less evil or blameworthy. They do not lower the crime to a less serious one, but do tend to reduce punishment.

External financing   A corporation's raising money by selling **stock** or by borrowing.

External memorandum   An analysis of the law written to convince someone outside the office to do something.

Exterritoriality   The freedom from a foreign country's local laws enjoyed by **ambassadors** and many subordinates when living in that country. (*Not* **extraterritoriality;** see that word.)

Extinguishment   The ending of a right, power, contract, or property interest. It may end because of a merging with a bigger thing. For example, a right of **tenancy** *extinguishes* not only if the tenant moves out, but also if the tenant buys the house.

Extort   *1.* To compel, force, or coerce; for example, to get a confession by depriving a person of food and water. *2.* To get something by illegal threats of harm to person, property, or reputation. *3.* The process is called *extortion* (pronounce: ex-tor-shun).

Extra   *1.* Outside of. *2.* In addition to.

Extra legem   (Latin) "Extralegal" or "outside of the law." Something that is illegal or, if not illegal or "wrong," is outside the law's protection.

Extradition   One country (or state) giving up a person to a second country (or state) when the second requests the person for a trial on a **criminal** charge or for punishment after a trial.

Extrajudicial   *1.* Unconnected with court business; outside of court. *2.* Beyond the proper scope of court business. *3.* Not having legal effect, though said or done by a judge. See **dictum.**

Extralateral right   See **apex rule.**

Extraneous evidence   **Evidence** about the meaning of the terms of a **contract** or other document that comes from other than the document itself. Also called *evidence* **aliunde.**

Extraordinary remedy   An action a court will take only if a more usual legal **remedy** will not suffice. These include **habeas corpus** and **mandamus** (see those words).

Extraterritoriality   The operation of a country's laws outside of its physical boundaries; for example, the U.S.'s right to bring to trial and punish its soldiers in another country for crimes committed on a U.S. base there. (*Not* **exterritoriality;** see that word.)

Extremis   (Latin) Last illness or mortal injury.

Extrinsic evidence   **Evidence** drawn from things outside a **contract** (or other document). For example, the fact that a person was forced to sign a contract is *extrinsic* to the words (**"face"**) of the contract itself.

Extrinsic fraud   In a lawsuit, **fraud** that prevented the losing party from having a full, fair trial. It is *extrinsic* because it is "outside" the issues in the trial (which might involve *intrinsic fraud*), involving the way the loser was prevented from knowing his or her rights or was prevented from presenting his or her side of the case.

Eyewitness   A person with firsthand knowledge of an event. Someone who can testify as to what he or she saw or heard or smelled, etc.

Eyre   A court of traveling judges in old England. [pronounce: air]

F. *1.* Federal Reporter (see **National Reporter System**). "F.2d." is the second **series** of the Federal Reporter, and F.3d. is the third. *2.* Following; for example, "26f." means "page 26 and the next page," and 26ff. means page 26 plus the next pages.

F.A.A. Federal Aviation Administration; the branch of the U.S. Department of Transportation that regulates all air travel safety matters.

F.A.S. Free along side. Indicates that the stated price includes shipping costs and delivery along side the ship. Compare with **F.I.L.O.**

F.A.S.B. Financial Accounting Standards Board.

F.B.I. Federal Bureau of Investigation. The branch of the U.S. Justice Department that investigates violations of federal law not specifically handled by other agencies.

F.C.A. Farm Credit Administration. A federal agency that supervises the Farm Credit System of federal land banks and associated banks and **cooperatives.**

F.C.C. Federal Communications Commission. The U.S. agency that **regulates** television, telephone, radio, etc.

F.C.R.A. Fair Credit Reporting Act (15 U.S.C. 1601 (1970)).

F.D.A. Food and Drug Administration. The federal agency that **regulates** the safety of food, drugs, cosmetics, etc.

F.D.C.A. Food, Drug, and Cosmetic Act (21 U.S.C. 301 (1938)).

F.D.I.C. Federal Deposit Insurance Corporation. The U.S. agency that insures bank **deposits** for individual depositors.

F.E.C. Federal Election Commission. And the *F.E.C.A.* is the Federal Election Campaign Act (2 U.S.C. 431 (1971)).

F.E.P.C. Fair Employment Practices Commission. A state or local government agency that administers employment anti**discrimination** laws.

F.H.A. *1.* Federal Housing Administration. The U.S. agency that insures housing loans through approved lenders on approved homes. *2.* Farmers Home Administration. The U.S. agency that provides rural housing loans. Also abbreviated FmHA.

F.H.L.B. Federal Home Loan Bank. The system of, or any one of the many banks and other financial institutions that may borrow from, a regional Federal Reserve Bank to make home loans.

F.H.L.M.C. Federal Home Loan Mortgage Corporation. A federal agency that buys **first mortgages** (see that word) from members of the Federal Reserve System and other approved banks. Also called "*Freddie Mac.*"

F.I.C.A. "Federal Insurance Contributions Act." The federal law governing the Social Security program.

F.I.F.O. "First in, first out," a method of calculating the worth of **inventory.** Under this accounting method, if a merchant buys a blivit for a dollar, then buys another for two dollars, then sells either blivit, the remaining blivit is worth two dollars. Compare with **L.I.F.O.** and **N.I.F.O.**

F.I.L.O. "Free-in, liner-out." Indicates that the shipper will load the cargo onto a certain ship and will pay all loading costs. Compare with **F.A.S.**

F.L.R.A. Federal Labor Relations Authority. The U.S. agency that handles labor problems with the unions that represent federal employees.

F.L.S.A. **Fair Labor Standards Act.**

F.M.C.S. Federal Mediation and Conciliation Service. The U.S. agency that helps resolve labor disputes.

F.M.V. *Fair* **market value.**

F.N.M.A. Federal National Mortgage Association. A government sponsored, but privately owned, organization that buys home **mortgages.** Also called "*Fannie Mae.*"

F.O.B. "Free on board." Indicates that the stated price of goods includes transportation costs to the *F.O.B. point,* which is a specific place named in the contract.

F.O.I.A. **Freedom of Information Act.**

F.P.R. Federal procurement regulations. Rules for federal government buying.

F.R. *Federal Rules,* as in *F.R.A.P.* or *F.R.App.P.* (Federal Rules of Appellate Procedure), *F.R.C.P.* or *F.R.Civ.P.* (Civil Procedure), *F.R.Crim.P.* (Criminal Procedure), *F.R.E.* or *F.R.Evid.* (Evidence), and *F.R.D.* (**Federal Rules Decisions**).

F.R.B. Federal Reserve Board. See **Federal Reserve Act.**

F.T.C. Federal Trade Commission. The U.S. agency that enforces prohibitions against **unfair competition** in business and "unfair or deceptive acts or trade practices"; it also enforces other federal laws such as the **Consumer Credit Protection Act.**

F.T.C.A. **Federal Tort Claims Act.**

F.Y.   Fiscal *year.*

F.Cas.   Federal Cases. A series of federal case reports that predate the **National Reporter System.**

F.Supp.   Federal Supplement.

Fabricated evidence   "Facts" that have been created or changed in an attempt to present false **evidence** in a trial or "facts" that have been faked to mislead officials.

Face   All things seen in normal inspection of a document; primarily the language of the document. For example, a **contract** can be valid "*on its face*" even though a person was forced to sign it at gunpoint and no court would uphold it.

Face value   The formal cash-in value written on a **note** or other financial document. *Face value* does not include **interest** or other charges normally added on, nor does it reflect fluctuating value in the marketplace.

Facial   Having to do with the words of a document, as opposed to the way the words apply to a specific situation.

Facilitation   Doing something intentionally to make it easier for another person to commit a crime.

Facility of payment clause   An agreement in an **insurance** contract allowing the insurer to make payments to a particular person to hold for the person ultimately entitled to the money.

Fac<u>simile</u>   Exact copy.

Fact   *1.* An act; a thing that took place; an event. *2.* Something that exists and is real as opposed to what *should* exist. For example, a "*question of fact*" is about what is or what happened, while a "*question of law*" is about how the law affects what happened and what should have happened according to law. *3.* Something that exists and is real as opposed to opinion or supposition. *4.* For *types* of facts, such as **adjudicative facts** and **legislative facts,** see those words.

Fact pleading   Code pleading. See that word for the definition and see **pleading** for examples.

Fact situation   A summary of the facts of a case without any comments or legal conclusions.

Factfinder   *1.* See **trier of fact.** *2.* A person (or group of persons) appointed by a government agency or court to collect facts, clarify issues, and make recommendations, often by holding a hearing.

Facto et animo   See **animus et factum.**

Factor   A person who is given goods to sell and who gets a **commission** for selling them.

Factoring Buying **accounts receivable** from a business. The business gets immediate cash for the money owed by its clients and the buyer gets the accounts at a discount.

Factor's (or agent's) acts State laws that protect buyers of goods sold by **agents,** whether or not the owner approved the sale.

Facts & Findings A **National Association of Legal Assistants** publication.

Factum (Latin) *1.* Act; fact; central fact or act upon which a question "turns." *2.* Old word for an appeal **brief** or for a statement of facts. *3. Factum probandum* is a "fact to be proved" or one at issue in a case, and *factum probans* is an **evidentiary fact** (see that word) used to prove a main issue.

Failure of consideration The situation that exists when something that is offered as part of a deal (the "**consideration**") becomes worthless or ceases to exist before the deal is completely carried out.

Failure of issue Dying without children.

Faint pleader A **pleading** in a lawsuit that is false or that has false or misleading information, usually to trick someone not participating in the lawsuit.

Fair comment The **common law** (pre**constitutional**) right to comment, within limits, upon the conduct of public officials without being **liable** for **defamation** (see that word).

Fair Credit Billing Act (15 U.S.C. 1666) A federal law regulating billing disputes and making credit card companies partially responsible for items bought by **consumers.**

Fair Credit Reporting Acts Federal (15 U.S.C. 1681) and state laws regulating the organizations that investigate, store, and give out **consumer credit** information, organizations that collect bills, etc. Consumers are given rights to know about investigations, see and dispute their files, etc.

Fair hearing The word many **administrative agencies** use for their trial-like decision-making process, which is used when a person **appeals** an administrative decision. The **hearing** does not have to use full trial rules or procedures and is "fair" because it follows rules, not because persons always get what they need or deserve.

Fair Labor Standards Act (29 U.S.C. 2011) The 1938 federal law that set minimum wages and maximum hours for workers in industries engaged in interstate commerce, prohibited the labor of children under sixteen, etc.

Fair market value See **market value.**

Fair trade practices   *1.* General practices of fairness in business, such as truth in advertising. *2.* Fixing retail prices. When done by manufacturers or distributors acting together, it is generally illegal. When done by a single manufacturer who is not also the retailer, it is generally illegal if done with any retailer's agreement.

Fair trial   *1.* A trial before a competent, **impartial** judge (and, if applicable, an impartial jury) in an atmosphere of judicial calm. *2.* A criminal trial that is conducted without violating any of the defendant's **constitutional** rights.

Fair use   The limited copying, quoting, displaying, adapting, or other use of another's copyrighted work permitted by **copyright** law even if no fee is paid and no permission is granted. Such *fair use* is often permitted when the copyright owner does not suffer financial loss and when the work is used for purposes such as criticism, news reporting, parody, or teaching.

Fair warning (or notice)   The rule that a criminal law must define the offense clearly enough for a reasonable person to know what conduct to avoid.

Fairness doctrine   A former Federal Communications Commission rule that broadcasters must present, or give others a chance to present, all sides of major public issues if they present one side. See also **Equal Time Act.**

False   *1.* Intentionally or knowingly untrue. *2.* Untrue.

False arrest   Any unlawful restraint or deprivation of a person's liberty, usually by a public official. It is a **tort.**

False imprisonment   **False arrest.**

False light   False or misleading statements about a person that are part of an **invasion of privacy.**

False pretenses   A lie told to cheat another person out of his or her money or property. It is a crime in most states, though the precise definition varies.

False representation   Similar to **false pretenses,** but the basis for a lawsuit rather than a crime. To sue for *false representation,* you must prove that a person told a lie to cheat you and that you were hurt financially by relying on that lie.

False return   *1.* A **sheriff's** or other court officer's certification that something false is true or that something not done was done. See **sewer service** for an example. *2.* A **tax return** that is intentionally (or grossly, negligently) wrong.

False swearing (or oath)   Lying on an **affidavit** or under **oath** in an official proceeding other than a court proceeding. A less serious form of **perjury** (see that word).

False verdict   A jury's **verdict** that is so unjust or out-of-line from the facts that the judge may set it aside. See judgment **non obstante veredicto.**

Falsus in uno doctrine   (Latin) The principle that if a jury believes that any part of what a witness says is deliberately false, the jury may disregard it all as being false.

Family   A broad word that can mean, among other things: *1.* Any household or group of persons living together as a single group. *2.* Parents and children. *3.* Persons related by blood or marriage. "*Family*" is usually defined differently for different purposes. For example, it might have one meaning in a state's zoning laws and another meaning in its tax laws.

Family car doctrine (or family purpose doctrine)   The rule that the owner of a car will usually be **liable** for damage done by a family member driving the owner's car. This rule has been limited or rejected by most states.

Family corporation (or partnership)   A **corporation** (or **partnership**) set up to spread income among family members, usually reducing the total tax bill.

Family court   *1.* A court that may handle proceedings for child **abuse** and **neglect, support, paternity suits, custody,** juvenile delinquency, etc. A specific *family court* is usually referred to by its formal name, often something like "Juvenile and Domestic Relations Court." *2.* A **domestic** relations court that handles **divorces, separations,** etc.

Family farmer bankruptcy   See **Chapter Twelve.**

Family law   See **domestic** *relations.*

Fannie Mae   See **F.N.M.A.**

Fascism   **Absolutism** (see that word) as practiced by a central state that allows private ownership of property, but makes all economic and social decisions from the top. Under *fascism,* individuals exist to serve the state.[pronounce: fash-izm]

Fatal   Causing the failure, invalidity, or unenforceability of a court claim, contract, or other legal effort. For example, a *fatal* **error** (see that word) can be the reason for granting a new trial.

Fatico hearing   A pre-sentencing hearing (named after *Fatico v. U.S.,* 603 F.2d.1055 (1971)), sometimes granted to someone convicted of a crime, in which the conclusions of a sentencing report may be disputed and other sentencing evidence offered.

Fault _1._ Lack of care; failure to do a duty; responsibility for a wrong; cause of harm. _2._ Defect or imperfection. _3._ According to the **Uniform Commercial Code,** _fault_ means a "wrongful act, omission, or breach."

Fauntleroy doctrine The rule that a state must enforce a **judgment** of a court in another state even if it is based on a lawsuit that would not be legal or valid in the state asked to enforce it. The doctrine (from _Fauntleroy v. Lum,_ 210 U.S. 230) is a specialized application of the **full faith and credit** requirement.

Favored beneficiary A person who has a hand in preparing a **will** and is favored in the will over others who have an equal claim to inherit. This _favored_ **beneficiary** may have **undue** _influence_ over the **testator** (the person whose will it is).

Feasance Doing an act; performing a duty. [pronounce: fee-zence]

Featherbedding A popular name given to the practice (usually done in response to an employee or union demand) of employing more persons than a job requires. This may include creating or maintaining "busy work."

Fed _1._ "The Fed" is short for the Federal Reserve System, the central U.S. bank that sets monetary policy. _2._ Short for _federal,_ as in _Fed. Reg._ for **Federal Register.**

Fed.R. _Federal Rules,_ as in _Fed.R.App.P._ (Federal Rules of Appellate Procedure), _Civ.P._ (Civil Procedure), _Crim.P._ (Criminal Procedure), and _Evid._ (Evidence).

Federal _1._ A _federal union_ is two or more states uniting into one strong central government with many powers left to the states. _2._ The U.S. _federal government_ is the national, as opposed to state, government. _3._ For the various _federal_ **agencies** that are not listed here or by name, look under their initials at the start of the letter.

Federal Circuit See _Federal Circuit_ under **United States Courts.**

Federal common law Federal judge-made law, now restricted to areas (such as interstate commerce and federal labor and antitrust laws) that are governed by the federal Constitution and federal statutes, or that require a nationally uniform rule.

Federal courts See **United States Courts.**

Federal question A legal issue directly involving the U.S. **Constitution, statutes,** or **treaties.** Federal courts have **jurisdiction** in cases involving a _federal question._

Federal Register   The first place that the rules and **regulations** of U.S. **administrative agencies** are published. Abbreviated "Fed. Reg."

Federal Reporter   A publication with the **opinions** of many federal courts below the U.S. Supreme Court level. Those lower federal court opinions not published in the *Federal Reporter* are published in the **Federal Supplement.**

Federal Reserve Act   The law that created the *Federal Reserve banks,* supervised by the *Federal Reserve Board,* to maintain money reserves; issue *Federal Reserve notes* (dollar bills, fives, etc.); lend money to banks; and supervise banks. The *member banks* of the system, one in each region of the country, are the working centers of the *Federal Reserve System.*

Federal rules   The *Federal Rules* of **Civil Procedure, Criminal** *Procedure,* **Appellate** *Procedure,* and **Evidence.** (These rules also serve as models for many state rules.) Specialized rules also cover **bankruptcy, admiralty,** and other proceedings, as well as proceedings before U.S. **magistrates.**

Federal Rules Decisions   A **reporter** that contains federal court decisions having to do with the courts' procedural rules.

Federal Supplement   A publication with the **opinions** of many federal courts below the Supreme Court level. Those lower federal court opinions not published in the *Federal Supplement* are published in the **Federal Reporter.**

Federal Tort Claims Act   (28 U.S.C. 1346) The 1946 federal law that abolished the federal government's **immunity** from lawsuits based on **torts.** Suits based on some kinds of intentional torts, or on some kinds of discretionary acts by federal officials, are still not permitted.

Federalism   A system of political organization with several different levels of government (for example, city, state, and national) co-existing in the same area with the lower levels having some independent powers.

Federalist Papers   Essays advocating adoption of the U.S. **Constitution** that still help interpret what it means.

Federation   A formal group of persons, organizations, or governments loosely united for a common purpose.

Fee   *1.* A charge for services. *Fee splitting* is a lawyer sharing a legal fee with another person. This is ethically permissible if both lawyers who work on a case split the fee, but not if only one has done work or if the fee is split with a non-lawyer. *2.* Any **estate** in **land** that can be conveyed by gift, sale, and inheritance. *Fee* is often used to mean *"fee simple absolute,"* a full estate in land with no ownership limitations.

Fee simple   The same as **fee** (see that word) in **land** and **inheritance** law. A *fee simple* **estate** can be **absolute, conditional,** or **defeasible.**

Fee tail   An **estate** that can be passed on only to children (or only to those in a set line of **inheritance**).

Feint pleader   **Faint pleader.**

Fellow servant rule   A rule, abolished in most states by **employers' liability acts,** that an employer is not responsible for the injuries one employee does to another employee if the employees were carefully chosen.

Felon   A person convicted of a **felony.**

Felonious   *1.* Done with the intent to commit a major crime; of or pertaining to a **felony.** *2.* Evil; malicious; unlawful.

Felony   *1.* A serious crime. *2.* A crime with a **sentence** of one year or more.

Felony-murder rule   The principle that if a person (even accidentally) kills another while committing a **felony,** then the killing is murder. The *misdemeanor-manslaughter rule* is similar: if a person (even accidentally) kills another while committing a **misdemeanor,** then the killing is at least **manslaughter.**

Feme couvert   (French) A married woman. Married women in the past had legal disabilities, such as an inability to make **contracts.** *Feme couvert* was used in comparison to *feme sole* (a woman alone; an unmarried woman). [pronounce: fem coov-er]

Feoffment   The old method of transferring full ownership of land in England. [pronounce: feef-ment]

Ferae naturae   (Latin) "Of wild nature." Naturally wild animals. Naturally tame animals are *dometae naturae. Dometae naturae* are considered to be owned by the landowner, while *ferae naturae* are owned by no one.

Fertile octogenarian rule   The rule that you cannot assume that merely because persons are beyond normal fertility age that there will be nobody new to **inherit** from them.

Feudal law   The law of property from the Middle Ages in England. It was based on the *feudal system* of rights and duties tying people to the land in a rigid **hierarchy** from the king on down to the serfs.

Ff   An expression such as "p. 26ff." means "found on page 26 and on the pages immediately following."

Fi. fa.   Abbreviation for **fieri facias.**

Fiat   (Latin) "Let it be done"; a command, especially an authoritative yet arbitrary command.

Fictio   (Latin) A *legal* **fiction.**

Fiction   A *legal fiction* is an assumption that something that is (or may be) false or nonexistent is true or real. Legal fictions are assumed or invented to help do justice. For example, bringing a lawsuit to throw a nonexistent "John Doe" off your property used to be the only way to establish a clear right to the property when legal **title** was uncertain. See **constructive trust** for another example of a legal fiction.

Fictitious   *1.* Fake (and usually in bad faith); but see no. 2. *2.* Nonexistent; made up, often for a legal, useful purpose. For example, see **John Doe.**

Fidelity bond   Insurance on a person protecting against that person's dishonesty. A company must often buy this type of insurance when an employee is in a position of trust, handles large sums of money, and is seldom checked on by others.

Fides   (Latin) Faith, honesty.

Fiduciary   *1.* A person who manages money or property for another person and in whom that other person has a right to place great trust. *2.* A relationship like that in definition no. 1. *3.* Any relationship between persons in which one person acts for another in a position of trust; for example, lawyer and client or parent and child. *4.* The *fiduciary shield doctrine* is the principle that acts performed by an employee solely for the corporation do not form the basis for **jurisdiction** over that person as an individual, only as a corporate employee. Compare with **corporate veil.**

Field search   A search restricted to part of a **database.**

Field warehousing   An arrangement by which a lender takes formal control of goods stored in the possession of a borrower. The borrowing merchant, wholesaler, or manufacturer gets access to the goods, and the lender gets a **security** *interest* and close watch over the goods.

Fieri facias   (Latin) A **writ** of **execution** commanding a **sheriff** to seize and sell the personal property of a debtor and use the proceeds to pay off a **judgment** against the debtor. [pronounce: fie-er-e fay-she-as]

Fifteenth Amendment   The U.S. **constitutional** amendment that guarantees the right to vote regardless of race, color, or prior slavery.

Fifth Amendment   *1.* The **constitutional** amendment that guarantees an **indictment** or grand jury **presentment** for persons accused of major crimes; **due process of law** (see that word) before depriving a person of life, liberty, or property; and just compensation in taking private property for public use. The amendment also prohibits **double jeopardy** and forcing a person to be a **witness** against him or herself. *2. "Taking the Fifth"* means refusing to answer a question because it might implicate you in a crime.

Fighting words   Speech that is *not* protected by the **First Amendment** to the U.S. **Constitution** because it is likely to cause violence by the person to whom the words are spoken.

File   *1.* The complete court record of a case. *2.* "To file" a paper is to give it to the court clerk for inclusion in the case record. *3.* A folder in a law office (of a case, a client, business records, etc.). *4.* A *file wrapper* is the entire record of a **patent** office proceeding in a patent application, from first application, through all negotiations and objections, to an issued patent. *File wrapper estoppel* is the limitation placed on a patent holder's attempt to get a broad interpretation of the patent once the patent holder accepts a more narrow patent to avoid a patent examiner's objections.

Filiation proceeding   Same as **paternity suit.**

Filibuster   A tactic used in a legislature by which long, often irrelevant speeches are made to delay vote on a proposed bill, often in the hopes of "killing" it. *Filibusters* can be cut off by a **cloture** vote or by outlasting the talker.

Final agency action   An administrative agency decision that is sufficiently concrete in its effect on a person's rights that it is properly subject to review by a court. Compare with **exhaustion of remedies.**

Final argument   A last statement made to the jury (or to the judge when there is no jury) by each side in a trial. Each side presents what it thinks the facts are and how it thinks the law applies to those facts.

Final decision (or decree, determination, judgment, opinion, or order)   Each of these words has opposite uses: *1.* The last action of a court; the one upon which an **appeal** can be based. *2.* The last decision of a court or a series of courts from which there are *no more* appeals.

Final passage   The last affirmative vote on a **bill** in one **house** of a **legislature** after it has gone through all preliminary procedures.

Final submission   The time when an entire case (**testimony,** each side's in-court **arguments** and written materials, etc.) is finished and the judge can make a **decision.**

Finance charge The interest or other payment made in addition to the price of goods or services paid off in installments or "on time." This does not include late charges, collection expenses, etc. It must often be expressed as an **annual percentage rate** (see that word).

Finance committee *1.* A U.S. **Senate committee** (see those words) that handles taxation and related matters. It is comparable to the House Ways and Means Committee. *2.* A committee of a company's **board** *of directors* that makes major financial decisions.

Financial institution Any **bank, trust company, credit union, savings and loan association,** or similar organization licensed by a state or the U.S. government to do financial business.

Financial lease A long-term property **lease** that cannot be canceled and that provides no maintenance or other services.

Financial planning Integrated planning that includes such things as investment, insurance, tax, retirement, and estate planning.

Financial responsibility acts State laws requiring **insurance,** posting a **bond,** or a cash payment by applicants for a motor vehicle **license** or **registration.**

Financial statement A summary of what a company or other organization owns and what it owes. It may be in the form of a **balance sheet,** a profit and loss statement, or an **annual report.** This is *not* a **financing statement.**

Financing statement A paper, filed on the proper public records, that shows a **security** *interest* in goods. This is *not* a **financial statement.**

Finder A person who brings together two companies for a **merger,** who secures a **mortgage** for a borrower, who locates an underwriter (see **underwrite**) for a company issuing **stock,** etc., usually for a fee, often called a "*finder's fee.*"

Finder of fact See **trier of fact.**

Finding A decision (by a judge, jury, **hearing examiner,** etc.) about a question of fact; a decision about **evidence.** It is often called a "*finding of fact*" upon which a "*conclusion of law*" may be based.

Fine Payment of a sum of money imposed by a court. A *fine* may be a **civil** or a **criminal** penalty.

Fire sale A sale at reduced prices due to fire or water damage or, sometimes, any emergency. Fire sales often require special **licenses** and are regulated to protect **consumers.**

Firefighter's rule The principle that an owner or occupant of property is not **liable** to firefighters or police officers for unintentional injuries caused by the problem that brought them to the property.

Firm offer   A merchant's written **offer** (see that word) to buy or sell _goods,_ that will be held open for a certain length of time. It is a type of **option** that requires no **consideration** (see that word) to be valid.

First Amendment   The U.S. **constitutional** amendment that guarantees _freedom of speech, religion, press,_ and _assembly_ as well as the right to **petition** the government.

First chair   Head lawyer of an in-court legal team.

First degree   The most serious form of a particular crime that has more than one type. For example, _first degree_ **murder** includes **premeditation** or extreme atrocity or cruelty, or is done in the commission of a major **felony.**

First impression   New. A case or a question is "_of first impression_" if it presents an entirely new problem to the court and cannot be decided by **_precedent._**

First instance   A _court of first instance_ is a **trial** court as opposed to an **appeals** court.

First mortgage (or lien)   The **mortgage** (or **lien**) that has the right to be paid off before all others. This is not necessarily the first in time.

First offender   A person who has never before been convicted of a crime and who may be entitled to more lenient treatment, such as a short sentence, **diversion** rather than prosecution, or **expunge**ment of the arrest record.

First refusal   See **right of first refusal.**

First sale doctrine   The right to sell or display something obtained lawfully under **copyright** law.

Fiscal   Financial. The _fiscal year_ is a period of time, equal in length to a calendar year, but starting on the day that the state or company uses as "day one" for its business records. This is often January, April, July, or October first.

Fishing trip (or expedition)   _1._ Using the courts to find out information beyond the fair scope of the lawsuit. _2._ The loose, unfocused questioning of a **witness** or the overly broad use of the **discovery** process.

Fitness for a particular purpose   If a merchant knows or should know that an item is to be used by a buyer for a particular purpose, the merchant is responsible (absent a statement to the contrary to the buyer) for that item's fitness for the purpose. Such "**warranty** _of fitness for a particular purpose_" is in most cases an **implied warranty.**

Fix bail   Determine the amount of bail or the bail bond required for a defendant to go free pending trial. A judge or magistrate does this.

Fixation   See **fixed work.**

Fixed assets   Property such as land and machinery used in a company's business. *Fixed assets* are not part of a company's merchandise; are used up slowly, if at all; and are sometimes referred to as "property, plant, and equipment."

Fixed capital   *1.* **Fixed assets.** *2.* The money permanently invested in a business.

Fixed charges (or fixed costs)   Business costs that continue whether or not business comes in; for example, rent.

Fixed opinion   **Bias** or prejudgment about a person's guilt or **liability** that should disqualify a juror for lack of impartiality.

Fixed sentence   See **sentence** no. 2.

Fixed trust   A *non*discretionary trust.

Fixed work   Under **copyright** law, a new work is "*fixed*" or "*created*" when it is put in stable, tangible form, such as written on paper, recorded on film, sculpted in clay, etc. This *fixation* gives the author of the work an "automatic" copyright, whether or not the correct formalities are followed (although registering the work with the Copyright Office and putting proper copyright notice on it gives the work added protections).

Fixture   Anything attached to land or a building. The word sometimes refers to attached things that, once attached, may *not* be removed (by a tenant or by a person selling a building) and sometimes refers to those things attached that *may* be removed. A *trade fixture* is a fixture attached by a tenant for reasons of commercial gain.

Flag of convenience   The flag of a merchant ship **registered** in a country that has low costs or low safety requirements rather than registration in the country where it is owned or does most of its business.

Flagrante delicto   (Latin) *1.* In the act of committing the crime. *2.* Popularly used to mean lovers caught together in bed.

Flat rate   A fixed amount of money paid each time period rather than paying at fluctuating levels (for electricity used, for services used, etc.).

Flat sentence   See **sentence** no. 2.

Flat-benefit plan   A **pension plan** (see that word) or other employee **benefit** plan with a value to each employee that is unrelated to that employee's salary level (pays the same to everyone, pays more by years of service, etc.).

Flee to the wall doctrine   The principle that a person must try every reasonable way of escape before killing an attacker. Compare with **true person doctrine.**

Flight Leaving or hiding to avoid arrest or prosecution.

Flipping *1.* Popular word for refinancing **consumer** loans, often at higher rates of interest. *2.* Popular word for purchasing and quickly reselling real estate for profit. *3.* Popular word for buying a large block of a new stock to drive up the price, then selling it at a profit. This often works because those who **underwrite** the stock temporarily support its price.

Float *1.* The time between the deposit of a check in one bank and its subtraction from an account in another bank. This is "free" use of the money by the person who wrote the check. *2.* To let a national currency's value against other currencies change freely depending on supply and demand rather than by one or both countries' fixing or "**pegging**" the "exchange rate" by law or otherwise. *3.* See the six *floating* words following this definition, in most of which "floating" means "changeable."

Floating capital Money available to pay short-term debt and other current expenses.

Floating debt Short-term debt.

Floating interest rate An interest rate that varies according to changes in some external financial measure, such as the **prime** *rate.*

Floating lien An arrangement in which later property purchased by someone with a **secured** debt or **lien** (see those words) on property becomes **subject** to that debt or lien, and the original property remains subject to the lien until all debts are paid.

Floating (or floater) policy A supplemental **insurance** policy to cover items such as jewelry that frequently change location or quantity.

Floating stock (or bonds) Issuing and selling **stock** (or **bonds**).

Floor *1.* The right to speak in a meeting or **legislature** is called *holding the floor. 2.* The central meeting place of a legislature or **stock** (or similar) **exchange.** *3.* A lowest limit.

Floor plan financing A loan to a retail seller that is **secured** by the items to be sold and that is paid off as each sells.

Flotsam The wreckage of a ship or its goods found floating in the water or washed up on land. Compare with **jetsam.**

Fluctuating clause See **escalator clause.**

Fm.H.A. See **F.H.A.**

Followed A **case** is *followed* by a later case if it is relied upon as **precedent** (see that word) to decide the later case.

For cause   For a sound legal reason, as opposed to merely a stated reason. To remove an official from a job *for cause* may require a better reason than "because we didn't like certain actions he took or like the way he handled his job." It usually requires proof that the official lacked the ability or fitness to do the job right.

Forbearance   *1.* Refraining from action (especially action to enforce a right). *2.* Holding off demanding payment on an overdue debt. *3.* The *"forbearance rule"* or *"patient forbearance rule"* is the principle that, in most circumstances, a person does not lose a right merely because the person did not enforce the right quickly. For example, if a wife puts up with abuse, this does not automatically stop the wife from getting a **divorce** based on that abuse.

Force   *1.* A cause of something, such as an **intervening cause** or **force majeure**. *2.* Violence or compulsion, whether lawful or not. *3.* Unlawful or wrongful violence. For example, *forcible entry* is taking possession of or entering another person's property against that person's will or by using "force" in its ordinary meaning. *4.* "*In force*" means "*in effect and valid.*"

Force majeure   (French) Irresistible, natural, or unavoidable force; for example, an earthquake. See **act of God** for further discussion. [pronounce: force ma-zhur]

Forced heir   A person who cannot be deprived of a share of an **estate** unless the **testator** (person making a will) has a recognized legal cause for disinheriting the person.

Forced sale   *1.* A court-ordered sale of property, especially a sale in which the proceeds are to be used to pay a **judgment** or otherwise pay a debt. *2.* Popular term for a sale caused by financial hardship.

Forcible detainer   *1.* The act of a person who refuses to give up occupancy of land or a building to the rightful owner or tenant; most often the refusal of a person to leave when occupancy rights end. *2.* The summary (quick) court process for getting back land or a building held as in no. 1. Also called *forcible entry and detainer.*

Foreclosure   An action by a person who holds a **mortgage** to: 1) take the property away from the mortgagor (such as the homeowner); 2) end that mortgagor's rights in the property; and 3) sell the property to pay off the mortgage debt. Both the process (which is usually but not always done by lawsuit) and the result are called "*foreclosure.*"

Foreign   Belonging to, coming from, or having to do with another country or another state. For example, a Maine court would call a **corporation** incorporated in and based in Ohio a "*foreign corporation.*"

Foreign agent   *1.* A person who must register with the federal government as a lobbyist, advertising agency, or other representative of a foreign country or company. See also **lobbying acts.** *2.* A spy or other person who works for a foreign country.

Foreign exchange   Trading or exchanging the money of one country for that of another.

Foreign service   The part of the State Department, including **ambassadors** and their staffs, that represents the U.S. to foreign governments.

Foreign situs trust   A **trust** that exists because of foreign laws.

Foreign substance   A substance or thing found where it should not be and where it does not occur naturally, such as a sponge left behind by a doctor in a patient's body or a nail in a can of beans.

Foreign trade zone   An area of a country where component parts and raw materials may be imported tax-free until the finished product enters that country's market or is re-exported. See also **free port.**

Forensic   Having to do with courts and law. For example, *forensic medicine* is medical knowledge or medical practice involved with court **testimony** or other legal matters. And *forensics* refers to both firearms evidence and to the skill of making reasoned arguments.

Foreperson (man, woman)   The leader chosen to speak for the **jury.**

Foreseeability   The degree to which the consequences of an action *should* have been anticipated, recognized, and considered beforehand. *Not* hindsight.

Forestall the market   **Abbroachment.**

Forfeit   To lose the right to something due to neglect of a duty, due to an offense, or due to a **breach of contract.** For example, if a criminal **defendant** fails to show up for trial, the judge may order a *forfeiture* of the defendant's bail bond. [pronounce: for-fit]

Forgery   *1.* Making a fake document (or altering a real one) with intent to commit a **fraud.** *2.* The document itself in no. 1.

Foris   (Latin) On the outside; put out. For example, *forisfactura* is a "putting out" or forfeiture.

Form   *1.* A model to work from (or a paper with blanks to be filled in) of a legal document such as a **contract** or a **pleading.** *2.* The language, arrangement, conduct, procedure, or legal technicalities of a legal document or a legal **proceeding,** as opposed to the "**substance**" (subject, meaning, and legal importance) of the document or proceeding. *3.* See **forms of action.**

Forma pauperis   **In forma pauperis.**

Formal   *1.* In form only. For example, a *formal party* is a person who is involved in a lawsuit in name only and has no real interest in the proceedings. The opposite of *real, substantial,* etc. *2.* Fully formalized. For example, a *formal contract* is written, as opposed to oral, and contains all the necessary legal language, signatures, etc. The opposite of *informal.*

Formbook   A collection of legal forms with summaries of relevant law and information on how to use the forms.

Formed design   A deliberate and set intention to commit a crime (particularly a killing).

Former adjudication   Either **estoppel by judgment** or **res judicata.**

Former jeopardy   See **double jeopardy.**

Forms of action   Once, the special, individual, technical ways each different type of lawsuit was brought in court. If a legal problem did not fit into one of the *forms of action* (such as **assumpsit, debt, detinue, ejectment, replevin, trespass,** *trespass on the* **case,** and **trover**), it could not be brought to court. These have all been replaced under state and federal rules of civil procedure. Under the **Federal Rules** *of Civil Procedure,* they are now all **civil actions.**

Formula instructions   Jury **instructions** of the type: "if you find *these* facts to be true, then your **verdict** must be for *that* party." Compare with **affirmative charge.**

Fornication   Sexual intercourse between a man and a woman not married to each other.

Forswear   *1.* Swear to something you know is untrue. This is broader than **perjury** (see that word), but not as serious. *2.* Formally deny or deny under oath.

Forthwith   An unnecessarily formal word meaning "immediately" or "as soon as possible."

Fortiori   (Latin) See **a fortiori.**

Fortuitous   Happening by chance or accident; unexpected; unforeseen; unavoidable; *not* the same as "lucky."

Fortune 500   A ranked list of the 500 largest U.S. industrial corporations.

Forum   (Latin) A court. For example, *forum domicilii* is a court in the place where a person lives, and *forum rei* is a court where either the thing involved with the suit is or where the **defendant** lives.

Forum non conveniens   (Latin) "Inconvenient court." If two or more courts both have proper **venue** (see that word) for a case, a judge may rule that a lawsuit must be brought in the _other_ court for either the convenience of or fairness to the parties.

Forum shopping Choosing the one court, among two or more that may legally handle a lawsuit, that you think may look most favorably at your side.

Forward _1._ Set a rate (such as an **interest** or exchange rate) today for a future transaction. _2._ Send on. For example, a _forwarding fee_ is money paid to a lawyer who **refers** a client to another lawyer. The money is paid by the lawyer who receives the client. Some forms of this type of arrangement are unethical.

Forward contract See **futures.**

Foster child A child living with, cared for, and under the control of someone other than his or her own parents, but not **adopted** by this other person. A _foster home_ is a home for children without parents or who have been taken away from parents by a court.

Foul bill A **bill of lading** that says that the goods are damaged or partly missing.

Foundation _1._ Basis. For example, the _foundation_ of a trial is the group of issues in dispute between the sides (as set out in the **pleadings**). _2._ The preliminary questions to a **witness** that establish the admissibility (legal usability) of that person's **testimony** (or of other things) as **evidence** in a trial are called "_laying the foundation._" _3._ An organization funded by **will,** by **trust,** or by contributions and set up to give money to charitable, educational, and other nonprofit organizations and projects. However, _any_ organization may legally call itself a "foundation" without meeting the actual definition, and a "private foundation," according to the **I.R.S.,** is one that does _not_ meet several technical requirements for the _most_ favorable charitable organization tax treatment.

Four corners Same as **face** (see that word) of a document; that is, the document itself without outside information about it.

Four corners rule _1._ The principle that the meaning of an _unambiguous_ document should be determined from the document alone, not, for example, from oral **testimony** about what the writer "really" meant. _2._ The general rule that the meaning of a phrase should be interpreted in the context of the entire document, not from the phrase in isolation.

Fourteenth Amendment The U.S. **constitutional** amendment that forbids the states from enforcing laws that "_abridge the privileges and immunities_" of U.S. citizens, forbids the states from depriving any person of **due process** or **equal protection of law,** and changes the **apportionment** of congressional **representatives.**

Fourth Amendment   The U.S. **constitutional** amendment that forbids unreasonable searches and seizures and requires **probable cause** for **search warrants.**

Frame   *1.* Popular word for incriminating someone on false **evidence.** *2.* Draw up; put into words. For example, to *frame* a **complaint** is to choose the legal form it will take, fit the facts to the form, and choose the actual wording.

Franchise   *1.* A business arrangement in which a person buys the right to sell, rent, etc., the products or services of a company and use the company's name to do business. The person who buys the rights is a *franchisee,* and the person who sells the rights is a *franchisor. 2.* A special right given by the government, such as the right to vote or to form a **corporation.** *3.* A sports team granted a particular territory by the league. [pronounce: <u>fran</u>-chize]

Franchise tax   A tax on the right of a company to do business. It may be based on a fixed fee, on the amount of business done, on **assets,** etc.

Frank   *1.* The right, primarily of the federal government, to mail things without charge. Also called a *franking privilege. 2.* An old English word for *free.* For example, a *frank-pledge* was the responsibility of all free persons (the community as a whole) for the good conduct of each adult in the community.

Fraternal benefit association   A group of persons, often in the same line of work, who band together for such things as *group* **insurance** coverage.

Fraud   Any kind of trickery used to cheat another of money or property. See, for example, **tax fraud.** [pronounce: frawd]

Fraud on the market theory   The principle that if a broker, stock issuer, or company gives out false information about the company that probably changed the value of the company's stock, and if a person loses money by relying on that stock price to buy or sell the stock, the person was cheated by the information-giver even if the person did not rely on the false information itself. See also **efficient market.**

Fraud order   A decision by the postmaster general to deny a person the use of the mail. This is done to prevent the person from continuing to obtain money fraudulently.

Frauds, statute of   See **statute of frauds.**

Fraudulent   Cheating. For example, a *fraudulent conveyance* is a **debtor's** transfer of property to someone else in order to cheat a **creditor** who might have a right to it.

Freddie Mac See **F.H.L.M.C.**

Free agency The right of some veteran professional athletes to play for any team that wants them.

Free and clear With **clear title** (unrestricted, doubt-free legal ownership) to property with no **encumbrances** (liens, mortgages, etc.).

Free and equal election *Free* means that each person has a reasonable chance to qualify as a voter and, once qualified, a reasonable chance to vote without coercion of any kind. *Equal* means that each voter has the same rights as any other voter to have his or her vote count equally in the election.

Free exercise clause That part of the **First Amendment** to the U.S. **Constitution** that states, "Congress shall make no law . . . prohibiting the *free exercise [of religion]."* See **freedom of religion.**

Free on board See **F.O.B.**

Free port An area of a country (usually of a marine port, but sometimes a railroad crossover, airport, etc.) set aside for bringing in and selling foreign goods without paying import taxes. See also **foreign trade zone.**

Free ride Popular phrase for a riskless action that may result in a profit or for getting the benefit of **union** representation without having to join the union or pay dues.

Free speech See **freedom of speech.**

Free trade zone **Foreign trade zone.**

Freedom of association (or assembly) The **First Amendment** right to gather together in groups for any lawful purpose.

Freedom of choice Among other general meanings, the right to attend the school of your choice within a school district so long as there is no **de jure** segregation. This "right" often produces **de facto** segregation.

Freedom of contract The constitutionally protected right to make and enforce **contracts,** as limited only by reasonable laws about health, safety, and consumer protection.

Freedom of expression The **First Amendment** freedoms of religion, speech, and press combined.

Freedom of Information Act (5 U.S.C. 552) A 1966 federal law that makes all records held by the federal government, except for certain specific types of records (such as certain military secrets), available to the public. Procedures are set up to get these records and to **appeal** decisions to withhold them, but these procedures are often slow and cumbersome.

Freedom of religion The **First Amendment** right to hold any religious beliefs and to practice these beliefs in any way that does not infringe on public safety or infringe on important rights of others. Also, the right of all citizens to be free of the exercise of religious control by or through the government. See **establishment clause.**

Freedom of speech The **First Amendment** right to say what you want as long as you do not interfere with others' rights. These other rights are protected by the laws of **defamation,** public safety, etc.

Freedom of the press The **First Amendment** right of the press to publish most things "without **censorship** or **prior restraint,**" to be free from unreasonable attempts to punish what has already been published, and other rights.

Freedom of the seas A merchant ship's right to travel the **high seas** at all times.

Freehold Ownership of land, either unrestricted or limited by no more than a time limit.

Freeze A halt to changes in prices, wages, hiring, etc.

Freeze-out The use of **corporate** power by a majority of the stockholders (owners) or of the **board** *of directors* to either get rid of **minority** stockholders and board members or to strip them of all power. See also **squeeze-out.**

Fresh complaint rule The idea, used infrequently now, that a rape or other sexual assault complaint may not be believable unless the complainant went for help within a short time.

Fresh (or hot) pursuit rule *1.* The right of a police officer to cross state (or county or other) lines to continue an unbroken chase of a suspected criminal. This right is limited to those states which allow it. *2.* The right of a person who has had property taken to use reasonable force to get it back after a chase that takes place immediately after it was taken.

Friend of the court See **amicus curiae.**

Friendly fire A fire that remains contained where intended, but may do damage anyway.

Friendly suit A lawsuit brought by agreement to settle a point of law that affects opposing persons.

Friendly takeover One company gaining control of another with the approval of the second company's **board** and officers.

Fringe benefits Things besides salary that either compensate a person for working (such as paid medical insurance or **profit-sharing** plans) or make it pleasant to work (such as on-site recreational facilities).

Frisk   A superficial running of hands over a person's body in order to do a quick search, especially for weapons.

Frivolous   Legally worthless. For example, a **pleading** that clearly has no legal leg to stand on, even if every fact it claims is true, is *frivolous*. Also, an **appeal** that presents no legal question or is so lacking in substance that it could not possibly succeed is *frivolous*.

Frolic   An employee's deviation from a mission to do something for himself or herself.

Front name   **Street name.**

Front wages   Prospective payments made to a victim of job **discrimination** who cannot yet be given the job to which he or she is entitled. These payments, made until the job comes through, make up the difference between money earned now and money that would be made now if the new position were immediately available.

Frontage assessment   A tax to pay for improvements (such as sidewalks or sewer lines) that is charged in proportion to the frontage (number of feet bordering the road) of each property.

Front-end load   Charging a large part of the commissions and selling costs at the *start* of a deal to buy insurance, to invest in a mutual fund, to lease property, etc.

Frozen account   An **account** (usually a bank account) from which no money may be removed until a court or administrative **order** is lifted.

Frozen assets   The property of a business that cannot be easily sold without damaging the business. This includes financial assets which, if sold, will hurt the company's financial structure. The opposite is *liquid assets.*

Fructus   (Latin) **Fruit** or profit.

Fruit   Product of; material result. For example, rental income is the *fruit* of renting land out and stolen money is the "fruit of crime."

Fruit and tree doctrine   The rule that income tax cannot be avoided by merely assigning income to another person. The only way to transfer the income tax to another person is to give away the income-producing property itself (such as by giving it to a child who may pay lower taxes).

Fruit of the poisonous tree doctrine   The rule that **evidence** gathered as a *result* of evidence gained in an illegal search or questioning cannot be used against the person searched or questioned even if the later evidence was gathered lawfully. Compare with **independent source rule.**

Frustration   "*Frustration of contract*" occurs when carrying out a bargain has become impossible because of some change or occurrence that is not the fault of the persons making the deal. The change must remove something (or change some condition) that the persons who made the contract knew from the beginning was necessary for the contract to be carried out. "*Frustration of purpose*" occurs when, even if a bargain can be carried out, some change has wiped out the real reasons for the contract. In some cases, promises need not then be carried out.

Fugitive from justice   A person accused of committing a crime who leaves the area or hides to avoid prosecution.

Full coverage   Insurance that pays for every dollar of a loss with no maximum and no **deductible** amount.

Full faith and credit   The **constitutional** requirement that each state must treat as valid, and enforce where appropriate, the laws and court decisions of other states. There are exceptions to this rule, especially those cases in which the other state lacked proper **jurisdiction.**

Functional   In **trademark** law, essential to a product's use or purpose, or affecting the product's cost or performance. A *functional* product feature cannot get trademark protection unless it has a **patent.**

Functus officio   (Latin) A person whose official job is finished and who has no further authority to act.

Fund   *1.* A sum of money set aside for a particular purpose. *2.* Money and all other **assets** (such as stocks or bonds) on hand.

Fundamental   Basic or crucial. For example, *fundamental rights* are the basic rights, such as the right to vote and right to travel, that are most strongly protected by the **Constitution.** See also **strict scrutiny test.**

Fundamental analysis   Deciding whether to buy or sell a particular **stock** or other **security** based on the company itself, the industry in general, etc. Compare with **technical analysis.**

Fundamental law   A country's **constitution** or its basic governing principles.

Funded debt   *1.* State or local debts that have either a fund of money or a specific tax plan set aside for payment. *2.* A company's long-term debt, such as a **bond** *issue,* replacing other short-term debts.

Fungible   Able to be easily replaced one for another. For example, pounds of a particular grade and type of rice are *fungible* because one may be substituted for another, but different paintings are not fungible. [pronounce: fun̲ji-ble]

Furandi animus   (Latin) See **animo.**

Furman v. Georgia   (408 U.S. 238) The 1972 U.S. Supreme Court decision that found certain state laws and practices imposing the death sentence to be violations of the **Eighth Amendment's** prohibition of cruel and unusual punishment. Many state death penalty laws and practices were changed because of this case, but later cases have limited its effect.

Furtherance   Helping something move forward.

Furtum   (Latin) A theft or the item stolen.

Future advances   Money lent on the same **security** as a previous loan. Some open-ended **credit** and **mortgage** contracts allow additional loans like this.

Future-acquired property   See **after-acquired property.**

Future damages   Money awarded in some lawsuits to compensate for the likely future effects (such as long-term medical expenses, pain, and loss of earnings) of an injury. Contrast **speculative damages.**

Future earnings   Estimated money that would have been made in the future if an injury had not occurred.

Future interests   Present rights in property that give the right to future possession or use; for example, the right to own property and use it after ten years go by.

Futures   Contracts promising to buy or sell standard commodities (rice, soybeans, etc.) or **securities** at a future date and at a set price. These are "paper" deals that involve profit and loss on promises to deliver that do not depend on possession of the actual commodities.

G.A.A.P. *Generally Accepted Accounting Principles* published by the Financial Accounting Standards Board.

G.A.A.S. *Generally Accepted Auditing Standards* published by the American Institute of Certified Public Accountants.

G.A.O. General Accounting Office. The federal agency that assists the U.S. Congress in financial matters; **audits** and investigates federal programs; settles claims against the U.S.; etc.

G.A.T.T. General Agreement on Tariffs and Trade. An international agreement that lowers import taxes and otherwise makes international trade flow more smoothly.

G.D.P. Gross domestic product. The value of all goods and services produced in a nation in one year.

G.M.I. *Guilty, but mentally ill.* A jury's recommendation of treatment after it rejects a defendant's **insanity** defense.

G.N.M.A. Government National Mortgage Association. A government organization that operates special programs in which housing **mortgages** are bought and sold to encourage private lending in certain types of housing. Also called "*Ginnie Mae.*"

G.N.P. See **G.D.P.**

G.P.M. **Graduated payment mortgage.**

G.P.O. Government Printing Office. The agency that publishes all the laws, **regulations,** etc., of the federal government.

G.S. Short for general schedule or government service. The abbreviation precedes most federal civil service ranks, which range from G.S. 1 to G.S. 18.

G.S.A. General Services Administration. The federal agency that manages U.S. property.

Gag order *1.* A judge's **order** that a wildly disruptive **defendant** be bound and gagged during a trial. *2.* A judge's order to lawyers and **witnesses** that they discuss the trial with no outsiders, reporters in particular. *3.* A judge's order, usually held **unconstitutional,** to reporters that they not report certain court proceedings.

Gag rule *1.* A **gag order.** *2.* Any law or rule that prohibits the expression of ideas or that cuts off debate.

Gage   An old word for **pledge,** pawn, or **security.**

Gambling policy   An insurance policy issued to a person who has no **insurable interest** in the person or property insured. These policies are unenforceable, and sometimes illegal.

Gaol   (Old English) Jail.

Gap-filler   An essential contract term that is supplied by a court or by a law because the parties failed to include it.

Garnishee   A person who holds money or property belonging to a **debtor** and who is subject to a **garnishment** (see that word) proceeding by a **creditor.**

Garnishment   A legal process, taken by a **creditor** who has received a money **judgment** against a **debtor,** to get the debtor's money. This is done by **attachment** of a bank account or by taking a percentage of the debtor's regular income. State laws set a limit on the percentage (often 25 percent) of a person's *wages* that may be *garnished* through a person's employer. The garnishment of federal wages is limited by the *Federal Wage Garnishment Act,* which, in addition, gives some protection from dismissal due to garnishment.

Gault decision   The Supreme Court case (*In the Matter of Gault,* 387 U.S. 1 (1967)) that gave juvenile **defendants** the rights of adult criminal defendants (such as the right to **counsel,** the privilege against **self-incrimination,** etc.).

Gay rights   A general term for the prevention of **discrimination** based on sexual orientation.

Gearing   See **leverage.**

Gebser v. Lago Vista   (524 U.S. 274) The 1998 U.S. Supreme Court decision that a school district is not liable for sexual harassment of a student by a teacher when no responsible official had actual notice of or was deliberately indifferent to the teacher's misconduct.

Gele   An old word for a rent or a public license similar to a **royalty** payment for mining.

Gen.   **General.**

Gender discrimination   See **discrimination.**

General   *1.* A whole group (as opposed to only a part of the group or only one individual in the group); applying to all (as opposed to only some or only one); broad or unlimited. The opposite of "*general*" is often "**special**" or "**limited.**" *2.* For *general* **election, instructions, partner, verdict,** and others that do not follow here, see those words. See also **special** and **limited** for the *opposite,* especially if the word cannot be found here or under the base word.

General appearance   Coming before a court and submitting to its **jurisdiction** in a case. Compare with **special appearance.**

General assembly   *1.* The entire **legislature** in many states. *2.* The lower **house** of many state legislatures. *3.* The meeting of representatives of all the member nations of the United Nations.

General assignment for creditors   A transfer of all rights to a **debtor's** property to a **trustee** who settles the debtor's affairs and distributes money to the **creditors.**

General assistance (or general relief)   A local form of aid to the poor that sometimes has state backing, but involves no federal funds. It is usually temporary.

General average loss (or contribution)   A loss at sea that will be shared by the shipowner and all owners of cargo shipped. This happens if the lost or damaged items (often thrown overboard) were intentionally lost to save the ship and the rest of the cargo.

General building scheme   A development plan involving the division of a piece of land into separate building lots that are sold with identical restrictions on each as to how the land may be used.

General cash issue (or offer)   A sale of **stock** or other **securities** open to all buyers.

General (or prime) contractor   A person who contracts for a whole project (such as a building job) and hires subcontractors (such as plumbers) to do specialized work.

General creditor   A person who is owed money, but who has no **security** for the debt.

General digest   See **American Digest System.**

General execution   A court **order** to a sheriff or another court official to take any personal **property** of a **defendant** in order to pay off a **judgment** against that person.

General jurisdiction   The power of a court to hear and decide any of a wide range of cases that arise within its geographic area.

General lien   A right (arising from a **contract**) to hold personal **property** of another person until payment of a debt is made.

General strike   A work stoppage by a large part of the workers in a geographic area. The strike may be spontaneous, and its goals are often political rather than economic.

General warranty deed   A document used for the transfer of land that includes the promise to protect the buyer against all claims by others to ownership of the property transferred. Compare with **quitclaim.**

General welfare clause　The provision of the U.S. **Constitution** (Article I, Section 8, Clause 1) that Congress may tax and pay debts to provide for the country's "*general welfare.*"

Generation-skipping trust　A **trust** in which, for example, a grandmother gives the income from the trust property to her children and then the trust **assets** to her grandchildren. By not passing the trust assets directly to her children, then on to the grandchildren, one *transfer tax* is avoided, but there are now tax rules that impose a special *generation-skipping tax* on this.

Generic citation　Public domain *citation.*

Generic name　A general name for a type of product that does not distinguish between the various brands of the product; the non**trademark** name of a product.

Genericide　A court or Patent and Trademark Office decision that there has been an **abandonment** of a **trademark** right because the trademarked name (such as *aspirin*) was permitted to come into common use as the generic name for the product.

Genetic marker testing　See **DNA fingerprinting** and **HLA testing.**

Geneva Convention　An international agreement for the conduct of war that includes the proper care of enemy wounded, the safety of hospitals and medical crews, etc.

Gentleman's agreement　A deal that cannot be enforced in court and that depends solely on the good faith of the persons making it. See **informal agreement.**

Germane　Close on point, relevant, pertinent.

Gerrymander　Create unusually shaped (or otherwise odd or unnatural) political boundaries or districts in a state or country in order to accomplish an improper purpose, such as to give a voting advantage to one political party.

Gideon v. Wainwright　(372 U.S. 335) The 1963 U.S. Supreme Court decision that gave criminal defendants in state **felony** trials the right to **counsel.**

Gift　*1.* Any willing transfer of money or property without payment close to the assumed value of the thing transferred. *2.* Any willing transfer of money or property without payment and with no thought of any possible financial benefit to the giver. *3.* For *gift causa mortis,* see **causa mortis.**

Gift over　A property transfer that takes effect automatically when another ends; for example, a gift "to Linda for life, then to David."

Gift tax   A tax on **gifts** (see that word) that is paid by the giver (federal and some state taxes) or by the person receiving the gift (some states). Once, federal *gift tax* was separate from **estate tax** but now there is a *"unified estate and gift tax."* See **unified transfer tax** (and compare with **inheritance** *tax*).

Gifts to Minors Act   A **uniform act,** adopted by most states, that simplifies the transfer of property to **minors.** In a transfer under the act, the adult keeps **title** to and control over the property, and the child gets the **interest** or **dividends,** which may be used for the child's support.

Gilt edge   A popular term describing a **stock, bond,** other **security,** or **negotiable instrument** with the highest rating (for safety of investment).

Ginnie Mae   See **G.N.M.A.**

Gist   The main point, issue, or argument. [pronounce: jist]

Giveback   An arrangement in which a union negotiates a new contract with lower salaries or benefits, usually to preserve jobs.

Gloss   An explanation of a passage in a book or document that is usually put on the same page.

Glossary   *1.* Dictionary. *2.* Small dictionary; specialized dictionary.

Go bare   *1.* **Self-insurance** (see that word). *2.* Making a risky investment or doing a risky deal without **hedging** against the risk.

Go forward   Proceed.

Go to protest   See **protest.**

Going and coming rule   The principal that while a person is commuting to or from work the person is not usually covered by **workers' compensation laws,** and the person's **torts** are not usually within the **scope of employment,** so in neither case must employers pay for such things as collision injuries.

Going concern   A company that is transacting its usual business in its usual way (even if in a weak financial condition).

Going private   *1.* A company's taking its **stock** off a stock **exchange.** *2.* A company's rebuying of its own stock or otherwise rearranging its financial affairs so that it is no longer owned by many persons (for example, by merging with or being bought by a larger company).

Going public   Selling **shares** in a **corporation** to the general public for the first time.

Goldberg v. Kelly   (397 U.S. 254) A 1970 Supreme Court decision that called **welfare** a **right,** not a **privilege,** thus requiring a **hearing** before termination of benefits.

Goldbricking *1.* An organized work slowdown. *2.* Shirking work; "goofing off" while pretending to work.

Golden parachute An employment contract or termination agreement that gives a top executive a big bonus or other major benefits if the executive loses his or her job (usually due to a change in corporate control).

Golden rule *1.* **Plain meaning rule.** *2.* "Do unto others as you would have them do unto you." A moral, not legal rule. *3.* The *golden rule argument* is a request by a lawyer (or instructions by a judge) that **jurors** imagine themselves or their family members in the place of the person hurt (who is suing), and then make a decision. This request is no longer permitted in any trial.

Good Valid; legally sufficient. For *good consideration,* see **consideration.**

Good behavior A vague term, applied differently to the conduct required for public officials to keep their jobs, for criminals to get out of jail early, etc.

Good cause Legally sufficient; not arbitrary.

Good faith *1.* Honest; honesty in fact. *2.* For a merchant, *good faith* also means "the observance of reasonable commercial standards of fair dealing in the trade" according to the **Uniform Commercial Code.** *3. Good faith bargaining* is the obligation of an employer to hold honest negotiations about wages, hours, and employment conditions with a **union** that has been **certified** to represent its employees. *4.* A *good faith purchaser* in commercial law is a person who buys something honestly, pays good value, and knows of no other person's claim to the thing bought. *5.* There is a *good faith exception* to the **exclusionary rule.**

Good Samaritan doctrine *1.* The principle that a person who helps another in great danger cannot be held **liable** for that person's injuries unless the help was **negligent** and definitely worsened the person's condition. *2.* See also **emergency doctrine** and **rescue** *doctrine.*

Good title **Marketable** *title* (see also **marketable title acts**).

Goods A general word that can have a meaning as broad as "all property excluding **land**" or as narrow as "items for sale by a merchant." *Durable goods,* such as refrigerators, have a long life; *fungible goods,* such as pounds of rice, are interchangeable; *hard goods* are durable goods sold to consumers; and *soft goods* are nondurable goods, such as clothing, sold to consumers.

Goodtime The amount of time that may be credited against a prison sentence for the early release of a prisoner who has behaved well.

Goodwill The reputation and patronage of a company. The monetary worth of a company's _goodwill_ is roughly what a company would sell for over the value of its physical property, money owed to it, and other **assets.**

Government instrumentality doctrine The rule that an organization run by a branch of government may not be taxed. See also **sovereign immunity.**

Governmental function An action performed for the general public good by a government agency (such as an arrest by a police officer) or by a private organization closely tied to government (such as a primary election by a political party). These functions are _state action_ subject to the **due process of law** and **equal protection** clauses of the Constitution. If performed by a government agency, they are usually free from **tort** lawsuits unless the suits involve constitutional issues or are otherwise authorized by **statute.**

Governmental trust A **charitable trust** for things like maintenance of historic government buildings and city playgrounds.

Grab law See **aggressive collection.**

Grace _1._ A favor. _2._ A holding off on demanding payment of a debt or enforcing some other right. Often called "_grace days_" or a "_grace period,_" such as the short period of time an insurance policy stays in effect after the **premium** is due, but unpaid. _3._ A permission to do something in a lawsuit is "_of grace_" if it is not automatic, but is given because the judge thinks it is the fair thing to do.

Graded offense A criminal offense divided into **degrees** (see that word).

Graduated lease A commercial **lease** with rent payments that vary according to the money made by the renter or by some other standard such as the number of people who enter the store.

Graduated payment mortgage A **mortgage** in which payments go up by a set formula over the years. Compare with **variable rate mortgage.**

Graduated tax See **tax rate.**

Grand jury See **jury.**

Grand larceny A **theft** of money or property worth above a certain amount set by law.

Grandfather clause An exception to a restriction or requirement that allows all those already doing something to continue doing it even if they otherwise would be stopped by the new restriction or obligated to meet the new requirement.

Grant *1.* Give or confer. *2.* A transfer of land, usually by **deed.** *3.* A gift or subsidy. *4.* A transfer of any property or right.

Gran<u>tee</u>   A person to whom a **grant** is made or land is deeded.

Grant-in-aid   A sum of money given for a particular purpose and with some "strings attached."

Grantor   A person making a **grant** or deeding over land.

Grantor trust   A **trust** with income that is taxed to the person who created it because he or she kept certain rights to the **assets.**

Grantor-grantee index   A reference list to the recorded documents, such as **deeds,** in a county's land records, organized by both the names of the person transferring the property and the person to whom it was transferred. See also **tract index.**

Gratis   (Latin) Free; for example, a *gratis dictum* is a free (voluntary) statement to which a person may not be strictly held. [pronounce: grah-tis]

Gra<u>tui</u>tous   *1.* Without payment or other **consideration.** *2.* Without being requested; without being wanted.

Gratuitous licensee   A nonbusiness visitor; a social guest.

Gra<u>va</u>men   The basis, gist, "heart," or material part of a **charge, complaint,** etc.

Gray market goods   Goods made lawfully outside the U.S. that are imported into the U.S. and that by importation are an **infringement** of a copyright, trademark, or patent.

Great Writ   **Habeas Corpus.**

Green card   Popular name for the *permanent resident* **visa** that is a requirement for noncitizens to hold many jobs in the U.S. The card is no longer green.

Green river ordinance   A local law that protects residents against peddlers and door-to-door salespersons.

Greenmail   Payment by a corporation of a price above **market value** for stock held by someone threatening a hostile *takeover.*

Grievance procedure   An orderly, regular way of handling problems between workers and employers, prisoners and guards, etc.

Griswold v. Connecticut   (381 U.S. 479) The 1965 Supreme Court decision that invalidated state anti-contraceptive laws as applied to married persons. See **zone of privacy** and **penumbra.**

Gross   *1.* Great or large. *2.* Flagrant or shameful. *3.* Whole or total.

Gross estate   The total value of a dead person's property from which **deductions** are subtracted (and to which certain gifts made during life are added) to determine the amount on which federal **estate** and **gift taxes** will be paid.

Gross income   *1.* Money taken in (as opposed to "**net** *income,*" which is money taken in minus money paid out). *2.* Under the federal tax laws, *gross income* is all money taken in minus **exclusions** (such as interest on tax-free **bonds**).

Gross lease   A **lease** in which the landlord pays all ownership and maintenance expenses, and the tenant pays rent. Compare with **net lease.**

Gross receipts   The total amount of money received (or the monetary value of anything received) from running a business, selling property, performing services, etc.

Gross up   Add back into the value of property or income the amount that has already been deducted or paid out (usually for taxes).

Ground rent   Rent paid for raw land, usually under a long-term lease, by a tenant who puts up a building (usually a commercial building).

Grounds   Basis, foundation, or points relied on. For example, "*grounds*" for a **divorce** may include **adultery, cruelty,** etc.

Group insurance   *1.* Insurance for employees paid by or through the employer. *2.* Any insurance bought through an organization, rather than directly from the insurance company, with the organization holding the "*master policy.*"

Group legal services   Legal help given to members of an organization or employees of a company. It is paid for in advance on a group basis, often similar to group health insurance.

Growth rate   The rate at which a company increases its revenues and its **earnings per share.**

Growth stock   A stock invested in primarily for an increase in value (**capital** gains) rather than for income payments (**dividends**).

Guarantee   Same as **guaranty.**

Guarantee clause   The provision of the U.S. **Constitution** (Article 4, Section 4) promising the states a republican (see **republic**) form of government and protection from invasion and domestic violence.

Guaranteed mortgage   *1.* A **mortgage** made by a mortgage company that then sells the mortgage to an investor, guarantees payments to the investor, and manages the mortgage for a fee. *2.* A mortgage with payments guaranteed by the government.

Guaranty   *1.* The same as a merchant's **warranty** (promise) that goods are of a certain quality, will be fixed if broken, will last a certain time, etc. *2.* A promise to fulfill an obligation (or pay a debt) if the person who has the obligation fails to fulfill it. For example, John contracts with Ron that if Ron lends Don five dollars and Don fails to pay it back in a week, John will pay it. *3.* Any promise.

Guardian   A person who has the legal right and duty to take care of another person or that person's property because that other person (for example, a child) cannot. The arrangement is called "*guardianship.*"

Guardian ad litem   A **guardian** (see that word), usually a lawyer, who is appointed by a court to take care of the interests of a person who cannot legally take care of himself or herself in a lawsuit involving that person.

Guest statute   Laws in a few states that do not permit a person who rides in another person's car as a *guest* (without payment or other business purpose) to sue that person if there is an accident, unless the accident involves more than ordinary **negligence.**

Guilt by association   Being penalized (by loss of job, prosecution for a crime, etc.) merely for belonging to a particular group or by being personally associated with certain people. Except in cases of a **conspiracy,** criminal prosecutions of this type are not permitted.

Guilty   *1.* Responsible for a crime. *2.* Convicted of a crime. *3.* Responsible for a civil wrong (**tort** or **breach of contract**).

H.A.L.T.   Help Abolish Legal Tyranny, a group devoted to lessening the public's dependence on lawyers.

H.B.   House Bill. A **bill** in the process of going through the **House of Representatives.**

H.D.C.   **Holder in due course.**

H.H.S.   The U.S. Department of Health & Human Services. The cabinet department that handles health, welfare, and Social Security.

H.I.D.C.   **Holder in due course.**

H.L.   **House** *of Lords.*

H.L.A. testing   Human leukocyte antigen testing. A blood test used to help determine paternity for a **paternity suit.**   It is not as accurate as **D.N.A. fingerprinting.**

H.M.O.   Health Maintenance Organization. A group health insurance plan that requires use of specific doctors, hospitals, and other medical services. Compare **P.P.O.**

H.O.W.   **Home owners warranty.**

H.R.   **House of Representatives.**

H. Res.   House **Resolution.**

H.R.-10 Plan   **Keogh Plan.**

H.U.D.   Department of Housing and Urban Development. The U.S. **cabinet** department that coordinates federal housing and land use policy and funds housing construction through a variety of programs.

Habeas corpus   (Latin) "You have the body." A judicial **order** to someone holding a person to bring that person to court. It is most often used to get a person out of unlawful imprisonment by forcing the captor and the person being held to come to court for a decision on the legality of the imprisonment or other holding (such as keeping a child when someone else claims **custody**). [pronounce: hay-bee-as core-pus]

Habendum clause   The part of a **deed** that describes the ownership rights being transferred.

Habitability   The requirement that a rented house or apartment be fit to live in, primarily that it can pass building and sanitary code inspections.

Habitual Regular, common, and customary; more than just frequent. Some states have "*habitual criminal*" laws that may apply to a person who has been convicted of as few as two prior crimes (often violent or drug-related crimes) and that greatly increase the penalties for each succeeding crime.

Habitual intemperance Regular drunkenness that is serious enough to interfere with a normal home or job. This is grounds for a **divorce** in many states. Some states consider drug addiction to be *habitual intemperance.*

Haeres/haereditas (Latin) **Heir/inheritance.** Also, *haeredes proximi* are "nearest heirs" or **next of kin;** *haereditas testimentaria* is inheritance by **will;** and *haereditas legitima* is **intestate** (by law) inheritance.

Hague Convention Any of the many international treaties that begin with these words may be called "the" Hague Convention by specialists. Many Conventions standardize legal procedures in areas such as **service** of **process** in a foreign country or taking **evidence** there.

Hague Tribunal See **International Court of Justice.**

Hallmark A stamp put on gold, silver, and other items to prove their genuineness. The word is used in a legal sense to mean any official mark of genuineness.

Hammer A **forced sale;** any sale by auction.

Hammurabi, Code of One of the oldest sets of laws, prepared in Babylonia almost four thousand years ago.

Hand down Decide. A judge *hands down* an **opinion** or a **decision** (usually in a case that has been appealed or one in which the judge has delayed a decision) by announcing it or filing it.

Handicap *1.* See **disability.** *2.* An impairment that substantially limits performance of an important life function. *3. Handicap* is defined differently in different **statutes.**

Harassment *1.* Words and actions that unlawfully annoy or alarm another. Harassment may include anonymous, repeated, offensively coarse, or late-night phone calls; insulting, taunting, or physically challenging approaches; words or actions by a debt collector that serve no legitimate purpose; etc. *2.* See also **sexual harassment.**

Harbor *1.* Shelter, house, keep, or feed. *2.* Shelter or conceal a person for an illegal purpose, such as to hide a criminal from police arrest.

Hard cases Cases where fairness requires being loose with legal principles. The phrase "hard cases make bad law" comes from this idea.

Harmless error See **error.**

Harmonize   Reconcile differences between points of view to reach a good result; for example, interpret two **statutes** that seem in conflict in a way that eliminates the conflict.

Harter Act   (46 U.S.C. 190) An 1893 federal law prohibiting **bills of lading** that relieve negligent or otherwise at-fault shipowners from **liability** for lost or damaged cargo. The law also protects from liability shipowners whose crews act responsibly.

Hatch Act   (5 U.S.C. 1501) A 1939 federal law to prevent certain types of political activity (such as holding public office) by federal employees and by certain state employees who are paid with federal funds. States have similar laws.

Hate   A *hate crime* is a crime that violates a person's civil rights and is motivated by hatred for a particular group, such as the person's race or national origin. And *hate speech* expresses hatred for one of these groups, expresses nothing protected by the First Amendment, and is likely to provoke violence.

Have and hold   A common formal phrase in a **deed** that is no longer necessary to make the deed effective. *To have and to hold* is the first phrase of a typical **habendum clause.**

Hazard   Any risk or danger of loss or injury. In **insurance** law, *hazard* is the probability that something may happen, and *moral hazard* is the risk of fire or similar destruction as measured by the carefulness, integrity, etc., of the person whose property is insured plus the person's possible loss or gain from the destruction of the insured property.

Head money   *1.* A tax based on each person counted. A "head tax," "**capitation tax,**" **poll tax,** immigration tax, etc. *2.* A bounty or reward for enemies or outlaws killed or brought in alive.

Head of family   A person who financially supports a group of related persons living together.

Head of household   A special category of federal taxpayer. To be taxed at *head of household* rates, you must meet several tests; for example, unmarried or legally separated, pay over half the support of your **dependents,** etc.

Head tax   Capitation tax.

Headnote   A summary of a **case,** or of an important legal point made in the case, placed at the beginning of the case when it is published. A case may have several headnotes.

Healthcare proxy   A document that allows another person to make healthcare decisions for you if you cannot make them for yourself. It is a type of **advance directive.**

Hearing   *1.* A court proceeding. *2.* A trial-like proceeding conducted by an **administrative agency** or in another noncourt setting. *3.* A meeting of a legislative **committee** to gather information. *4.* A "*public hearing*" may involve an agency's showing a new plan or proposed action to the public and allowing public comment and criticism.

Hearing examiner (or hearing officer)   A judgelike official of an **administrative agency.** Also called *administrative law judge.*

Hearsay   A statement about what someone else said (or wrote or otherwise communicated). *Hearsay evidence* is **evidence,** concerning what someone said outside of a court proceeding, that is offered in the proceeding to prove the truth of what was said. The *hearsay rule* bars the admission of hearsay as evidence *to prove the hearsay's truth* unless allowed by a **hearsay exception.**

Hearsay exception   An exception to the *hearsay rule* (see **hearsay**). There are *hearsay exceptions* for **business records, declarations** *against interest, dying* **declarations, excited utterances, party admissions, present sense impressions, public records,** etc.

Heart balm acts   State laws that either eliminate or restrict lawsuits based on **alienation of affection, breach of promise to marry, criminal conversation,** and seduction of an adult.

Heat of passion   A state of violent and uncontrollable provoked anger. Killing someone in the *heat of passion* may constitute **manslaughter** rather than **murder.**

Hedge fund   An investment group (not licensed by the **S.E.C.** to sell shares to the general public) that makes risky investments based on the **leverage** of financial instruments such as **derivatives** that are more traditionally used to reduce risk through **hedging.**

Hedging   Safeguarding a deal or speculation by making counterbalancing arrangements. For example, if a dealer contracts to deliver a hundred ounces of gold at a future time, then thinks that the price of gold may go up, the dealer might contract to *buy* fifty, or even a hundred, ounces of gold for that same future delivery date. Contrast **hedge fund.**

Hedonic damages   Money awarded in some lawsuits for loss of the ability to enjoy life's pleasures.

Height density controls   Control of an area's population density by limiting the maximum height of buildings through **zoning** laws.

Heir   A person who **inherits** property; a person who has a *right* to inherit property; or a person who has a right to inherit property only if another person dies without leaving a valid, complete **will.** An *heir ap-*

parent is a person who will inherit property if the ancestor who owns the property dies first without a valid will, and an *heir presumptive* is an heir apparent who will not inherit the property if a child is born with a better claim to inherit it. [pronounce: air]

Held   Decided; as in "the court held that"; see definition no. 2 of **hold.**

Henceforth   An unnecessarily formal word meaning "from now on."

Hereafter   An unnecessarily formal word meaning "in the future."

Hereditaments   Anything that can be inherited. Objects that can be inherited are called "*corporeal hereditaments*" and rights that can be inherited are called "*incorporeal hereditaments.*"

Hereditary succession   **Intestate succession.**

Herein   A vague word meaning "in this document." ("*Hereinabove*" and "*hereinafter*" are just as vague, adding only "before this" and "after this" to the definition.)

Heresy   Holding or advocating opinions contrary to established religion. This is punishable in some foreign countries, but the U.S. **Constitution** prohibits governmental involvement in religion.

Hereto   An unnecessarily formal word meaning "to this."

Heretofore   A vague and unnecessary word meaning "before" or "in times past."

Hereunder   A vague word meaning either "in this document" or "in accordance with this document."

Herewith   An unnecessarily formal word meaning "in this" or "with this."

Hermeneutics   The study of the rules and techniques used to interpret documents.

Hidden asset   An **asset** with a much higher value than the value stated in the company's financial records.

Hierarchy   An ordering of persons, things, or ideas by rank or level, especially with "more at the bottom than at the top." A typical *hierarchy* is the army (many privates, some majors, very few generals, etc.). Most **bureaucracies** are hierarchies. [pronounce: hi- er-ark-ee]

High crimes and misdemeanors   The basis for **impeachment** in the U.S. **Constitution** (Article 2, Section 4). Opinions differ as to the exact meaning of the phrase. It may include **felonies;** it may include offenses against the U.S. that have serious governmental or political consequences; or it may be whatever the U.S. **Congress** decides it is.

High seas   International waters, beyond any one country's control.

Highest and best use   The potential use of **land** that would bring in the most money. For example, a real estate **assessor** valuing a piece of farm land inside an urban area might say that its *highest and best use* is an office complex and, thus, that the land should be valued more highly for tax purposes.

High-low settlement   An agreement that if the jury awards below a certain minimum amount of **damages,** the defendant will pay that minimum amount, and if the jury awards above a certain maximum, the defendant will pay that maximum. In between, the defendant pays the jury award.

Hijack   Take over a vehicle or plane by illegal force, threat of force, or theft.

Hire-purchase   See **lease-purchase.**

Hit and run law   A law that requires a motorist involved in an accident to stop and give identification and other information to others involved in the accident and to the police.

Hitherto   An unnecessarily formal word that means "in the past" or "until now."

Hobbs Act   See **Anti-Racketeering Act.**

Hobby loss   A non**deductible** loss from a *hobby,* rather than a deductible loss from a business activity. Under federal tax law, an activity is presumed to be a hobby unless the activity made a profit in two of the last five years.

Hoc   (Latin) This.

Hodgepodge   See **hotchpot.**

Hold   *1.* To possess or own something lawfully and by good **title.** *2.* To decide. A judge who decides how law applies to a case or "declares **conclusions of law**" is said to "*hold that. . . .*" *3.* Conduct or have take place; for example, to "*hold court.*"

Hold harmless   Agree to pay certain claims that might come up against another person.

Hold over   *1.* Keep possession as a **tenant** after the **lease** period ends. *2.* Stay in office after the **term** of office is up.

Hold (or held) self out   Claim you have a legal status (usually without having it) or act as if you have it. "She held herself out as the homeowner, but she was a renter."

Holdback   A percentage of the amount owed under a contract that is retained until all work is satisfactorily completed and, in the case of construction work, until it is certain that there are no **mechanic's liens.**

Holder   A person who has legally received possession of a **negotiable instrument** (see that word), such as a **check,** and who is entitled to get payment on it.

Holder in due course A **holder** (see that word) who buys a **negotiable instrument** thinking that it is **valid,** and having no knowledge that any business involving it is "shady." The Uniform Commercial Code defines it as "a holder who takes the instrument for value, in good faith and without notice that it is overdue or has been dishonored or of any defense against or claim to it." But this definition is limited to the "usual course of business" and does not normally apply to *judicial sales,* **inheritance,** etc. A *holder in due course* has more rights than a mere holder. For example, except in **consumer** sales and credit, a holder in due course cannot be sued for defective goods by a buyer of merchandise involving the negotiable instrument.

Holding The core of a judge's **decision** in a case. It is that part of the judge's written **opinion** that applies the law to the facts of the case and about which can be said "the case means no more and no less than this." When later cases rely on a case as **precedent,** it is only the *holding* that should be used to establish the precedent. A *holding* may be less than the judge said it was. If the judge made broad, general statements, the holding is limited to only that part of the generalizations that directly apply to the facts of that particular case. Contrast **dicta.**

Holding company A company that exists primarily to control other companies by owning their **stock.** A *personal holding company* is formed by a few persons and is subject to a special federal income tax.

Holding period The length of time a **capital** asset is owned. Federal tax law categorizes certain assets as short-term or long-term depending on the length of the *holding period.*

Holograph A **will, deed,** or other legal document that is entirely in the handwriting of the signer. Some states require a *holographic* **will** to be signed, witnessed, and in **compliance** with other formalities before it is valid. Other states require less.

Homeowners policy A standard type of **insurance** that insures a home against losses due to fire, water, theft, **liability,** etc.

Homeowners warranty A **warranty/insurance** program that protects a home buyer against loss due to major defects for a set time period.

Home port doctrine *1.* The general rule that a ship in interstate or foreign commerce may be taxed only in its home port. *2.* The general rule that a provider of repairs for a ship anywhere other than in the home port can get a **lien** for these repairs, but in the home port, local law decides whether a lien is allowed.

Home relief See **general assistance.**

Home rule   Local self-government.

Homestead exemption   State laws allowing a head of a family to keep a home and some property safe from **creditors** other than mortgage holders, or to allow certain persons (such as those over a certain age) to avoid paying real estate or inheritance taxes on their homes.

Homicide   Killing another person (not necessarily a crime). *Justifiable homicide* is the *rightful* killing of another person, such as in time of war or in self-defense. *Excusable homicide* is the *wrongful* killing of another person that is not a crime, such as when a defendant is found "not guilty by reason of **insanity.**" Two types of **criminal** *homicide* are **murder** and **manslaughter.**

Homo   (Latin) A man; a human being.

Homologation   *1.* Approval by a court. *2.* **Estoppel.**

Hon   Short for "honorable," often placed before a judge's name.

Honor   To **accept** (or pay) a **negotiable instrument,** such as a **check,** when it is properly presented for acceptance (or payment).

Honorarium   A free gift; a free payment as opposed to a payment for services. But merely calling a payment (for example, for a speech) an *honorarium* does not necessarily make it nontaxable.

Honorary trust   A **trust** that gets no special tax advantages, but is not quite a private, ordinary trust; for example, a trust set up to "feed the pigeons in Clark Park." Some states allow these trusts, but most do not.

Horizontal merger   One company acquiring another that produces the same or similar products for sale or has a similar type and level of operation in the same geographic area.

Horizontal price fixing   An agreement among competing producers, wholesalers, or merchants to set the price of goods. These agreements are prohibited by law.

Horizontal property acts   Laws dealing with **cooperative** housing or **condominiums.**

Hornbook   A book summarizing the basic principles of one legal subject, usually for law students. For **hornbook law, see black letter law.**

Hose and spray   An expression for the power of some **trustees** to decide how much each person named in a will should get.

Hostile environment   A workplace in which an employer permits regular intimidating or offensive words or actions based on sex, race, religion, etc.; for example, the sexual harassment that exists if repeated sexual jokes make it difficult for a woman to perform her job.

Hostile fire A fire that either escapes from where it was contained or a fire that was never intended to exist at all.

Hostile possession Claiming ownership of land against the whole world (including the person whose name appears on the land records as owner), but not necessarily in an angry, aggressive, or emotionally "hostile" way. It is a part of **adverse possession.**

Hostile witness A **witness** called by one side in a trial who shows so much **prejudice** or hostility to that side that he or she can be treated as if called by the other side.

Hot blood See **heat of passion.**

Hot cargo *1.* Goods produced or handled by an employer with whom a **union** has a **labor dispute.** *"Hot cargo agreements,"* in which a company promises to put pressure on another company with which a union has a dispute, are now illegal. *2.* Stolen goods.

Hot pursuit See **fresh pursuit rule.**

Hotchpot Combining properties belonging to different persons to redistribute them fairly, especially the practice of counting in any **advancement** (see that word) when dividing a *decedent's* **estate.**

House *1.* One of the branches of a **legislature;** either the *"upper house"* (for example, the British House of Lords) or the *"lower house"* (for example, the British House of Commons). *2.* The lower chamber of a two-part legislature. For example, "the House" is short for the U.S. **House of Representatives.**

House arrest Requiring a person accused or convicted of a crime to remain home for all but certain approved purposes, such as work or medical care.

House counsel A lawyer who is an employee of a business and does its day-to-day legal work.

House of Representatives *1.* The lower **house** of the U.S. **Congress,** with members elected according to state population to two-year terms. *2.* The name for the lower chamber of certain **legislatures,** including those of several states.

Housebreaking Breaking into and entering a house to commit a crime. Some states call it **burglary** if done at night.

Household A **family** (see that word) living together (plus, sometimes, servants or others living with the family).

Humanitarian doctrine See **last clear chance doctrine.**

Hung jury A **jury** that cannot reach a **verdict** (decision) because of disagreement among jurors.

Hurdle rate   The minimum acceptable rate of profit expected on a project for it to be started. See **opportunity cost.**

Husband-wife privilege   See **marital communications privilege.**

Hybrid security   A cross between an *equity* **security** (such as a stock) and a *debt* security (such as a bond).

Hybrid state (or hybrid theory jurisdiction)   Any state in which a **mortgage** is considered a cross between a **lien** and a transfer of **title.** In a *hybrid state* the **creditor** must use **foreclosure** to force the sale or return of a mortgaged property when payments fall behind or stop. In a hybrid state, a **mortgage** may take the form of a **deed of trust,** by which a **trustee** holds legal title as **security** for repayment of the debt incurred in the purchase of real estate.

Hypertext   A direct link from information in a computerized document to information elsewhere.

Hypothecate   *1.* To **pledge** or **mortgage** a thing without turning it over to the person making the loan. *2.* Securing repayment of a loan by holding the **stock, bonds,** etc., of the **debtor** until the debt is paid, with the power to sell them if it is not paid.

Hypothesis   A theory or working assumption, especially one that is to be tested by experiment or observation.

Hypothetical question   Posing a *hypothetical question* involves setting up a series of facts, assuming that they are true, and asking for an answer to a question based on those facts. In a trial, *hypothetical questions* may be asked of **expert witnesses** only. For example, a gun expert might be asked "If this gun had a silencer, could a shot be heard from a hundred feet away?"

I.C.J. **International Court of Justice.**

I.e. (Latin) That is. Short for *id est.*

I.F.P. **In forma pauperis.**

I.L.P. Index of Legal Periodicals.

I.M.F. International Monetary Fund. A United Nations agency that helps stabilize international exchange rates and promotes world trade.

I.N.S. **Immigration and Naturalization Service.**

I.O.L.T.A. Interest on Lawyers' Trust Accounts. State programs that set up accounts into which lawyers deposit funds held for clients. The interest on these funds sometimes supports legal services to the poor.

I.O.U. "I owe you." A written acknowledgment of a debt.

I.R.A. **Individual Retirement Account.**

I.R.B. Internal Revenue Bulletin. The **I.R.S.** publication that contains most important new information about the tax laws.

I.R.C. **Internal Revenue Code.**

I.R.S. Internal Revenue Service. The U.S. tax collection agency.

I.T.C. Investment tax credit. See **investment credit.**

Ibid. (Latin) The same; in, from, or found in the same place (same book, page, case, etc.). Short for *ibidem.*

Id. (Latin) Exactly the same thing; the same **citation** as the one immediately before. Short for *idem.*

Idem sonans (Latin) "Sounds the same." The *idem sonans rule* is the principle that if a person's wrongly spelled name sounds the same as the correctly spelled name, a legal document with the name spelled wrong will usually be valid.

Identity *1.* In **patent** law, *identity of invention* means exact sameness as to looks, parts, method of operation, and results. *2.* In **civil procedure**, *identity of interest* means two persons joined so closely (usually in a business sense) that suing one serves as **notice** of the lawsuit to the other, and a **judgment** against one **bars** another judgment against the other. *3.* In **evidence** law, *identity* means that something (or someone) is authentic, that it is the thing (or person) it is represented to be.

Idiopathic Caused by a person's infirmity, disease, or personal condition, rather than by the person's employment or by unexplained outside causes.

Ignoramus (Latin) "*We are ignorant (of a reason).*" The formal words that used to be said by a grand **jury** that failed to find a reason to charge someone with a crime. Now they say "*no bill,*" "*not found,*" or something similar.

Ignorantia legis neminem excusat (Latin) Ignorance of the law is no excuse.

Illegal Contrary to the criminal law; breaking a law (not merely improper, a **tort,** or civilly wrong).

Illegal entry *1.* A foreigner is guilty of *illegal entry* into the U.S. if he or she comes in at the wrong time or place, avoids examination by immigration officials, or gets in by **fraud.** *2.* Entering a building with the intent to commit a crime.

Illegal purpose doctrine The rule that an otherwise legal act is illegal if done to further an illegal purpose. This rule is **constitutional** only in certain limited situations.

Illegally obtained evidence **Evidence** obtained by violating a person's **constitutional** or **statutory** rights; for example, by searching without a **warrant,** with a legally defective warrant, or with no **probable cause** to arrest and search. This evidence cannot be used in a **criminal** trial. See **exclusionary rule** and **fruit of the poisonous tree doctrine.**

Illegitimate *1.* Contrary to law; lacking legal authorization. *2.* Describes a child born to an unmarried mother. The law in many states is changing as to who may be defined as *illegitimate,* as to **inheritance** and other rights of illegitimate children, and as to use of the word itself.

Illicit Prohibited; unlawful. [pronounce: il-liss-it]

Illusory promise A statement that looks like a promise that could make a **contract,** but, upon close examination of the words, promises nothing real or legally binding.

Imagination test The principle that the more that consumer imagination, thought, or perception is needed to associate a **trademark** (or **service** *mark*) with a particular product (or service), the stronger the mark is and the more it will be protected against **infringement.**

Imbargo See **embargo.**

Imbezzle See **embezzlement.**

Imitation Something made intentionally to resemble something else. In **trademark** law, if a use of words, letters, signs, etc., is close enough to a trademark to fool much of the general public (not necessarily when placed side by side, but when there is no chance to compare the two), it is an *imitation* and usually forbidden.

Immaterial   Not necessary; not important; without weight; trivial.

Immediate   *1.* Close, closest, or touching, depending on the context, when referring to distance. *2.* As fast as (reasonably) possible, when referring to time. *Immediately* does not usually mean *instantly.*

Immediate cause   *1.* The last event in a series of events, which, without any further events, produced the result in question. *2.* **Proximate cause.**

Immediate issue   Children.

Immemorial   See **time immemorial.**

Immigrant   *1.* A foreigner who comes into a country. *2.* A foreigner who comes into a country with the intention of living there permanently. *3.* In U.S. law, a foreigner who comes to the U.S. to live permanently and who meets several specific requirements of the *Immigration and Naturalization Act.*

Immigration and Naturalization Service   A U.S. government agency that handles the admission, **naturalization,** and **deportation** of foreigners. It is also responsible for preventing the illegal entry of **aliens.** The *Immigration Appeals Board* handles mostly **appeals** from deportation orders.

Imminent   Just about to happen; threatening; *not* "eminent." The *imminent peril doctrine* is the **emergency doctrine.**

Immoral   A vague word that can mean anything from "contrary to the accepted conduct of one religious sect" to "flagrant and shameless disregard for the welfare of the community or the opinions of most of its members" to "violating community standards as expressed by law." For a **contract** to be **invalid** or **void** due to *immoral* **consideration** or for a lawyer to be disbarred due to *immoral conduct,* immorality usually means serious illegality.

Immovables   **Land** and things naturally and permanently a part of the land.

Immunity   *1.* An exemption from a legally imposed duty, freedom from a duty, or freedom from a penalty. See also **privilege.** *2.* The freedom from prosecution (based on anything the witness says) that is given by the government to a **witness** who is forced to **testify** in a trial, before a **grand jury,** before a **legislature,** etc. *Transactional immunity,* the broadest form, is freedom from prosecution for all crimes *related to* the compelled testimony, so long as the witness tells the truth. *Use immunity,* less broad, is freedom from prosecution *based on* the compelled testimony and on anything the government learns from following up on the testimony. *Testimonial immunity,* the narrowest form, is freedom from prosecution based on the compelled testimony only. *3.* The freedom of a national, state, or local *government* from all taxes and from most **tort** lawsuits. See **government instrumentality doctrine** and **sovereign immunity.** *4.* The freedom of national, state, and local government *officials* from prosecution for, or arrest during, most official acts, and their freedom from most tort lawsuits resulting from their official duties. See also **diplomatic immunity.**

Impact rule   The rule (used today in very few states) that **damages** for emotional distress cannot be had in a **negligence** lawsuit unless there is some physical contact or impact.

Impair   Weaken, make worse, lessen, or otherwise hurt.

Impanel   Make up a list of possible **jurors** for a trial or select those who will actually serve.

Imparl   Delay proceedings in a lawsuit so that the two sides can discuss settlement of the dispute. Both the delay and the discussion used to be called an *imparlance.*

Impartial   Unable to see any personal advantage from taking one side rather than another. To be *impartial,* an **expert witness** or a **jury** must not favor one side over the other or prejudge any of the facts or theories involved in the case. A **juror** in particular must be fair, open-minded, unbiased, and just, so that decisions are based only on proper **evidence.**

Impasse   A breakdown in negotiations with no definite plans for further efforts to break the deadlock, after both sides have tried hard to negotiate in good faith to reach agreement. An *impasse* permits either side in a labor dispute to then take certain unilateral actions.

Impeachment   *1.* Showing that a **witness** is untruthful, either by **evidence** of past conduct, or by showing directly that the witness is not telling the truth. When you do this, you *impeach* the witness. *2.* The first step in the removal from public office of a high public official such as a governor, judge, or president. In the case of the president of the United States, the House of Representatives makes an accusation by drawing up "*articles of impeachment,*" voting on them, and presenting them to the Senate. This is *impeachment.* But *impeachment* is popularly thought to include the process that may take place after impeachment: the trial of the president in the Senate and conviction by two-thirds of the senators.

Impediment   A thing causing the legal inability to make a contract. For example, an *impediment to marriage* might be a prior marriage that is still **valid.**

Imperfect   *1.* Incomplete or **executory.** *2.* Defective or missing an essential legal requirement. *3.* Unenforceable (or enforceable only in certain circumstances).

Impersonation   Pretending to be a police officer, a public official, or a person (such as a doctor or lawyer) whose occupation requires a state license. Such behavior is often criminal.

Impertinence   Irrelevance in the sense that the proof offered may be relevant to an issue, but the issue itself is irrelevant to the trial.

Implead   Bring into a lawsuit. For example, if A sues B and B sues C in the same lawsuit, B *impleads* C, and the process is *impleader.*

Implicate   Show that a person is involved with a crime or other misdeed.

Implied   Known indirectly. Known by analyzing surrounding circumstances or the actions of the persons involved. The opposite of **express.** For example, *implied authority* is the authority one person gives to another to do a job even if the authority is not given directly (such as the authority to buy and charge gas if you run out while making a delivery for your boss). And *implied terms* are parts of a **contract** that do not exist on paper, but are part of the contract nonetheless (because the law requires them, because usual contracts in that business have them, etc.).

Implied acquittal   Conviction of a **lesser included offense** is an *implied acquittal* of the greater offense, and thus bars a trial on that offense because of **double jeopardy.**

Implied consent laws   State laws that permit law officers to require a blood alcohol test even if the driver does not consent. Consent is implied from the use of the public roadway.

Implied contract   Either an **implied-in-fact contract** or a **quasi contract.**

Implied powers   See **necessary.**

Implied remedy   A **remedy** (to compensate a violation of a **constitutional** right) that is not specifically provided by law but is **implied** from the existence of the right itself.

Implied trust   **Resulting trust.**

Implied warranty   An unstated promise, imposed on a merchant, that what is sold is fit for normal use, or, if the merchant knows what the buyer wants the thing for, that it is fit for that particular purpose. Unless these *implied warranties* are expressly excluded (for example, by clearly labeling the thing sold **"as is"**), a merchant will be held to them.

Implied-in-fact contract   A **contract** with existence and terms determined by the *actions* of the persons involved, not by their words. Compare with **express contract** and **quasi contract.**

Implied-in-law contract   A **quasi contract.**

Import-export clause   The provision of the U.S. **Constitution** (Section 10, Clause 2) that no state may tax imports and exports unless the tax is absolutely necessary for inspection laws or otherwise permitted by Congress.

Impossibility   That which cannot be done. A contract is not binding and cannot be enforced if it is *physically impossible* (for example, to be in two places at once); *legally impossible* (for example, to make a contract at age four); or *logically impossible* (for example, to sell a car for one thousand dollars when the buyer pays two thousand for it). These are all examples of "*objective impossibility*." However, "*subjective impossibility*" (such as not having enough money to pay for something you have contracted to buy) will not get you out of a contract.

Imposts   Taxes; import taxes.

Impound   *1.* Take a thing into the **custody** of the law until a legal question about it is decided. *2. Impoundment* is an action by a president or governor to prevent the spending of public money that the **legislature** has ordered spent. *3.* An *impound account* is money set aside for future use. *4.* Seal a legal record. See **sealed.**

Impracticability   Less than an **impossibility** and more than a big inconvenience; difficult, to the point where it would be unreasonable or unfair to require something.

Impressment   The act of forcibly taking for public use or service, such as forcing a person into the army or forcing a merchant seaman or merchant ship into the navy.

Imprest   *1.* A loan or advance. *2.* An *imprest fund* contains "petty cash."

Imprimatur   (Latin) "Let it be printed." Official government permission to publish a book. This is not needed in the U.S.

Imprisonment   *1.* Putting a person in prison. *2.* Depriving a person of personal liberty in any physical way.

Improper accumulation   Too much profit that is kept by a business to shield the owners from personal taxes. See **accumulated earnings tax.**

Improvement   *1.* An addition or change to land or buildings that increases the value. More than a repair or replacement. See **repair** for the *tax* difference. *2.* Any development of land.

Improvident   A judge's **decision, judgment,** or **order** is "*improvidently granted*" if the judge later thinks that he or she made a mistake.

Imputed   Something is "*imputed*" to you if, even though you do not know a fact, you *should* have known it (both legally and actually) or if, even though you are not *physically* responsible for something, you are *legally* responsible. See the words following for examples.

Imputed income   If you do certain kinds of activities, **income** will be imputed to you for tax purposes whether or not money was actually paid.

Imputed knowledge   If the facts are available to you and if it is your duty to know those facts, knowledge may be *imputed* to you and you are treated legally as if the facts are known.

Imputed negligence   If David is **negligent** and Paul is responsible for David's actions, David's negligence is *imputed* (carried over or attributed) to Paul.

Imputed notice   If Linda is given **notice** of something (a fact, a lawsuit, etc.) and Linda is Ruth's **agent** (lawyer, manager, etc.), then notice to Linda can be *imputed* as notice to Ruth.

In autre droit   (French) "In another's right." Representing someone else (as an **executor, trustee,** etc.) in a legal proceeding. [pronounce: in oh-tra dwat]

In banc   See **banc.**

In being   Existing now. See **life in being.**

In blank   Without restriction. Signing a **negotiable instrument,** such as a **check,** without making it **payable** to anyone in particular (leaving the "pay to" space empty).

In camera   (Latin) "In chambers"; in a judge's private office; also describes a **hearing** in court with all spectators excluded.

In common   With others; by all without division; together. Describes something shared on equal terms. For example, if two people own a house "*in common,*" they both own all of it.

In eadem causa   (Latin) In the same condition. [pronounce: in e-a-dem cow-sa]

In esse   (Latin) In being; now existing.

In evidence   *1.* Facts or things that are already before the court as **evidence.** *2.* "*Facts in evidence*" may be those facts already fully proved (but not necessarily believed, or believed to be important, by the jury).

In extremis   (Latin) In the last illness before dying.

In faciendo   (Latin) While doing something.

In fieri   (Latin) Incomplete. In the process of happening or being made. [pronounce: in fa-yer-e]

In forma pauperis   (Latin) "As a pauper." Describes a court filing that is permitted without payment of the customary fees or court costs if the person filing proves that he or she is too poor to pay.

In futuro (Latin) In the future; at some future time.

In genera **In kind.**

In haec verba (Latin) In these (same) words.

In hoc (Latin) In this; concerning this.

In integrum (Latin) To the original or former state.

In invitum (Latin) Against an adversary.

In jure (Latin) In law or by right. *In jure alterius* means "by another's right."

In kind The same type of thing. For example, a loan is returned "*in kind*" when a closely similar, but not identical, object is returned. An *in kind contribution* is of labor, materials, etc., rather than money.

In lieu of Instead of; in place of.

In limine (Latin) "At the beginning"; preliminary. A **motion** *in limine* is a (usually pretrial) request that prejudicial information be excluded as trial **evidence.**

In litem (Latin) See **ad litem.**

In loco parentis (Latin) In the place of a parent; acting as a parent with respect to the care and supervision of a child; acting with the power to discipline a child as a parent can.

In medias res (Latin) Into the heart or middle of a subject without introduction or preface.

In pais (French) *1.* Describes an act done informally, as opposed to one done by taking legal action or by making a formal document. *2.* Outside of the courtroom. See **pais.** [pronounce: in pay]

In pari delicto See **pari delicto.**

In pari materia See **pari materia.**

In perpetuity Forever.

In personam (Latin) Describes a lawsuit brought to enforce rights against another person, as opposed to one brought to enforce rights in a thing against the whole world (**in rem**). For example, a suit for automobile accident injuries is *in personam* because it is against the driver or owner only. A suit to establish **title** to land is *in rem* because, even if there is a person fighting the claim on the other side, a victory is binding against the whole world and a "thing" is primarily involved.

In pleno lumine (Latin) "In daylight"; common knowledge.

In posse (Latin) "In possibility"; not now or yet existing.

In praesenti (Latin) Right now.

In principio (Latin) At first; at the start.

In promptu (Latin) *1.* Now ready; in readiness. *2.* Without preparation.

In propria causa nemo judex (Latin) No one can be a judge in his or her own case.

In propria persona (or in pro. per.) **Pro se.**

In re (Latin) "In the matter of." This is a prefix to the name of a case "concerned with something," rather than a lawsuit directly between two persons. For example, *"In re Brown's Estate"* might be the name of a proceeding in **probate** court to dispose of the property of a dead person. The words are also sometimes used when a child is involved. For example, *"In re Mary Smith"* might be the name of a child **neglect** proceeding even though it is really against the parents. *"In re"* should *not* be used in an ordinary sentence as a substitute for "concerning." [pronounce: in ray]

In rem (Latin) Describes a lawsuit brought to enforce rights in a thing against the whole world as opposed to one brought to enforce rights against another person. For an example of each type of suit, see **in personam.** Also, there is a type of lawsuit "in between" *in rem* and *in personam* called *"quasi in rem"* or "sort of concerning a thing." *Quasi in rem* **actions** are really directed against a person, but are formally directed only against property (or vice versa); for example, a mortgage **foreclosure.**

In se (Latin) In and of itself. [pronounce: in say]

In solido (Latin) "As a whole"; **joint and several** (see that word). Each of several persons liable for an *in solido* debt can be held responsible for the entire debt.

In specie (Latin) *1.* In the same or similar form or way; **in kind.** But see no. 2. *2.* In specific; specific. For example, *"performance in specie"* usually is given the same meaning as *"specific* **performance."**

In terrorem (Latin) "In threat"; "in terror"; "by threat." An *in terrorem clause* in a will "threatens" a **beneficiary** with revocation of that person's **bequest** if he or she contests the will.

In testimonium (Latin) As a **witness** to; as **evidence** of.

In the black (red) Making a profit (taking a loss).

In toto (Latin) In whole; completely.

In transitu (Latin) While in transit.

Inadmissible Refers to facts or things that cannot be admitted into **evidence** in a trial; for example, evidence from an illegal search or most **hearsay.**

Inadvertence *1.* Lack of attention or carelessness. *2.* Excusable mistake or oversight.

Inalienable Something that cannot be given away, taken away, or sold. For example, "*inalienable rights*" are those basic **constitutional** rights that cannot be taken away.

Inc. Incorporated; for example: "Pink Ink, Inc." is the Pink Ink Corporation.

Incapacity *1.* Lack of legal ability or power to do something. For example, a child has a legal *incapacity* to vote or make **contracts**. *2.* An injury bad enough to prevent working.

Incarceration Confinement in a jail or prison.

Incest Sexual intercourse between a man and woman who, according to state law, are too closely related by blood or adoption.

Inchoate Partial, unfinished, unripened. For example, an "*inchoate instrument*" is a document, such as a **deed,** that is **valid** between the **parties,** but will not give the holder full rights or protections against most others until it is registered or recorded with the proper officials. [pronounce: in-<u>ko</u>-ate]

Incident of ownership An indication that a right or some property has been kept rather than fully given away; some measure of control kept over something.

Incidental Depending upon or relating to something else more important. "*Incidental damages*" are the "side costs" of a broken contract, such as storing the goods you thought were sold. A search is *incidental* to an arrest (and thus permissible) only if it is at the same time, limited in scope, and for a definite purpose.

Incite Urge, provoke, strongly encourage, or stir up.

Included offense A crime with a legal definition that is part, but not all, of the legal definition of a more serious crime. For example, **manslaughter** is a lesser crime included in *murder.* Also called "*lesser included offense.*"

Inclusio unius See **expressio unius.**

Income *1.* Money gains from business, work, or investments. *2.* All financial gain. *3. Accrued income* is earned but not necessarily received; *earned income* is from work or a business, rather than from investments; *gross income* is what is taken in before **deductions;** *imputed income* is a benefit that will be taxed as income even though it doesn't look like income; and *ordinary income* is from wages, interest, etc. (everything except **capital** gains, such as from the sale of stocks that go up, etc.).

Income averaging Reducing your taxes by showing that your income in prior years was far lower and by paying tax on the basis of your average income for several years. _Income averaging_ is currently available only for certain farmers.

Income basis   A way of figuring out the _rate of return_ (payoff) of a **security** (such as a stock or bond) by dividing the **interest** income or **dividend** paid in that time period by what you paid to buy the security.

Income splitting (or shifting)   See **assignment** _of income._

Income statement   See **statement** _of income._

Income tax   A tax on profits from business, work, or **investments,** but not on the increase in value of investments or property before they are sold. For income tax **return,** see **tax return.**

Incompatibility   _1._ Describes two or more ideas or things that cannot logically, physically, or legally coexist. _2._ The inability of a husband and wife to live together in marriage. _"Incompatibility"_ is **"grounds"** for a **divorce** in some states. In these states, a divorce may be granted without either person being at fault.

Incompetency   The lack of legal ability to do something; the condition of persons who lack the mental ability to manage their own affairs and who have someone appointed by the state to manage their finances.

Incompetent evidence   Facts, objects, **testimony,** etc., that may not be admitted into (used as) **evidence** in a legal proceeding.

Incomplete transfer   A gift or other transfer of property made by a person who keeps some of the control or benefits. If the person then dies, the value of that property may be included in his or her **estate** for tax purposes. See also **incident of ownership.**

Inconsistent   Contradictory, so that if one thing is **valid,** another thing cannot be valid. Or, if one thing is allowed to happen, another thing cannot be.

Incontestability clause   A provision in a life or health **insurance** policy that after a certain number of years the insurance company cannot get out of the contract by claiming that statements made in the original application were wrong.

Inconvenience   A broad word meaning anything from trivial problems to serious hardship or injustice. See also **forum non conveniens.**

Incorporate   Formally create a **corporation,** usually by filing _articles of incorporation_ and paying a fee. The persons who do this are called _incorporators._

Incorporate by reference   Make a part of something else by mere mention. For example, if document A says that "document B is _incorporated by reference,_" then document B becomes a part of document

A even though the words in document B are not rewritten into document A.

Incorporation doctrine   The principle that the **Bill of Rights,** which protects persons against certain actions of the federal government, also protects against most, but not all such actions by a state government because the **Fourteenth Amendment** requires it.

Incorporeal   Intangible; without physical substance. Rights such as **patents** are called *incorporeal property.*

Incorrigible   Uncorrectable or unmanageable. An *incorrigible* **juvenile** is a child who cannot be managed or controlled by parents or **guardians.**

Increment   *1.* One piece or part of a piece-by-piece increase (or decrease, which is also called a *decrement*). *2.* Anything gained or added. *3.* The process of gaining or adding to something.

Incriminate   Implicate in a crime or show involvement in a crime.

Incriminatory   Tending to show guilt.

Incroachment   See **encroachment.**

Inculpate   *1.* Accuse of guilt or crime. *2.* Involve in guilt or crime.

Incumbent   *1.* A person who presently holds an office (usually an elective public office). *2.* Required.

Incumber   See **encumber.**

Incumbrance   See **encumbrance.**

Incur   Get. Get something bad, such as a debt or **liability,** because the law places it on you. For example, you *incur a liability* when a court gives a money **judgment** against you.

Indebitatus assumpsit   See **assumpsit.**

Indecent   A general term meaning "offensive to public morality." For example: *indecent assault* (fondling or otherwise touching an unwilling person but with no intent to commit **rape**); *indecent exposure* (showing genitals in a public place); *indecent liberties* (fondling or otherwise taking sexual advantage of a child); and *indecent speech* (words, visuals, or symbolic actions that depict or describe, in an offensive way, sexual or excretory activities or organs). Indecent speech is not necessarily **obscene.**

Indefeasible   Describes a right that cannot be defeated, **revoked,** or taken away.

Indefinite sentence   See **indeterminate** *sentence.*

Indemnify   Compensate or promise to compensate a person who has suffered a loss or may suffer a future loss.

Indemnity A contract to compensate or reimburse a person for possible losses of a particular type; a type of **insurance.**

Indenture *1.* The written agreement of sale for **bonds** that contains the **maturity** date, interest rate, etc. *2.* Any **mortgage** or similar agreement in which there is a **lien** or similar **security** *interest. 3.* An apprenticeship agreement. *4.* An old word for a formal paper, such as a **deed,** with identical copies for each person signing it. *5.* An old word for a **deed** to real estate containing promises by both the **grantor** and **grantee.**

Independent agency A federal **agency, board** or **commission** that is not a part of one of the **cabinet** departments. These include the *Environmental Protection Agency, Federal Trade Commission, Federal Reserve Board,* and many others.

Independent contractor A person who contracts with an "employer" to do a particular piece of work by his or her own methods and under his or her own control.

Independent counsel An outside lawyer hired for special tasks, such as to give impartial advice or to conduct an investigation. When a government agency hires the lawyer for a criminal investigation, the word used is sometimes "special prosecutor." (The chief investigator in the Nixon impeachment was a special prosecutor and in the Clinton impeachment an independent counsel.)

Independent source rule The general rule that if new **evidence** can be traced to a source completely apart from the illegally gathered evidence that first led to the new evidence, it may be used by the government in a criminal trial. Compare with **fruit of the poisonous tree doctrine.**

Indestructible trust A **Claflin trust.**

Indeterminate With the exact time period not set. For example, an *indeterminate sentence* is a criminal sentence with a maximum or minimum set, but not the exact amount of time. Some states allow judges to set only indeterminate sentences, and have special **boards** to decide the exact sentence later.

Index fund A **mutual fund** that invests in stocks in the proportion that those stocks make up an index, such as the Dow Jones 30, Standard & Poor's 500, or Russell 3000. Its returns should generally parallel those of the index.

Index offenses The major crimes reported to the **F.B.I.,** such as **murder, rape, robbery,** etc.

Indexing Linking the level of payments (on **bonds,** wages, pension benefits, etc.) to an index such as the **Consumer Price Index.**

Indian   The word used for **Native American** in statutes and judicial decisions before about 1975. For *Indian reservation,* see **reservation.**

Indicia   Indications; pointers; signs; circumstances that make a certain fact probable, but not certain. For example, *indicia of partnership* are those circumstances that tend to show that a particular business arrangement is a partnership, and *indicia of title* are documents, such as photocopies of bills of sale, that show, but not conclusively, who holds title to personal property. [pronounce: in-<u>dish</u>-ee-a]

Indictment   A sworn written accusation of a crime, made against a person by a **prosecutor** to a *grand* **jury.** If the grand jury approves it as a *true bill,* the indictment becomes the document used against the person as a **defendant** in pretrial and trial proceedings. [pronounce: in-<u>dite</u>-ment]

Indigent   A poor person. An indigent criminal defendant is entitled to a free court-appointed lawyer.

Indignity   In **divorce** law, a type of mental cruelty that makes a marriage intolerable. *Indignity* includes continued abusive language and ridicule, and is **grounds** for divorce in some states.

Indirect attack   **Collateral attack.**

Indirect contempt   See **contempt.**

Indirect cost   **Fixed charges.**

Indirect evidence   **Circumstantial evidence.**

Indirect tax   *1.* A tax on a right, privilege, or event (such as the granting of the right to **incorporate**) rather than a tax on a purchase or on income, etc. *2.* The opposite of a **direct tax** (see that word).

Indispensable party   A person who has such a stake in the outcome of a lawsuit that the judge will not make a final decision unless that person is formally joined as a **party** to the lawsuit.

Individual Retirement Account   A bank or investment account into which some persons may set aside a certain amount of their earnings each year and have the interest taxed only later when withdrawn. (Some spouses without income may have I.R.A.s, and some persons who have tax-deferred pension or profit-sharing plans have limited or no use of I.R.A.s, depending on their income.) See also **Keogh Plan** and **S.E.P.**

Indorse   Sign a paper or document.

Indorsement   *1.* Signing a document "on the back" or merely signing it anywhere. *2.* Signing a **negotiable instrument,** such as a check, in a way that causes the piece of paper, and the rights it stands for, to transfer to another person. A *qualified indorsement* limits rights (for example, signing "without **recourse**") and a *restrictive indorsement* limits its purpose or the person who may use it (for example, signing "for deposit"). For **accommodation, blank,** and **conditional** indorsements, see those words. *3.* The signatures themselves in definitions no. 1 and no. 2.

Inducement   *1.* A statement or promise by a person that convinces another person to make a deal. A benefit or advantage of a deal. *2.* A thing that convinces someone to do something. The motive for an action.

Industrial relations   All employer-employee matters, such as safety, **benefits,** union recognition and bargaining, etc.

Industrial union   A labor union whose members may have different skills, but who work for the same type of industry (printing, clothing manufacture, etc.).

Industry   Any type of trade or business.

Ineffective counsel   See **effective counsel.**

Inevitable discovery   The principle that even if criminal **evidence** is gathered by unconstitutional methods, the evidence may be **admissible** if it definitely would have come to light anyway.

Infamy   The loss of a good reputation because of **conviction** of a major crime, and the loss of certain legal rights that accompanies this loss of reputation. An *infamous crime* used to be defined by *type* (such as **treason**), but is now defined by punishment possible (such as over a year in prison).

Infancy   A general word for being a very young child. In some states, however, this means the same as **minority.** An *infant* is either a very young child or a **minor** (see that word).

Inference   A fact (or proposition) that is *probably* true because a true fact (or proposition) leads you to believe that the *inferred* fact (or proposition) is also true. For example, if the first four books in a set of five have green covers, it is a reasonable *inference* that the fifth book has a green cover.

Inferior court   *1.* Any court but the highest one in a court system. *2.* A court with special, limited responsibilities, such as a **probate** *court.*

Infeudation   An obsolete word for granting a **freehold.**

Infirmative   Describes **evidence** or theories that weaken the impact of other evidence or theories. In **criminal** law, tending to **exculpate.**

Infirmity   A defect. For example, if the papers that transfer a **title** are defective, the title transferred has an *infirmity.*

Informal agreement   *1.* An agreement that is not fully formalized, but *is* valid; for example, some types of **oral contract**. But see no. 2. *2.* Not fully formalized, so *not* valid; for example, a **gentleman's agreement**. But see no. 1.

Informant   A person who gives information to law enforcement officers. For certain legal purposes, however, only persons who come forward with information on their own, rather than witnesses and persons questioned in the course of an investigation, are considered to be *informants.*

Information   *1.* A formal accusation of a crime made by a proper public official such as a prosecuting attorney. *2.* A sworn, written accusation of a crime that leads to an **indictment**. *3.* Personal knowledge of something. (But *"information and belief"* may mean no more than a person's good faith opinion.)

Informed consent   A person's agreement to allow something to happen (such as surgery) that is based on a full disclosure or full knowledge of the facts needed to make the decision intelligently.

Informed intermediary   In *product liability* law, a person in the chain of distribution (between manufacturer and user) who has been informed of product risks. In some cases (particularly those involving prescribing doctors) the manufacturer may not be liable for harm to the ultimate user (such as a patient) when the product is obtained from an *informed intermediary.*

Informer's privilege   The government's right in some situations to withhold the identity of persons who give information about illegal activity.

Infra   (Latin) *1.* Below or under. *2.* Within. *3.* Later in this book. For example, *"infra p. 236"* means "look at page 236, which is further on."

Infraction   *1.* A violation of a minor law. *2.* A violation or **breach** of a contract or a duty.

Infringement   *1.* A **breach** or violation of a right. *2.* The unauthorized making, using, selling, or distributing of something protected by a **patent, copyright,** or **trademark.**

Infuedation   See **infeudation.**

Ingross   See **engrossment.**

Inherent   Derived from and inseparable from the thing itself. For example, *"inherent danger"* is the danger some objects have by merely existing. A bomb is probably inherently dangerous, while a hammer is probably not.

Inherent powers   The powers a government must have to govern, even if not explicitly stated in its governing documents; for example, the constitutional power of the federal government to conduct foreign affairs or the power of the federal courts to protect constitutional rights.

Inherent vice   A basic defect that exists in an item no matter how it is used, or exists in a law no matter how it is applied.

Inherit   To legally receive ownership of property from the **estate** of a person who has died. Property can be *inherited* by **will** or, if the person died without a valid will, by **intestate succession.**

Inheritance   Property **inherited** by a person (or property that the person assumes will be inherited.) An *inheritance tax* is the tax that the person who inherits pays. This is not an **estate tax** (see that word).

Initial disclosure   The information that each **party** to a lawsuit must make available to all other parties without the need for a **discovery** request by those parties. In **federal courts,** this includes such things as a copy or description of relevant documents.

Initiative   The power of the people to directly enact laws by voting, without the need for passage by the **legislature.** *Initiative* also describes the *process* of direct enactment and the *proposed law* to be enacted.

Injunction   A judge's order to a person to do or to refrain from doing a particular thing. For example, a court might *issue an injunction* to "**enjoin**" (prevent) a company from dumping wastes into a river. An injunction may be *preliminary* or *temporary* (until the issue can be fully tried in court) or it may be *final* or *permanent.*

Injure   *1.* Hurt or harm. *2.* Violate the legal rights of another person. See **injury.**

Injuria   (Latin) A wrong or injury. *Injuria absque damno* means "a wrong done that does not result in harm or damage." The phrase describes a wrong that cannot support a lawsuit because no harm exists for the law to compensate. *Damnum absque injuria* means "a harm without legal injury." The phrase describes damage that cannot support a lawsuit because the damage was not caused by actions that the law forbids. *Injuria non excusat injuriam* means "one wrong does not excuse another." [pronounce: in-joo-ree-a]

Injury   *1.* Broadly, any wrong, hurt, or damage done to another person's rights, body, reputation, or property. *2.* As a technical legal word, a violation of another person's rights. In this sense, the *injury* causes **damage** (the loss or harm commonly called an "injury") and results in **damages** (payment for the *damage* suffered). For example, wrongfully hitting a person is an *injury,* the wound is the *damage,* and the court-ordered payment is the *damages.*

Innocent *1.* Not guilty. *2.* Not responsible for an action or event. For example, a person who does not know or suspect that the package he or she has been asked to deliver contains illegal drugs may be an *innocent agent*. *3.* Honestly; without knowledge. *4.* The *innocent construction rule* is the principle that if allegedly **libelous** words can be interpreted innocently, they should be read that way, especially if reading the statement as a whole makes the words less defamatory. Compare with **innuendo**. *5.* For *innocent purchaser,* see **bona fide** *purchaser.*

Inns of court Associations that govern the education and **admission** to the **bar** of prospective trial lawyers (called "**barristers**") in England.

Innuendo (Latin) "Meaning." The clause in some **complaints** for **defamation** that states the defamatory *meaning* given by the plaintiff to the words that were written or spoken by the defendant. Compare with **innocent** *construction rule.*

Inoperative Not now in effect.

Inquest *1.* A **coroner's hearing** (see those words) into the cause of a person's death, when that death was either violent or suspicious. *2.* Any formal inquiry; for example, into a person's sanity or into the validity of a **title**.

Inquisitorial system A method of trial in which the judge actively participates in fact-finding and in prosecution for the government. The *inquisitorial system* is different from the **adversary system** that exists in the U.S.

Insane See **insanity**.

Insanity *1. Insanity* is a legal, not a medical word, but it is no more precise than "crazy." It has different meanings in different situations: *2.* In various state proceedings to put a person into a mental hospital against his or her will because of *insanity,* the person may have to be "a danger to self or others," "incapable of caring for self and property," or "a fit subject for treatment." The definitions are often circular, allowing the locking up of "insane persons" and defining "insane persons" as those who need locking up. *3.* In a test of **capacity** to stand trial on a **criminal** charge, the definition of *insanity* is usually "an inability to understand the **charge** or to help in the **defense**." *4.* There are several different definitions of *insanity* when deciding whether a person is "not guilty (of a crime) by reason of insanity" (at the time it was committed). These include **M'Naghten's rule** and the **Durham Rule** (see those words). The *A.L.I. Model Penal Code* says, "A person is not responsible for criminal conduct if at the time of such conduct, as a result of mental disease or defect, he lacks *substantial capacity* either to appreciate the criminality (wrongfulness) of his conduct or to conform his conduct to the requirements of law." *5.* When deciding the capacity of a person to make a valid **will,** some of the signs of *insanity* are "inability to understand the property being given away, the purpose and manner of its distribution, and the persons who are to receive it." *6.* Other areas of law that may involve definitions of *insanity* include: **defenses** to a **contract, annulment** of a marriage, **divorce,** appointment of a **guardian,** etc.

Inscription   *1.* Formally placing (**"recording"**) a document, such as a mortgage, into the public record. *2.* Anything written on a durable surface such as on a ring, a tombstone, etc.

Insecurity clause   A section of a **note** or **contract** that gives a **creditor** the right to make an entire debt come due if there is a good reason to think that the **debtor** cannot or will not pay. Compare with **acceleration** *clause.*

Insider   *1.* A person who is an **officer** or **director** of a **corporation** or who owns over 10 percent of it. *Insider trading* is the illegal act of buying or selling a corporation's **securities** by an insider (or by a **tippee** "tipped off" by an insider) using *insider information* not available to the general public. *2.* Anyone who has information not available to the general public.

Insolvency   The condition of being **insolvent** (see that word).

Insolvent   *1.* Unable to pay debts as they come due. *2.* Having **liabilities** far greater than **assets.**

Inspection   *1.* Looking at things, documents, land, etc., often during the **discovery** process. *2.* *Inspection laws* allow site visits to determine such things as the cleanliness of serving food, the safety of work conditions or buildings, etc. See also *administrative* **search.**

Inspector General   The title of an official in various government agencies who supervises investigations and audits.

Installment   *1.* A separate delivery or payment. For example, an *installment contract* usually involves the delivery of goods in separate lots with payment made for each. *2.* A regular, partial payment of a debt. *Installment credit* is an arrangement in which a buyer pays the price (and, usually, interest and other finance charges) in regular (usually monthly) payments. *Installment* sales, loans, etc., are usually subject to **usury** laws (which set interest rate maximums) and *truth-in-lending laws* (which set disclosure requirements).

Instance   *1.* A forceful request. *2.* A situation or occurrence.

Instant   Present or current. The "*instant case*" means the current lawsuit.

Instanter   (Latin) Immediately.

Instigate Push into action (especially illegal action); **abet.**

Institutes An old word for various textbooks about the law.

Institution *1.* A public organization such as a college or a prison. *2.* The start of anything; for example, the commencement of a lawsuit. *3.* A basic system of laws.

Instructions Directions given by a judge during a trial, especially directions telling the jury how they should go about deciding the case. The *jury instructions* may include a summary of the questions to be decided and the laws that apply, plus an explanation of the **burden of proof.** These instructions may be *general* (applying to the whole case) or *special* (applying to part or to one legal point). For *instructed verdict,* see **directed verdict.**

Instrument *1.* A written document; a formal or legal document such as a **contract** or a **will.** *2.* Short for "**negotiable instrument**" (see that word). *3.* A tool, especially one with a definite purpose.

Instrumental trust A **ministerial** trust.

Instrumentality *1.* An organization that is totally controlled by another organization. *2.* See **instrument** no. 3.

Insubordination A **willful** failure or refusal to obey the reasonable orders of a superior who has the right to give such orders.

Insurable interest A person's real financial interest in another person or in an object. The "interest" is the fact that a person will suffer financially if the insured person dies or the insured object is lost. An **insurance** contract must involve an *insurable interest,* or it may be a form of gambling and unenforceable.

Insurance *1.* A **contract** in which one person pays money and the other person promises to reimburse the first person for specified types of losses if they occur. The person agreeing to compensate for losses is usually called the "*insurer*" or "*underwriter*"; the person who pays for this protection is the "*insured*"; the payment to the insurer is a "*premium*"; the written contract is a "*policy*"; the *insured's* financial interest in another person or in an object is the **insurable interest;** and the types of harm protected against are "*risks*" or "*perils.*" *2.* A few of the more common types of insurance (and the situations they cover) are as follows: *automobile liability* (injury to other persons or their property from an accident involving a car you own or drive); *casualty* (accidents and injuries); *credit life* (to pay off a car or other major purchase in case of death while installments are still owed); *group* (insurance provided at lower rates through an employer or other defined group of persons); *homeowners* (a set of different types of insurance that usually include fire, theft, and liability); *self* (putting aside money into an account that will be used to pay claims if they come up or merely being *prepared* to pay for possible losses or claims); *straight life* (life insurance with continuing payments); *term* (insurance that ends at the end of a certain time period); *title* (protection against claims disputing the title to land you own); *unemployment* (a government program through your job) and **workers' compensation.** *3.* There are hundreds of types of insurance and dozens of ways of arranging it. Some of these are defined under their own words, but many are too technical or too little used to be included.

Insured *1.* A person who buys insurance on property or life. *2.* A person whose life is insured.

Insurer The person or company that provides insurance.

Insurrection A violent rebellion against the government. Participating in an *insurrection* is a federal crime.

Intangibles Property that is really a right, rather than a physical object; for example, bank accounts, **stocks, copyrights, "goodwill"** of a business, etc.

Integrated *1.* Made whole or complete. *2.* See **integration.**

Integrated agreement A written contract in which the persons making the contract state that it is their full, complete, and final agreement. All the persons' previous discussions, promises, writings, and statements are said to be *merged* into the agreement, sometimes called an "*integration.*" See **parol evidence rule.**

Integrated bar A system in which all lawyers who practice before the courts of a geographical area must belong to one organization (the "bar"), which is supervised by the highest court of that area.

Integration *1.* The process of making something whole or complete. See **integrated** and the words following it. *2.* Bringing together different groups (such as races) as equals. *3.* Combining different businesses.

Intellectual property *1.* A **copyright, patent, trademark, trade secret,** or similar intangible right in an original tangible or perceivable work. See also **property.** *2.* The works themselves in no. 1. *3.* The right to obtain a copyright, patent, etc. for the works in no. 1.

Intelligible Clear; easily understood.

Intemperance See **habitual intemperance.**

Intended use doctrine The principle that the manufacturer of a product is responsible for any harm caused by the product when it is used as intended by the manufacturer, especially if used as shown or implied in the manufacturer's advertising. A manufacturer is also liable for harm caused by *foreseeable, unintended* uses.

Intendment   *1.* True, correct meaning. *2.* Intention.

Intent   *1.* The resolve or purpose to use a particular means to reach a particular result. "*Intent*" usually explains *how* a person wants to do something and *what* that person wants done, while "**motive**" explains *why*. These words often get confused. *2.* In **criminal** law, *intent* is divided into two types: *general* (intent to do something that the law prohibits); and *specific* (intent to do the exact thing **charged**). Also, if a person does something knowing that a certain result is likely, there is an *intent* to cause that result whether or not the person *desires* it.

Intention   Determination to do a certain thing (see **intent**).

Inter   Among or between. Compare with **intra.**

Inter alia   (Latin) "Among other things." The phrase is usually used when what is being mentioned is only part of what there is; for example, "In the box was, *inter alia,* a book."

Inter se   (Latin) Among or between themselves only. [pronounce: in-ter say]

Inter vivos   (Latin) "Between the living." An *inter vivos* **gift** is an ordinary gift, as opposed to a gift made shortly before dying. An *inter vivos* **trust** is an *ordinary* trust as opposed to one created under a **will** upon death.

Interdict (or interdiction)   *1.* A prohibition; a **decree** prohibiting something. *2.* A guardianship.

Interesse   (Latin) A legal interest or right. For example, an *interesse termini* is a **lease** held by a **tenant** who has not yet taken possession of the property.

Interest   *1.* A broad term for any right in property. For example, both an owner who **mortgages** land and the person who lends the owner money on the mortgage have an *interest* in the land. *2.* The extra money a person receives back for lending money to another person; money paid for the use of money. *3.* A basic right, especially the **constitutional** rights of ("*interests in*") *liberty* and *property* that require **due process** for their deprivation. *4.* For the various types of interest, such as: **compound, future, public,** or **security** interest, see those words.

Interested   Having a stake in the outcome of a decision or a dispute.

Interference   In **patent** law, a hearing between two (or more) persons, each claiming the same invention or discovery, to determine who has *priority of invention.*

Interim   Temporary; meanwhile. For example, *interim financing* may be a short-term construction loan, with final financing provided later by a **mortgage.**

Interior   Short for Department of the Interior. The U.S. **cabinet** department that manages public lands, Native American affairs, natural resources, etc.

Interlineation   Writing between the lines.

Interlocking directorates   **Boards** *of directors* that have some of the same directors.

Interlocutory   *1.* Provisional; temporary; while a lawsuit is still going on. An *interlocutory order* is an **intermediate order** (see that word). The *Interlocutory Appeals Act* (28 U.S.C. 1292 (1948)) is a federal law that provides for an **appeal** while a trial is going on if the trial judge states in writing: 1) A legal question has come up that directly affects the trial. 2) There are major questions as to how that point of law should be resolved. 3) The case would proceed better if the appeals court answers the question.

Intermediate court   An **appellate** court that is subject to **judicial review** by a higher appellate court.

Intermediate order   An **order,** made by a judge during a trial, that is not a **final decision,** so you cannot **appeal** it.

Intermediation   Investing through a bank or other financial institution.

Intermingling   See **commingling** and **confusion.**

Internal financing   Raising money for projects by keeping earnings, by using tax savings due to **depreciation** deductions, and by other methods that do not involve selling **stock** or borrowing.

Internal law   The law of a country (or state) that applies to disputes wholly within that country; a country's laws excluding its **conflict of laws** rules.

Internal Revenue Code   (26 U.S.C. 1) The primary United States **tax** laws.

Internal security acts   (8 U.S.C. 1101) Federal laws controlling the subversive activities of communist organizations and others whose purpose it is to overthrow or disrupt the government.

International Court of Justice   A branch of the United Nations that settles voluntarily submitted disputes between countries and also gives **advisory opinions** to the branches of the United Nations.

International law   *1. Public international law* is the customary law that applies to the relationships and interactions between countries. *2. Private international law* is the set of principles that determines which country's courts should hear a dispute and which country's laws should apply to each situation. It is sometimes called **conflict of laws.**

International Shoe doctrine See **minimum contacts doctrine.**

Internment The confining of enemy foreigners or persons suspected of disloyalty during war.

Interpellation *1.* Questioning. *2.* A short-term agreement. *3. Not* **inter*po*lation.**

Interpleader *1.* A procedure in which persons having conflicting claims against a third person may be forced to resolve the conflict before seeking relief from the third person. For example, if A is sued by B for a debt and A thinks that C might have a legitimate claim against A for the same debt, A may *interplead* C (bring in or "join" C as a **party**) to the suit. *2. Interpleader* also refers to the settling or deciding of claims between **defendants** in order to then settle or decide claims between the **plaintiff** and the defendants.

Interpol An international criminal police organization that coordinates various law enforcement agencies from various countries.

Interpolation *1.* The insertion of words into a completed document. *2. Not* **inter*pel*lation.**

Interpose *1.* Intervene in a dispute. See **intervention.** *2.* Interject or present. To *interpose* a **defense** is to present one (interject it between what the plaintiff asks for and possibly gets). *3. Interposition* is the principle, now dead, that a state may reject a federal government demand if the state considers the demand **unconstitutional.**

Interpretation *1.* The process of discovering or deciding the meaning of a written document by studying only the document itself and not the circumstances surrounding it. But see no. 2. *2.* Studying the document *and* surrounding circumstances to decide the document's meaning. See **construction.**

Interpretive rule An **administrative agency's** statement about what it thinks a **statute** or **regulation** means, rather than a change of an existing regulation. (A change is a *substantive rule,* which is usually subject to procedural requirements such as publication and the right of interested persons to comment before the rule takes effect.)

Interrogation Questioning by police, especially of a person suspected or accused of a crime. A *custodial interrogation* involves a restraint of freedom, so it requires a **Miranda warning.** A routine *investigatory interrogation* involves no restraint and no accusation of a crime.

Interrogatories *1.* Written questions sent from one side in a lawsuit to another, attempting to get written answers to factual questions or seeking an explanation of the other side's legal contentions. These are a part of the formal **discovery** process in a lawsuit and usually take place before the trial. *2.* In some states, written questions addressed to any **witness.** *3.* See **special interrogatories.**

Interspousal immunity   A prohibition against **tort** actions by one spouse against the other. *Interspousal immunity* has been abolished or greatly limited in most states. *Not* **marital communications privilege.**

Interstate Commerce Act   A federal law that **regulates** the surface transportation of goods and persons between states; regulates rates for railroads, pipelines, etc., formerly through the Interstate Commerce Commission, now through the Surface Transportation Board of the Department of Transportation.

Interstate compact   An agreement between or among states that has been passed as law by the states and has been approved by Congress.

Interval ownership   Property ownership for part of each year; for example, ownership of a vacation condominium unit for two weeks each year. Also called *timeshare.*

Intervening cause   A cause of an accident or other injury that will remove the blame from the wrongdoer who originally set events in motion. It is also called an "*intervening act,*" "*intervening agency,*" "*intervening force,*" "*superseding cause,*" "*supervening negligence,*" etc.

Intervenor   A person who voluntarily **enters** (becomes a **party** in) a lawsuit between other persons (see **intervention**).

Intervention   A proceeding by which a person is allowed to become a **party** to a lawsuit by joining the **plaintiff,** joining the **defendant,** or making separate claims. See also **joinder.**

Intestacy   See **intestate.**

Intestate   *1.* Without a **will.** *Dying intestate* is dying without having a valid will or without having a will that covers all of the dead person's property. *2.* A person who dies without a valid will.

Intestate succession   The distribution of **inheritances** to **heirs** according to a state's laws about who should collect. This is done when there is no valid **will** or when the will does not cover some of a dead person's property.

Intolerable cruelty   Same as **cruelty.**

Intoxication   A greatly lessened ability to function normally caused by alcohol or drugs. *Involuntary intoxication* (caused by others against your will) is a defense against **criminal** charges and **negligence** suits, while *voluntary intoxication* is only relevant in determining a state of mind when proving a particular state of mind as part of a criminal charge.

Intra "Within." For example, *intrastate commerce* is business carried out entirely within one state, as opposed to *interstate commerce* (see **Interstate Commerce Act**). *Intra* is usually contrasted with either *inter* (meaning between or among) or with **ultra** (see that word).

Intrinsic evidence Facts learned from a **document** itself, not from outside information about it.

Intrinsic fraud Fraud that directly involves the issues in a lawsuit. Compare with **extrinsic fraud.**

Intrinsic value Value of a thing itself, not the **market value.** For example, the intrinsic value of a rare stamp, measured by the value of the materials, is next to nothing.

Introduction of evidence **Admission** *of evidence.* (Sometimes used to mean the **offer** or **submission** of something for admission.)

Inure Take effect; result. For example, if "benefits *inure* to Mr. Smith," they will come to him and take effect for him. "*Inurement*" usually means taking effect by **operation of law,** rather than by a person's actions.

Invade (or invasion) *1.* Infringe (or **infringement**). *2. Invade the principal* means make payments out of **principal** that are normally made only out of **interest.**

Invalid *1.* Inadequate; useless. *2.* Not binding; lacking legal force.

Invasion of privacy Publicizing someone's private affairs that are of no legitimate public concern; using a person for publicity without permission; eavesdropping; or violation of the right to be left alone. This may be a **tort.**

Invention In **patent** law, the process of producing, by independent work, something not previously known or existing. *Invention* also refers to the thing produced. While the term is sometimes used to include *discovery,* the mere discovery of something existing but previously unknown is not patentable.

Inventory *1.* A detailed list of articles of property. *2.* Goods or materials held for sale or lease. *3.* Materials used in, or partially completed products of, a business.

Inverse condemnation A lawsuit against the government to demand payment for an informal or irregular taking of private property.

Inverse order of alienation doctrine The rule that when a piece of land has been sold off in separate parcels and a person must collect on a **mortgage** or **lien** on the original land, the person must now collect first on the piece still held by the original owner, then on the piece sold last, then next to last, and so on until paid off.

Investment Using money to make money (buying **stocks,** putting cash in a savings account, etc.).

Investment banker An underwriter (see **underwrite**) or a middleman between a **corporation** putting out new **stocks** and **bonds** and the buying public. The *investment banker* may form a group of bankers to buy the stocks outright and then resell them or merely buy some and act as **agent** for the rest.

Investment Company Act (15 U.S.C. 80) A federal law that **regulates** persons and companies: that trade in **securities** such as **stocks, bonds,** and *commodity* **options** (or claim to trade in them); that invest in large blocks of securities; that invest in other companies; etc.

Investment contract Under federal law, any agreement that involves an investment of money pooled with others' money to gain profits solely from the efforts of others.

Investment credit A tax **credit** (see that word) for some property (such as buildings and major machines) bought for a business.

Investment securities **Stocks, bonds,** etc. See **security.**

Investment trust A company that sells its own stock and invests the money in stocks, real estate, etc. A **mutual fund** is one example, as is a **real estate investment trust.**

Invidious discrimination See **discrimination** no. 2.

Invitation *1.* Asking someone to come onto your property for a particular purpose involving your benefit or keeping land or a building in such a way as to make persons think that you want them to come in. For example, a store owner "*invites*" the public to come in by actions, signs, and ads. The person who comes in is an **invitee** rather than merely a **licensee** (see that word).

Invited error doctrine The principle that when one side in a lawsuit gets away with using **inadmissible** evidence, the other side may use similar evidence to refute it.

Invitee A person who is at a place by **invitation** (see that word). Note: a social caller may not be an "*invitee*," but a "**licensee**" (see that word).

Invoice A list sent by a merchant that details goods sent to another person (often a purchaser) and usually gives prices item by item.

Invoke *1.* Enforce; put into operation or legal effect. *2.* Use as a source of **authority.**

Involuntary commitment See **civil commitment.**

Involuntary confession A confession to a crime that cannot be used because the way it was obtained violates the **constitutional right**

against compelled **self-incrimination.** A confession is *involuntary* if the government got it by force, threats, promises, or undue influence.

Involuntary conversion   Loss of property by theft, casualty, or public condemnation. Most financial gain (from insurance on the lost property, payment for the condemnation, etc.) due to an *involuntary conversion* will not be taxed as income until a later time if property similar to what was lost is bought soon after.

Involuntary intoxication   See **intoxication.**

Involuntary manslaughter   See **manslaughter.**

Involuntary servitude   The forcing of one person to work for another.

Involuntary trust   A **constructive trust.**

Ipse dixit   (Latin) "He himself said it." Describes a statement that depends for its persuasiveness on the authority of the person who said it. Something asserted, but not proved.

Ipso facto   (Latin) "By the fact itself"; "by the mere fact that."

Ipso jure   (Latin) By **operation of law** alone.

Irreconcilable differences   **Grounds** for a **divorce** in some states because the marriage has simply broken down. Compare with **no fault** *divorce.*

Irrecusable   Cannot be challenged or rejected.

Irregularity   The failure to proceed properly. The failure to take the proper formal steps in the proper way while involved in a lawsuit or doing some official act. An *irregularity* is not an illegal act, but it may be serious enough to invalidate or otherwise harm what a person is trying to accomplish.

Irrelevant   Not related to the matter at hand. For example, *irrelevant evidence* is proposed **evidence** that will not help to either prove or disprove any point that matters in a lawsuit.

Irreparable injury   Probable harm that cannot be properly remedied by money alone, and that is serious enough to justify an **injunction** (see that word) or other unusual court action.

Irresistible impulse   The loss of control due to **insanity** that is so great that a person cannot stop from committing a crime. This is one of many vague "*tests*" used to decide whether a person will be treated as a criminal (and put away in jail) or treated as a mental patient (and put away in a mental hospital).

Irrevocable   Incapable of being called back, stopped, or changed. See **revocation** and **revoke.**

Issuable   *1.* Describes a **security** that can be offered for sale legally. *2.* Can be litigated; especially referring to a legal **issue** that is stated with enough specificity to allow its **adjudication.** *3.* Open to dispute. *4.* A possible outcome.

Issue   *1.* To send forth, put out, or **promulgate** officially. For example, when a court *issues* a **writ** or other legal paper, it gives it to a court officer to be served on (delivered to) a person. *2.* One single point in dispute between two sides in a lawsuit. An issue may be "*of law*" (a dispute about how the law applies to the case) or "*of fact*" (about the truth of a fact). *3.* Descendants (children, grandchildren, etc.). *4.* A group of **stocks** or **bonds** that are offered or sold at the same time. *5.* The first transfer of a **negotiable instrument** such as a check.

Issue preclusion   See **collateral estoppel** and **res judicata.**

Ita est   (Latin) "So it is." A formal statement put on a copy of a document by a **notary public** when the original document was notarized by an earlier notary.

Item   *1.* A separate **entry** in an **account** or list. *2.* One single sum of money for a particular purpose in an **appropriation.**

Itemize   *1.* List by separate articles or items; break down something by listing its separate parts. *2.* For *itemized deductions,* see **deduction.**

Iter   (Latin) Right of way.

J *1.* Judge (or Justice). For example, *"Johnson, J."* means Judge (or Justice) Johnson. *2.* Journal.

J.A.G. Judge advocate general. See **military law.**

J.D. Short for "Juris Doctor" or "Doctor of Jurisprudence." This is now the basic law degree, replacing the "LL.B." in the late 1960s. There are many other law degrees offered in other countries and many advanced law degrees offered here and elsewhere. These include the LL.M., LL.D., B.L., J.C.D., D.C.L., etc.

J.J. Judges or Justices. See **J.**

J.N.O.V. Judgment **non obstante veredicto.**

J.P. Justice of the peace. A local judge.

Jackson-Denno hearing A criminal case **suppression** hearing (named after *Jackson v. Denno,* 378 U.S. 368 (1964)) in which a confession (or other statement by a defendant) is challenged as involuntary, and thus excluded as evidence.

Jactitation False boasting or false claims.

Jail A place of confinement for time periods longer than those usual for a police station lockup and shorter than those usual for a **prison.** A jail is usually used to hold persons either convicted of **misdemeanors** (minor crimes) or persons who cannot get out on **bail** while awaiting trial.

Jailhouse lawyer A popular name for a prisoner who helps other prisoners with legal problems, such as getting **sentences** reduced.

Jane Doe The female version of **John Doe** (see that word).

Jason clause A provision in a **bill of lading** that requires a cargo owner to contribute to the **general average loss** (see that word), even if the loss was caused by **negligence,** as long as the shipowner was careful in outfitting and crewing the ship.

Jay walking Crossing a street in any but a safe, legal way.

Jencks rule (18 U.S.C. 3500) A federal criminal **defendant** must be given government documents needed to **cross-examine** witnesses (for prior statements inconsistent with current **testimony,** etc.).

Jeofaile statute A law that allows **pleadings** to be freely corrected. [pronounce: ja-fail]

Jeopardy *1.* Danger; hazard; peril. *2.* The risk of **conviction** and punishment faced by a **defendant** in a criminal trial. [pronounce: jep-er-dee]

Jeopardy assessment The right of the **I.R.S.** to **assess** and collect a tax immediately if tax **evasion** is probable (for example, if the taxpayer plans to leave the country).

Jetsam *1.* Goods thrown off a ship to lighten it in an emergency. *2.* Any goods jettisoned (thrown off) a ship that float on the water or are washed up on land. Compare **flotsam.**

Jim Crow **Segregation** laws, now **unconstitutional.**

Job action A **strike** or work slowdown, usually by public employees.

Jobber *1.* A person who buys and sells for other persons. *2.* A **wholesaler.**

John Doe A made-up name used in some types of lawsuits in which there is no real **defendant,** in a legal proceeding against a person whose name is not yet known, to protect a person's identity, or as a name for a person in an example used to teach law. (He tends to have many legal dealings with Richard Roe, the owner of Whiteacre.)

Joinder Joining or uniting together. For example, *joinder of parties* is the bringing in of a new person who joins together with the **plaintiff** as a plaintiff or the **defendant** as a defendant; *joinder of issue* is when a lawsuit gets past the preliminary stages and issues are clearly laid out, with one side asserting the truth of each point and the other side asserting its falsity; *nonjoinder* is the failure to bring in a person who is necessary as a **party** to a lawsuit; *misjoinder* is improper or mistaken joinder; and *collusive joinder* is bringing in an unnecessary party from another state in order to have the case brought in federal court. If a party or an issue *must* be included in a case, it is called *compulsory joinder;* otherwise it is *permissive joinder.*

Joint Together; as a group; united; undivided. For example, a "*joint return*" is a combined reporting of income taxes by a husband and wife, and a *joint work* in **copyright** law is written by two or more authors with the intention that their contributions be merged into one whole.

Joint adventure (or joint venture) A "one-shot" grouping together of two or more persons in a business. If they have a continuing relationship, it may be a **partnership** (see that word).

Joint and several Both together and individually. For example, a **liability** or debt is *joint and several* if the **creditor** may sue the **debtors** either as a group (with the result that the debtors would have to split the loss) or individually (with the result that one debtor might have to pay the whole thing).

Joint and survivor See **annuity.**

Joint authorship An act of creation of a work by more than one creator. See _joint work_ under **joint.** Mere additions or improvements do not give a person the right to claim _joint authorship_ of a book, a song, etc.

Joint bank account A bank account held in the names of two or more persons, each of whom has full authority to put money in or take it out.

Joint committee Any committee (other than a **conference committee**) made up of members of both **houses** of a **legislature.**

Joint debtors acts _1._ State laws that allow a judge to grant a **judgment** for or against some **defendants** who owe money and allow the trial to go on against the others. _2._ State laws that allow a **plaintiff** to go ahead with a lawsuit when only some of the defendants who owe money have been served with **process** (formally told to show up in court), and to get a judgment against all of them.

Joint enterprise A **joint adventure.**

Joint estate The ownership of property by _joint_ **tenants** (see that word).

Joint lives A phrase used in certain **deeds** to define the length of a **life estate.** For example, "to Beau for the _joint lives_ of Mac and Otto" means that Beau has a right until _either_ Mac _or_ Otto dies.

Joint resolution See **resolution.**

Joint stock company A company that is "more than" a **partnership,** but "less than" a **corporation** (see those words). It is similar to a corporation in most ways, but all owners are **liable** for company debts.

Joint tenancy See _joint_ **tenant.**

Joint through rate The charge for shipping something from a point on one transportation line to a point on another.

Joint venture See **joint adventure.**

Jointure An old **common law** marriage settlement of a **life estate** in land received instead of **dower.**

Joker A clause or phrase inserted in a _legislative_ **bill** (or a contract or other document) that is superficially harmless, but actually destroys the bill's effectiveness.

Jones Act (46 U.S.C. 688) A federal law that permits ship employees (such as merchant seamen) to sue for **damages** if injured and provides other protections.

Journal _1._ A book that is written in regularly, such as an **account** book, in which all expenses paid and all money taken in are written down as they occur. _2._ A periodical magazine such as a _law journal._

Journalists' privilege *1.* The right of a publisher or writer to make "**fair comment**" upon the actions of public officials without being **liable** for **defamation.** This privilege exists so long as the writer and publisher didn't know (and didn't recklessly disregard their obligation to find out) that the statements were false. *2.* See **shield law.**

Journey worker (or journeyman or woman) *1.* A person who has completed apprenticeship training in a trade or craft. *Journey worker's pay* (or "union scale") is the minimum wage paid to an experienced worker in a particular job in a geographic area. *2.* A day worker or hired hand.

Joyriding Stealing a car to ride around, rather than to keep it.

Judex (Latin) A judge.

Judge *1.* The person who runs a courtroom, decides all legal questions, and sometimes decides entire cases by also deciding factual questions. *2.* Decide.

Judge advocate A military legal officer who may act as a judge or a lawyer. A *judge advocate general* heads the legal system of each service (army, navy, etc.).

Judge-made law *1.* Law that results from judicial **precedent** rather than from **statutes.** *2.* **Judicial activism.**

Judgment *1.* The official decision of a court about the rights and claims of each side in a lawsuit. *"Judgment"* usually refers to a final decision that is based on the facts of the case and made at the end of a trial. It is called a *judgment on the merits. 2.* There are, however, other types of judgments. For example, a *consent judgment* is the putting of a court's approval on an agreement between the sides about what the judgment in the case should be; a *default judgment* is one given to one side because the other side does not show in court or fails to take proper procedural steps; and an *interlocutory judgment* is one given on either a preliminary issue or a side issue during the course of a lawsuit. For other types of *judgments,* such as **cognovit note, confession of, declaratory, default, deficiency, non obstante veredicto,** etc., see those words.

Judgment book (or docket) A list of court **judgments** kept for public inspection. Also called a *civil docket* or *criminal docket,* depending on the type of case.

Judgment creditor A person who has proven a debt in court and is entitled to use court processes to collect it. The person owing the money is a *judgment debtor.*

Judgment note The paper a debtor gives to a creditor to allow **confession of judgment.**

Judgment-proof Persons against whom a money **judgment** will have no effect (persons without money, persons protected by wage-protection laws, etc.).

Judicature Relating to the **judicial** branch of government; the judicial branch of government itself. For example, in England, the _Judicature Acts_ set up their modern system of courts.

Judicia (Latin) **Trials, judgments,** or **decisions.** [pronounce: ju-<u>dish</u>-ee-a]

Judicial _1._ Having to do with a court. _2._ Having to do with a judge. _3._ Describes the branch of government that interprets the law and that resolves legal disputes. _4. Not_ "**judicious.**" [pronounce: ju-<u>dish</u>-al]

Judicial act Any act, whether proper or improper, taken by a judge in his or her official capacity. Although improper judicial acts may be subject to **judicial review** or to discipline, judges usually have absolute **judicial immunity** from lawsuits based on these acts.

Judicial activism A judge's decision that ignores strict **precedent** in order to bring about a result the judge thinks is just and that is in keeping with the judge's view of how society as a whole should operate. The opposite is **judicial restraint.**

Judicial admission See **admissions.**

Judicial discretion The right of a judge to have great leeway in making decisions, so long as he or she follows the law and proper procedures and refrains from arbitrary action.

Judicial fact See **judicial notice.**

Judicial immunity A judge's complete protection from personal **liability** in lawsuits based on the judge's official duties, even in situations where the judge acted in bad faith.

Judicial notice The act of a judge in recognizing the existence or truth of certain facts without bothering to make one side in a lawsuit prove them. This is done when the facts are either common knowledge and undisputed (such as the fact that Argentina is in South America) or are easily found and cannot be disputed (such as the text of the Constitution).

Judicial question An issue that the courts may decide, as opposed to one that only the **executive** branch may decide (a **political question**) or that only the **legislature** can decide (a _legislative question_). A _judicial question_ is also different from a _moot question_ (an issue that has no practical effect on the case being decided).

Judicial restraint A judge's decision and decision-making that excludes the judge's personal views and relies strictly on **precedent.** Contrast **judicial activism.**

Judicial review *1.* A court's power to declare a statute **unconstitutional** and to interpret laws. *2.* An **appeal** from an **administrative agency** decision. In the federal government the general rules governing this are in the *Judicial Review Act. 3.* A higher court's examination of a lower court's decision.

Judicial sale A sale held under a court **judgment** or **order** or held under court supervision. See also **execution.**

Judiciary The branch of government that interprets the law; the branch that judges. For example, the Judiciary Act of 1789 set up the system of federal courts. [pronounce: ju-<u>dish</u>-ee-ary]

Judicious With the use of good judgment. *Not* "**judicial.**" [pronounce: ju-<u>dish</u>-us]

Jump bail *1.* Leave the area or hide to avoid going to court while "out on **bail.**" *2.* Fail to show up in court while on bail.

Jump citation See **pinpoint citation.**

Junior Describes an **interest** or a right that collects after, or is subordinate to, another interest or right. See **subordination.**

Junk bond A high-yield, high-risk **bond** with no credit rating or with a rating below "investment grade."

Jura (Latin) Rights or laws.

Jural *1.* Having to do with the basic or fundamental law of rights and obligations. *2.* Describes legal rather than moral rights and obligations.

Jurat Name for the written statement on an **affidavit** about where, when, and before whom it was sworn to.

<u>Jure</u> (Latin) Right; by the right or law of. See **de jure.**

Jur<u>i</u>dical *1.* Having to do with the court system or with a judge. *2.* Regular; conforming to law and court practice. *3.* Intended to have legal consequences. *4.* For a *juridical person* see **juristic person.**

Juris (Latin) Of right or of law.

Juris doctor *Doctor of laws.* The basic U.S. law degree. See **J.D.**

Juris et de jure (Latin) "By law and right." Describes a **conclusive** *presumption.*

Jurisdiction *1.* The geographical area within which a court (or a public official) has the right and power to operate. *2.* The persons about whom and the subject matters about which a court has the right and power to make decisions that are legally binding. For types of jurisdiction, such as **ancillary, appellate, in personam, in rem,** etc., see those words.

Jurisdictional *1.* Having to do with **jurisdiction** (see that word). *2.* Essential for jurisdiction. For example, the "*jurisdictional amount*" is the value of a claim being made in a case. Some courts take only those cases that have jurisdictional amounts above or below a certain money limit. _Jurisdictional facts_ are those things a court must know before taking and keeping a case (such as whether the **defendant** has received proper **service,** etc.).

Jurisdictional dispute   A conflict between unions, either as to which union should represent certain workers or as to which union's members should do a certain type of work. Strikes based on these disputes are generally illegal.

Jurisprudence   The study of law and legal philosophy.

Jurist   _1._ A judge. _2._ A legal scholar.

Juristic act   Something done that is intended to have (and capable of having) a legal effect.

Juristic person   A person for legal purposes. This includes both natural persons (individuals) and **artificial persons (corporations),** but sometimes refers only to corporations.

Juror   A person who is a member of a **jury.**

Jury   A group of persons selected by law and sworn in to consider certain facts and determine the truth. The two most common types of juries are a _grand jury_ (persons who receive complaints and accusations of crime, hear preliminary evidence on the complaining side, and make formal accusations or **indictments**) and a _petit jury_ or _trial jury_ (usually twelve, but sometimes as few as six persons who decide questions of **fact** in many trials). There are also **coroner's** juries, **advisory juries,** and other types.

Jury box   The enclosed place where the jury sits during a trial.

Jury commission   A committee of private citizens that picks **jurors.** In some places, this job is done by a _jury_ **clerk.**

Jury fixing (or tampering)   Illegally influencing a juror or jurors (often through bribery) to influence the outcome of a trial.

Jury list   _1._ A list of those **jurors** selected to try a case. _2._ A list of all jurors commanded to be in court to be selected for various cases. _3._ A list of all possible jurors.

Jury nullification   A jury's rejection of the evidence it was instructed to consider or the law it was instructed to follow, usually because the jurors do not want to reach a verdict they consider unfair.

Jury trial   A trial with a judge and jury, not just a judge. This is a **constitutional** right in **criminal** cases and in many **civil** cases. In some states, the lowest court does not use a jury, but these states allow an "appeal of right" to another trial, or an initial choice between two courts, the higher of which offers the *jury trial* option.

Jury wheel   A device for randomly selecting jurors from a list of eligible citizens.

Jus   (Latin) *1.* Right or justice. *2.* Law, or the whole body of law. For example: *jus belli* (the law of war, wartime rights); *jus civile* (**civil law,** Roman law, or the law of one country); *jus commune* (**common law**); *jus gentium* (the law of nations or **international law**); *jus naturae* (the "law" of nature); *jus naturale* (**natural law**); *jus privatum* (the law of private rights); *jus publicum* (public or governmental law); and *jus soli* (the law of a person's birthplace; also, citizenship in a country because you are born there). *3.* A particular right. For example: *jus disponendi* (the right to do what you want with your own property or the right of a seller to let **title** pass or keep it until all payments are made); *jus dividendi* (the right to give property by **will**); *jus habendi* (the right to possess something); *jus sanguinis* ("law of the blood"; citizenship in a country because your parents are citizens); and *jus tertii* (the right of someone not involved in a lawsuit to property that is involved in the suit).

Just   *1.* Legal or lawful. *2.* Morally right; fair. Words like "*just cause*" and "*just compensation*" include both meanings (no. 1 and no. 2) of "just."

Justice   *1.* Fairness in treatment by the law. *2.* Short for *Department of Justice.* The U.S. **cabinet** department that manages the country's legal business. It represents the U.S. in both **civil** and **criminal** matters, runs the federal prison system, and has specialized departments that handle antitrust, civil rights, the Federal Bureau of Investigation, immigration and naturalization, etc. *3.* A judge, especially an appellate judge such as a justice of the U.S. Supreme Court.

Justice of the peace   One type of local judge.

Justiciable   Proper to be decided by a particular court. For example, a "*justiciable controversy*" is a real, rather than hypothetical, dispute. Federal courts may handle only cases that present a justiciable controversy. [pronounce: jus-<u>tish</u>-able]

Justification   A legally valid reason that frees a person from **liability** for intentional acts that would otherwise have been unlawful. For example, **self-defense** may be *justification* for a killing. Compare with **excuse.**

Juvenile   *1.* Not yet an adult for the purpose of the criminal law. *2.* Not yet an adult. A minor. This may be a different age than no. 1.

Juvenile court   A court set up to handle cases of either **delinquent** or neglected children.

K Abbreviation for **contract.**

K.B. King's Bench.

Kangaroo court A popular expression for a mock court with no legal powers.

Kansas v. Hendricks (521 U.S. 346) A 1997 U.S. Supreme Court decision that permitted indefinite **civil commitment** for repeat violent offenders.

Keep To carry on or manage (a hotel); to tend or shelter (a dog); to maintain continuously (a record book); to store (a box); to continue without change (a ship's course); or to protect (a child).

Keogh Plan ("H.R.10 Plan") A tax-free retirement account for persons with self-employment income. [pronounce: key-oh]

Key numbers A reference system that classifies legal subjects by specific topics and subtopics, using a "Key Number" (such as "theaters and shows 6(18) athletic events") attached to each topic. Key numbers help you to find cases by subject in the **American Digest System** and the **National Reporter System** (see those words). The Key Number system was developed by West Publishing Company.

Key person insurance Life or disability insurance bought by and for a company that insures a vital employee.

Key-word search A search using words specified by a **database** rather than using words that might be there.

Kick out clause A contract provision that lets one side end the contract if a specific thing happens or fails to happen.

Kickback Something given to a company (or government) employee for doing a favor for another company. This may be a crime if done, for example, by a federal **contractor.**

Kicker *1.* Any loan charge in addition to interest. *2.* Any extra charge or penalty.

Kiddie tax Slang for a federal tax on certain unearned income (over a certain amount) of children under fourteen. The income is taxed at the parent's highest rate to discourage *income* **shifting.**

Kidnapping Taking away and holding a person illegally, usually against the person's will or by force.

Kin (or kindred) *1.* Persons with a blood relationship. *2.* Persons with any relationship by blood or marriage.

Kind See **in kind.**

King's Bench (or Queen's Bench) An English court that developed most of the "**common law**" (see that word) that has become the basis for the law in the United States.

Kiting Writing checks on an **account** before money is put in to cover them.

Kleptocracy Slang for a government that is looted by those who run it.

Knock and announce rule The rule that a police officer making a legal arrest or search may break down a door only after first stating his or her authority and purpose for being there and after entrance is refused or avoided. This rule has exceptions such as if knocking is a *useless gesture* (because the officer is sure that the occupant knows the purpose of the visit) or if a search is conducted with a *no-knock warrant* (granted because, without surprise, evidence will probably be destroyed).

Knock down An auctioneer's acceptance of a **bid** as final. This gives the bidder the right to the property once it is paid for.

Knowingly With full knowledge and intentionally; **willfully.**

Kovel accountant An accountant hired by a lawyer, so the accountant's work is usually covered by the lawyer-client **privilege.** Turning prior accounting work over to a lawyer does not get the privilege. The name comes from the 1961 Second Circuit case *Kovel v. U.S.* (296 F.2d. 918).

L.A.M.A.   Legal Assistant Management Association.

L.B.O.   Leveraged buyout. See **leverage.**

L.I.F.O.   "Last in, first out." Describes a method of calculating the worth of a merchant's **inventory.** Under this method if a merchant buys a blivit for a dollar, then buys another for two dollars, then sells either blivit, the remaining blivit is worth one dollar. Compare with **F.I.F.O.** and **N.I.F.O.**

L.J.   *1.* **Law journal.** *2.* Law judge. *3.* Lord Justice.

L.K.A.   Last known address.

LL.B.   "Bachelor of Laws." The basic U.S. law degree until the late 1960s. Replaced by **J.D.** (see that word).

L.L.C.   **Limited liability company.**

LL.M. and LL.D.   Advanced law degrees (masters and doctorate). Other initials are also used for some advanced law degrees (see **J.D.** for a list of examples).

L.L.P.   **Limited liability partnership.**

L.P.   **Limited partnership.**

L.R.   *1.* **Law reports.** *2.* Law review (see **law journal**).

L.R.I.   Legal Resources Index. A large, computerized and microfilmed listing of law review articles and law-related articles in general newspapers and magazines.

L.S.   Short for "locus sigilii" or "the place of the seal." These letters once were placed next to a signature to make a **contract** formally binding.

L.S.A.T.   Law School Admission Test.

L. Ed.   *Lawyer's Edition* of the U.S. Supreme Court Reports. A set of books containing all of the written **opinions** of the U.S. Supreme Court, plus **annotations.**

L. Rev.   Law review (see **law journal**).

Label   *1.* Any writing added onto a larger document. *2.* Product and package label honesty is covered by the Federal Fair Packaging and Labeling Act and label content is covered by various food and drug laws. *3.* A brand name.

Labor Department of Labor. The U.S. **cabinet** department that **regulates** working conditions, labor-management relations, human resources development, etc. The National Labor Relations Board (**N.L.R.B.**), however, is an **independent agency.**

Labor contract A **collective bargaining agreement.**

Labor dispute A controversy between an employer and employees or an employer and a union involving wages, hours, working conditions, or the question of who has the right to speak for the employees.

Labor organization Any group, whether or not a labor **union,** and whether or not it is formally organized, that deals with pay, hours, or any other working conditions.

Labor Relations Act **National Labor Relations Act.**

Labor Relations Board See **N.L.R.B.**

Labor Standards Act **Fair Labor Standards Act.**

Labor union A formal organization of employees formed to improve compensation and working conditions. See **union** for types.

Labor-Management Relations Act The **Taft-Hartley Act.**

Labor-Management Reporting and Disclosure Act The **Landrum-Griffin Act.**

Laborer's lien See **mechanic's lien.**

Laches The legal doctrine that a delay (in pursuing or enforcing a claim or right) can be so long that the person against whom you are proceeding is unfairly hurt or *prejudiced* (see **prejudice**) by the delay itself. This may keep you from winning. *Laches* (or **estoppel** *by laches*) is an **equitable defense** (see those words), used when a plaintiff delays unfairly in starting a lawsuit. [pronounce: latch-es]

Laden in bulk Carrying loose cargo such as grain rather than carrying containers of grain or individual items such as chairs.

Lading See **bill of lading.**

Laesa majestas (Latin) **Treason.**

Laissez-faire (French) Describes the theory or practice of a free economy in which the government does not interfere with private economic decisions. [pronounce: lay-say fair]

Lame duck *1.* An elected official who is serving out the end of a **term** after someone else has been elected to take his or her place. A *lame duck session* is a **legislative** session held after an election and before new members of the legislature are to begin their terms. The **Twentieth Amendment** to the U.S. **Constitution** is called the *Lame Duck Amendment* because it abolished the short post-election congressional session. _2._ Any public or private officeholder who cannot continue beyond the current term of office. _3._ An investor in **stock** who has over-bought and cannot meet his or her financial commitments.

Land   In the law, land is not just the surface. It includes everything underneath plus the airspace above and usually means the same thing as **real estate,** which includes buildings and intangible rights in the land such as leases.

Land bank   _1._ Describes a federal program in which land is taken out of agricultural production and used for conservation or trees. Also called _soil bank. 2._ A federally created bank that makes low-interest farm loans.

Land grant (or land patent)   A gift (usually with conditions attached) of land from the government to a private person, organization, business, or another government. Many state colleges are _land grant_ institutions.

Land sales contract   A **contract** for the sale of real estate (often not recorded in the land records) in which the seller keeps **title** to the property until an agreed future time. This is often done to keep a low interest rate on an existing **mortgage** or when conventional financing cannot be obtained. Also called a _contract for deed_ and _installment land contract._

Land tech. (or landman or landwoman)   A **paralegal** who works in oil and gas land and leasing law.

Land use planning   A general term that can mean **zoning** laws, real estate development and use laws, environmental impact studies, state and local master plans, etc.

Landlord   The owner of land or a building that is rented or leased to a **tenant.**

Landmark case   A court case that makes major changes in the law, especially a U.S. Supreme Court case that resolves a major issue and has substantial practical impact.

Landrum-Griffin Act   (29 U.S.C. 401) A 1959 federal law that gave several new rights to individual union members (such as the requirement that unions must have a fair **constitution**). It also changed the **Taft-Hartley Act** in some pro-union, some pro-employer ways. See also **secondary boycott** and **hot cargo.**

Lanham Act   (15 U.S.C. 1051) A 1946 revision of the federal **trademark** laws.

Lapping   Stealing or "borrowing" from an employer by taking money paid by a customer, not recording the payment, then covering the theft by putting the next customer's payment into the first's account, and so on.

Lapse *1.* The end or failure of a right because of the neglect to enforce or use it within a time limit. *2.* The failure of a gift by **will.** *3.* See **antilapse statutes.**

Larceny Stealing of any kind. Some types of larceny are specific crimes, such as *larceny by trick* or **grand larceny.**

Larger parcel rule When a piece of land taken by **eminent domain** (see that word) is part of a larger piece of land, the price paid by the government may be higher than it would have been for an identical piece of land standing alone.

Lascivious Tending to excite lust; impure; obscene; immoral. [pronounce: la-<u>siv</u>-ee-us]

Last antecedent rule The principle that a phrase that *can* be read as referring to the immediately preceding words *should* be read that way unless the document as a whole makes it clear that the phrase should refer to words farther away or should be read more broadly.

Last clear chance doctrine The legal principle that a person injured in (or having property harmed by) an accident may win **damages** even when **negligent** if the person causing the damage, while also negligent, could have avoided the accident after discovering the danger and if the person injured could not have. This rule is not accepted in every state and, where accepted, has many different forms (and names).

Last injurious exposure rule The principle that when an occupational disease was caused by a succession of jobs, or could have been caused by any one of a succession of jobs, the most recent employer with the risk exposure is liable.

Last resort A *court of last resort* is one from which there is no **appeal.**

Last will and testament **Will.**

Latent *1.* Hidden. A *latent defect* is something wrong (with an article sold or with the validity of a legal document) that cannot be discovered by ordinary observation or care. In this sense, its opposite is **patent.** A *latent* **ambiguity** is an uncertainty that arises when seemingly unambiguous words in a document are applied to the factual situation at issue. *2.* Dormant, **passive,** or "put away." For example, a *latent deed* is one kept for twenty (or thirty) years in a secret place. *3.* "*Latents*" is police slang for fingerprints found in a criminal investigation.

Lateral support The sideways support of land provided by adjoining land, and the right to such continued support. For example, if a landowner digs a drainage ditch that causes a cave-in of another's land, the landowner is usually financially responsible for the damage. Compare with **subjacent support.**

Laudum (Latin) A **judgment** or **award.**

Laughing heir A person who inherits unexpectedly from a distant relative.

Laundering Exchanging money gained illegally for money that cannot be traced to crime.

Law *1.* That which must be obeyed. *2.* A **statute;** an act of the **legislature.** *3.* The whole body of principles, standards, and rules put out by a government. *4.* The principles, standards, and rules that apply to a particular type of situation; for example, *"juvenile law."* *5.* See **fact** for the difference between fact and law. *6.* For the many different types of law, such as **caselaw, constitutional law, military law, substantive law,** etc., see those words.

Law and Economics The study of law based on the idea that legal principles, laws, and court decisions should be subject to cost-benefit analyses to see whether they are economically efficient.

Law day (law date) *1.* A court-set day after which a *mortgagor* (see **mortgage**) can no longer pay off a debt on real estate and get the real estate back from **foreclosure.** *2.* May First. A day for special school and public programs honoring the U.S. legal system.

Law directory A **law list.**

Law enforcement officers Police, **F.B.I.** agents, **sheriffs,** etc.

Law French The Norman French language used in the law in England for several centuries. Many words survive.

Law journal (or law review) A publication put out by a law school (or bar association, etc.) with articles on legal subjects such as court decisions and legislation.

Law Latin The changed form of Latin that developed in the English courts. Many words survive.

Law list A directory of lawyers practicing in a particular area, such as the *Martindale-Hubbell Law Directory.*

Law merchant The generally accepted customs of merchants. These customs have standardized over the years and become a part of the formal law.

Law of nations See *public **international law.***

Law of nature *1.* **Natural law.** *2.* The "law" of survival in the wild.

Law of the case Any **decision** or **ruling** in a case by a trial or **appeals** court. The *law of the case* may not usually be changed in any later phase of that same case, except by review of a higher court. Compare with **res judicata.**

Law of the land   *1.* A law or rule that is in force throughout the country or, sometimes, throughout a geographical area. *2.* A country's customs, which gradually become as important legally as written law. *3.* The fundamental rights of persons, and the laws that protect those rights, such as **due process of law** and **equal protection of laws.**

Law of the road   Safety customs, such as "keep to the right," that have become law.

Law reform   Using a case in court to make a basic change in the law, often by bringing a **test case.**

Law reports   Published books in a series that contain the written **opinions** in cases decided by various courts.

Law review   See **law journal.**

Law week   Short for *U.S. Law Week.* A **looseleaf service** with "hot off the press" news from the Supreme Court, other courts, and some **legislatures.**

Lawful   Legal; authorized by law; not forbidden by law.

Lawsuit   A **civil action.** A court proceeding to enforce a right between persons (rather than to **convict** a **criminal**).

Lawyer   A person licensed to practice law. Other words for "lawyer" include: **attorney, counsel, solicitor,** and **barrister.**

Lay   Nonprofessional. For example, a lawyer would call a nonlawyer a layperson and a doctor would call a nondoctor a layperson. A *lay advocate* is a nonlawyer (often a **paralegal**) who specializes in representing persons in **administrative** hearings. A *lay judge* is either a nonlawyer who acts as a low-level judge such as a justice of the peace or who acts as an assistant judge to a trial judge. A *lay witness* is any witness other than an **expert witness** (see that word).

Layaway   Putting down a deposit to hold a purchase for later pickup. (This is *not* necessarily an "**installment** sale" involving **credit**.)

Laying foundation   Establishing the preliminary **evidence** needed to make later, more important evidence **relevant** and **admissible.**

Layoff   A temporary or indefinite loss of a job due to a reduction in work to be done. The last person "laid off" often gets rehired first due to **seniority.**

Lead counsel   The head of a team of lawyers on one side of a case, especially when the lawyers are from different law firms.

Leading case   A **case** that either established a legal principle or is otherwise very important in an area of law.

Leading object rule   The **main purpose doctrine.**

Leading question   A question that shows a **witness** how to answer it or suggests the preferred answer; for example, "Isn't it true that you were in Boston all last week?" _Leading questions_ are generally permitted on **cross-examination** of the other side's witness in a trial, but not on **direct examination** of your side's witness.

Learned intermediary   A professional who is given information on a product's dangers. Giving this information may reduce the manufacturer's liability to the final user.

Lease   _1._ A **contract** for the use of land or buildings, but not for their ownership. The **lessor** is called the **landlord** and the **lessee** is the **tenant.** _2._ A contract for the use of something, but not for its ownership. _3._ A long-term loan of something in exchange for money. _4._ For special types of _leases_ such as **mineral lease, percentage lease,** and **subletting,** see those words. [pronounce: leess]

Leaseback   A sale of property with a **lease** of the same property from the buyer back to the seller. This is often done with land or industrial equipment for tax purposes, is usually long term, and may be called a _sale-leaseback._

Leasehold   The property rights a **tenant** has in land or buildings held by **lease.**

Lease-purchase   A rental agreement in which making all the contract payments gives ownership. Also called _rent-to-own._

Least and latest rule   Pay the least amount of taxes legally possible as late as legally possible.

Least fault divorce   (See **comparative rectitude rule.**)

Leave   _1._ To give by **will.** _2._ Permission. For example, _"leave of court"_ is permission from a judge to take an action in a lawsuit that requires permission (to file an amended **pleading,** for example).

Ledger   A business **account** book, usually recording the day-to-day transactions, and usually showing **debits** and **credits** separately.

Legacy   _1._ A gift of money by **will.** _2._ A gift of personal property (anything but **real estate**) by will. _3._ A gift of anything by will.

Legacy tax   A tax on the privilege of inheriting something. This may be an **inheritance** _tax_ based on the value of the property or it may be a flat fee.

Legal   _1._ Required or permitted by law. _2._ Not forbidden by law. _3._ Concerning or about the law. _4._ Having to do with a _court of law_ as opposed to a _court of_ **equity** (see that word). _5._ See the list of _legal_ words that follows for various examples and other meanings. (Many words _preceded_ by the word "legal" will be found only under the word itself; for example, _legal_ **person** or _legal_ **separation.**)

Legal acumen doctrine   The principle that, if it takes special legal skills to figure out that there may be something wrong with the **title** to a piece of land, a court may be asked to use its **equity** power to do what is fair to resolve the property's ownership.

Legal age   The age at which a person becomes old enough to make contracts to which the person can be held. This is eighteen in most states, but it may be lower for specific purposes. The phrase is sometimes used to mean the age at which a person can legally buy alcoholic beverages or legally consent to sexual intercourse.

Legal aid   Describes an organization or service that provides free legal help to poor persons.

Legal assistant   See **paralegal.**

Legal cap   Long legal stationery with a wide left-hand margin and a narrow right-hand margin.

Legal capital   *1.* The **par** or stated value of a company's **stock.** *2.* The amount of money a company must keep to protect its **creditors.** *3.* Property with enough value to balance a company's stock **liability.**

Legal cause   See **proximate cause.**

Legal certainty test   *1.* The principle that if a **plaintiff's** claim is challenged as being less than the court's **jurisdictional** *amount* (see that word), the amount claimed in the **complaint** will be accepted by the court unless there is a *legal certainty* that the amount that can be claimed *is less*. But see no. 2. *2.* The *opposite* principle, use in the **removal** of a case from state to federal court, that if a claim is challenged as being less than the court's jurisdictional amount, the challenge will succeed unless there is a legal certainty that the amount that can be claimed *is more.*

Legal conclusion   *1.* A statement about legal rights, duties, or results that is not based on specific facts. A **conclusory** statement. *2.* A conclusion about legal rights, duties, or results that is drawn from specific facts, but those facts do not include the facts legally necessary to draw the conclusion. *3.* Used loosely to mean a **conclusion of law,** the *opposite* of the meanings in no. 1 and no. 2.

Legal cruelty   See **cruelty.**

Legal death   See **brain death rule, civil death,** and **death** for various uses of the word.

Legal description   The identification of a piece of land that is precise enough to locate it without ambiguity and to show any **easements** or *reservations* (see **reserve**). This may be done by government survey, recordation of precise measurements, lot numbers on a recorded **plat,** or similar formal means.

Legal detriment A **liability,** duty, or change in financial position that results from making a contract or relying on a promise. See **promissory estoppel.**

Legal entity A living person, a **corporation,** or any organization that can sue and be sued or otherwise function legally.

Legal ethics *1.* The moral and professional duties owed by lawyers to their clients, to other lawyers, to the courts, and to the public. *2.* The study of legal ethics. *3.* The written rules of ethics such as the **Rules of Professional Conduct.**

Legal executive In England, a highly trained **paralegal.**

Legal fiction See **fiction.**

Legal heirs *1.* Persons who will inherit if a person dies without a will. *2.* Any **heirs.**

Legal holiday A day on which normal legal business may not be transacted. This varies widely from state to state, but the work prohibited on that day may include **service** of **process,** court proceedings, banking, etc.

Legal investments (or legal list) See **prudent person rule.**

Legal necessity (for mistrial) The inability of a jury to agree on a **verdict,** or a physical cause of a **mistrial** such as the death of the judge. *Legal necessity* permits a retrial without violating a criminal defendant's right to avoid **double jeopardy.**

Legal positivism The view that **positive law** (law enacted by **legislatures)** is the only valid law, so **natural law** (rules of conduct that are basic to human behavior or morality) is not.

Legal proceedings Any actions taken in court or formally connected with a lawsuit.

Legal realism A philosophy of law that takes psychology, sociology, economics, politics, etc., into account in order to explain how legal decisions are made (and should be made).

Legal representative *1.* A person, such as an **executor** or **administrator** of **wills,** who takes care of another person's business involving courts. *2.* A family member entitled to bring a **wrongful death action.**

Legal reserve The percentage of total funds that an insurance company or a bank must set aside to meet possible claims.

Legal residence See **domicile.**

Legal Services Corporation An organization that runs a federally funded program of **legal aid.**

Legal technician A **paralegal,** often self-employed.

Legal tender   Official money (dollar bills, coins, etc.).

Legal value   See **par** *value,* **book value,** and **face value.**

Legal worker   See **paralegal.**

Legalese   Legal jargon or overly complicated language in laws, **regulations,** contracts, etc.

Legalism   *1.* A judge's adherence to the exact wording or narrowest interpretation of a law, rather than basing a decision on what would be fair or on what was probably intended by the law's passage. *2. Legalese.*

Legalized nuisance   A **nuisance** that may not be objected to as a nuisance because it exists due to specific laws. For example, a hospital might be permitted by law to cause neighborhood problems (such as traffic noise and congestion) that a factory would not be permitted to cause.

Legatee   A person who **inherits** something by **will.**

Legation   All the persons making up one country's embassy in another country.

Leges (or legis or legem)   (Latin) Laws; plurals of **lex.**

Legislate   To enact or pass laws. A *legislator* (person who makes laws) works in the *legislature* (lawmaking branch of government) on *legislation* (laws, **statutes, ordinances,** etc.). This work of *legislation* (passing laws) is a *legislative* function (lawmaking, as opposed to "**executive,**" which is carrying out laws, or "**judicial,**" which is interpreting laws). [pronounce: ledge-eh-slate]

Legislation   *1.* The process of thinking about and passing or refusing to pass **bills** into law (**statutes, ordinances,** etc.). *2.* Statutes, ordinances, etc.

Legislative   Lawmaking, as opposed to "**executive**" (carrying out or enforcing laws), or "**judicial**" (interpreting or applying laws). Concerning a **legislature.**

Legislative council   A group of officials that studies state laws, **legislative** problems, etc. *Not* **legislative counsel.**

Legislative counsel   A person or office that helps **legislators** and legislative committees research and write **bills,** as well as help with other technical aspects of lawmaking. *Not* **legislative council.**

Legislative courts   Courts that have been set up by **legislatures** (Congress, state legislatures, etc.), rather than those set up originally by the U.S. **Constitution** or by state constitutions.

Legislative facts General facts that help an **administrative agency** to decide general questions of law and policy and to make rules. They are different from **adjudicative facts** (see that word).

Legislative history The background documents and records of **hearings** related to the enactment of a **bill**. These documents may be used to decide the meaning of the law after it has been enacted. See **legislative intent rule.**

Legislative immunity The constitutional right of a member of Congress to say almost anything for almost any reason while performing an official function (speeches, debates, newsletters, etc.), and to be free from most lawsuits based on what was said.

Legislative intent rule The principle that when a **statute** is ambiguous, a court should interpret the statute by looking at its **legislative history** to see what the lawmakers meant or wanted when they passed the statute. This is one of several possible ways of interpreting statutes. Compare with **legislative purpose rule.**

Legislative purpose rule The principle that when a **statute** is ambiguous, a court should interpret the statute by looking at what the law was before the statute was passed and then deciding what the statute means by looking at both the statute itself and at what the statute was trying to change. This is one of several possible ways of interpreting statutes. Compare with **legislative intent rule.**

Legislator A lawmaker, such as a U.S. Senator, a member of a city council, etc.

Legislature A lawmaking body such as the U.S. Congress, a city council, etc.

Legitimate _1._ Lawful or legal (also, a child born to a married couple is sometimes described as _legitimate_). _2._ To make lawful.

Legitime An **inheritance** that must go to a **forced heir** (see that word).

Lemon law A state law permitting the return of a defective product, usually a car, within a limited time period if there are substantial defects that cannot be fixed.

Lese majesty (French) **Treason** or **rebellion.**

Lesion corporelle (French) Bodily injury.

Lessee A person who **leases** or rents something _from_ someone. A lessee of land is also called a **tenant.**

Lesser included offense A crime with a legal definition that is a part (but not all) of the legal definition a more serious crime. For example, **manslaughter** is a lesser crime included in **murder.**

Lessor   A person who **leases** or rents something *to* someone. A lessor of land is also called a **landlord.**

Let   *1.* **Award** a contract (such as for construction work) to one of several bidders. *2.* **Lease.**

Letter   *1.* The strict, precise, literal meaning of a document. The exact language (of a law, for example) rather than the **spirit** or broad purpose. *2.* A formal document. For example, a *"letter of attorney"* is a document giving a person **power of attorney** (see that word).

Letter of advice   A **drawer's** (for example, a person who makes out a check) notice to a **drawee** (for example, a bank) that a **draft** (a check for a certain amount to a certain person) has been *drawn* (made out).

Letter of attornment   A letter from a landlord to a tenant saying that the property has been sold and telling the tenant to send the rent payments to the buyer.

Letter of comment   A letter from the **S.E.C.** to persons registering a proposed sale of **securities (stocks,** etc.) that the **registration** *statement* does not comply with law and must be changed.

Letter of credence   The document that **accredits** a new **ambassador** or other foreign **minister** (recommends and certifies him or her to another country).

Letter of credit   A written statement by a bank or other financier that it will back up or pay the financial obligations of a merchant involved in a particular sale. It may be a **negotiable instrument** to pay a certain sum, a letter that the person's **credit** is good to a certain amount, or something in between. *Import, export,* and *travelers' letters* authorize a foreign bank to cash checks or make other payments in local currency to be reimbursed by the bank that writes the letter.

Letter of intent   *1.* A preliminary written understanding that is meant to be the basis for a **contract.** *2.* A letter (often from a government **agency**) to a **contractor** stating that a contract **award** will be made. This gives the contractor some, but not all, the rights of a signed contract.

Letter of request   **Letters rogatory.**

Letter ruling   A written answer by the **I.R.S.** to a taxpayer about how the tax laws apply to a specific set of facts (often a proposed transaction). Sometimes this is called a *"private letter ruling"* because it is advice for one specific situation and one specific person only.

Letter stock   **Stock** that does not need to be **registered** with the **S.E.C.** because buyers give the seller a letter saying that the stock will be held for investment and not resold for a long time.

Letters   Formal, written permission to do something. See the following words for examples.

Letters of administration (or letters testamentary)   Court papers appointing a person to take charge of the property of a dead person in order to distribute it. Generally, _letters of administration_ appear an **administrator** (someone _not_ chosen as **executor** in the person's will) and _letters testamentary_ appoint an executor (someone chosen in the will).

Letters of marque and reprisal   See **marque and reprisal.**

Letters patent   A government document giving a person exclusive rights to a piece of land or granting a new **patent.**

Letters rogatory   A request made by one court to another in a different **jurisdiction** that a **witness** answer the **interrogatories** sent with the letter.

Lettres de cachet   (French) Documents signed by the king that allowed persons to be imprisoned or excused persons from crimes for no reason at all. These were abolished during the Revolution of 1789. [pronounce: <u>let</u>-re de ca-shay]

Leverage   _1._ The power of a small amount of money to buy things of far greater value through borrowing. This power is often expressed as the _ratio_ of total purchase price to actual money used to buy property. _2._ Putting down a small investment (usually as a down payment) to control a large amount of **stock** (and usually borrowing the rest). This makes the eventual profit or loss quite large when compared to the money actually put up if the price of the stock changes. _3._ Any borrowing to buy an asset, especially as an investment. _4._ The proportion of a company's **bonds** and _preferred_ **stock** compared to its **common stock.** The common stock is called "_highly leveraged_" if there is proportionately little of it, because small changes in the company's income can result in big changes in the stock's value, since payments that must be made on bonds and preferred stock are large, but unchanging. _5._ A "_leveraged lease_" is a deal in which leased items are financed by a third person. This is often done to shift tax benefits from the persons who lease and actually use the property to the owners who gain more. See **equity investor.** _6._ A _leveraged buyout_ is using borrowed money to buy a **controlling interest** in a company.

Levy   _1._ To **assess,** raise, or collect. For example, to _levy a tax_ is to either **pass** one in a **legislature** or to collect one. _2._ To seize or collect. For example, to _levy on a debtor's property_ is to put it aside by court **order** in order to pay **creditors.** _3._ The **assessment** or seizure itself in no. 1 and no. 2. _4._ To _levy war_ is to start a rebellion against the government. It is an act of **treason** under the U.S. **Constitution.**

Lewd   Morally impure in a sexual sense; **lascivious.**

Lex   (Latin) *1.* Law (or a collection or body of laws). For example: *lex mercatoria* (**law merchant**); *lex naturale* (**natural law**); *lex ordinandi* (**procedural law,** as opposed to **substantive law**); *lex scripta* (written law; **statutes**); *lex talionis* (law of retaliation; "eye for an eye"); and *lex terrae* (law of the land; **due process of law**). *2. Lex loci* is the "law of the place." For example, *lex loci actus* (law of the place where the act was done); *lex loci contractus* (law of the place where the **contract** was made or the place with the most important legal connections to the contract); *lex loci criminis* or *delictus* (law of the place where the crime was committed); *lex loci domicilii* (law of the **domicile** or permanent home of the person involved); *lex loci rei sitae* or *situs* (law of the place where the thing, usually land, is); etc. Many of these are abbreviated without the "*loci,*" but that changes the Latin ending of the words. See no. 3 for contrast. *3. Lex fori* is the "law of the **forum**" or court, the law of the state or country where the case is decided. Judges must often choose whether *lex fori* or *lex loci* (see no. 2) is the law that decides a case. See also **conflict of laws.**

LEXIS   A computerized legal research source.

Leze majesty   (French) **Treason** or **rebellion.**

Liability   A broad word for legal obligation, responsibility, or debt. *Liability insurance* is **insurance** against claims based on others' bodily injury, against claims based on others' property damage, or against specified claims involving any type of *liability.*

Liable   Responsible for something (such as harm done to another person); bound by law; having a duty or obligation enforceable in court against you by another person. *Not* "**libel.**"

Libel   *1.* Written **defamation.** Publicly communicated, false written statements that injure a person's reputation, business, or property rights. To *libel* certain public figures, the written statement must also be made with at least a "reckless disregard" for whether the statement is true or false. *2.* Formerly the first **pleading** in an admiralty (maritime or ocean-ship) court, corresponding to the **complaint** of an ordinary **civil** lawsuit. Also, the name for some specialized complaints in some places, such as a "*divorce libel.*" *Not* "**liable.**"

Libelant   **Plaintiff.**

Libelous   Defamatory; tending to injure a reputation.

Liberal construction   Interpretation of the meaning of a **statute** that permits the statute to apply to situations within its general scope, but not explicitly covered. See **equity of a statute** for more detail and compare with **strict** *construction.*

Liberty *1.* Freedom from illegal personal restraint. *2.* Personal rights under law. *3.* A *liberty interest* is a right protected by **due process of law** (see that word). *4.* For *liberty of* contract, speech, the press, etc., see **freedom of** that word.

Library of Congress system A method of finding books, first by subject area (law is "K") and then by a number assigned in time order by the Library of Congress. Compare with the **Dewey decimal system.**

License *1.* Formal permission to do something specific; for example, a state driver's license or the license given by one company to another to manufacture a patented product. But see no. 3. *2.* The document that gives the formal permission. *3.* Acting without any legal restraint; disregarding the law entirely.

Licensee *1.* A person who holds a **license.** *2.* A person who is on property with permission, but without any enticement by the owner and with no financial advantage to the owner; often called a *"mere,"* *"bare,"* or *"naked" licensee* as opposed to an **"invitee"** in **negligence** law. In some situations, an invited personal guest is a *licensee, not* an *invitee.*

Licentiousness *1.* Doing what you want with total disregard for ethics, law, or others' rights. *2.* Lewdness or lasciviousness; moral impurity in a sexual context.

Licit Permitted by, authorized by, or not forbidden by law.

Lie Exist; be supported by. For example, the phrase "the action *lies* in **tort**" means that the right way to bring a lawsuit based on a particular subject is as a tort case.

Lie detector A machine that reads blood pressure, heart rate, and other body signs (such as the skin's electrical resistance) and gives a rough indication of whether or not a person is telling the truth while questions are asked. Lie detector (also called *polygraph*) tests are not admitted as evidence, except in some states that allow them when both sides of a case agree to use the results. (Other machines, such as "voice stress analyzers," have also been used as lie detectors.)

Lien A claim against specific property that can be enforced in court to secure payment of a **judgment,** duty, or debt. Sometimes *lien* is defined to *exclude* claims due to contracts or mortgages. A *lienee* is an owner of property with a lien against it and a *lienor* (or *lienholder*) is a person who owns a lien against property. A *mechanic's lien* is the right of a worker to hold property worked on until paid for the services. A *tax lien* is the government's placing on a piece of property a financial obligation that must be paid because taxes have not been paid. Other types of *liens* include **landlord's,** maritime, etc. [pronounce: leen]

Lien creditor   See **lien** and **secured** *creditor.*

Lien state (or theory jurisdiction)   A state in which a **mortgage** is considered a mere **lien** on property, with the result that the creditor who holds the mortgage cannot get title to the property until a foreclosure sale is completed. Compare with **title** *theory state.*

Lieu   (French) "Place." "*In lieu of*" means "instead of."

Lieutenant   *1.* A **deputy,** substitute, or second in command, such as a *lieutenant governor. 2.* A military or police middle rank; closer to the bottom than the top in the military, about the middle for the police.

Life   *1.* Human *life* begins at different times for different legal purposes. It may begin at conception, at the time when a child is capable of living outside the womb, at the moment of birth and first breath, etc. For definitions of the end of life, see **death.** *2. Life* is also short for *"for life"* or *"for the duration of life."* For example, a *life* **estate, interest,** or **tenancy** lasts until a named person or persons die. And a *life* **annuity** is a type of **insurance** or **pension plan** (see that word) that pays from a certain point until the end of the person's life.

Life care contract   An agreement (usually between an elderly person and a nursing home) in which the person turns over all property in return for all support from then on.

Life estate (or interest or tenancy)   An ownership interest in property (an **estate**) that lasts until a named person or persons die.

Life expectancy   The length of time a person of a given age, sex (and sometimes health) is expected to live. This is computed from life (or actuarial) tables, sometimes adjusted for individual health-related history and characteristics, and used in figuring **insurance** rates, **damages** for injuries, etc.

Life in being   The lifetime of a specific person already born, or the lifetime of a person who *will* be alive when a **deed** or **will** takes effect. A *life in being* is used in the calculations used in the *rule against perpetuities* (see **perpetuity**).

Lift   Remove an obstacle or obligation. Stop the effect of something, such as a court **order.**

Like-kind exchange   A trade of ownership of certain property by one person for property of the same type owned by another person. With certain exceptions and limitations, a gain or loss on the trade is not *recognized* (see **recognition**) as a currently *taxable event.*

Limine   (Latin) See **in limine.**

Limit order   See **order.**

Limitation   *1.* A restriction. *2.* A time limit. For example, a *statute of limitations* is a law that sets a maximum amount of time after something happens for it to be taken to court, such as a "three-year statute" for lawsuits based on a contract, or a "six-year statute" for a criminal prosecution. (A distinction is sometimes made between a *statute of limitations,* which ends the **remedy** of going to court, and a *statute of repose,* which ends the underlying **right** or **cause of action.**) *3.* See **limited.**

Limited   *1.* Partial or restricted. For example, *limited liability* is the legal rule that the owners (shareholders) of a **corporation** cannot usually be held accountable for **corporate** actions or losses and, thus, the most they can usually lose is the value of their investment. But see **piercing the corporate veil.** The *limited partners* but not the *general partners* of a **limited partnership** also have limited liability. See also **limited liability company** and **limited liability partnership.** *2.* "*Limited*" is the British and Canadian word for "incorporated." It is abbreviated "Ltd." *3.* A previously decided case is said to be *limited* by a subsequent case if the court in the subsequent case reduces the scope or applicability of a **rule of law** (without *overruling* it) established in the previous case. *4.* For other examples, see the words following.

Limited admissibility   The principle that a judge may allow **evidence** to be used for one purpose in a trial, but not another. If it is a jury trial, the judge should instruct the **jury** carefully about what the evidence may and may not prove and how the jurors may consider it.

Limited divorce   See **separation.**

Limited fee simple   See **fee simple.**

Limited liability company   A cross between a **partnership** and a **corporation** (see those words) owned by *members* who may manage the company directly or delegate to officers or managers who are similar to a corporation's *directors.* Governing documents are usually a publicly filed *articles of organization* and a private *operating agreement.* Members are not usually **liable** for company debts, and company income and losses are usually divided among and taxed to the members individually according to share.

Limited liability partnership   A **partnership** (see that word) in which the partners have less than full **liability** for the actions of other partners, but full liability for their own actions. In a *limited liability* **limited partnership,** the *general partners* have less than full liability for the actions of other general partners.

Limited partnership A **partnership** (see that word) formed by *general partners* (who run the business and have **liability** for all partnership debts) and *limited partners* (who partly or fully finance the business, take no part in running it, and have no liability for partnership debts beyond the money they put in or promise to put in). See also **limited liability partnership** and **limited partnership association.**

Limited partnership association A business organization with many of the characteristics of a **limited liability company** (see that word) and the restriction of membership to persons elected by current members.

Limited publication Communication of a work to a few people. This is not a **dedication** of the work to the public that results in a loss of the work's **copyright.**

Limited trust A **trust** set up for a specific time period.

Line item veto See **veto.**

Line of credit The promise to lend money up to a certain maximum that a merchant or bank will give to a customer, usually for an ongoing series of transactions.

Line of descent A **direct** *line of descent* includes grandparents, parents, children, etc., and a **collateral** *line of descent* includes brothers, aunts, nieces, etc.

Line of duty Acts performed by military or law enforcement officers to carry out their assigned tasks.

Lineal In a line. For example, *lineal relationships* are those of father and son, grandson and grandmother, etc. [pronounce: lin-ee-al]

Lineup A group of persons, placed side-by-side in a line, shown to a witness of a crime to see if the witness will identify the person suspected of committing the crime. A *lineup* should not be staged so that it is suggestive of one person.

Link financing The process by which one person deposits a **compensating balance** in a bank to help another person get a loan.

Link-in-chain Describes the principle that the **constitutional** privilege against **self-incrimination** (see that word) includes protection against questions that could lead even indirectly to a linking of the person and criminal activity.

Liquid *1.* Having enough money to carry on normal business. *2.* Easily turned into cash.

Liquidate *1.* Pay off or settle a debt. *2.* **Adjust** or settle the amount of a debt. *3.* Settle up affairs and distribute money, such as the money left by a dead person or by a company that goes out of business.

Liquidated   *1.* Paid or settled up. *2.* Determined, settled, or fixed. For example, a *"liquidated claim"* is a claim or debt with a definite amount fixed either by agreement or by a court's action, and *liquidated damages* is a specific amount of money agreed to in a contract as compensation for a **breach** of that contract. Contrast **penalty clause.** *3.* Sold for cash. The assets of a dead company may be *liquidated* (to pay creditors, owners, etc.).

Liquidation   *1.* See **liquidate.** *2.* *Winding up* (see **wind up**) a company's affairs in order to end its existence.

Liquidity   *1.* See **liquid.** *2.* The ability to turn **assets** easily into cash.

Lis pendens   (Latin) *1.* A pending lawsuit. *2.* A warning notice that **title** to property is in **litigation** and that anyone who buys the property gets it with legal "strings attached."

List   *1.* See **listing.** *2.* See **docket.** *3.* *List price* is a suggested retail price of goods set by the manufacturer. It may be reduced for many reasons.

Listed security   A **stock** (or other **security**) that has met the requirements of a stock **exchange** (financial reports, supervision, etc.) and is traded on that exchange.

Listing   *1.* A **real estate** agent's right to sell **land.** An *open* (or *general*) *listing* is the right to sell that may be given to more than one agent at a time. An *exclusive agency listing* is the right of one agent to be the only one other than the owner who may sell the property during a period of time. An *exclusive (authorization to sell) listing* is a written **contract** that gives one agent the sole right to sell the property during a time period. This means that even if the owner finds the buyer, the agent will get a **commission.** *Multiple listing* occurs when an agent with an exclusive (or exclusive agency) listing shares information about the property (and its availability for sale) with many members of a real estate association and agrees to share the commission with an agent who finds the buyer. And, a *net listing* is an arrangement in which the seller sets a minimum price he or she will take for the property, and the agent's commission is the amount the property sells for over that minimum selling price. *2.* See **listed security.**

Literacy test   A reading test that must be passed to vote. Most state literacy tests have been ended by the *Federal Voting Rights Act.*

Literal construction   See **interpretation** definition no. 1.

Literary property   *1.* A written work, such as a novel or screenplay, protected by **copyright.** *2.* Ownership rights in a **literary work.**

Literary work   Under **copyright** law, any work (except audiovisual) expressed in words, numbers, or symbols, regardless of its physical form (books, manuscripts, tapes, etc.).

Litigant A **plaintiff** or **defendant** in a lawsuit.

Litigate *1.* Actively carry on a lawsuit. *2.* Carry on the **trial** part of a lawsuit.

Litigation A lawsuit or series of lawsuits.

Litigious *1.* Prone to bringing lawsuits; bringing too many lawsuits. *2.* Disputable; subject to disagreement. [pronounce: le-tij-es]

Littoral Having to do with a shore, bank, or side of a body of water.

Live storage The temporary parking of a car in a garage.

Livery An old word for the formal transfer and either actual or symbolic delivery of something (especially land).

Living trust A **trust** that will take effect while the person setting it up is still alive, as opposed to one created under a **will** upon death.

Living will An **advance directive** by which you authorize your possible future removal from an artificial life support system.

Lloyd's of London The world's largest association of **insurance** underwriters (persons and companies that insure things).

Load *1.* That part of **insurance, mutual fund,** or other business charges that represents **commissions** and selling costs. *2.* An unreasonable additional charge.

Loadstar method See **lodestar method.**

Loan commitment A promise by a bank, **mortgage** company, etc., to lend someone a certain amount of money at a certain rate of interest for a certain length of time. A loan commitment to finance a real estate purchase will usually be held open long enough to give the buyer time to complete the purchase and provides that the property purchased will be **collateral** for repayment of the loan.

Loan for consumption A loan such as a cup of sugar that gets returned as a different cup of sugar. See **loan for use.**

Loan for use A loan such as a lawnmower that gets returned as exactly the same lawnmower. See **loan for consumption.**

Loan ratio (or loan-to-value ratio) A comparison of the amount of a loan to either the market value of the property on which the loan is made or to the property's purchase price. The use of one "ratio" phrase or the other is imprecise, so look for the specification of market value or purchase price.

Loan shark A person who lends money at an **interest** rate higher than the legal maximum or who uses **extortion** to force repayment.

Loan value The highest amount a lender will lend (or can safely lend) on a piece of property, on a life **insurance** policy, etc.

Loaned servant doctrine   The legal principle that in most cases when an employer lends a person to another employer, that person becomes an employee of the second employer for many purposes, such as **liability** to others.

Lobbying   Attempting to persuade a **legislator** to vote a certain way on a bill or to introduce or change a bill.

Lobbying acts   Federal and state laws requiring the **registration** of *lobbyists,* the reporting of money spent by lobbyists, and other things. See also **foreign agent.**

Local action   A lawsuit that may be brought in only one place. Compare with **transitory action.**

Local agent   A person who takes care of a company's business in a particular area. Many states require a company doing business in the state to **register** a *local agent* for the **service** of **process** for lawsuits against the company.

Local assessment (or local improvement assessment)   A tax on only those properties benefiting from an improvement such as a sidewalk or sewer.

Local court   A vague term meaning a **municipal** court, a particular **foreign** court, a state rather than a **federal** court, etc.

Local law   A vague term for a law that operates only in one geographic area, that affects only one type or group of persons or things, that operates "here" rather than "there," etc.

Local option   *1.* The choice given to a city, county, etc., under state law to choose whether to allow such things as the sale of alcoholic beverages, the existence of racetracks, etc. *2.* **Home rule.**

Location   Taking actions to make a claim for the mineral rights to land. There are detailed requirements that can include posting of signs to give notice of the claim and marking the boundaries on which the claim is made.

Locative calls   The description of land in a **deed** or other document by using landmarks, physical objects, and other things by which the land can be precisely located and identified.

Lockbox system   First a company's customers send payments to a local post office box, then a local bank collects the payments and sends them on to the company's main bank. This is a common form of *concentration banking,* in which local payments feed into local banks for transfer.

Locked in   *1.* Describes someone who has profits on **stocks** or other **securities** that will require a high tax payment if the stocks are sold now.

2. Describes someone who has an **option** to purchase something at a certain price even if the price goes up, or who has a mortgage-application interest rate guaranteed for a specific time period.

Lockout An employer's refusal to allow employees to work. This is not an individual matter between an employer and a single employee, but a tactic in employer-union disputes.

Lockup A place of detention in a police station or courthouse.

Loco parentis See **in loco parentis.**

Locus (Latin) *1.* Place. For example, *locus contractus* (the place where the contract was made); *locus criminis* or *delicti* (the place where the crime was committed); *locus regit actum* (the place where the act is done); etc. See **lex** *loci* for more examples. *2. Locus sigilii* is "the place of the seal." See **L.S.** *3. Locus poenitentiae* is the "place of repentance," a final chance to change your mind before making a deal or committing a crime.

Lodestar method *1.* Calculating the award of attorney's fees in a case by multiplying the reasonable hours spent (which may be less than the actual hours) by the reasonable hourly rate (which may be less than the requested rate). *2.* Any **statutory** attorney's fees calculated by what is reasonable, rather than by what is claimed.

Lodger A person who pays to live in a part of a dwelling managed by another and who does not have total control over the rooms lived in.

Log rolling *1.* Including many different things in one legislative bill to get many different people to vote for it, thus voting for things they might have voted against if the things were separate. *2.* Legislative favor-trading in general.

Logging in Recording the names of persons as they are brought to a police station. The *logging in* process may be combined with **booking** (see that word).

Loitering Hanging around with no apparent purpose. Many anti-loitering laws are **unconstitutional.**

Long (or long position) A person who has large amounts of **stock** or who has contracted to buy large amounts of a stock for future delivery in expectation of a price rise is called *long* and has *a long position.*

Long-arm statute A state law that allows the courts of that state to claim **jurisdiction** over (decide cases directly involving) persons outside the state who have allegedly committed **torts** or other wrongs inside the state. Even with a *long-arm statute,* the court will not have jurisdiction unless the person sued has certain minimum contacts with the state.

Loophole   A technical way to avoid the intent or main thrust of a law or contract, such as legally avoiding taxes by taking advantage of an ambiguity or omission in the tax laws.

Looseleaf service   A set of books in looseleaf binders that gives up-to-the-minute reports on one area of law, such as federal taxes. As the law changes, new pages replace old ones. Three big publishers of these are Prentice-Hall, Commerce Clearing House, and Bureau of National Affairs.

Lord Campbell's Act   *1.* Shorthand name for a law that sets the maximum amount that can be recovered in a **wrongful death action** (see that word). *2.* The first law that allowed truth published for the public benefit to be a **defense** to **libel.**

Lord Mansfield's Rule   The principle, used in some states, that neither spouse may **testify** about the husband's **access** to the wife at the time a child was conceived.

Loss   A broad word that can mean anything from *total loss* (dropping a coin in the ocean accidentally) through *partial loss* (a drop in the value of a **stock**) to *technical loss* ("loss of an eye" might mean "not able to see well enough to work"). In general, the legal use of the word is close to its ordinary use. For various types of *loss,* such as **casualty, general average, hobby,** etc., see those words.

Loss leader   Merchandise sold below cost to attract customers who may buy other items. When this is advertised with no intention of selling the promised items, it may be **bait and switch.**

Loss of bargain rule   **Benefit of bargain rule.**

Loss payable clause   *1.* A provision in an **insurance** policy that lists the order of payments if the insurance is insufficient to pay everyone involved. *2.* A provision in an insurance policy that permits payment to someone other than the person named as the policy owner.

Loss ratio   The proportion of **insurance** premiums collected to loss claims paid.

Lost grant doctrine   The principle that if a person holds land as the owner and the previous owner knew about it for a long time, then it is assumed that there must have been a document transferring ownership even if it cannot be found.

Lost volume seller   A seller who has goods because a buyer has broken a contract to buy them, and who then sells the goods to a second buyer who would have otherwise given the seller additional sales volume by buying identical goods. The seller may collect lost profits from the first buyer.

Lost will A **will,** known to have been *executed* (see **execute**), but that cannot be found after the **testator's** death. In some states, the content of a *lost will* can be proved by **evidence** about it. In some states, the fact that there is a lost will creates a **rebuttable** *presumption* that the will was revoked and is **void.**

Lot *1.* An individual piece of land. *2.* A thing or group of things that is part of one separate sale or delivery. *3.* One sale of **stock** or other **security.** See **odd lot** and **round lot.**

Louisiana Law Law based primarily on the French **Code Civil** rather than British **common law.**

Love and affection See **consideration.**

Low docs See **no docs.**

Loyalty oath A pledge of allegiance required of many public employees, mostly of those in jobs having access to secrets. If the oath is vague or requires swearing to things in a way that violates a person's **civil rights,** it is usually **unconstitutional.**

Ltd. **Limited.**

Lucid interval A period of "temporary sanity" or clearheadedness, during which an insane or mentally infirm person can lawfully marry, write a valid will, or enter into binding contracts.

Lucrative title An old phrase for rights to property received by gift or **inheritance.**

Lucri causa (Latin) In order to gain or profit; profit motive.

Lump-sum settlement *1.* Payment of an entire amount of owed money at one time, rather than in installments. Such settlement may be for less than the entire amount owed or in dispute. *2.* Payment of a fixed amount of money to take care of an obligation that might otherwise have gone on forever. For example, "*lump-sum alimony*" might be a payment of one large sum to avoid having to pay a changeable, potentially greater, amount of money on a regular basis for a long time.

Lunacy See **insanity.**

Luxury tax A tax on things considered unnecessary, such as jewelry over a certain price, cigarettes, or liquor. A *luxury tax* is a type of **excise.**

Lying by Describes a person who remains silent during a transaction that affects his or her interests. The right to protest the transaction may be forfeited if the person's *lying by* indicates **acquiescence** to the transaction. See also **estoppel.**

Lynch law Illegal actions by persons who claim to take the law into their own hands to punish someone, usually by death.

M.A.C.R.S. Modified accelerated cost recovery system.

M.B.E. Multistate **Bar Examination.**

M.D. Middle **district.**

M.J. Military Justice Reporter.

M.L.P. Master Limited Partnership. A publicly traded **limited partnership,** often in real estate or natural resources, that has certain tax advantages.

M.O. Modus operandi.

M.S.P.B. Merit Systems Protection Board.

M.&A. Mergers and acquisitions. See **merger** no. 2.

Made See **make.**

Magisterial precinct (or district) The part of a county in which a magistrate, constable, or justice of the peace has official power.

Magistracy *1.* All public officials. *2.* All judges and law enforcement officials. *3.* All judges. *4.* All low-level judges such as **justices of the peace.** *5.* The office of **magistrate** (see that word).

Magistrate A judge, usually with limited functions and powers; for example, a **police court** judge. *U.S. magistrates* conduct pretrial proceedings, try minor criminal matters, etc. [pronounce: maj-eh-strate]

Magna Charta (or Carta) A document, signed by the English king in 1215, that defined and gave some individuals many basic rights for the first time in England. These included personal and property rights, limits on taxation, certain freedoms from religious interference, etc.

Magnuson-Moss Act (15 U.S.C. 2301) A 1975 federal law that set standards for **warranties** on **consumer** products. The act requires clear, simple written warranties, defines what "full warranty" means, etc.

Mail fraud The federal crime of using the mails in any way to deliberately cheat another person.

Mail order divorce Popular name for a **divorce** granted by a country in which neither person lives and to which neither person has traveled to get the divorce (or to which only one person with no **domicile** in that country has traveled). *Mail order divorces* are not valid in the United States.

Mailbox rule   The rule that an **acceptance** of an **offer** is made (and forms a valid **contract**) when it is mailed, so neither the person making the offer nor the person accepting it can take it back after the acceptance is in the mail. This rule applies only in situations where mailing is a reasonable practice. The general principle (that sending, not receipt, makes an acceptance) applies to other ways of communicating also. The *mailbox rule* does not apply to *making* an offer or to the **revocation** of an offer.

Maim   Seriously wound, disfigure, or disable a person.

Main purpose doctrine   The principle that if the *main purpose* of a person's promise to pay another's debt is the person's own benefit, that promise need not be in writing to be enforceable. (This is an exception to the general rule under the **statute of frauds** that the promise to pay another's debts must be in writing.)

Maintain   Carry on; keep from **lapse** or failure; support; keep in good shape; continue; do repeatedly. See also **maintenance.**

Maintenance   *1.* Acting to **maintain** (see that word). *2.* Meddling with a lawsuit that doesn't concern you; for example, by paying a person to continue a lawsuit he or she would have dropped. See also **champerty.** *3.* Supplying the necessities of life. See also **separate maintenance.** *4.* For *maintenance call,* see **margin call.**

Major and minor fault rule   The principle that when one ship's fault is uncontradicted and clearly could have caused the collision, any doubts about the other ship's possible fault should be resolved in its favor.

Major dispute   A *major dispute* in transportation *labor law* concerns the creation or change of a labor contract, while a *minor dispute* concerns the meaning of an existing contract as it applies to specific situations.

Major federal action   A project that requires substantial planning, time, spending, or resources by the U.S. government. These actions may require an **Environmental Impact Statement.**

Majority   *1.* Full legal age to manage your own affairs. *2.* More than half. Fifty-one is a *majority* of votes when one hundred persons vote. A distinction is sometimes made between an *absolute majority* (more than half of the voters who come to vote) and a *simple majority* (more than half of the voters who actually vote on one particular issue or election contest). *3.* For majority *opinion,* see **opinion.** A *majority view* is a legal principle agreed to by most of the courts that have considered the question or by the highest court in most of the states that have considered it. And *majority-consent* is the procedure in some states by which a majority of a company's stockholders can give written consent to **waive** the annual meeting and take various actions by written agreement.

Make *1.* Sign a document to make it legally valid, as in *"made and executed."* *2.* Prove a legal point, as in *"make your case."* *3.* Create something. For example, to *make a record* is to create a basis *"in the* **record***"* for a decision in your favor (or for a possible appeal) by presenting **evidence;** or to create and assemble the physical record of a case (**transcript, pleadings, exhibits,** etc.). And a judge *makes law* by deciding a case (or interpreting a statute) in a way that creates a new and different **precedent.**

Make whole Put a person who has suffered a loss because of another's wrong back into the financial position he or she was in before the wrong was done.

Maker *1.* A person who initially signs a **negotiable instrument,** such as a **note,** and by doing so promises to pay on it. *2.* A person who signs, creates, or performs something.

Mala fides (Latin) Bad faith. [pronounce: <u>mal</u>-a <u>fee</u>-dez]

Mala in se See **malum in se.**

Mala praxis **Malpractice.**

Mala prohibita See **malum prohibitum.**

Malefactor A person who is guilty of a crime.

Malfeasance *1.* Wrongdoing. *2.* Doing an illegal act (especially by a public official). Compare with **misfeasance** and **nonfeasance.**

Malice *1.* Ill will. *2.* Intentionally harming someone; having no moral or legal justification for harming someone. *3.* In **defamation** law, with knowledge of falsity or with reckless disregard for whether or not something is false. [pronounce: <u>mal</u>-iss]

Malice aforethought An intention to seriously harm someone or to commit a serious crime.

Malicious Done intentionally, from bad motives and without excuse. For example, *malicious prosecution* is the **tort** of bringing criminal **charges** against someone in order to harm that person and with no legal justification for doing it. Some states recognize a similar tort, *malicious institution of civil proceedings*. See also **abuse** *of process.* [pronounce: ma-<u>lish</u>-us]

Malicious mischief The criminal offense of intentionally destroying another person's property.

Mallory rule The **McNabb–Mallory rule.**

Malloy v. Hogan   (387 U.S. 1) The 1964 U.S. Supreme Court decision that used the **Fourteenth Amendment** to extend the *federal* **Fifth Amendment** protection against **self-incrimination** to criminal defendants in *state* courts.

Malo animo   (Latin) "With evil mind"; **malice.**

Malo grato   (Latin) Unwillingly.

Malpractice   Professional misconduct or unreasonable lack of skill. This word usually applies to bad, incomplete, or unfaithful work done by a doctor or lawyer.

Malum (or mala) in se   (Latin) "Wrong in and of itself"; morally wrong; describes **common law** crimes. [pronounce: ma-lum in say]

Malum (or mala) prohibitum   (Latin) "Prohibited wrongs"; describes **statutory** crimes, especially those *not* **malum in se.**

Manager   *1.* A person chosen to run a business or a part of one. *2.* A member of the House of Representatives who is chosen to prosecute an **impeachment** trial in the Senate. *3.* See **conference committee.**

Managing agent   A corporate employee for whose actions the corporation may be held responsible; a corporate employee who may serve as a corporate representative; etc. What type or level of employee is a *managing agent* differs from state to state and from situation to situation (employee fraud, service of process on the corporation, testimony about corporate affairs, etc.).

Mandamus   (Latin) "We command." A *writ of mandamus* is a court **order** that directs a public official or government department to do something. It may be sent to the **executive** branch, the **legislative** branch, or a lower court. [pronounce: man-day-mus]

Mandatary   An **agent.** *Not* **manda*tory.***

Mandate   *1.* A judicial command to act; see **mandamus.** *2.* An authorization to act. *3.* Require. See **mandatory.** *4.* Strong voter approval for a political position. *5.* For *mandated reporter,* see **child abuse.**

Mandatory   Required; must be followed or obeyed.

Mandatory authority   **Binding authority.**

Mandatory injunction   All **injunctions** are **mandatory** in the sense that they must be obeyed, but *mandatory injunction* refers to an injunction that requires a person to do something, as contrasted with a *prohibitory injunction,* which requires a person to refrain from doing something.

Mandatory instruction   See **formula instruction.**

Mandatory sentence   See **sentence** no. 2.

Manifest *1.* Clear, visible, indisputable, or requiring no proof. *2.* A written document that lists goods being shipped or stored, giving descriptions, values, shipping information, etc. *3.* A list of passengers carried by a ship or a plane. *4. Manifest necessity,* is **legal necessity.**

Manifesto *1.* A formal written statement by the head of a country concerning a major international action. *2.* A public declaration of political principles.

Man-in-the-house rule Any state regulation (now **unconstitutional**) used to deny **welfare benefits** (see those words) to poor families solely because a man lives with them.

Manipulation A series of **stock** (or other **securities**) transactions intended to raise or lower the price of the stock or to convince others to buy or sell. This is usually done by creating a false impression of active trading or by trying to trigger a major trading trend.

Mann Act (8 U.S.C. 1557) A 1910 federal law prohibiting the transport of women across state lines for immoral purposes (especially prostitution).

Manslaughter A crime, less severe than **murder,** involving the wrongful but non-malicious (see **malice**) killing of another person. There are various categories of *manslaughter.* In some states *voluntary manslaughter* is a killing in a sudden rage such as occurs during a quarrel and fight, and *involuntary manslaughter* is a killing with no intention to cause serious bodily harm, such as by acting without proper caution.

Manufacturer's liability See **strict liability.**

Manumission A release from slavery.

Mapp rule The principle, from the 1961 U.S. Supreme Court case of *Mapp v. Ohio* (367 U.S. 218 (1961)), that **evidence** obtained in violation of a criminal defendant's **constitutional** rights may not be used against the defendant in a state criminal trial. The *Mapp rule* is an **exclusionary rule.** A *Mapp hearing* is a criminal case *suppression hearing* to determine whether evidence should be excluded because it was illegally obtained.

Marbury v. Madison (5 U.S. 137) The 1803 U.S. Supreme Court decision that established the right of the **judiciary** to decide whether an act of **Congress** is **constitutional.** This is one type of **judicial review.**

Margin *1.* A boundary or boundary line. *2.* The percentage of the cost of a **stock** (or other **security**) that must be paid in cash by the buyer. A **broker** who offers such a *margin* transaction then makes a loan for the balance of the cost, keeping the stock as **collateral** in a *margin account. 3.* For *margin of profit,* see **profit margin.**

Margin call   *1.* A stockbroker's (see that word) demand for more cash or more **collateral** for a stock bought on **margin** because the stock has gone down in value. This is also called a *maintenance call* or *re-margining* and is done by others, such as **commodity** dealers. *2.* A stockbroker's notice to a buyer that a certain stock has been bought and that the purchase price must now be paid.

Marginal cost   The cost of adding one more identical item to a bulk purchase, of manufacturing one more item in a production run, of borrowing one more dollar in a loan, etc.

Marginal rate   The **tax rate** applied to a person's or organization's highest **tax bracket.**

Marital   Having to do with marriage. For example, the *marital deduction* is the amount of money a wife or husband can inherit from the other without paying **estate** or gift taxes; and *marital property* is any property owned by a husband and wife together, including most things purchased during the marriage.

Marital agreements   *1.* All **contracts** between persons married to each other. *2.* Contracts between persons about to get married or about to separate. These usually concern the division of property, custody, and support in the event of divorce or legal separation. When entered into prior to marriage, these contracts are known as *premarital, prenuptial,* or *antenuptial agreements.* When entered into during the marriage (after the marriage ceremony), the contracts are known as *separation agreements* or *postnuptial agreements.*

Marital communications privilege   *1.* The right of a husband and wife to keep the contents of their private conversations secret. *2.* The right of a husband or wife to keep the other from testifying against him or her in a **criminal** trial. This right may not apply if the crime is by one spouse against the other. *Not* **interspousal immunity.**

Maritime (or marine) belt   See **territorial** *waters.*

Maritime law   The law of ships, ocean commerce, and sailors. See also **admiralty.**

Mark   *1.* A sign, such as a cross-mark (X), used by a person who cannot sign a name. To be valid, it usually requires **witnesses** who sign the document. *2.* See **marque and reprisal.** *3.* An indication; proof or evidence. For example, a *mark of fraud* is a sign or indication that something is phony. *4.* A **trademark, service** *mark,* **collective mark** or **certification mark** (see those words) that can be **registered** under federal law because it is "used in commerce" by being displayed on or with a product or service sold or advertised in more than one state or country.

Market *1.* The geographical region in which a product can be sold, or the economic and social characteristics of potential buyers. *2.* Short for "stock market" or "commodities market." *3.* The demand for something or the price it will sell for if sold. *4.* The range of **bid and asked** (see that word) prices for **over-the-counter** stocks.

Market making Establishing a sales price for **over-the-counter** stocks and other securities by placing **bid and asked** (see that word) quotations.

Market order See **order.**

Market power A company's (or group of companies') ability to raise prices by lowering output because it controls a large amount of the trade in an item. This may be a violation of **antitrust acts.**

Market price *1.* The price at which something has just sold in a particular market. *2.* **Market value.**

Market share The percentage of sales that one company controls of a particular item in a particular market.

Market value The price to which a willing seller and a willing buyer would agree for an item in the ordinary course of trade. It is also called "actual market value," "actual value," "cash market value," "clear market value," "current market value," "fair cash value," "fair market value," "fair value," "just compensation," etc.

Marketable *1.* Easily sold for cash. For example, a *marketable security* is a **stock, bond,** etc., that can be sold in the proper **exchange** or through normal business channels. *Marketable securities* also refers to a company's temporary investments of extra cash in such short-term, low-risk things as **treasury bills** and **commercial paper.** *2.* Commercially valid. For example, a *marketable title* to land is ownership that can be freely sold because it is clear of any reasonable doubts as to its validity.

Marketable title acts State laws that make it possible to determine whether or not a **title** to land is good by searching the public records for a limited time only (for example, back to forty years ago).

Marketing contract *1.* Any agreement between an **agent** (or a **broker** or merchant) and a producer by which goods, **securities,** etc., are sold. *2.* An agreement between a producers' **cooperative** and its members in which the members promise to sell through the co-op and the co-op promises to get the best possible price. *3.* An **output contract** or a **requirements contract.**

Marketing order   A federally approved limit on the amount of a particular vegetable or other agricultural commodity that can be sold by farmers in a particular area.

Marketplace of ideas   A goal of **freedom of speech:** the best ideas can find acceptance if unhindered by the government.

Markup   *1.* The meeting in which a **committee** of a **legislature** goes through a **bill** section-by-section to revise and finalize it. *2.* An amount of money added to the cost of an item to give the merchant selling costs plus a profit. If a merchant buys a shirt for ten dollars and sells it for fifteen, it has a "50 percent markup," or a "five dollar markup."

Marque and reprisal   The request made to the ruler of one country to seize the citizens or goods of another country until some wrong done by that other country is righted.

Marriage   Legal union as husband and wife. For **ceremonial marriage,** see that word. For *informal, consensual,* or *common law* marriage, see **common law marriage.**

Marriage settlement   *1.* See **marital agreements.** *2.* A transfer of title to property that firmly fixes the right of **succession** to protect the wife or the inheritance rights of existing or future children. For example, an aunt might "*settle*" the title to a house on the bride and her children as of the date of the proposed marriage.

Marshal   A person employed by a federal court to keep the peace, deliver legal orders, and perform duties similar to those of a state **sheriff.** *Not* "**martial.**"

Marshaling   *1.* Arranging, ranking, or disposing of things in order. For example, *marshaling assets and claims* is collecting them up and arranging the debts into the proper order of priority and then dividing up the **assets** to pay them off. This is done by a **trustee** when someone goes **bankrupt** and by an **executor** or **administrator** of a dead person's **estate.** *2.* In general, if one **creditor** could collect from either of two pots of a **debtor's** money and a second creditor can collect from only one of them, the first creditor will be required to take from the singly-claimed pot first. This is called the *rule of marshaling assets,* the *rule of marshaling remedies,* the *rule of marshaling securities,* and the *two funds doctrine.* The *rule of marshaling liens,* is also called the **inverse order of alienation doctrine.**

Martial law   Government completely by the military; control of the domestic civilian population by the military in wartime or during a breakdown of civilian control. Not "**marshal.**" Compare **military government** and **military law.** [pronounce: <u>mar</u>-shall]

Martin v. Hunter's Lessee (14 U.S. 304) The 1816 case that established the U.S. **Supreme Court's** right to review all state court decisions involving the U.S. **Constitution** or laws.

Martindale–Hubbell Short for the *Martindale-Hubbell Law Directory,* a multivolume book that lists many lawyers by location and type of practice. Other volumes contain summaries of each major area of the law in each state and most foreign countries.

Mary Carter agreement An agreement between a plaintiff and one (or more, but not all) of the co-defendants that gives the co-defendant a financial interest in the plaintiff's **recovery.**

Mask work A series of related images that represent the design of a semiconductor chip. *Mask works* are protected from **infringement** by the *Semiconductor Chip Protection Act of 1984.*

Mass picketing **Picketing** in large numbers. If it disrupts a business it may be an **unfair labor practice** or subject to an **injunction** or a lawsuit for **damages.**

Massachusetts trust A **business trust.**

Master *1.* An employer who has the right to control the actions of an employee (the "*servant*"). The term "*master*" is not applied to one who hires an **independent contractor.** *2.* A *special master* is a person appointed by a court to carry out the court's orders in certain types of lawsuits. A special master might, for example, supervise the sale of property under a **decree (order)** that it be sold. Federal courts and many state courts have *masters* to perform a wide variety of information-gathering jobs for a trial. *3.* Overall or controlling; for example: a *master agreement* is an agreement between a large **union** and the leaders of one industry that becomes a model for **labor contracts** with each individual company; a *master contract* is a basic agreement to buy or lease equipment as needed, each time under the same general terms; a *master deed* is the overall plan containing the obligations of, and restrictions on, each unit of a **condominium;** a *master limited partnership* is a **limited partnership** that sells its shares as **securities;** a *master plan* is the overall plan of a city for housing, business, recreation, etc., as laid out in a map and in materials on **zoning** laws, environmental impacts, etc; and a *master policy* is an insurance policy for persons in a **group insurance** plan.

Material Important; probably necessary; having effect; going to the heart of the matter. For example, a *material allegation* in a legal **pleading** is a statement that is essential to the **claim** or **defense** being used and without which the pleading would have little or no legal effect, and a *material alteration* is a change in a document that affects its meaning or legal effect. For other examples, see the words following. Also see **relevant.**

Material breach   A **breach of contract** that involves a failure to *substantially perform* (see **substantial** *performance*) a contractual promise. A breach of contract must be *material* for a lawsuit based on the breach to succeed.

Material evidence   See **relevant.**

Material fact   *1.* A basic reason for a contract, without which it would not have been entered into. *2.* A fact that is central to winning or deciding a case. *3.* A fact which, if told to an **insurer,** would have influenced the insurer to refuse insurance, cancel insurance, or raise its cost.

Material issue   A question that is formally in dispute between persons properly brought before the court and that is important to determining the outcome of the lawsuit.

Material witness   A person who can give **testimony** no one else can give. In an important **criminal** case, a *material witness* may sometimes be held by the government against his or her will in order to assure that person's availability to testify.

Materialman   A person who supplies building materials for a construction or repair project. A more general word is "*supplier.*"

Mathematical evidence   A phrase sometimes misused to mean **demonstrative evidence.**

Matrimonial actions   **Annulments, divorces,** legal **separations,** etc.

Matter   *1.* A central, necessary, or important fact. *2.* An event, occurrence, or transaction. *3.* The subject of a lawsuit. *4.* The name for certain special types of legal proceedings. For example, "*In the matter of John Jones*" might be the name for a child **neglect** case.

Matter of fact   A question that can be answered by using the senses or deduced from the **testimony** of **witnesses** or other **evidence.**

Matter of law   A question that can be answered by applying the law to the facts of a case.

Matter of record   Anything that can be proved by merely checking a court record. The word is sometimes broadened to include anything that can be proved by checking any official record.

Matured   *1.* See **liquidated.** *2.* See **maturity.**

Maturity   The time when a debt or other obligation becomes due or a right becomes enforceable.

Maxim A general statement about the law that works when applied to most cases.

Mayhem The crime of violently, maliciously, and intentionally giving someone a serious permanent wound. In some states, a type of **aggravated assault.** Once, the crime of permanently wounding another (as by dismemberment) to deprive the person of fighting ability.

Mayor The head of a city, town, or other local government. Mayors may be elected or appointed, important or ceremonial. A _mayor's court_ is usually a police or traffic court in a small town, with the mayor serving as judge.

McCarran Act _1._ See **internal security acts.** _2._ A federal law (15 U.S.C. 1011) that permits states to tax and **regulate** out-of-state **insurance** companies that have in-state customers.

McCulloch v. Maryland (17 U.S. 316) The 1819 Supreme Court decision that upheld the **implied** power (not stated directly in the **Constitution**) of the federal government to take certain actions, such as establishing banks, and denied the states the right to tax any part of the federal government, confirming that the national government was supreme in all matters allowed it by the Constitution.

McNabb–Mallory rule The rule (used in federal court and many state courts, and found at 318 U.S. 322 and 354 U.S. 449) that if someone has been held too long by the police before bringing the person before a judge, no **confession** obtained during the holding period may be used against that person.

McNaghten rule See **M'Naghten's rule.**

Mean high tide The long-term average, highest line that the tide reaches on waterfront land. This is often considered the private property line; anything on the seaward side may be used by the public.

Means _1._ Money, property, or income available to support yourself, to support your family, to pay a debt, etc. _2._ Laws, **acts,** and **initiative** and **referendum** measures (the _means_ to accomplish what the people want the government to accomplish). _3._ A cause; an agent of change; a method of accomplishing something.

Means test _1._ A financial requirement that a person have or make either more or less than a certain amount of money to qualify for something. _2._ The requirement that if a company makes choices that are potentially _discriminatory_ (see **discrimination**), the company's purpose must be legally justified and the _means_ it uses to accomplish that purpose (or "end") must be the least drastic possible.

Mechanical equivalents   Two things that do the same work in the same basic way and produce the same result.

Mechanic's lien   A worker's legal claim to hold property (such as a car) until repair charges are paid or to file formal papers securing a right to property (such as a car or a house) until charges for work done are paid.

Med-Arb   **Arbitration** that follows unsuccessful **mediation.**

Mediate   *1.* "In between"; secondary; incidental. *2.* See **mediation.** *3.* Indirect or deduced.

Mediation   Outside help in settling a dispute. The person who does this is called a *mediator.* This is different from **arbitration** (see that word) in that a mediator can only persuade, not force, people into a settlement. The Federal Mediation and Conciliation Service (**F.M.C.S.**) helps to settle **labor disputes.**

Medicaid   A government program of medical payments for low-income persons who meet federal and state requirements.

Medical directive   See **advance directive.**

Medical examiner   A public official who investigates violent or unexplained deaths, performs autopsies, and helps **prosecute homicide** cases. Compare with **coroner.**

Medical jurisprudence   See **forensic** *medicine.*

Medicare   A federal government program of medical payments for elderly persons.

Meeting of creditors   In **bankruptcy** law, a hearing involving the bankrupt person (the debtor), the bankruptcy **trustee,** and the bankrupt person's **creditors.** In this meeting, the debtor is questioned by the trustee and creditors. Only the *first meeting* is held in simple cases, but *interim* and *final meetings* may be needed in complex cases. *Contested matters* may be heard by a judge in an *adversary proceeding.*

Meeting of minds   Agreement among all persons entering into a deal on the basic meaning and legal effect of the **contract.** Compare **mutual assent.**

Megan's law   A law requiring registration of convicted sex offenders and permitting law enforcement officials to notify the communities where they live.

Melioration   Improvement to, rather than repair of, property.

Member   *1.* One of the persons in a family, **corporation, legislature, union,** etc. *2.* A bank that is affiliated with one of the federal reserve banks, or a brokerage firm that is affiliated with a stock or other securities **exchange.** *3.* Short for member of a **house of representatives.** *4.* An "external" part of a body, such as an arm.

Membership corporation A nonprofit, nonstock **corporation** created for social, charitable, political, etc., purposes.

Memorandum *1.* An informal note; a written summary of a meeting or **contract.** *2.* A note from one member of an organization to another. *3.* A written document that proves a contract exists. See **statute of frauds.** *4.* A **brief** (see that word) of law. It is often submitted to a judge in a case.

Memorandum decision A court's *decision* that gives the **ruling** (what it decides and orders done), but no **opinion** (reasons for the decision). A *memorandum opinion,* however, is a **per curiam** (see that word) opinion.

Memorial *1.* A **petition** or written statement presented to a **legislature** or to the head of a country or state. *2.* A rough draft, **abstract,** or **memorandum** of a court's **order,** setting it down in writing until it can be put into the public records in final form. *3.* See **memorandum** no. 3.

Men of straw See **straw man.**

Mens rea (Latin) Guilty mind; wrongful purpose; criminal intent. *Mens rea* is a state of mind which (when combined with an **actus** *reus,* or "criminal act") produces a crime. This state of mind is usually to *intentionally* or *knowingly* do something prohibited, but is occasionally to *recklessly* or *grossly negligently* do it. See also **strict liability** for crimes that do not require *mens rea.*

Mensa et thoro (Latin) "Bed and board." Describes a type of limited **divorce** (see that word) or legal separation.

Mental anguish (or mental suffering or distress) Nonphysical harm that may be compensated for by **damages** in some types of lawsuits. *Mental anguish* may be as limited as the immediate mental feelings during an injury or as broad as prolonged grief, shame, humiliation, despair, etc.

Mental cruelty See **cruelty.**

Mental disease (or disability, illness, (in)capacity, or (in)competent) See **insanity** and **competency.**

Mental element **Mens rea.**

Mercantile Commercial; having to do with buying and selling, etc.

Merchant banker A broad term for an institution that may perform some of the functions of commercial **banks** (that make loans), some of **investment bankers** (that **underwrite** securities), and other functions such as putting their own money directly into business deals.

Merchantable *1.* Fit to be sold; of the general type and quality described and fit for the general purpose for which it was bought. *2.* **Marketable,** as in **marketable title acts.**

Mercy killing Causing the death of a person who is near death from a terminal disease and who is thought to desire death. It may be *active* (such as by lethal injection, and often subject to prosecution) or *passive* (such as by withdrawing a feeding tube). Also called *euthanasia.* See also **death, brain death rule,** and **natural death acts.**

Merger *1.* The union of two or more things, usually with the smaller or less important thing "ceasing to exist" once it is a part of the other. Companies, rights, contracts, etc., can *merge.* The following definitions divide these mergers by type: *2.* When **corporations** merge, it is a *horizontal merger* if business competitors selling the same product in the same area join, a *vertical merger* if a company joins with its customers or suppliers, and a *conglomerate merger* if unrelated companies join. *Conglomerate mergers* are of three types: it is a *pure merger* when two totally unrelated companies join; a *geographical extension merger* when companies selling similar products in different **markets** join; and a *product extension merger* when two companies selling related, but different products join. Finally, many states allow a quick, cheap *short-form* merger when a **subsidiary** merges with its *parent company. 3.* In **contract** law, if the persons who make a contract intend it, one contract may end and become a part of another through *merger.* Also, all prior oral agreements may be ended by establishing a written contract as the entire agreement by including a *merger clause.* See **integration.** *4.* Two rights, or **estates** can merge. For example, if a tenant buys the house, the right of **tenancy** *merges* and is ended with the start of the right of ownership. Merging of rights occurs in many other areas of the law, such as **divorce** law, **judgment** law, etc. *5. Merger* also occurs in **criminal** law when a person is charged with two crimes (based on the exact same acts), one of which is a **lesser included offense** of the other. The lesser crime *merges* because, under the prohibition against **double jeopardy,** the person may be tried for only one of them.

Merit system A method of hiring, firing, and promoting used by governments and based on specific rules. It is meant to ensure competence in the **civil service** and to limit **patronage.**

Merits *1.* The central part of a case; the "meat" of one side's legal position. *2.* The substance or real issues of a lawsuit, as opposed to the form or the legal technicalities it involves. *Judgment on the merits* is a final resolution of a lawsuit after full *discussion* of the **evidence** (in a **summary judgment**) or after *presentation* of the evidence in a trial.

Mesne Middle; intermediate. For example, "_mesne process_" includes the legal papers and court **orders** _in between_ the start and finish of a lawsuit. [pronounce: men]

Messuage A home plus its surrounding land and outbuildings. See also **curtilage.**

Metes and bounds Boundary lines and fixed points and angles used to describe and measure the perimeter of land.

Metropolitan district An area that includes more than one city, such as a city and its suburbs, that is set up by state law to handle regional problems such as public transportation, water supply, and sewage disposal. It may be a _general district,_ headed by a _metropolitan council,_ or a _specific district_ such as a "transportation district" run by a **board.**

Mexican divorce See **mail order divorce.**

Middleman (or intermediary) _1._ A person who brings others together and helps them make deals. _2._ A person who buys from one person and sells to another. _3._ An **agent** or **broker.**

Migratory divorce A **divorce** gained by a person who has moved (often temporarily) to another place in order to get the divorce.

Military government Government by the military, under the direction of the civilian head of state, of either territory outside the country or within the country during an insurrection or civil war. Compare **martial law** and **military law.**

Military jurisdiction Martial law, military government, and **military law.**

Military law The law that **regulates** the armed forces and its members. U.S. _military law_ is contained in a comprehensive **Code of Military Justice,** administered by military officers under the supervision of the **judge advocate** _general_ of each service and decided by a system of _military courts_ (**courts martial** for trials, _courts of military review_ for major cases on **appeal,** and the _U.S. Court of Military Appeals_ for **civilian** review of the most major cases). There are also _military boards,_ which act as fact-finders, advisory boards, and courts in cases involving personnel matters such as promotion and in matters such as property damage, loss of funds, etc. Typical _military offenses_ (in addition to those which would also be civilian crimes) include **desertion, insubordination,** or sleeping while on guard.

Military will A **will** made by a member of the armed forces while on active duty. Many of the usual requirements for a will to be valid (such as those involving writing, witnesses, and age) are eliminated or reduced.

Militia   A part-time military force, called to active duty during a crisis. This job is now primarily performed by state National Guard units and various armed forces reserve units. [pronounce: mil-<u>ish</u>-a]

Mill   One-tenth of a cent. Some property taxes are expressed in mills. A *mill rate* of "one" indicates that one dollar is to be paid for each thousand dollars of **assessed valuation.**

Miller v. California   See **obscene.**

Mind and memory   A phrase describing adequate mental **capacity** to make a **will** (know what you're doing, know what you're giving away, and to whom).

Mineral   As defined in land laws, any nonanimal, nonvegetable substance found on or in the ground; any commercially valuable, naturally occurring chemical substance.

Mineral lease   An agreement giving a right to explore for **minerals** and then to take out those found (upon payment of rent for use of the land or **royalties** based on what is taken).

Mineral right   A right to either take minerals out of the ground or to receive payment for minerals taken out.

Minimal diversity   See **diversity of citizenship.**

Minimum contacts doctrine   The principle that a person must carry on a certain minimum amount of activity within a state, or have formal ties to the state, before that person can be sued in the state.

Minimum fee schedules   The lowest fee for a particular service that a **bar association** will permit a lawyer to charge. *Minimum fees* have been abolished because they violate **antitrust acts.**

Minimum wage   The lowest wage that may be paid to certain employees as set by federal law.

Mining lease   A type of **mineral lease** (see that word).

Mining location   See **location.**

Minister   *1.* A person acting for another person or carrying out that person's orders. *2.* A diplomatic representative such as **ambassador** or **envoy.** *3.* The head of a **cabinet** department or government organization in many countries. The job is similar to that of a **secretary** (of defense, of labor, etc.) in the United States.

Ministerial   *1.* Done by carrying out orders, rather than by personally deciding how to act. In this use of the word, a police *chief's* actions would be *discretionary* and a police *officer's* actions *ministerial.* But see no. 2. *2.* Done by carrying out a general **policy** (whether or not there is much choice of action) rather than by setting or making policy. In this sense of the word, a police *chief's* actions would be *ministerial* and the police *board's* would be *discretionary.*

Minitrial **Alternative dispute resolution** by a panel of executives from two companies engaged in a complex dispute. A neutral moderator helps the two sides sort out factual and legal issues to reach a voluntary settlement. Compare **summary jury trial.**

Minor *1.* A person who is under the age of full legal rights and duties. *2.* Less or lower. *3.* Legally insignificant.

Minor dispute See **major dispute.**

Minority *1.* Being a **minor** (see that word). *2.* Less than half. *3.* Describes groups with only a small percentage of the total population. *4.* For *minority view,* contrast **majority** *view.*

Minority opinion A *dissenting opinion.* See **opinion** (or **dissent**).

Minority stockholder A person who holds too few **shares** of **stock** to control the way the **corporation** is managed (or to elect any **directors**).

Minor's estate Property that must be looked after by a **trustee** because its owner is not yet of legal age to manage it.

Minute book The record book kept by the **clerk** of some courts that lists a summary of all **orders** by case and case number.

Minutes Written notes of a meeting.

Miranda warning The warning that must be given to a person **arrested** or taken into **custody** by a police officer or other official. The warning includes the fact that what you say may be held against you and that you have the rights to remain silent, to contact a lawyer, and to have a free lawyer if you are poor. If this warning is not given properly, no statements made by the **defendant** during custody may be used by the police or by the **prosecutor** in court. The warning is required by the 1966 case *Miranda v. Arizona* (384 U.S. 436).

Mirandize Slang for giving a **Miranda warning.**

Mirror image rule The **common law** rule that an **offer** and **acceptance** must state identical terms to make a valid contract. The **Uniform Commercial Code,** however, upholds the validity of commercial contracts that have minor differences in the "fine print" of the offer and acceptance.

Misadventure An accident; an unintentional injury, often with no one legally at fault.

Misapplication Improper spending or use of another's funds by a person having rightful possession or control over the funds.

Misappropriation Taking something wrongfully, but not necessarily illegally.

Misbranding Any intentionally false information on a product label.

Miscarriage of justice Unfair harm to a person; unfair legal proceeding or other official action.

Mischief *1.* Intentionally or recklessly done harm. *2.* The problem or danger that a legislative **act** is designed to correct.

Misconduct *1.* Doing a forbidden act intentionally or willfully. *2. Official misconduct* includes **malfeasance, misfeasance,** and **nonfeasance.** *3.* The act done in no. 1.

Misdemeanant A person who commits a **misdemeanor** (see that word).

Misdemeanor A criminal offense less than a **felony** that is usually punishable by a **fine** or less than a year in jail. For *misdemeanor-manslaughter rule,* see **felony-murder rule.**

Misfeasance The improper doing of an otherwise proper or lawful act. Compare with **malfeasance** and **nonfeasance.**

Misfortune An accident that could not have been guarded against.

Misjoinder See **joinder.**

Mislaid Put somewhere by someone who then forgets where. *Mislaid property* may not be technically "lost" so different legal rules may apply to the finders of mislaid and lost property.

Misprision *1.* The failure to carry out a public duty, such as the duty to properly carry out a high public office. *2.* The failure to prevent or report a crime. *3.* The crime of concealing another's crime, including *misprision of felony* and *misprision of treason. 4.* An old meaning of *misprision* included **contempt** of court, **sedition,** and other open rejections of proper authority.

Misrepresentation *1. Innocent misrepresentation* is a false statement that is not known to be false. *2. Negligent misrepresentation* is a false statement made when you should have known better. *3. Fraudulent misrepresentation* is a false statement known to be false and meant to be misleading.

Mistake An unintentional error or act. A *mistake of fact* is a mistake about facts that is not caused by a **negligent** failure to find out the truth. A *mistake of law* is knowledge of the true facts combined with a wrong conclusion about the legal effect of the facts.

Mistrial A trial that the judge ends and declares will have no legal effect because of a major defect in procedure or because of the death of a **juror,** a deadlocked **jury,** or other major problem. Compare with **retrial.**

Mitigating circumstances Facts that provide no **justification** or **excuse** for an action, but that can lower the amount of moral blame, and thus lower the criminal **penalty** or civil **damages** for the action.

Mitigation of damages _1._ Facts showing that the size of a claim for **damages** is unjustified. _2._ The _doctrine of mitigation of damages_ is the principle that a person suing for damages must have taken reasonable steps to minimize the harm done, or the amount of money awarded will be lowered.

Mittimus The name for a court **order** sending a convicted person to prison, or transferring records from one court to another.

Mixed action A legal proceeding that is both **in personam** and **in rem** (see those words). This is not the same as _quasi in rem._

Mixed nuisance A **nuisance** (see that word) that is both _public_ and _private._

Mixed property _1._ **Property** (see that word), such as **fixtures,** that is both _real_ and _personal._ _2._ See **hotchpot.**

Mixed questions Legal questions involving both **fact** and **law** or involving both local and **foreign** law.

Mixed trust A trust set up for both charities and private persons.

M'Naghten's rule One of many different definitions of **insanity,** proposed over the years in different cases, to determine whether a person will be held criminally responsible for an act. According to the "_Rule in M'Naghten's Case,_" a person is "not guilty because of insanity" if, at the time of the offense, "a defect of reason produced by a disease of the mind" caused the person to "not know the nature of the act" or to "not know right from wrong." Some parts of this rule are included in the _Model Penal Code._

Model Acts Proposed laws put out by the _Commission on Uniform State Laws_ and the _American Law Institute_ (but not those proposed as **uniform acts**); for example, the _Model Penal Code._

Model Code of Ethics and Professional Responsibility Ethical guidelines of the **National Federation of Paralegal Associations.**

Model Penal Code test _Substantial capacity test._ See **insanity** no. 2.

Model Rules of Professional Conduct See **Rules of Professional Conduct.**

Modification A change or alteration. "_Modification_" is often used for a minor change, but a _modification of judgment_ under most court rules includes a **judgment** changed in major ways and for major reasons such as fraud.

Modified accelerated cost recovery system A tax **accounting** method that uses a range of time, usually shorter than an **asset's** useful life, during which a business may take fixed yearly **depreciation** deductions on the asset.

Modus (Latin) Method, means, manner, or way. For example, "*modus operandi*" is a method of operation (that usually refers to a distinct pattern of criminal behavior).

Moiety *1.* Half. *Moiety acts* are criminal laws that allow up to half of the **fine** paid by a convicted person to be paid to the informant whose information helped trigger the prosecution. *2.* A part; a fractional part. [pronounce: moy-ity]

Monarchy A government by a king, queen, or other royal head. Monarchies may be **absolute** or **constitutional.**

Monetary aggregates Subcategories of the **money supply** (see that word).

Money market The institutions that deal with short-term loans and near-term transfers of funds. Also short for **money market fund** or **money market certificate.**

Money market certificate A type of savings certificate, sold by banks and other savings institutions, that is usually held for a short, definite time period such as six months. It pays the buyer interest at a rate based on the rate paid by U.S. **treasury bills.**

Money market fund A **mutual fund** that invests in safe short-term **securities** such as **treasury bills.**

Money order A type of **draft** (like a check) sold by banks, post offices, and others, to persons who use it to make payments.

Money supply The amount of money, or the amount of certain "types" of money, in circulation within a country. In the U.S., the *Federal Reserve Board* has defined several categories (M-1A, M-1B, M-2, M-3) to help measure the money supply. M-1A, for example, includes all paper money and coins plus all **demand** deposits held in banks.

Money-purchase plan A **pension plan** in which an employer contributes a fixed amount each year. The ultimate value of the **benefits** paid will vary, depending on how much the invested sums earn.

Monition A judge's order or warning.

Monopoly Control by one or a few companies of the manufacture, sale, distribution, or price of something. A *monopoly* may be prohibited if, for example, a company deliberately drives out competition.

Monopsony A situation in which there is only one buyer in a product market. *Monopsony power* is the ability of some buyers who buy a large percentage of a producer's output to control the price they will pay.

Monroe doctrine   The assertion (first made in 1823 by U.S. President James Monroe) that the U.S. will oppose any European interference in the affairs of any Western Hemisphere country.

Monument   A post, pile of stones, natural boundary, marked tree, etc., used to mark the boundaries of land.

Moot   _Moot_ has several conflicting and overlapping definitions, including: _1._ No longer important or no longer needing a decision because _already decided._ For example, a federal court will not take a case if it is _moot_ in this sense. _2._ For the sake of argument or practice. For example, _moot court_ is a mock court in which law students practice by arguing **appellate** cases. _3._ Abstract. Not a real case involving a real dispute. _4._ A subject for argument; undecided; unsettled. In this sense, _moot_ means roughly the opposite of the first definition.

Moral   _1._ Having to do with the conscience and with principles of good conduct. _2._ Having to do with only the conscience and not enforceable by law, as in "only a moral obligation." _3._ Depending upon a belief, rather than being complete proof. In this sense, **testimony** is _moral evidence,_ and _moral certainty_ is a very strong belief that something is correct. _4._ For _moral hazard,_ see **hazard.**

Moral rights   In **copyright** law, the rights that protect an artist's professional reputation, such as the right, under some circumstances, to prevent a work's modification or to disclaim its authorship if modified.

Moral turpitude   Describes any crime, such as **larceny,** that involves immorality or dishonesty.

Moratorium   _1._ An enforced delay. For example, a city may impose a _moratorium_ (a suspension or temporary delay) in giving out building permits in order to protect the environment. _2._ Any deliberate delay, whether or not enforced, required, or agreed to.

More definite statement   See **motion.** Also see **bill of particulars.**

More favorable terms clause   A labor contract provision in which a **union** promises a company that it will not give more favorable terms (as to wages, benefits, hours, working conditions, etc.) to competitors of the company. Compare with **most favored nation** _clause._

More or less   A contract **term** meant to keep the delivery of small variations in quantity from being a **breach.** What is "_more or less_" the right amount varies with what is customary in the trade and between the persons.

Morgue   The place where unidentified or as yet unclaimed dead bodies are taken for identification. [pronounce: morg]

Mortality tables   Actuarial tables (or mathematical formulas) that predict how many persons from a group of a certain age, sex, and other characteristics will die in each succeeding year.

Mortgage   *1.* One person putting up land or buildings (or, in the case of a **chattel mortgage,** personal **property**) as security for a loan. The property is **collateral** for repayment of the loan. A mortgage usually takes one of three forms: A. The ownership of the property actually transfers in whole or in part to the lender. B. The ownership does not change at all, and the mortgage has the same effect as a **lien** (see that word). C. The property is put into **trust** with an independent person until the debt is paid off. *2.* For various types of mortgages, such as **closed-end, conventional, first, purchase money, wraparound,** etc., see those words. *3.* Some "mortgage words" include the following: A *mortgage banker* makes mortgage loans with its own or others' money, usually on a short-term basis. A *mortgage bond* is a **bond** with property put up for **security.** A *mortgage certificate* is a document showing a share owned in a mortgage. A *mortgage commitment* is a letter agreeing to a specific loan on specific terms. A *mortgage company* makes mortgage loans, then sells them to others. A *mortgage contingency clause* makes a sale depend on finding mortgage money. A *mortgagee* is a lender who takes a mortgage. *Mortgaging out* is 100 percent financing, or buying property without using any of your own money. A *mortgagor* is a borrower who gives a mortgage in return for the loan. [pronounce: mor-gidj]

Mortgage market   The granting of real estate **mortgages** to individuals and businesses by banks and other financial institutions, the resale of these mortgages to investors, and the packaging of these mortgages into groups to back **bond**-like **securities.** The federal government oversees the process through its banking regulators and supports both the granting and resale markets through organizations such as the **F.H.A., V.A., Ginnie Mae,** and **Fannie Mae.**

Mortis causa   See **causa mortis.**

Mortmain   (French) *1.* "Dead hand." Describes property controlled "by the hand" of a dead person, especially when the property is transferred with resale restrictions to a corporation. *Mortmain acts* in England restricted the church practice of controlling land indefinitely by transferring the land to a corporation. *2. Mortmain statutes,* in those states that still have them, invalidate some deathbed gifts to charity.

Most favored nation   *1.* An agreement between two countries that says that each will treat the other as well as it treats the country it treats best. The main effect of "most favored nation" status is lowered import taxes. *2.* A *most favored nation* **clause** in a **labor contract** is a company's promise to give union members any benefits later given to any union's members. Compare with a **more favorable terms clause.**

Most suitable use **Highest and best use.**

Mother Hubbard clause *1.* A **dragnet clause.** *2.* The name for many types of statements in a document that other things not specifically described in the document are *included* in its effect or *excluded* from its effect.

Motion *1.* A request that a judge make a **ruling** or take some other action. For example, a *motion to dismiss* is a request that the court throw the case out; a *motion for more definite statement* is a request that the judge require an opponent in a lawsuit to file a less vague or ambiguous **pleading;** a *motion to strike* is a request that **immaterial** statements or other things be removed from an opponent's pleading; and a *motion to suppress* is a request that illegally gathered **evidence** be prohibited. *Motions* are either *granted* or *denied* by the judge. *2.* The formal way something is proposed in a meeting.

Motive The reason why a person does something. *Not* **intent** (see that word for the difference).

Mousemilking Great effort to trivial effect. Wasting a court's time with massive amounts of evidence or a long-winded argument to prove a trivial point.

Mouthpiece Slang for "lawyer."

Movables Personal property.

Movant Person who makes a **motion** (see that word). [pronounce: move-ant]

Move Make a **motion** (see that word).

Moving cause See **proximate cause.**

Moving papers Court papers to make or support a **motion** or a lawsuit.

Mugging A street robbery, particularly one using or threatening physical violence.

Mugshot A picture taken for an official police record during a **booking.** These pictures are collected in *mugbooks* to help identify criminals in the future.

Mulct *1.* A **fine** or **penalty,** or to fine someone. *2.* A **fraud,** or to commit a fraud.

Mulier An old word for a **legitimate** child.

Multidistrict litigation Lawsuits involving the same facts that come up in several different federal **district courts** may all be transferred to one court by a special federal panel according to special rules. The types of complex cases that get transferred this way include **antitrust** cases, airplane crash suits, **patent, trademark,** and **securities** cases, etc.

Multifariousness   Several unconnected claims combined in one lawsuit or several unconnected subjects in one legislative **bill** (sometimes called an **omnibus** *bill*).

Multilateral agreement   An agreement among several persons, companies, or governments.

Multinational   *1.* A company with major centers of operation or **subsidiaries** in several countries. *2.* A company that merely does business in several countries.

Multiple access   The **defense** to a **paternity suit** that the woman had several lovers. **DNA fingerprinting** has reduced the usefulness of this defense.

Multiple evidence   Facts that may be used in a trial to prove only certain things and no others.

Multiple listing   See **listing.**

Multiple offense   An act that violates more than one law and in ways that do not totally overlap.

Multiple party account   A **joint bank account** or a **trust** account, but not an account for an organization.

Multiple sentences   See **cumulative sentence.**

Multiplicity of actions   Two or more lawsuits against the same defendant about the same issues. The suits should usually be combined into one.

Multiplicity of charges   Charging the same offense in more than one **count** of an **indictment.** This violates the constitutional provision against **double jeopardy.**

Mun.   **Municipal.**

Muni   A **municipal** *bond.*

Municipal   Having to do with a local government. For example, *municipal bonds* are **bonds** issued by a local government to raise money, and a *municipal ordinance* is a local law or regulation. [pronounce: mu-niss-eh-pul]

Municipal corporation   A city or other local government unit that has been set up according to state requirements.

Municipality   A **municipal corporation.**

Muniments   Documents such as **deeds** that are **evidence** of **title.**

Murder   The unlawful killing of another human being that is premeditated (planned in advance) or is with **malice aforethought** (see that word). Most states divide murder into first and second **degrees.** *First degree murder* usually involves a **willful** and deliberate killing, such as by torture or lying in wait, or killing during the commission of another **felony** such as **arson, rape, robbery,** and **kidnapping.** *Second degree murder* is less serious, but still worse than **manslaughter.**

Mutatis mutandis   (Latin) With necessary changes in detail.

Mutilation   *1.* Cutting, tearing, erasing, or otherwise changing a document in a way that changes or destroys its legal effect. *2.* **Mayhem.**

Mutiny   *1.* A revolt in the armed services. *2.* A revolt of sailors aboard any ship.

Mutual   Done together or **reciprocal.** See that word for further definition and examples of such things as *mutual* (**reciprocal**) *wills.*

Mutual assent   An **offer** and **acceptance** or other definite intention of both parties to make a valid **contract.** Compare **meeting of minds.**

Mutual benefit association (or company, corporation, or society)   See **nonprofit organization.**

Mutual company   *1.* A company in which the customers are also the owners, with profits often passed on in proportion to the dollar value of each customer's business. *2.* A company in which the employees are the owners, with profits often passed on in proportion to each employee's job level or work. *3.* See also **nonprofit organization.**

Mutual fund   An investment company that pools investors' money and buys **securities** (often **shares** of **stock** in many companies). It does this by selling its own shares to the public. Mutual funds are *open-end* (the number of shares held by investors changes), but there are also investment companies like mutual funds that are *closed-end* (the number of shares issued is fixed).

Mutual mistake   A mistake, by both parties to a contract, about a subject that was important to both in their decisions to enter into the contract. It is a *mutual mistake* if both make the same mistake or if each makes a different mistake about the same important thing. A contract may be **voidable** if there was mutual mistake.

Mutual strike aid   Financial help given by a group of companies in an industry to those companies in the group that are struck by a union.

Mutuality of contract (or obligation)   Describes the principle that, for a binding **contract** to exist, each side must have some obligation or duty to perform under the contract.

N.A. Nonacquiescence; not allowed; not available; not applicable; etc.

N.A.A.C.P. National Association for the Advancement of Colored People. A group that brought many landmark civil rights cases.

N.A.F.T.A. North American Free Trade Agreement.

N.A.L.A. **National Association of Legal Assistants.**

N.A.L.S. **National Association of Legal Secretaries.**

N.A.R. National Association of Realtors.

N.A.S.A. National Aeronautics and Space Administration.

N.A.S.D. National Association of Securities Dealers. An association of dealers in **over-the-counter** stocks and other **securities.**

N.A.S.D.A.Q. National Association of Securities Dealers Automatic Quotations System. The primary **over-the-counter** stock and bond trading system.

N.B. (Latin) "Nota bene." Mark well, note well, or observe. The phrase is used to give special emphasis to the comment that follows.

N.C.D. (Latin) "Nemine contra dicente." No one dissenting.

N.C.I.C. National Crime Information Center. Computerized records of criminals, **warrants,** stolen vehicles, etc.

N.D. Northern **district.**

N.E. North Eastern Reporter (see **National Reporter System**).

N.E.P.A. **National Environmental Policy Act.**

N.F.P.A. **National Federation of Paralegal Associations.**

N.G.O. Nongovernmental organization.

N.I.F.O. "Next in, first out." Describes a method for valuing current **inventory** by its replacement cost. Under this accounting method, if a merchant buys a blivit for a dollar, but knows that once it is sold a replacement blivit will cost two dollars, the owned blivit is worth two dollars. Compare with **F.I.F.O.** and **L.I.F.O.**

N.L.A.D.A. National Legal Aid and Defender Association.

N.L.R.A. **National Labor Relations Act.**

N.L.R.B. National Labor Relations Board. A federal agency that **regulates** labor-management activities such as **collective bargaining,** union elections, **unfair labor practices,** etc.

N.O.V. See **non obstante veredicto.**

N.O.W. Negotiable order of withdrawal. A **negotiable instrument,** such as a check, that is payable on **demand** from funds in a financial institution, such as a bank. A *N.O.W. account* is a type of checking account that pays interest.

N.P. Notary public.

N.R. New reports; not reported; nonresident.

N.R.C. Nuclear Regulatory Commission.

N.S. New series.

N.S.A. National Security Agency. It conducts communications security and intelligence gathering.

N.S.F. *1.* National Science Foundation. *2.* Not sufficient funds.

N.Y.S.E. New York Stock Exchange.

Naked Incomplete; without force; unjustified. See also **bare** and **nude.**

Napoleonic Code **Code Civil.**

Narcotic *1.* Any substance that dulls senses, induces sleep, or becomes addictive. *2.* A substance, like those in no. 1, that either federal or state law prohibits or regulates as possibly harmful to public health or safety. However, substances such as caffeine and nicotine are not defined as *narcotics.*

Narr Abbreviation for the Latin "narratio" (a **declaration** in a lawsuit) and used in the phrase "narr and cognovit," which means **confession of judgment** (see that word).

Narrative evidence A witness's **testimony** that is given without interruption or the usual questions by a lawyer.

Narrow interpretation Giving a law or **constitutional** provision a meaning that restricts it to a literal reading, rather than "broadly" expanding its application. See **strict** *construction.*

National Association of Legal Assistants A group that certifies **paralegals** and other legal assistants through its *C.L.A.* exam, offers professional responsibility standards, and provides continuing legal education and other services.

National Association of Legal Secretaries A group that certifies legal secretaries through its *P.L.S.* exam and provides continuing legal education and other services.

National bank A bank incorporated under the laws of the U.S., rather than under state laws. A bank can be a *national bank* even if it has branches in only one state. National banks are usually members of the *Federal Reserve System* and are insured by the **F.D.I.C.**

National Conference of Commissioners on Uniform State Laws See **Commission on Uniform State Laws.**

National consultation right The right of certain large unions of federal employees to be consulted with by the government concerning changes in federal personnel policies.

National Endowment for the Arts v. Finley (524 U.S. 569) The 1998 U.S. Supreme Court decision that a federal agency's refusal to make a grant because a performance does not conform to "general standards of decency" does not violate the performer's **First Amendment** *freedom of speech* rights and is not *void for vagueness* under the **Fifth Amendment.**

National Environmental Policy Act (42 U.S.C. 4321) The 1969 federal law requiring **Environmental Impact Statements** (see that word) on major building and development projects and setting out the major environmental goals of the United States.

National Federation of Paralegal Associations A group of organizations that offers professional responsibility standards for legal assistants and provides continuing legal education and other services. It publishes the *National Paralegal Reporter.*

National Labor Relations Act (29 U.S.C. 151) The federal law that set up the National Labor Relations Board (**N.L.R.B.**) and established rules for all types of employer-employee contact (union **recognition,** strikes, secret ballots for selection of a union, union elections, **unfair labor practices,** etc.). It is a combination of the **Wagner, Taft-Hartley** and **Landrum-Griffin Acts.**

National Reporter System A system of sets of books that collect all cases from state supreme courts by region. (For example, the North Eastern Reporter has Illinois, Indiana, Massachusetts, New York, and Ohio. It is abbreviated "N.E." and its more recent books are N.E.2d or North East Reporter, Second Series.) The Reporter System also has sets for all federal cases, some lower court cases state-by-state, and a **digest** for each region. It has become the official place for some states to publish the decisions of their courts. The system is published by West Publishing Company.

Nationality The country of which a person is a citizen. (In some cases, a person could be a *"U.S. national"* without being a citizen as are, for example, the residents of a U.S. **territory.**) Nationality gives a person a political base, while **domicile** gives a person a **civil** base (a place to sue and be sued, pay taxes, claim benefits, etc.). A person gains nationality by birth or **naturalization.** The *U.S. Nationality Act* is the shortened name for the U.S. law dealing with immigration, naturalization, and entry of foreigners to the country.

Nationalization A country taking over a private industry, owning, and running it, with or without payment to the ex-owners.

Native A **citizen** by birth (including persons born overseas to parents who are citizens).

Native American Inhabitants of the U.S. since before the voyage of Columbus. This term generally replaced the term *Indian* about 1975, but earlier laws and court decisions retain the prior term.

Natural affection Love or family ties between persons directly related (parent-child, husband-wife, sister-brother). *Natural affection* alone may be enough **consideration** for a contract.

Natural born citizen A person born in the United States or, perhaps, a person born *to* U.S. citizens.

Natural death acts State laws that allow a person to give binding written instructions that doctors should not prolong the person's life by artificial means if he or she is near death from a terminal condition. See also **mercy killing** and **living will.**

Natural heir (or object) *1.* A child. *2.* A close relative. *3.* Anyone who would **inherit** if there were no **will.**

Natural law *1.* Rules of conduct that are thought to be the same everywhere because they are basic to human behavior. *2.* Basic moral law.

Natural monument See **monument.**

Natural object (of bounty) **Natural heir.**

Natural person A human being, as opposed to a corporation (see **artificial person**).

Natural resources *1.* Materials, still in their original state, that would have economic value if extracted (timber, oil, minerals, etc.). *2.* Any natural place or product that is of benefit to people (those things in no. 1 plus lakes, parkland, etc.).

Naturalization The formal process of becoming a **citizen** of a country.

Navigable waters Water in or adjacent to the U.S. that forms a continuous passage for commercial ships from the sea.

Ne exeat (Latin) A court paper forbidding a person from leaving the area. [pronounce: ne ex-ee-at]

Ne varietur (Latin) "Do not alter it." Words sometimes written by a **notary public** after authenticating a document.

Near v. Minnesota (382 U.S. 679) The 1931 U.S. Supreme Court decision that struck down as **prior restraint** (see that word) a state law that prohibited publication by a newspaper that prints malicious **defamation.**

Near-money Quick assets.

Necessaries doctrine The rule that a seller may collect from a parent (or a spouse) the price of goods sold for the basic support of the parent's child (or the other spouse).

Necessarily included offense Lesser included offense.

Necessary Physically or logically required. For example, a *necessary cause* is an event or action without which something would not have happened. *2.* Legally required. For example, a *necessary party* is a person without whom a lawsuit cannot proceed or cannot proceed with complete fairness. *3.* Appropriate or helpful, whether or not absolutely required. For example, the *necessary and proper clause* (Article I, Section 8, Clause 18) of the U.S. **Constitution** gives **Congress** the power to pass all laws appropriate to carry out its functions. See also **penumbra doctrine.**

Necessity Anything from an irresistible force or compulsion to an important, but not required action. *Necessity* often refers to a situation that requires an action that would otherwise be illegal or expose a person to **tort** liability. A *public necessity* that triggers a person's actions required for the public good provides more protection than a *private necessity* that triggers actions required for the person's own good. See also **necessary, necessaries doctrine,** and **legal necessity.**

Negative averment Something stated in the negative form that is really a positive statement to be proved, rather than a denial of someone else's positive statement. For example, "he was not old enough to make a valid contract when he signed the papers" is a *negative averment* (because it's something he must prove), while "the signature is not his" is a simple denial (because the other side must prove the signature is his).

Negative covenant A promise, in a contract, to refrain from doing something; for example, a promise by the seller of a business, in the sale contract, to refrain from competing with the business sold.

Negative easement See **easement.**

Negative enforcement Using a court **order** to restrain a person who has **breached** an exclusive employment contract from performing for others services like those required under the contract.

Negative option An option that takes effect if you *fail* to do something; for example, a book club selection you buy if you fail to send back a rejection card.

Negative pregnant   A denial that really admits what seems to be denied. For example, in response to the question "Did you go to New York?", "I didn't go yesterday" would be a *negative pregnant* because it implies going some other time.

Neglect   *1.* Failure to do a thing that should be done. *2.* Absence of care in doing something. *3.* Failure to properly care for a child.

Negligence   *1.* The failure to exercise a reasonable amount of **care** in a situation that causes harm to someone or something. It can involve doing something carelessly or failing to do something that should have been done. Negligence can vary in seriousness from *gross* (recklessness or willfulness), through *ordinary* (failing to act as a reasonably careful person would), to *slight* (not much). *2. Criminal negligence* is the careless state of mind that can make an action a crime; for example, the extreme carelessness in driving a car that might change a noncriminal **homicide** into **manslaughter.** For **comparative, contributory, imputed,** etc., negligence, see those words.

Negligent   Careless (see **negligence**). For example, *negligent entrustment* is leaving a gun with a child, a car with a drunk, a surplus with a legislator, etc.

Negotiable   *1.* Capable of being transferred. Describes something that can have its ownership transferred by signing it over to someone else. *2.* See **negotiate.**

Negotiable instrument   A signed document that contains an unconditional promise to pay an exact sum of money, either when demanded or at an exact future time. Further, it must be marked **payable** "to the **order** of" a specific person or payable "to **bearer**" (the person who happens to have it). *Negotiable instruments* include **checks, notes,** and *bills of* **exchange.** There is a whole branch of law concerning them and a special vocabulary of ordinary sounding words (such as "**holder**") that have specialized meanings in this area. You can, however, gain a basic understanding of negotiable instruments by looking at what is printed on a check, thinking about the reasons for each phrase or blank, and reading the bank's rules for cashing the check.

Negotiate   *1.* Discuss, arrange, or bargain about a business deal. *2.* Discuss a compromise to a situation. *3.* Transfer a **negotiable instrument** (see that word) from one person to another.

Negotiation   See **negotiate.**

Nem. con.   Abbreviation for **nemine contradicente.**

Nemine contradicente   (Latin) "No one dissenting." Describes a unanimous decision or vote.

Nemo (Latin) No one; no person. *Nemo* is used in many legal phrases such as "nemo est supra leges" (no one is above the law).

Nepotism Giving jobs or contracts to your own relatives.

Net The amount remaining after subtractions. For example, *net assets* (or net worth) are what is left after subtracting what you owe from what you have; *net weight* is the weight of a product not counting the container; and the *net cost* of a car might be what you pay the dealer minus what you get back from the automaker as a **rebate.**

Net book value (or net asset value) *1.* The amount of a company's property backing each share of **stock** or **bond** it puts out. Calculating this amount is complex. *2.* The market value of a **mutual fund,** usually the value of all securities held, minus any liabilities, all divided by the number of shares held by investors.

Net contract (or listing) A sales (or **listing**) contract in which the broker's **commission** is equal to the amount by which the sale price exceeds a particular amount.

Net lease A **lease** in which the tenant pays rent plus all the costs of ownership, such as taxes and maintenance.

Net position The difference between short and **long positions** held in one **commodity** or **security;** more simply, the amount that a person will gain or lose by a change in the value of a commodity or a stock.

Net worth method A way the **I.R.S.** proves that a person has understated taxable income by showing that the person has acquired more **assets** than could be bought by the stated income.

Neutral *1.* Impartial or lacking bias. *2.* Not a part of the prosecutorial system. *3.* Independent.

Neutrality laws Laws prohibiting the U.S. government or U.S. citizens from giving military help in a war against any country with which the U.S. is at peace.

Neutralize Lessen the effect of harmful **testimony** by showing that the **witness** has made conflicting statements. See also **impeachment.**

New and useful In **patent** law, describes an invention that accomplishes a practical result in a new way.

New value In **bankruptcy** law, something given to or done for a debtor by a creditor, after bankruptcy proceedings have started, that is sufficiently unrelated to past debts that it may be compensated by the debtor without being a *preferential transfer* subject to challenge by other creditors.

New York Times v. Sullivan (376 U.S. 967) The 1964 U.S. Supreme Court decision that established the rule that, under the **First Amendment,** a public official cannot get **damages** from a newspaper (or others) for **libel** unless the publisher knew the material was false or published it with a **reckless** disregard for whether or not it was true.

Newly discovered evidence Facts about something crucial to the outcome of a trial that were not known (nor should have reasonably been known) by a **party** to the trial. If these facts are discovered by the party after the **verdict,** but existed before the verdict, they may be the basis for requesting a new trial.

Newsperson's privilege See **journalist's privilege** and **shield law.**

Next cause See **proximate cause.**

Next friend A person who acts formally in court for a child without being that child's legal **guardian.**

Next of kin *1.* Persons most closely related to a dead person. *2.* All persons entitled to **inherit** from a person who has not left a **will.**

Nexus A direct, clear, and substantial interconnection.

Nice question A question that is hard to answer; a decision that is hard to make.

Nihil (Latin) Nothing. For example, *nihil dicit* ("he says nothing") is a **default** *judgment* given by a court to the **plaintiff** because the **defendant** does not answer the **complaint;** and *nihil est* ("there is nothing") is used by a **sheriff** to describe a court paper that cannot be served (formally delivered) to the proper person.

Nil (Latin) Nothing.

Nineteenth Amendment The U.S. **constitutional** amendment that gave women the right to vote.

Ninety day letter A notice from the **I.R.S.** that claims you owe more taxes. During the ninety days after receiving the notice, you must pay the taxes, pay the taxes under protest and claim a refund, or challenge the I.R.S.'s decision in **Tax Court.**

Ninth Amendment The U.S. **constitutional** amendment that states that merely because certain rights are specifically given by the Constitution to the people, there is no implication that other unlisted rights do not exist.

Nisi (Latin) "Unless." A judge's **rule, order,** or **decree** (see those words) that will take effect *unless* the person against whom it is issued comes to court to "show cause" why it should not take effect. [pronounce: ni-si]

Nisi prius   (Latin) "Unless before." In American law, describes a trial court as opposed to an **appellate** court. [pronounce: <u>ni</u>-si pri̠-us]

Nitro (glycerine) instruction   **Allen charge.**

Nixon v. United States   (418 U.S. 683) A 1974 Supreme Court decision that refused to allow a claim of **executive privilege** (see that word) to keep tape recordings made by the president from being produced for an important **criminal** trial.

No action clause   A provision in many **liability** *insurance* policies that the insurance company need not pay anything until a lawsuit against the insured person results in a **judgment** or agreement about the amount owed.

No action letter   A letter from a government **agency** lawyer that, if the facts are as represented in a request by a person for an agency decision, the lawyer will recommend that the agency take no action against the person.

No bill   The statement made by a *grand* **jury** that finds insufficient evidence for an **indictment** against a person on a criminal charge. Also called "not found," "not a true bill," or "ignoramus."

No contest   *1.* See **nolo contendere.** *2.* A *no contest clause* is a provision in a **will** that, if a person challenges the will or anything in it, that person loses what he or she was to be given in the will.

No docs (and low docs)   Describes loans that can be approved with no (or few) credit checks, tax statements, or other documentation because the buyer puts up more than the usual down payment.

No evidence   There is *no evidence* to support a contention or a lawsuit if facts to support any crucial part of the case are completely missing, are barred from **admission,** are so trivial that they amount to nothing, or are indisputably contradicted by contrary facts. (If any of these situations exist, a judge may give a judgment **non obstante veredicto,** a **summary judgment,** or a **directed verdict.**)

No eyewitness rule   The principle that if there is no **direct evidence** (see that word) of what a dead person did to avoid an accident, the **jury** may assume that the person acted with care for his or her own safety.

No fault   *1.* Describes a type of automobile **insurance,** required by some states, in which each person's own insurance company pays for injury or damage up to a certain limit no matter whose fault it is. *2.* A *no fault divorce,* available in most states, is granted upon proof that a husband and wife have lived apart without marital relations for a period of time, usually six months or one year.

No knock warrant   See **knock and announce rule.**

No limit order   Instructions from a client to a **broker** to buy or sell a certain amount of **stock** or other **securities** without any limits on price.

No load fund   A **mutual fund** that charges no sales commissions (but may charge a management fee).

No retreat rule   See **true person doctrine.**

Noerr-Pennington doctrine   The principle that the **First Amendment** permits companies to join together to lobby any part of the government even if the result is anticompetitive under the **antitrust acts.**

Nol. Pros.   Short for **nolle prosequi.**

Nolens volens   (Latin) Willing or unwilling.

Nolle prosequi   (Latin) The ending of a criminal case because the **prosecutor** decides or agrees to stop prosecuting. When this happens, the case is "*nolled,*" "*nollied,*" or "*nol. prossed.*" (This is *not* **nolo contendere** or **non prosequitur,** although it is sometimes used as a synonym for *non prosequitur.*)

Nolo contendere   (Latin) "I will not contest it." A defendant's **plea** of "*no contest*" in a **criminal** case. It means that he or she does not directly admit guilt, but submits to sentencing or other punishment. A defendant may plead *nolo contendere* only with the judge's permission because, unlike a **"guilty"** plea, this cannot be used against the defendant in a later **civil** lawsuit.

Nominal   *1.* In name only. For example, a *nominal defendant* is a person sued in a lawsuit, not to get anything but because the lawsuit would be formally defective without including that person. And a *nominal interest rate* is the interest stated on a **stock** or other **security,** rather than the actual interest earned as computed by the cost of the stock and other factors. *2.* Not real or substantial; slight; token or symbolic only. For example, *nominal damages* are often set at six cents or one dollar because *actual damages* have not been proved.

Nominal trust   A **dry** *trust* (see that word).

Nominee   *1.* A person chosen as a candidate for public office. *2.* A person chosen as another person's representative (**deputy, agent, trustee,** etc.). *3.* A *nominee* **trust** is an arrangement in which one person agrees in writing to hold property for the benefit of another undisclosed person. See also **street name.**

Non   *1.* A prefix meaning "no" or "not." Its use may be separate ("non contestable"), hyphenated ("non-contestable"), or together with the base word ("noncontestable"). *2.* Most English words beginning with "non" can be found by looking up the base word. (For example, to understand "Nonacceptance," look up "**acceptance.**") These words include: _non_**access,** _non_**assessable,** _non_**cancelable,** _non_**contribution,** _non_**insurable,** _non_**joinder,** _non_**recognition,** _non_**stock,** etc. _3._ Some English "non" words (such as **nonacquiescence, noncontestable, nonintervention,** etc.) have technical meanings not found in the base word definitions. These are separately defined after this word. _4._ A Latin word meaning "no," "not," "do not," "should not," "did not," etc. It appears in many legal phrases (such as "**non compos mentis,**" "**non obstante veredicto,**" "**non prosequitur,**" etc.). These are separately defined after this word. _5._ "He did not." The first part of the name for many **defenses** to old lawsuits, such as _non acceptavit_ ("he did not accept" a _bill of_ **exchange**); _non assumpsit_ ("he did not promise" to make a **contract**); _non concessit_ ("he did not **grant**" by **deed**); _non demisit_ ("he did not **demise**" a property lease); _non detinet_ ("he did not detain" the property of another); and _non est factum_ ("it is not his deed or act" that is being sued on).

Non compos mentis   (Latin) "Not of sound mind." This includes idiocy, **insanity,** severe drunkenness, etc.

Non obstante veredicto   (Latin) "Notwithstanding the verdict." A _judgment non obstante veredicto (J.N.O.V.)_ is a judge's giving **judgment** (victory) to one side in a lawsuit even though the jury gave a **verdict** (victory) to the other side.

Non pros   Short for **non prosequitur.**

Non prosequitur   (Latin) "He does not follow up." Describes a **judgment** given to a **defendant** because the **plaintiff** has stopped pursuing the case. This is now usually replaced by a "**motion** _to dismiss_" or a **default** _judgment,_ but where still used is often called a _non pros._ (This is _not_ **nolle prosequi** _or_ **nolo contendere.**)

Non sui juris   (Latin) "Not of his own law or right." Describes a **minor,** an insane person, etc.

Non vult contendere   **Nolo contendere.**

Nonacquiescence   The **I.R.S.**'s announced disagreement with a decision of the U.S. **Tax Court.**

Nonage   Not yet of legal age; still a **minor** (see that word).

Nonclaim law   _Statute of_ **limitations.**

Nonconforming goods   Goods that fail to meet contract specifications.

Nonconforming lot   A piece of land with a size or shape that would not be permitted by current **zoning** laws.

Nonconforming use   The use of a piece of land that is permitted, even though that type of use is not usually permitted in that area by the

zoning laws. This can come about either because the use (building size, use, etc.) existed before the zoning law or because a **variance** has been granted.

Noncontestable clause   A provision in an **insurance** policy that prohibits the insurance company from refusing (on the basis that there was a **mistake** or **fraud** committed in the application for insurance) to pay a claim if a certain amount of time has passed since the application was made.

Nonfeasance   The failure to perform a required duty (especially by a public official). Compare with **malfeasance** and **misfeasance.**

Nonintervention will   Any **will** that contains a provision allowing the **executor** to handle the dead person's property without court supervision. Only a few states recognize the validity of such a provision.

Nonprofit organization   Any group that is not organized for the primary purpose of making a profit and that does not distribute profits to shareholders, directors, etc. Most are **tax exempt** under section 501(c) of the Internal Revenue Code. 501(c) organizations include social, business, labor, **mutual** financial benefit, and other organizations, but most are 501(c)(3) **charitable** and religious organizations. Some 501(c) organizations primarily benefit their members and some primarily benefit the public. Many are organized under state laws based on the Revised Model Nonprofit **Corporation** Act. Many different combinations of words are used to mean "*nonprofit organization.*" "Beneficial," "benefit," "benevolent," "charitable," "eleemosynary," "mutual," "not-for-profit," "philanthropic," "voluntary," and other words are used for "*nonprofit,*" and "**association,**" "corporation," "**foundation,**" "society," and other words are used for "*organization.*" These words often have overlapping or conflicting uses. See the **bold** words (especially **charitable**) for more information, and contrast **business organization.**

Nonrecourse loan   Any loan for which the borrower is not personally liable and for which the lender may only take and sell the **collateral** (if any) if the loan is not repaid. This type of loan is used in surplus crop price support programs in which the crop is the only **security** for the loan. Some **mortgage** loans are also *nonrecourse.* Current tax law limits **deductions** for some types of nonrecourse loans.

Nonsuit   The ending of a lawsuit because the **plaintiff** has failed to take a necessary step or accomplish a necessary action. In most places now, this will be a **dismissal,** a **default** *judgment,* or a **directed verdict.**

Nonsupport   The failure to provide financially for a spouse, child, or other dependent. It is **grounds** for a **divorce** in some states and may be a crime if **willful.**

Nonuser   The failure to use a right, such as an **easement,** for so long that the right may be lost.

Normal law   The law as it affects normal persons "of sound mind" who can manage their own affairs and act for themselves in legal situations.

Norris-LaGuardia Act   (29 U.S.C. 101) A 1932 federal law to prevent many types of **injunctions** against strikers and to prohibit **yellow dog contracts** (see that word).

Noscitur a sociis   (Latin) "It is known from its associates." _1._ Describes the principle that a word's meaning, if unclear, may be determined from the meaning of surrounding words. _2._ Describes the assumption that a person's character is similar to that of his or her friends.

Not found   **No bill.**

Not guilty   See **guilty.**

Notary public   A person given power by a state to administer **oaths,** certify the authenticity of signatures, witness wills, etc., within the state.

Notation voting   Voting (by a **board, legislature,** etc.) without any meeting. It is not permitted in most situations.

Note   _1._ A written promise to pay a debt. See **promissory note.** _2._ A short explanation in a **law journal** of a legal point or a set of cases.

Notes of decisions   References to cases that discuss the laws printed in an **annotated statutes** book.

Not-for-profit organization   See **nonprofit organization.**

Notice   _1._ Knowledge of certain facts. "_Constructive notice_" means a person is treated as if he or she knew certain facts. _2._ Formal receipt of the knowledge of certain facts. For example, "_notice_" of a lawsuit usually means that formal papers have been delivered to a person (_personal notice_) or to the person's **agent** (_imputed notice_). _3._ Various **trial** notices include _notice: of_ **motion,** _of_ **orders,** _of_ **judgments,** _of_ **trial,** _to appear, to_ **plead,** etc. _4._ For various types of real estate transaction _notice_ laws (such as _race statutes, notice statutes,_ and _race-notice statutes_), see **recording acts.** _5._ **A** "_notice to creditors_" is the _notice_ in a **bankruptcy** proceeding that a **meeting of creditors** will be held, that claims must be **filed,** or that **relief** has been granted. _6._ A "_notice to quit_" is the written notice from a **landlord** to a **tenant** that the tenant will have to move.

Notice and comment period **Comment period.**

Notorious *1.* Well known or publicly known. *2.* Well known and scandalous, perhaps also illegal.

Novation The substitution by agreement of a new **contract** for an old one, with all the rights under the old one ended. The new contract is often the same as the old one, except that one or more of the **parties** is different.

Novelty Newness. For an invention to be *novel* enough to get a **patent,** it must not only have a new form, but also perform a new function or perform an old one in an entirely new way.

Nude Lacking something basic to be legally valid. See also **naked** and **bare.**

Nudum pactum (Latin) "Nude pact" or bare agreement. A promise or action without any **consideration** (payment or promise of something of value). [pronounce: new-dum pack-tum]

Nugatory Invalid; without force or effect.

Nuisance *1.* Anything that annoys or disturbs unreasonably, hurts a person's use of his or her property, or violates the public health, safety, or decency. *2.* Use of land that does anything in no. 1. *3.* A *private nuisance* is a **tort** that requires a showing of special harm to you or your property and allows the recovery of **damages** for the harm as well as an **injunction.** A *public nuisance* is a general, widespread problem that can be opposed by an **injunction** or criminal prosecution. A *nuisance* can be both public and private.

Null No longer having any legal effect or validity.

Nulla bona (Latin) "No goods." The name for a type of **return** (see that word) a sheriff uses to inform a judge that the goods the sheriff has been ordered to seize cannot be found.

Nullification *1.* Ending something's legal effect and validity. *2.* **Jury nullification.** *3.* The principle advocated by southern states before the Civil War that a state can declare a federal law **unconstitutional.**

Nullity "Nothing." Of no legal force or effect.

Nunc pro tunc (Latin) "Now for then." Describes something done "now" that has the same effect as if done "then," so that it has retroactive effect. For example, a judge may issue a *nunc pro tunc* **order** to correct a trial **record** made earlier, with the effect that the record is considered correct as of the date it was first made, in effect backdating the order.

Nuncupative will An oral **will.** It is valid in a few states. See also **military will.**

O.A.S.   Organization of American States.

O.A.S.D.I.   Old Age, Survivors' and Disability Insurance.

O.M.B.   Office of Management and Budget. The federal agency that assists the U.S. president in financial matters, oversees the federal budget, etc.

O.P.I.C.   Overseas Private Investment Corporation.

O.P.M.   The U.S. Office of Personnel Management.

O.R.   Short for "own recognance" (see **recognizance**).

O.S.H.A.   Occupational Safety and Health Administration.

O.T.C.   Over-the-counter.

Oath   A formal swearing that you will tell the truth (an *assertory oath*) or will do something (a *promissory oath*). Oaths of truthfulness are required of **witnesses,** and oaths of **allegiance** and faithful performance of duty are required of many public office-holders, soldiers, etc.

Obiter dictum   See **dictum.**

Object   *1.* Purpose. *2.* Claim that an action by your adversary in a lawsuit (such as the use of a particular piece of **evidence**) is improper, unfair, or illegal, and ask the judge for a **ruling** on the point. *3.* Formally state a disagreement with a judge's ruling, usually to preserve the right to appeal based on that ruling.

Objection   *1.* The process of objecting (see **object**). *2.* Disapproval.

Objective theory of contracts   The principle that a court should resolve most **contract** issues by considering only the actions, writings, and other *objective* evidence of what the parties did (and meant to do) rather than also considering what the parties *subjectively* meant to do (by asking them what they were thinking, etc.).

Obligation   A broad word that can mean any **duty,** any legal duty, a duty imposed by a **contract,** a formal written promise to pay money (such as a government bond), a duty to the government, a tax owed, etc.

Obligee   Person to whom a **duty** is owed.

Obligor   Person who owes a **duty** to another person.

Obliteration   Erasing or blotting out written words. (Sometimes lining out or writing over is *obliteration* even if the words still show.)

Oblivion An act of forgiving and forgetting such as granting a **pardon** or **amnesty** (see those words).

Obloquy *1.* Abusive language. *2.* A bad reputation.

Obscene Lewd and offensive to accepted standards of decency. The "test" of whether something is *obscene* (as stated in the 1973 U.S. Supreme Court case of *Miller v. California*, 413 U.S. 15) includes such things as whether a book, movie, etc., "violates contemporary community standards," "appeals primarily to prurient interest," "describes sexual conduct in a patently offensive way," "is without redeeming social importance," etc. If a court finds **speech** to be *obscene,* it loses its protection under the **freedom of speech** and **freedom of the press** clauses of the **First Amendment** to the **Constitution** and may be banned, regulated, or prosecuted under state law.

Obscenity See **obscene.**

Obstructing justice Interfering by words or actions with the proper working of courts or court officials; for example, trying to keep a **witness** from appearing in court. This can be a crime.

Obviate Prevent or make unnecessary.

Occupancy *1.* Physical possession of land or buildings, either with or without legal right or **title.** *2.* **Occupying the field.**

Occupation *1.* **Occupancy.** *2.* Business or profession. *3.* **Occupying the field.**

Occupational disease A disease that is widespread among workers in a particular job, such as "black lung" disease among miners. **Workers' compensation laws** and special federal programs authorize payment for workers who contract these diseases if the disease is peculiar to the industry or if the job puts workers at high risk of contracting the disease.

Occupational Safety and Health Administration A federal agency that sets and enforces health and safety standards in many industries. The *O.S.H.A. Review Commission* handles appeals from O.S.H.A. rulings.

Occupying claimant act See **betterment.**

Occupying the field The federal government's prohibiting all state laws in a subject area because the subject is of national importance. *Occupying the field* is total federal **pre-emption** (see that word).

Occurrence policy An insurance policy that pays for acts or losses that occur within a specified time period even if the claim is not made within that period. Contrast **claims made policy.**

Odd lot *1.* A number of shares of **stock** less than the number usually traded as a unit. This is often fewer than one hundred shares. *2.* The *odd lot doctrine* in **workers' compensation law** is the principle that a person is totally disabled even if the person can perform limited services, as long as the accident or injury has removed the possibility that a reasonable market for these services exists.

Odium Widespread hatred or dislike.

Of age No longer a **minor.** A person who has reached the legal age to sue, vote, drink, etc.

Of counsel *1.* A person employed as a lawyer in a case. *2.* A lawyer who helps the primary lawyer in a case. *3.* A lawyer who advises a law firm or who is a temporary member.

Of course As a matter of right. Actions that a person may take in a lawsuit, either without asking the judge's permission, or by asking and getting automatic approval.

Of grace See **grace.**

Of record Entered on the proper formal records. For example, "*counsel of record*" is the lawyer whose name appears on the court's records as the lawyer in a case.

Of the essence Critically important. See **time is of the essence.**

Off Postponed indefinitely.

Off point See **on point.**

Off-board Describes a **stock** or other **securities** transaction that does not take place through a national securities **exchange.** *Off-board* exchanges are either between private individuals or **over-the-counter.**

Offense A **crime** or other violation of the law. An **offender** is a person who has committed a crime.

Offer *1.* Make a proposal; present for acceptance or rejection. An "*offer*" in contract law is a proposal to make a deal. To be capable of **acceptance,** the offer must be communicated from the person making it to the person to whom it is made, and it must be reasonably definite and certain in its terms. *2.* The thing proposed in no. 1 (a "thousand dollar offer for the car"). *3.* Attempt the **admission** (see that word) of something into **evidence** in a trial.

Offer of compromise An offer to settle a dispute without admitting **liability.**

Offer of proof When a question to a witness has not been allowed by the judge, the lawyer who wanted to ask the question may tell the judge, out of the jury's hearing, what the answer *would* have been. This *offer of proof* creates a more complete trial **record** for the possible **appeal** of the refusal to allow the question.

Offering   A coordinated attempt to sell a specified amount of a company's **securities.** A *primary offering* sells previously unsold, unissued securities ("new **issues**"). A *secondary offering* resells previously issued securities. A *private offering* is made to a small group of persons who know something about the company. A *public offering* is made to the general public.

Office   *1.* A power to act plus a duty to act in a certain way; for example, the *office* of **executor** of an **estate.** *2.* Short for "public office," the description of mid- and upper-level elected and appointed government jobs. *3.* A bureau, department, or other government **agency.** The place where this bureau works.

Office audit   See **audit.**

Officer of the court   A court employee such as a **judge, clerk, sheriff, marshal, bailiff,** and **constable** (see these words). Lawyers are also *officers of the court* and must obey court rules, be truthful in court, and generally serve the needs of justice.

Officers   The persons who run and control the day-to-day operations of an organization. The *officers* of a **corporation** include a *president,* usually *vice presidents,* a *treasurer,* and a *secretary.*

Official Gazette   A weekly publication of the *U.S. Patent and Trademark Office,* formally listing **patent** and **trademark** applications and notices.

Official notice   The same as **judicial notice** (see that word), except that it is granted by a **hearing examiner,** not a judge.

Official records   Reports, statements, data files, etc., kept by a federal government agency. These may be used as **evidence** in a federal trial without need for the record keeper as a **witness.** The *Official Records Act* allows this same use of government documents in federal administrative proceedings. Some states have similar laws.

Officiousness   Performing services or paying money where they are not needed, requested, or required. A person who does this may be called an *officious intermeddler* and denied payment for the actions.

Offset   *1.* Any claim or demand made to lessen or cancel another claim. When done in a lawsuit, it may be a **setoff,** a **counterclaim,** or a **recoupment,** depending on whether or not it is an entirely separate claim, whether it exceeds the original claim, and other factors. *2.* An *offset account* is a **bookkeeping** device to **balance** one set of figures against another to make the books "come out even" at the end.

Old Age, Survivors' and Disability Insurance   The federal program, commonly known as "Social Security" and funded by employer and employee payments, that pays retirement, disability, dependent, and death benefits.

Oligarchy   Government by a small group of people.

Oligopoly   A situation in which a few sellers dominate the market for a particular product. *Oligopsony,* in contrast, is a situation in which a few *buyers* dominate the market.

Olograph   See **holograph.**

Ombudsman   (Swedish) *1.* A person who acts as the government's "complaint bureau" and who has the power to investigate official misconduct, help fix wrongs done by the government, and, sometimes, prosecute wrongdoers. *2.* A similar person in a nongovernmental organization.

Omission   *1.* Leaving something out or the thing left out. *2.* Failing to do something that should be done.

Omnibus   (Latin) Containing two or more separate and independent things. For example, an "*omnibus bill*" is a legislative **bill** containing proposed laws concerning two or more entirely different subjects.

Omnibus clause   *1.* A provision in a **will** (or in a judge's **order** to distribute a dead person's property) that gives out all property not specifically mentioned. *2.* A provision in an auto **insurance** policy that extends insurance to all drivers operating the insured vehicle with the owner's permission.

Omnis (or omne, omni, omnia, etc.)   (Latin) *All;* as in the phrase "*omnis definitio in lege periculosa*" (all legal definitions are dangerous).

Omnium   The total value of several different things.

On account   As a part payment for something bought or owed.

On all fours   Two cases or decisions are "*on all fours*" if they are generally similar and are exactly alike in all legally important ways.

On demand (or on call)   Payable immediately when requested.

On its face   See **face.**

On or about   *1. On or about May first* is a phrase used to avoid being pinned down to the exact May first date. *2. On or about the person* means kept nearby, usually referring to a concealed weapon or hidden drugs.

On pain of   At the risk of a specified punishment.

On point   A law or prior case is *on point* if it directly applies to the facts of the present case.

On the merits   See **merits.**

Oncale v. Sundowner Offshore Services   (523 U.S. 75) The 1998 U.S. Supreme Court decision that Title VII of the federal civil rights laws prohibits same-sex workplace sexual harassment.

One "Someone by the name of" or "something called a." A useless word when put in front of a word that needs no number; for example, "one Marcie Evans testified that . . ."

One person, one vote The rule, established in *Reynolds v. Sims* (377 U.S. 533 (1964)), that one **house** of a state **legislature** must be apportioned (and regularly reapportioned) by population, so that each person's vote for a member of that house has approximately equal power.

Onerous *1.* Unreasonably burdensome or one-sided. Compare with **unconscionability.** *2.* In some countries (and in Louisiana) *onerous* means *properly* burdensome. In these countries, an *onerous contract* is one with benefits and burdens on both sides, and an *onerous title* is the right to property that is paid for or otherwise gained in exchange for something of value.

Onus probandi (Latin) **Burden of proof.**

Open *1.* Begin. *2.* Make visible or available. *3.* Remove restrictions. *4.* Visible or apparent. *5.* With no limit as to time or as to amount. *6.* For examples of these meanings, see the words following.

Open a judgment Keep a **judgment** from going into effect until a court can reexamine it.

Open account (or open credit) A "charge account" in which purchases (or loans) can be made without going through separate **credit** arrangements each time. This is often done on credit cards and "revolving charges" on which you can pay a part of what you owe each month on several different purchases. See also **open-end mortgage.**

Open and obvious doctrine The principle that clear dangers do not normally support lawsuits for injuries due to these dangers.

Open bid An offer to do work or supply materials (usually in the construction business) that reserves the right to lower the bid to meet the competition.

Open court *1.* A court that is formally open for business that day. *2.* A court that allows public spectators.

Open fields doctrine The principle that a search **warrant** is not usually required for a search of an open area far from an occupied building. See also **curtilage.**

Open listing See **listing.**

Open mortgage A **mortgage** that can be paid off without a penalty at any time before **maturity** (the time it ends). See also **open-end mortgage** and **closed-end mortgage.**

Open order An **order** placed by a customer with a **broker** to buy **stock,** other **securities,** or **commodities** at or below a certain price. The order remains active until canceled.

Open policy An *unvalued policy.* See **valued policy.**

Open price term An unspecified price in a contract. Although the failure to specify a price may invalidate a contract, an *open price term* will not invalidate a sale of *goods* between businesses if the price is based on a standard market indicator or if the persons intend "reasonable price" to be set at time of delivery.

Open shop A business where nonunion persons may work.

Open-end company A **mutual fund.**

Open-end contract A **requirements contract.**

Open-end mortgage A **mortgage** (see that word) allowing future borrowing (often of unspecified amounts but with a total dollar ceiling) against the same **collateral.** See also **open account, open mortgage,** and **closed-end mortgage.**

Open-end settlement An agreement under which workers' compensation benefits are paid until a person can work again.

Opening statements The introductory statements made at the start of a trial by lawyers for each side. The lawyers typically explain the version of the facts best supporting their side of the case, how these facts will be proved, and how they think the law applies to the case.

Operating Relating to the running of a business. *Operating expenses* include such things as rent and electricity required to keep a business running normally. *Operating profit* is sales minus the cost of the goods sold and operating expenses. *Net operating assets* is the worth of assets (such as machines) used in the ordinary course of business minus the business tax **deductions** taken for **depreciation** on the assets and minus business **bad debts.** *Net operating income* (*or loss*) is income (or loss) minus depreciation deductions taken for operating assets, but not yet accounting for any interest gained or income taxes paid. *Operating margin* is *net operating income* divided by sales. Also, an *operating lease* is a short-term business **lease** that can be canceled.

Operation of law Describes the automatic effect some laws have on rights and responsibilities. For example, the wife of a man who dies without a will may gain ownership of her husband's property (under **intestate succession** laws) by *operation of law* without taking any action.

Operative words (or part) That part of the text of a document (such as the granting clause of a **deed**) by which rights are actually created or transferred. The legal "heart" of a document, as opposed to its introduction, explanations, etc.

Opinion   *1.* A judge's statement of the decision he or she has reached in a case. *2.* A judge's statement about the conclusions of that judge and other judges who agree with the judge in a case. A *majority opinion* is written when over half the judges in a case agree about both the result and the reasoning used to reach that result. A *plurality opinion* is written when a majority of the judges agree with the result, but not with the reasoning. A *concurring opinion* agrees with the result, but not the reasoning. A *dissenting or minority opinion* disagrees with the result. (Concurring, dissenting, and minority opinions are all *separate opinions.*) A *per curiam opinion* is unanimous and anonymous. A *memorandum opinion* is unanimous and briefly states only the result. *3.* A document prepared by a lawyer for a client that gives the lawyer's conclusions about how the law applies to a set of facts in which the client is interested.

Opinion evidence   Evidence of what a witness thinks, believes, or concludes about facts, rather than what the witness saw, heard, etc. *Opinion evidence* is usually accepted only from an **expert witness** (see that word).

Opportunity cost   The profit you could get by investing your money, rather than putting it into a particular project. See **hurdle rate.**

Oppression   *1.* **Unconscionability.** *2.* **Duress.** *3.* Harm (usually bodily harm) done by a public official acting beyond the scope of authority.

Opprobrium   Shame or disgrace.

Option   *1.* A **contract** in which one person pays money for the right to buy something from, or sell something to, another person at a certain price and within a certain time period. For example, a *commodity option* gives a person the right to buy (a "*call*") or the right to sell (a "*put*") a certain **commodity** (such as a ton of rice) at a certain price (the "*striking*" price) by a certain time. The option holder pays a fee (a "*premium*") for this right and may use ("*exercise*") it or not depending on **market** conditions. A combined right to either buy or sell is called a *straddle.* And an option sold by a person who owns no stock or commodities to back it up is called a *naked option. 2.* Any right to choose, such as the right to pick from a list of ways an **annuity** benefit can be paid.

Optional bond   A **callable** bond.

Optional writ   A **show cause order.**

Oral argument   The presentation of each side of a case before an **appeals** court. The presentation typically involves oral statements by a lawyer, interrupted by questions from the judges.

Oral contract   A **contract** that is not entirely in writing or not in writing at all. (Similarly, an *oral* **will** is either partly in writing or not in writing at all.)

Ordeal   An ancient form of trial in England by which God was supposed to make the decision. Ordeals were by fire or water and uniformly nasty. The cold water ordeal, for example, involved throwing a tied-up person into a pond. Floating meant guilt (and often death); sinking meant innocence (and often death).

Order   *1.* A written command or direction given by a judge. For example, a *restraining order* is a judicial command to a person to temporarily stop a certain action or course of conduct. *2.* A command given by a public official. *3.* "*To the order of*" is a direction to pay something. These words (or "*pay to the* **bearer**") are necessary to make a document a **negotiable instrument** (see that word). A document with these words on it is called *order paper. 4.* For "*order nisi,*" see **nisi.** *5.* "*Order of the* **coif**" is an award, often for law school achievement. *6.* Instructions to buy or sell something. In **stock** sales, for example, a "*day order*" is an instruction from a customer to a **broker** to buy or sell a stock on one particular day only; a "*limit order*" is an instruction to buy only under a certain price or sell only over it; a "*market order*" is an instruction to buy or sell right away at the current **market price;** a "*scale order*" is an instruction to buy or sell a certain amount of stock at each of several price levels; and a "*split order*" is an instruction to buy or sell some stock when it reaches one price and some when it reaches another. For **stop order,** see that word.

Ordinance   *1.* A local or city law, rule, or **regulation.** *2.* A name occasionally used for an important statute, such as the *Ordinance of 1787* (providing for the government of the Northwest Territory).

Ordinary   Regular or usual. This word means the same thing in most legal and nonlegal contexts. In tax law, however, *ordinary income* means income from business profits, wages, **interest, dividends,** etc., as opposed to income from the sale of things. See **capital** *gains tax.*

Organic   Basic. For example, an *organic act or statute* is a law that gives self-government to a geographical area or that establishes an **administrative agency,** and *organic law* is the basic, fundamental law of a government, such as its **constitution.**

Organization   Any group of persons with legal or formal ties.

Organized labor   Workers represented by **labor unions.**

Original document rule   The rule that the best evidence (see **best evidence rule**) of what a document says is the original document. A copy may not be acceptable for use in court, especially if the original is available.

Original jurisdiction   The power of a court to take a case, try it, and decide it (as opposed to *appellate jurisdiction,* the power of a court to hear and decide an **appeal**).

Original package doctrine   The federal rule that a state can tax an imported item only after the original package is broken because this takes the item out of interstate commerce.

Origination fee   A charge for finding, placing, or giving a loan.

Orphans court   **Probate** court.

Ostensible   Apparent. For *ostensible authority,* see **apparent** *authority.*

Ouster   Throwing someone off land who has a right to possess it. [pronounce: ow-ster]

Outcome test   When a case is in federal court solely because of **diversity of citizenship** (see that word), the result should be the same as it would be in the proper state court. If it is not, an appeals court may decide that the trial judge used the wrong law to decide the case or otherwise acted incorrectly.

Out-of-court settlement   A private compromise or agreement that ends a lawsuit without official help from, or orders by, the judge.

Out-of-pocket   *1.* Describes a small cash payment. *2.* Describes a loss measured by the difference between the price paid for an item and the (lower true) value of that item. The "*out-of-pocket rule*" allows this to be the measure of **damages** when something has been bought as a result of **fraudulent** statements. *3.* Describes payments that must be made by a contractor before the job is completed or describes all costs except the contractor's own time.

Output contract   An agreement in which a manufacturing company agrees to sell everything it makes to one buyer, and the buyer agrees to take it all. This is a valid **contract** even though the amounts are indefinite. Compare with **requirements contract.**

Outs   Conditions or promises which, if not complied with by a customer, allow a banker or a company to get out of a deal.

Outside director   See **director.**

Outside salesperson   A person whose full-time job is making sales from a location different from the employer's place of business.

Outstanding   *1.* Still unpaid; not yet collected. *2.* Remaining in existence; not brought in or gathered up.

Outstroke   A mineshaft that penetrates into someone else's adjoining property.

Over   *1.* Continued from one time or day to another. For example, when a court case gets a **continuance,** the case is said to be "*over*" (to another day, to an unspecified time, etc.). *2.* Shifting or passing on from one person or thing to another. For example, a "*gift over*" or "*estate over*" takes place when someone leaves property in a will first to one person and then to another person (if the first one should die after a certain number of years, etc.). *3.* See the "over" words that follow and see **over-the-counter.**

Overbreadth   A law will be declared **void** for *overbreadth* if it attempts to punish **speech** or conduct that is protected by the **Constitution** and if it is impossible to eliminate the unconstitutional part of the law without invalidating the whole law.

Overdraft (or overdraw)   Taking out more money by check from a bank account than you have in the account.

Overhead   *1.* **Fixed charges** (see that word) and all those costs that cannot be allocated to a particular department or product. *2.* An *overhead rate* is calculated by apportioning fixed costs to the costs of producing products and services.

Overissue   Putting out more shares of a company's **stock** than are permitted by the company's incorporation papers or by the law.

Overlying right   A landowner's right to take and use water from under the surface of his or her own land.

Overreaching   Taking unfair commercial advantage by **fraud** or **unconscionability.**

Override   *1.* Set aside; for example, the U.S. Congress may *override* the president's **veto** of a **bill** by a two-thirds vote of both houses, causing the bill to become law without presidential signature. *2.* A **commission** paid to a supervisor when an employee makes a sale or a commission paid to a **real estate** (see that word) agent when a landowner sells directly to a purchaser who was found by the agent before the **listing** was ended.

Overrule   *1.* To reject or supercede. For example, a case is *overruled* when the same court, or a higher court in the same system, rejects the legal principles on which the case was based. This ends the case's value as **precedent.** *2.* To reject an **objection** made during a trial. This is done by the judge.

Oversubscription   A situation in which more orders for **shares** of **stock** exist than there are shares of stock to fill the orders.

Overt   Open; clear. For example, an *overt act* in **criminal** law is more than mere preparation to do something criminal; it is at least the first step of actually attempting the crime. The overt act itself need not be unlawful to be the first step in such crimes as *treason* and *criminal conspiracy,* or in an "attempt crime" such as *attempted murder.*

Over-the-counter   *1.* Describes **securities,** such as **stocks** and **bonds,** sold directly from **broker** to broker or broker to customer rather than through an **exchange.** *2.* Describes a drug that may be sold without a prescription.

Owelty   *1.* A court-ordered payment to equalize an unequal division of land. *2.* Money paid to equalize an exchange of land with different values. See also **boot.**

Owner   A general term for the person who holds the legal or "paper" **title** to property; for the person who has a right to property no matter what the "papers" say; or for several other shades of control over, or rights to benefit from, property.

Owners' equity statement   See **statement.**

Oyer and terminer   (French) "Hear and decide." Describes certain higher state **criminal** courts. [pronounce: oy-yay and term-i-nay]

Oyez   (Law French) "Hear ye." The word cried out by a court official in some courtrooms to get attention at the start of a court session. [pronounce: oy-yay]

P. *1.* Pacific Reporter (see **National Reporter System**). *2.* **Plaintiff.** *3.*℗ is the symbol for **copyright** in a sound recording.

P.A. *1.* **Professional association.** 2. **Partnership Association.** See **limited partnership association.**

P.A.C. Political action committee. A federally **regulated** organization that raises funds to support candidates in an election.

P.A.C.E. *Paralegal Advanced Certification Exam* of the National Federation of Paralegal Associations.

P.B.G.C. Pension Benefit Guaranty Corporation. The federal agency that collects payments from most private **pension plans** (see that word) to protect against insufficient pension funds through a plan similar to insurance.

P.C. **Professional corporation; patent** cases; **penal** code; personal computer; politically correct; **probable cause; protective custody;** etc.; plus many British phrases such as Pleas of the Crown and Privy Council.

P.C.R. **Postconviction remedies.**

P.D. *1.* Private detective. See **private investigator.** *2.* **Public defender.** *3.* Police department.

P.-H. Prentice-Hall (see **looseleaf service**).

P.H.C. **Personal holding company.**

P.H.V. **Pro hac vice.**

P.I. *1.* **Private investigator.** *2.* **Personal injury.**

P.I.T.I. Principal, interest, taxes, and insurance—the basic components of a typical monthly mortgage payment.

P.J. Presiding judge.

P.L. **Public law**(s) or **pamphlet law**(s).

P.L.I. Practicing Law Institute. A nonprofit organization that publishes books and holds seminars to educate lawyers.

P.L.S. A *Professional Legal Secretary,* professionally certified by the **National Association of Legal Secretaries.**

P.M.I. **Private mortgage insurance.**

P.O.D. *1. "Payable on death."* Describes a bank or other account payable to a person (or a group of persons) and, on that person's death, payable to someone else. *2.* Pay(able) on delivery.

P.P.O. Preferred Provider Organization. A group health insurance plan that gives discounts for using certain doctors, hospitals, and other health services. Compare **H.M.O.**

P.S. Public **statute.**

P.S.C. **Public service commission.**

P.S.I. Pre**sentence** investigation report (of a **defendant's** personal history and background).

P.T.I. *1.* Previously taxed income. *2.* Pretrial intervention. See **diversion.**

P.U.C. Public Utilities Commission. See **Public Service Commission.**

P.U.D. **Planned unit development.**

Package mortgage A **mortgage** that makes appliances or other listed items part of the **security** for the repayment of a real estate loan.

Package settlement The total money value of wage and **benefit** changes in a new union-employer **contract.**

Packager *1.* A **broker.** *2.* An **underwriter.** *3.* A person who puts together deals, such as group travel, a television series, etc.

Packing Trying to get a favorable decision from a jury (or a court, an agency, etc.) by improperly placing specific persons on the jury, court, etc.

Pact A bargain or agreement.

Pactum (Latin) A bargain or agreement. See **nudam pactum.**

Paid-in Supplied by the owners. For example, *paid-in capital* is money or property paid to a company for its **capital** stock, and *paid-in surplus* is that part of a company's **surplus** supplied by the stockholders rather than generated from profits.

Pains and penalties See **bill of pains and penalties.**

Pairing *1.* Two persons (one for and one against a **bill** in a **legislature**) agreeing to refrain from voting. This allows them both to be absent for the vote. This is also called *"pairing off."* *2.* Sending all the children from two school areas to one or the other school by grade.

Pais (French) The countryside; outside the court. For example, a matter *"in pais"* (see that word) has to do with facts (that happened outside the courtroom), not with law (that is applied to facts inside the courtroom). [pronounce: pay]

Palimony **"Alimony"** (see that word) paid between persons who are not and never were married. Any payments based on an **express** or

implied contract between two persons who lived together in a sexual relationship. The law as to the validity of these contracts is still changing.

Palm off   Sell goods made by one manufacturer as if they are made by another (usually better or more famous) manufacturer.

Palpable   Plain, clear, easily seen, or notorious. (The word usually refers to an **error,** an **abuse** of authority, or something else wrong.)

Palsgraf doctrine   The rule (from _Palsgraf v. Long Island R.R., 169_ N.E. 99) that a person is responsible for those results of a **negligent** action that are foreseeable but not for everything that happens to follow.

Pamphlet law   A new state law distributed in temporary form before it is published in the state **code.**

Pandect   A country's complete legal **code** with history, explanations, and case annotation.

Pander   _1._ To pimp or solicit for prostitution. _2._ Openly advertise **obscene** material to appeal to erotic interest.

Panel   _1._ A jury list. _2._ A group of judges (smaller than the entire court) that decides a case. _3._ _"Open panel legal services"_ is an arrangement (usually a type of insurance or an employee benefit) that pays in advance for legal representation by a lawyer of a person's own choice. _"Closed panel legal services"_ is the same except that representation is provided by a specific group of lawyers.

Paper   _1._ "The papers" are all the documents connected with a lawsuit. _2._ "Paper" may be short for "**commercial paper**" or a **negotiable instrument** (see those words). _3._ "Paper" may mean "only paper." For example, a _"paper title"_ is a **document of title** (see that word) that may or may not be valid; and a _"paper profit"_ is an increase in value (of an investment) that might be lost again if the value goes down before sale. _4._ When a prosecutor _"papers"_ a case, it means, in some places, that it _will_ be formally prosecuted, and, in other places, that it will _not_ be formally prosecuted.

Par   _1._ **Face value.** If a hundred dollar **bond** sells in the bond market for one hundred dollars, it sells _"at par."_ _2._ _"Par items"_ are things a bank will process and send on without charge to another bank.

Paralegal   The **American Bar Association** restricts the term _"paralegal"_ to legal assistants with special education, training, or work experience who work under a lawyer's "ultimate" supervision on "substantive" legal work that the lawyer would otherwise do. _Introduction to Paralegalism_ (Statsky, 1997) also includes those who are "otherwise authorized to use legal skills," but restricts the tasks performed to those that do not require all the skills of an attorney. More generally, persons who do law-related work for government agencies and businesses, nonlawyers who represent others before administrative agencies, legal secretaries, and others are sometimes called *paralegals.*

Parallel citation   An alternate reference to a case (or other legal document) that is published in more than one place. There is usually one official publication of a court case or a statute. If so, that is the *official* or *primary* citation, and all others are *parallel citations.*

Parallel jurisdiction   See **pendent jurisdiction.**

Paramount title   *1.* Best right of ownership. A **holder in due course** (see that word) has *paramount title* to a document (and to all the money or property it stands for). The primary exception is that the original owner has paramount title over even a *holder in due course* if the document was stolen from the original owner. *2.* In **real estate** law, *paramount title* previously meant original title, but has come to mean "better" title or "superior" title.

Parcener   An old word for a person who, along with another person, inherits property with each person inheriting the whole thing. "*Coparcener*" means the same thing as "parcener." A *parcener* is now usually called a *joint* **heir.**

Pardon   A president's or governor's release of a person from punishment for a crime. Compare with **reprieve** and **commutation.**

Parens patriae   (Latin) "Country as parent." Refers to the right of the government to take care of minors and others who cannot legally take care of themselves. The use of this power to deprive a person of freedom has been limited by laws and court decisions. [pronounce: pa-rens pat-ree-i]

Parent corporation   A **corporation** that fully controls or owns another company.

Parental liability and responsibility laws   Laws in some states requiring parents to pay for some **torts** (liability) or pay fines for some crimes (responsibility) committed by their minor children, especially if the child's actions resulted from a lack of parental control.

Parental rights   Such things as the parent's right to discipline and control a child, to manage the child's property, to be supported by an adult child, etc.

Pari causa   (Latin) With (or by) equal right or equal cause.

Pari delicto   (Latin) Equal fault or equal guilt. *1.* The "*doctrine of pari delicto*" in **contract** law is the principle that a court should not help enforce an illegal or invalid contract except in some cases where one party is much less at fault than the other or has been manipulated by the other. *2.* There are several "*doctrines of pari delicto*" in **tort** law. One is that in cases of approximately equal mutual fault, the defendant wins. Another is that joint **tortfeasors** may not get **indemnity** from each other (but may get **contribution**). A third is the requirement of **clean hands** in bringing a lawsuit requesting **equitable** *relief.*

Pari materia (Latin) "On the same subject"; interdependent. For example, two laws *in pari materia* must be read together as if one law.

Pari passu (Latin) Equally; without preference. For example, persons receiving *profits pari passu* get equal amounts.

Parish The word for "**county**" in Louisiana.

Parity *1.* Equality, equivalence, even-exchangeability. *2.* Government **price support** of farm products based on a comparison with the farmer's equivalent purchasing power during a prior "base period." *3. Parity* may also refer to proportional job opportunities and fair wages for minorities, to equality of pay between police and firefighters, etc.

Parking Making safe, temporary short-term investments. If this investment involves an agreement to buy back **securities** at the price sold it may be a sham transaction that violates tax or securities laws.

Parliamentarian A person who advises a **legislature** or other group about the rules and procedures for holding a legislative or other meeting. These include the rules and customs of the particular meeting plus general rules such as **Robert's Rules.**

Parliamentary law Rules, such as **Robert's rules,** and customs by which **legislatures** (and many other types of meetings) are run.

Parliamentary system A government by an elected **legislature,** from which a prime minister and **cabinet** are selected by the majority party. This system, based on the one developed in England, does not have the **separation** *of powers* between the **legislative** and **executive** branches that exists in the U.S.

Parol Oral; not in writing. For example, *parol evidence* is oral **evidence** (the evidence a **witness** gives). It usually refers to evidence about an agreement's meaning that is not clear from the written **contract.** See **parol evidence rule** for a meaning that includes *written* statements. Not **parole.**

Parol arrest An "on-the-spot" **arrest** without a **warrant.**

Parol evidence rule The principle that the meaning of a written agreement, in which the parties have expressly stated (in a "*merger* *clause*") that it is their complete and final agreement, cannot be contradicted or changed by using prior oral *or written* statements or agreements as **evidence.** Exceptions to the rule include situations in which there was **duress, fraud,** or **mistake.**

Parole A release from prison, before a **sentence** is finished, that depends on the person's "keeping clean" and doing what he or she is supposed to do while out. If the person fails to meet the *conditions of parole,* the rest of the sentence must be served. *Parole* decisions are made by a state or federal *parole board* or *corrections board,* and persons out on parole are supervised by *parole officers.* Compare with **probation.** *Not* **parol.**

Pars (Latin) *1.* A **party;** as in *pars rea* (*party* **defendant**). *2.* A part.

Part performance See **performance.**

Partial average **Particular average loss.**

Partial disability (or incapacity) An injury that disables a worker from doing part of his or her job or that lowers the value of that person's labor. The word does not mean the loss of part of an arm, part of the use of an arm, part of the ability to lift things, etc., which are usually called *partial losses.*

Partial insanity See **diminished responsibility doctrine** and **insanity.**

Partial verdict *1.* A **verdict** in which a criminal defendant is found guilty on some **counts** but not guilty on others. *2.* Any verdict in which the jury's decision is for one side on some counts, and for the other side (or unable to reach a decision) on others.

Particeps criminis (Latin) An **accomplice.**

Participation *1.* An **insurance** policy in which the person insured pays a certain percentage of any loss. *2.* A loan arrangement in which several banks combine to make a large loan. *3.* A **mortgage** agreement in which the lender gets a share of the profits of the venture (in addition to interest on the loan). *4.* Short for *profit participation* (sharing in the profits of a venture).

Particular average loss A loss of property at sea that is the result of **negligence** or accident and that must be borne by the owner of the property.

Particular lien A right to hold specific property because of a claim against that property; for example, a garage's right to hold a car until its repair bill is paid.

Particulars *1.* The details of a legal **claim** or of separate items on an **account.** See also **bill of particulars.** *2.* A detailed description of property to be sold at auction.

Parties   See **party.**

Partition   Dividing land owned by several persons into smaller parcels owned by each person individually.

Partner   A member of a **partnership** (see that word). A *"full"* or *"general"* partner participates fully in running the company and sharing the profits and losses. A *"dormant," "silent,"* or *"sleeping"* partner is a person who is in a partnership, but is not known as a partner by the public, does not take an active hand in the business, and, if also a *"special"* or *"limited"* partner, puts in a fixed amount of money, gets a specified amount of profit, and is usually not **liable** for anything beyond the investment itself. Finally, a *"nominal"* or *"ostensible"* partner is *not* a partner, but only someone who *looks like* a partner to an outsider.

Partnership   An *unincorporated* business organization co-owned by two or more persons. Partnerships are usually owned and managed according to a *partnership agreement* and each partner usually has full **liability** for all partnership debts. Partnership income and losses are usually allocated among the partners according to their shares, with taxes paid by the partners individually. See also **limited partnership, limited liability partnership,** and **partner.** For *partnership association,* see **limited partnership association.** See **business organization** for other organizations set up to make a profit.

Partnership association   **Limited partnership association.**

Party   *1.* A person concerned with or taking part in any contract, matter, affair, or proceeding. For various types of *parties,* such as **accommodation party, third party,** etc., see those words. *2.* A person who is either a **plaintiff** or a **defendant** in a lawsuit. A *real party* is a person who actually stands to gain or lose something from being a part of the case, while a *formal* or *nominal party* is one who has only a technical or "name only" interest. *3.* A person who *must* be included in a lawsuit, whether or not currently included (an *indispensable party,* without whom the lawsuit must be dismissed) or who *should* be included if at all possible (a *necessary party,* although the term is sometimes used to mean *indispensable*). *4.* A *party wall* is a wall, on a property line, that is part of the structure of adjoining buildings. *5.* A group organized to nominate and elect persons to public office, to influence government policy, etc.

Party admission   An out-of-court statement by a **party** (or a party's representative) to a lawsuit. A relevant party admission can usually be used by an opposing party as **evidence** under a **hearsay exception.**

Party of the first part   A wordy and unnecessary phrase used instead of repeating the name of a **party** to a document. For example, if a **contract** is between Freeway Motors and John Driver, the contract should use "Freeway Motors," "Freeway," or "seller" rather than "party of the first part" (and use "John Driver," "Driver," or "buyer" rather than "party of the second part") each time the names must be repeated.

Pass   *1.* Say or pronounce. For example, a judge may *pass sentence* on a convicted defendant. *2.* Enact successfully. For example, a **bill** "passes" when enough members of a **legislature** vote "yes" on it. *3.* Examine and determine. For example, a jury *passes upon* the issues in a lawsuit. *4.* Transfer or become transferred. For example, when a **deed** is properly written, signed, and delivered, property *passes* from one person to another. *5.* Approve. For example, when **account** books are examined and determined accurate, they are said to "pass." *6.* Put out, especially to put out fraudulently; for example, "*pass*" **counterfeit** money.

Passage   Enactment or approval of a **bill** by one **house** of a **legislature**; enactment by both houses; or enactment plus signature by the president or governor.

Passbook   A document in which the deposits and withdrawals of savings accounts may be recorded.

Passenger   *1.* Any rider in, other than the driver of, a motor vehicle. *2.* A rider in a vehicle who pays for the ride or a rider whose ride involves some possible financial benefit to the driver.

Passim   (Latin) "Here and there"; found in various places; everywhere (indicating a general mention or overall reference to a book or document).

Passion   Rage, anger, or terror (not love or lust). See **heat of passion.**

Passive   *1.* Inactive. *2.* Submissive or permissive, rather than actually agreeing to or participating in something.

Passive trust   A **dry** *trust.*

Passport   *1.* A document giving a person his or her country's permission to travel, and that country's request that other countries permit the person to pass through safely. *2.* A document issued in time of war to give a person or a ship safe conduct.

Past consideration   Something of value given, which the giver later calls **consideration** (see that word) in an attempt to create a valid **contract.**

Past recollection recorded   See **recollection.**

Pat. Pend.   Short for *"patent pending,"* a phrase placed on things that may be patentable to give notice that a **patent** has been applied for.

Patent   *1.* Open, evident, plainly visible. Compare with **latent.** For *patent defect,* compare with **latent** *defect. 2.* A grant of a right (given by the federal government to a person) to exclusively control, for a limited number of years (usually seventeen), the manufacture and sale of something that person has discovered or invented. *3.* A **grant** of land by the government to an individual.

Patent and copyright clause   The provision of the U.S. **Constitution** (Article I, Section 8, Clause 8) that gives Congress the power to promote science and the arts by passing laws, such as the **patent** and **copyright** laws, which give creators exclusive rights to their creations for limited time periods.

Patent and Trademark Office   A federal agency in the **Commerce** Department that decides on and keeps track of **patent** and **trademark** applications, keeps a complete public reference file, publishes related information, etc.

Patent pooling   An agreement among companies (usually manufacturers) to share **patent** information and rights. It is extensive **cross-licensing.**

Patentable   Able to meet the requirements for securing a **patent.** For an invention or discovery to be *patentable,* it must be *new and useful,* not a mere description of some physical law, and *non-obvious* in light of prior inventions and discoveries.

Paternity suit   A court action to prove that a person is the father of an **"illegitimate child"** and to get **support** for the child from the father.

Patient forbearance rule   See **forbearance.**

Patient Self-Determination Act   (42 U.S.C. 1395) A 1991 federal law that requires most hospitals to ask patients if they have an **advance directive,** to post these directives on the patient's chart, and to advise patients of their right to reject, and sometimes to choose, treatment.

Patient-physician privilege   See **doctor-patient privilege.**

Patrimony   *1.* All rights and property that have passed or will pass to a person from ancestors (parents, grandparents, etc.). *2.* All of a person's property, rights, and liabilities that can be given a dollar value.

Patronage   *1.* All the customers of a business; giving a company your business. (A *patronage dividend* is the refund given to a member of a **cooperative** based on purchases made from the cooperative.) *2.* The privilege of some public officials to give out some jobs at their own **discretion,** without going through a **civil service** process. This privilege is often limited at higher levels to jobs of a "political or confidential" nature and at low levels to small governments without a full civil service system.

Pattern or practice   A regular, repeated, intentional course of conduct.

Pauper   A poor person who cannot support him or herself and who requires financial help from the government (to live, to carry on a lawsuit or defend a criminal trial, etc.).

Pawn   *1.* To give personal **property** (such as a camera) to a commercial lender (usually called a *pawnbroker*) as **security** for a loan. A pawned item is held until the money loaned is paid back. If the money is not paid back within a certain time, the item is sold. *2.* The property itself in no. 1.

Payable   *1.* Owing, and to be paid in the future. *2.* Owing, and due for payment now. *3.* For *payable to bearer* and *payable to the order of,* see **bearer** and **order.**

Payables   **Accounts** *payable.*

Payee   The person to whom a **negotiable instrument** (such as a check) is made out; for example, if a check is made payable "to the **order** of John Doe," John Doe is the payee.

Payout ratio   The **dividend** a company pays on each share of **common stock** divided by the stock's **earnings per share** (see that word). The ratio shows how much money a company pays its investors compared to how much is available to put back into the business.

Payroll tax   A tax collected from a company's payroll. It is often a payroll subtraction made by the employer from the employee's salary.

P/E ratio   **Price-earnings ratio.**

Peace bond   A **bond,** required by a judge of a person likely to "breach the peace," to guarantee the person's good behavior for a period of time.

Peace officer   Any public official (such as a **sheriff,** police officer, **marshal,** etc.) with the authority to make **arrests.**

Peaceable possession   Holding land or a building continuously, with no attempt by others (such as a lawsuit) to remove the possessor from the land. *Peaceable possession* is one requirement for gaining legal ownership of land by **adverse possession** or by an action to **quiet title.**

Peculation   **Embezzlement.**

Pecuniary   Monetary; related to money. A *pecuniary interest* is a right that has monetary value. A judge should not decide a case that could affect the judge's pecuniary interests.

Pederasty   Anal (and in some states oral) intercourse between males, especially between man and boy.

Peers   Equal persons. However, a trial "by a jury of peers" does not mean "by persons exactly equal to the **defendant**," but merely "by citizens chosen fairly."

Pegging   Officially, arbitrarily, or artificially fixing or setting the value of something. For example, a country can "*peg*" the relative value of its currency or allow it to **float** relative to other countries' currency. Also, an underwriter selling a new stock **issue** can "*peg*" (try to set) the price by placing repeated orders to buy at a certain price in the stock **market**.

Peine fort et dure   (French) "Punishment strong and hard." Describes a punishment in ancient England involving pressing to death under a great weight a person who refused to speak when accused of a major crime.

Penal   *1.* Concerning a penalty. In this sense, a *penal action* is a **civil** lawsuit to make a wrongdoer pay a fine or penalty to the person harmed, and a *penal bond* is a **bond** put up as a promise to pay money if a certain thing is not done. *2.* Criminal. In this sense, a *penal action* is a **criminal** prosecution, a *penal law* is a criminal law, a *penal code* is a collection of federal or state criminal laws, and *penal servitude* is imprisonment for committing a crime or imprisonment with forced labor. *3.* For *penal damages,* see *punitive* **damages.**

Penalty   *1.* A punishment imposed by law. *2.* A sum of money promised by one person to another, to be paid if the first person fails to do something.

Penalty clause   A contract clause that calls for payment of a specific amount of money to *punish* a **breach.** Unlike **liquidated** *damages,* it is not based on the money that would *compensate* for the breach, but is arbitrarily set. If it greatly exceeds liquidated damages, a court will not enforce it.

Pendency   *1.* While **pending** (see that word). *2.* A *notice of pendency* is a formal warning, recorded in the land records, that a claim has been made against a property. The notice warns that anyone who buys the property does so subject to the claim.

Pendent jurisdiction   A federal court's right to decide a claim based on a nonfederal **issue** if this claim depends on the same set of facts as does a federal claim in the case before the court.

Pendente lite (Latin) "Pending the suit"; while a lawsuit is in progress. For example, *support pendente lite* is temporary support while a divorce case is in progress. [pronounce: pen-<u>den</u>-te lee-te]

Pending As yet undecided; begun but not finished.

Penitentiary A **prison** for **felons.**

Pennoyer v. Neff (95 U.S. 714) The 1877 U.S. Supreme Court decision that a state court cannot take **jurisdiction** over a person unless the person has been served with **process** in that state. This rule has been greatly modified (see, for example, **long-arm statute**), but the general principle that a court must have jurisdiction over a person to give a **judgment** or **decree** against that person is still valid.

Pennsylvania rule The principle that if a person who breaks a traffic law is in a collision, that person must prove that the violation did *not* cause the accident in order to be free of fault.

Penny stock **Stock,** often speculative, selling at less than a dollar a share.

Penology The study of prisons and criminal punishment.

Pension Benefit Guaranty Corporation See **P.B.G.C.**

Pension plan A plan set up by an employer to pay employees after retirement. This may be either a fund of money (called "funded" if it is fully paid-in to meet the promised pension needs) set up by the employer or payments by the employer to the employee. A *qualified plan* is one that meets **I.R.S.** requirements for the payments to be deducted by the employer and initially tax-free to the employee. A *defined-benefit plan* has benefits specified in advance, usually as a percentage of salary and related to years of service, with no individual account kept for each employee. A *money-purchase plan* (or *defined-contribution plan*) has a specified amount of money periodically contributed to a retirement fund by the employer, by the employee, or by both. The money is invested, with earnings divided proportionally among all plan participants. See also **Individual Retirement Account, Keogh Plan, Employee Retirement Income Security Act, vested,** and **annuity.**

Penumbra doctrine *1.* The principle that the "**necessary** *and proper clause*" of the U.S. **Constitution** allows the federal government to take all actions to carry out legitimate government purposes, even if the powers needed to carry out these purposes are only **implied** from other powers (which themselves are not specifically mentioned in the Constitution, but only implied). *2.* The principle that specific **constitutional** rights have less clear, but still real, **implied** rights, such as the right to **privacy.**

Peona (Latin) Punishment.

Peonage Slavery or forced labor to pay off a debt.

People *1.* A nation or state. *2.* All persons in a nation or state regarded as a single group. *3. Not* the plural of "**person**" in the law.

Peppercorn Something of actual, but very insignificant, value.

Per (Latin) By; through; by means of; during. For example, *per annum* means "by the year" or "yearly" and *per autre vie* means "during the life of another person."

Per capita (Latin) "By heads." By the number of individual persons, each equally. Compare with **per stirpes.**

Per curiam (Latin) "By the court." Describes an **opinion** backed by all the judges in a particular court and usually with no one judge's name on it. [pronounce: per cure-ee-am]

Per diem (Latin) *1.* By the day; day by day; each day. *2.* A fixed amount of money paid to a person each day for either a salary or expenses (such as food and lodging). [pronounce: per dee-em]

Per pais See **pais.**

Per procuration In English law, acting as an **agent** with only limited authority. Abbreviated "per. proc." or "p.p."

Per quod (Latin) "By that"; "by which acts." A specification of necessary details; requiring specific proof. Sometimes used as the opposite of **per se.**

Per se (Latin) In and of itself; taken alone; inherently. For example, some types of business arrangements are "*per se violations*" of **antitrust acts** because, even without specific proof that **monopoly** power has hurt competition, the arrangements are in and of themselves considered bad. Compare **rule of reason** no. 3 and **per quod.** [pronounce: per say]

Per stirpes (Latin) "By roots"; by right of representation. Describes a method of dividing a dead person's **estate** by giving out shares equally "by representation" or by family groups. For example, if John leaves three thousand dollars to Mary and Sue, and Mary dies, leaving two children (Steve and Jeff), a *per stirpes* division would give fifteen hundred dollars to Sue and seven hundred and fifty dollars each to Steve and Jeff. A "**per capita**" (see that word) division would give one thousand dollars each to Sue, Steve, and Jeff.

Percentage depletion See **depletion allowance.**

Percentage lease A **lease** of a building with the rent, above a certain minimum rent, based on the dollar value of sales by the tenant in the building.

Percentage order   Instructions from a customer to a **broker** to buy or sell a certain number of shares of stock after a specific number of shares have been traded on the **market.**

Perception   An old word for taking something into possession or for counting out money and paying a debt.

Peremptory   *1.* Absolute; conclusive; final; or arbitrary. *2.* Not requiring any explanation or cause to be shown. For example, a *peremptory challenge* to a potential **juror** is the automatic elimination of that person from the jury by one side before trial without needing to state the reason for the elimination. Each side has the right to a certain number of peremptory challenges, and all other attempts to eliminate a potential juror must be for a reason (which may or may not be accepted by the judge).

Peremptory ruling   A judge's ruling that "takes the final decision away" from the jury; for example, a **directed verdict** or *judgment* **non obstante veredicto.**

Peremptory writ   *1.* See **mandamus.** *2.* See **summons.**

Perfect   *1.* Complete; enforceable; without defect. Also called "perfected." *2.* To tie down or "make perfect." For example, to *perfect a title* is to record it in the proper place so that your ownership is protected against all persons, not just against the person who sold to you. This is called "*perfection.*" And *perfecting bail* is meeting all the qualifications to "go **bail**" for someone and get him or her out of jail.

Perfect tender rule   The rarely-applied rule that exact **performance** of the details of a commercial **contract** is required to make the contract enforceable.

Performance   Carrying out a **contract,** promise, or other **obligation** according to its terms, so that the obligation ends. *Specific performance* is being required to do exactly what was agreed to. A court may require specific performance of a contract if one person fails to perform and **damages** (money) will not properly compensate the other side for harm done. *Part performance* is carrying out some, but not all, of a contract, or doing something in **reliance** on another's promise. Part performance of an *oral* contract that should have been in writing to be enforceable (see **statute of frauds**) usually makes the contract enforceable. Part performance in reasonable reliance on another's promise may make the promise irrevocable.

Performance (or completion) bond   A **bond** that guarantees that a **contractor** will do a job correctly and finish it on time.

Performance right　A **copyright** holder's right to control who will perform or broadcast the work.

Peril　*1.* A **risk** or **accident** insured against in an **insurance** policy. *2.* A natural, as opposed to human-caused danger.

Periodic　Happening after regular, fixed amounts of time. For example, *periodic alimony* is payment of a certain sum of money to an ex-spouse once a month, once a week, etc.; and *periodic tenancy* is a **lease** that continues from month-to-month or year-to-year unless ended (usually by someone giving a notice that it will be ended).

Perjury　Lying while under **oath,** especially in a court proceeding. It is a crime. See also **false swearing.**

Perk　Short for **perquisite.**

Permanent　*Permanent* can mean anything from "for an indefinite time" (as in *permanent employment*), to "definitely right now" (as in *permanent residence*), to "definitely for a long time" (as in *permanent disability*).

Permissive　*1.* Allowed or endured, as opposed to actively approved of. *2.* By right. *3.* Lenient or tolerant. *4.* For *permissive counterclaim,* see **counterclaim.**

Permit　*1.* An official document that allows a person to do something (usually something legal that is not allowable without the permit). *2.* A *permit card* is a document given by a union to a nonmember allowing that person to work on a job for which there are not enough union members.

Pernancy　An old word for the taking or receiving of something.

Perp　Slang for **perpetrator.**

Perpetrator　The person who commits a particular crime.

Perpetual succession　The continuous existence of a **corporation** as the same "being," even though its owners, **directors,** and managers may change.

Perpetual trust　A **trust** that continues as long as the need lasts (the life of a person or a charity, etc.).

Perpetuating testimony　A procedure for taking and preserving **testimony** (usually by **deposition**) of persons who are in very bad health, very old, about to leave the state, or might otherwise be unavailable for a later trial.

Perpetuation of evidence　Making sure that **evidence** is available for a possible trial later.

Perpetuity　*1.* Forever. *2.* An investment that gives equal future payments essentially forever. *3.* Any attempt to control the **disposition** of your property by **will** that is meant to last longer than the life of a person alive when you die (or at least conceived by then) plus twenty-one years. Most states prevent such control by a law known as the *rule against perpetuities.*

Perquisite   A benefit of a job in addition to the salary; for example, a company car for personal use. A "*perk*." [pronounce: <u>per</u>-qui-zit]

Person   *1.* A human being (a "natural" person). *2.* A **corporation** (an "artificial" person). Corporations are treated as persons in many legal situations. Also, the word "*person*" includes corporations in most definitions in this dictionary. *3.* Any other "being" entitled to sue as a legal entity (a government, an association, a group of **trustees,** etc.). *4.* The plural of person is *persons, not* **people** (see that word).

Persona non grata   (Latin) "Persons not wanted." Describes a person rejected as an **ambassador** or other government representative by the country to which he or she is sent.

Personal   *1.* Having to do with a human being. *2.* Having to do with movable property, as opposed to land and buildings. *Personal effects* means anything from "all movable property" to "only that property normally carried on the person." *3.* For *personal* **holding company, property, recognizance,** etc., see those words. A few other "personal" words follow this word.

Personal injury   *1.* Any harm done to a person's rights, except for property rights. *2.* Describes **negligence** and other **tort** actions brought to get compensation for bodily and other harm done.

Personal representative   A general term for the **executor** or **administrator** of a dead person's property.

Personal trust   A **trust** for individuals and their own families, as opposed to business-related trusts or trusts set up to benefit a charity.

Personality   *1.* A person's mental characteristics. In this sense, a *personality disorder* is a continuing behavioral or emotional problem, rather than a mental illness. *2.* The condition of being a person. In this sense, a **corporation** has *legal personality.* See **person.** *Not* **personalty.**

Personalty   **Personal** property; movable property. *Not* **personality.**

Persuasive authority   All sources of law that a judge might use, but is not required to use, in making up his or her mind about a case; for example, legal encyclopedias or related cases from other states. A case may be strongly persuasive if it comes from a famous judge or a nearby, powerful court.

Pertinent   Relevant to an **issue** that itself is relevant to the outcome of a trial.

Perverse verdict   A jury's **verdict** (see that word) that did not follow (or could not have been in accordance with) a judge's **instructions** about a **point** of law.

Petit jury (or petty jury)   "Small jury." Describes the standard trial jury as opposed to a *grand* **jury.**

Petit larceny   "Small **larceny.**" The crime of stealing something worth less than a certain amount set by law.

Petition   *1.* A written request to a court that it take a particular action. In some states the word is limited to written requests made when there is no other side in a case (**ex parte** cases, see that word), and in some states, "*petition*" is used in place of "**complaint**" (the first **pleading** in a lawsuit). *2.* A request made to a public official.

Petition in bankruptcy   A paper filed to start a **bankruptcy** (see that word) by a **debtor** requesting **relief** from debts. It can also be filed by **creditors** asking that a person be put into bankruptcy involuntarily.

Petitioner   Same as "**plaintiff**" in many states.

Petitory action   A lawsuit to establish **title** to land, as opposed to a lawsuit to gain physical possession of the land.

Pettifogger   An old word for a lawyer who is either incompetent or who tries to win by clouding the issue and drowning it in trivia.

Petty   Small or unimportant. For example, *petty cash* is money kept on hand to meet small expenses, and a *petty offense* is one punishable by only a **fine** or a short jail term. For *petty jury,* see **petit jury.**

Phantom jury   **Shadow jury.**

Phantom stock   Employee compensation that is similar to a nontransferable, nonvalued, nonvoting stock option that can be cashed in at a later date for the value of a certain number of shares of company stock as of that later date (but not for the shares themselves).

Philadelphia lawyer   Originally, a skillful lawyer; now, a sly or tricky lawyer.

Philanthropic organization   See **nonprofit organization.**

Physical   *1.* Having to do with the body, rather than the mind; for example, a *physical incapacity* is either an injury that prevents working or impotence due to a physical cause. *2.* Real as opposed to imaginary. *3.* See **physical fact.** *4.* See *physical impossibility* under **impossible.** *5. Physical necessity* means being compelled to do something by an irresistible force.

Physical fact   *1.* An indisputable law of nature or a scientific fact. *2.* Something visible, audible, or otherwise "graspable" by the senses.

3. The "*physical fact rule*" is the principle that **evidence** contrary to a known law of nature may justify a judge's decision to take a case away from the **jury.** This evidence may also be disregarded by an **appeals** court even if the judge accepted it. *4.* Another different "*physical fact rule*" is the principle that a driver is **negligent** if he or she did not see what should have been seen.

Physician-patient privilege See **doctor-patient privilege.**

Physician's directive See **advance directive.**

Picketing Persons gathering outside a place to disturb its activities or to inform persons outside of grievances, opinions, etc., about the place. This usually takes place when a **labor union** tries to publicize a **labor dispute** with a company, influence customers to withhold business, etc. For **chain, common situs, cross, mass,** and other types of *picketing,* see those words.

Piercing the corporate veil A judge's holding individual owners, **directors, officers,** etc., **liable** for a **corporation**'s debts or wrongdoing. This is done in unusual circumstances such as to punish **fraud** or when the corporation's stock is not fully paid for.

Pinkerton rule See **conspiracy.**

Pinpoint citation The page number of a specific quote, as opposed to the general **citation** (see that word). It follows the page number on which the quoted document begins. In the general citation 17 U.Dl.L.R.247, 250, the *pinpoint citation* is page 250. Also, some *pinpoint citations* are to a page plus a specific paragraph number, and some are to a paragraph number alone.

Pioneer patent A **patent** for an invention or device that is entirely new, rather than a small improvement; or a patent that may open up a whole new area of experimentation or development.

Piracy *1.* Attacking and looting or stealing a ship or airplane. *2.* Reprinting all or part of a copyrighted book, movie, etc., without permission.

Pit A commodity **exchange's** trading area.

Place *1.* Arrange a sale or other financial transaction. *Placement* could be arranging the sale of a new **issue** of **stock,** arranging a loan or **mortgage** by matching up borrower and lender, or finding a job for a person. *2. Place of business* and *place of employment* have no precise definitions in the law.

Placer claim A public land claim to mine minerals deposited in loose sand or rock, along the bank of or under a river, etc.

Placitory Having to do with **pleading** or **pleas.**

Placitum   (Latin) An old word for a wide variety of different things including agreements, laws, court decisions, public meetings, courts, lawsuits, **pleadings,** etc.

Plagiarism   Taking all or part of the writing or idea of another person and passing it off as your own. See also **infringement.** [pronounce: play-jar-ism]

Plain error rule   The principle that an **appeals** court can **reverse** a **judgment** because an obvious error affecting substantial rights was made by the trial court during trial, even if the error was not objected to at the time.

Plain meaning rule   _1._ The principle that if a law seems clear, you should take the simplest meaning of the words and not read anything into the law. This is one of several possible ways of interpreting **statutes.** _2._ The principle that if a contract, statute, or other writing seems clear, the meaning of the writing should be determined from the writing itself, not from other **evidence** such as **testimony.**

Plain view doctrine   The rule that if police officers see or come across something while acting lawfully, that item may be used as **evidence** in a criminal trial even if the police did not have a **search warrant.**

Plaintiff   A person who brings (starts) a lawsuit against another person.

Plaintiff in error   An **appellant.**

Planned unit development   An area of land to be developed as one unit of various housing groups plus commercial or industrial development. This development may be approved even if the **zoning** requirements for one part of the land might not allow the buildings planned for that piece.

Plant patent   A **patent** given to the first person who recognizes the distinctive characteristics of a plant and reproduces it any way but by seed. This could include grafting, genetic engineering, etc.

Plat   A map showing how a piece of land will be subdivided (divided up) and built upon. A _platmap_ gives the legal description of pieces of property by lot, street, and block numbers.

Plea   _1._ The **defendant's** formal answer to a criminal **charge.** The defendant says: "guilty," "not guilty" or "**nolo contendere**" (no contest). _2._ For the use of the word in most modern **civil** lawsuits, see **pleading.** _3._ An older word for several types of civil motions, such as a _plea in abatement,_ that have been largely replaced by a "**motion** _to dismiss._" Other types of old pleas include _pleas in_ **bar,** _pleas in_ **discharge,** and _pleas of_ **release.** [pronounce: plee]

Plea bargaining   Negotiations between a **prosecutor** and a criminal **defendant's** lawyer, attempting to resolve a criminal case without trial. For example, during *plea bargaining,* the defense lawyer may suggest that the defendant plead guilty in exchange for the prosecutor's agreeing to accept a **plea** to a less serious **charge,** to drop some charges, or to promise not to request a heavy **sentence** from the judge.

Plead   *1.* Make or file a **pleading** or a **plea.** *2.* Argue a case in court.

Pleading   *1.* The process of making formal, written statements of each side of a **civil** case. First the **plaintiff** submits a paper with "facts" and claims; then the **defendant** submits a paper with "facts" (and sometimes counterclaims); then the plaintiff responds; etc., until all issues and questions are clearly posed for a trial. *2. A pleading* is any one of the papers mentioned in no. 1. The first one is a **complaint,** the response is an **answer,** etc. *The pleadings* is the sum of all these papers. Sometimes, written **motions** and other court papers are called *pleadings,* but this is not strictly correct. *3.* The old forms of **common law** *pleadings* (which were so rigid that one small technical mistake could lose the suit) included a *declaration, defendant's plea, replication, rejoinder, surrejoinder, rebutter, surrebutter,* etc. See **theory of pleading doctrine.** *4.* In modern legal practice under the *Federal Rules of Civil Procedure,* pleading is no longer inflexible, and pleadings may be amended freely to fit facts as they develop. Modern *pleadings* include complaints, answers (which may include **counterclaims** or **cross-claims**), replies (or answers) to these claims, and **third party** *complaints* and *answers.*

Plebicite   A vote by the people for or against a proposed new major law or expressing an opinion on a major public issue.

Pledge   Handing over physical possession of a piece of personal **property** (such as a radio) to another person, who holds it as **security** (see that word) for a debt.

Plenary   Full; complete; of every person or every thing. For example, *plenary jurisdiction* is the full power of a court to make decisions about all the people and property involved in a case, and a *plenary session* is a meeting of all the members of a **legislature** or other large group.

Plenipotentiary   Possessing full powers. *Ministers plenipotentiary* are diplomatic representatives slightly below the rank of **ambassador.**

Plessy v. Ferguson   (163 U.S. 537) The 1896 U.S. Supreme Court decision that permitted racial segregation in *"separate but equal"* facilities. This case was not overturned until the 1954 **Brown decision.**

Plottage   The area of a piece (*plot*) of land. *Plottage value (plottage,* for short) refers to the extra value two or more pieces of land may have because they are side-by-side and can be sold as a unit.

Plow back   Reinvest profits into a business rather than pay them out to owners.

Plurality   The greatest number. For example, if Jane gets ten votes and Don and Mary each get seven, Jane has a *plurality* (the most votes), but not a **majority** (more than half of the votes).

Pluries   Many. Many interrelated things.

Pocket part   An addition to a lawbook that updates it until a bound supplement or a new edition comes out. It is found inside the back (or occasionally, front) cover, secured in a "pocket," and should always be referred to when doing legal research.

Pocket veto   See **veto.**

Point   *1.* An individual legal proposition, argument, or question raised in a lawsuit. *Points and authorities* is the name for a document prepared to back up a legal position taken in a lawsuit (for example, to support or oppose a **motion**). *2.* One percent. A term used by **mortgage** companies to describe an initial charge made for lending money, and by **bond** traders for one percent of **face value.** *3.* One unit of measure. For example, if a **stock** goes up in price one dollar, it has gone up "one point," since stocks are usually expressed in dollar amounts; and a speeding violation might cost a driver "three points" towards the suspension of a driver's license (when licenses are taken away for the accumulation of a certain number of "points" that reflect the severity of driving tickets). Also see **basis point.** *4.* A *point of error* is an **error** used as the basis for an **appeal.**

Point reserved   See **reserve** *decision.*

Poison pill   Any of several tactics used by a company to make itself less attractive as a *takeover* target.

Poisonous tree   See **fruit of the poisonous tree doctrine.**

Polar star rule   The principle that the intent of a document should be determined from the document alone unless it violates laws or public policy. See also **four corners rule.**

Police court   A local court with widely different functions in different places. *Police courts* usually have the power to handle minor criminal cases.

Police power   The government's right and power to set up and enforce laws to provide for the safety, health, and general welfare of the people; for example, *police power* includes the power to **license** occupations such as hair cutting.

Policy   *1.* The general operating procedures and goals of an organization. *2.* The general purpose of a **statute** or other law. *3.* A type of lottery that involves betting on numbers; a "numbers game." *4. Public policy* is the general good of the state and its people. A contract is "against public policy" if carrying out contracts of that type is considered harmful to the public. *5.* For various types of *insurance policies,* see **insurance.**

Political crime (or offense)   A **crime** against the government, such as **treason** or **sedition.** It is often a crime of violence against the established order. *Political crimes* are usually excluded from **extradition** treaties.

Political question   An issue that a court may refuse to decide because it concerns a decision properly made by the **executive** or **legislative** branch of government and because the court has no adequate standards of review or no adequate way to enforce the court's judgment. Most *political questions* are international diplomatic issues (such as whether or not a foreign country is an independent nation) that are considered by the federal courts to be best left to the president of the United States.

Political rights   Rights concerning a citizen's participation in government; for example, the right to vote.

Poll tax   A tax, now illegal, paid to vote or for the right to vote.

Polling the jury   Individually asking each member of a **jury** what his or her decision is. This is done by the judge, at the defendant's request, immediately after the **verdict.**

Polls   A *challenge to the polls* is an objection to the selection of a particular **juror,** made before the jury (often a *grand* **jury**) convenes.

Polygamy   Having more than one wife or husband. It is a crime in the U.S.

Polygraph   A **lie detector.**

Ponzi scheme   A fake investment company in which fake profits are paid from money paid in, so more investments, and more investors, are lured in.

Pool   *1.* Join together resources of individuals or companies in a common commercial venture. *2.* Describes an agreement between companies to not compete and to share profits. These types of arrangements are usually illegal under **antitrust acts.** *3.* A pot of money bet on a horse race, a football game, etc.

Pooling of interest   Directly combining the **balance sheets** of two companies when the companies merge. (This **accounting** procedure disregards **goodwill** as a measure of the difference in company values.)

Popular   Belonging to the people.

Popular name tables   Reference charts that cross-reference the common name of a **statute** with its official name and number. For example, you could find the official name and **citation** of the "Sherman Act" from a *popular name table.*

Popular sense   The meaning that persons familiar with the subject area of a **statute** would give to it. This is not necessarily the common-language meaning of the words.

Pornographic   Depicting sexual behavior to cause sexual excitement. Non-**obscene** (see that word) pornography is protected by the **First Amendment,** but **child pornography** is not.

Port authority   Various federal, state, or interstate agencies that **regulate** boat traffic, promote port business, and maintain other services such as airports, tollroads, bus terminals, etc.

Port of entry   A port where immigrants and imported goods may enter the country and where **customs** offices are located.

Portal-to-Portal Act   (29 U.S.C. 251) A 1947 federal law requiring payment for some types of employees' time getting to and from work.

Portfolio   All the investments (usually **stocks** and other **securities**) held by one person or organization.

Position classification   Formal job categorization and description that determines job salaries, duties, and powers.

Positive evidence   See **direct evidence.**

Positive law   Law that has been enacted by a **legislature.**

Posse comitatus   (Latin) "The power of the state." The group of citizens who may be gathered by the **sheriff** or other law officer to help enforce the law, usually on an emergency basis. It is abbreviated "*posse.*"

Possession   Control of **property.** For example, a **tenant** may have *possession* of land, and someone with an illegal drug in a pocket has *possession.*

Possession is nine-tenths of the law   *1.* The principle that to get a court to give you something held by another person, you must have a strong legal **title** to it. *2.* The perception that court procedures are too costly and cumbersome to get something held by someone else even if you have a legal title to it. *3.* The perception that forcible possession may defeat legal right.

Possessory action A lawsuit to gain control of property, as opposed to one that attempts to get legal ownership to property. For example, an **eviction** is a *possessory action.*

Possibility of issue See **fertile octogenarian rule.**

Post *1.* Announce something to the public by putting up signs in prominent places; for example, giving notice of a legal proceeding by *posting* in town hall, announcing construction by *posting* a permit, or announcing that land or water is off limits to hunting by *posting* signs around the borders. *2.* Put something in the mail. *3.* See **posting.**

Postconviction remedies (or relief) Procedures for prisoners to challenge their **convictions** or **sentences.** These procedures include asking the convicting court to correct the sentence, **habeas corpus** petitions, and other forms of court action. There are federal and state laws that apply to this area.

Postdate To put a date on a document that is later than the date the document is signed.

Posthumous After death. For example, a *posthumous child* is one born after the death of the father.

Posting *1.* Writing down an **entry** (such as the amount of money spent for a lamp) into an **account** book or writing down a financial entry by transferring information from an original record or notation. *2.* The procedure a bank follows when paying a check (verifying the signature and that the account has sufficient funds, charging the account, etc.). *3.* Placing a notice in a public place, such as a place legally specified for **service of process,** or placing a notice at the border of a private property to forbid hunting.

Postmortem (Latin) "After death." A *postmortem examination (postmortem,* for short) is an **autopsy** (see that word).

Postnuptial agreement An agreement between spouses, such as a **separation** *agreement* or *a property settlement agreement.* Compare with **antenuptial** *agreement.*

Post-obit "After death." Describes an agreement in which a borrower of a sum of money promises to repay a larger sum after the death of someone from whom the borrower expects an **inheritance.**

Postponement *1.* **Subordination** of a **lien, mortgage,** or **judgment** when it would normally have **priority** over the lien, mortgage, or judgment now given priority. *2.* A rescheduling, such as a **continuance** of a court proceeding.

Post-trial discovery Information gathering (such as taking a **deposition**) after a trial but before an appeal, often done to prepare for a possible retrial.

Poundage *1.* A charge imposed on an item according to its weight. *2.* **Impound**ment, or an amount paid to end an impoundment. *3.* Describes fees paid to a **sheriff** or other public official who conducts a court-ordered **execution** on property. The fees are usually a percentage of the property's value or selling price.

Pourover A **will** that gives some money or property to an existing **trust** is called a *pourover will,* and a trust that does the same thing is a *pourover trust.*

Poverty affidavit A document signed under **oath** that a person is poor enough to qualify for public assistance, a free lawyer, **waiver** of court fees, etc.

Power *1.* The right to do something. *2.* The ability to do something. *3.* A combination of no. 1 and no. 2. For example, a *power of acceptance* is the right and ability of a person who has been made an offer to agree to the offer's terms and create a binding **contract.** For specific powers, such as the *commerce power* under the **commerce clause** and *reserved powers* under **reserved,** see those words. *4.* A *power coupled with an interest* is a power to take an action that affects something in which you have an **interest** (see that word). This is a stronger right than a *power* or *interest* alone.

Power of appointment The power to decide who gets certain money or property or how it will be used. This power is usually given to a specific person in a **deed** or **will.**

Power of attorney A document authorizing a person to act as **attorney** *in fact* for the person signing the document.

Power of sale The right of a **mortgage** holder or mortgage **trustee** to sell the real estate **secured** by the mortgage if payments are not made.

Pp. Pages.

Practicable A stuffy word meaning "feasible"; can be done.

Practice *1.* Custom, habit, or an act regularly repeated. *2.* Formal court procedure; the way a lawsuit is taken to and through court as opposed to what it is about. For example, a *practice manual* is a book of forms and procedures to use in **pleading** and court practice, and *practice rules (or acts)* are rules of court practice such as the **Federal rules** (see that word). *3.* Engage in a profession, such as law. *4.* Doing things that are only permitted to be done by a member of a profession. For example, giving legal advice or arguing a case in court is the *practice of law.*

Praecipe (Latin) A formal request that the court **clerk** take some action. Any **motion** that can be granted by the signature of a court clerk without a judge's approval. A lawyer can "**enter** an appearance" in a case by *praecipe*. [pronounce: <u>pres</u>-i-pee]

Praedial *1.* "From the ground." Crops, trees, and other plants. *2.* A *praedial servitude* is a requirement put on one piece of land that it may be used in some way by the owner of another piece of land. [pronounce: <u>pred</u>-i-al]

Prayer Request. That part of a legal **pleading** (such as a **complaint**) that asks for **relief** (help, money, specific court action, an action from the other side, etc.).

Preamble An introduction (usually saying why a document, such as a **statute,** was written).

Preappointed evidence Proof that is required in advance. For example, a **statute** may say that proof of a certain crime requires *preappointed evidence* of a specific set of facts.

Precatory Expressing a wish; advisory only; not legally binding in most situations. [pronounce: <u>prek</u>-a-tory]

Precedent *1.* A court decision on a *question of law* (how the law affects the case) that is **binding authority** (see that word) on lower courts in the same court system for cases in which those courts must decide a similar question of law involving similar facts. (Some legal scholars include as *precedent* court decisions that are merely **persuasive authority.**) The U.S. court system is based on judges making decisions supported by past precedent, rather than by the logic of the judge alone. See **stare decisis.** *2.* Something that must happen before something else may happen; see **condition** *precedent.* [pronounce: <u>press</u>-i-dent]

Precept *1.* A command by a person in authority, usually in the form of a written **order** or **warrant** from a judge to a **peace officer.** *2.* A rule of conduct.

Precinct A police or election district within a city or county.

Precipe See **praecipe.**

Preclusion order A judge's **order,** issued when one side in a lawsuit doesn't produce something requested in **discovery,** which forbids that side from making (or opposing) legal arguments based on what was not produced.

Precognition The examination of a **witness** before trial.

Precontract A **contract** that keeps you from entering into a similar contract with someone else.

Predatory intent Describes lowering prices (usually to below cost) solely to put a competitor out of business.

Predial See **praedial.**

Predisposition Previous tendency or desire. See **entrapment.**

Pre-emption *1.* Describes the first right to buy something. For example, *pre-emptive rights* are the rights of some stockholders to have the first opportunity to buy any new stock the company issues. Also see **right of first refusal.** *2.* Describes the first right to do anything. For example, when the federal government *pre-empts the field* by passing laws in a subject area, the states may not pass conflicting laws and sometimes may not pass any laws on the subject at all.

Preexisting duty rule The rule that the promise or performance of something already promised, or the threat of nonperformance, is not **consideration** for a contract change.

Preference *1.* A **creditor's** right to be paid by a **debtor** before non-preferred creditors are paid. *2.* The act of an **insolvent** (broke) debtor in paying off a creditor more than a fair share of what is left. For example, if John owes Mary ten dollars and Don ten dollars, but has only ten dollars left and pays it all to Mary, this is a *preference.* If a debtor gives a creditor preference shortly before going into **bankruptcy,** the bankruptcy court may be able to get that money back so that it can be divided fairly.

Preferential shop A place of business where **union** members will be hired first and laid off last.

Preferential voting An election in which voters may (or must) list first, second, third, etc., choices. If no one gets over half the first place votes, second place choices are added in (then, if needed, third place, etc.) until someone gets over 50 percent of the votes.

Preferred risk A person who pays lower **premiums** for insurance (because of a good safety record, not smoking, etc.).

Preferred stock See **stock.**

Prehire agreement An agreement by which a **union** may **bargain** with an employer even though it has not proved that it represents a majority of the employees.

Prejudice *1.* Bias; a preconceived opinion. Leaning towards one side in a dispute for reasons other than an evaluation of the justice of that side's position. *2.* A judge's bias for or against a **party** in a case, rather than an opinion about the subject of the case. *3.* If a case is *dismissed with prejudice,* it cannot be brought back into court again. *4.* Substantially and improperly harmful to rights. For example, *prejudicial error* is serious enough and wrong enough to be appealed, and *prejudicial publicity* includes news reports that deprive a **defendant** of a fair trial.

Preliminary complaint   The process in some states by which a court can conduct a **probable cause** (see that word) hearing for **binding over** a criminal defendant to another court that has the power to hold criminal trials. See **preliminary hearing.**

Preliminary evidence   *1.* Those facts needed to begin a hearing or trial; not necessarily those needed to ultimately win. *2.* Facts required to be shown before other things are **admissible.**

Preliminary hearing   *1.* The first court proceeding on a **criminal** charge, in federal courts and many state courts, by a **magistrate** or a judge to decide whether there is enough evidence for the government to continue with the case and to require the defendant to post **bail** or be held for trial. It is also called a *preliminary examination,* **probable cause** *hearing,* and *bind over hearing. 2.* In some states, a preliminary hearing is a court session for hearing **motions** before the actual trial.

Preliminary injunction   See **injunction.**

Premeditation   Thinking about something before doing it; thinking in advance about how to commit a crime.

Premises   *1.* Buildings and the surrounding land under the same control. *2.* The part of a document that explains the "who, what, where, how, and when" of a transaction and precedes the words actually putting the transaction into effect. *3.* The basis for a logical deduction. The facts or arguments upon which a conclusion is based.

Premium   *1.* The money paid for **insurance** coverage. *2.* An extra amount of money paid to buy something; a bonus. *3.* The amount by which a **stock** or other **security** sells above its **par** (**face** or **nominal**) *value.*

Prenuptial agreement   An **antenuptial** *agreement.*

Prepaid expense   Any expense or debt paid before it is due or incurred. Prepaying expenses may have special tax consequences.

Prepaid income   Money received, but not yet earned or due. Prepaying income may have special tax consequences.

Prepaid legal services   See **panel.**

Prepayment penalty   Extra money that must be paid if you pay off a loan early. This is said to compensate the lender for lost interest or extra paperwork.

Preponderance of evidence   The greater weight of evidence, not as to *quantity* (in number of witnesses or facts) but as to *quality* (believability and greater weight of important facts proved). This is a *standard of proof,* generally used in **civil** lawsuits. It is not as high a standard as **clear and convincing evidence** or **beyond a reasonable doubt.**

Prerogative *1.* A special privilege. *2.* Special official power.

Prerogative writs **Writs** a court will issue only under special circumstances. These include, for example, *writs* of **mandamus** and **habeas corpus** (see those words). In most courts, *prerogative writs* are no longer used, but have been replaced by regular **motions** or **complaints.**

Prescription *1.* A method of getting legal ownership of *personal* **property** (everything but *land*) by keeping it in your possession openly, continuously, and with a claim that it belongs to you. This must be done for a length of time set by state law. *2.* The right of access to a path, a waterway, light, open air, etc., that is gained because of longtime continuous use. *3.* An order or direction. *Not* **proscription.**

Presence "View," "earshot," or general observation. A police officer may make an **arrest** without a **warrant** if the **offense** was committed in the officer's *presence.* This may include hearing a disturbance at a distance or finding out in many other direct, immediate ways that there was an offense committed and that a particular person probably did it.

Present *1.* Immediate; for example, a *present interest* is a property **interest** that gives the owner the right to immediate use or possession of the property. Compare with **future interest.** *2.* See **presentment.**

Present recollection revived (or present memory refreshed) See **recollection.**

Present sense impression A statement made during or immediately after an event by a participant or an observer. A person may testify about someone else's *present sense impression,* even though such testimony is **hearsay,** in those courts that recognize the "present sense exception" to the hearsay rule.

Present worth (or value) The value of future payments, earnings, or debts discounted to their value today (as if a sum of money were invested today to make the future payments).

Presentence investigation An investigation by court-appointed social workers, **probation** officers, etc., into a criminal's background to determine the criminal's prospects for rehabilitation. The report of the investigation, which usually includes recommendations, is considered by a judge at a *presentence (or sentencing) hearing.*

Presentment (or presentation) *1.* A grand **jury's** charging a person with a crime that it has investigated itself (not by an **indictment** given to it by a prosecutor). In some states it is a suggestion to the prosecutor, not a formal charge. *2.* Offering for payment a **negotiable instrument,** such as a check.

Presents *"These presents"* is an obsolete phrase for "this legal document."

Presidential electors See **electoral college.**

Presumed intent Describes the legal rule that a person means to cause any natural or probable results of his or her **voluntary** acts. A person legally *intends* not only a crime, but its consequences.

Presumption A conclusion or inference drawn. A *presumption of fact* is a conclusion that because one fact exists (or one thing is true), another fact exists (or another thing is true). If no new facts turn up to prove the presumption wrong, it is **evidence** as good as any direct proof of the fact. A *presumption of law* is an automatic assumption required by law that whenever a certain set of facts shows up, a court must automatically draw certain legal conclusions. For example, the *presumption of innocence* is that all persons are innocent of all crimes unless proven guilty **beyond a reasonable doubt.** Presumptions can be *rebuttable* (good until destroyed by more facts) or *conclusive, absolute,* or *irrebuttable* (an inference that must be drawn from a set of facts no matter what). Other *presumptions* include the *presumption of death* (if a person disappears and is gone for a certain number of years, that person is presumed dead); the *presumption of legitimacy* (if a child is born to a married woman, the husband is presumed to be the father); and the *presumption of survivorship* (in those states that do not have **simultaneous death acts,** the younger, stronger, healthier, etc., person is presumed to have been the later one to die in an accident if it is not known who really died last).

Presumptive May be inferred. *Presumptive* **evidence** is either a **presumption** *of fact* or **prima facie** *evidence.*

Presumptive trust A **resulting trust.**

Pretermitted heir A child (or sometimes any descendant) either unintentionally left out of a **will** or born after the will is made. Some states have *pretermission statutes* that allow a child left out by mistake to take a share of the parent's property.

Pretext arrest The arrest of a person for a minor offense when the real purpose is to search for evidence of serious crime for which there is no justification to search.

Pretrial conference A meeting of lawyers and judge to narrow the issues in a lawsuit, agree on what will be presented at the trial, and make a final effort to **settle** the case without a trial. Procedural agreements can be put in writing in a *pretrial order.*

Pretrial diversion (or intervention) See **diversion.**

Prevailing party The person who wins a lawsuit (even if the person is awarded far less money than he or she sued for).

Prevention (of performance) Doing something that prevents the other side from performing a **contract** duty. This normally does not create a **breach** by the other side.

Preventive detention Holding persons against their will, usually by order of a judge, because they are likely to commit a crime or to harm themselves or others. This practice is **constitutional** only in certain situations.

Preventive justice A general term for actions such as issuing a **peace bond** (see that word), taken by judges to prevent future lawbreaking.

Preventive law Legal help and information designed to help persons to avoid future legal problems rather than to solve existing legal problems.

Previous question In **parliamentary law,** the main motion (proposal) being considered (*not* a prior or subsidiary motion). To "call the *previous question*" or to "move that the *previous question* be considered" is a binding request for a vote on whether to now vote on the main motion under consideration.

Previously taxed income Earnings that have been taxed, but not yet received. This usually happens, for example, when an **S corporation** holds onto earnings rather than distributing them to its owners who are taxed on the earnings.

Price discrimination Different prices for the same quantity of the same goods charged to different buyers. This is illegal if done with **predatory intent.**

Price fixing *Horizontal price fixing* is different companies (or associations of companies) agreeing to charge similar prices for similar things. *Vertical price fixing* is controlling the resale price of something (usually by requiring a retailer to sell at no lower than a certain price, etc.). These arrangements often are violations of **antitrust acts.**

Price leadership A situation in which one large company regularly sets selling prices for something, and the rest of the industry then sets the same price. This is not a violation of **antitrust acts** unless the companies worked together on the pricing or tried to drive other companies out of the market.

Price supports Government loan, subsidy, and buying programs designed to keep prices (usually farm prices) above a certain level.

Price-earnings ratio The cost of a **share** of **stock** divided by the yearly **dividend** paid by that stock. For example, a $20 stock that paid $2 has a ten-to-one ratio. The *price-earnings ratio* is one measure of a stock's investment quality.

Priest-penitent privilege   See **clergy's privilege.**

Prima facie   (Latin) At first sight; on the face of it; presumably. Describes something that will be considered to be true unless disproved by contrary **evidence.** For example, a *prima facie case* is a case that will win unless the other side comes forward with evidence to disprove it. [pronounce: pri-ma fay-sha]

Primary activity   A **strike, boycott,** or **picketing** against an employer with which a **union** has a dispute. (In contrast, a boycott directed against, for example, a store that handles the employer's products is a **secondary boycott.**)

Primary authority   *1.* **Binding authority.** *2.* Laws, court decisions, regulations, and other similar sources of law rather than interpretive or indirect information from legal encyclopedias, **treatises,** etc.

Primary election   An **election** in which a political **party** chooses its candidates for public office (to run in the *general election*).

Primary evidence   *Best evidence* (see **best evidence rule**).

Primary jurisdiction doctrine   The principle that even if a court has the right and power to take a case, if the case involves issues that are better decided by an **administrative agency,** the court should give the agency the first opportunity to resolve the issue.

Primary market   *1.* The place in which, or the method by which, the first sale of a stock or other securities issue is made. *2.* A company's or a product's most important source of customers (geographic, demographic, etc.).

Prime   *1.* Original. *2.* Most important. *3.* For *prime contractor,* see **contractor.** *4.* The *prime rate* is the lowest **interest** rate a bank will charge its best customers for short-term, unsecured loans. This is an indicator of what the bank's other interest rates will be, and the *prime rates* of **national banks** (see that word) are one of the major economic indicators.

Primogeniture   *1.* The first child born to a husband and wife. *2.* Describes the former rule that the first son inherited everything.

Principal   *1.* Chief; most important; primary. *2.* The sum of money invested, as opposed to the income or profits (often **interest**) made with the money. *3.* An employer or anyone else who has another person (an **agent**) do things for him or her. *4.* A person directly involved with committing a crime, as opposed to an **accessory** (see that word). *5.* Not "**principle.**"

Principal residence exemption The exemption from **capital gains** tax of some or all of the profits from the sale of a primary home. There are detailed rules for how often you can use the exemption and how much it is.

Principle A basic legal truth, doctrine, or generalization. *Not* "**principal.**"

Printers ink statute A state law that makes it illegal to advertise anything that is false or deceptive.

Prior art In **patent** law, all previously patented devices and processes against which the device or process described in a patent application is compared. The comparison is to determine whether the device or process is *new* and *non-obvious* (requirements for issuing a new patent).

Prior consistent statement A witness's statement, made before the trial, that seems to support what he or she now says in the trial. This statement may be used to support the believability of the witness if it is challenged.

Prior hearing A **hearing** by an **administrative agency** that must sometimes be given to a person before taking any action that harms the person.

Prior inconsistent statement A witness's statement, made before the trial, that seems to contradict what he or she now says in the trial. This statement may be used to discredit the believability of the witness, but not to prove the truth of what was said unless made under oath in a prior proceeding.

Prior mortgage (or lien) See **priority.**

Prior restraint The government stopping someone from saying, publishing, or otherwise communicating something. *Prior restraint* of speech is **unconstitutional** under the **First Amendment** unless the speech is a "clear and present danger" to the country or is **obscene** or violates a person's legally recognized right to **privacy.**

Prior use doctrine The rule that one governmental organization cannot take property for a public use if the property is already devoted to a public use by another government organization unless there are specific laws allowing it.

Priority The right to be first. The right to have a claim paid first and completely, whether or not the deal on which the claim is based came first and whether or not the claim itself was made first. (When these claims are **liens,** the first person to **perfect** the lien has *priority.*)

Prison A place for long-term incarceration for a crime. Compare with **jail.**

Prisoner   Anyone deprived of liberty by the government, either because of an accusation of a crime or **conviction** of a crime.

Privacy   Describes the right to be left alone. The *right to privacy* is sometimes "balanced" against other rights, such as *freedom of the press.*

Privacy acts   Federal and state laws restricting access to personal and financial information (tax returns, mental health records, etc.) and prohibiting many types of electronic and other surveillance (wiretapping, etc.).

Private   *1.* Concerning individuals, not the general public and not the government. *2.* For *private* **foundation, international law, letter ruling, offering,** etc., see those words. Others follow here.

Private attorney general   A private individual who goes to court to enforce a public right for all affected citizens.

Private investigator   A person who is not a law enforcement officer, but who is licensed to do detective work.

Private law   *1.* A **statute** passed to affect one person or group, rather than the general public. This is also called a *private bill. 2.* The law of relationships among persons and groups (such as the law of **contracts,** divorce, etc.) as opposed to **public law,** which concerns relationships between individuals and the government or the operation of government.

Private mortgage insurance   **Insurance** to protect the lender on many loans where the **mortgage** represents over 80 percent of the home's **market value.**

Privateer   A ship owned and armed by a private individual that is empowered by a government to fight with enemy ships and capture enemy shipping in time of war. There is an international **treaty** abolishing *privateering,* but the U.S. never signed it.

Privatize   Convert a business from governmental to private ownership. Compare **take private.**

Privies   See **privity** and **privy.**

Privilege   *Privilege* has conflicting and overlapping meanings, including: *1.* An advantage; a right to preferential treatment. *2.* An exemption from a duty others like you must perform. *3.* The right to speak or write defamatory (personally damaging) words because the law allows them in certain circumstances. For example, most words are *privileged* if spoken completely "in the line of public duty." *4.* A basic right, such as **privileges and immunities.** *5.* A special advantage, as opposed to a right; an advantage that can be taken away. *6.* The **right** to prevent disclosure, or the **duty** to refrain from disclosing, information communicated within a specially recognized confidential relationship. See, for example, **attorney-client privilege, clergy's privilege, doctor-patient privilege, executive privilege, journalists' privilege,** and **marital communications privilege.** *7.* See also **immunity.**

Privileged communication   See **confidentiality** and **privilege.**

Privileges and immunities   Describes the **constitutional** requirement (Article 4, Section 2, Clause 1) that a state must treat a person from another state as fairly as it treats its own citizens.

Privity   *1.* Private or "inside" knowledge. *2.* A close, direct financial relationship. For example, both the **executor** (person who **administers** a **will** and hands out property) and an **heir** (person who gets the property) are in **privity** with the **testator** (person who wrote the will and gave away the property). Also, *privity of contract* exists among those persons who actually took part in making the deal. These persons have special rights and duties because of their privity, including the right to enforce the contract. For example, a manufacturer and a seller may be "in privity," but not the manufacturer and an ultimate buyer.

Privy   *1.* A person who is in **privity** (see that word) with another person. The plural is *privies. 2.* **Private.**

Prize   A ship taken by one country (or by a **privateer** from that country) from another with which it is at war. When a ship is brought in as a *prize,* a *prize court* determines who gets it.

Pro   (Latin) For.

Pro bono publico   (Latin) "For the public good." Describes free legal work done by a lawyer to help society. Abbreviated *"pro bono."*

Pro confesso   (Latin) As if confessed. A *decree pro confesso* is like a **judgment** given to a plaintiff by **default** because the defendant did not appear in court or did not answer the **complaint,** so the complaint is accepted "as if confessed."

Pro forma   (Latin) *1.* As a matter of form; a mere formality. *2.* Projected. A *pro forma* financial **statement** is one that is projected on the basis of certain assumptions.

Pro hac vice   (Latin) "For this one particular occasion only." For example, when an out-of-state lawyer wants to represent someone before a state court in a case without being permanently admitted to the state **bar,** the court has the power to permit representation *pro hac vice.* [pronounce: pro hock <u>vee</u>-chay]

Pro interesse suo   (Latin) "According to his interest." For example, a person who claims a right to property that is burdened with a **mortgage, judgment, lease,** etc., may ask a court to decide whether or not (or how much of) the property is his or hers. This is an *examination pro interesse suo.*

Pro. per.   Pro se.

Pro rata   Proportionately; by percentage; by a fixed rate; by share. For example, if Tom, Dick, and Harry are owed two, four, and six dollars respectively by John, but John has only six dollars to give out, a *pro rata* sharing would be one, two, and three dollars respectively. A *pro rata clause* in an **insurance** policy says that the company will not pay a higher percentage of a loss than the percentage that company covers of the total insurance coverage from all companies. And a *pro rata distribution clause* in an insurance policy says that the amount of insurance on each piece of property is in proportion to the value of that property compared to the total value of all property covered.

Pro se   (Latin) For himself or herself; in his or her own behalf. For example, *pro se representation* means that a person will handle his or her own case in court without a lawyer. [pronounce: pro say]

Pro tanto   (Latin) For that much; to the extent of; describes a partial payment.

Pro tem   (Latin) Short for "*pro tempore*"; for the time being.

Probable cause   *1.* The U.S. **constitutional** requirement that law enforcement officers present sufficient facts to convince a judge to issue a **search warrant** or an **arrest** *warrant,* and the requirement that no warrant should be issued unless it is more likely than not that the objects sought will be found in the place to be searched or that a crime has been committed by the person to be arrested. *2.* In certain situations where an officer *cannot* obtain a warrant (for example, when the **evidence** to be searched for might be destroyed or the person to be arrested might escape) an officer may search or arrest if, from what the officer knows, it is more likely than not that a crime is being (or has been) committed. *Probable cause* does not depend on what the officer finds out after the search or arrest, but on what the officer knew before taking action ("*reasonable belief*"). If there was no probable cause to search or arrest, the search or arrest was probably not proper. In each case, it depends on the nature of the suspicion, the need for immediate action, and the intrusiveness of the search.

Probate   The process of handling the **will** and the **estate** of a dead person. A *probate court* handles these matters and sometimes handles the problems of **minors** and others who are not legally **competent** to manage their affairs.

Probation   *1.* Allowing a person convicted of a criminal offense to avoid serving a jail sentence imposed on the person, so long as he or she abides by certain conditions (usually including supervision by a *probation officer*). Compare with **parole.** *2.* A trial period. A period during which a person's continued employment is conditioned on "making good" in the job and during which the person has fewer job rights than permanent employees. The period is often called the *probationary period* and the person is often called the *probationary employee* during the period.

Probationer   A person on **probation** (see that word).

Probative   Tending to prove or actually proving something.

Probative facts   Facts that prove other facts that are needed to resolve a valid issue in a lawsuit; **evidentiary facts** (see that word).

Probity   Honesty; integrity.

Procedural due process   See **due process** and **procedural law.**

Procedural law   The rules of carrying on a civil lawsuit or a criminal case (how to enforce rights in court) as opposed to **substantive law** (the law of the rights and duties themselves).

Procedure   The rules and methods of carrying on a civil lawsuit or a criminal case (**pleading,** making **motions,** presenting **evidence,** etc.). Federal trials are governed by the *Federal Rules of Civil Procedure* and the *Federal Rules of Criminal Procedure.*

Proceeding   *1.* A **case** in court. *2.* The orderly progression of a case in court. *3.* The recorded history of a case. *4.* Any official action taken by a governmental body (an agency **hearing,** a police investigation, etc.).

Proceeds   Money or property gained from a sale or other transaction.

Process   *1.* A court's ordering a **defendant** to show up in court or risk losing a lawsuit; a **summons.** *2.* Any court **order** that "takes **jurisdiction** over" (brings formally under the court's power) a person or property. *3.* A regular, legal method of operating.

Process patent   A **patent** for a new way of making something or of bringing about a result that has commercial value.

Process server   A person with legal authority to formally deliver court papers such as **writs** and **summonses** to **defendants.**

Prochein ami   (French) **Next friend.** [pronounce: pro-shen ah-mee]

Proclamation   A type of formal government statement meant for immediate widespread announcement.

Proctor   *1.* Someone appointed to manage another person's affairs. *2.* A lawyer or representative.

Procuration   *1.* Making someone else your **agent,** lawyer, or representative. See **proctor.** *2.* Doing something as someone's agent, buyer, or representative. See **proctor.** *3.* Pimping; soliciting for prostitutes. See **procure.**

Procure *1.* Make something happen; get something for someone. *2.* Solicit customers for a prostitute.

Procurement *1.* Government purchasing; usually by special rules, forms, contracts, etc. *2.* **Procuration.**

Procuring cause *1.* See **proximate cause.** *2.* Describes a **broker** who has started in motion a chain of events leading to the sale of real estate and who is entitled to a **commission** for this service.

Prodition **Treason.**

Produce Bring forward; show; yield up. For example, a *motion to produce* or a *motion for production* is a request that the judge order the other side to show you specific documents, physical objects, or real estate.

Producing cause *1.* See **proximate cause.** *2. See* **procuring cause.**

Product liability The responsibility of manufacturers (and sometimes sellers) of goods to pay for harm to purchasers (and sometimes other users or even bystanders) caused by a defective product.

Production payment An advance payment for a purchase that is really a loan to allow the manufacture of the thing purchased.

Profer (or profert) See **proffer.**

Professio juris A made-up Latin word for an agreement in a **contract** to have the law of one particular state or country decide all questions involving the contract.

Professional association *1.* Any group of professionals organized for social, educational, or other purposes; for example, a **bar association.** *2.* A group of persons formed to practice a licensed profession. The term has been used to both include and exclude a **professional corporation.**

Professional corporation A special type of **corporation** (see that word) that may be set up by lawyers, doctors, and other licensed professionals. It limits each participant's **liability** for the others' actions and has special tax advantages.

Professional legal secretary A person certified by the **National Association of Legal Secretaries.**

Professional limited liability company (or partnership) **A limited liability company or limited liability partnership** (see those words) set up by a group of licensed professionals.

Professional responsibility See **Rules of Professional Conduct.**

Proffer *1.* To offer or present. *2.* **Avowal.** *3.* Do something (such as build some low-cost units in a proposed residential complex) in exchange for a right (such as a permit to build the complex) granted by a government agency. *4.* Formally offer a physical object as **evidence** in a trial.

Profit All gains, including both money and increases in the value of property.

Profit and loss statement See **statement** *of income.*

Profit margin *1.* Sales minus costs and expenses (including taxes). *2.* Sales minus the cost of sales and **operating** *expenses,* that figure then divided by sales. A company's *gross profit margin* (also called *operating margin*) is its **operating** *profit* divided by its money made on sales. Its *net profit margin* (also called *net ratio*) is its *net profit* divided by its sales. These percentage figures can be used to compare the company with others and to compare efficiency and profitability with prior years.

Profit sharing Describes a plan set up by an employer to distribute part of the firm's profits to some or all of its employees. A *qualified plan* (one that meets requirements for tax benefits) must have specific criteria and formulas for who gets what, how, and when.

Profiteering Making unreasonable profits by taking advantage of unusual circumstances; for example, by selling scarce goods at high prices during a war.

Profits a prendre (French) Describes the right to take the growing crops of another person's land. [pronounce: a prahn-d]

Profits a rendre (French) Describes that which must be rendered or paid; usually rent. [pronounce: a rahn-d]

Programmed costs **Fixed charges** (see that word), such as those for long-term research, that do not directly produce or sell goods and services. Compare with **capacity costs.**

Progressive tax A tax that is proportionately greater on higher incomes or greater assets. The federal *income tax* is progressive, at least in theory. The opposite of a progressive tax is a *regressive tax.* This hits the poor harder. An example is a sales tax. Even though everyone pays the same tax, it takes a larger part of a poor person's money to pay it.

Prohibited degrees Blood relations too close to legally marry; for example, brother and sister, grandfather and granddaughter, in most states first cousins, etc.

Prohibition *1.* An order to stop certain actions or a warning not to engage in them. For example, a *writ of prohibition* is an order from a higher court telling a lower one to stop proceeding with a lawsuit. *2.* The popular name for the period in U.S. history from 1919 to 1933 when the manufacture or sale of alcoholic beverages was illegal.

Prohibitory injunction See **mandatory injunction.**

Prolixity Use of too many words, facts, theories, etc., in court papers or **evidence.**

Promise *1.* A statement that morally, legally, or in some other way may bind the person who makes it to do something. *2.* In **contract** law, an oral or written statement from one person to another, given in exchange for something of value (which can be another promise). It binds the person making the promise to do something and may give the other person the legal right to demand that it be done.

Promissory estoppel The principle that when Person A makes a promise and expects Person B to do something in **reliance** upon that promise, then Person B does act in reliance upon that promise, the law will usually help Person B enforce the promise because Person B has *relied* upon the promise to his or her *detriment.* Person A is "stopped" from breaking the promise even when there is no **consideration** to make the promise binding as part of a contract.

Promissory note *1.* A document that contains an acknowledgment of a debt and a promise to pay the debt. A promissory note is **negotiable** if by its terms it can be sold. *2.* A *negotiable promissory note* typically requires the borrower to pay an exact sum of money immediately, when asked for, or by a certain date either "to the **order** of" a specific person or "to **bearer**" (the person who physically has it).

Promoter *1.* A person who arranges an event or a deal, usually for a percentage of the profits. *2.* A person who forms a **corporation.**

Promulgate Publish; announce officially; put out formally.

Pronounce To say formally and officially. For example, a judge *pronounces* **sentence** by solemnly saying in open court what sentence a convicted **defendant** will have to serve.

Proof A body of **evidence** supporting a contention. Those facts from which a conclusion can be drawn. In this sense, *proof* can be convincing or unconvincing. But see no. 2. *2.* The result of convincing **evidence.** The conclusion drawn that the evidence is enough to show that something is true or that an argument about facts is correct. There are various **standards** *of proof* including: *beyond a reasonable doubt* (how convincing evidence must be in a **criminal** trial); *by clear and convincing evidence;* and *by a preponderance* (greater weight) *of the evidence.* In this sense, proof is always convincing. But see no. 1.

Proof of claim A sworn statement in a **bankruptcy** or **probate** proceeding of how much a **creditor** is owed.

Proof of loss A sworn statement made to an **insurance** company of a loss thought to be covered under an insurance policy with the company.

Proper Fit, suitable, or appropriate. For example, a *proper party* to a lawsuit is a person who has a real, substantial interest in the suit's outcome, who can conveniently be added to the suit as a **party,** but without whom the suit can still be decided.

Property *1.* Ownership of a thing; the legal right to own a thing. *2.* Anything that is owned or can be owned, such as land, automobiles, money, **stocks, patents,** the right to use a famous actor's name or picture, etc. Property is usually divided into *real* (land and things attached to or growing on it) and *personal* (everything else), but some property is hard to categorize as *real* or *personal.* See also **intellectual property.**

Property tax A state or local tax based on the value of certain property (homes, cars, etc.) owned.

Prophylactic Designed to prevent something.

Proponent The person who offers something, puts something forward, or proposes something.

Proposal *1.* An **offer** that can be accepted to make a **contract.** *2.* A preliminary or exploratory idea for discussion that is *not* an offer as in no. 1.

Propound To offer, propose, or put forward something. For example, to *propound a will* is to put it forward and request that it be accepted as valid by the **probate** court.

Proprietary Having to do with ownership. *Proprietary rights* or interests are the rights or interests that a person has because of property ownership, or that are an integral part of property ownership. For example, if one person has the sole right to make and sell a medicine, it is a *proprietary drug.* And the right to vote a **share** of **stock** is a *proprietary interest* of owning it. The *proprietary functions* of a city (as opposed to its public functions) include such things as sidewalk repair and trash pickup. And a *proprietary lease* is between tenant-owners of a **cooperative** apartment building and the owners' association.

Proprietorship *1.* The running of a business. *2.* **Sole** *proprietorship* (see that word).

Prorate To divide or share proportionately or by shares; see **pro rata.**

Prorogation *1.* An agreement in a **contract** to allow the courts of one particular state or country to decide all disputes involving the contract. *2.* A delay, putting off, or **continuance.**

Proscription   Prohibiting or restricting something (or the prohibition or restriction itself). *Not* **prescription.**

Prosecute   *1.* Formally start and pursue a **civil** lawsuit. *2.* Charge a person with a crime and bring that person to trial. The process is called *prosecution,* the person who was harmed by the crime or who made the complaint is a *prosecuting witness,* and the public official who presents the government's case is called a **prosecutor.** *3.* Start and carry out any plan or action. For example, to *prosecute* a **patent** is to apply for one and follow through on the application until a patent is granted. This application process is documented in a *prosecution history* (also called a **file** *wrapper*).

Prosecutor   *1.* A public official who presents the government's case against a person accused of a crime and who asks the court to **convict** that person. *2.* The private individual who accuses a person of a crime is sometimes called the *private prosecutor.*

Prosecutorial discretion   The power of the **prosecutor** to decide whether or not to prosecute a **charge** against a person, how serious a charge to press, how large a penalty to request, what kind of a **plea bargaining** *agreement* to accept, etc.

Prospective   Looking forward; concerning the future; likely or possible. For example, a *prospective law* is one that applies to situations that arise after it is enacted. Most laws are *prospective* only.

Prospectus   *1.* A document put out to describe a **corporation** and to interest persons in buying its **stock.** When new stock is sold to the public, the **S.E.C.** requires a *prospectus* that contains such things as a **statement** *of income,* a **balance sheet,** an auditor's report, etc. *2.* Any offer (written, by radio or television, etc.) to interest persons in buying any **securities,** such as stock. *3.* A document put out to interest persons in any financial deal (such as the offer to sell a building or the offer of shares in a limited partnership).

Prostitution   A person offering her (in most states, his or her) body for sexual purposes in exchange for money. A crime in most states.

Protected class   *1.* A group of persons protected by **statute.** *2.* A *suspect class.* See **suspect classification.**

Protection   Most legal uses of "*protection*" are based on its ordinary language meaning. For *protection order,* see **protective order.**

Protective committee   A group of stockholders appointed to protect the interests of all holders of that type of stock during the **reorganization** or **liquidation** of a **corporation.**

Protective custody   Putting someone in jail, in a mental hospital, in a secret house, etc., for the person's own safety, whether or not the person wants it. This can happen to a **witness** in a case involving dangerous **defendants,** to a drunk, to a mentally ill person, etc.

Protective (or protection) order   _1._ A court **order** that temporarily allows one side in a lawsuit to hold back from showing the other side documents or other things that were (or might be) requested. _2._ Any court order protecting a person from **harassment, stalking, service** _of process,_ etc. _3._ A court order putting someone in **protective custody** (see that word).

Protective (or protection) theory   _1._ The principle that a government can **condemn** more property than is needed for a public project if a "buffer zone" is useful to protect the environment or the surrounding neighborhood. _2._ The principle that a country can assert **jurisdiction** over a person whose conduct outside the country threatens the country's security or could interfere with the country's governmental functions.

Protectorate   A country whose international affairs are managed by another country.

Protest   _1._ A written statement that you do not agree to the legality, justice, or correctness of a payment, but you are paying it while reserving your right to get it back later. _2._ A formal certificate of the **dishonor** of a **negotiable instrument** (see those words) that has been presented for payment. The document, which must normally be _acknowledged_ by a **notary public,** is meant to give **notice** to all persons **liable** on the negotiable instrument that they may have to pay up on it.

Prothonotary   Head **clerk** of some courts.

Protocol   _1._ The first draft of an agreement between countries or the preliminary document opening an international meeting. _2._ Formalities. _3._ The etiquette of international diplomacy, including the ranking of officials. _4._ A short summary of a document. _5._ The **minutes** of a meeting (usually initialed by all to show their accuracy).

Prove up   **Prove.**

Province   Duty, or area of responsibility.

Provision   Money or property held by or sent to the **drawee** of a **bill** of exchange in order to pay it upon **presentment.**

Provisional   Temporary or preliminary. For example, a _provisional remedy_ is a court **order** or an action permitted by a court that helps to enforce the law on a temporary basis. These include temporary **injunctions** and **attachments** (see those words).

Pro͟viso A **condition, qualification,** or **limitation** in a document.

Provocation An act by one person that triggers a reaction of rage in a second person. *Provocation* may reduce the severity of a crime. It may also be a **defense** to a **divorce** based on **cruelty.**

Proximate cause The "legal cause" of an accident or other injury (which may have several actual causes). The *proximate cause* of an injury is not necessarily the closest thing in time or space to the injury and not necessarily the event that set things in motion because "proximate cause" is a legal, not a physical concept. Some other names for the same idea are "causa causans," "causa proxima," and "dominant," "efficient," "immediate," "legal," "moving," "next," or "producing" cause.

Proxy *1.* A person who acts for another person (usually to vote in place of the other person in a meeting the other cannot attend). *2.* A document giving the right mentioned in no. 1. *3.* A *proxy marriage* is a marriage ceremony in which someone "stands in" for either the bride or groom (or both). *4.* A *proxy statement* is the document sent or given to stockholders when their voting *proxies* are requested for a **corporate** decision. The S.E.C. has rules for when the statements must be given out and what must be in them.

Prudent person rule The principle that a **trustee** (see that word) may invest **trust** funds only in traditionally safe investments or risk being personally responsible for losses. These safe investments may be restricted by state law to a specific group of **securities** called *legal investments* or the *legal list.*

Pr͟urient interest A shameful or obsessive interest in immoral or sexual things. "*Appealing to prurient interest*" is one of many factors involved in deciding whether *speech* is **obscene.**

Psychotherapist-patient privilege Some states' extension of the **doctor-patient privilege** to certain psychological counsellors.

Pub. L. Public law.

Public *1.* Having to do with a state, nation, or the community as a whole. For example, a tax or a government function that will benefit the community as a whole and not merely individual members has a *public purpose.* *2.* Open to all persons.

Public defender A lawyer, paid directly or indirectly with government funds, who represents poor persons accused of a crime.

Public domain *1.* Land owned by the government. *2.* Describes something free for anyone to use or something not protected by **patent** or **copyright.** *3.* A *public domain* **citation** (see that word) is one that can be found and used without reference to a commercial publisher's volume and page number system. An online document's public domain citation is an _electronic citation._

Public duty doctrine   The principle, applied in some states, that to win a **tort** suit against the government, the plaintiff must show that the government breached a **duty** that was owed to the plaintiff (or to a particular class of persons like the plaintiff), not merely owed to the general public.

Public figure   Anyone who is famous (or infamous) for what he or she has done or who has come forward to take part in a public controversy. A _public figure_ is given less legal protection against **defamation** and **invasion of privacy** than is an ordinary person.

Public function   **Governmental function.**

Public interest   _1._ A broad term for anything that can affect the general public's finances, health, rights, etc. For example, a business that is on public property and that the public must deal with is called "affected with" or "clothed by" a _public interest. 2._ The practice of _public interest law_ is often done on a nonprofit basis for a public cause, such as protection of the environment.

Public lands   _1._ Land owned by the government. _2._ Land owned by the government and not set aside for a particular purpose, so subject to possible sale without any change in the laws.

Public law   _1._ The study of law that has to do with either the operation of government or the relationship between the government and persons. Examples are **constitutional law, administrative law, criminal** _law,_ etc.). _2._ A name given at time of **enact**ment to most U.S. laws (and to some state laws), reflecting (by _public law number_) when the law was enacted. For example, "Public Law No. 100–33" refers to the 33d U.S. law passed by the 100th Congress. U.S. _public laws_ are later collected by subject area in the **United States Code** and given additional **citations.**

Public office   A vague term for a government job that requires independent decision-making. A mayor is a _public official;_ a police chief might be, and a police officer is probably not.

Public policy   A vague word that can be as broad as "what is good for (or will not harm) the general public" or "the law."

Public records exception   A **hearsay exception** (see that word) for most documents that are actively produced by a government agency (but not for most documents that are submitted by others and passively filed).

Public service (or utilities) commission A state agency that **regulates** private businesses that have a state **charter,** perform a necessary public function, and need special government help. These private businesses (such as railroads or power companies) are called *public utilities,* are often **monopolies,** and must provide service to all persons fairly.

Public utility *1.* See **public service commission.** *2.* The *Public Utility Holding Company Act* is a federal law that broke up large power and other companies and forced them under state or local control.

Public works Government construction projects.

Publication Making public. For example, in **copyright** law, *publication* is offering a book, a movie, etc., to the public by sale or other distribution; in the law of **defamation,** *publication* usually means communicating defamatory information to a person other than the person defamed; in the law of **wills,** *publication* is telling a **witness** that you intend a document to be your will; in the law of court procedure, *publication* is printing a legal notice in a newspaper; and in banking law, *publication* is trying to collect money on a forged check, a counterfeit dollar bill, etc.

Publici juris (Latin) "Of public rights." Describes common public rights or property, such as the right to breathe the air.

Publicly held corporation A **corporation** with **stock** sold to a large number of persons.

Publish *1.* See **publication.** *2.* Try to collect on a forged document (check, dollar bill, etc.).

Puffing *1.* Salesmanship by a seller that is mere general bragging about what is sold, rather than definite promises about it or intentionally misleading information. *2.* Secret bidding for the seller at an auction to raise the price.

Puis (or puisne) Lower ranking or **junior.**

Pullman doctrine The principle that federal courts should usually **abstain** from deciding cases that involve unsettled state law questions when state court resolution of the questions might end the need to decide federal **constitutional** questions. Compare with **Burford doctrine** and **Younger doctrine.**

Punitive damages See **damages.**

Pur autre vie See **autre** *vie.*

Purchase *1.* Buy. *2.* According to the **Uniform Commercial Code,** "any voluntary transaction creating an interest in property," including a gift, a mortgage, etc.

Purchase money mortgage A buyer's financing of part of a purchase by giving a **mortgage** on the property to the seller as **security** for the loan.

Purchase money resulting trust When a person puts up money to buy something for him or herself, but held in another person's name, **title** to that property is held by a *purchase money resulting trust* in favor of the person putting up the money.

Purchase order A purchaser's document that authorizes a person or a company to deliver goods or perform services. The use of a *purchase order* implies a promise to pay for the goods or services.

Pure plea *1.* An **affirmative defense.** *2.* A legal **pleading** that requires no further paperwork to be acted upon by a judge.

Pure race statute (or act) See **recording acts.**

Purge *1.* Cleanse, clear, or exonerate from a charge, from guilt, or from a **contract.** *2.* In the law of wills, *"purge"* means to omit the gift to a person named in a will (because that person is legally prohibited from getting anything) without destroying the rest of the will.

Purport *1.* Imply, profess outwardly, or give an impression (sometimes, a false impression). *2.* The meaning, intent, or purpose of something.

Purpresture Taking something public for private use; for example, fencing in part of a public park to use as if part of your private land.

Pursuant In accordance with; in carrying out. For example, "pursuant to my authority as governor" means "I have the authority to do what I am about to do because I am governor."

Pursuit of happiness The phrase used in the **Constitution** to summarize those rights not specifically mentioned, such as freedom of contract and occupation, domestic rights, etc.

Purview The purpose, scope, and design of a **statute** or other enacted law.

Put An **option** (see that word) to sell a particular **stock** or **commodity** at a certain price for a certain time. The person who buys a *put option* expects prices to fall. If they don't, he or she loses the purchase price of the *put,* but does not have to **exercise** (use) it.

Putative Alleged, supposed, or commonly known as. For example, a *putative father* is the alleged father of an "**illegitimate** child."

Putative marriage A marriage in which a technical legal defect, unknown to the husband and wife, is discovered. These marriages are usually considered to be still valid.

Pyramid sales scheme A type of sales plan under which, once you become a "distributor" or "qualified," you get **commissions** not only for products you sell but also for products sold by persons you bring into the business ("under you in the pyramid"). It is also known as a "referral sales plan," a "chain referral plan," and a "multilevel distributorship." It is illegal in some forms.

Pyramiding The use of a small amount of money or of "paper profits" to finance buying large amounts of **stock,** to control companies, etc. This is using things bought with **leverage** to purchase more things, gaining greater leverage and taking greater risk.

Q   *1.* Quarterly. *2.* Question.

Q.B.   Queen's Bench (see **King's Bench**).

Q.D.R.O.   *Qualified Domestic Relations Order.* A court **judgment, decree,** or **order** that gives a spouse, ex-spouse, or **dependent** child rights in the spouse's or parent's **pension plan.**This is an exception to the pension protection rules of **E.R.I.S.A.**

Q.T.I.P.   Qualified Terminable Interest Property. Property that may be designated as part of the *marital deduction* from the federal **estate** tax because the surviving spouse has a *life income interest* that qualifies under the tax code.

Q.V.   (Latin) Quod vide; "which see" or "look at." This is a direction to the reader to look in another place in the book (or in another book) for more information. This dictionary uses the phrase "*see that word*" where most lawbooks would say "*Q.V.*"

Qua   (Latin) As; considered as; in and of itself. For example, "the *trustee qua trustee* is not **liable**" means that the **trustee** is not liable as a trustee (but might be liable as an individual).

Quae   (Latin) Things; those things; things already mentioned; etc.

Quae est eadem   (Latin) "Which is the same." Describes two apparently different things that are the same.

Quaere   (Latin) A **question,** query, or doubt. When used before a phrase *quaere* means that what follows is an open question. *Not* **quare.** [pronounce: quee-ree]

Qualification   *1.* Meeting specific requirements or conditions, such as possessing the personal qualities, property, or other necessary things to be eligible to fill a public office or take on a particular duty. *2.* **Limitation** or restriction.

Qualified acceptance   In **contract** law, a **counteroffer** (see that word) that resembles an **acceptance** of another's **offer.** For example, if a person says in response to an offer, "I accept your offer, but I'll pay you only $1,000, not $1,200," this is a *qualified acceptance* since it is phrased like an *acceptance,* and is a *counteroffer* because the price is not agreed to.

Qualified indorsement   See **indorsement.**

Qualified privilege   *1.* The right to say or publish something derogatory about a person if done without **malice** (see that word). Also see **privilege.** *2.* The right, under certain limited circumstances, to withhold information from the other side in a lawsuit. *"Attorney work product"* is usually given a *qualified privilege* that protects it from disclosure.

Qualify (or qualified)   *1.* See **qualification.** *2.* For *qualified plan,* see **pension plan.**

Quality of estate   *When* a person gets property rights, and the *type* of rights (**joint, common,** etc.) that the person gets in a **deed.**

Quando   (Latin) When.

Quantum meruit   (Latin) "As much as he deserved." An old form of **pleading** used in a lawsuit for compensation for work done. The *theory of quantum meruit* (fair payment for work done) is still used in modern contract law. See also **quasi contract.** [pronounce: quan-tum mer-u-it]

Quantum valebant   (Latin) "As much as they were worth." An old form of **pleading** used in a lawsuit for payment for goods sold and delivered. The *theory of quantum valebant* (fair payment for goods delivered) is still used in modern contract law. See also **unjust enrichment.**

Quarantine   A holding or isolation period. The government usually has the right to hold and isolate a ship, isolate a person, forbid the transportation of goods, etc., in order to prevent the spread of a disease, of a pest, etc.

Quare   (Latin) "Wherefore." For example, *"quare clausum fregit"* means "wherefore he broke the close," which describes an old form of **pleading** in a lawsuit that requests **damages** from someone who committed a **trespass** ("broke the close") on your land. *Not* **quaere.** [pronounce: kwa-re]

Quarters of coverage   The number of quarters of the year (January–March, April–June, July–Sept., Oct.–Dec.) that a person has made payments into the Social Security fund. Retirement (and other) benefits depend on this.

Quash   Overthrow; **annul;** completely do away with. (*Quash* usually refers to a court stopping a **subpoena,** an **order,** or an **indictment.**)

Quasi   (Latin) "Sort of"; "as if."

Quasi contract   An obligation "sort of like" a **contract** that is created, not by an agreement, but by law. The principle of *quasi contract* is used to bring about a fair result when a person's actions or the relationship between persons makes it clear that one *should* owe an obligation to the other that is similar to a contract. For example, if a doctor in a hospital treats an unconscious person in an emergency, the person cannot contract for the help. Since it would be unfair for the doctor to be unpaid and since the victim probably would have agreed to pay, the law imposes an obligation to pay the amount deserved (**quantum meruit**). *Quasi contract* is also called *constructive contract* and *implied-in-law contract.* Compare with **implied-in-fact contract.**

Quasi corporation   A **joint stock company.**

Quasi in rem   See **in rem.**

Quasi-judicial   Describes the case-deciding function of an **administrative agency** when it acts like a court.

Quasi-legislative   Describes the rule-making function of an **administrative agency** when it acts like a **legislature.**

Quasi-suspect classification   See **suspect classification.**

Queen's Bench   See **King's Bench.**

Query   **Question** (see that word). Also see **quaere.**

Question   *1.* A subject or matter to be investigated, looked into, debated, etc. *2.* A point in dispute in a lawsuit; an issue for decision by judge or jury. *3.* For **leading question, hypothetical question,** *questions of* **fact** *and law,* etc., see those words.

Questman (or questmonger)   In old England, a person who started lawsuits or prosecutions, checked weights and measures, and investigated public **fraud** and **abuse.**

Qui   (Latin) He or she (who). For example, *qui non negat fatetur* means "he or she who does not deny something admits it."

Qui tam   (Latin) "*Who* (for himself) *as well as* (for the government)." Describes a lawsuit brought by an individual on behalf of the government, or brought by the government based on an informer's tip. If the government collects a fine or penalty from the lawsuit, the informer may get a share. See also **whistleblower.**

Quia timet   (Latin) "Because of fears." Describes a request to a court, similar to a request for an **injunction** (see that word).

Quick assets   A company's cash, plus its **liquid** assets (those that can be quickly and easily sold for cash). *Quick assets* are **current** *assets minus* **inventory** (see those words). "*Net quick assets*" are quick assets *minus* **current** *liabilities* (what the company owes that comes due soon). The "*quick asset ratio*" (or "*quick ratio*" or "*acid test ratio*") is quick assets *divided by* current liabilities. These are measures of whether a company can meet unexpected obligations, can take advantage of unexpected opportunities, and has good short-term prospects and survivability.

Quid pro quo   Something for something; this for that. The giving of one valuable thing for another. A *quid pro quo* can be the **consideration** (see that word) required for a valid **contract.**

Quiet   Free from interference or disturbance. For example, an *action to quiet title* is a way of establishing clear ownership of land, and a *covenant for quiet enjoyment* is, among other things, a promise in a **deed** that the seller will protect the buyer against claims or lawsuits based on ownership rights.

Quietus   A final **discharge** from a debt or obligation.

Quit   *1.* Leave and give up possession of a place. *2.* Free or clear of a debt, of a criminal charge, etc.

Quitclaim deed   A **deed** that passes on to the buyer all those rights or as much of a **title** as a seller actually has. A *quitclaim deed* does not **warrant** (promise) that the seller actually has any rights at all to sell.

Quittance   Release from a debt or obligation.

Quo animo   (Latin) "With what intention or motive." See **animo** for other phrases with "animo."

Quo warranto   (Latin) "With what authority." Describes a proceeding in which a court questions the right of a person (usually a public official) to take a certain action or to hold a certain office.

Quod   (Latin) *1.* That which; that. *2.* For *quod vide,* see **Q.V.**

Quorum   The number of persons who must be present to make the votes and other actions of a group (such as a **board**) valid. This number is often a majority (over half) of the whole group, but is sometimes much less or much more.

Quota   *1.* An assigned goal or minimum requirement, such as a certain minimum amount of sales a salesperson must make. *2.* A limit, such as the maximum number of cars that may be imported from a particular country. *3.* A proportional share of a **liability.**

Quotation (or quote)   The selling or asking price of a **stock,** other **security,** or **commodity.**

Quotient verdict   A jury's decision about the amount of **damages** to **award,** which is arrived at by each juror's writing down a dollar amount, then adding them all up, and dividing by the number of jurors. This type of **compromise verdict** may be permitted to help discussion, but not as a way of computing an amount for a final decision. [pronounce: <u>kwo</u>-shent]

R

R ® is the symbol for federally registered as a **trademark, service** *mark,* or **certification mark.**

R.A.R. Revenue agent's report. An **I.R.S.** document explaining changes in tax owed resulting from an **audit.**

R.E.I.T. **Real estate investment trust.**

R.E.L.P. Real estate **limited partnership.**

R.E.M.I.C. Real estate mortgage investment conduit. A financial device that packages the rights to interest paid on many individual real estate mortgages for sale to investors as **bonds.**

R.E.S.P.A. Real Estate Settlement Procedures Act (12 U.S.C. 2601). A 1974 federal law requiring **disclosure** of **settlement (closing)** costs in real estate sales financed by federally insured lenders.

R.F.P. Request for proposals. A government notice soliciting applicants to perform a contract or receive a grant.

R.I.C.O. Racketeer Influenced and Corrupt Organizations Act (19 U.S.C. 1961). A broadly applied 1970 federal law that creates certain "racketeering offenses," which include participation in various criminal schemes and conspiracies, and that allows government seizure of property acquired in violation of the act. A *R.I.C.O. pattern* is two or more crimes from a specified list (forgery, murder, unauthorized use of explosives, etc.), committed by the same person within a ten-year period. See also **racketeering.**

R.I.F. Reduction in force. A **layoff** done by eliminating specific jobs. See also **bumping.**

R.I.L. **Res ipsa loquitur.**

R.O.I. Return on investment. See **yield.**

R.O.R. Release on own **recognizance** (see that word).

R.S. Revised **statutes.**

R.U.R.E.S.A. *Revised Uniform* **Reciprocal Enforcement of Support Act.**

Race statutes (or race-notice statutes or race recording acts, etc.) See **recording acts.**

Racketeering *1.* **Extortion** by organized crime (usually threats of violence against a person or business to stop competition or to extract "protection money"). *2.* The charging of illegal interest on loans or the large-scale, organized conduct of illegal gambling, narcotics traffic, prostitution, etc. See also **R.I.C.O.**

Rack-rent Exorbitantly high rent.

Raid *1.* One company's attempt to take over another company by buying its **stock** to gain control of its **board** *of directors.* This is often accomplished by a **tender** *offer.* The takeover is more often called a *raid* when the "raiders" want something the company *has* (such as **retained earnings** or a salable **asset**) rather than wanting to run the company as an ongoing business. *2.* Steal another company's employees or business. *3.* See also **bear raiding.**

Railroad Rush something through; for example, force a **bill** through a **legislature** over the objections of some of its members or **convict** a person without **due process.**

Railway Labor Act (45 U.S.C. 151) A 1962 federal law that established **mediation** and other procedures for handling labor disputes between railroad companies and their employees.

Rainmaker Slang for a person who brings a lot of new business into a firm.

Raise *1.* To *raise funds* is to solicit or collect money. *2.* To *raise an issue* is to make it a subject of discussion or a problem for decision in a lawsuit. *3.* To *raise a* **presumption** is to say or do something that creates an **inference** that something else happened or is true. *4.* To *raise a check* is to alter it fraudulently so that the amount paid on it is higher.

Raising portions An old word (from the time when the oldest son inherited all land) referring to the duty of the oldest son to give money to the other children.

Rake-off An illegal bribe, payoff, or skimming of the profits of a business.

Range *1.* A straight row of **townships** running North-South within a state on government maps. Compare with **tier.** *2.* A large, open grazing area, whether public or private.

Ransom *1.* Money or property paid to free a kidnapped person or to free persons or property captured during war. *2.* In old English law, money paid to obtain a **pardon** for a major crime.

Rap sheet A police or other government document listing a person's **arrest** and **conviction** record.

Rape The crime of a man imposing sexual intercourse by force or otherwise without legally valid consent. Also, *statutory rape* is the crime of a man having sexual intercourse with a girl under a certain state-set age (whether or not the girl consents). The definition of what precise acts constitute rape (and whether or not a man can be raped or a woman can rape) differs from state to state, as does the terminology (aggravated sexual abuse, criminal sexual conduct, first degree sexual assault, sexual battery, etc.). For *rape shield law,* see **shield law.**

Rapine An old word for the act of taking a person's property by force.

Rasure *1.* Scraping a paper to remove letters or words. *2.* Any obliteration of a document, including erasure, lining over, etc.

Ratable *1.* Proportional; adjusted by some formula or percentage. *2.* Describes a proportional, but usually unequal division. *3.* Capable of being evaluated. *4.* Taxable.

Rate *1.* An amount fixed by mathematical formulas or adjusted according to some standard; for example, an **interest** *rate. 2.* A charge that is the same to all persons for the same service; for example, a shipping rate. *3.* A classification by quality; for example, a "*first-rate* **insurance** *risk.*" *4.* For **discount rate, prime** *rate,* etc., see those words.

Rate base The property value (or investment amount) upon which a **public service commission** calculates a utilities profit.

Rate fixing The power of some **administrative agencies** (such as state power commissions) to set the charges a company may get for its services. This is *not* the same as **price fixing,** which is done by sellers of goods or services and is often illegal.

Rate of return Profit as a percentage of money or property value invested.

Ratification Confirmation and acceptance of a previous act done by you or by another person. For example, when the president signs a **treaty,** the Senate must *ratify* it (make it valid from the moment it was signed). Also, if a child makes a **contract,** it is probably not enforceable against the child, but if the child *ratifies* it after becoming an adult, it becomes a binding contract. Compare with **reaffirmation.**

Ratio decidendi (Latin) "Reason for decision." The *rationale* for a judge's **holding;** the basic ideas a judge uses to come to a **decision** in a case. [pronounce: ra-shee-o des-i-den-dee]

Ratio legis (Latin) *1.* The reason or purpose for passing a law; the problem or situation that makes a law necessary. *2.* The basic reasoning or principle behind a law; the legal *theory* on which it is based.

Rational basis (or purpose) test The principle that a court should not second-guess a **legislature** (or an **administrative agency**) about the wisdom of a law (or of an administrative decision) if the law (or decision) has some *rational basis.* Compare with **strict scrutiny test.**

Ravishment *1.* **Rape.** *2.* An old word for unlawfully taking away a person who is in the care of another.

Re (Latin) "Concerning"; see **in re.**

Reacquired stock **Treasury stock.**

Readjustment A **reorganization** of a company in financial trouble that is done voluntarily by the owners without court or other intervention.

Reaffirmation Agreement to something previously agreed to, especially if the prior agreement is not enforceable. *Reaffirmation* may make the following types of agreements enforceable: debts for which the *statute of* **limitations** has run; agreements that must be in writing but are not; and debts under an agreement *discharged* in **bankruptcy.** Compare with **ratification.**

Real *1.* Having to do with land and things permanently attached to the land, such as buildings. *2.* Having to do with a thing, rather than with a person. For example, a *real defense* against a lawsuit to enforce a document is a defense that challenges the validity of the document, rather than challenging the circumstances surrounding it. Real defenses include **forgery,** the fact that the person signing was a **minor, alteration** of the document, etc., but not such things as **duress.**

Real estate Land, buildings, and things permanently attached to land and buildings. Also called *realty* and *real property.*

Real estate investment trust An arrangement in which investors buy shares in a **trust** that invests in **real estate.** To qualify for special **income tax** benefits, a *R.E.I.T.* must meet certain requirements, such as being unincorporated, having fewer than a certain number of investors, and gaining most of its income from real estate and related financial ventures.

Real Estate Settlement Procedures Act See **R.E.S.P.A.**

Real evidence Objects seen by the jury; for example, wounds, fingerprints, weapons used in a crime, etc.

Real party in interest *1.* Someone who has a legal right to bring a lawsuit, whether or not the person is the one who will ultimately benefit from winning. But see no. 2. *2.* The person who will ultimately benefit from winning a lawsuit, whether or not that person brought it initially.

Realized Actual; "in hand"; cashed in. For example, a *realized profit* is a cash-in-hand gain as opposed to a **paper** *profit.* A *realized gain or* *loss* is the difference between the **net** sale price of something and its net cost (or, in tax terms, its **adjusted basis**). Income or loss is *realized* when a *"taxable event"* takes place, typically a sale or exchange of property. Not all gain that is *realized* is *recognized*. Non**recognition** provisions of the tax law allow taxation of certain gains to be deferred.

Realtor® A *real estate* **broker** who belongs to the National Association of Realtors.

Realty **Real estate.**

Reapportionment Changing the boundaries of *legislative* **districts** to reflect changes in population and ensure that each person's vote for **representatives** carries roughly equal weight. See also **gerrymander.**

Reargument Additional **argument** to clarify a prior legal point or to consider a legal point that should have been considered previously. Compare **rehearing.**

Reasonable A broad, flexible word used to make sure that a decision is based on the *facts* of a particular situation, rather than on abstract legal principles. It has no exact definition, but can mean "fair," "appropriate," "moderate," "rational," etc. When reading the following examples, remember that the definitions tend to be circular and depend on the actual situation, not on the precise words used. For example, *reasonable care* has been defined as "that degree of care a person of ordinary prudence (the so-called *reasonable person*) would exercise in similar circumstances"; and *reasonable doubt* "is not mere conjecture, but doubt that would cause prudent persons to hesitate before acting in matters important to themselves."

Reasonable belief See **probable cause** no. 2.

Reasonable inference rule The principle that a **jury** may draw any reasonable inferences from **evidence** and use those inferences in deciding a case.

Reasonable person (or man) doctrine See **reasonable** and **foreseeability.**

Reasonable woman test The **Equal Employment Opportunity Commission's** standard for whether a man's conduct is so offensive as to create either **sexual harassment** or a **hostile environment** for a woman to work: what would a *reasonable woman* (as opposed to a reasonable man) think?

Reassessment The government's reestimating of the value of property and changing the official value it gives to that property for tax purposes.

Rebate A discount, deduction, or refund.

Rebellion   Organized, armed resistance to the government. If it succeeds, it may be a **revolution.**

Rebus sic stantibus   (Latin) "At this state of affairs." A principle of **international law** that if conditions change greatly after making a **treaty** or other agreement, the treaty is **voidable.**

Rebut   Dispute, defeat, or take away the effect of facts or arguments. *Rebuttal* is formal contradiction of statements made by an adversary.

Rebuttable   Disputable. For example, a *rebuttable presumption* is a conclusion that will be drawn unless **evidence** is presented that counters it.

Rebutter   A *common-law* **pleading,** the third by the **defendant.**

Recall   *1.* Remove an elected official from office by a vote of the people. *2.* Take away a diplomat's job and bring him or her back from a foreign country. *3.* Notify car (or other product) owners of a safety defect and offer to fix it. *4.* **Revoke,** cancel or **vacate** a **judgment** because facts originally relied upon to grant it are found to be wrong.

Recapitalization   Readjusting the types, amounts, values and priorities of a corporation's **stocks** and **bonds.**

Recaption   Taking something back that has been taken away.

Recapture   *1.* An **I.R.S.** recovery of a tax benefit of a prior **deduction** or **credit** taken by a taxpayer, usually when circumstances have changed from those that were assumed when the original benefit was claimed. *2.* A **contract** provision that limits profits or provides for the recovery of goods in special situations. *3.* A **lease** provision giving the landlord a percentage of profits and allowing the landlord to end the lease if profits are not high enough.

Receipt   *1.* A written document acknowledging that something has been received or put into your hands. *2.* The act of getting or receiving.

Receipts   Money that comes into a business (usually through sales).

Receivables   See **accounts receivable.**

Receive evidence   See **admission** *of evidence.*

Receiver   *1.* An outside person appointed by the court to manage money and property during a lawsuit. *2.* A person who gets stolen goods.

Receivership   A court putting money or property into the management of a **receiver** (see that word) in order to preserve it for the persons ultimately entitled to it. This is often done when the **creditors** of a business suspect **fraud** or gross mismanagement and ask the court to step in and watch over the business to protect them.

Receiving stolen goods (or property)   The criminal offense of getting or concealing property known to be stolen by another.

Recent theft rule The principle that if a person is found with recently stolen property, there is a **presumption** that he or she is the thief.

Recess *1.* A brief break taken by a court, usually lasting an hour or two at most. *2.* A break in a **legislative** session, sometimes lasting many weeks.

Recidivist *1.* A repeat **criminal** offender. *2.* A **habitual** criminal.

Reciprocal Mutual (done together) and bilateral (two-sided, two-way, or done one for the other). For example, *reciprocal wills* are **wills** made by two persons, and enforceable against each other because each person put something in his or her will that the other asked for; *reciprocal sales* involve a company that gets unusually good prices when it buys things from a company to which it also sells (or a company that favors customers by buying goods from the customer), in possible violation of **antitrust acts;** and *reciprocal trade agreements* are agreements between countries to lower import taxes on goods traded between the countries.

Reciprocal Enforcement of Support Act A law, adopted in most states, that allows a spouse (or parent of a child) in one state to enforce **support** *obligations* on the other spouse (or parent) in another state. The latest version of the law is the Revised Uniform Reciprocal Enforcement of Support Act (R.U.R.E.S.A.).

Reciprocity *1.* Two states (or countries) giving identical privileges to the citizens of the other state. *2.* See **reciprocal.**

Recision See **rescission.**

Recital *1.* A formal statement in a document that explains the reasons for the document or for the transaction involving the document. *2.* Any formal listing of specific facts.

Reckless *"Reckless"* can mean anything from "careless and inattentive" or "indifferent to consequences" to a "willful disregard for danger to the life or safety of others," but usually involves more than **negligence** and can lead to both **civil** and **criminal** penalties.

Reclamation *1.* A seller's right, under certain circumstances, to take back goods sold to a buyer who cannot pay for them. *2.* A *reclamation act* is a federal law setting up a system of water storage and diversion projects in Western states, primarily for making dry lands productive.

Recognition *1.* Designation of a gain or loss due to a *taxable event* (such as a sale of property) as "taxable" in the current tax year. Gains upon sale of property are taxable in the current year unless there is an applicable *nonrecognition provision.* See **realized** for further discussion. *2.* Acknowledgment that something done by another person in your name was authorized by you. *3. Recognition picketing* is **picketing** to force an employer to bargain with a particular **union**. This is usually not permitted.

Recognizance   A formal obligation to do a certain act that is recorded in court. For example, a person accused of a crime may be allowed to go free before trial without putting up a **bail bond.** The person gives the court a formal written statement acknowledging that failure to show up will mean payment to the court of a certain amount of money. This is called getting out on your *own recognizance.*

Recollection   The act of remembering. This may be done by a **witness** who *refreshes the memory* by using an object or a document. This is called "*present memory refreshed*" or "*present recollection revived.*" For example, the witness might look at a document to remember what it was about, then put it down and **testify** about events mentioned in the document. If the witness still cannot remember clearly, the document might then need to be introduced into **evidence** under an exception to the **hearsay** *rule* after the witness testifies as to its authenticity and accuracy. This is called "*past recollection recorded*" or "*recorded past recollection.*"

Reconciliation   *1.* The renewal of a broken relationship with forgiveness on both sides. See also **condonation.** *2.* Bringing two differing **accounts** into agreement; for example, adjusting the balance in your checking account records to agree with the bank's monthly **statement.**

Reconduction   The forcible return of undesirable **aliens** to their native countries.

Reconstruction   The process of making changes in the governments of the Southern states in order to bring them back into the United States after the Civil War.

Recontinuance   An old word for a person's getting inherited rights that had been wrongfully taken away.

Reconveyance   The return of **title** to property; for example, the return of title to a car when the bank loan is paid off.

Record   *1.* A formal, written account of a case, containing the complete formal history of all actions taken, papers filed, **rulings** made, **opinions** written, etc. The *record* also can include all the actual **evidence** (**testimony,** physical objects, etc.) as well as the evidence that was *refused* **admission** by the judge. *Courts of record* include all courts for which permanent records of proceedings are kept. *2.* A *public record* is a document filed with, or put out by, a government agency and open to the public for inspection. For example, a *title of record* to land is an ownership interest that has been properly filed in the public land records. The official who keeps these records is usually called the *recorder of deeds,* and the filing process is called *recordation. 3.* A corporation's *records* include its **charter, bylaws,** and **minutes** of meetings. The *record date* for payment of a company's stock **dividends** or for voting is the date on which stockholders must be **registered** on the company's books to vote or to receive dividends.

Recorded past recollection   See **recollection.**

Recorder   *1.* A person who keeps public records. See **record** no. 2. *2.* The name for some local judges who hear minor cases, often in a *recorder's court.*

Recording acts   State laws establishing rules for **priority** among persons who claim the same **interests** in **real estate** (and sometimes other property). These laws have many different forms and time limits in different states, but the three basic types are: *1. Race statutes.* In a state with a "race statute," a person who first **records** (files) a claim (such as a **deed**) has the legal right to that claim. For example, if Tom sells a house to Dick, then sells it again to Harry, then Harry files the deed, Harry's deed will probably be good against Dick because he won the "race." *2. Notice statutes.* In these states, the person with a *later* valid claim (whether or not recorded) has priority over an earlier unrecorded claim unless the later person knew about the earlier claim. For example, if Tom sells to Dick (who does not record the deed), then sells to Harry, Harry's deed will probably be good against Dick *even if* Dick then records the deed and Harry doesn't, *unless* Harry knew about the prior sale. *3. Race-notice statutes.* In these states, the first person to record without knowledge of a prior unrecorded claim wins. For example, if Tom sells to Dick (who does not record), then sells to Harry, who then records without knowing about Dick's claim, Harry wins.

Recoupment   *1.* Keeping or holding something back that you owe because there is a fair, just reason to do so. *2.* Taking or getting something back (especially money lost). *3.* A **counterclaim.**

Recourse   *1.* The right of a person who holds a **negotiable instrument** (see that word) to get payment on it from anyone who indorsed (signed) it. *Recourse* is available unless the signer signs it "no recourse" or "without recourse." *2.* The means of enforcing a **right.**

Recovery   The thing received when a lawsuit is decided in your favor, such as the amount of money given by a **judgment** in a successful lawsuit.

Recrimination   *1.* The principle that if a person seeking a divorce is guilty of the same conduct on which **grounds** for the divorce are based, no divorce will be granted. *2.* An accusation made by an accused person against the accuser.

Recross examination   See **examination.**

Rectum   (Latin) *1.* A right. *2.* A trial or accusation.

Recuperatio   (Latin) Recovery by court action of something wrongfully kept from you.

Recusation (or recusal)   The process by which a judge is disqualified (or disqualifies himself or herself) from hearing a lawsuit because of **prejudice** or because the judge is **interested.**

Red circle rate   A pay rate equal to that of a person's past job when the person is transferred to what would otherwise be a lower paying job.

Red herring   *1.* A preliminary **prospectus,** used during the "waiting period" between filing a *registration statement* with the S.E.C. and approval of the statement. It has a red "for information only" statement on the front and states that the **securities** described may not be offered for sale until S.E.C. approval. The *red herring* must be filed with the S.E.C. before use. *2.* An interesting point or important issue raised to distract attention from the question under discussion.

Redaction   A revision or editing, especially to remove confidential information or to remove references to a **co-defendant** in a confession. [pronounce: ree-dak-shun]

Reddendum   Describes a **clause** in a **deed** that reserves (keeps) some right of **reversion.**

Reddition   An old word for giving something back or being told by a court that something must be given back.

Redeem   *1.* Buy back. Reclaim property that has been **mortgaged** or **pledged.** *2.* Turn in for cash.

Redeemable bond   *1.* A **callable** *bond* (one that can be called in by the company and paid off at any time before **maturity**). *2.* Any bond that has a maturity date (as opposed to a **consol**).

Redemption   Repurchase or turn in for cash (see **redeem**). A *redemption period* is the time during which a **mortgage** or similar debt that has gone into **default** can be paid off without losing the property. Some states have **mandatory** redemption periods for home mortgages.

Redhibition   An old word for getting out of a deal because of a serious defect in the thing bought. In Louisiana, this is a *redhibitory defect.*

Redirect examination   See **examination.**

Rediscount rate   The rate at which a *federal reserve bank* can make loans to *member banks* on **commercial paper** (**bills, notes,** etc.) already discounted (resold) by those banks. See also **discount rate.**

Redlining   *1.* A bank or **mortgage** company's refusing to make loans in a particular neighborhood, "because" of deteriorating conditions, which *results* in discrimination. *2.* Showing possible revisions next to original text.

Redraft   *1.* A second **note** or **bill** offered for payment after the first has been refused payment. The *redraft's* total includes the costs of delayed payment and collection in addition to the original amount. *2.* A second writing (of a **legislative** bill, etc.).

Redress   Satisfaction or payment for harm done. *2.* Access to the courts to get no. 1.

Reductio ad absurdum   (Latin) "Reduce to the absurd." Disproving an argument by showing that it leads to a ridiculous conclusion.

Reduction   Turning something abstract into something concrete. For example, *reduction to possession* is turning a right to something (such as a debt) into the thing itself (the money owed), and *reduction to practice* is turning an idea for a device or process into an actual, working device or process. See also **conception.**

Redundancy   Unnecessarily repetitive, superfluous, or irrelevant matter in a **pleading** (see that word).

Reed v. Reed   (404 U.S. 71) The 1971 U.S. Supreme Court decision that was the first to strike down a state law as discrimination against women because it violated the **equal protection of laws** under the **Fourteenth Amendment.**

Reenactment rule   The principle that if a **legislature** *reenacts* a law (to prevent it from expiring or to make minor changes), the legislature automatically **adopts** any well-established interpretation of the law made by the courts or the **executive** branch.

Re-entry   Taking back possession of land by asserting a right you reserved (kept) when you left the land. Depending on the situation, this may be done by a lawsuit for **eviction,** for **ejectment,** or to **quiet title.**

Reexchange   The expenses caused by the refusal to pay a *bill of* **exchange** in a foreign country.

Refer   *1.* Point to; direct attention to. *2.* A judge's action of turning a case (or part of a case) over to a person who has been appointed to sort things out by taking **testimony,** examining documents, and making decisions and recommendations. This person is often called a "*referee*" or "*special master.*"

Referee in bankruptcy   An old word for a federal judge who ran **bankruptcy** hearings.

Reference   *1.* An agreement in a **contract** to submit certain disputes to an **arbitrator** for decision. This may be an *arbitration clause. 2.* The act of sending a case to a referee for a decision (see **refer**). *3.* A person who will provide information for you about your character, credit, etc. *4.* Mention in a book or document of another place to find information on a subject or of the place from which the information used was taken. See also **citation.** *5.* See **incorporate by reference.**

Referendum   Putting an important law to a direct vote of the people rather than passing it through the **legislature** (or in addition to passing it through the legislature).

Referral plan (or referral sales scheme)   **Pyramid sales scheme.**

Refinance   Exchange one debt arrangement for another; usually by paying off a loan with part or all of the money from a new loan.

Reformation   A procedure in which a court will rewrite or correct ("*reform*") a written agreement to conform with the original intent of the persons making the deal. The court will usually do this only if there was **fraud** or **mutual mistake** in writing up the original document.

Reformatory   A prison for **youthful offenders.**

Refoulement   (French) Turning back an immigrant to the country of origin. [pronounce: re-fowl-ment]

Refreshing memory   See **recollection.**

Refunding   Refinancing a debt.

Reg.   *1.* **Regulation.** *2.* **Registered.**

Regalia   (Latin) A king's or queen's royal rights.

Regent   *1.* A person who governs a kingdom while the king or queen is too young, disabled, or away for a long time. *2.* The name for the heads of some public institutions such as the persons on the *Board of Regents* of a state university system.

Regional reporter   A **reporter** that contains the state court **opinions** of one region of the U.S. A *regional* **digest** summarizes these opinions.

Register   *1.* A book of public facts, such as births, deaths and marriages (also called a "*registry*"). *2.* The public official who keeps the book mentioned in no. 1. *3.* To place information into the book in no. 1. *4.* Examples of public record books include the *register of patents* (a list of all patents granted) and the *register of ships* (a list of ships and the countries where they are registered that is kept by **customs**). *5.* Examples of public record keeping officials include the *register of deeds* (an official who keeps land records) and the *register of wills* (usually the **clerk** of the **probate** court). An official who keeps records is often called "*recorder*" or "*registrar.*" *6.* A chronological list; for example, a *check register* of checks written.

Registered Listed on an official record. For example, a *registered stock* is either a stock listed with the S.E.C. and sold to the public according to its rules or a stock that can only be cashed in by the person whose name is officially recorded as the owner. Each time ownership changes, that fact is recorded. A *registered bond* has the bond (or only the interest payments) registered this way. (See also **registration statement**.) A *registered check* is an un**certified** check for which a record is kept by the bank that sells it. And a *registered representative* is a person listed and approved by the government to sell **securities** after a training period and after passing **N.A.S.D.** and **N.Y.S.E.** tests.

Registrar *1.* See **register** definition no. 5. *2.* A **transfer agent.**

Registration *1.* Recording (see **record**). *2.* Making up a list. *3.* Putting yourself on a list of eligible voters. *4.* A *registration statement* is a financial and ownership **statement,** often including a **prospectus** and other documents, required by the S.E.C. of most companies that want to sell **stock** or other **securities** and of all companies that want their securities traded in **markets** such as the New York Stock Exchange. Some stocks sold to certain limited groups of persons may meet lesser S.E.C. registration requirements or be exempt from registration.

Registry See **register** definition no. 1.

Regnal years Refers to the years or dates of a king's or queen's reign. For example, law cases and **statutes** in England are usually dated in *regnal years* according to the name of the king or queen on the throne at the time and the year of their reign.

Regressive tax Opposite of **progressive tax.**

Regs. Abbreviation for **regulations.**

Regular *1.* Steady; uniform: with no unusual variations. *2.* Lawful; legal; in conformity with usual practice. *3.* *Regular course of business* refers to actions (such as business record keeping) of a business that are in **good faith** and that conform to the usual practice of that business.

Regulate Control. For example, a government *regulates* businesses (such as power companies) by writing laws and setting up government organizations called "*regulatory agencies*" (or **administrative**

agencies) to write rules and **regulations** that explain what the *regulated* businesses can and cannot do, how they may operate, and, often, what they may charge. The agencies also administer and enforce the rules by giving **orders,** holding **hearings, etc.**

Regulation   A rule that is put out by a local government or an **administrative agency** to **regulate** (see that word) conduct. For example, **I.R.S.** *regulations* are rules about how the tax **code** applies to specific situations, and local governments put out *parking regulations.* Many regulations are known by name to insiders in the field. For example, see *regulation* **Z.**

Regulatory agency   See **regulate.**

Regulatory offense   *1.* A **statutory crime.** But see no. 2. *2.* A minor offense, defined by **regulation** rather than by **statute.**

Rehabilitation   *1.* The restoring of former rights, abilities, authority, credibility, etc. For example, *rehabilitating a witness* means asking questions to restore the witness's believability after the other side has destroyed it or put it in question, and *rehabilitating a prisoner* means preparing him or her for an honest productive life once released. *2.* See **Chapter Thirteen** for a *rehabilitation in bankruptcy.*

Rehearing   A new **hearing** to reconsider an action that may have been wrongly taken or overlooked in a prior hearing. Compare **reargument.**

Reinstate   Place back in a condition that has ended or been lost. For example, to *reinstate a case* is to put it back into court after it has been dismissed (thrown out).

Reinsurance   A **contract** by which one **insurance** company insures itself with another insurance company to protect itself against all or part of the **risk** it took on by insuring a customer.

Rejoinder   A *common law* **pleading.**

Relation   "Relating back" or having retroactive effect.

Relative fact   *1.* An **evidentiary fact.** *2.* **Circumstantial evidence.**

Relator   A person in whose name a state brings a legal action (the person who "relates" the facts on which the action is based). The name of the case might be *State ex rel* ("on the relation of") *Smith v. Jones.* [pronouce: re-late-or]

Relaxatio   (Latin) A **release.**

Release   *1.* Give up or relinquish a claim or right to the person against whom it might have been enforced. *2.* A document by which a claim or right is relinquished; for example, a *release* from further **liability** received in exchange for paying money to settle an accident claim.

Release on own recognizance   See **recognizance.**

Relevance (and relevancy)   See **relevant.**

Relevant   Tending to prove or disprove a fact that is important to a claim, charge, or defense in a court case. Information must be *relevant* to be admitted as **evidence** in a case. (In evidence law, "relevant" and "**material**" are sometimes used as synonyms, but here *material* means "important to a claim, charge, or defense in a court case.") All *relevant* evidence is **admissible** into a case unless excluded by a specific rule, such as the **hearsay** *rule*. Relevant evidence may also be excluded if its value as evidence is outweighed by the possibility of unfair prejudice, the time wasted by presenting it, the possibility of confusing the issues, etc.

Relevant market   The geographic area in which a particular type, price, and quality of product is sold.

Reliance   Belief in something, plus acting on that belief. See also **promissory estoppel.**

Relict   An old word for widow or widower.

Reliction   Slow **dereliction** (see that word).

Relief   *1.* The help given by a court to a person who brings a lawsuit. The "relief asked for" might be the return of property taken by another person, the enforcement of a contract, money, etc. *2.* Public assistance to poor persons.

Religion   See **freedom of religion** and **establishment clause.**

Rem   (Latin) "Thing"; see "**in rem.**"

Remainder   *1.* An interest or **estate** in land or **trust** property that takes effect only when another interest in land or trust property ends. For example, if Mary's **will** says "I leave my house to Joe for ten years and then to Jane," Jane's interest is a *remainder*. A *contingent remainder* is a remainder that goes to a person not yet alive, to a person as yet unascertained, or to a person whose rights depend on some uncertain future event. Compare **reversion.** *2.* Used as language *in* a will, "remainder" means "what's left"; for example, "my house and clothing to Joe and the remainder to Jane" means that Jane gets what's left after Joe gets the house and clothing.

Remainderman   *1.* An old word for a person who will (or may) get an interest in land at a future time. *2.* An old word for a person who gets what is "left over" under a will or when a **trust** ends.

Remand   Send back. For example, a higher court may *remand* (send back) a case to a lower court, directing the lower court to take some action. Also, a prisoner is *remanded to custody* when sent back to jail after failing to meet, or being denied release on, **bail.**

Remargining See **margin call.**

Remedial statute *1.* A law that is passed to correct a defect in a prior law. *2.* A law passed to provide (or modify) a **remedy** (for example, to create a new **lien**).

Remedy The means by which a right is enforced or satisfaction is gained for a harm done. The means by which a violation of rights is prevented, redressed, or compensated. For example, Ron's *remedy* against Don if Don refuses to give back Ron's book might be to take it back, to argue with Don until he gives it back, or to go to court to either get it back or make Don pay for it. "Legal remedies" or "court remedies" include such things as **injunctions** and **damages.**

Remise **Release,** give up, or forgive.

Remission *1.* **Release** (ending or forgiving) of a debt. *2.* Forgiving an offense, injury, or harm done. See also **condonation.**

Remit *1.* Send; send in or send back. *2.* Give up or pay. *3.* Refer for decision, especially to **remand.** *4.* Mitigate or lessen. *5.* Pardon or forgive.

Remittance Money (or a check, etc.) sent by one person to another, often as payment for a debt owed.

Remitter *1.* Being "sent back" to an earlier, better right. For example, if a person who owns property and **leases** it to another is left the lease rights in the renter's **will,** the owner gets full original rights to the property by *remitter. 2.* **Remittitur** no. 3.

Remittitur *1.* The power of a trial judge to decrease the amount of money awarded by a **jury** to a **plaintiff.** *2.* The power of an **appeals** court to deny a new trial to the **defendant** if the plaintiff agrees to take a certain amount of money less than that given in the trial. Compare with **additur.** *3. Remittitur of record* is the return of a case from appeals court to trial court for the trial court to carry out the higher court's decision.

Remonstrance A formal protest against government policy or government actions.

Removal The movement of a person or thing from one place to another. For example, "removal from the state" means absence from the state long enough to be a change of residence, and "removal of a case" is the transfer of a case from one court to another (most commonly, from a state to a federal court, often for **civil rights** reasons). For *removal from office* or *removal for cause,* see **for cause.**

Render *1.* **Pronounce,** state, or declare. For example, a judge *renders judgment* by formally making a decision in a case in court. *2.* Give up or return. For example, *rendition* is a state's returning a **fugitive from justice** (see that word) to a state seeking the fugitive's return. *3.* Pay or perform.

Renegotiation board A temporary federal agency that **negotiates** with **contractors** on federal projects to lower payments when it decides that costs to the government have been unfairly high or excessive.

Renewal *1.* The act of extending contractual relations beyond a contract's original term, often by entering into a new contract (on the same or similar terms) that begins when the old one ends. *2.* The act of extending any legally binding arrangements for an additional time period.

Reno v. A.C.L.U. (521 U.S. 844) A 1996 U. S. Supreme Court decision striking down as violations of **freedom of speech** the provisions of the federal Communications Decency Act that attempted to regulate "indecent" material on the Internet.

Renounce Reject, cast off, or give up openly and in public.

Rent strike An organized **tenant** refusal to pay rent in order to force the **landlord** to do something.

Rent-a-judge **Alternative dispute resolution** in which two sides in a dispute choose a person to decide the dispute. The two sides may agree to make the procedure informal or formally similar to a real trial, and they may agree to make the decision advisory only or binding and enforceable.

Renunciation *1.* **Abandonment** of a right; giving up a right without transferring it to anyone else or dedicating it to public use. *2.* **Withdrawal from conspiracy or criminal action** (see that phrase).

Renvoi (French) Returning; reflecting. Describes the principle that the laws in your own state or country should be applied to a case when your laws direct you to abide by another state's or country's laws but those laws in turn direct the use of your laws. *2.* **Reconduction.** [pronounce: ron-vwa]

Reorganization *1.* See **Chapter Eleven** for *reorganization* in **bankruptcy.** *2.* Any restructuring of an organization. The **I.R.S.** labels **corporate** reorganizations by type (A–G) depending on possible tax consequences.

Rep. Short for **reporter, reports** or **representative.**

Repair Fix a defect. *Repairs* and **improvements** are treated differently for tax purposes. A *business* repair can be taken as a tax **deduction,** while a personal residence repair has no tax benefits unless made soon before sale of the home. Both business and home *improvements* can be added to the property's **basis.**

Reparable injury   A wrong that can be compensated by money.

Reparation   Payment for an injury; redress for a wrong done.

Repeal   Wipe out an earlier **statute** by passing a later one. This is usually **prospective** only.

Repetition   Trying to get back a payment made by mistake.

Replacement cost   The cost of buying something that does the job of something lost; for example, the cost of building a house roughly comparable to one that burned down. Compare with **reproduction cost.**

Repleader   **Motion** for a new trial.

Replevin   A legal action to get back personal **property** wrongfully held by another person.

Replevy   To give back personal **property** to a person who has brought a lawsuit for **replevin** of the property.

Replication   An old form of **pleading** similar to the modern **reply** (**plaintiff's** response to a **defendant's** first pleading).

Reply   In federal **pleading,** the **plaintiff's** response to the **defendant's answer** or **counterclaim.** The usual order is: complaint, answer, reply. The reply denies some or all of the facts in the answer. Sometimes, it adds new facts, but only to counter facts in the answer.

Repo   *1.* Short for a *repurchase agreement* in which a **dealer** agrees to buy back a **security** at a set time and price. *2.* Short for **repossession.**

Report   An official or formal statement of facts or proceedings.

Report out   The action of a committee in sending a **bill** to the **legislature** for action.

Reporter   *1.* **Reports.** *2.* A person who compiles reports. *3.* The *court reporter* is the person who records court proceedings in court and later makes good copies of some of them. *4.* A **looseleaf service.**

Reports   Published volumes of case decisions by a particular court or group of courts.

Repose   See **limitation.**

Repossession   Taking back something sold, usually because payments have not been made.

Represent   *1.* To say or to state certain facts. *2.* To act for, do business for, or "stand in" for another person. See also **agent.** *3.* To act as another person's lawyer.

Representation *1.* See **represent**. *2.* In the law of **contracts,** any statement made (or any impression given about a state of facts) to convince the other person to make a contract. *3.* In the law of **inheritance,** *taking by representation* is the same as taking **per stirpes** (see that word).

Representative *1.* A person who **represents** (see that word) another. *2.* A voting member of the lower **house** of a **legislature.**

Representative action *1.* A lawsuit brought by one stockholder in a **corporation** to claim rights or to fix wrongs done to many or all stockholders in the company. It is also called a **derivative action.** *2.* Any **class action.**

Reprieve Holding off on enforcing a criminal **sentence** for a period of time after the sentence has been handed down. Compare with **pardon** and **commutation.**

Reproduction cost The cost of replacing a lost or destroyed item with an *exact* duplicate. Compare with **replacement cost.**

Reproduction right The right of a **copyright** holder to decide who will make copies or recordings of the work.

Reproductive rights The rights of a woman to control, under most circumstances, whether to become pregnant, whether to have an abortion, etc. *Not* **reproduction right.**

Republic A country with a government by elected officials and, in theory, with ultimate power in the hands of the citizens.

Republication Reestablishing the validity of a **will** that has been revoked.

Repudiation Rejection or refusal. For example, *repudiation of a* **contract** is the refusal to go through with it, usually with a legal right to refuse.

Repugnancy *1.* Inconsistency. A condition which occurs if one part of a document is true (or correct), so that another part cannot be true (or correct). *2.* The *repugnancy doctrine* is the principle that if two parts of a document contradict each other, the first clear one will be given effect.

Reputation What people in a community think about a person.

Request for admissions One side in a lawsuit giving a list of facts to the other and requesting that they be admitted or denied. Those admitted need not be proved at the trial.

Request for instructions Either side in a lawsuit giving the judge a written list of **instructions** about the law that it would like the judge to give to the jury.

Request for production   See *motion for production* under **produce.**

Required records   Business records that must be kept to comply with government regulations. These records are not protected by a person's privilege against **self-incrimination.**

Requirements contract   A **contract** for the supply of goods in which the exact amount of goods to be bought is not set, but is agreed to be all that the buyer reasonably needs while the contract is in force. Compare with **output contract.**

Requisition   *1.* A demand or a request for something to which you have a right; for example, a request by one state governor to another to hand over a **fugitive from justice** (see that word, and see **extradition**). *2.* The taking of private property by the government during an emergency. *3.* A routine written request for supplies or services, made by one department of an organization to another.

Requisitory letters   **Rogatory letters.**

Res   (Latin) *1.* A thing; an object; things; a status. *2.* The subject matter or contents of a **will** or **trust.** [pronounce: race]

Res adjudicata   **Res judicata.**

Res controversa   (Latin) "A thing in controversy." Contrast with **res judicata.**

Res derelicta   (Latin) Abandoned property.

Res fungibiles   (Latin) **Fungible** goods.

Res gestae   (Latin) "Things done"; an entire occurrence. Everything said and done that is part of a single occurrence. An **assault's** *res gestae* might include, for example: **excited utterances,** threats that are part of the assault, **present sense impressions,** and other words that are an integral part of the occurrence. Words spoken by others can usually be testified about even if **hearsay** if the words are part of the *res gestae.* Compare with **verbal acts.** [pronounce: race guest-i]

Res immobiles   (Latin) Immovable things such as land and buildings.

Res integra   (Latin) "A whole thing." An undecided point of law. A legal question without **precedent,** and probably without any discussion in prior cases.

Res inter alia acta   (Latin) "A thing done among strangers." Describes the principle that a **party** to a lawsuit should not be affected by the words or deeds of persons with whom the party has no connection and for whom the party has no legal responsibility.

Res ipsa loquitur   (Latin) "The thing speaks for itself." A **rebuttable** *presumption* (a conclusion that can be changed if contrary **evidence** is introduced) that a person is **negligent** if the thing causing an accident was in his or her control only, and if that type of accident does not usually happen without negligence. It is often abbreviated "res ipsa" or "R.I.L." [pronounce: race ip-sa low-kwe-tur]

Res judicata (Latin) "A thing decided"; "a matter decided by **judgment.**" If a court decides a case, the subject of that case is firmly and finally decided between the persons involved in the suit, so no new lawsuit on the same subject may be brought by the persons involved. See also **collateral estoppel, double jeopardy,** and **law of the case.** [pronounce: race ju-di-ca-ta]

Res nova See **res integra.**

Res publicae (Latin) "Public things"; things belonging to the public.

Resale price maintenance See **fair trade practices.**

Resale rights The right of a seller to resell (usually perishable) goods if the buyer does not pay or does not claim them in time.

Rescind To take back or **annul.** To cancel a **contract** and wipe it out "from the beginning" as if it had never been. [pronounce: re-sind]

Rescission _1._ The **annulment** of a **contract** (see **rescind**). _2._ The president's request to Congress that certain money already appropriated not be spent. [pronounce: re-si-zhon]

Rescript _1._ A judge's short note to a clerk explaining how to dispose of a case. _2._ An **appeals** court's short, usually unsigned, written **decision** in a case that is sent down to the trial court.

Rescue _1._ The _rescue doctrine_ is that if one person negligently puts a second person in danger, and a third person is hurt while attempting a rescue, the third person can collect **damages** from the first person and cannot be charged with **contributory negligence** unless he or she acted recklessly. See also **emergency doctrine** and **Good Samaritan doctrine.** _2._ The forcible and unlawful freeing of a prisoner or the taking back of goods that have been lawfully taken away.

Reservation _1._ See **reserve.** _2._ Land owned by a Native American nation as a whole for the use of its people.

Reserve _1._ Hold back a thing or a right. For example, a **deed** to land can _reserve_ the right to cross the land for the person selling it, and to _reserve_ **title** is to keep an ownership right as **security** that the thing will be fully paid for. Also, a judge may _reserve_ **decision** of a legal question in a case by putting it off until some later time. _2._ A fund of money set aside to meet future needs, losses or claims (such as a **sinking fund** _reserve_ to repay long-term debt or a **bad debt** _reserve_ to cover losses). _3._ A _reserve bank_ is a member of the _Federal Reserve System_ and the _Reserve Board_ is the Federal Reserve _Board of_

Governors. 4. A *reserve clause* in an athlete's **contract** puts restrictions on his or her right to change teams. *5. Reserved powers* are all powers not given to the U.S. government by the Constitution and, under the **Tenth Amendment,** given (*reserved*) to either the states or the people. *6. With reserve* in an auction means that the thing will not be sold unless the highest **bid** exceeds a certain amount (the *reserve price*) and *without reserve* means that the thing will be sold at whatever is the highest price bid.

Resettlement   A judge's reopening of an **order** or **decree** to include something accidentally left out.

Residence   A place where a person lives all or part of the time. Sometimes this is the same as **domicile.** *Residency requirements* are state laws on how long a person must live in a state to get a **divorce, welfare, admission** to the bar, etc.

Resident agent   A person living in a state who is authorized to accept **service** of **process** for another (usually a **corporation**).

Resident alien   A foreigner whose residence in the U.S. is legal and who intends to become a U.S. citizen.

Residential cluster   A piece of land developed as a unit with open common land and grouped housing.

Residual   *1.* **Residuary.** *2.* A payment to a writer, actor, etc., for re-use of a TV movie, etc. *3.* A *residual security* is a **bond** or *preferred* **stock** that can be exchanged for **common stock.**

Residuary   The part left over. For example, a *residuary clause* in a will disposes of all items not specifically given away (the "leftovers").

Residuum   (Latin) Leftovers.

Resisting an officer   The criminal act of attempting to stop or hinder a police officer from performing a duty such as making an **arrest,** serving a **writ,** or keeping the peace. This may be a crime whether or not force is used.

Resolution   A formal expression of a decision made by an organized group (such as a club, a professional organization, a **legislature,** a public assembly, etc.). Congressional resolutions may be by one **house** only, **concurrent,** or **joint.** A *concurrent resolution* is passed by one house, agreed to by the other, and expresses the "sense of Congress" on a subject though it does not become a law. A *joint resolution* is passed by both houses of Congress and, in general, is the same as a **bill** that has been passed by both houses.

Resolve   *1.* See **resolution.** *2.* A firm decision to do something; a strong will to achieve a goal.

Resort   A *court of last resort* is a court whose decision cannot be appealed within the same court system.

Respondeat superior   (Latin) "Let the master answer." Describes the principle that an employer is responsible for most harm caused by an employee acting within the **scope of employment.** In such a case, the employer is said to have **vicarious liability.**

Respondent   *1.* The person against whom an **appeal** is taken. (This person might have been either the **plaintiff** or the **defendant** in the lower court.) Also called the "**appellee.**" *2.* The person against whom a **motion** is filed (who then responds).

Responsibility   Guilt (for a crime or **tort**), **liability** (for a payment, contract **breach** or tort), or **competency** (to stand trial).

Responsible bidder   A company, competing by bid for public work, that is financially sound, honest, and competent to do the work. A government agency soliciting bids will usually reject bids, no matter how low, from all "unresponsible" bidders.

Responsive   Answering. A *responsive pleading* is a court paper that directly answers the points raised by the other side's **pleading.** Also, if a **witness** does not answer a question directly, the answer may be objected to as *not responsive.*

Rest   To *rest a case* is to formally end your side's presentation of evidence for a major phase of a case in court. For example, in a criminal case, the prosecution presents its evidence (witnesses, documents, etc.) first. After the prosecutor *rests,* the defense may then present its evidence.

Restatement of Law   Books put out by the **American Law Institute** that tell what the law in a general area is, how it is changing, and what direction the authors think this change should take; for example, the *Restatement of the Law of Contracts.*

Restitution   *1.* Giving something back; making good for something. *2.* There are various rules for how much "giving back" is full *restitution.* For example, in **contract** law, restitution is usually the amount that puts the **plaintiff** back in the financial position he or she was in before the contract. *3. Restitution programs* in some states make a convicted **criminal** pay back the crime victim in money or work.

Restrain   *1.* Prohibit from action; hold back. *2.* Hinder or obstruct.

Restraining order   A **temporary restraining order** or a **protective order.**

Restraint of marriage   Describes a provision in a **will,** gift, or **trust** that prohibits the person getting the gift from marrying. Such provisions are rarely enforced by courts.

Restraint of trade   An illegal agreement or combination of companies that eliminates competition, sets up a **monopoly,** or artificially raises prices. See **antitrust acts.**

Restricted security   Letter stock.

Restrictive covenant   A **clause** in a **deed** that forbids the new owner (and all later owners of the deeded land) from doing certain things with the land; for example, a clause that prohibits use of the land for commercial purposes. *2.* A clause in an employment contract that prohibits the employee from working for the employer's competitors for a certain time period after the contract ends.

Restrictive indorsement   Signing a **negotiable instrument** (see that word) in a way that ends its negotiability; for example, marking a check "Pay to Robert Smith only."

Restructure   Change the terms of a debt; for example, the payment schedule.

Resulting trust   A **trust** created by law (rather than by agreement) for reasons of fairness when one person holds property for another. For example, if Peter gives money to Paul to be held "in trust," but no formal trust document is signed, Paul may be found to hold the money in a *resulting trust* for Peter's benefit. And if Peter buys a house for himself but puts the **title** in Paul's name, a court may decide that the house is held in a *purchase money resulting trust* for Peter's benefit.

Retainage   Holdback.

Retained earnings   A company's yearly **net** *profit* minus the **dividends** it paid out that year. *Accumulated retained earnings* is that year's *retained earnings* plus retained earnings left over from prior years. It is a measure of what a company can use for future improvements and expansions as well as to ride out possible bad years. A *retained earnings statement* is a part of most corporate **annual reports.** See **statement.** Most payments to shareholders made by a company with "*retained earnings and profits*" will be taxed as dividends, no matter what they are called.

Retainer   *1.* Employment of a lawyer by a client. *2.* The specific agreement in no. 1. *3.* The first payment in no. 1, either for one specific case or to be available for unspecified future cases. *4.* Holding something back when you have a right to hold it back.

Retaliatory eviction   A landlord's attempt (prohibited in most states) to throw out a tenant for complaining to the health department, forming a tenants' union, etc.

Retaliatory law   A state law "evening up" taxes or restraints placed by other states on businesses from the first state. For example, if Maryland taxes Virginia insurance companies at a higher rate than Virginia does, Virginia might pass a *retaliatory law* that raises the tax rate on Maryland insurance companies.

Retirement   Making the final payment owed on a **bond, note,** or other **security** and ending its existence and all obligations under it.

Retirement plan   See **pension plan** and **profit sharing.**

Retorsion (or retortion)   Treating the citizens of a foreign country harshly because that country treats your citizens harshly.

Retraction   Taking something back, especially taking back something you said and admitting that it was false.

Retraxit   A **plaintiff's** complete and voluntary **abandonment** of a lawsuit. In federal practice, this would be done by a *voluntary dismissal.*

Retreat to the wall   See **flee to the wall doctrine.**

Retrial   A new trial in the court that completed the original trial and made the original decision. A *retrial* is usually ordered because the original trial was improper or unfair due to, for example, procedural errors. Compare with **mistrial.**

Retribution   The process of "getting even." One theory justifying punishment of criminals is that society should have *retribution* for the wrongs done to it. Compare with **rehabilitation.**

Retro   Back; backwards; behind; past. For example, a *retrospective* or *retroactive* law is one that changes the legal status of things already done or that applies to past actions. See also **ex post facto** laws.

Retrocession   Giving a person back a **title** to property that the person once held, but lost.

Return   *1.* The act of a **sheriff** or other **peace officer** in delivering back to a court a brief account of whether or not (and how) he or she served (delivered) a court paper to a person. *2.* **Yield** or profit. *3.* See **tax return.**

Return day (or date)   *1.* The date by which a **sheriff** or other **peace officer** must make a **return** (see that word). *2.* The day by which a **defendant** must file a **pleading** after receiving a **summons** to come to court.

Return on equity   *1.* The profit a company makes compared to its value; especially the annual profit made compared to the total cost of its **common stock.** See also **statement** and **equity.** *2.* The profit an investor makes on shares of stock or other investments, such as rental housing, compared to the owner's original investment.

Reus (Latin) **Party.** [pronounce: <u>ree</u>-us or <u>ray</u>-us]

Rev. *1.* Short for *review* (as in **law review**). *2.* Short for *revised* (as in **revised statutes**). *3.* Short for *revenue* (as in **revenue ruling**).

Revaluation Raising the value of a country's money relative to other countries' money.

Revendication *1.* Demanding that someone return something you sold. *2.* **Replevin.**

Revenue *1.* Income. *2.* **Profit** on an investment. *3.* Describes things that raise money for the government. For example, *revenue bills* raise tax money, *revenue bonds* are sold by governments and backed by money-making public projects, *revenue stamps* are placed on something (such as a recorded deed) to prove that a tax was paid, and "*revenue enhancer*" is a euphemism for a tax or tax increase.

Revenue officer *1.* A tax collector. *2.* A tax investigator, such as a person who hunts for illegal whiskey stills.

Revenue procedures and rulings *Revenue procedures* (Rev. Proc.) are **I.R.S.** opinions on procedural tax matters and *revenue rulings* (Rev. Rul.) are I.R.S. interpretations of the tax law as it applies to specific cases. They are first published in an *Internal Revenue Bulletin* (IRB), then collected in *Cumulative Bulletins* (C.B.). They have slightly less legal "weight" than tax **regulations** and slightly more than *private* **letter rulings.**

Reverse *1.* Set aside. For example, when a higher court *reverses* a lower court on **appeal,** it sets aside the **judgment** of the lower court and either substitutes its own judgment for it or sends the case back to the lower court with instructions on what to do with it. *2.* A *reverse stock split* is a corporation's calling in of all **stock** to reduce the number of **shares.** This increases the value of each share without changing the total value of all the stock.

Reverse discrimination The inference that if a school admission slot, a promotion, or other benefit is reserved for minorities, that benefit is then denied to non-minorities. *Reverse discrimination* is a rationale for court decisions restricting **affirmative action** programs.

Reverse engineering Analyzing something (usually produced using a **trade secret**) to duplicate the process that produced it. This may be a legitimate way to learn and use these secrets.

Reverse mortgage (or reverse annuity mortgage or reverse equity mortgage) A **mortgage** in which the homeowner (usually an older, retired person), rather than making interest payments, gets regular payments for income, so the loan balance increases.

Reversible error   See **error.**

Reversion   Any **future interest** (see that word) kept by a person who transfers away property. For example, if John rents out his land for ten years, his ownership rights during those years, his right to take back the property after ten years, and his **heirs'** right to take back the property after ten years if he dies are _reversionary interests._ Compare **remainder.**

Reverter   The process of **reversion.** See also **remainder.**

Review   See **judicial review.**

Revised statutes   _1._ A **code.** _2._ A book of **statutes** in the order they were originally passed, with temporary and repealed statutes removed. Abbreviated Rev. Stat., Rev.St., or R.S.

Revival   Restoration to original force or legal effect. An expired **contract** can be _revived_ by acknowledging it and making a new promise to perform it. A **will** can be _revived_ if a later will that revoked or invalidated it is itself revoked or invalidated. And a dead person's **lawsuit** can be _revived_ and carried on by the executor or administrator of the person's estate.

Revocation   _1._ The taking back of some power or authority. For example, _revoking_ (taking back) an **offer** before it is accepted ends the other person's power to accept. _2._ The ending or making **void** of a thing. For example, _revocation_ of a **will** takes place when a person tears it up intentionally or makes another will.

Revoke   Wipe out the legal effect of something by taking it back, canceling, rescinding, etc. (see **revocation**). If something can be revoked, but has not been revoked, it is _revocable._

Revolution   The complete overthrow of a government. A successful revolt, **insurrection,** or **rebellion.**

Revolving charge   Credit, often provided through credit cards or department stores, by which purchases may be charged and partially paid off month-by-month. New purchases may be made, charged, and paid off during the same period.

Rex   (Latin) King.

Reynolds v. U.S.   (98 U.S. 145) An 1879 Supreme Court decision that excluded the right to do illegal acts from the protection of **freedom of religion** (see that word).

Richard Roe   A common name used for a **fictitious** party or a name used along with "**John Doe**" to illustrate a legal situation.

Rider   An additional piece of paper attached to a larger document. For example, a _rider to a bill_ is an addition made late in the **legislative**

process and usually unrelated to the subject of the **bill,** but "tacked on" anyway.

Rigging the market   Artificially driving up the price of a **stock** by making a series of **bids** that make it look like demand for the stock has soared.

Right   *1.* Morally, ethically, or legally just. *2.* One person's *legal* ability to control certain actions of another person or of all other persons. Most *rights* have a corresponding **duty.** (When lawyers speak of "a right," they mean a legal, not moral right.) *3.* For **Bill of Rights, riparian** *rights,* **stock rights,** the *right to* **privacy,** *right to* **counsel,** *right to* **travel,** or the *rights of* **election, redemption, survivorship,** etc., see those words. For *right to die,* see **advance directive.**

Right from wrong test   **M'Naghten's rule.**

Right of action   A claim that can be enforced in court.

Right of first refusal   The right to have the first chance to buy property when it goes on sale, or the right to meet any other offer.

Right of way   *1.* The right to cross another person's property. *2.* The part of a property that others have a right to cross. *3.* The land on which a railroad is built. *4.* The right of a vehicle (or person) that has a legal right to proceed or go first. The right might be to enter an intersection, use a waterway, etc.

Right to work laws   State laws that forbid: labor agreements requiring **union** membership, forced payment of union dues by nonmembers of a union, preferential hiring, or similar provisions. See also **union shop.**

Rights issue (or offer)   An **issue** of stock (or other **securities**) that is sold only to current stockholders.

Ringing up   **Brokers** exchanging sales **contracts** in order to cancel them out, with leftover differences paid.

Riot   A vague word for a public disturbance, especially a violent one created by three or more persons acting together.

Riparian   Having to do with the bank of a river or stream. *Riparian rights* are a landowner's rights to use water and the land around and under it. Compare with **water rights.** [pronounce: ri-<u>pare</u>-ee-in]

Ripe   *1.* A case is *ripe for selection and decision* by the U.S. Supreme Court if the legal issues involved are clear enough and well enough evolved and presented so that a clear decision can come out of the case. Any court or agency that has the power to turn down cases may use *ripeness* as a way of deciding whether to take the case. *Ripeness* also includes the idea that the case involves a real **controversy,** not merely potential harm. _2._ A case is _ripe for decision_ by a **trial** court if everything is completed and in order, and nothing remains but the **decision** itself.

Rising of court   _1._ The final **adjournment** of a court **term.** _2._ Any break in the court's work (for the day, for a **recess,** etc.). _3._ The start or stop of court business when a court official calls out "all rise" and the judge enters or exits.

Risk   _1._ In insurance: A **hazard** (fire); the danger of hazard or loss (one chance in ten thousand per year); the specific possible hazard or loss mentioned in an **insurance** policy (John's house burning down); or the item insured itself (the house). _2._ In investing: _financial (or credit) risk_ is the risk that the issuer of a security will not be able to pay the investors; _market risk_ is the risk that an investment will go down in value because the whole market for that type of investment goes down; _inflation risk_ is the risk that an investment payout will buy less in the future; _economic risk_ is risk associated with changes in national and world events; _interest rate risk_ is the risk that as interest rates rise, most investment values fall; etc. _3. Risk capital_ is money or property invested in a business (usually as **stock** or a share of the business) as opposed to loans or bonds (even "risky" bonds are not _risk capital_). Also see **venture capital** and _risk_ **arbitrage.** _4. Risk of loss_ usually refers to the responsibility for loss or damage during a property transfer between seller and buyer.

Robbery   The illegal taking of property from the person of another by using force or threat of force.

Robert's rules   Short for _Robert's Rules of Order._ A set of rules by which many **legislatures** and other meetings are conducted. They are _official_ **parliamentary law** only where they have been specifically adopted.

Robinson-Patman Act   (15 U.S.C. 13 & 21) A 1936 federal law that prohibits **price discrimination** and other anticompetitive practices in business.

Roe v. Wade   (410 U.S. 113) A 1973 Supreme Court decision that said that the _right of privacy_ (that is possessed by all, implied by the Constitution, and recognized in earlier cases) includes the right of a woman to get an abortion in the first trimester of pregnancy.

Rogatory letters   A request from one judge to another asking that the second judge supervise the examination of a **witness** (usually in another state and usually by **interrogatories**).

Roll *1.* A record of official proceedings. *2.* A list of persons or property subject to a tax. *3.* A *roll call* is calling off a list of names, usually to take a vote or to see if there is a **quorum** to vote.

Rollback A temporary lowering of an amount of money regularly paid.

Rolling over *1.* Extending a short-term loan for another short period. *Rollover paper* is a short-term **note** that can be extended. *2.* Refinancing a debt. *3.* Making certain nontaxable transfers from one retirement fund to another.

Roman law Laws of the Roman Empire that form the basis for the **civil law** of several European countries and for many legal words and ideas in the U.S., especially in Louisiana.

Romer v. Evans (517 U.S. 620) A 1995 U.S. Supreme Court decision that struck down as a violation of **equal protection of laws** a Colorado state law that prohibited local laws protecting homosexuals against discrimination.

Roomer A lodger. A person who rents rooms in a house, as opposed to a **tenant** (see that word). Roomers have fewer legal rights than tenants, especially with respect to **eviction** and the right to deny others access to the room.

Root of title The **record**ed land transaction (usually the most recent one that is at least forty years old) relied on as the original basis for a claim to land ownership.

Rota (Latin) The order of rotation or **succession** for a job or temporary office.

Round lot A normal unit of trading in **stocks** or **bonds.** Fewer shares are an **odd lot.**

Royalty A payment made to the creator of a work or the owner of a natural material for the use of that work or material. For example, a publisher might pay an author a *royalty* of 10 percent of the retail price of each book sold, a manufacturer might pay an inventor a *royalty* of $10 per invention sold, and a mining company might pay a landowner 10¢ per pound of a mineral extracted.

Rubric *1.* Overall purpose. *2.* Title. *3.* Category. *4.* **Rule** no. 2.

Rule *1.* To settle a legal issue or decide a **motion, objection,** etc., raised by one side in a dispute. The *ruling* is made by the person in charge (judge, hearing officer, chairperson, etc.). *2.* An established standard, principle, or guide. A *rule* may be accepted in one **jurisdiction,** rejected in another, and modified in a third. *3.* A **regulation** made by a group or by an **administrative agency,** often to govern its internal workings.

Rule against accumulations   A state law that prevents a **trust** from storing up money for too long. It is similar to the *rule against perpetuities*. See **perpetuity**.

Rule against perpetuities   See **perpetuity**.

Rule in Shelley's case   See **Shelley's case**.

Rule in Wild's case   See **Wild's case**.

Rule of completeness   See **rule of optional completeness**.

Rule of four   The principle that if at least four of the nine U.S. Supreme Court justices vote to take a case, the court will hear the case. The Court uses the *rule of four* for cases that reach the Court by **certiorari** (see that word).

Rule of law   *1.* A general legal principle, often stated as a maxim or "rule of thumb," that is used as a guide in deciding legal issues. *2.* A general statement that is intended to guide conduct, applied by government officials, and supported by an authoritative source. *3.* The principle that the highest authority is the law, not the government or its leaders.

Rule of lenity   The principle that if it is not clear how greatly a law punishes conduct, a judge should choose the more lenient interpretation.

Rule of marshaling assets (and liens)   See **marshaling** (and **inverse order of alienation**).

Rule of optional completeness   The rule that when one side in a lawsuit uses part of a document (such as a **deposition** transcript) as evidence, the other side may require that the rest of the document be made part of the evidence as well.

Rule of reason   *1.* The principle that actions must be **reasonable** to be legal. *2.* The principle that a conclusion must be based on logical reasoning. *3.* The principle that some kinds of *restrictive trade practices* are not **per se** (see that word) violations of the **Sherman Act** unless the facts of that particular case show that they are an *unreasonable restraint of trade.*

Rule of 78   A method of computing **interest** on a loan, especially on an installment loan that is repaid early. It is calculated as follows: the sum of the months in a year (1–12) is 78. If repayment is made in the first month of a one-year loan, 12/78ths of the total interest must be paid; in the second month, another 11/78ths, etc. This is more than paying 1/12th for each month the money was used.

Rule of 72   A way to calculate how many years of a certain percentage rate of **compound interest** will double an investment (divide the interest into 72 to get the number of years) or what compound interest is needed to double an investment in a certain number of years (divide the number of years into 72 to get the interest).

Rule of the sum of the digits   **Rule of 78.**

Rulemaking   **Legislative** activity by an administrative agency that sets future policy, as opposed to an **adjudication** of past actions.

Rules committee   A **committee** of a **house** of a **legislature** that acts as a preliminary sifting place to decide which **bills** from the various committees will be voted on by the house, and in which order.

Rules (federal)   See **federal rules.**

Rules of Decisions Act   The 1948 federal law (28 U.S.C. 1652) that makes state **substantive law** applicable to federal lawsuits based on **diversity of citizenship.**

Rules of Professional Conduct   **American Bar Association** rules stating and explaining what lawyers must do, must not do, should do, and should not do. They cover the field of *legal ethics* (a lawyer's obligations to clients, courts, other lawyers, and the public) and have been adopted in modified forms by most of the states.

Ruling   A judge's decision on a legal question raised during a trial.

Run   *1.* To have legal validity. For example, the law *runs* throughout the state. *2.* To continue to count. For example, "the *statute of* **limitations** is running" means that days are being counted against the maximum allowable number of days before the statute prohibits a lawsuit. (But see no. 3.) *3.* A specified time period has expired. For example, "*the statute of limitations has run*" means that it has been too long since the acts on which a lawsuit is based for the lawsuit to be permitted. (But see no. 2.) *4.* To be attached to another thing. For example, a **covenant** (see that word) may *run with the land* and stay with the land even if the land's ownership changes.

Runaway shop   A business that closes and moves away to avoid unionization, high union wages, etc.

Running account   An open, as yet unsettled account; a charge account.

Rylands v. Fletcher   The old English case that established the principle of **strict liability** for inherently dangerous things and abnormally dangerous activities.

S *1.* **Section.** *2.* **Statute.** *3.* **Senate.**

S.A. Abbreviation for *incorporated* in French and Spanish. The same as "Inc." after a company's name. See **corporation.**

S.B. *Senate bill.* A **bill** in the process of going through the U.S. Senate.

S.B.A. Small Business Administration. A U.S. agency that provides loans and advice for small businesses.

S.C. *1.* **Supreme Court.** *2.* Same **case.**

S.D. Southern **district.**

S.E. South Eastern Reporter (see **National Reporter System**).

S.E.C. **Securities and Exchange Commission.** See also **securities acts.**

S.E.P. Simplified Employee Pension. An employer's contribution to an employee's **I.R.A.** (Individual Retirement Account) that meets certain federal requirements. Self-employed persons often use a S.E.P.

S.E.S. Senior Executive Service. The federal government's top management.

S.G. **Solicitor General.**

S.I.P.C. Securities Investor Protection Corporation. A semi-private government agency that protects, up to a certain amount, investor accounts in brokerage firms.

S.J.T. **Summary jury trial.**

S.L. *1.* **Session laws.** *2.* **Statute** law.

S.M. **Service** *mark.*

S.P. *1.* **Sine prole.** *2.* Same principle or point.

S.S. *Sworn statement.* A symbol found on many **affidavits.**

S.S.A. Social Security Administration. The U.S. agency that runs the federal program of retirement and disability insurance.

S.S.S. **Selective Service System.**

S.U.B. Supplemental unemployment benefits. Benefits from a private unemployment insurance plan, especially those in addition to state benefits.

S.W. South Western Reporter (see **National Reporter System**).

S.&L. **Savings and Loan Association.**

S corporation   A small (defined by number of owners) business **corporation** that has chosen a tax status that allows it to be taxed essentially as a **partnership** to avoid the **corporate** income tax.

Sabotage   *1.* The intentional destruction of or interference with national defense production, material, or premises. *2.* The intentional destruction of or interference with an employer's property or operations during a **labor dispute** (see that word).

Saenz v. Roe   (119 S.Ct. 1518) The 1999 U.S. Supreme Court decision that a state violates the **privileges and immunities** clause by limiting first-year welfare benefits to what would have been received in the recipient's home state.

Safe harbor   *1.* An approved way of complying with a **statute** when the statute is phrased in general terms. For example, S.E.C. **regulations** (see that word) list ways that are sure to keep you out of trouble when making certain types of stock **offerings** (even though other ways might be legal also). *2.* A statement in a statute or regulation that a **good faith** attempt to comply is sufficient, even if the attempt has failed.

Safe investment rule   *1.* **Prudent person rule.** *2.* A method of calculating **future earnings** by estimating what sum of money, safely invested, would equal the earnings.

Said   An unnecessary word for "the one mentioned before"; for example, "*said table.*" Avoid the phrase because "the" or "this" will usually do.

Sailor's will   See **military will.**

Salary   Fixed annual compensation earned by an employee (often a manager or other professional) and paid weekly, monthly, etc. Compare **wage.**

Sale   *1.* An exchange of property for money (or the contract that expresses the exchange). *2.* For **approval, bootstrap, bulk transfer, consignment, foreclosure, judicial, short,** and other types of *sales,* see those words. *3.* A *sale and return* is a sale in which the buyer may return any unused items if bought for resale; a *sale-note* is a summary of a sale, given by a **broker** to the seller and buyer; and a *sale against the box* is a **short sale** in which the seller actually owns that **stock.** *4.* "*Sales*" is a field of law, now covered primarily by the **Uniform Commercial Code,** which governs the sale of **goods.**

Sales finance company   *1.* A company that buys the rights to **accounts receivable** (money owed by customers to a merchant) at a discount and then tries to collect the debts. *2.* A finance company that specializes in financing **consumer** sales.

Sales tax   A state or local tax on goods sold, equal to a certain percentage of the sale price. It is usually collected by the merchant. Some states tax items (such as cars) at different rates, and some states do not tax some items (such as food) at all. Compare with **excise.**

Salvage   *1.* Property recovered after an accident or other damage or destruction. *2.* Business property that has only scrap value, or, sometimes, business property that is disposed of simply because it has been replaced or is of no further use to the company, whether or not it is still valuable. *3.* Money paid to someone who rescues property from destruction at sea. *4. Equitable salvage* is a **lien** in favor of the last person to make a payment that prevents the loss of property through **lapse, foreclosure,** etc.

Same evidence test   The principle that if exactly the same evidence would **convict** a person in two separate prosecutions, the second prosecution is prohibited because of **double jeopardy.**

Sample   An item representative of other items. A *sale by sample* usually means that the items bought must "conform to" the sample. In commercial law, this may mean "substantially identical," and it may mean "similar and accepted in the trade as of equal quality."

Sanction   *1.* To agree to or confirm another person's actions. *2.* A penalty or punishment attached to a law to make sure it is obeyed.

Sanctions tort   A court-ordered payment by the side in a lawsuit that abused the **discovery** process, made to the side that was hurt by the abuse.

Sandwich lease   A **lease** in which the person who rents a property rerents (sublets) it to another for more money; for example, leasing a shopping center and renting out the stores in it.

Sanitary code   Local laws regulating the cleanliness of places where food is handled or where medical services are provided.

Sanity   *1.* Soundness of mind; the opposite of **insanity** (see that word). *2.* A *sanity hearing* is a court proceeding to determine whether a person is mentally fit to stand trial, is committable to a mental hospital, etc. Also called a **competency proceeding,** a *sanity trial* (where it is a separate proceeding), and other names. *Competency* may be different from *sanity.*

Satellite   Related, but secondary or peripheral.

Satisfaction   *1.* Taking care of a debt or **obligation** by paying it. See also **accord** and *satisfaction. 2.* A *satisfaction contract* is one in which one person promises to do work or supply goods that will satisfy another. "Satisfactory" in this sense does not usually mean "to every personal whim" but "to any reasonable need" or "according to the judgment of an impartial expert." *3.* A *satisfaction* of **judgment, lien,** or **mortgage** is a written document signed by the person paid, stating that an obligation has been paid. A *satisfaction piece* is a written document, made to be recorded, similar to the one above or stating that two sides in a lawsuit have agreed that payments have been made, and the lawsuit should be ended.

Satisfactory A general word for "enough" or "good enough."

Save Hold until later; reserve; preserve.

Save harmless **Hold harmless.**

Saving (or separability or severability) clause *1.* A **clause** in a **statute** (or a **contract**) that states that if part of the statute (or contract) is declared **void,** the remainder stays in effect. See also **severable.** *2.* A clause in a statute that preserves certain rights, responsibilities, or liabilities that are in existence as of the adoption of the statute but would otherwise be lost upon its adoption. Sometimes, a **grandfather clause.**

Saving property rule The little-used principle that a person is liable not only for damage done to an owner's property, but also for the owner's injuries caused by an attempt to save the property.

Saving to suitors clause A federal law (28 U.S.C. 1333) that allows persons to bring **admiralty** (maritime) lawsuits in either a state or federal court, but that requires state courts to use federal **substantive law** for these lawsuits. (Other types of cases that can be brought in either state or federal court must use *state* substantive law in either place.)

Savings and loan association A financial institution, similar to a bank, that historically engaged primarily in making loans to home buyers. They are federally and state-chartered.

Savings bank (or account) trust A **Totten trust.**

Sc. **Scilicet.**

Scab Slang for a person who works for less than union wages, works under conditions prohibited under a union contract, takes the place of a striking union worker, passes through a union picket line, etc.

Scale order See **order.**

Scale-down A **composition.**

Scalper *1.* A small-scale speculator in **stocks, bonds,** theater tickets, etc. See **speculate.** *2.* An investment advisor who buys **securities** such as stocks, and then recommends them without disclosing the fact that a price rise will be to his or her benefit.

Scandal Defamation.

Scènes a faire General ideas or common themes (such as sequences of events that obviously follow from a given situation) that cannot be **copyrighted.** [pronounce: senz ah fair]

Scenic easement A type of government restriction on private land use imposed to preserve natural areas.

Schedule *1.* A list. *2.* A list attached to a document that explains in detail things contained in the document. For example, *scheduled property* is items on a list attached to an **insurance** policy, with the value of each item and what the company will pay if it is lost or hurt. The supporting pages of calculations attached to the main sheet of a **tax return** are called *schedules,* as are the charts for looking up the amount of tax owed.

Scheme *1.* Any general plan or system, especially a *business plan.* *2.* A plan to trick or **defraud** someone. *3.* See **common scheme.**

Schempp v. Abington School District (374 U.S. 203) A 1963 Supreme Court decision that forbade Bible reading and prayer in public school classes.

Schenck v. U.S. See **clear and present danger test.**

Scienter (Latin) Knowingly; with guilty knowledge. [pronounce: si-en-ter]

Scilicet (Latin) "That is to say." An unnecessary word, often used after a general statement to introduce a list of specific examples. [pronounce: sill-is-it]

Scintilla A very little bit. The word is often used in the phrase "a mere scintilla of evidence" ("*is* enough to let the jury decide the case"; "is *not* enough to let the jury decide the case").

Scire facias (Latin) Describes a judge's command to a public official to come to court and explain why a record in that person's possession should not be disclosed, given force, wiped out, etc. [pronounce: si-ree fay-she-es]

Scope of employment The range of actions within which an employee is considered to be doing work for the employer. See **respondeat superior.**

Scope of review The issues a court may handle and the actions it may take when reviewing the decisions of a lower court or administrative agency.

Scorched earth policy A company policy that, in the event of a hostile takeover, it will sell off those assets that make the company attractive for takeover.

Scott v. Sanford   See **Dred Scott case.**

Scrip   A piece of paper that is a temporary indication of a right to something valuable. *Scrip* includes paper money issued for temporary use; partial **shares** of **stock** after a stock split; **certificates** of a deferred stock **dividend** that can be cashed in later, etc.

Script   A manuscript, especially the original copy.

Scrivener   "Writer." An old word for a person who drew up **contracts, deeds,** and other legal papers; also for a person who managed **securities** and investments for a percentage of the profits.

Seal   An identification mark pressed in wax. Originally, for a document to be valid, it had to have a wax seal on it to show that it was done seriously, correctly, and formally. Later, the use of the letters "**L.S.**" took the place of wax. Now, there is little use for a seal, except to formalize certain **corporate** documents and documents witnessed by a **notary public.** See also **sealed** and **contract under seal.**

Sealed   *1. Sealed bidding* is a way of taking offers to do work, supply materials, purchase at auction, etc. Each **bid** is submitted in a sealed envelope; all are opened at the same time, and the best bid is chosen. *2. Sealed records* are a way of keeping some criminal, juvenile, divorce, adoption, etc., records secret unless opened by a court **order.** *3.* A *sealed verdict* is a way of allowing jury members to go home after they have made a decision while the court is out of session. They seal it in an envelope and have it read when the court is in session again. *4. "Sealed and delivered"* are old, now unnecessary, words following the signatures on a **deed.** *5.* A *sealed instrument* is a document that is signed and bears a **seal** (see that word). *6.* See **contract under seal.**

Seaman's will   See **military will.**

Search   *1.* An examination of a person's clothing, car, house, body, etc., by a law officer to discover a weapon or **evidence** of a crime. If done without either **probable cause** or a **search warrant** (or without its being a very limited, necessary search at the time of legal arrest or on suspicion of a concealed weapon), the search may be forbidden by the **Fourth Amendment** to the U.S. Constitution and any evidence obtained excluded from use in a **criminal** trial. *2.* An *administrative (or regulatory) search (or inspection)* is usually done to enforce health or safety laws and **regulations.** An administrative search may not be used to circumvent the stronger **probable cause** requirements of a search for evidence of a crime. *3.* A *title search* is an examination of all proper land records to see who legally owns property and whether there are any **mortgages, liens,** etc., on it.

Search warrant Written permission from a judge or **magistrate** for a police officer (or **sheriff**, etc.) to search a particular place for **evidence**, stolen property, etc. The police must give a good reason for needing these items, a likely reason why they might be in the place they want to search, and some indication that the information on which they are basing their search request is reliable.

Seasonable *1.* In a reasonable amount of time. *2.* Within the agreed time.

Seasoned Having experience. A **stock** is *seasoned* if it has already sold in a stock market, and a company or business venture is *seasoned* when it has been in existence for a while and has made some money.

Seat Capital, or place where the main government offices are located.

Seated land Land that is used in any way (farmed, occupied, etc.).

Seaworthy Describes a ship that is properly constructed, maintained, supplied, and crewed, and with proper instructions from its owners.

Sec. Short for **section.**

Secede Withdraw from membership in a group; break away from a governmental union. The process is called *secession.*

Second Lower ranking; coming later; farther away. For example, a *second degree crime* is less serious than a *first degree crime* (*second degree* **murder** is without **premeditation** so it is less serious than *first degree murder*); a *second mortgage* ranks below a *first mortgage* in its right to be paid; and *secondhand evidence* (not **secondary** *evidence*) is **hearsay** evidence (that has passed through other persons or media to the witness). See also **secondary.**

Second Amendment The U.S. constitutional amendment that grants to the people the right to keep and bear arms. This right has been defined restrictively by state and federal laws.

Second chair Primary assistant lawyer of an in-court legal team.

Second look statute A **wait and see statute.**

Secondary Lower ranking; coming later; farther away. For example, a *secondary distribution or offering* is the sale of a large block of **stock** that is not a new **issue,** but one that has been held by the company or an investment firm; *secondary evidence* (not **second***hand evidence*) such as a photocopy of a document is not as good as *best evidence* (see **best evidence rule**); and *secondary liability* is a duty that does not come due unless someone else fails to perform his or her primary duty. Other "secondary" words follow. See also **second.**

Secondary authority *1.* **Persuasive authority.** *2.* Writings about the law, such as articles, treatises, and encyclopedias.

Secondary boycott   A **boycott** (see that word) aimed at a business that does business with the one a union is actually having a dispute with. *Secondary* **picketing** and *secondary* **strikes** are other types of indirect pressure.

Secondary easement   The right to do what it takes to fully use or maintain an **easement. Implied** rights that go with an easement.

Secondary market   An organized method for buying and selling existing financial documents, such as a stock **exchange** for buying already issued securities or the *secondary mortgage market* in which financial institutions buy and sell existing mortgages.

Secondary meaning   A strong association in the "public mind" between a name and a company's product (or service). To get **trademark** (or **service** *mark*) protection for a name that is a common or *descriptive* one (as opposed to one that is *fanciful* or *arbitrary*), a company must establish a *secondary meaning* through use of the name in connection with the product (or service).

Secret Service   The federal organization that investigates offenses against the currency, **securities,** or banks of the U.S. and protects the president, vice president, ex-presidents, presidential candidates, visiting heads of state, etc.

Secret trust   A **trust** in which the **trustee** gives only a verbal promise to hold the property in trust.

Secretary   *1.* An organization's official record keeper, such as a **corporate** secretary *2.* The head of a government department, such as the *secretary of defense. 3. Secretary general* is the name given to the head of the United Nations and of some other public organizations.

Secretary of state   *1.* In the U.S. government, this is a **cabinet** member who heads the State Department and is in charge of foreign relations. *2.* In most state governments, this is the official who takes care of many types of formal state business, such as the licensing of **corporations.**

Secrete   Hide something away, especially to keep it from **creditors** by putting **title** in someone else's name.

Secta   (Latin) **Lawsuit.**

Section   *1.* A subdivision of a law, regulation, or other document, such as a subdivision of an **article** of the U.S. Constitution or a chapter of a book. Often abbreviated s, sec, or §. *2.* A subdivision of a **township** that is one mile on a side, containing 640 acres. *3.* A subdivision in some **bureaucracies.**

Secundum (Latin) *1.* "According to," as in the phrase *secundum regulam* ("according to the rule"). *2.* **Second.**

Secure To give **security** (see that word). To guarantee the payment of a debt or the keeping of a promise by giving a **mortgage, lien, pledge,** etc.

Secured Protected by a **mortgage, lien, pledge,** or other **security** *interest.* The person whose money is protected is called a "*secured* **creditor**" or "*secured* **party,**" and the deal is called a **security** *agreement.* A *secured transaction* is a *secured* deal involving **goods** or **fixtures** that is governed by Article Nine of the **Uniform Commercial Code.**

Securities *1.* See **security.** *2.* **Stocks, bonds, notes,** or other documents that show a share in a company or a debt owed by a company.

Securities acts Federal and state laws regulating the sale of **securities (stocks, bonds,** etc.). These include the federal *Securities Act of 1933* (which requires the **registration** of securities that are to be sold to the public and the disclosure of complete information to potential buyers); the *Securities and Exchange Act of 1934* (which regulates stock **exchanges** and **over-the-counter** stock sales); the *Uniform Securities Act* (a model law adopted in part by many states); **blue sky laws** (see that word); *broker-dealer provisions* (those parts of the securities laws that regulate those who sell stock on behalf of others); the *Investment Advisors Act* (the federal law that regulates those who give investment advice); etc. Federal securities acts are administered by the **Securities and Exchange Commission.**

Securities and Exchange Commission A federal agency that administers the federal **securities acts** (see that word), primarily by regulating the sale and trading of stocks and other securities.

Securities Investor Protection Corporation See **S.I.P.C.**

Securitize Turn *assets* (such as mortgage loans) into *asset-backed securities* (such as bonds) by transferring them to a special trust or organization that pools them together, then reissues them in changed form to sell to investors.

Security *1.* Property that has been pledged, mortgaged, etc., as financial backing for a loan or other obligation. A *security interest* is any right in property that is held to make sure money is paid or that something is done. Most property **secured** this way may be sold by the **creditor** if the debt it backs is not paid. *2.* A person who is a **surety** or gives a **guaranty** (see those words). *3.* A share of **stock,** a **bond,** a **note,** or one of many different kinds of documents showing a share in a company or a debt owed by a company or a government. There are different technical definitions of *security* in the various **securities acts,** the **Uniform Commercial Code,** the *Uniform Probate Code,* the *Federal Bankruptcy Act,* the *Internal Revenue Code,* etc. The U.S. Supreme Court has defined a security as any investment in a common enterprise from which the investor is "led to expect profits solely from the efforts of a promoter or a third party." *4.* For **assessable, equity, hybrid, listed,** etc., *security,* see those words.

Security Council The **executive** body of the United Nations. It has eleven members from eleven countries with five permanent members, including the U.S.

Security deposit Money paid by a **tenant** to a landlord and held in trust as **security** for the tenant's obligations under the lease (including the tenant's duty to refrain from damaging the property and to pay rent).

Security for costs Money, property, or a **bond** given to a court to pay **costs** in case you lose. This is sometimes done, for example, when the **plaintiff** is from another state.

Sed vide (Latin) "But see." A reference to something that conflicts with the statement just made.

Sedition Stirring up persons to armed resistance against the government. [pronounce: se-<u>dish</u>-un]

Seditious libel Publishing something to stir up class hatred or contempt for the government. The **First Amendment** invalidated *seditious libel* laws in the U.S.

Seduction Inducing (usually by deception or promise to marry) a person (usually a chaste, unmarried woman) to have sex. Most states have **heart-balm acts** that prohibit lawsuits and prosecutions based on *seduction.*

Segment search A search restricted to part of a **database.**

Segregation *1.* The separation of property into groups. *Segregation of assets* involves identifying and setting aside the property belonging to one person from a common fund or pot. *2.* The **unconstitutional** practice of separating persons in housing, schooling, and public accommodation, based on race, color, nationality, etc.

Seisin Full and complete present ownership and possession of land. Someone with *seisin* is "*seised.*" [pronounce: seez-in]

Seize *1.* See **seisin.** *2.* See **seizure.**

Seizure *1.* The act by a public official (usually a **peace officer**) of taking property because of a violation of the law, because of a **writ** or **judgment** in a lawsuit, or because the property will be needed as **evidence** in a criminal case. *2.* The act of a peace officer taking a person into

custody and detaining the person in a way that interferes with freedom of movement. See also **Fourth Amendment.**

Select committee   A **legislative** *committee* set up for a limited time and purpose. Compare with **standing** *committee.*

Select council   The upper branch of some city councils, corresponding to the **senate** in state or U.S. government.

Selective prosecution   Prosecuting fewer than all the persons who are guilty of a crime. This may violate the **equal protection** rights of those prosecuted.

Selective Service System   The federal agency that handles registration for compulsory military service and selects those to serve during times when a draft is used to supplement voluntary recruitment.

Selective tax   A sales or use tax on particular items, such as tobacco products.

Selectperson (man, woman)   A member of some local **legislatures** or town councils. When a town is too small to have a mayor, the role of mayor may be taken by the *first selectperson.*

Self-authentication (or self-proving)   Proof that a document is genuine, contained within the document. For example, many states allow a will to be *self-authenticated* if a **notary public,** two witnesses, and the will-maker all sign at the same time and place. This avoids the need to present testimony or other evidence that the will is genuine. Some official documents need not be authenticated to be used as evidence.

Self-dealing   A **trustee** (or other person with a **fiduciary** duty) acting to help himself or herself, rather than the person for whom he or she is supposed to be working.

Self-defense   Physical force used against a person who is threatening the use of physical force or using physical force. This is a right if your own family, property, or body is in danger, but sometimes only if the danger was not provoked. Also, deadly force may (usually) be used only against deadly force. See also **true person doctrine** and **flee to the wall doctrine.**

Self-employment tax   The Social Security tax on the earnings of self-employed persons.

Self-executing   Describes laws or court decisions that require no further official action to be carried out.

Self-help   Taking an action yourself without obtaining official help or authorization when that action may need authorization. For example, a *self-help eviction* may be a **landlord's** removing the **tenant's** property from an apartment and locking the door against the tenant. In many states, some forms of *self-help* are illegal.

Self-incrimination   Anything said or done by a person that implicates the person in a crime. It is **unconstitutional** to force or require a person to do this or to be a **witness** *against self,* except in limited circumstances such as when a **criminal** defendant voluntarily **takes the stand** to **testify.**

Self-insurance   Setting aside a fund of money to pay for future losses (rather than purchasing an insurance policy to cover possible losses) or merely not providing for such losses at all.

Self-liquidation   Paying off a loan by the short-term sale of the items bought with the loan money. For example, a loan to a car dealer might *self-liquidate* through the sale of the cars bought by the dealer with borrowed money.

Self-proving   See **self-authentication.**

Self-serving declaration   An out-of-court statement by a **party** to a lawsuit that, if admitted as **evidence** in the lawsuit, would tend to be helpful to the party. *Self-serving declarations* are usually inadmissible **hearsay.**

Selling short   See **short sale.**

Semble   (French) "It seems that." An introduction to an uncertain point of law.

Senate   The upper **house** of a state or of the U.S. **legislature.** The members are *senators.*

Senatorial courtesy   The informal right of U.S. senators to have the **Senate** reject presidential nominations for judges and other important federal jobs within the senator's state.

Senior interest   An **interest** or right that takes effect or that collects ahead of others; for example, a *senior mortgage* has preference or priority over all others.

Senior judge   Either the judge who has served on a court the longest or a judge who takes "semi-retirement," accepting special assignments.

Seniority   Preference or priority; often, but not always, given because the person or thing came first in time.

Sentence   *1.* The punishment, such as time in jail, given to a person convicted of a crime. The process is called *sentencing* and is usually done by the trial judge, but sometimes by a jury or a *sentencing council* of judges. *2.* A *determinate, fixed, straight,* or *flat sentence* is an exact penalty set by law. A *mandatory sentence* is a determinate sentence that cannot be suspended and that does not allow the judge to order **probation.** An *indeterminate sentence* is one having a minimum and maximum, with the decision of how long the criminal will serve depending on the criminal's behavior in prison and other things. *3.* For **concurrent** and **cumulative** *sentences,* see those words.

Separability clause   See **saving clause** and **severable.**

Separable controversy rule   The principle that even if only one claim (out of several in some lawsuits in state courts) is of the type that can be removed to a federal court, the whole case can be removed. The federal judge may then decide whether to keep the whole case or only that one claim.

Separate but equal doctrine   The rule, established in the 1896 Supreme Court case **Plessy v. Ferguson** and then rejected as **unconstitutional** in the 1954 **Brown decision,** that when races are given substantially equal facilities, they may lawfully be segregated.

Separate estate (or property)   The property owned by a person as an individual, rather than owned jointly as a partner in a business or marriage.

Separate maintenance   **Alimony** or **support** paid by one married person to the other if they are no longer living as husband and wife. In some states, this term refers to only *temporary* alimony or support.

Separate sovereigns   The rule that the constitutional protection against **double jeopardy** does not apply to prosecutions by two different states or by a state and the federal government.

Separation   *1.* A husband and wife living apart by agreement, either *before* a **divorce** or *instead of* a full divorce. A formal *separation* is sometimes called a *divorce a mensa et thoro* (a "divorce" "from bed and board" only). There is often a *separation agreement,* a document about child **custody, support, alimony,** property division, etc. If it is by **order** of a court, it is a *judicial* or *legal separation. 2. Separation of powers* is the division of the federal government (and state governments) into **legislative** (law making), **judicial** (law interpreting), and **executive** (law carrying-out) branches. Each acts to prevent the others from becoming too powerful. *3. Separation of witnesses* is a court **order** that **witnesses** stay out of the courtroom unless called to **testify.** Separation of witnesses usually occurs upon a request by one of the lawyers to invoke *"the rule on witnesses." 4. Separation of church and state* is a combination of the requirements of the **establishment clause** and **free exercise clause** of the **First Amendment** to the U.S. **Constitution.** See **freedom of religion.**

Sequester To isolate, hold aside, or take away. For example, to *sequester* a **jury** is to keep it from having any contacts with the outside world during a trial, and to *sequester property* is to have it put aside and held by an independent person during a lawsuit. This process is called *sequestration* and may also apply to such things as the judicial **impounding** of a bank account and the governmental taking of property belonging to citizens of another country with which the first country is at war.

Sergeant-at-arms A person appointed to keep order in a **legislature,** court, or large meeting.

Serial bonds Groups of **bonds** put out at the same time, but with different cash-in times for each group. *Not* **series bonds.**

Serial note A **promissory note** that is paid back in **installments.**

Serial right The right to publish a book by installments in, for example, a magazine.

Seriatim (Latin) One at a time; in proper or logical order.

Series A set of lawbooks in numerical order. A new (second, third, etc.) *series* follows, not replaces, an older one.

Series bonds Groups of **bonds** put out at different times with different cash-in times, but all part of the same deal. *Not* **serial bonds.**

Servant A person employed by another person and subject to that person's control as to *what* work is done and *how* it is done. An employee is called a *servant* and an employer is called a **master** in the law of **agency** and of **negligence.**

Service *1.* The delivery (or its legal equivalent, such as publication in a newspaper in some cases) of a legal paper, such as a **writ,** by an authorized person in a way that meets certain formal requirements. It is the way to notify a person of a **lawsuit.** *2.* Regular payments on a debt. The process is called *servicing* the debt or *debt service. 3. Service charges* for **consumer credit** include all costs that have anything to do with the credit no matter what they are for or what they are called. These include *time-price differentials,* credit investigations, **carrying charges,** creditor insurance, etc. *4. Service establishments* include any place that sells services to the public (barbershops, laundries, auto repair shops, etc.). *5.* The *service life* of property is how long it should be useful. This is not necessarily the same as its **depreciable life.** *6.* A *service mark* is a mark used in the sale or advertising of services (including such things as the character names on television programs), usually to identify the service by a distinctive design, title, character, etc.; for example, Lazy Transport Company's federally protected service mark *"Slotruk Service ®."* See also **trademark.**

Servient Describes land subject to a **servitude** (see that word).

Servitude *1.* A **charge** or burden on land in favor of another. For example, the owner of a piece of land may be required by the **deed** to allow the owner of adjoining land to walk across a part of the land. This type of *servitude* is called an **easement.** The land so restricted is the *servient estate* and the land (if any) benefiting from the restriction is the **dominant** *estate. 2.* The condition of being a slave or servant.

Session Either a day or a period of days in which a court, a **legislature,** etc., carries on its business.

Session laws **Statutes** printed in the order that they were passed in each session of a **legislature.** See also **statutes at large.**

Set aside *1.* Cancel, **annul,** or **revoke** a court's **judgment.** *2.* Keep potential cropland out of production to conserve soil and stabilize crop prices. *3.* Describes any program of saving **assets** for future use. *4.* Reserve a portion of something for one specific use.

Set down Put a case on the list (or court **docket**) for a **hearing.**

Set of exchange An original and copies of a foreign **bill** *of exchange.*

Set up Raise an issue, such as a specific **defense,** or present the facts and law needed to raise the issue.

Setback A distance from a street, property line, building, etc., within which building is prohibited by **zoning** laws, **building codes,** etc.

Setoff A defendant's **counterclaim** that has nothing to do with the plaintiff's lawsuit against the defendant.

Setting The date and time of a court hearing.

Settle *1.* To come to an agreement about a price, a debt, payment of a debt, or disposition of a lawsuit. *2.* Finish up; take care of completely. *3.* Transfer property in a way that specifies a succession of owners. *4.* Set up a **trust.**

Settlement *1.* See **settle.** A *settlement workup (or brochure)* is a summary of facts designed to get the other side to settle a case. *2.* The meeting in which the ownership of real **property** actually transfers from seller to buyer. All payments and debts are usually adjusted and taken care of at this time or immediately thereafter. These financial matters are written on a *settlement sheet,* which is also known as a **closing** *statement.*

Settlor A person who sets up a **trust** by providing the money or property for it.

Seventeenth Amendment   The U.S. **constitutional** amendment that changed the election of senators from a vote by state **legislature** to a vote directly by the people.

Seventh Amendment   The U.S. **constitutional** amendment that guarantees a **jury** trial in most federal **civil** cases.

Sever   Cut off or separate into parts. For example, to *sever* the trial of a person from others who might otherwise be in the same trial is to **try** that person's case separately and at another time. The process is often called *severance.*

Severability clause   See **saving clause.**

Severable   Capable of carrying on an independent existence. For example, a *severable statute* is one that can still be valid even if one part of it is struck down as **invalid** by a court. A *severable contract* is one that can be divided into separate contracts, each valid even if the other is not. Some **statutes** and **contracts** have a **saving clause** (see that word). See also **divisible.**

Several   *1.* More than one. *2.* Separate, individual, independent. See also **joint and several.**

Severally   Distinctly; separately; each on its own.

Severalty ownership   Sole ownership; ownership by one person.

Severance   Separation. For example, *severing* (separating) **joint** rights in property into individual rights to pieces of it, harvesting crops or taking minerals from land, ending a person's employment, separating the **claims** of various **parties** in a lawsuit, etc.

Severance tax   A tax on the volume or value of a **natural resource** (oil, coal, etc.) taken from the land.

Sewer service   Slang for the practice of telling the court that you have properly served (officially delivered) a court paper when it has actually been thrown away.

Sex discrimination   See **discrimination.**

Sexual abuse, battery, or assault   See **rape.**

Sexual harassment   In a narrow sense, using a position of power over a person's job, salary, etc., to gain sexual favors or punish the refusal of such favors. More broadly, sexual harassment includes unwarranted sexual innuendoes, maintaining a workplace where employees feel sexually threatened, etc.

Shadow jury   A group of persons (selected to be similar to the real jurors) paid by one side in a lawsuit to observe the trial and give their reactions.

Shadow stock   **Phantom stock.**

Shall   *1.* Must. *2.* May, should, will, or can, but *only* if these alternative meanings to *must* are clear from the surrounding words.

Sham   False or fake. For example, a *sham pleading* is a court paper that is formally correct, but that is so clearly false as to the facts that it is rejected, and a *sham transaction* is one that is disregarded by the **I.R.S.** because it was done *solely* for tax advantage. Compare with **simulate.**

Share   *1.* A portion. *2.* One unit of **stock** in a **corporation.** *3.* A *share certificate* (or *warrant*) is a document certifying that a person is entitled to own (or buy) a certain number of shares of stock.

Shared equity   A **real estate** purchase arrangement in which an investor puts up part of the purchase price and pays part of the **mortgage** in exchange for tax benefits and a share of the eventual profits of a sale.

Shareholder   A person who owns **stock** in a corporation.

Shark repellant   An action (such as a **bylaws** change or implementing a **scorched earth policy**) taken to make a company less attractive for, or susceptible to, a hostile takeover.

Sharp   Quickly and easily collectible. A **mortgage** or other **security** document is *sharp* if it allows the **creditor** to take quick **summary** action to collect if the debtor fails to pay.

Shaving   A slang expression for buying **notes** or other **securities** at a discount; for cutting prices secretly to a few persons; for illegally holding down the score in a sporting event to help certain bettors; or for using **extortion** to get something.

Shelf registration   **Securities and Exchange Commission** approval of a stock sale **registration** (see that word) with a delayed sale.

Shell company   A company with no stated business or a company with no business at all. Sale of stock (usually **penny stock**) in a *shell company* is called a *blank-check offering* because the company has a free hand to do almost anything it wants to do with the money.

Shelley's Case   The *Rule in Shelley's Case* is that when a **life estate** is given to a person, followed by a **remainder** given to **heirs,** the heirs take nothing, but the holder of the life estate gets an interest in **fee** (see those words). For example, under the rule, if John gives land to Sue to use for life and, in the same document, gives it to someone else after that and then to Sue's children, Sue gets it all to do with as she pleases. This rule is *no longer followed*; life estates and remainders *are* permitted.

Shelter *1.* Describes the principle that a buyer has as good a **title** to property as the seller had. For example, under the U.C.C. *shelter doctrine,* the *holder* of a **negotiable instrument** has the rights of a **holder in due course** if the person who sold the instrument was a holder in due course. *2.* A way of investing money to gain tax advantage. *3.* For *shelter trust,* see **bypass trust.**

Shepardizing Using a Shepard's **citator** (see that word) to trace the history of a case *after* it is decided to see if it is **followed, overruled, distinguished,** etc.

Sheriff The chief law officer of a county, who, with the help of deputies, is in charge of serving **process,** calling **jurors,** keeping the peace, executing **judgments,** operating a county jail, etc.

Sheriff's deed A document giving ownership rights to property sold at a *sheriff's sale* (a sale held by a **sheriff** to pay a court **judgment** against the owner of the property).

Sheriff's jury An old form of a **coroner's** inquest.

Sherman Act (15 U.S.C. 1) The first **antitrust** (antimonopoly) law, passed by the federal government in 1890 to break up *combinations in restraint of trade.*

Shield law *1.* A state law that protects ("shields") a writer's sources of information. *2.* A law that protects a government informer's sources or protects anonymity. *3.* A state law that prohibits use of most **evidence** of a rape (or other sexual crime) victim's past sexual conduct, or that protects the victim's identity.

Shifting Changing; varying; passing from one person to another. For example, *shifting income* is transferring income but not ownership from the person who owns the property that is earning the income to someone else, usually a family member who is in a lower tax bracket. The **I.R.S.** rarely allows a tax advantage gained by *shifting income.*

Shipping *1.* Transporting goods for a charge. *Shipping documents* include **bills of lading, letters of credit,** etc. *2.* Having to do with ships or moving goods by sea. *Shipping articles* are a written agreement between a sailor and the ship's master concerning the voyage, the pay, etc.

Shop right rule The principle that if an employee gets a **patent** on an invention worked on during work hours and using the employer's materials, the employer has a right to *use* the invention for free, but the employee owns the patent.

Shop steward A **union** official elected to represent workers and collect dues in one department of a business.

Shop-book rule   An older, more limited version of the **business records exception** (see that word) in **evidence** law.

Short cause (or short calendar)   A lawsuit, or part of a lawsuit, that must be heard by a judge, but is usually scheduled early because it can be disposed of quickly.

Short sale   A **contract** for the sale of something, such as a stock, that the seller does not own. It is a method of profiting from the expected fall in price of a stock, but is risky because if the stock goes up the person will have to buy at whatever price it reaches to *cover* the short sale. A person is called *short* or in a *short position* if he or she owns less of a **stock,** a **commodity,** or a **futures** *contract* than may be needed to meet future obligations. The number of shares *short* is called the *short interest.*

Short summons   A **summons** that may bring a **debtor** to court quickly if the court agrees that the debtor may run away or fraudulently dispose of property.

Short-swing profits   Profits made by a company **insider** on the **short-term** sale of company **stock.**

Short-term   Less than a week, less than six months, less than a year, etc., as defined by various **statutes.** For example, *short-term* **capital** *gains* are increases in value of property held less than a year that may be taxed as ordinary income.

Short-term trust   A **Clifford trust.**

Shotgun charge   An **Allen charge.**

Show cause order   A court **order** to a person to show up in court and explain why the court should not take a proposed action. If the person fails to show up or to give sufficient reasons why the court should take no action, the court will take the action.

Shower   A person who takes a **jury** to a crime scene, an accident scene, or other place and *shows* them things.

Show-up   A pretrial identification procedure in which only one suspect and a **witness** are brought together. Compare with **lineup.**

Shut-in royalty   Money paid to keep a mineral **lease** active when nothing is being produced.

Shyster   Slang for a dishonest lawyer.

Si   (Latin) If.

Sic   (Latin) Thus; so; in such a way. (Usually used in parentheses after a misspelled word quoted exactly from the original source.)

Sidebar conference   An in-court discussion among lawyers and the judge that is out of the hearing of witnesses and the jury. Sidebar conferences are usually *on the* **record**.

Sight   *At sight* means **payable** when shown and requested. A **bill** or **draft** payable when shown is a *sight bill* or *sight draft*. *Sight drafts* can be sent by a seller to a new, faraway buyer's bank. When the buyer tells the bank to pay the draft, the ownership documents for the goods are given to the buyer.

Signature   *1.* A hand-signed name. *2.* In some commercial situations, any mark that normally serves as a hand-signed name. *3.* A *signature loan* is an un**secured** (see that word) loan given to a creditworthy borrower who promises to repay the loan. *4.* A *signatory* is any **party** to a signed agreement. *5.* A criminal's recurring method of committing crimes.

Silent partner   See **partner.**

Silent witness theory   The principle that once a photograph has been fully authenticated, the photograph can stand alone as **substantive evidence** of what it shows rather than be limited to use as **demonstrative evidence** in conjunction with **testimony.**

Silver platter   Describes the use by federal officials of **evidence** that was gathered illegally by state officials. This is no longer permitted.

Simple   *1.* Pure, unmixed, or uncomplicated. For example, *simple interest* is **interest** paid on an amount of money invested, borrowed, etc. ("the principal"), but not on any earnings or interest that accumulate (compound interest). *2.* Not aggravated. (See **aggravated assault.**) *3.* A *simple contract* was one not under **seal** (see that word and see **contract under seal**). A *simple trust* is a **trust,** benefiting an individual, that pays out the income as it is made instead of either accumulating the income or reducing the trust **corpus.**

Simulate   Take on the appearance of; imitate; fake. For example, a *simulated sale* is a fake sale to make it look to **creditors** as if the property is out of their reach. This is also called a *fraudulent conveyance* and will not be recognized by a court. Compare with **sham.**

Simultaneous death act   A law, adopted in most states, that if there is no **evidence** as to who died first in an accident, each dead person's property will pass as if that person survived longer. Some state laws create a **presumption** that the younger, healthier, etc., person lived longer. See also **common disaster.**

Sine   (Latin) Without. For example, *sine die* means "without day," which describes a final ending or **adjournment** of a **session** of a court or a **legislature.** [pronounce: si-ne dee-A]

Sine prole   (Latin) "Without children"; abbreviated *s.p.*

Sine qua non   (Latin) A thing or condition that is indispensable.

Single juror charge   A judge's **instruction** to a jury that if even one **juror** does not agree that the **plaintiff** should get something, the plaintiff gets nothing.

Single name paper   A **negotiable instrument** (see that word) that has only one **maker** (original signer) or, if more than one original signer, persons signing for exactly the same purpose (for example, as **partners**). This is opposed to **accommodation paper** (where one person signs as a favor to another) or a **surety**ship (where, usually for a fee, one person cosigns to back up another person's debt).

Single proprietorship   An unincorporated business owned by one person. It is also called a *sole proprietorship.*

Single publication rule   The principle that if a person sues for **libel,** the number of copies of the book or magazine containing the libelous statement may influence the dollar *amount* of **damages,** but multiple copies may not normally be the basis for multiple lawsuits.

Sinking fund   Money or other **assets** put aside for a special purpose, such as to pay off **bonds** and other long-term debts as they come due or to replace, repair, or improve machinery or buildings when they wear out or become outdated.

Sister corporations   Two (or more) companies with the same or mostly the same owners. Compare with **interlocking directorate.**

Sistren   "Sisters" or female colleagues on a court. "Colleagues" is more usual.

Sit   *1.* Hold court as a judge. *2.* Hold any session of a court, **legislature,** etc.; to be formally organized and carry on official business.

Sit-down strike (or stay-in strike)   A **strike** during which employees refuse to leave the job site and refuse to work.

Sitting   In **session;** meeting; carrying on official business.

Situs   (Latin) Site or fixed location; place. Usually the place where a thing has legal ties.

Sixteenth Amendment   The U.S. **constitutional** amendment, ratified in 1913, that gave the U.S. Congress the power to tax income.

Sixth Amendment   The U.S. **constitutional** amendment that gives those accused of a crime various rights, such as the right to a prompt public trial by an impartial **jury,** the right to know the accusation, the right to confront **witnesses,** the right to a lawyer's help, etc.

Sixty-day notice   Describes the federal requirement that both employers and unions must give a notice sixty days before reopening or ending a labor contract. During this time **strikes** and **lockouts** are prohibited.

Skeleton bill   A **bill** *of exchange* written or signed **in blank** (see those words).

Skip   *1.* Slang for a person who has "skipped" or cannot be found. A *skiptracer* is a detective service that finds missing debtors, heirs, witnesses, etc. *2.* A person more than one generation after another when a generation has been "skipped" in transferring a property **interest.**

Slander   Oral **defamation.** The speaking of false words that injure another person's reputation, business, or property rights.

Slating   Booking.

Slayer's rule   The principle that a killer cannot inherit from a victim.

Sleeping partner   *Silent* **partner.**

Slip decision (or slip sheet or slip opinion)   A printed copy of a U.S. Supreme Court **decision** (or certain other court decisions) that is distributed immediately.

Slip law   A printed copy of a **bill** passed by Congress that is distributed immediately once signed by the president.

Small business   A general word for a company that has few employees, a low sales volume, few **stock**holders, etc. The definition differs, depending on who (Small Business Administration, the I.R.S., etc.) defines it.

Small claims court   A state court that handles only cases for which the **damages** sought are under a certain monetary limit (often about one thousand dollars). These courts have a more streamlined procedure, faster action, and fewer formalities than regular courts have. They were originally set up to help the "little person" get a day in court, but are mostly used by stores and collection companies to collect overdue bills. Not all places have *small claims courts.*

Small loan acts   State laws setting maximum interest rates on **consumer** loans or on small short-term loans.

Smart money   *1.* Slang for *punitive* **damages.** *2.* Money profitably invested, especially if invested based on inside information. See **insider.**

Smorgasbord plan   A **cafeteria plan.**

Smuggling   The crime of secretly bringing into or taking out of a country things that are either prohibited or taxable.

So.   Short for Southern Reporter (see **National Reporter System**).

Social contract theory   The theory that the only legitimate basis for the existence of a government is the consent of those governed.

Social Security Administration   A federal agency, set up by the *Social Security Act* and the *Federal Insurance Contribution Act (FICA),* that administers a national **Old Age, Survivors, and Disability Insurance** program and other **insurance** and **welfare** programs.

Socialism   A government system in which many of the means of production and trade are owned or run by the government and in which many human welfare needs are provided directly by the government. *Socialism* may be democratic, or it may be a form of **absolutism.**

Societé   (French) *1.* **Society.** *2.* A **partnership.** *3.* A *societé anonyme* is a **corporation.**

Society   *1.* Any group of persons organized for a common purpose. Often an unincorporated business. *2.* The love, care, companionship, help, and earning power of a family member. See also **consortium.**

Sodomy   A general word for an "unnatural" sex act or the crime committed by such act. While the definition varies, *sodomy* can include oral sex, anal sex, homosexual sex, or sex with animals.

Soil bank   Describes a federal program in which farmers are paid to keep cropland idle or in noncrop use to preserve the soil and make crop surpluses less likely.

Soldiers' and Sailors' Civil Relief Act   (50 U.S.C. 501) A 1991 federal law that suspends or modifies a military person's **civil** liabilities, or requires persons who want to enforce their **claims** against persons in the service to follow certain procedures.

Soldier's will   See **military will.**

Sole   Single, individual, or separate. For example, a *sole proprietorship* is an unincorporated business owned by one person.

Sole actor doctrine   The rule that a **principal** (such as an employer) will be held legally responsible for knowing what his or her **agent** (such as an employee) knows and for what that agent does.

Solemn   Formal, correct, and serious. To *solemnize* is to perform a formal ceremony, and *solemnity of contract* is the principle that any **contract** is enforceable, no matter how seemingly unfair, if it is correctly formalized (and there are no **defenses,** such as fraud, illegality, or unconscionability).

Solicitation   *1.* Asking for; enticing; strongly requesting. This may be a crime if the thing being urged is a crime. *2.* A lawyer's drumming up business in too aggressive a way. This is prohibited by the lawyer's **Rules of Professional Conduct.**

Solicitor   *1.* A lawyer in England who handles all legal matters except trial work (which is done by a **barrister**). *2.* The name for the head lawyer for many towns and other government bodies. *3.* A person who seeks business or contributions.

Solicitor general The second-ranking U.S. government lawyer, in charge of all **civil** suits involving the U.S.

Solidarity A contract with **joint and several** (see that word) liability on one or both sides.

Solvency *1.* The ability to pay debts as they come due. *2.* Having more **assets** than **liabilities.**

Solvent See **solvency.**

Son of Sam law A law that prevents a convicted criminal from profiting by selling story rights. These state laws, intended to compensate victims, have been greatly restricted on **First Amendment** grounds.

Sophisticated (or accredited) investor A person who has the background and knowledge to understand what he or she is getting into when buying shares in a business venture. Some **stock** sales can avoid S.E.C. **registration** and **disclosure** requirements by selling to only *sophisticated investors* who can afford the investment in a *private* **offering.**

Sound *1.* Whole; in good condition; healthy. *2.* "*Sounds in*" means "relates to" or "is primarily." For example, a lawsuit *sounds in damages* if the only **remedy** requested is **damages** (money), as opposed to other remedies such as *specific* **performance.** ("Sounds in" is sometimes used to mean that the *facts* presented by a **plaintiff** can support only one possible remedy, so the lawsuit "sounds in" that remedy.)

Sovereign immunity The government's freedom from being sued. In many cases, the U.S. government has **waived** immunity by a **statute** such as the Federal Tort Claims Act. See also **government instrumentality doctrine.**

Speaker The chairperson or head of a **legislative** body, such as the *speaker* of the U.S. **House of Representatives.**

Speaking Bringing up matters that are not found within the legal papers of the case. This was not previously allowed (such things as *speaking demurrers* and *speaking motions* were prohibited), but bringing up new matters is now usually permitted by the *Federal Rules of Civil Procedure.*

Special *1.* Limited. For example, a *special indorsement* is the signing over of something to one particular person; and a court of *special jurisdiction* can handle only limited matters, such as **probate** cases. *2.* Unusual; not regular. For example, a *special session* is an extra meeting of a court or **legislature.** *3.* For *special* **court martial, mas-**

ter, partner, verdict, etc., see those words. Some other "special" words follow.

Special act (or law)   A **private law.**

Special appearance   Showing up in court for a limited purpose only, especially to argue that the court lacks **jurisdiction** (see that word) over you or your client. *Special appearances* have been replaced in federal courts and many state courts by **motions** or **pleadings** for the same purpose.

Special assessment   A **real estate** tax that singles out certain landowners to pay for *special benefits* (improvements such as a sidewalk that will, at least in theory, benefit all of those owners, but not the rest of the taxpayers).

Special damages   See **consequential damages.**

Special exception   *1.* See special use permit. *2.* An **exception** (see that word) based on the wording, rather than the content, of an opponent's claim.

Special facts rule   The rule that corporate **insiders** must reveal certain types of financial and ownership information to stockholders, especially when fairness would be served by revealing the information.

Special interest   A group with members who share a common goal or interest, especially a group that lobbies the government to influence the passage or enforcement of laws.

Special interrogatories   Written questions asked by a judge to a **jury** to see if the jury's answers conflict with the jury's **verdict.**

Special law   A **private law.**

Special pleading   See **pleading.**

Special trust   Any **trust** that is either a **ministerial** *trust* or a **discretionary trust** (see those words).

Special use permit (or permit of exception)   Government permission to use property in a way that is allowed by **zoning** rules, but only with a permit. (This is *not* a **variance.**)

Special use valuation   The valuation of **real estate,** especially of farmland, according to its current use as opposed to its **highest and best use.** *Special use valuation* is sometimes allowed when calculating **estate tax.**

Special warranty deed   *1.* A **deed** (having fewer promises and protections than a **general warranty deed**) that includes the formal, written promise to protect the buyer against claims of ownership of the property that are based on relationships with or transfers from the seller. *2.* The same as a **quitclaim deed** (see that word) in a few states.

Specialist *1.* Generally, a person with expertise in a particular field; often, a person who has been **board certified.** *2.* A member of a securities **exchange** who is assigned the duty of fair **market making** in a particular stock or other **security.**

Specialty *1.* A **contract under seal.** *2.* A building that can be used only for limited purposes unless greatly modified.

Specie *1.* Coins, especially gold and silver coins. *2. In specie performance* of a **contract** means doing exactly what the contract says to do; and return of an item *in specie* means return of the exact, not a similar or replacement, item.

Specific Exact. For example, *specific intent* is an intent to commit the exact crime charged, not merely a general intent to commit some crime or merely a generally guilty mind; and a *specific bequest* is a gift in a **will** of a precisely identifiable object such as "the family Bible."

Specific performance See **performance.**

Specification *1.* A detailed description or list of particulars, such as the list of things a soldier is accused of in a military trial or the "description of the invention" part of a **patent** application. *2.* Changing raw material into a product (such as grapes into wine), with the effect that **title** to the raw materials passes, and the owner of the raw materials is left with only financial rights (such as the right to sue for their value if the raw materials were not paid for).

Spectrograph A machine used to produce **voice prints** (see that word).

Speculate *1.* Make a risky (*speculative*) investment in the hopes of making a big profit. A person who does this is a *speculator. 2.* Conjecture; theorizing. *Speculation* is usually accepted in a trial only from **expert witnesses** and only in limited ways.

Speculative damages **Damages** that will *not* be awarded by a court because they are based on possible, but unlikely future events. Contrast **future damages.**

Speech In regard to **freedom of speech:** speaking, writing, gesturing, and any other way of communicating ideas. See also **symbolic speech.**

Speech or debate clause The provision of the U.S. **Constitution** (Article I, Section 6, Clause 1) that protects U.S. senators and congressmen against suits and arrests for almost everything they say in the legislative chambers.

Speedy trial   A trial free from unreasonable delay. A trial conducted according to regular rules as to timing; not necessarily a fast trial or a trial as soon as you want one. The federal government has a *Speedy Trial Act* (18 U.S.C. 3162 (1975)) to implement this **Sixth Amendment** requirement in **criminal** cases. Many states have similar laws.

Spendthrift   A person who spends money wildly and whose property the state may allow a **trustee** to look after. This protection of a person's property against himself, herself, or **creditors** is called a *spendthrift trust*. These trusts are also set up privately through **wills** and **trusts** to enable one person to give money or property to another without fear that it will be squandered.

Spin-off   A new **corporation** created from an existing corporation that sets up and funds the new corporation and gives the **shares** of the new corporation to the old corporation's stockholders. The process is also called a *spin-off*. Compare with **split-off** and **split-up.**

Spirit   Broad purpose or meaning. See **letter** for contrast and details. Also see **liberal construction.**

Split   See the following words and see **stock split.**

Split action   A lawsuit to recover only part of a single claim. When this is done, the rest of the claim usually may not be raised in a second lawsuit.

Split decision   An **appellate** court decision with at least one **dissent**ing judge. Also see **opinion.**

Split income   Allowing a married couple to pay taxes as if each earned his or her income separately or as if each earned half the total income separately.

Split order   See **order.**

Split sentence   A criminal **sentence** in which one part is enforced and another part is not.

Split-off   A new **corporation** created from an existing corporation that sets up and funds the new corporation and gives the **shares** of the new corporation to the old corporation's stockholders in exchange for some of their shares in the old corporation. The process is also called a *split-off*. Compare with **spin-off** and **split-up.**

Split-up   The process of dividing a **corporation** into two or more separate new corporations, giving its shareholders the shares of these new corporations, and then going out of business. Compare with **spin-off** and **split-off.**

Spoliation   *1.* Destruction by an outsider; for example, alteration of a check by someone who has nothing to do with it. *2.* The failure by one side in a trial to come forward with **evidence** in its possession (and the inferences that the other side may ask the judge and jury to draw from this failure). *3.* Destruction of evidence. *4.* Violent and illegal seizure of property.

Spontaneous statement (or declaration or exclamation) rule   The rule that makes most statements about an event or condition **admissible** as **evidence** (even though they are **hearsay**) if they were spoken during or immediately after the event or condition. The older rule was that the statement had to be an **excited utterance** (made while still under stress), but most courts now allow **present sense impressions** (no need for excitement).

Spot   Immediate. For example, a *spot* exchange rate is the conversion rate for money exchanged at the time the rate is quoted.

Spot trading   Selling something for immediate delivery with immediate payment. The *spot price* is the price of things sold this way.

Spot zoning   Changing the **zoning** of a piece of land without regard for the zoning plan for the area.

Spread   The difference between two prices, amounts, dates, or numbers; for example, between **bid and asked** (see that phrase) prices in **commodity** trading. *Spread* is also the name given to many complex transactions involving **commodity** trading or **arbitrage** (see that word).

Sprinkling trust   A **trust** that gives income to many persons at different times.

Spurious   Not genuine. For example, a *spurious class action* is a joining together of several persons' claims in one lawsuit for the sake of the court's efficiency, even though the claims are different and couldn't normally be part of a **class action;** and a *spurious* $5 bill is one that has some things right about it (such as the fact that it was made on proper plates), but some things wrong (such as the signature). It is not genuine, but only partly **counterfeit.**

Squatter's right   The "right" to ownership of land merely because you have occupied it for a long time. This is different from **adverse possession** (see that word) and is not recognized as a right in most places.

Squeeze-out   A **merger** or other change in a corporation's structure that is done by majority owners to get rid of (or further reduce the power or claims of) **minority stockholders** (see that word). See also **freeze-out.**

Stakeholder   *1.* A person with an interest at stake. A **corporation's** stakeholders include its owners, officers, employees, and, more loosely, its suppliers and customers or even the communities in which it operates. *2.* A person chosen by others to hold something that is in dispute between them while the dispute is worked out in court or in some other way, or a person who holds a bet for others.

Stale   Too late, so without legal effect; for example, a *stale check* has been made uncashable because it has been held too long. State law often sets this time period. See *statute of* **limitations** and **laches.**

Stalking   The crime of repeatedly following, threatening, or harassing another person in ways that lead to a legitimate fear of physical harm. Some states define *stalking* more broadly as any conduct with no legitimate purpose that seriously upsets a targeted person, especially conduct in violation of a **protective order.**

Stamp tax   A tax on transactions such as real estate sales, paid (or once paid) by purchasing stamps to put on the transaction document.

Stand   *1.* The place where a witness sits to **testify.** *2.* Remain valid or effective. *3.* Refuse to change. *4.* To *stand trial* is to be a **defendant** in a trial, usually a **criminal** trial. *5.* To *stand mute* is to raise no objections in a trial, to assert a privilege against **self-incrimination** in a criminal trial, or to refuse to **plead** "guilty" or "not guilty" in a criminal trial. In this last situation, the judge usually enters a "not guilty" plea for the defendant. *6.* A *stand-still* is an agreement in which one or both sides agree to not proceed with some action for a stated or indefinite time period.

Standard   *1.* Conforming to accepted practice. *2.* A model; something accepted as correct. *3.* A minimum requirement against which something is judged or measured. For example, the *standard of care* in **negligence** cases is the level of care a reasonable person would use in similar circumstances, and the *standard of need* for receiving **welfare** is the total need of that size and type of family as determined by the state. See also **standard of proof.**

Standard deduction   A specified dollar amount subtracted from **taxable income** by persons who do not *itemize* **deductions** on their income **tax returns.**

Standard of proof   A level of certainty to which something must be proved. In a **criminal** prosecution, a defendant's guilt must be proved **beyond a reasonable doubt.** And in a **civil** lawsuit, claims must usually be proved by a **preponderance of the evidence,** but sometimes to the higher standard of **clear and convincing evidence.**

Standard Oil Co. of N.J. v. U.S.   (221 U.S. 1) The 1911 U.S. Supreme Court decision that broke up the world's largest monopoly as a violation of the **Sherman Antitrust Act.**

Standing   *1.* A person's right to bring (start) or join a lawsuit because he or she is directly affected by the issues raised. This is called "standing to sue." *2.* Reputation. *3.* A *standing committee* of a **house** of a **legislature** is a regular **committee,** with full power to act within a subject area. *4.* See **stand.**

Star chamber   A court in old England that had the power to arbitrarily punish persons who disobeyed the king. The phrase *star chamber law* is used to describe a lack of procedural fairness or the handing out of overly harsh punishments by a judge.

Star page   *1.* An asterisk or star plus a page number next to text in an unofficial (often *annotated*) **reporter** to show where the same text appears in the *official reporter. 2.* A reference to a page in an earlier edition of a book. *3. Star paging* is also a way to show the page breaks in a printed document on a computer screen or to request a specific document page in a computer search.

Stare decisis   (Latin) "Let the decision stand." The rule that when a court has decided a case by applying a legal principle to a set of facts, the court should stick by the principle and apply it to all later cases with clearly similar facts unless there is a strong reason not to, and that courts **below** *must* apply the principle in similar cases. This rule helps promote fairness and reliability in judicial decision making. See also **precedent.** [pronounce: star-e de-si-sis]

Starker exchange   A delayed, tax-deferred exchange of real estate held for business purposes. It works like this: first sell business property #1 and have the sales proceeds held beyond your **constructive receipt** by a third party such as a bank trust department, then designate business property #2 within the required time limit, and finally complete the purchase within another time limit. There will be no tax due on profit from property #1 until #2 is sold or taken out of business use.

Stat.   *1.* **Statute(s).** *2.* Immediately! (Short for the Latin *statim.*) (*Not* **stet.**)

State   *1.* Say; set down; or declare. *2.* The major political subdivision of the U.S. (*State action* is action by a state, such as New York, or private action that must be enforced by the government.) *3.* A nation. (An *act of state* is by a country, such as France.) *4.* Condition; situation. *5.* Short for the Department of State, the U.S. **cabinet** department that handles relations with foreign countries.

State of mind exception   An **exception** to the **hearsay** *rule:* An out-of-court statement by a person, which reveals or explains the reason why that person did something, spoken when the thing was done, may be used as **evidence** even if the person is available to **testify.**

State of the case   The procedural status of a case: not ready for trial, ready for trial, in trial, or awaiting **appeal.**

State secrets   Facts that the U.S. need not reveal to a court (or to anyone else) because they might hurt national security or another equally important national interest.

Stated   *1.* Regular. For example, a *stated meeting* of a **board** *of directors* is one held at regular intervals according to law or **charter.** *2.* Settled or agreed upon. For example, a *stated account* is an agreed amount owing.

Statement   *1.* Any assertion, whether oral, written, or implied by conduct, intended to be an assertion of fact, of intent, etc. *2.* A document laying out facts. For example, a *statement of account* or *bank statement* lists all the transactions made by a customer for that month, and a *statement of affairs* in a **bankruptcy** proceeding is meant to be a complete list of the debtor's financial records, assets, and debts. *3.* There are several technical **accounting** *statements* that supplement a corporation's basic **balance sheet** in its reports. These include: *statements of* **income** (profits and losses; **earnings per share;** money in and out for such things as wages, supplies, interest, taxes, etc., all compared with prior years); *changes in financial position* or *sources and application of funds* (cash **balances, working capital,** etc.); *changes in accounting* (the way **inventory** is valued, the way **assets** are depreciated, etc.); *owners' equity* (basically, **assets** minus **liabilities,** but for a corporation, it is measured by **paid-in** *capital* plus **retained earnings**); and *retained earnings* (basically, profit kept by a corporation after paying out profits as **dividends,** etc.).

State's attorney   See **district attorney.**

State's evidence   A general word for **testimony** for the prosecution, given by a person who was involved in a crime, against others who were involved in the same crime, especially if the testimony is given in return for a grant of **immunity,** for a reduction of charges, etc. Giving such testimony is called *"turning state's evidence."*

States' rights   All rights of the states of the U.S., especially those rights reserved to the states by the **Tenth Amendment.** The *philosophy* of states' rights is that the U.S. **Constitution** should be interpreted to give the greatest possible powers to the states rather than to the federal government.

Station house   Police station.

Statuable   **Statutory.**

Status   *1.* A basic condition. The basic legal relationship of a person to the rest of the community. A *status crime* is one that depends solely on a person's status (what the person *is*) rather than on something he or she has done. Most status crime laws are no longer **constitutional**, but states have gotten around the problem by defining a prohibited *status* (for example, being an alcoholic) as a prohibited *act* ("found intoxicated in a public place"), or by restricting behavior without calling it a crime (for example, putting a child in an institution for being "beyond parental control"). A youth who is under court supervision for repeated acts that are not crimes is a *status offender. 2.* The state of things. For example, *status quo* is the existing state of things or the way things are at a particular time. *Status quo ante* means "the way things were before"; for example, before a contract was made.

Statute   A law passed by a **legislature.** [pronounce: stah-chute]

Statute of frauds   Any of various state laws, modeled after an old English law, that require many types of **contracts** (such as contracts for the sale of **real estate** or of goods over a certain dollar amount, contracts to guarantee another's debt, and certain long-term contracts) to be signed and in writing to be enforceable in court.

Statute of limitations (or repose)   See **limitation.**

Statute of uses   See **use.**

Statute of wills   Any of various state laws, modeled after an old English law, that require a **will** to be in writing, signed, and properly witnessed to be valid. See also **holograph.**

Statutes at large   A collection of all **statutes** passed by a particular legislature (such as the U.S. Congress), printed in full and in the order of their passage. The U.S. *Statutes at Large* also contains *joint* **resolutions,** constitutional **amendments,** presidential **proclamations,** etc.

Statutory   Having to do with a **statute;** created, defined, or required by a statute. [pronounce: stah-chu-tory]

Statutory construction   See **construction.**

Statutory crime   An act that is a crime because a law or regulation was passed against it, not necessarily because it is morally evil. See also **malum prohibitum** and **strict liability.**

Statutory employer   A company that may be responsible under **workers' compensation laws** for the employees of an **independent contractor** if the work done is a regular part of the company's business.

Statutory rape   See **rape.**

Stay   *1.* Stop or suspend. For example, when a judge *stays* a **judgment,** the judge stops or delays its enforcement. *2.* A stoppage or suspension. For example, stoppage of the enforcement of the judgment in definition no. 1 is called a "_stay of judgment._" _3. Stay laws_ are **statutes** that suspend legal actions, usually to protect **debtors** in times of national financial crisis.

Stenographic recording   The taking down of **testimony** by a court reporter who uses a paper-punching device, a tape recorder, a shorthand notebook, or other device to record testimony and court proceedings, and then types an exact copy later. _Nonstenographic_ recording involves the use of a tape recorder, videotape, etc., without a court reporter to run or transcribe it.

Step transaction   A series of transactions that are viewed by the **I.R.S.** as one transaction for tax purposes.

Step up (or down) basis   An increase (or reduction) in the **basis** (see that word) of a property for income tax purposes that usually occurs when **heirs** take a dead person's property. The property's basis then becomes the **market value** (or the **alternative valuation date** value).

Stet   Undo the deletion. (Let it stand, from the Latin _stare,_ "to stand.") _Stet_ is written near marked deleted words to have them put back in. (_Not_ **stat.**)

Steward   A **shop steward.**

Stifling a prosecution   Taking money for agreeing not to **prosecute** a person for a criminal offense. This may be a crime.

Stipulation   _1._ An agreement between lawyers on opposite sides of a lawsuit. It is often in writing and usually concerns either court procedure (for example, an agreement to extend the time in which a **pleading** is due) or agreed-upon facts that require no proof. _2._ A demand. _3._ One point in a written agreement.

Stirpes (or stirpital or stipital)   See **per stirpes.**

Stock   _1._ The **goods** held for sale by a merchant. _2._ Shares of ownership in a **corporation.** Stock is often divided into _preferred_ (getting a fixed rate of income before any other stock) and _common_ (the bulk of the stock). _3._ There are various types of **corporate** stock. Some of these are: _assessable_ (the owner may have to pay more than the stock's cost to meet the company's needs); _blue-chip_ (has excellent investment ratings); _callable_ or _redeemable_ (can be bought back by the company at a prestated price); _control_ (describes that amount of stock, often much less than a **majority,** that can control the company); _cumulative_ (gets unpaid **dividends** before any **common stock** is paid); _donated_ (given back to the company for resale); _floating_ (on the open market for sale); _growth_ (bought for an increase in value, not dividends); *guaranteed* (dividends guaranteed by another company); *letter* (a letter is required stating that the buyer will not resell before a certain time); *listed* (traded on an **exchange**); *participation* (gets a share of profits); *penny* (sells for less than one dollar and is often speculative); and *registered* (**registered** with the **Securities and Exchange Commission**). *4.* For **capital, convertible,** etc., *stock,* see those words. *5.* For *stock:* **dividend, market, option, warrant,** etc., see those words. *6.* Other "stock" words follow here.

Stock association A **joint stock company.**

Stock control Maintaining records of **inventory** (goods held or for sale).

Stock dividend Profits of **stock** ownership (**dividends**) paid out by a corporation in more stock rather than in money. This additional stock reflects the increased worth of the company.

Stock law district An area where cows, sheep, etc., are prohibited from running free.

Stock rights Rights to buy more **stock** in a **corporation** at a future time, given to existing stockholders (or to their successors) by a document (usually a **warrant**). See also *pre-emptive rights* under **pre-emption.**

Stock split A dividing of a company's **stock** into a greater number of shares without changing each stockholder's proportional ownership.

Stockholder's derivative suit A lawsuit in which a shareholder of a corporation sues in the name of the corporation because a wrong has been done to the company and the company itself will not sue.

Stockholder's equity A **corporation's** net worth (**assets** minus **liabilities**) expressed, not in terms of the assets themselves (buildings, **inventory,** etc.), but in terms of the corporation's **capital** *stock,* **capital** *surplus,* and **retained earnings** (see those words).

Stop and frisk A quick, temporary detention and "pat down" by a police officer of a person whom the officer suspects of being armed. This is called a "*Terry-type stop*" for the case (*Terry v. Ohio*) establishing less stringent rules for less than a full search.

Stop order *1.* A customer's instruction to his or her bank to refuse payment on a check the customer has written to another person. *2.* An instruction from a customer to a stockbroker to buy a particular stock at a price above the current market price or sell it at a price below the current price. A *stop-limit order* states a price above which it can't be bought and below which it can't be sold, and a *stop-loss order* is an instruction to buy or sell at a particular price. *3.* An **order** from a judge, from an **administrative agency,** etc., that tells a person to stop doing something, such as building a house without a **permit.** See also **injunction** and **cease and desist order.**

Stoppage in transit   Halt the delivery of goods even after they have been given to a **carrier** (railroad, etc.), especially when done as a matter of right by the seller when the buyer is **insolvent** or is otherwise unable or unwilling to pay for the goods.

Straddle   Buy both **put** and **call** (see those words) _options_ for the same stock.

Straight sentence   See **sentence** no. 2.

Straight-line depreciation   Dividing the cost of a thing used in a business by the number of years in its **useful** _life_ and deducting that fraction of the cost each year from **taxable income.** See also _accelerated depreciation_ under **depreciation deduction.**

Stranger   A person who takes no part in a deal in any way; a **third party.**

Straw (or straw man, woman, or person)   _1._ A "front;" a person who is put up in name only to take part in a deal. This is sometimes done to transfer property more easily or to conceal a true participant in a deal. See also **street name.** _2._ A man who stood around outside a court in old England and was hired by lawyers to give false **testimony.** _3._ An argument set up purely to be knocked down. This is sometimes done to divert attention from the real point because your opponent will win that one.

Stream of commerce   Goods held within a state for a short while, but which come from another state and will go to another state, are in the _stream of commerce_ and cannot be taxed by the state.

Street certificate   A **share** of **stock** signed **in blank,** so anyone can transfer it.

Street name   _1._ The name of a stock brokerage company. **Stock** or other **securities** held in the stockbroker's own name instead of the customer's (for convenience, to hide the owner's name, because the stock was bought on **margin,** etc.) are held in a _street name._ See also **book entry.** _2._ The made-up name used by investment companies, banks, etc., to hide the real owners of stock, of a business, etc. Also called "_straw_," "_front name_," and "_nominee._"

Stretchout   More work for the same pay.

Strict   Exact; precise; governed by exact rules. _Strict construction_ of a law means taking it literally or "what it says, it means" so that the law should be applied to the narrowest possible set of situations. Compare with **liberal construction.** Also see **letter of the law** and **construction.** _Strict construction_ of a contract means that any ambiguous words in the contract should be interpreted in the way least favorable to the side that wrote the words.

Strict foreclosure A **creditor's** right, in some circumstances, to take back property and cancel the debt. In these situations, the property acts as an exact cancellation of the debt, and neither the creditor nor the **debtor** can sue the other for any additional money.

Strict liability *1.* The legal responsibility for damage or injury, even if you are not at fault or **negligent.** For example, a manufacturer may be **liable** for injuries caused by certain defective products even if the person hurt cannot prove exactly how the manufacturer was careless. *2.* Guilt of a **criminal** offense even if you had no criminal intention (**mens rea**). Only minor offenses (such as speeding) and special **regulatory offenses** (such as polluting) can be *strict liability offenses.* See also **statutory crime.**

Strict scrutiny test The principle that a state law (or an administrative agency regulation) that affects **fundamental** individual rights is valid only if it accomplishes important state objectives in the least restrictive way possible. Compare with **rational basis test.**

Stricti juris (Latin) Determined by **strict** *construction* (see that word).

Strike *1.* Take out. For example, to *strike* a word is to remove it from a document. *2.* Employees stopping, slowing down, or disrupting work to win demands from an employer. *3.* An *economic strike* is a strike that attempts to improve such things as wages, hours, and working conditions, as opposed to a strike precipitated by an employer's **unfair labor practices;** a *general strike* is throughout an industry or country; a *jurisdictional strike* protests assignment of work to members of another union; a *secondary strike* is by one union against an employer who does business with another employer whose employees are on strike; and a *wildcat strike* is unauthorized by union officials. *4.* See also **sit-down strike, sympathy strike, blue flu, job action, recognition,** and **work-to-rule.** *5.* In some states, a *motion to strike (the* **evidence***)* is similar to a **motion for** judgment (*of* **acquittal**).

Strike suit A **stockholder's derivative suit** (see that word) brought purely for the gain of the stockholder or to win large lawyer's fees for a stockholder who is a lawyer.

Striking a jury Forming a **jury** for a particular case by choosing persons from among those on a jury **panel.** See also **struck jury.**

Striking price The price at which a person can *exercise* an **option** (see that word) to buy or sell a **commodity.**

String citation   A series of case names and **citations** (see that word) that is printed after an assertion or legal conclusion in order to back it up.

Strip   The principal-only or interest-only part of a **security** that has been split into two parts.

Strong-arm provision   A part of the federal **bankruptcy** law that gives a bankruptcy **trustee** powers equal to those of a powerful **secured** *creditor* (whether or not such creditor actually exists) to help the trustee gather all of the bankrupt person's property.

Struck jury   *1.* A jury, not from the regular jury **panel,** chosen for a special case. But see no. 2. *2.* The jury as chosen, as opposed to the panel from which it is chosen. *3.* A jury chosen after each side has a chance to delete a certain number of names from a list of potential jurors.

Style   Official name.

Sua sponte   (Latin) *1.* Of his or her own will; voluntarily. *2.* On a judge's own **motion,** without a request from one of the **parties.**

Sub   Under, below, secondary, a smaller part.

Sub judice   (Latin) "Under judicial consideration." As yet undecided because a judge is considering it. [pronounce: sub joo-di-see]

Sub modo   (Latin) Subject to a restriction.

Sub nom.   (Latin) Abbreviation for *sub nomine,* meaning "under the name of."

Sub silentio   (Latin) "Under silence"; in silence; without taking any notice or giving explicit consideration; having an unstated effect. To **overrule** *sub silentio* is to give a result that invalidates a prior case without mentioning that case.

Subchapter C and S corporations   See **C corporation** and **S corporation.**

Subcontractor   A person who contracts to do a piece of a job for another person who has a contract for a larger piece of the job or for the whole job.

Subdelegation   Same as **delegation** (see that word) of authority.

Subdivision   Land divided into many lots by a developer and sold to different persons under a common plan.

Subinfeudation   The process in the middle ages of kings owning all the land and granting only the use of it to nobles, who then gave use only of smaller parts to others, and so on down several layers. The *statute of quia emptores* ended this process in England, leaving the power of *infeudation* (granting *feuds,* the basis for feudal law) only to the king and making all lower land transfers more similar to modern sales and **grants.**

Subjacent support   The support given to the surface of land by the soil and other material lying below the surface. There usually exists a right to have land supported from below, so if a person digs a hole on the person's own land that causes another's land to cave in far from the hole, the person will be responsible for the damage. Compare with **lateral support.**

Subject   *1.* "Subject to" means subordinate to, governed by, affected by, limited by, and other similar things. Use a more precise word if possible. *2.* "Subject" in front of another word ("the subject contract") is jargon used to indicate that the other word was previously mentioned. Use the word alone ("the contract") or the precise thing ("the Sept. 1 Jones contract"). *3.* For *subject matter jurisdiction,* see **jurisdiction.**

Subletting   A **tenant's** renting of property (or part of a property) to another person (a *subtenant* or *sub***lessee**), either for the rest of the tenant's own lease or for a portion such as a "summer *sublet.*"

Submission agreement   **Evaluation agreement.**

Submit   *1.* Put into another's hands for a decision. If a case is good enough to be submitted for decision, it is *submissible. 2.* Allow; yield to another's authority. *3.* Attempt to introduce **evidence.** *4.* Offer something for approval.

Subordination   *1.* Making something weaker or lesser than something else. For example, agreeing, in a signed document, that your **claim** or **interest** (for example, a **lien**) is weaker than another one and can collect only after the other one collects. *2.* Any ranking of rights. *3. Not* **subornation** (see next entry).

Subornation of perjury   *1.* The crime of asking or forcing another person to lie under **oath.** *2. Not* **subordination.** [pronounce: sub-or-nay-shun]

Subpoena   A court's **order** to a person that he or she appear in court to **testify** (give **evidence**) in a case. Some **administrative agencies** may also **issue** subpoenas. [pronounce: suh-pee-na]

Subpoena duces tecum   A **subpoena** (see that word) by which a person is commanded to bring certain documents to court or to an **administrative agency.** [pronounce suh-pee-na due-kes tay-kum]

Subrogation   The substitution of one person for another in claiming a lawful right or debt. For example, when an **insurance** company pays its policy holder for damage to his or her car, the insurance company becomes *subrogated to* (gets the right to sue on or collect) any claim for the same damage that the policy holder has against the person who hit the car.

Subscribe *1.* Sign a document (as the person who wrote it, as a **witness,** etc.). *2.* Formally agree, usually by signing a *stock subscription agreement,* to purchase some initial **stock** in a company. *3.* The person who does no. 1 or no. 2 is a *subscriber* and the act is *subscription. 4.* For *subscription right,* see *pre-emptive right* under **pre-emption.** *5.* A *subscription warrant* is a long-term **option** to buy stock at a fixed price. It may come with a **bond** or a share of *preferred* **stock.** *6.* Agree to contribute to a charity.

Subsidiary *1.* Under another's control; lesser. *2.* Short for *subsidiary corporation,* a **corporation** that is owned by another corporation (the **parent corporation**).

Substance *1.* Reality, as opposed to mere appearance. *2.* Subject, meaning, or legal importance. Contrast **form.** *3.* See **substantive law.**

Substantial *1.* Valuable; real; worthwhile. *2.* Complete enough. For example, *substantial performance* of a building contract may exist when there are defects but the building is fit for its intended use. *3.* "A lot," when it is hard to pin down just how much "a lot" really is. For example, *substantial evidence* is more than a mere **scintilla** of evidence but less than a full **preponderance of evidence.** *Not* **substantive evidence.** *4.* For *substantial capacity,* see *Model Penal Code* under **insanity** no. 2.

Substantiate Establish the existence of something or prove its truth; verify. See also **corroborate.**

Substantive due process See **due process** and **substantive law.**

Substantive evidence Evidence used to prove facts rather than to discredit or back up a **witness's** believability. *Not* **substantial** *evidence.*

Substantive law The basic law of **rights** and **duties** (**contract** law, criminal law, accident law, law of **wills,** etc.) as opposed to **procedural law** (law of **pleading,** law of **evidence,** law of **jurisdiction,** etc.).

Substantive rule A change in an existing regulation. Compare with **interpretive rule** for more detail.

Substituted basis The cost of a property for tax purposes when it is transferred in a **like-kind exchange** (or certain other ways) and the old owner's **basis** becomes the new owner's basis.

Substituted service **Service** of **process** by any means other than personal delivery; for example, by mail, publication in a newspaper, or service on a member of the family at the person's usual residence.

Subtenant See **subletting.**

Subtraction   The old offense of keeping from another person money, rights, or services that the person was entitled to.

Subversive activities   Espionage, **treason, sedition, sabotage,** and other acts to undermine a government.

Succession   *1.* The transfer of a dead person's property. *Intestate succession* (or *hereditary succession*) is the transfer of a dead person's property by law to **heirs** if the person does not leave a **will.** A *succession law* is an **inheritance** law, and a *successor* is a person who gets a dead person's property. *2.* Taking over a predecessor's official duties. *3.* The continuation of a **corporation** even though its owners, **directors,** and managers change.

Sudden emergency (or peril) doctrine   See **emergency doctrine.**

Sudden heat of passion   See **heat of passion.**

Sue   To start a **civil** lawsuit.

Sue out   Ask a court to **issue** a **writ,** a court **order,** or other court papers.

Suffer   Allow or permit something to happen. To *suffer* something usually means to willingly permit it, but in the case of *sufferance,* it may imply neglecting to enforce a right.

Sufficient cause   *1. Legal cause* to remove a public official from office. It must be for something basic to the person's job qualifications as they affect an important public interest. *2.* **Probable cause.** *3.* A good legal reason to do something.

Suffrage   The right to vote.

Suggestion   A mere hint or insinuation that does not make a fact probable or even possible, but only introduces the idea that it *might* be possible; less than an **inference** or **presumption.**

Sui generis   (Latin) One of a kind. [pronounce: sue-ee jen-er-is]

Sui juris   (Latin) "Of his or her own right." Possessing full **civil** and **political rights** and able to manage his or her own affairs.

Suicide   *1.* Killing yourself. *Attempted suicide* may be a crime, as may be the accidental killing of another person during an attempt or persuading another person to attempt suicide. *2.* A person who kills him or herself.

Suit   A lawsuit; a **civil action.**

Suit money   Lawyer's fees and costs that a judge orders one side in a lawsuit to pay to the other.

Suitor   A **party** or **litigant** in a lawsuit; usually the **plaintiff.**

Suits in Admiralty Act   (46 U.S.C. 741) A 1920 statute, similar to the **Federal Tort Claims Act,** that permits maritime (seagoing) suits against the U.S. government.

Sum certain   An exact amount of money, usually of money owed. An amount owed may be a *sum certain* even if it includes interest, costs, etc., so long as these added amounts are exactly computable. Having a *sum certain* is a legal requirement for such things as the *negotiability* of a **negotiable instrument** or for granting certain **judgments.**

Summary   Short, concise, and immediate, with formalities reduced or eliminated.

Summary judgment   A final **judgment** (victory) for one side in a lawsuit (or in one part of a lawsuit), without **trial,** when the judge finds, based on **pleadings, depositions, affidavits,** etc. that there is no genuine factual issue in the lawsuit (or in one part of the lawsuit).

Summary jury trial   **Alternative dispute resolution** in which the judge orders the two sides in a complex case to present their most important facts to a small jury, with **admission** *of evidence* either agreed to or decided by the judge in advance. The two sides may agree in advance to be bound by the verdict or may interview the jurors and use the results to negotiate a settlement. Compare **minitrial.**

Summary proceeding   A **proceeding** in which normal formalities are either reduced or eliminated; for example, a court proceeding without **pleadings** or a **jury,** such as a **contempt** hearing or the procedure in most **small claims courts.**

Summary process   *1.* **Summary proceeding.** *2.* **Summary judgment.** *3.* Taking action to assert a legal right without using the courts at all; for example, by **recaption.** *4.* Slang for an **eviction** by no. 1, no. 2, or no. 3.

Summing up (or summation)   Each lawyer's presentation of a review of the **evidence** at the close of a trial.

Summons   *1.* A **writ** (a notice delivered by a **sheriff** or other authorized person) informing a person of a lawsuit against him or her. It tells the person to show up in court at a certain time or risk losing the suit without being present. *2.* Any formal notice to show up in court (as a witness, juror, etc.).

Sumptuary laws   Laws controlling the sale or use of certain socially undesirable, wasteful, and harmful products.

Sunk costs   Past spending that no longer directly affects current decisions. For example, the original (sunk) cost of a fully paid car is not as important as its current sale value or its tax value.

Sunset law   A law that puts an **administrative agency** automatically out-of-business unless the law is renewed after a careful reexamination of the agency by the **legislature.**

Sunshine law A law requiring open meetings of government agencies or allowing (or assisting) public access to government records. See also **Freedom of Information Act.**

Suo nomine (Latin) In his or her name.

Superfund The pot of money, originally established by the Comprehensive Environmental Response, Compensation, and Liability Act (CERCLA) of 1980, to help clean up toxic waste sites. CERCLA also made all contributors to the sites liable for cleanup.

Superior *1.* Higher. However, a *superior court* is sometimes a state's *lowest* court, sometimes its highest, and sometimes an intermediate court. *2.* Having control. For example, a *superior estate* (which might be quite small) might have an *easement* against an *inferior estate* (which might be quite big). These are generally called *dominant* and *servient estates.* See **easement** and **dominant.**

Supermajority A majority far above 50 percent. This vote total is required for many important, unusual actions, such as change to a **constitution.**

Superpriority A **priority** (see that word) higher than first priority. The **bankruptcy** code has an even higher *super-superpriority.*

Supersede *1.* Set aside; wipe out; make unnecessary. *2.* Replace one law or document by another later one.

Supersedeas (Latin) Describes a judge's **order** that temporarily holds up another court's proceedings or, more often, temporarily **stays** a lower court's **judgment.** For example, a *supersedeas bond* may be put up by a person who **appeals** a judgment. The bond delays the person's obligation to pay the judgment until the appeal is lost. [pronounce: sue-per-<u>see</u>-dee-as]

Superseding cause **Intervening cause.**

Supervening New; newly effective; interposing. For *supervening cause,* see **intervening cause,** and for *supervening negligence,* see **last clear chance doctrine.**

Supervisor *1.* An individual or a member of a **board** that runs a county or town in some states. *2.* Anyone with authority over others, but in labor law this does not include low-level persons who do not need to use "independent judgment" in their supervision of others.

Supplemental pleading A **pleading** that brings up events that happened after the start of the lawsuit.

Supplementary proceedings A **judgment creditor's** (see that word) in-court examination of the **debtor** and others to find out if there is any money or property available to pay the debt.

Support *1.* A *support obligation* is the obligation to provide for your immediate family. *2. Support payments* are payments made to a wife, husband, child, etc. (with or without court supervision or formal agreement) to meet your *support obligations. 3.* See **lateral support** and **subjacent support.**

Suppress *1.* To *suppress evidence* is to keep it from being used in a **criminal** trial by showing that it was gathered illegally. This can happen at trial or at a pretrial *suppression hearing. 2.* Refuse to give evidence in a criminal trial. This may be a crime. *3.* Hold back evidence favorable to a defendant. This may be **unconstitutional** if done by the prosecution.

Sup-pro   Short for **supplementary proceedings.**

Supra   (Latin) Above; earlier (in the page, in the book, etc.).

Supremacy clause   The provision in *Article VI* of the U.S. **Constitution** that the U.S. Constitution, laws, and **treaties** take precedence over conflicting state constitutions or laws.

Supremacy of law   Describes a government in which the highest authority is in law, not in persons.

Supreme Court   The highest of the **United States courts** (see that word) and the highest court of most, but not all, of the states.

Surcharge   *1.* An extra charge on something already charged. *2.* A special payment, such as the personal payment a **trustee** must make to a **trust** if he or she has negligently handled the account and it has lost money. *3.* An overcharge. A charge beyond what is right or legal. *4.* See also **surtax.**

Surety   A person or company that insures or guarantees that another person's debt will be paid by becoming **liable** (responsible) for the debt when it is made. The relationship among debtor, creditor, and *surety* is a *suretyship.* See also **guaranty.** [pronounce: <u>shoor</u>-e-tee]

Surface   A vague word which, when used in land **deeds,** may mean anything from "the top few feet of land with no **mineral rights**" to "all the land and minerals except oil and gas."

Surplus   Money left over. A corporation's surplus, or its "**capital** *surplus,*" is defined in several different, overlapping, and sometimes conflicting ways including "**assets** minus **liabilities,**" "assets minus **stock** value," etc.

Surplusage   *1.* Extra, unnecessary words, or matter not relevant to the case, in a legal document. *2.* **Surplus.**

Surprise   *1.* The situation that occurs when one side in a trial, through absolutely no fault of its own, is faced with something totally unexpected that places an unfair burden on its case. When this happens, a

continuance is often granted and, occasionally, a new trial is granted. *2.* The situation that occurs when a **witness** gives unexpected **testimony** that hurts the side that called the witness. That side may then **impeach** its own witness with **prior inconsistent statements.**

Surrebutter and surrejoinder   Two old forms of **pleading** no longer used. Modern court practice usually stops with two or three pleadings, not the five or more it would take to reach these.

Surrender   Give back; give up; hand back; return.

Surrender value   The value of a life insurance policy if it is cashed in or borrowed against.

Surrogate   *1.* The name for the judge of a **probate** court in some states. *2.* A person who stands in for, takes the place of, or represents another.

Surtax   *1.* An additional tax on what has already been taxed. *2.* A tax on a tax. For example, if you must pay a hundred dollar sales tax on a one thousand dollar purchase (10 percent), a 10 percent *surtax* would require an additional ten dollar payment, not an additional hundred dollar payment.

Survey   *1.* Measure or map land boundaries. *2.* An investigation, examination, or questioning, such as an opinion poll.

Survival statute   A state law that allows a lawsuit to be brought by a relative for a person who has died. The lawsuit is based on the **cause of action** the dead person would have had. See also **wrongful death action.**

Survivorship   The *right of survivorship* is the right of certain property owners, such as **joint** owners of real estate who outlive other joint owners, to own the property. Joint renters and other joint property holders may have similar survivorship rights.

Suspect classification   Making choices (in employment, etc.) based on factors such as race or nationality. These choices, only rarely legitimate, must be strongly justified if challenged. (*Gender* is a *quasi-suspect classification* that must be justified, but not as strongly, if challenged.)

Suspended sentence   A **sentence** (usually "jail time") that the judge allows the convicted person to avoid serving (usually if the person continues on good behavior, completes community service, etc.). See also **probation.**

Suspicion   *1.* More than a guess, but less than full knowledge. *2. Held on suspicion* is being temporarily held by the police without specific charges against you.

Sustain *1.* Grant. When a judge *sustains an* **objection,** he or she agrees with it and gives it effect. *2.* Carry on; bear up under. *3.* Support or justify. If the evidence fully supports a **verdict,** it is said to *sustain* the verdict.

Swear Take an **oath;** for example, the *swearing in* of a **witness** or a person about to become a public official in an official oath-taking ceremony, or the *swearing out* of a criminal **warrant** by making a charge under oath.

Sweat equity The increase in property value due to an owner's own labors.

Sweating Harsh, threatening, or overly aggressive questioning of a **criminal** suspect.

Sweetheart contract A labor contract containing unusually favorable terms for one side or the other. *Sweetheart contracts* are occasionally gained by actions unrelated to the employment relationship, such as bribery.

Swift witness A **witness** who seems overeager to give information or who shows a **bias** toward one side.

Syllabus A **headnote,** summary, or **abstract** of a case.

Symbolic delivery A legally **implied** delivery of a thing when only a symbol of the thing is actually delivered. For example, delivering a key to a safety deposit box is sometimes considered to be *symbolic delivery* of the box's contents.

Symbolic speech Gestures and actions that are meant to communicate a message; for example, holding your nose. *Symbolic speech* is protected as if actual speech under the **First Amendment** to the U.S. Constitution.

Sympathy strike A **strike** by one **union** to help another union's strike. These are now mostly prohibited.

Synallagmatic contract **Bilateral contract.**

Syndicalism The theory that trade unions should control the means of production and, ultimately, the government. *Criminal syndicalism* is advocating a crime, **sabotage,** etc., to take over an industry or affect the government.

Syndicate *1.* A **joint adventure.** *2.* Any business venture, whether permanent or temporary, incorporated or not. *3.* "The syndicate" is slang for organized crime.

Synopsis A summary of a document, book, etc.

T *1.* An old abbreviation for the Latin "testamentum" (**will**). *2.* Short for term; territory; title; etc. *3.* Short for U.S. Treasury, as in T-bill, T-bond, and T-note. See **Treasury bill.**

T.A.M. Technical advice memorandum. An **I.R.S.** publication that explains a complex tax issue.

T.C. Tax Court. A *T.C. Memo* is a **memorandum decision** of the U.S. Tax Court.

T.M. Short for **trademark,** but "TM" is *not* an official designation and does *not* mean "registered® trademark."

T.R.O. Temporary restraining order.

Table *1.* Suspend consideration of a *legislative* **bill** but put it "on the table" for *possible* future consideration. *2.* A list of figures, such as a federal precomputed tax-rate table. *3.* A *table of authorities* is an alphabetical index of cases, statutes, articles, etc. used in a book with the page numbers on which they are referenced.

Tacit *1.* Understood without being openly said; done in silence; implied. *2.* Customary.

Tacking Attaching something later, smaller, or weaker to something earlier, larger, or stronger. For example, if the owner of a third **mortgage** buys the first mortgage on a property and joins them together to get **priority** over the owner of the second mortgage, this is called *tacking.* The term is also used for combining rights to make **adverse possession** (see that word) claims, to avoid the effect of *statutes of* **limitations,** to extend trucking routes, etc.

Taft-Hartley Act (29 U.S.C. 141) A 1947 federal law that added several employers' rights to the union rights in the **Wagner Act.** It established several union "unfair labor practices" (such as attempting to force an employee to join a union).

Tail Limited; limited to only children, grandchildren, etc. See **fee tail.**

Taint *1.* **Attainder** or **attaint.** *2.* The loss of reputation that results from **conviction** of a serious crime. *3.* *Tainted* **evidence,** money, or property is that gained by illegal means or resulting from something gained by illegal means.

Take   *Take* has a wide variety of meanings in the law, but most are close to the ordinary language meaning. For example, in criminal law, to *take* something is to take it without the owner's consent and with the intent to cheat or steal; the government is said to *take* a person's property even when the government action only lowers the value of the property; when you **inherit** property, you *take by descent; take-home pay* is pay after deductions for such things as taxes, insurance, savings plans, etc.; a *takeover* is the gaining of control, but not necessarily **majority** ownership of a company (see **tender** *offer*); and to *take up* a **note** or other **negotiable instrument** is to pay or **discharge** it.

Take private   Convert a business that is held by a large number of stockholders, with shares traded in a market, to one held by a few owners. Compare **privatize.**

Take the Fifth   See **Fifth Amendment.**

Take the stand   **Testify** as a **witness** in court.

Take-down   *1.* The time when a deal is actually performed, such as when goods have been both delivered and paid for. *2.* The time when prearranged credit is actually used.

Take-out loan   A permanent **mortgage** loan that pays off a construction loan.

Taking clause   The last clause of the **Fifth Amendment:** "nor shall private property be taken for public use without just compensation."

Talesman   Originally, a person taken from off the street or inside the courthouse to serve as a **juror;** now, a member of a **jury panel.** [pronounce: <u>taliz</u>-man]

Tamper   Make changes by meddling; interfere. For example, *jury tampering* is attempting to bribe, threaten, or otherwise illegally influence a **juror.**

Tangible   Capable of being touched; real.

Tare   Box or container weight subtracted from the total weight of goods.

Target   The thing aimed at. For example, a *target company* is the subject of a takeover by a **tender** *offer;* a *target offense* is the contemplated crime in a **conspiracy;** and a *target witness* is a person called before a grand **jury** because the government wants to get an **indictment** against that person.

Tariff   *1.* An import tax or a list of articles and the import tax that must be paid on items on that list. A *protective tariff* is meant to protect local businesses from foreign competition; a *retaliatory tariff* is in response to a foreign country's tax on goods from your country; and an *antidumping tariff* is to prevent foreign countries from selling their goods in the U.S. at a lower price than the goods sell for in the foreign country or at a price lower than manufacturing cost. *2.* A public list of services, rates, charges, and rules of a public utility, such as an electric company.

Tax *1.* A required payment of money to support the government. Some of the hundreds of different types of taxes are listed in no. 2. *2.* Types of taxes defined in this dictionary include: **ad valorem; capital** *gains;* **capital** *stock;* **capitation; collateral inheritance; direct; estate; excess profits; gift; holding company; income; indirect; inheritance; luxury; payroll; poll; progressive; property;** *regressive* (see **progressive); sales; selective; severance; stamp; surtax; tonnage; transfer; undistributed profits; unified transfer; use; withholding;** etc. (see those words). *3.* For *tax* **certificate, foreclosure, lease, lien, sale,** and **title,** see **tax deed,** then refer to the base word (certificate, etc.). *4.* For *tax* **assessment, audit, credit, deduction, exclusion, exemption, roll, schedule, shelter, table,** etc., see those words. *5.* Other *tax* words follow.

Tax avoidance Planning finances carefully to take advantage of all legal tax breaks, such as **deductions** and **exemptions.** *Not* **tax evasion.**

Tax benefit rule The principle that if a loss or expense deducted from taxes in one year is recovered in another year, the recovery will be taxed as income in that later year to the extent of the deduction.

Tax bracket A specified interval of income to which a specific **tax rate** is applied. For example, to income between X and Y dollars, a tax rate of Z percent is applied.

Tax Court A **United States court** that takes **appeals** from taxpayers when the **I.R.S.** has charged them with deficiencies (underpayments) in their payments of **income, estate,** or **gift taxes.** (The *U.S. District Courts* also handle tax cases.) There are also specialized *tax courts* in some states.

Tax deed A proof of ownership of land given to the purchaser by the government after the land has been taken from another person by the government and sold for failure to pay taxes. Also, a *tax certificate* is a temporary proof of ownership that can be turned into a **deed** if the original owner does not **redeem** the property by paying the taxes due by a certain date; and a *tax lease* is a proof of ownership for a number of years when state law prohibits **absolute** sales for tax reasons. (All of these are *tax* **titles** given at a *tax* **sale** after a *tax* **warrant** has been issued for a *tax* **foreclosure** on a *tax* **lien;** see those words.)

Tax evasion See *criminal* **tax fraud.** *Not* **tax avoidance.**

Tax exempt(s) *1.* Property (such as that belonging to schools, churches, etc.) that is not subject to property taxation. *2.* Investments (such as **municipal** *bonds*) that give income that is not subject to (in this case, federal) income taxation. *3.* Income that is free from taxation, such as income *received* by a **charitable** organization. *4.* See **nonprofit organization.**

Tax ferret A person who searches out property that has not been taxed (for a state fee) or who turns in tax cheaters (for a percentage of the tax recovered).

Tax fraud The deliberate nonpayment or underpayment of taxes that are legally due. *Tax fraud* can be **civil** or **criminal,** with criminal fraud (*"tax evasion"*) having higher fines and the possibility of a prison sentence upon the showing of "willfulness." The line between the two types of fraud is blurred.

Tax haven A place that attracts foreign investment because of low or nonexistent taxes.

Tax home That base of business operations from which, if you travel on business, travel expenses may be deducted from taxes as business expenses.

Tax preference items Certain **income, credits, deductions,** etc., that may give certain high-income persons and organizations very low taxes. The **alternative minimum tax** is imposed on these items.

Tax rate The percentage of **taxable income** (or of inherited money, things purchased subject to sales tax, etc.) paid in taxes. For income tax, the percentage that must be paid within a specific **tax bracket.**

Tax return The form used to report income, **deductions,** etc., and to accompany tax payments and requests for refunds.

Tax stamp See **revenue** *stamp.*

Tax (taxable) year See **fiscal** *year.*

Taxable estate (or gift) The property of a dead person (or a gift) that will be taxed after subtracting for allowable expenses, **deductions,** and **exclusions.**

Taxable income Under federal tax law, this is either the "**gross income**" of businesses or the "**adjusted gross income**" of individuals (see those words) minus **deductions** and **exemptions** (see those words). It is the income against which **tax rates** are applied to compute tax paid before any **credits** are subtracted.

Taxing costs Making one side in a lawsuit pay the other side's costs of the suit. This is sometimes required, sometimes forbidden, and sometimes at the judge's discretion.

Taxpayer suit   A lawsuit brought by an individual to challenge the spending of public money for a particular purpose.

Teaser rate   A low initial interest rate on a loan that is soon replaced by a much higher rate.

Technical   *1.* Having to do with an art or a profession. Technical terms are often called "**words of art.**" *2.* Minor; merely procedural. For example, *technical errors* are mistakes in trial procedure that cause no real harm to either side.

Technical analysis   Deciding whether to buy or sell a particular **stock** or other **security** based on its price and its sales patterns. Compare with **fundamental analysis.**

Teller   A person whose duties include counting money (a *bank teller*), counting votes (a legislative *vote teller*), or counting other things.

Temporary restraining order   A judge's **order** to a person to not take a certain action during the period prior to a full **hearing** on the rightfulness of the action. Abbreviated *T.R.O.*

Tenancy   The condition of being a tenant; the **interest** a tenant has; the **term** (amount of time) a tenant has. See **tenant.**

Tenant   *1.* A person who holds land or a building by renting. A *tenant at will* has a **lease** that can be terminated at any time ("at will") by either the tenant or the landlord. A *tenant by sufferance* is a person who wrongly stays in property after the lease has expired. This is not a true tenant. *2.* A person who holds land or a building by any legal right including ownership. For example, *tenants in* **common** each hold a share of land that can be passed on to **heirs** or otherwise disposed of; **joint** *tenants* are like tenants in common except that they must also have *equal* interests in the property and, if one dies, that person's ownership interest passes to the other owner(s); and *tenants by the* **entireties** are like joint tenants except that they must also be husband and wife and that neither has a share of the land, but both hold the *entire* land as one individual owner. Different states vary these definitions slightly.

Tender   *1.* An **offer,** combined with a readiness to do what is offered. *2.* An offer of money. *3.* "Cash on the line." Actually putting money forward, as opposed to merely offering it. In this sense, U.S. cash is *legal tender* in the U.S. *4.* A *tender offer* is an offer (usually public) to buy a certain amount of a company's **stock** at a set price. This is often done to get control of the company.

Tender years doctrine   The principle, used in some courts, that in a **custody** dispute the custody of a very young child should be given to the mother unless the mother is unfit.

Tenement *1.* Any house, apartment, or place where people live. *2.* A particular kind of living place, such as an apartment house. The word may be defined differently by different **statutes** or **regulations.** *3.* In its original sense, anything that could be held, including offices, rights, etc., but especially an **estate** in land.

Ten-K (10-K) The annual report required by the S.E.C. of publicly held **corporations** that sell **stock.**

Tenor A vague word that can mean anything from "the exact words" to "the general meaning" or "train of thought."

Tentative trust A **Totten trust.**

Tenth Amendment The U.S. constitutional amendment that says all powers not specifically given to the federal government are kept by the states and the people.

Tenure *1.* Term of office. The length of time ("four years," "life and good behavior," etc.) a person may hold a job. *2.* A right to lifetime employment, subject to specific restrictions. *3.* The **feudal law** right to hold property as a subject of a higher lord.

Term *1.* A word or phrase (especially a "*term of art,*" one that has a fixed technical meaning). *2.* A fixed period; the length of time set for something to happen. For example: a *term of court* is the time period in which the court may hear cases (hold **sessions**); a *term loan* is a bank loan for a specific time period over a year; and a **lease** or *jail term* is how long each lasts. *3.* A part of an agreement that deals with a particular subject; for example, a *price term.* *4.* For *term* **bonds** and *term* **insurance,** see those words.

Termination Any ending; an ending before the anticipated end; an ending as specifically defined under some law. For example, under the **Uniform Commercial Code,** *termination* marks the end of a **contract** without its being broken by either side.

Terra (Latin) Land.

Territorial *1.* Having to do with a particular country. For example, *territorial waters* are inland waterways and the oceans surrounding a country. These waters "belong" to the country out to a certain distance. *2.* Having to do with a particular area. For example, *territorial jurisdiction* is the power of a court to take cases from within a particular geographical area.

Territorial courts Courts in each U.S. **territory,** such as the U.S. Virgin Islands. They serve as both federal and state courts.

Territory A general word meaning a geographical area, especially land that is administered by a country, but not a permanent part of that country or completely integrated into its governmental workings.

Terry v. Ohio (392 U.S. 1) The 1968 Supreme Court decision that a police officer may stop and **frisk** a person acting suspiciously (a "*Terry stop.*")

Test case *1.* A **lawsuit** brought to establish an important legal principle or right; or breaking a law to challenge it in court. *2.* One case selected from many similar ones to be tried first, with all persons involved in the other cases agreeing to be bound by the **decision.** *3.* An **amicable action.**

Test oath A **loyalty oath.**

Testacy (or testate) Having a valid **will** at time of death. *Testate succession* is the giving and receiving of property by a will.

Testament A **will.**

Testamentary Having to do with a **will.** For example, *testamentary capacity* is the mental ability needed to make a valid will; and a *testamentary class* is the group of persons who will eventually **inherit** from a will, especially when group size is not known.

Testator A person who makes a **will.**

Teste The statement in a document of the witnesses' names and the fact that they are witnesses.

Testify Give **evidence** under **oath.**

Testimonium clause The part of a **deed** or other document that contains who signed and when and where it was signed.

Testimony **Evidence** given by a **witness** under **oath.** This evidence is "*testimonial*" and is different from **demonstrative evidence.**

Testis (Latin) **Witness.**

Thayer theory See **bursting bubble theory.**

Theft Stealing of any kind. In many states, various **common law** crimes involving stealing, such as **larceny** and **embezzlement,** have been merged into a single offense called *theft.*

Theocracy Government by the dominant religious group in which church law is the highest law.

Theory of pleading doctrine The **common law** principle that a person must prove a case *exactly* as alleged in the **pleadings** to win the case. The doctrine is now of limited applicability because in modern practice pleadings may usually be amended to match the proof.

Theory of the case *1.* An interpretation of facts and law that fits the facts of a case. It may be one of several theories based on the **evidence** or it may be *the* legal theory that properly explains the evidence. *2.* The facts on which a case is based; the **cause of action** (see that word).

Therapeutic relief (or therapeutics)   A court order (or an agreement to settle a case) that requires an action (such as a revision of corporate procedures) to solve a problem rather than to compensate the plaintiff or punish the defendant.

Thereabout (and other "there" words)   A vague, overly formal word meaning "approximately there." Like most other "there" words (*thereafter, thereat, thereby, therein, thereof, thereto, theretofore, thereunder, thereupon, therewith,* etc.), it is best left out of a sentence or replaced by the exact thing referred to.

Thin corporation   A **corporation** that owes its **shareholders** so much money that the **I.R.S.** will treat some of the debt as **equity** and treat some of the debt payments as **dividends,** thus raising the owners' taxes.

Thin market   Very few items for sale or very few offers made for these items.

Third amendment   The **constitutional** prohibition against quartering soldiers in private homes during peacetime without the owner's permission.

Third degree   *1.* Illegal methods of interrogation to force a person to confess to a crime. *2.* The third most serious form of a crime.

Third market   Sale of **stocks** or other **securities** by a method other than sale through one of the established **exchanges.** This is also called "*off-board*" and is sometimes done by institutional traders of large blocks of stock.

Third part (or one-third portion)   See **election** no. 2.

Third party (or person)   A person unconnected with a deal, lawsuit, or occurrence, but who may be affected by it. For example, a *third party beneficiary* is a person who is not part of a **contract,** but for whose direct benefit the contract was made. A *third party complaint* is a **complaint** brought by a **defendant** in a lawsuit against someone not in the lawsuit. It brings that person into the lawsuit because that person may be **liable** for all or part of what the **plaintiff** is trying to get from the defendant.

Thirteenth Amendment   The U.S. **constitutional** amendment that abolished slavery and other forms of *involuntary servitude.*

Thirty-day letter   An **I.R.S.** letter to a taxpayer stating a tax **deficiency** (or refusing a refund request) and explaining **appeal** rights.

Threat   A communicated **intent** to harm another person by an illegal act. *Threats* against the president, threats of terrorism, threats using the mails, and certain other threats are federal crimes.

Three strikes law   A criminal **statute** with a severe required punishment (such as life imprisonment) for a defendant's third **felony** conviction (sometimes restricted to violent crimes and drug sales).

Three-judge court   A federal *trial* court that hears a case using three judges (rather than the customary one judge or judge plus jury) because a federal **statute** requires it in the type of case being heard. **Appeal** from the judgment of a *three-judge court* goes directly to the U.S. **Supreme Court.**

Through bill   A **bill of lading** for goods that will be carried in sequence by more than one shipper.

Throwback rule   The principle that if the **beneficiary** of a **trust** receives income from the trust in excess of the trust's income that year, and the trust has not in previous years paid out all of its income, the excess will be taxed to the beneficiary that year minus a **credit** for tax previously paid by the trust.

Ticket   *1.* A unified group or list of candidates, usually from one political party, with each candidate running for a different political office. *2.* A traffic law violation notice. *3.* A certificate showing a **right** (theater tickets, train tickets, lottery tickets, etc.).

Tie-in   See **tying in.**

Tier   A straight row of **townships** running East-West within a state on government maps. Compare with **range.** [pronounce: teer]

Time draft (or time bill or time loan)   A **draft** (or **bill** or loan) payable at a certain time.

Time immemorial   *1.* Since before the memory of anyone now alive. *2.* Since before any oral or written records on the subject.

Time is of the essence   A phrase used in a **contract** to make timeliness of performing a contractual promise **material,** thus making a failure to do what is required by the time specified a **breach** (breaking) of the contract.

Time, place, or manner restriction   Government restriction of when, where, or how a speech may be made or a group may assemble in public. The restriction does not violate **First Amendment** rights if it serves a legitimate government purpose, permits reasonable alternate speech or assembly, and does not restrict the subject matter.

Time-barred   Prohibited by a *statute of limitations.* (See **limitation.**)

Timely   Done within the required or promised time. A *timely* **suit** is one that is brought to court soon enough to be valid (for example, within the time specified by a *statute of* **limitations**).

Time-price doctrine   The principle that courts may allow a higher price to be charged for things bought on **credit** than for the same things paid for in cash. This is a way for a seller to get around state **usury** (see that word) laws.

Timeshare   See **interval ownership.**

Tippee   A person given information about a company by an **insider** whose duty to the company and the general public forbids giving out such information.

Title   *1.* The name for a part of a **statute.** For example, Title VII of the 1964 Civil Rights Act is known to specialists in the field as "Title Seven." *2.* Formal ownership of property. *3.* A document that shows no. 2. *4.* For **abstract** *of;* **chain of; clear; color of;** *defective* (see **defect**); **document of; lucrative; marketable; onerous; paper; perfect; record; root of; torrens,** etc., *title,* see those words. *5.* A *title search* is a search of the land records to see if title is good or restricted; a *title guaranty company* makes this search, then guarantees the title for the buyer; *title standards* are criteria set up by state organizations of banks, real estate lawyers, etc., to evaluate whether or not a title is good; and a *title state* or *title theory jurisdiction* is a state in which the title to mortgaged property is held by the lender until the debt is paid. See also **lien state** and **hybrid state.**

To have and to hold   A phrase used in some **deeds** to make a transfer of land valid. The phrase is no longer necessary.

To wit   An unnecessary phrase meaning "that is to say" or "namely." It can usually be replaced by a colon (:).

Toll   *1.* A fee to use a road, bridge, etc. *2.* To *toll* a *statute of* **limitations** (see that word) is to do something to delay it from taking effect, to "stop the clock from running."

Tombstone ad   A **stock** (or other **securities**) or land sales notice that clearly states that it is informational only and not itself an offer to buy or sell. It has a black border that resembles one on a death notice.

Tonnage tax   A tax on a ship based on its weight or on its carrying capacity.

Tontine   A type of **insurance,** now illegal, in which many persons pay into a fund and only those living by a certain date split it up.

Torrens title system   A system of land ownership **registration,** used in some states, in which the owner receives a conclusive "*certificate of title*" to land after a successful hearing. Use of the *Torrens system* is voluntary and is supplementary to the mere recording of a **deed,** which provides only *evidence* of land ownership.

Tort   A **civil** (as opposed to a **criminal**) **wrong,** other than a **breach of contract.** For an act to be a *tort,* there must be: a legal **duty** owed by one person to another, a **breach** (breaking) of that duty, and harm done as a direct result of the action. Examples of torts are **negligence, battery,** and **libel** (see those words).

Tort reform   Any attempt to reduce **tort** litigation by limiting the amount of **damages** or by limiting court access for certain types of cases.

Tortfeasor   A person who commits a **tort** (see that word). [pronounce: tort-fee-zor]

Tortious   Having to do with a **tort.** [pronounce: tor-shus]

Total   Complete for legal purposes. For example, a *total disability* may not be "total" in the common language sense, but merely be that which stops a person from doing his or her normal work; and *total loss* by fire need not be a burning to the ground, but merely be a complete commercial loss.

Totalitarianism   **Absolutism** (see that word) in which the government controls most of the small details of each person's life. This is done through propaganda, an intrusive military and police, etc.

Totten trust   A **trust** created by putting money into a bank account in your name as **trustee** for another person. You can take it out when you want, but if you do not take it out before you die, it becomes the property of that other person.

Touch and stay   A ship's right, under its **insurance** policy, to stop and stay at certain ports, but not to carry on any trade there.

Town   Describes a community of persons, a geographical area, or a type of local government. "*Town*" means different things in different states.

Township   *1.* A division of state land having six miles on each side and varying in importance as a unit of government from state to state. *2.* A division of a **county,** having different meanings and powers in different states.

Tract index   A public record containing references to all recorded **deeds, mortgages, liens,** etc., organized according to numbered lots with map references, so if you know exactly where a particular parcel of land is located, you can easily find references to all the recorded transfers of ownership and many other recorded matters concerning the parcel. Compare with **grantor-grantee index.**

Trade   *1.* Buying and selling; commerce. *2.* A job or profession. *3.* Barter; swap. *4.* A *trade agreement* is an agreement among countries to allow the sale of certain items in those countries (and at certain import tax rates); a *trade association* is a group of similar businesses organized for idea exchange, maintaining standards, and **lobbying;** *trade credit* is **credit** sales made by one business to another (commercial **accounts receivable**); *trade debt* is credit purchases by one business from another (commercial **accounts payable**); a *trade discount* is a price reduction to certain types of business customers (for example, from a lumber dealer to building **contractors**); a *trade dispute* is any **labor dispute** (excluding such things as the refusal to cross picket lines); and *trade usage* is common, regular practice or custom within a type of business or trade.

Trade acceptance   See **acceptance.**

Trade dress   A product's total appearance (size, shape, color, etc.) and its packaging and advertising. A court may prohibit a product's *trade dress* that is too similar to a more established product's trade dress.

Trade name   The name of a business. It will usually be legally protected in the area where the company operates and for the types of products in which it deals.

Trade secret   A process, tool, chemical compound, etc. that is used confidentially by a company and that is not generally known to the public or **patented.**

Trade usage   See **usage.**

Trademark   A distinctive mark, brand name, motto, or symbol used by a company to identify or advertise the products it makes or sells. *Trademarks* (and *service* **marks**) can be federally **registered** and protected against use by other companies if the marks meet certain criteria. A federally registered mark bears the symbol®.

Traditionary evidence   **Evidence** of what a dead person said long ago.

Traffic   Regular commerce, trade, or transportation.

Tranche   A part or "slice" of a whole; often applied to one set of **bonds** separated from all the others in a series by **maturity** date. [pronounce: transh or trahnsh]

Transaction   *1.* A business deal. *2.* An occurrence; something that takes place. A group of facts so interconnected that they can be referred to by one legal name, such as a "crime," a "contract," a "wrong," etc.

Transactional immunity   See **immunity.**

Transcript   A copy; especially the official copy of the **record** of a court proceeding.

Transfer   Change or move from person to person (sell, give, sign something over, etc.) or from place to place (court to court, etc.).

Transfer agent   A person (or an institution such as a bank) who keeps track of who owns a company's stocks and bonds. Also called a *registrar*. A *transfer agent* sometimes also arranges **dividend** and **interest** payments.

Transfer payments   Government payments (such as welfare or Social Security) for which the government gets nothing directly in return.

Transfer tax   A name given to different types of taxes in different contexts. For example, the term *transfer tax* is sometimes used to refer to an **estate tax**, a **gift tax**, a tax on the sale of **stocks**, etc. See also **unified transfer tax.**

Transferred intent rule   *1.* In **tort** law, the principle that if a person intended to hit another but hits a third person instead, he or she legally *intended* to hit the third person. This "*legal* **fiction**" sometimes allows the third person to sue the hitter for an *intentional tort*. *2.* In criminal law, the similar principle that if an unintended illegal act results from the intent to commit a crime, that act is also a crime.

Transgressive trust   A **trust** that violates the *rule against perpetuities.* (See **perpetuity.**)

Transitory action   A **lawsuit** that may be brought in any one of many places.

Transmutation   Changing one type of property **interest** into another, such as separate property into **community property.**

Transportation   Short for the U.S. Department of Transportation, the **cabinet** department that **regulates** interstate transportation through such agencies as the Federal Highway Administration. It also supervises the Coast Guard in peacetime. Some state transportation agencies use the same "*D.O.T.*" initials.

Trauma   *1.* An injury to the body caused by an external blow. *2.* Sudden psychological damage. *3.* Severe psychological damage caused by a specific past event.

Travel Act   (18 U.S.C. 1952) The 1961 law that makes it a federal crime to travel interstate to commit a crime or to use any interstate or foreign means of transportation, communication, or commerce to commit a crime.

Travel rights   The **constitutional right** to be free of unreasonable restraints on personal travel. These rights range from absolute rights (such as the absence of a passport requirement to travel between states of the U.S.) to relatively more fragile **penumbra doctrine** rights (such as the restriction on unreasonable state residency requirements for receipt of welfare benefits).

Traveler's check   A **cashier's check** (see that word) bought from a bank to safeguard travel money. It can be cashed only when signed a second time with a matching signature by the purchaser of the traveler's check.

Traverse   An old form of **pleading** in which facts in the other side's pleading are denied.

Treason   The **crime,** defined in the U.S. **Constitution,** committed by a U.S. citizen who helps a foreign government to overthrow, make war against, or seriously injure the U.S.

Treasurer   The person in charge of keeping track of an organization's money (taking in, paying out, etc.), but not usually the person who makes the organization's financial decisions.

Treasure-trove   Hidden money or other valuables with no known owner. Depending on state law, it may belong to the finder, to the land owner, to the state, or part to each.

Treasury   Short for the Department of the Treasury, the U.S. **cabinet** department that handles most national financial, monetary, and tax matters. It runs the Internal Revenue Service (which collects many taxes), the Mint (which makes coins), the **Secret Service** (which investigates counterfeiting of currency and performs certain nonfinancial tasks), etc.

Treasury bill, bond, certificate, or note   Documents showing that the U.S. Treasury has borrowed money. A *treasury bill* comes due in three, six, nine, or twelve months, paying its **face** amount (which is more than the purchase price) at the end of the set term; a *treasury certificate* comes due in one year and pays interest by **coupon;** a *treasury note* is like a *certificate* but comes due in two to ten years; and a *treasury bond* is issued for long-term borrowing.

Treasury stock (or treasury shares)   Shares of **stock** that have been rebought by the **corporation** that issued them.

Treatise   A large, comprehensive book on a legal subject.

Treaty   A formal agreement between countries on a major political subject. The *treaty clause* of the U.S. **Constitution** requires the approval of two-thirds of the **Senate** for any treaty made by the president.

Treble damages   Damages three times as great as the amount of proven financial harm caused, authorized by **statute** to strongly discourage certain kinds of wrongful actions in certain types of lawsuits.

Trespass   *1.* A wrongful entry onto another person's property. *2.* An old term for many types of civil wrongs or **torts.** For example, the *trespass* in no. 1 was called *trespass quare clausum fregit* (see **quare**); modern **contract** lawsuits grew out of *trespass on the case;* and *tres-*

pass vi et armis (force and arms) became modern lawsuits for both **negligence** and **battery** (see those words).

Trial   The process of deciding a case (giving **evidence,** making **arguments,** deciding by a judge and **jury,** etc.). It occurs if the dispute is not resolved by **pleadings,** pretrial **motions,** or **settlement.** A trial usually takes place in open court, and may be followed by a **judgment,** an **appeal,** etc.

Trial balance   Separate totals of all **credit** entries and of all **debit** entries in an **account** (or of all accounts with a *credit balance* and all accounts with a *debit balance*) calculated to compare the two. If they are not equal, there is a **bookkeeping** error.

Trial brief (or manual or book)   See **brief** no. 4 for *brief, manual,* and *book,* and no. 2 for *brief* only.

Trial list (or calendar)   See **calendar.**

Tribe   A Native American nation. *Tribal lands* (or a *reservation*) are lands held by a Native American nation as a whole. And a *tribal court* is a court that has **jurisdiction** over criminal offenses committed on tribal lands by a member of the nation, and over many types of civil cases between members or between members and nonmembers.

Tribunal   Court.

Trier of fact   *1.* The **jury,** or the judge if there is no jury. *2.* An **arbitrator,** an **administrative law judge,** etc.

Trover   An old type of lawsuit, now rarely used, in which a piece of property was claimed to be lost by you and then found by the person from whom you want it back. This got around the problem of proving the thing was wrongfully taken because all you had to prove was that it was yours and that the other person had it.

True bill   An **indictment** approved and made by a *grand* **jury.**

True lease   A **lease** that under **I.R.S.** rules qualifies the **lessor** to claim ownership benefits (such as *tax* **credits** and **deductions** for **depreciation**) and qualifies the **lessee** to deduct payments from income. *True leases* may resemble **installment** *contracts,* but they are different.

True person doctrine   The principle that a totally blameless person need not try to escape before killing a person who suddenly attacks with deadly force. Compare with **flee to the wall doctrine.**

True value rule   The principle that if corporate **stock** is not fully paid for in "real money" or its equivalent, stockholders may be **liable** to **creditors** of the company for the difference.

Trust   *1.* A group of companies that has a **monopoly** (see that word). *2.* An arrangement by which one person holds legal **title** to money or property for the benefit of another. For example, a *trust* is created when a mother signs over **stocks** to a bank to manage for her daughter with instructions to give the daughter the income each year until she turns thirty and then to give it all to her. In this example, the mother is the **settlor** or **grantor** of the **trust,** the bank is the **trustee,** and the daughter is the **beneficiary.** A trust, however, need not be set up explicitly; for example, if a father gives a son some money saying "half of this is for your brother," this arrangement may be a trust. Also, a trust can be set up in a **will;** created by formally stating that you *yourself* hold money in trust for another person; and created several other ways, both intentional and unintentional. *3.* There are hundreds of types of trusts. Some of those defined in this dictionary are: **accumulation; active; blind; business; charitable; charitable remainder; Clafin; Clifford; common law; community; complete voluntary; complex; constructive; direct; directory; discretionary; dry; equipment; estate; fixed; foreign; foreign situs; generation-skipping; governmental; grantor; honorary; imperfect; indestructible; instrumental; inter vivos; investment; involuntary; limited; living; Massachusetts; mixed; nominal; nominee; passive; perpetual; personal; pourover; real estate investment; resulting; savings bank; secret; short-term; simple; special; spendthrift; sprinkling; tentative; Totten; transgressive; unitrust; vertical; voluntary;** and **voting.** (See those words.) *4.* Many other kinds of *trusts,* such as **alimony; annuity; bond; contingent; executory; express; implied; insurance; irrevocable; ministerial; naked; precatory; private; public; reciprocal; shifting;** and **testamentary** are not in the dictionary as *trusts,* but can be understood by learning *trust* plus the listed word. *5.* Other *trust* words follow here.

Trust account See **trust deposit.**

Trust allotment Land given to Native Americans but held in **trust** for them by the government for a certain time.

Trust certificate A document showing that property is held in **trust** as **security** for a debt based on money used to buy the property. See also **deed of trust.**

Trust company A bank or other organization that manages **trusts,** acts as **executor** of **wills,** and performs other financial functions.

Trust deed A **deed of trust.**

Trust deposit Money or property put in a bank to be kept separate (often for ethical or legal reasons) or used for a special purpose.

Trust estate *1.* The legal **title** that is held by the **trustee** of a **trust.** *2.* The legal rights of the **beneficiary** of a trust. *3.* A property held in trust.

Trust ex delicto (or ex maleficio or invitum)   (Latin) "Trust from crime or wrongdoing." A **constructive trust** (see that word) that exists because legal title to property was obtained through a crime or other wrongdoing and another person is entitled to the property.

Trust fund   *1.* Money or property set aside in a **trust** or set aside for a special purpose. *2.* Money or property that *should* be treated as a trust. For example, the *trust fund theory* (or doctrine) says that certain funds (such as those improperly used by a corporation's **directors** or others) will be considered as held in trust for **creditors** or others.

Trust indenture   *1.* A document that spells out the details of a **trust.** *2.* The *Trust Indenture Act* is a federal law requiring certain investor-protection provisions in documents used to **issue** some kinds of **bonds.**

Trust instrument   A **deed of trust** (see that word) or a formal **declaration of trust.**

Trust officer   A person in a **trust company** who manages **trusts.**

Trust receipt   A document by which a lender puts up money to buy something and the borrower promises to hold the thing in **trust** for the lender until the debt is paid off. These arrangements are now usually handled by **security** agreements.

Trust state (or trust theory jurisdiction)   A state in which **title** to mortgaged property is transferred to a **trustee** to hold until the debt is paid. See also **title** *state* and **lien state.**

Trust territory   An area put under one country's administration by the United Nations.

Trustee   *1.* A person who holds money or property for the benefit of another person (see **trust**). *2.* A person who has a **fiduciary** duty to another person; for example, a lawyer or an **agent** who must act for another in a position of trust. *3.* A *trustee in bankruptcy* is a person appointed by a court to manage a **bankrupt** person's property and to decide who gets it; and a *trustee de son tort* (French) is a person who is held responsible for his or her wrongful or **negligent** acts that are performed while improperly claiming the right to take on, or while taking on, the duties of a trustee.

Trustees of Dartmouth College v. Woodward   (17 U.S. 518) The 1819 Supreme Court decision that a state **charter** given to a school is a **contract** with a private **corporation** that is protected by the **contract clause** of the Constitution. This established protection for business contracts.

Trusty   A prisoner whose good behavior has earned a position of trust.

Truth-in-Lending Act   The **Consumer Credit Protection Act.**

Try   Prosecute; litigate; attempt. To *try* a case is to argue it in court as a lawyer, decide it as a judge, or participate in the case in any of several other ways.

Turncoat witness   A **witness** who is expected to give helpful **testimony,** but who **testifies** for the other side.

Turning state's evidence   See **state's evidence.**

Turnkey contract   *1.* A **contract** in which a builder agrees to complete a building to a specific point, usually "ready to move in," and in which the builder assumes all construction risks. *2.* A drilling contract in which the driller does all the work up to the point when a well can begin production and in which, for a set fee, the driller assumes all construction risks except the risk of a dry hole.

Turnover (or turnover rate)   The rate at which **inventory** or financial **assets** are replaced during a time period.

Turnover order   A court **order** that something be given to someone else (property from a **defendant** to a **plaintiff** who has won the case, property that is in dispute to the court for safekeeping, a **bankrupt's** property to the **trustee,** etc.). This is a general word for many different orders, **writs,** etc.

Turntable doctrine   See **attractive nuisance.**

Turpitude   Dishonesty or immorality.

Twelfth Amendment   The U.S. **constitutional** amendment that requires separate voting by **electors** for president and vice president.

Twelve mile limit   An imaginary line, twelve miles off the coastline of the U.S., that separates international waters from those claimed by the U.S.

Twentieth Amendment   The U.S. **constitutional** amendment that moved up the presidential inauguration and the congressional session from March to January, eliminating a "**lame duck**" legislative session.

Twenty-fifth Amendment   The U.S **constitutional** amendment that set up procedures for appointing a president and vice president in case of death, removal, or resignation.

Twenty-first Amendment   The U.S. **constitutional** amendment ending national **prohibition** (the banning of alcoholic beverages).

Twenty-fourth Amendment   The U.S. **constitutional** amendment forbidding a **poll tax.**

Twenty-second Amendment   The U.S. **constitutional** amendment prohibiting a person from being elected U.S. president more than twice and prohibiting a person from being elected president more than once if the person has previously served more than two years of a presidential term to which another was elected.

Twenty-seventh Amendment   The U.S. **constitutional** amendment prohibiting congressional pay changes within the same House term they are enacted.

Twenty-sixth Amendment   The U.S. **constitutional** amendment that made the voting age eighteen.

Twenty-third Amendment   The U.S. **constitutional** amendment that gave Washington, D.C. residents the right to vote in presidential elections.

Twisting   Misrepresenting policies to convince a person to switch insurance companies.

Two dismissal rule   The rule (used in federal court and some state courts) that when a plaintiff voluntarily dismisses a lawsuit in two different courts it is a final _dismissal with prejudice_ (see **dismissal**).

Two issue rule   The principle that if a judge made an **error** in a jury **charge** on one **issue,** but there was more than one issue in the trial, and it cannot be proved that the jury based its **verdict** on that issue, the verdict should be allowed to stand. This rule is not followed in all states.

Two tier method   Describes the system in the U.S. of taxing a corporation's income twice, first as corporate income and second as income of persons who receive dividends (or certain other income from the corporation).

Two witness rule   The rule that a person cannot be convicted of **perjury** (or, in some states, of _first degree_ **murder** or other crime with a possible death penalty) unless two witnesses **testify** that the person's statement was false (or that the person committed the crime).

Tying in   Linking the sale of one product or service to the sale of another product or service. _Tying in_ may involve a seller's refusal to sell a product unless another product is bought with it. If a seller has a **monopoly** on a product, _tying in_ the sale of another product may be a violation of the **antitrust acts,** especially if the _right_ to sell a **patented** product is tied into selling a non-patented product.

U.C.C. **Uniform Commercial Code.**

U.C.C.C. **Uniform Consumer Credit Code.**

U.C.M.J. *Uniform* **Code of Military Justice.**

U.F.T.A. Uniform Fraudulent Transfer Act.

U.G.M.A. Uniform Gifts to Minors Act.

U.L.A. Uniform Laws Annotated.

U.L.P.A. Uniform Limited Partnership Act.

U.N. United Nations.

U.P.A. Uniform Partnership Act.

U.P.C. Uniform Probate Code.

U.R.E.S.A. *Uniform* **Reciprocal Enforcement of Support Act.**

U.S. **United States Reports.**

U.S.C. **United States Code.**

U.S.C.A. *1.* **United States Code Annotated.** *2.* United States Court of Appeals.

U.S.C.C.A.N. **United States Code Congressional and Administrative News.**

U.S.C.S. United States Code Service. A set of lawbooks similar to **United States Code Annotated** (see that word).

U.S.D.A. United States Department of Agriculture. The **cabinet** department that **regulates** farm activities, sets agricultural policy, carries on agricultural research and education programs, etc.

U.S.D.C. United States District Court.

U.T.I. Undistributed taxable income.

U.T.M.A. Uniform Transfers to Minors Act.

Uberrima fides (Latin) "The greatest good faith." Refers to a type of contract in which one person must first disclose all important facts to the other.

Ubi (Latin) Where.

Ukase A wide-sweeping decree by a king or other person in full control of a country.

Ullage The amount of liquid missing from a closed container.

Ultimate facts   Facts essential to a **plaintiff's** or a **defendant's** case. Often facts that must be inferred from other facts and evidence.

Ultimate purchaser   A consumer or business purchaser who intends a product for use, not resale.

Ultra   (Latin) Beyond; outside of; in excess of. For example, *ultra vires* actions are things a **corporation** does that are outside the scope of powers or activities permitted by its **charter** or **articles of incorporation.**

Ultrahazardous activity   An activity so dangerous that the possibility of serious harm cannot be eliminated by exercising extreme caution. These activities, such as blasting, result in **strict liability** (see that word).

Umbrella policy   An **insurance** policy that provides **liability** coverage, to a set limit, of claims that exceed the limits of one or more other policies (such as a person's automobile and home owner's policies).

Umpire   Generally, a person chosen to decide a dispute such as a **labor dispute.** More often, a person chosen to decide a dispute when the **arbitrators** (or the experts) chosen by each side disagree.

Un   *Not.* Many compound words beginning with *un* are here, but some are defined at the root word only. For example, for *unvalued policy,* see **valued policy.**

Unauthorized practice of law   Nonlawyers doing things that only lawyers are permitted to do. Who and what fits into this definition is constantly changing and the subject of dispute. If, however, a clear case comes up (for example, a nonlawyer pretending to be a lawyer and setting up a law office), the practice may be prohibited and the person punished under the state's criminal laws.

Unavailable   Unable to **testify** as a witness because the person is dead, insane, or sometimes beyond the reach of the court's **subpoena,** or beyond the ability of the person who wants to use the witness's **testimony** to bring the witness to court. Once the witness's *unavailability* is shown, past testimony, *dying* **declarations,** and certain other types of **hearsay** by that witness may sometimes be used as **evidence** in court under a **hearsay exception** (see that word).

Unavoidable accident (or casualty, cause, danger, etc.)   An accident in which everyone was careful, yet it happened. In some states this could result in a lawsuit with no **damages** awarded, in the reopening of a lawsuit because the **defendant** was prevented by an accident from answering the court papers or showing up in court, etc.

Unclean hands   See **clean hands.**

Unconscionability Sales practices that are so greatly unfair that a court will not permit them. For example, a sales contract between a large company and a poorly educated person that contains unfair terms in small print and technical language, and involves an unfairly high sales price, is _unconscionable._ The **Uniform Commercial Code** permits **rescission** ("unmaking") of unconscionable contracts.

Unconscionable Grossly unfair. See **unconscionability.** [pronounce: un-_con_-shun-a-bul]

Unconstitutional Describes laws or actions that conflict with the U.S. **Constitution** (see that word). An _unconstitutional condition_ is a requirement that a person give up a **constitutional right** to get a government benefit.

Under advisement (or submission) See **advisement.**

Under color (or cover) of law See **color.**

Under protest See **protest.**

Undercapitalization Lacking enough cash or short-term profit to stay in business.

Undersigned The person (or persons) whose name is signed at the end of a document.

Understanding A vague word meaning anything from "silent agreement" to "a written **contract.**"

Undertaking _1._ A promise. _2._ A promise made in the course of a lawsuit to the judge or to the other side. _3._ **Bonds** or other financial **securities;** the process of putting out these bonds. _4._ A venture of any kind.

Underwrite _1._ Insure. An _underwriter_ is an insurer. _2._ Guarantee to purchase any **stock** or **bonds** that remain unsold after a public sale, or to sell an **issue** of stock or bonds _for_ a company or purchased _from_ a company. The person (or organization) who does this is an _underwriter._

Undistributed (or undivided) profits tax A tax on that portion of a company's profits that are kept (rather than paid to stockholders) in excess of reasonable needs (paying bills, expansion, contingencies, etc.). The federal tax on _undistributed profits_ is called the **accumulated earnings tax.**

Undivided right (or interest or title) A right to an entire property that is shared with one or more others. For example, two **joint** owners of a parcel of land each own an _undivided_ half interest in the entire land, meaning that each can use the whole parcel.

Undue *1.* Improper or illegal. For example, *undue influence* is pressure that takes away a person's free will to make decisions. Undue influence involves misusing a position of trust or improperly taking advantage of a person's weakness to change that person's actions or decisions. *2.* More than necessary.

Unearned income *1.* Income received before it is earned; for example, a landlord's getting a January rent payment in December. *2.* Income from investments, rather than from salary, wages, or self-earned income. Social Security tax (**F.I.C.A.**) is not paid on unearned income.

Unemployment benefits (or compensation or insurance) State payments to persons who have worked a certain minimum length of time, made to them when they are laid off or have lost their jobs. Plans have varying payment rates and different qualification rules, which often include the requirement that the person be "available for work."

Unethical conduct Actions that violate professional standards such as the lawyers' **Rules of Professional Conduct.**

Unfair competition *1.* Too closely imitating the name, product, or advertising of another company in order to take away its business. This is called *"passing off."* *2.* Certain dishonest trade practices, such as using someone else's work unfairly. *3. Unfair methods of competition* is a broad phrase, used by the *Federal Trade Commission,* which includes many forms of unfair trade practices.

Unfair labor practice An action by a **union** or by an employer that is prohibited by law; for example, an employer's attempt to force an employee to give up union organizing activities.

Unified bar See **integrated bar.**

Unified transfer tax A combined federal tax on transfers by **gift** or death. It replaced the separate federal gift and **estate** taxes. The *unified transfer credit* is a **credit** (see that word) against the unified transfer tax. It replaced the lifetime gift and estate tax **exemptions.**

Uniform Regular; even. Applying generally, equally, and evenhandedly.

Uniform acts (or uniform laws) Laws in various subject areas, proposed by the *Commission on Uniform State Laws* and the **American Law Institute,** adopted in whole or in part by many states. Some of these are the Uniform Anatomical Gifts Act, the **Reciprocal Enforcement of Support Act,** and the **Uniform Commercial Code.**

Uniform Code of Military Justice See **Code of Military Justice.**

Uniform Commercial Code A comprehensive set of laws on every major type of business law, including contract law as it applies to the sale of goods, banking law, and **negotiable instruments** law. It has been adopted by every state, in whole or in major part. It replaced many older uniform laws, such as the _Uniform Negotiable Instruments Act_ and the _Uniform Sales Act._

Uniform Consumer Credit Code A **uniform act** adopted by some states to regulate the way merchants and lending institutions give credit to consumers.

Unilateral One-sided. For _unilateral contract,_ see **contract.** A _unilateral mistake_ about a contract's _terms_ usually will not get a person out of the contract unless the other side knew about the mistaken idea when the contract was made.

Union _1._ Any joining together of persons, organizations, or things for a particular purpose. _2._ An organization of workers, formed to **negotiate** with employers on wages, working conditions, etc. _Labor unions_ include: _closed_ (highly restricted in number of members, long apprenticeships, high fees, etc.; compare with **closed shop**); _company_ (sponsored by an employer; now usually forbidden by labor laws); _craft_ or _horizontal_ (persons in the same craft, no matter where they work); _independent_ (persons working for one employer who form a union with no affiliations); _industrial_ or _vertical_ (working in one industry, regardless of job type); _local_ (workers in one company or place who affiliate their union with a larger one); _open_ (easy to get into; see also **open shop**); and _trade_ (refers to either a labor union generally or a craft union).

Union certification See **certification proceeding.**

Union security clause The provision in a **contract** between a **union** and an employer that sets out the union's status and explains which types of employees must belong to the union.

Union shop A business in which all workers must join a particular union. This violates federal law. Compare with **closed shop, agency shop,** and **open shop.**

Unit investment trust A fixed **portfolio** of **bonds,** held to **maturity,** and sold by financial institutions to investors in _units_ of one thousand dollars.

Unit of production One barrel of oil (or an equivalent measure of a different **natural resource**) out of the estimated number that will be produced from a particular well, **lease,** or property. The "unit" is each barrel's fractional part of the whole estimated production. The total costs and profits of each venture are divided among each barrel for tax purposes.

Unit ownership acts State laws on **condominiums.**

Unit pricing   Pricing by item and not by a flat **contract** price on a total deal involving many items. *Unit pricing* may also mean pricing by each unit of weight (per ounce of peanut butter rather than per jar), by length (by board-foot, rather than by board), etc.

Unit rule   *1.* A way of valuing a block of **stocks** (or other **securities**) by taking the sale price of one **share** sold on an **exchange,** multiplying it by the number of shares in the block, and ignoring all other facts and assumptions about value. *2.* A rule binding every member of a group to vote the way the majority of the group votes.

United States attorney   A lawyer appointed by the president to handle U.S. **civil** and **criminal** legal matters in a U.S. judicial **district** (all or part of a state). Also called **district attorney** (see that word).

United States Code   The official lawbooks containing federal laws organized by subject. They are recompiled every six years, and supplements are published when needed.

United States Code Annotated   The **United States Code** with explanations and annotations to cases for each set of laws.

United States Code Congressional and Administrative News   A series of books with the texts of, and cross-references to, all federal laws and some congressional committee reports and federal administrative **regulations.**

United States commissioner (or magistrate)   See **magistrate.**

United States Courts   **Federal** courts (as opposed to *state* courts) created by the U.S. **Constitution** and by **Congress.** U.S. courts are all part of one system with federal **jurisdiction** (based on such things as **diversity of citizenship, federal question, appellate jurisdiction,** and **certiorari**). These courts, from the top down, are the: *Supreme Court* (hears appeals from state courts and lower federal courts); *Courts of Appeals* (hear appeals from lower federal courts and administrative agencies; there is one court for each of twelve geographical *circuits* plus the *Federal Circuit,* which hears appeals nationwide from specialized federal courts and other appeals such as patent cases); *District Courts* (the U.S. **trial** courts; there are about one hundred around the country); and specialized courts such as *Federal Claims* (contract claims against the U.S.), *International Trade* (tariff-related claims), *Armed Forces Appeals, Veterans Appeals, Tax Court,* and *Territorial Courts* (in the U.S. territories).

United States Department of Commerce v. United States House of Representatives   (119 S.Ct. 765) The 1999 U.S. Supreme Court decision that statistical sampling techniques may not be used to supplement direct headcounts in federal census taking for the purpose of setting House districts.

United States Government Organizational Manual   An annual U.S. publication that summarizes most information on the branches, agencies, and persons running the U.S. government.

United States Reports   The official volumes in which decisions of the U.S. **Supreme Court** are collected.

United States Statutes at Large   See **statutes at large.**

United States v. _____   Case names that begin with "United States" are listed in this dictionary by the "versus" name, as in **Nixon v. United States.**

Unitrust   A **trust** (see that word) in which a fixed percentage of the trust property is paid out each year to the **beneficiaries,** after which the trust property is paid to a charity. To qualify for special tax benefits, a unitrust must comply with several **I.R.S.** requirements.

Unity   _1._ An identical interest in property held jointly. There are the _unities_ of: _time_ (the property was acquired by all **joint** owners at the same time), _title_ (the property was acquired by all through the same **deed** or event), _interest_ (each person got the same ownership rights), and _possession_ (each has the same right to possess the whole property). In addition, _unity of person_ refers to the way property is held "as one person" by **tenants** _by the entireties_ because they are married. _2. Unity of possession_ also refers to the **merger** (see that word) of rights in land.

Univ. of Calif. Regents v. Bakke   (438 U.S. 265) The 1978 U.S. Supreme Court decision that struck down fixed **affirmative action** quotas, but allowed race to be taken into account in making public college admissions decisions that remedy past **discrimination.**

Universal   Applying to everything or everyone.

Unjust enrichment   Obtaining money or property unfairly and at another's expense. This does not include merely driving a hard bargain or being lucky in a deal. The law provides several ways to avoid unjust enrichment, such as by imposition of **quasi contract** (see that word).

Unlawful   Contrary to law; unauthorized by law. Not necessarily a crime, but at least either a **tort** or disapproved of by the law.

Unlawful assembly   Three or more people gathered to commit a violent crime or a **breach of the peace** (see that word).

Unlawful detainer   Holding on to land or buildings beyond the time you have a right to them.

Unliquidated See **liquidated.**

Unmarketable title See **marketable** *title.*

Unnatural act *1.* See **sodomy.** *2.* Describes making a **will** that gives away most of a person's property, without apparent reason, to other than immediate relatives.

Unprofessional conduct *1.* Conduct that violates a profession's ethical code, such as the lawyer's **Rules of Professional Conduct** (see that word). *2.* Conduct that is generally considered immoral, unethical, or dishonorable. (This conduct must generally relate to the performance of the person's duties for it to be included in no. 1.)

Unrealized profit **Paper** *profit.*

Unreasonable See **reasonable.**

Unrelated business income Money made by a tax-exempt **nonprofit organization** that comes from its business activity, which has little to do with the purposes or activities that give the organization tax-exempt status. This income is usually taxed.

Unrelated offenses Crimes or other wrongdoings not related to the subject of a prosecution. These *unrelated offenses* may not be used to show a person's general character.

Unwritten law *1.* A "law" of decent behavior that most people follow because it is considered right, just, or usual to do so. *2.* Any one of several commonly held assumptions about the law that are *not* laws and will not be enforced by a court; for example, the "law" that a husband will not be punished if he kills his wife's lover. *3.* **Common law** or judge-made law as opposed to **statutes, regulations,** etc. *4.* Enforceable informal rules such as trade **usage.**

Upset price A **reserve** *price.*

Urban easement The right of most streetside property to get light, air, and free entrance from the street side. See also **ancient lights.**

Ursery v. U.S. (518 U.S. 267) A 1996 U.S. Supreme Court decision permitting the imposition of a criminal punishment and a civil **forfeit**ure for the same crime because it was not **double jeopardy.**

Usage A general, uniform, well-known course of conduct followed in a particular geographic area or type of business or trade. *Usage* is important in interpreting ambiguous **contracts.**

Use An old method of holding land, similar to a **trust,** in which one person got legal ownership, but another person got the use of the land. The *statute of uses* was a law in England that converted most uses into full ownership interests in property.

Use immunity   See **immunity.**

Use tax   Tax on some products brought into a state without paying the state's **sales tax.**

Useful   *1.* In **patent** law, something is *useful* if it actually *does* something (as opposed to merely existing for its own sake or conveying information) that can be "applied to some practical use beneficial to society." This is a prerequisite for something to be **patentable.** *2.* In **tax** law, *useful life* is one measure of the time period for the **depreciation** of business property. It need not be the actual length of time something will be used or how long it will last.

Useless gesture exception   See **knock and announce.**

Usufruct   An old word for the right to use something as long as it is not changed or used up.

Usurious   Involving **usury.**

Usury   Charging an illegally high rate of **interest.**

Utility   A requirement for a device or process to be **patented.** See **useful.** A *utility patent* is the most common type of patent: for an invention such as a machine, a new drug, or a new process.

Utter   *1.* Put into circulation. **Issue** or put out a **check.** *2.* Say. *3.* Enough so that it will be considered complete, total, or **absolute.**

Uxor   (Latin) Wife. Abbreviated *ux.*

v. *1.* An abbreviation for *versus* or "against" in the name of a case. For example, *Smith v. Jones* means that *Smith* is suing *Jones. 2.* Volume.

V.A. Veterans Administration. The U.S. agency that administers benefits and programs for armed services veterans. These programs include hospitals, college tuition assistance, etc.

V.A.T. **Value added tax.**

V.R.M. **Variable rate mortgage.**

Vacate *1.* **Annul;** set aside; take back. For example, when a judge *vacates a judgment,* it is wiped out completely. *2.* Move out or empty.

Vacco v. Quill (521 U.S. 783) A 1996 U.S. Supreme Court decision that said there is no **Fourteenth Amendment** right to physician-assisted suicide even though patients do have a right to refuse treatment.

Vadium (Latin) A **pledge.**

Vagrancy A vague, general word for "hanging around" in public with no purpose and no honest means of support.

Vague *1.* Indefinite; uncertain; imprecise. *2.* The *vagueness doctrine* is the rule that a **criminal** law may be **unconstitutional** if it does not clearly say what is required or prohibited, what punishment may be imposed, or what persons may be affected. A law that violates **due process of law** in this way is *void for vagueness.* See also **overbreadth.**

Valid *1.* Binding; legal; complying with all needed formalities. *2.* Worthwhile; sufficient.

Validation In employment law, the proof that a job test, selection procedure, or job requirement is related to job performance. *Content validity* is proof that a test measures skills or abilities needed for the job. *Construct validity* is proof that a test measures mental and psychological traits needed for the job. And *criterion validity* is proof that a selection procedure improves job performance by accurately measuring the results of the procedure against actual job performance.

Valuable consideration See **consideration.**

Value *1.* Worth. This may be what something *cost,* what it would cost to *replace,* what it would bring on the open market, etc. *Actual value, cash value, fair value, market value,* etc., may all mean the same. See

market value. *2. "For value"* or *"for value received"* means "for **consideration.**"

Value added tax   A tax based on the sale price of goods and services minus the cost of raw material and goods purchased to produce the goods and services. *V.A.T.s* are used in Europe.

Value rule   A way to measure **damages** that compares the value of what was promised to the value of what was actually received.

Valued policy   An **insurance** policy in which the items insured are given an exact value. This is in contrast to an *open (or unvalued) policy* in which a value need not be placed on items until they are lost, damaged, etc.

Vandalism   The intentional harming, defacing, or destroying of another person's property.

Variable annuity (or insurance)   An **annuity** (or **insurance** policy) with payments that depend on the income generated by particular investments. Also called **asset-**linked annuity (or insurance).

Variable rate mortgage   A **mortgage** with payments that change (every month, year, two years, five years, etc.) based on a standard index such as the **prime** *rate.*

Variance   *1.* A difference between what is alleged (said will be proved) in **pleading** and what is actually proved in a **trial.** *2.* Official permission to use land or buildings in a way that would otherwise violate the **zoning** regulations for the neighborhood.

Vel non   (Latin) Or not.

Vendee   Buyer.

Vendor   Seller.

Vendor's lien   A catchall phrase for various types of **liens** held by the seller of property, including the *purchase price lien* (not usually recognized by law) of a person who sells land with no **security** and the lien of a seller who holds goods until the price is paid.

Venire facias   (Latin) Describes a command to the **sheriff** to assemble a **jury.** [pronounce: ve-neer fay-she-as]

Venireperson (or member, man, or woman)   Juror or prospective juror (person on a jury **panel**).

Venture capital   Money invested in a young company with high risk and the potential for high reward.

Venue   The local area where a case may be tried. A court system may have **jurisdiction** (power) to take a case in a wide geographic area, but the proper *venue* for the case may be one place within that area for the convenience of the parties, etc. Jurisdiction is the subject of fixed rules, but venue is often left up to the **discretion** (good judgment) of the judge.

Verba (Latin) Words. *Verba artis* means "words of art" or technical terms.

Verbal Spoken; partly spoken and partly written; written but unsigned; or lacking some other formality.

Verbal act Words that have legal effect as part of a transaction. For example, the words "I give you this ring" are a verbal act if the ring is handed over at the same time, making the words part of the "gift transaction." (A gift requires both *intent,* supplied by the words, and *delivery,* supplied by handing over the ring.) *Verbal acts* are usually **admissible** as **evidence** because they are *conduct,* not mere words that might be barred as **hearsay.** Compare with **res gestae.**

Verdict *1.* The **jury's** decision. *2.* The usual verdict in a **civil** case, one where the jury decides which side wins (and how much, sometimes), is called a *general verdict.* When the jury is asked to answer specific *questions of* **fact,** it is called a *special verdict.* For **compromise, directed, partial, sealed,** etc., *verdicts,* see those words. *3.* The jury's verdict in a **criminal** case is usually "guilty" or "not guilty" of each **charge.** A jury might also make *sentencing* decisions.

Verify *1.* **Swear** in writing to the truth or accuracy of a document. *2.* Confirm; prove the truth of; back up; check up on.

Versus Against.

Vertical In a chain, such as from manufacturer to wholesaler to retailer (as opposed to among various manufacturers, among various retailers, etc.). In antitrust law, a *vertical trust* (or *vertical integration*) is the combination of several of these levels under one ownership or control.

Vertical union An **industrial union.**

Vest *1.* Give an immediate, fixed, and full right. *2.* Take immediate effect (see **vested**).

Vested *1.* **Absolute, accrued,** complete, not subject to any **conditions** that could take it away; not **contingent** on anything. For example, if a person sells you a house and gives you a **deed,** you have a *vested interest* in the property; and a pension is *vested* if you get it at retirement age even if you leave the company before that. *2.* There are several types of **pension plan** *vesting.* For example, *"cliff"* *vesting* (until you work a certain number of years, you get nothing; after that, you get all your accrued **benefits**); *"graded"* *vesting* (additional percentages of your accrued benefits are added the longer you work); and "*rule of 45*" vesting (after your age plus the number of years you have worked for the company equals 45, part of your accrued benefits become vested, with the rest vested in the next few years). There are variations on all of these methods.

Veterans Administration   See **V.A.**

Veterans preference   Federal and state laws giving honorably discharged war veterans various hiring preferences, with the strongest usually going to disabled veterans.

Veto   A refusal by the president or a governor to sign into law a **bill** that has been passed by a **legislature.** In the case of a presidential veto, the bill can still become a law if two-thirds of each **house** of Congress votes to *override* the veto. An *item veto* (or *line item veto*) is the veto by a state governor of only part of an **appropriations** bill, and a *pocket veto* is the failure by the president to sign a bill passed within ten days of the end of a legislative session (which has the same effect as a veto). Also, any member of the United Nations **Security Council** can *veto* a **resolution** of the Council.

Vexatious litigation   Lawsuits brought without any just cause or good reason. Also see **malicious** *prosecution.*

Vi et armis   (Latin) "Force and arms" (see **trespass**).

Via   (Latin) A right of way or road.

Viable child   A child developed enough to live outside the womb.

Viatical settlement   The purchase of a person's life insurance policy (or the transfer of rights to the person's death benefit) for less than the value of the death benefit because the person needs immediate money to cope with an illness that is likely terminal.

Vicarious liability   Legal responsibility for the acts of another person because of some relationship with that person; for example, the **liability** of an employer for certain acts of an employee. [pronounce: vi-care-ee-us]

Vice   *1.* Illegal (and considered immoral) activities such as prostitution. *2.* An imperfection or defect. *3.* Describes a second in command or substitute.

Victimless crime   A term often applied to illegal, but consensual, sexual acts or drug use.

Vide   (Latin) See. For example, *vide ante* means "look at the words or sections that come before this one." [pronounce: vee-de]

Videlicet   (Latin) "That is to say." Sometimes used to separate a general statement from the specific things that explain it. Usually abbreviated _viz;_ the term is unnecessary because a colon (:) can be used in its place.

View _1._ The right in some cases to have your windows free from new obstructions. See also **ancient lights.** _2._ An inspection by a jury, or by persons appointed by a court (called "_viewers_"), of an accident scene, a crime scene, a route for a proposed road, etc. _3._ For _majority_ or _minority view,_ see **majority.**

Vigilance   Watchfulness. Reasonable promptness in pursuing or guarding a **right,** enforcing a **claim,** etc.

Vinculo matrimonii   (Latin) See **a vinculo matrimonii.**

Violent presumption   Complete, even though indirect proof. For example, the fact that the sun was shining is a _violent presumption_ that an event did not take place at midnight in New York.

Vir   (Latin) A man; a husband.

Virtual adoption   See **equitable** _adoption._

Virtue   _1._ Something worthwhile or good (in a practical, rather than a moral sense). _2._ "_By virtue of_" means "by the power of" or "because."

Vis   (Latin) Force or violence. For example, _vis major_ is an irresistible force or a natural disaster. See also **act of God, force majeure,** and **trespass.**

Visa   Permission to travel in a country, given by officials of that country who usually mark it into a person's _passport._ A _visa_ is also sometimes required as permission from your _own_ country to travel to an otherwise "off-limits" country.

Visitation   _1._ Meeting with a person who is under the supervision of another. _Visitation rights_ usually refers to the right of a parent to see a child who is in the legal **custody** of the other parent. _2._ Inspection or supervision by an outsider.

Vital statistics   Data on births, deaths, diseases, marriages, divorces, etc.

Vitiate   Invalidate or make ineffective, **void,** or **voidable.** [pronounce: vish-ee-ate]

Viva voce   _1._ (Latin) "Living voice"; orally, as opposed to in writing. _2._ A _viva voce vote_ is usually taken on minor questions decided by a legislature or other assembly. The person leading the session decides who wins based on which side sounds louder.

Viz   See **videlicet.**

Voiceprint   A graph of the pitch, intensity, and timing of the sound waves that make up a person's voice. Some courts allow this graph, produced by a _spectograph_ machine, as **evidence** that identifies a speaker.

Void   Without legal effect; of no binding force; wiped out. For example, a *void contract* is an "agreement" by which no one is (or ever was) bound because something legally necessary is missing from it. Sometimes *void* is used imprecisely in legal documents to mean **voidable.**

Void for vagueness   See **vague.**

Voidable   Can be made **void.** Describes something that is in force but can be legally avoided. For example, a *voidable contract* is a **contract** that one or both sides can legally get out of, but is effective and binding if no one chooses to get out of it.

Voir dire   (French) "To see, to say"; "to state the truth." The preliminary in-court questioning of a prospective witness (or juror) to determine competency to testify (or suitability to decide a case). [pronounce: vwahr deer]

Volenti non fit injuria   (Latin) "A willing person cannot be injured legally." See **assumption of risk.**

Volstead Act   A defunct federal law that prohibited the manufacture and sale of alcoholic beverages. The law was passed under the repealed **Eighteenth Amendment** to the U.S. **Constitution.**

Voluntary   *1.* With complete free will; intentional. In this sense, a *voluntary trust* is one set up intentionally, rather than imposed by law. *2.* Free; without **consideration.** In this sense, a *voluntary trust* is set up as a gift, rather than as a way of protecting, for example, a **mortgage** holder. *3.* For *voluntary* **intoxication** and **manslaughter,** see those words.

Volunteer   A person who pays another's debt without being asked and with no requirement to pay it. See **officiousness.**

Voter   A person who has the legal qualifications to vote; a person who has **registered** to vote; a person who has actually voted.

Voting Rights Act   (42 U.S.C. 1973) A 1965 federal law that prohibited literacy and character tests, provided for federal voter **registration,** and prohibited states from certain other practices.

Voting stock   Any type of corporate stock (often only **common stock**) entitled to vote.

Voting trust   An arrangement by which stockholders in a company pool their **shares** of **stock** for the purpose of voting as a block at stockholders' meetings.

Vouch   Give personal assurance of the truthfulness, validity, or existence of something. A prosecutor is not permitted to *vouch* for a witness's trustworthiness to a jury.

Voucher   *1.* A document that authorizes the giving out of something, usually cash. *2.* A **receipt** or **release**; the **account** book that shows receipts and releases.

Vouching in   A procedure by which a **defendant** in a lawsuit notifies another person that the person may be liable for what the **plaintiff** asks. Under some circumstances, the person notified may be bound by the court's decision.

Vs.   Versus. See **v.**

W.D.   Western **district.**

Wade hearing   A criminal case **suppress**ion hearing (named after *Wade v. U.S.,* 388 U.S. 218 (1967)) that determines whether a witness's identification of the defendant was improper (usually due to unfairly suggestive procedures) and thus excludable as evidence. The term strictly refers to a hearing about the absence of counsel at a lineup, but has come to be used for hearings about all sorts of pretrial and in-court identifications.

Wage   *1.* Employee compensation by the hour, job, or piece as *opposed* to **salary** (see that word). But see no. 2. *2.* Under the federal Fair Labor Standards Act, *wages includes no. 1 plus salary,* bonuses, tips, commissions, board, and lodging.

Wage and hour laws   Federal and state laws setting minimum wages and maximum hours of work; the leading law is the federal *Fair Labor Standards Act.*

Wage assignment   An arrangement in which a person allows his or her wages to be paid directly to a **creditor.** It is illegal in most situations in many states. See also **garnishment.**

Wage earner's plan   See **Chapter Thirteen.**

Wager of law   A practice in old England by which a person accused of something, such as owing money, could swear that the money was not owed and could bring eleven neighbors (called *compurgators*) to swear to the person's general truthfulness.

Wager policy   A **gambling policy.**

Wagner Act   A 1935 federal law that established most basic union rights. It prohibited several employer actions (such as attempting to force employees to stay out of a union) and labeled these actions "*unfair labor practices.*" The *Wagner Act* (also known as the *National Labor Relations Act*) created the National Labor Relations Board to help enforce the labor laws. The Act was combined with other revised labor laws into a later **National Labor Relations Act** (see that word).

Wait and see statute   A state law that avoids some of the problems caused by the *rule against perpetuities* (see **perpetuity**) by allowing time to pass to find out if a **will** or **trust** violates the rule.

Waive Give up, renounce, or disclaim a privilege, right, or benefit with full knowledge of what you are doing. [pronounce: wave]

Waiver The voluntary giving up of a right (see **waive**). For example, *waiver of immunity* is the act of a **witness** who gives up the **constitutional** right to refuse to give evidence against himself or herself and who proceeds to **testify**. A criminal **defendant** waives **immunity** merely by going on the witness stand.

Waiving time Allowing a court to take a longer time than usual to **try** you on a criminal charge.

Walsh-Healey Act (41 U.S.C. 35) A 1936 federal law that set up minimum wage, hour, and work condition standards for employees working for **contractors** on federal jobs.

Want *1.* Desire. *2.* Lack.

Wanton *1.* **Reckless,** heedless, or **malicious.** *2.* Weighing about two thousand pounds. *3.* Floating in broth. *4.* In need.

War crimes Actions that violate **international laws** of the conduct of war. Individuals may be punished for war crimes by national or international courts. Since the Nuremberg trials following World War II, these crimes include *crimes against humanity* such as the systematic torture of civilians.

War powers clauses The U.S. **constitutional** clauses (Article I, Section 8, Clauses 11-14) that give Congress the power to declare war and raise armies and give the president the power to carry on the war.

Ward *1.* A division of a city for elections and other purposes. *2.* A person, especially a child, placed by the court under the care of a **guardian.**

Warehouse receipt A piece of paper proving that you own something stored in a warehouse. A warehouse receipt may be a **negotiable instrument.**

Warehouser (or warehouseman) A person in the business of storing goods. A *warehouser's lien* is the right of a person storing goods to keep them until storage charges have been paid.

Warrant *1.* Promise or guaranty, especially in a **contract** or in a **deed** (see **warranty**). *2.* Written permission given by a judge (or **magistrate,** etc.) to a police officer (or **sheriff,** etc.) to **arrest** a person, conduct a search, seize an item, etc. A warrant given directly from a judge to a police officer to arrest a person is a *bench warrant. 3.* See *subscription warrant* under **subscribe.** *4.* Promise that certain facts are true. *5.* The name for certain documents authorizing the payment or collection of money.

Warranty *1.* Any promise (or a presumed promise, called an *implied warranty*) that certain facts are true. *2.* In land law, a *warranty* is a promise or guaranty in a **deed** that the **title** of land being sold is good and is complete ("**marketable**"). (See **general** and **special warranty deeds.** See also **quitclaim deed.**) *3.* In the law of buildings, a *construction* or **home owners warranty** is the promise that it was built right, and a *warranty of habitability* is the implied promise to buyers or renters that a house is fit to live in. *4.* In commercial law, a *warranty* is either no. 2 or no. 3. *5.* In **consumer** law, a *warranty* is the same as in the previous definitions, plus any obligations imposed by law on a seller that benefit a buyer; for example, the *warranty* that goods are **merchantable** and the warranty that goods sold as *fit for a particular purpose* are fit for that purpose. Also, under federal law, if a written consumer warranty is not "full" (as to labor and material for repairs) it must be labeled *limited warranty* in the sales contract.

Wash sale *1.* Selling something and buying something else that is basically the same thing. The word often is used to describe the nearly simultaneous buying and selling of **shares** of the same **stock.** *2.* **Rescission** (see that word) is sometimes called a "wash" because all original rights, **liabilities,** and property (or their monetary equivalent) are returned. *3.* A sale with no profit or loss.

Waste *1.* Abuse or destruction of property in your rightful possession, but belonging to someone else, or in which someone else has certain rights. *2.* Loss of another's assets due to mismanagement. *3.* See also **wasting.**

Waste-book A merchant's log of rough notes of transactions as they occur. Also called a "*blotter.*"

Wasting Depleting; depletable; being used up. A *wasting asset* is some valuable natural resource (such as growing timber, mineral deposits, oil, etc.) which, when removed, normally qualifies for a **depletion allowance** (see that word) under income tax laws; a *wasting property* is a right to a *wasting asset,* a **lease** of limited duration, a **patent** right, etc.; and a *wasting trust* is a trust that gets used up by making scheduled payments to the trust's **beneficiary.**

Water rights The right to use water from a river, stream, ditch, pipe, etc. (sometimes for a specific purpose or amount). See also **riparian rights.**

Watered stock A stock **issue** that is sold as if fully paid for, but that is not (often because some or all of the shares were given out for less than full price).

Waybill   A document made out by a **carrier** that includes the "who, what, where, how, and when" of goods shipped. See also **bill of lading.**

Ways and Means   The name for the **committee** of the U.S. **House of Representatives** (and of some state **legislatures**) responsible for raising the tax revenue that funds all government activity.

Weight of evidence   **Evidence** that is more *convincing* than opponent's evidence, not necessarily the larger *quantity.*

Welfare   *1.* Public financial assistance to certain categories of poor persons. *2.* Health, happiness, and general well-being. *3.* See **general welfare clause.**

Well-pleaded complaint doctrine   The federal rule that a defendant cannot get **removal** of a lawsuit from state court to federal court unless the plaintiff's **complaint** shows that the case involves federal law. Compare with **artful pleading doctrine.**

WESTLAW   A computerized legal research source.

Wharton rule   **Concert of action rule.**

Whereas   A vague word, often used to mean "because." When placed at the beginning of a legislative **bill,** "whereas" introduces the explanation for why the bill should be passed and made law.

Whereby (and other "where" words)   A vague word meaning "by means of," "how?" or several other things. This word, like other vague, formal "where" words (*whereas, wherefore, whereof, whereon, whereunder, whereupon,* etc.), is usually best left out of a sentence or replaced by a specific thing, place, idea, etc.

Wherefore   A vague word, often used in a **complaint** to begin the section in which the **plaintiff** spells out exactly what he or she wants from the **defendant** or wants the court to do.

Whipsaw strike   *1.* A **strike** that is particularly harsh to convince other companies to give in to **union** demands. *2.* A strike against a company in which the union uses the added pressure of allowing the company's competitors to continue working by not striking them.

Whistleblower   An employee who brings organizational wrongdoing to the attention of government authorities. Government laws protect some whistleblowers. See also **qui tam.**

White Acre   See **Black Acre.**

White knight   A corporation that buys a company to save it from a *takeover* that the company's officers do not want.

White slave   The original word for a woman involved in a **Mann Act** (see that word) violation.

White-collar crimes *1.* Commercial crimes like **embezzlement, price fixing,** etc. *2.* Nonviolent crimes.

Whole law A state or country's **internal law** plus its **conflict of laws** rules. See also **renvoi.**

Whole life Life **insurance** with continuing **premium** payments (which stop if the policy becomes fully paid), a sum paid at death, and, usually, a **cash surrender value.**

Wholesale Sale (usually in quantity) to intermediaries or to retailers rather than to consumers of the product.

Widow's (or widower's) allowance That part of a dead spouse's money and property that a person may take free of all claims under some state laws.

Widow's (or widower's) election That part of a dead spouse's money and property that a person may choose to take under state law, rather than accepting what was given in the spouse's **will.** This is usually equal to what the person would get if there is no will. The process is sometimes called *waiving the will.*

Wildcat strike A strike without the consent of the union.

Wild's case An old English case that said if a person gives property in a **will** "to John and his children," unless the will clearly means something else, if John has children at the time the will is made, the children take the land jointly with John; but if John has no children when the will is made, John gets the land, but it goes to any children after he dies.

Will *1.* Desire; choice. For example, a *tenant at will* is a person who is permitted to use land or a building only as long as the owner desires the tenant to stay. *2.* A document in which a person tells how his or her property is to be handed out after death. If all the necessary formalities have been taken care of, the law will help carry out the wishes of the person making the will. For the various types of wills (**holograph, mutual, nuncupative, reciprocal,** etc.), see those words.

Will substitutes Refers to such things as life **insurance, joint** ownership of property, **trusts,** and other devices that partially eliminate the need for a **will.**

Willful *1.* Intentional; deliberate; on purpose. *2.* Obstinate; headstrong; without excuse. *3.* With evil purpose.

Wilson v. Lane (118 S.Ct. 2068) The 1999 U.S. Supreme Court decision that a police department violates the **Fourth Amendment** prohibition of unreasonable searches when it permits newspersons to accompany police into a home for a search or arrest.

Wind up   Finish current business, settle accounts, and turn property into cash in order to end a **corporation** or a **partnership** and split up the **assets**. See also **dissolution**.

Windfall profits   Profits that come unexpectedly, that come through no effort or financial cost, or that are much greater than deserved.

Wiretap   An electronic or other intercept of the contents of a communication. Government wiretaps must be authorized by a judge for **probable cause** and private wiretaps must have the consent of one participant (in some states, all participants).

Wish   Anything from "mildly desire" to "strongly command." Avoid or define the word in legal drafting.

With all faults   As is.

Withdraw   Remove a thing (*withdraw* money from an account), remove yourself (*withdraw* as a candidate for office), remove another person (*withdraw* a **juror** from a jury), remove from consideration (*withdraw* an **objection** in a trial), or remove all possible connections (see **withdrawal from conspiracy or criminal action**).

Withdrawal from conspiracy or criminal action   More than merely ceasing participation. To avoid **prosecution** for a **conspiracy,** a person must also disclose the conspiracy to law enforcement authorities, and to avoid prosecution for other criminal activity (often an **attempt**), a person must also try to prevent the crime through disclosure or direct action.

Withholding of evidence   Hiding, destroying, or removing objects, records, etc., because they may be needed by a court. This may be a crime.

Withholding tax   *1.* The money an employer takes out of an employee's pay and turns over to the government as prepayment of the employee's **income tax.** *2.* A tax on **dividends,** interest, and other income paid to certain people, including people in other countries.

Within the statute   Defined, prohibited, or permitted by the **statute.** Use a more precise term if possible.

Without day   See **sine** *die.*

Without recourse   A phrase used by an indorser (signer other than original "**maker**") of a **negotiable instrument** (check, etc.) to mean that if payment is refused, he or she will not be responsible.

Witness   *1.* A person who observes an occurrence (such as an accident), an event, or the signing of a document. *2.* A person who makes a sworn (under **oath**) statement that can be used as evidence (in a court, **legislature, hearing,** etc.). *3.* For **material witness** and **expert**

witness, see those words; and for "*witness against self,*" see **self-incrimination.**

Wobbler   *1.* A crime that "wobbles" between being a **felony** and a **misdemeanor,** so it can be punished as either.

Words and Phrases   A large set of lawbooks that defines legal (and many nonlegal) words by giving actual quotes from cases.

Words of art   Technical terms that are used in a special way by a particular profession. They are also called "*terms of art.*"

Words of limitation   The words in a **deed** or **will** that tell what type of **estate** or rights the person being given land receives.

Words of purchase   The words in a **deed** or **will** that tell who is to get the property.

Work (made) for hire   A **copyright**able work for which the employer (or hiring person), not the person hired to do the work, is the "*author*" and owner. Employee work is usually *work for hire* unless there is a signed writing to the contrary, but a "*specially commissioned work*" is a work for hire only if it is of a specified type and there is a signed writing that the work is "made for hire."

Work release program   Daytime release of prisoners to work, with return to the prison for nights and weekends.

Workers' compensation laws   Laws passed in most states to pay money to workers injured on the job, regardless of **negligence.** Businesses pay into a fund to support those payments.

Working capital   A company's **current** *assets* minus **current** *liabilities.* It is one measure of the company's ability to meet its obligations and to take advantage of new opportunities. See also **current** *ratio* and **quick assets.**

Working papers   Proof-of-age certificates to satisfy minimum age laws.

Workout   An agreement to **refinance, restructure,** or **discharge** a debt that is overdue or in **bankruptcy.**

Work-product rule   The principle that a lawyer need not show the other side in a case any facts or things gathered for the case unless the other side can convince the judge that it would be unjust for the things to remain hidden and that there is a special need for them. This is also called the "*qualified attorney work-product privilege.*" See also **qualified privilege.**

Work-to-rule   A work slowdown in which formal work rules are so closely followed that production slows down.

World Court   The **International Court of Justice.**

Worthier title doctrine   *1.* Historically, the rule that if persons who inherit something in a **will** would get exactly the same thing by being **intestate heirs** (see those words), their "*worthier title*" is to get it as if intestate heirs instead. *2.* Today, in different forms in those states that use it, the rule creates a **rebuttable** *presumption* that a person did not mean to limit a **remainder** interest to his or her heirs.

Wraparound   *1.* A **second** mortgage on a property that includes payments on a low-interest-rate first **mortgage.** This is done by buyers who don't want to lose the first mortgage and sellers who can't finance the sale without being willing to keep their names on the first mortgage. It is also done by lenders who finance work on older buildings. *2.* A new mortgage that makes payments on old mortgages on several properties at once.

Wrap-up clause   A **zipper clause.**

Writ   A judge's **order** requiring that something be done outside the courtroom or authorizing it to be done. The most common *writ* is a notice to a **defendant** that a lawsuit has been started and that if nobody comes to court to defend against it, the **plaintiff** may win automatically. If the writ cannot be served (delivered properly), a second one (called an "*alias writ*") may be used. Other types of writs include **prerogative** (unusual) **writs** such as **habeas corpus, mandamus, certiorari** and **quo warranto** (see those words), *writs of* **attachment, error, execution** (see those words) and many others. These include papers that are no longer strictly "writs" but have become part of the court's ordinary processes as **judgments** and **orders.**

Write up (down)   Update financial records to show the increased (decreased) value of property.

Writeoff   *1.* An uncollectible debt. *2.* A business or investment loss that can usually be claimed as a tax loss.

Writer   A person who sells **options.**

Writings   Anything expressed in words, symbols, and numbers, whether written, printed, photocopied, etc.

Written directive   See **advance directive.**

Written law   A **statute, constitution, treaty, regulation, ordinance,** etc., as opposed to **unwritten law** (see that word).

Wrong   A violation of a person's legal rights, especially a **tort.**

Wrongful birth action   A medical **malpractice** lawsuit, brought by the parents, based on a doctor's failure to provide proper information (to advise, diagnose, or test properly), which results in the birth of a child with serious birth defects. This is different from a malpractice claim based on procedures that *cause* birth defects.

Wrongful death action   A lawsuit brought by the **dependents** of a dead person against the person who caused the death. **Damages** (money) will be given to compensate the dependents for their loss if the killing was **negligent** or **willful**. See also **survival statute.**

Wrongful life action   A medical **malpractice** lawsuit, similar to a **wrongful birth action,** brought on behalf of the child. When the issue is life itself, rather than the defects, the suit usually fails.

Wrongful pregnancy (or conception) action   A medical **malpractice** lawsuit based on a doctor's failure to properly perform a sterilization or abortion (or a lawsuit based on a contraceptive drug or device failure).

Wyoming v. Houghton   (119 S.Ct. 1297) The 1999 U.S. Supreme Court decision that a police officer with probable cause to search a car may inspect a passenger's belongings found in the car because passengers have a reduced "expectation of privacy" regarding their belongings, as opposed to their person, in a car.

X *1.* A mark made by a person who cannot write a signature. It is usually followed by the person's name (and the signatures of witnesses if required by law). *2.* An abbreviation for *sold without something.* Depending on context, it might mean **ex dividend** (also abbreviated *xd*), **ex rights** (also abbreviated *xr*), etc.

Yates v. U.S. See **clear and present danger test.**

Year books **Reports** of old English cases.

Year-and-a-day rule The principle that a death cannot be attributed to another person's wrongful conduct unless the death occurred within a year and a day of the conduct. This principle has been abandoned in some states.

Yeas and nays Describes oral voting in a **legislature,** usually one-by-one, calling each name in turn.

Yellow dog contract An employment contract in which an employer requires an employee to promise that he or she will not join a **union.** These are now illegal.

Yield Profit as measured by a percentage of the money invested. For example, a ten dollar profit on a hundred dollar investment represents a 10 percent *yield. Current yield* is current interest or dividends divided by purchase price.

York-Antwerp rules Agreed international rules for **contract** provisions dealing with **bills of lading,** for settlement of disputes about maritime losses, etc.

Younger doctrine The principle that federal courts should usually **abstain** from deciding a case when there is a pending state court criminal case involving the same subject and the same people. Compare with **Burford doctrine** and **Pullman doctrine.**

Youthful offender An older adolescent treated as a *juvenile* **delinquent,** rather than as an **adult offender,** so eligible for special **diversion** programs.

Z 1. *Regulation Z* is the set of rules put out by the Federal Reserve Board under the **Consumer Credit Protection Act.** It describes exactly what a lender must tell a borrower and how it must be told. *2.* "Z" is a mark used to fill in unused blank spaces on a legal document to keep them from being filled in later.

Z.B.B. **Zero-base budgeting.**

Z bond A **bond** that pays no interest or principal until all earlier bonds in the **series** are paid.

Zealous witness A **swift witness.**

Zenger decision Short for the 1735 colonial case in which a man imprisoned for defaming New York's governor was freed. The case established the principle that truth is a valid **defense** to **libel.**

Zero-base budgeting Looking closely at an entire program's funding when planning its next budget, rather than looking only at that program's need for additional money.

Zero-coupon bond (or "zero") A **bond** sold at well below **face** value that pays no interest and can be redeemed at face value at **maturity.**

Zero-rate mortgage A **mortgage** in which a large down payment is made, and the rest of the purchase price is paid off in equal **installments** with no **interest.**

Zipper (or wrap-up) clause A statement in a contract that it is an **integrated agreement** (see that word).

Zone of danger rule The rule in some states that a **plaintiff** must be in danger of physical harm, and frightened by the danger, to collect **damages** for the **negligent** infliction of emotional distress that results from seeing another person injured by the **defendant.**

Zone of employment The physical area (usually the place of employment and surrounding areas controlled by the employer) within which an employee is eligible for worker's compensation benefits when injured, whether or not on the job at the time.

Zone of privacy A place or activity protected against government intrusion by the **Constitution.** See also **expectation of privacy.**

Zone pricing Charging everyone within a geographical area the same price for the same delivered goods.

531

Zoning *1.* The division of a city or county into mapped areas, with restrictions on land use, architectural design, building use, etc., in each area. *2. Cluster zoning* allows housing closer together than minimum lot size if open space is maintained; *Euclidean zoning* uses uniform residential lot sizes to get a desired land use density and usually excludes businesses, apartment houses, etc., from single family residential areas; *floating zoning* is the setting aside of a certain amount of land in each district for otherwise nonpermitted buildings, with the exact place for them not yet settled; and *spot zoning* is changing the zoning for a piece of land without regard for the zoning plan.

Appendix A
Where to Go for More Information

If you cannot find the word you want in this dictionary, if the definition given here does not fit the context in which you found the word, or if you need a more elaborate definition, there are several places to look. They are listed here with *the most convenient first and the most comprehensive last.*

1. Standard English Dictionaries

Try a regular dictionary. Legal documents often use an ordinary English word in its ordinary way, but because of some special emphasis or because of its use in an unfamiliar place, the word looks "legal." A regular dictionary may reassure you that the word's ordinary meaning fits perfectly. *American Heritage, Merriam-Webster,* and *Random House* are helpful dictionaries. For older words or for more detailed definitions try the *Oxford English Dictionary.*

2. Large Law Dictionaries

These books are especially helpful for long Latin phrases, old words and definitions, and situations in which you need several examples of how to use a word properly. Their definitions are sometimes confusing, but they have more words and more extensive definitions than this dictionary has. The three best known are *Black's, Ballentine's,* and *Bouvier's.*

3. Hornbooks

If you know the field of law your word comes from, a good starting place is a students' summary of the law in that field. This is called a "hornbook." For example, if the word belongs in the field of torts, try the index in the back of Prosser's *Law of Torts.*

4. Legislation and Cases

If the word comes from a statute (or ordinance or regulation), the statute may contain a specialized definition of the word, often in a "definition section" (or several definition sections scattered through it). This is always true of the "Uniform Laws" and usually true of major federal and state legislation. For example, the most important definitions for many commercial terms are found in the definition section of the Uniform Commercial Code. (If all you have is the popular name of a statute or a case, you can find it by using *Shepard's Acts and Cases by Popular Name,* found in most law libraries.)

5. Words and Phrases

If you want to be buried by every conceivable use of a term or if the word you want has not turned up in any of the preceding sources, go to a library and use the multivolume *Words and Phrases.* It has excerpts from almost every judge's decision that ever explained a word. It is the best place in a law library to get a start with complicated legal language. But be careful; the excerpts are frequently from cases that have been long overruled or discarded, from cases that were decided in the opposite way from what the quote would lead you to believe, or from "dicta" (words that have nothing to do with the basis for the decision). Also, do not forget to look in the supplement inside the back cover of each book for more recent uses of the word.

6. Descriptive Word Index

If the word you want is not a legal word, but you need to know if the word ever became entangled with the law, try the *Descriptive Word Index* to the *American Digest System.* For example, if you want to know whether there was ever a case about a pet skunk spraying a visitor (because your skunk gets edgy when the doorbell rings), you might try looking up "skunk," "pets," or "visitors." If you find nothing, try more general topics, such as "animals," "household liability," etc.

7. Legal Encyclopedias

If you want to get into the general legal subject that your word came from and if "hornbooks" are no help, try a legal encyclopedia. The two major ones are *Corpus Juris Secundum* and *American Jurisprudence.*

8. Computerized Legal Research

The word you want may be hard to find, but it's here. Some of the sources listed in numbers 1–7 are available in computerized form, and other computerized sources and research techniques are described at the end of Appendix C. Good hunting.

Appendix B
Lawyer Talk

This section is written primarily for lawyers, paralegals, law students, and others who use legal words in their work. Its message is simple: legal words are valuable technical tools, but they can complicate, confuse, and prolong any task. Legal jargon smothers clear thinking, clear writing, and clear speaking.

The section is also written for the "person on the street" who uses the dictionary to help with legal questions that come up in everyday life or to learn something about the law. The ability to sort out useful legal language from "legalese" is a big advantage.

Legal language is overused and misused for many reasons. Lawyers, paralegals, and legal writers often get carried away by legal jargon because of their training. Traditional law teaching is by the "case method." Students may spend much of their time studying how appeals judges (who have never seen the actual trial or any of the persons involved in the case) decide cases. This involves applying abstract legal concepts to abstract summaries of facts. After three years of dealing with legal words and abstract ideas, law students may have problems talking about the real world in clear English.

Even after working for real clients who have real problems, many lawyers and paralegals still use legal jargon either from habit or to cover up fuzzy thinking. Legal words are overused or misused in several different ways. Some of these ways include the following:

1. Using TECHNICAL legal words instead of clearly explaining legal concepts to nonlawyers

2. Using VAGUE legal words when clear English would be more precise

3. Using TOO MANY legal words

4. Using certain WORTHLESS legal words

1. Technical Words

Even when used accurately, legal words may be out of place when speaking or writing to nonlawyers. For example:

Lawyer talk	*English*
An "annulment" voids the marriage ab initio.	An "annulment" wipes the marriage off the books as if it never happened.
Plaintiff alleges defendant is the vendee.	Smith claims he sold it to Jones.
If you don't bequeath it in a codicil, it will go by intestate succession.	If you don't change your will to put it in, some cousin may get it.
I'll move for a continuance, but it may be denied as dilatory.	I'll try to put it off, but the judge will think we're stalling.
You hold the estate in fee, but if you alienate it, you activate the acceleration clause in the deed of trust.	You own the house, but if you sell it or give it away, the whole loan comes due.
You hold legal title on the face of the instrument, but extrinsic evidence shows that Smith has equitable title.	The papers are in your name, but a court would give it to Smith.

2. Vague Words

Some legal words have a "built in" vagueness. They are used when the writer or speaker does not want to be pinned down. For example, when a law requires that something be done within a "*reasonable* time," or with "*due* care," the law may be deliberately vague about *when* or *how* the thing must be done. This vagueness permits case-by-case judicial discretion about the time allowed or the care required. Vague words, however, just as often accompany vague thoughts. The following small list of vague words is drawn from many possibilities:

Sounds precise	*But is it?*
Above cited	Is it found earlier on the page? In the chapter? In the book?
Accident	Was it intentional? Negligent? By pure chance?
Adequate	For what? By what standard? Who decides?

Civil death	For all legal purposes? Just some? Permanent?
Community	The "block"? That section of town? The state?
Face	The whole document? The first page?
Facsimile	Exact copy? Close copy? How close?
Fair hearing	Fair in what way?
Final decision	Final before appeal? Final with no appeal?
Fixture	May be removed? May not be removed?
Foreign	Different country? Different state? Different city?
Heirs	Children? All who may inherit? Blood relatives?
Infant	Baby? Young child? Under legal age?
Reasonable person	By what standards? With hindsight?
Stranger	Not part of the deal? Knew nothing about it?
Substantial	A lot? More than a little? Above a cutoff?
Undue	A lot? Too much? By force? Illegal?

Some legal words have been in dispute in thousands of cases. Judges have decided that many of them "clearly" mean a dozen different, conflicting things. These words can rarely be avoided but should be replaced by specific objects, facts, or concepts whenever possible even if this requires using extra words. For example, lawyers almost never agree about the following words:

Consideration	Law
Conspiracy	Obscenity
Holding	Preponderance of evidence
Insanity	Proximate cause
Jurisdiction	Willful

3. Too Many Words

Doubling legal words that mean the same thing can be confusing. Good examples of legal word-doubling (and tripling) are found on pages 346 to 366 of *The Language of the Law* by David Mellinkoff (Boston, Mass., Little, Brown & Co., 1963). Some of these are:

Fit and proper	Mind and memory
Force and effect	Name and style
Give, devise, and bequeath	Null and void
Have and hold	Over and above

Known and distinguished as	Rest, residue, and remainder
Last will and testament	Written instrument

If the use of two similar words adds an important shade of meaning, use them with care. Most doublings, however, are just clutter.

4. Worthless Words

Many worthless words are used frequently in legal writing. Some are worthless because they are almost meaningless. Others mean exactly the same thing as a clear English word. Here are some examples of both types of worthless words:

Aforesaid	Issue (for "children")
Ambulatory	Party of the first part
And/or	Re (for "about")
Firstly	Said (as in "said table")
Forthwith	To wit
Four corners	Viz
Hitherto	Whereas

Here (or There)

-about	-inafter
-after	-to
-by	-tofore
-for	-upon
-from	-with
-in	-unto

What can a *legal professional* do about jargon? Before using a legal word, stop and think. Even if it is precise and useful, is it too technical for the situation? Is a vague word being used to smooth over vague thinking? Would fewer words do the job? Is the word on the "worthless list"?

What can a *nonlawyer* do about legal jargon? First, learn to recognize it. Legal language is less imposing once the "legalese" is stripped away. Next, ask for a translation when something you hear is confusing. And finally, don't use it.

Appendix C
Legal Research

How to Use This Appendix

Effective legal research requires practice, but some basic legal knowledge plus a reference guide will get you started.

This appendix is divided into three sections. *Concepts* introduces important legal ideas (such as "authority," "holding," and "jurisdiction") that you should keep in mind while doing legal research. *Techniques* explains basic skills of analyzing your problem, finding the law, and using the law you find to solve your problem. And *Sources* describes the places (such as statute books, case reporters, and the World Wide Web) where you will find the law, plus discussions about it and leads to it.

Here are some hints for using this appendix:

- If you need more detailed information than what is in this appendix, read the *Books on Doing Legal Research* section (page 570).

- If you have never used a law library, read the *Law Libraries* section (page 571) before going to one.

- *Take full advantage of the Internet.* Even if you lack access to fee-based, computer-assisted legal research, there is a wealth of free legal information a few keystrokes away. *Use this appendix* to help you get started.

- *Use this dictionary* while reading this appendix and while doing research. Words in **boldface** in this appendix are defined in the dictionary.

- *Use the following checklist* of things to consider while doing each research task:

Concepts in the Law

Legislative, judicial, or executive?

Statute or case?

Federal, state, or local?

Jurisdiction or not?
Civil or criminal?
Trial or appeal?
Binding or persuasive?

Techniques of Research

ANALYZING THE FACTS
Know your facts
Know your objectives
FINDING THE LAW
Create a word list
Do your search
ANALYZING THE LAW
Reading cases
Reading statutes and regulations
USING THE RESEARCH
Validate with a citator
Cite it right
Re-analyze, including both sides' positions
Write it up

Sources of the Law

PRIMARY SOURCES
Federal statutes and administrative regulations
State statutes
State administrative regulations and local ordinances
Case law: The National Reporter System
Case law: other sources
SECONDARY SOURCES
Martindale-Hubbell
Key Number Digests
American Law Reports (A.L.R.)
Citators: Shepards, Key-Cite, etc.
Legal encyclopedias

Other important secondary sources

(Words and Phrases; looseleaf services; treatises; law review articles; form, practice, and procedure books; etc.)

Books on doing legal research

LAW LIBRARIES

COMPUTER-ASSISTED LEGAL RESEARCH

Concepts in the Law

This section contains some basic concepts you should be familiar with before starting any serious legal research. You do not need to know these concepts in depth to do good research and you do not need to keep them in mind all at once. But you _do_ need to know what they mean when you come across them.

The concepts are presented as questions in the heading of each section. You can skim through these questions each time you are deciding how to approach a legal problem, how to look for the right books, or how to use the legal material you have found.

Legislative, Judicial, or Executive?

Which Branch of Government Is Involved?

The **legislative** branch of the U.S. government enacts **statutes**, the **judicial** branch decides court **cases** (in part by "interpreting" those statutes), and the **executive** branch "runs" the country (in part by "carrying out" those statutes). Figure 1 shows the three branches of the U.S. government.

Notice "The Constitution" in the top box. The U.S. Constitution is _not a statute_, but is the document establishing the basic principles for the entire government and setting up the basic structure and procedures for running it. Nothing done by the government (or by its citizens) may legally conflict with the Constitution.

Next notice the "Executive Branch" box below the Constitution. The executive branch produces several types of written laws (such as **executive orders** and **treaties**) that are also _not statutes._

And finally, look at the small boxes in the middle of the page and the one large box at the bottom. These show how the executive branch is divided into the **cabinet** departments and **administrative agencies** that run **(regulate)** specific parts of the government, primarily by issuing and enforcing **regulations** that _look like statutes._ These departments and agencies also hold **hearings** that *look like trials* but are governed by principles of **administrative law.** For these reasons, you must always know which branch of government produced the document you are using.

Statute or Case?

Is It Statutory Law or Case Law?

Most of "the law" you research will be clearly recognizable as **statutes** (enacted by the **legislative** branch of government) or **cases** (decided by the **judicial** branch). "**Statutory** law" is a **legislature**'s official statement about what it wants to encourage, permit, or forbid. Statutory law is collected in books and on-line, often in the form of **codes.**

A statute usually starts out as a **bill** that is voted on and passed (or rejected) by the legislature (with each **house,** if there are two, holding **hearings** in **committee** and sometimes holding **floor** debate). The bill becomes a statute when it is signed by (or passed over the **veto** of) the president of the United States (or a state governor).

"**Case law**" is a statement by a court that is based on legal principles developed from past case decisions. It is a judge's decision, plus the facts and reasoning behind that decision. It is called a court **opinion** and collected in books of case reports, reporters, and on-line.

See **statute, statutory, case,** and **caselaw** for more information.

Federal, State, or Local?

Which Level of Government Is Involved?

All three branches of government exist on the federal, state, and local levels. The state and local levels have divisions of authority similar to those of the U.S. government (Refer to Figure 1), but the terminology is sometimes different. For example, local constitutions are usually called **charters** and local statutes are usually called **ordinances.**

You must always know whether the constitution, statute, regulation, or case decision **(opinion)** you are dealing with is federal, state, or local.

Jurisdiction or Not?

Who Has the Power to Decide?

If a court "has jurisdiction" it has the power to decide a case. The decision of a court lacking jurisdiction has no legal effect. ("Jurisdiction" also describes a geographical area, such as a city or state, within which a government and its officials have the power to act.)

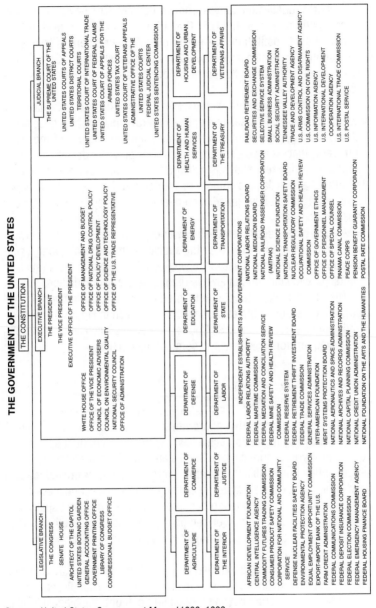

Source: *United States Government Manual* 1998–1999.

Figure 1 ■ Organization of the Federal Government

A court's jurisdiction derives from written law. The power of the federal courts derives from the U.S. Constitution and certain federal laws allowed by the Constitution. The power of state courts derives from state constitutions and certain laws allowed by these constitutions. Sometimes, more than one court has the power to decide a case; these courts have *concurrent jurisdiction.*

Federal courts operate within strict limits. These courts have the power to decide those cases that pose a **federal question** and those cases that have antagonists from different states and an amount of money in controversy that exceeds a particular sum. This power to decide cases with persons from different states is called *diversity jurisdiction.* State courts also often have dollar maximums or minimums. For example, a "small claims court" might have jurisdiction over only "money claims under one thousand dollars."

A court must usually establish power over the persons involved (*personal jurisdiction*) as well as over the subject matter in controversy (*subject matter jurisdiction*). Cases involving certain subject matters (such as disputed title to land) do not always require personal jurisdiction.

The jurisdiction of most courts is limited to a specific geographical area within the United States. For example, as seen in Figure 2, the numbered federal circuits for U.S. Courts of Appeals each include several states, with territories assigned to some of the circuits.

Civil or Criminal?
Which of Two Basic Categories of Law Is Involved?

The difference between **civil** and **criminal** cases is often easily seen. A crime is a wrong done "to society" which involves conduct specifically defined in a written criminal law. Crimes are usually either **felonies** (more serious, often punishable by a year or more in prison) or **misdemeanors** (less serious), with most states specifying degrees of seriousness (such as a "class two felony"). Most other cases are civil. They are usually lawsuits that involve one person or company in conflict with another person or company, although the government is involved in many civil cases (for example, zoning appeals).

The rules and procedures that apply to criminal cases are substantially different from those that apply to civil cases. For example, conviction of a crime requires proof **beyond a reasonable doubt** (the highest level of proof), while winning a civil lawsuit usually requires proof by the **preponderance of evidence.** Certain safeguards, such as the **Fourth Amendment** prohibition of unreasonable search and seizure, apply primarily to the government and only rarely apply to a civil case.

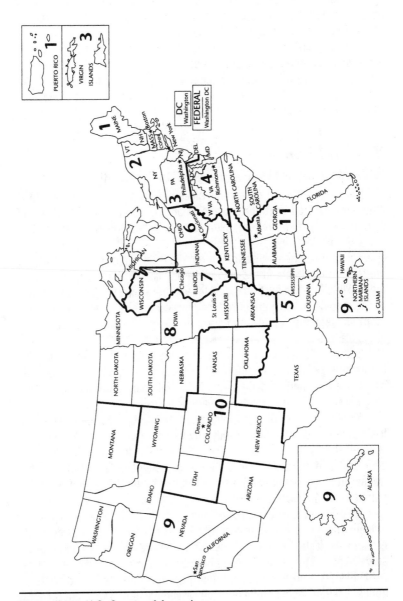

Figure 2 ■ U.S. Courts of Appeals

There is, however, a "gray area" between civil and criminal. For example, **civil commitment** involves confinement in a public institution even though no crime was committed. A minor traffic violation is not civil, but it is not a crime. The conviction of a juvenile offender for what would be a crime if the offender were an adult is not a crime, although it may be handled primarily as a "criminal" case.

Also, certain civil and criminal cases resemble each other. For example, **assault** is both a crime and the basis for a civil lawsuit, but civil and criminal assault may be defined differently and have different means of proof and defense. For all of these reasons, it is important to be sure whether you are dealing with a civil or a criminal case.

Trial or Appeal?
Which Procedural Phase of a Case Is Involved?

Most **hearings** in court cases take place in **trial** courts, but most of the **opinions** collected in **reporters** and in on-line sources are the result of hearings in courts of **appeal.** What are the differences between the two types of courts?

The purpose of a trial is to sort out the facts of a dispute and to apply the law to these facts in order to make a decision. Witnesses give **testimony** when they are questioned by lawyers for each side (and sometimes by the judge). The lawyers introduce physical objects as **evidence,** make **motions, objections,** and summary statements about the case, and sometimes file **briefs.**

Some trials are before a judge and **jury** (a jury trial) and some are before a judge alone (a **bench** trial). There are often preliminary hearings before the trial, and sometimes the judge will make a decision about the case based solely on these preliminary hearings.

A major purpose of an **appellate** proceeding is to decide whether the trial court applied the law correctly. Appeals are governed by special procedural rules. After an appeal is filed by a **party** dissatisfied with a trial court decision, the **record** from the trial (which includes part or all of the **transcript** and evidence accepted or refused by the trial judge) is transmitted to the appellate court. Briefs are submitted by both sides.

An **oral argument** is then presented before one or more appellate judges. There is no jury, no testimony, and no introduction of evidence because the factual findings made at trial usually cannot be altered. After study, appellate judges write the **opinions** contained in the reporters. *Note:* **administrative agencies** hold hearings that may be *called* trials or appeals, but they are administrative proceedings rather than court cases.

Hearing procedures are usually less formal than court procedures, and decisions can usually be appealed to (or replaced by a trial in) a trial court.

Binding or Persuasive?
Does a Prior Case Require a Judge to Rule a Certain Way?

Judges have wide discretion in deciding cases, but that discretion is limited by law. The decisions of a state court judge in Virginia, for example, must not conflict with the **statutes** and **constitutions** of Virginia and of the United States. Such written laws are one form of **binding authority** that a judge must follow in making a decision.

The other main form of binding authority is *an* **opinion** *by a higher court in the same court system.* This form of binding authority is called **precedent.** Judges must follow applicable precedent in much the same way that they must follow applicable statutes. This rule is expressed in the principle of **stare decisis** ("let the decision stand"). For example, the U.S. District Court for the Eastern District of Virginia (part of the 4th Circuit) may not make a decision that conflicts with decisions of the U.S. Court of Appeals for the 4th Circuit, the higher court to which appeals from the district court would go (see Figure 2). No court in any other circuit provides binding authority.

It is often important to know what nonbinding courts have decided, since this information (and other information, such as the views of legal experts expressed in **treatises** and **law journal** articles) can be persuasive to a judge. Such information is called **persuasive authority.**

Some information is more persuasive than other information. A judge from the U.S. Court of Appeals for the 4th Circuit will be interested in how similar cases were decided by the U.S. Courts of Appeals in other circuits. That judge, however, may care less about what a state court judge in Alaska decided.

You must find and analyze all binding authority. The less binding authority that exists, the more persuasive authority must be found. Persuasive authority also gives you a greater source from which to draw possible supporting arguments for your case.

Once all the binding authority has been identified—that is, once you have all the opinions and statutes that the judge in your case *must* follow—you must identify those *parts* of the cases that are binding. When a panel of judges decides a case, it is the written opinion of the majority of judges (the *majority opinion*) that must be followed, not any *dissenting* opinions. (A court such as the U.S. Supreme Court will often make a decision without a majority opinion. These decisions contain *concurring* opinions that complicate analysis of what is binding because you need to hunt through all the opinions to find what a majority of the judges agreed on.)

Even *within* the majority opinion, there is often material, known as **dicta,** that is *not* binding authority. Dicta are anything in the opinion that is *not a logically necessary part of the decision.* (Dicta, however, are often very persuasive.) The reason that dicta are not binding authority is that a judge's role is to resolve actual controversies; any words offered beyond such resolution are beyond the judge's official role, and are thus not binding on others. The resolution of the actual controversy, the logically necessary core of the judge's decision, is called the **holding.**

To summarize your search process for relevant cases:

■ From well over a million printed **opinions**

■ You *want* only opinions that are **binding** or **persuasive**

■ And *must have* all opinions that are **binding**

■ But can *rely on* only each majority opinion's **holding**

Techniques of Research

Analyzing the Facts

Know Your Facts

Much of research is listmaking. Your first, most important list will be of everything you know about the facts of your problem: The *things, happenings, persons,* and *places* involved. Note beside each fact what you know, how you know about it, and how sure you are about each of the subfacts. Avoid making assumptions about what the law might be at this stage.

Know Your Objectives

An ounce of thinking is worth ten pounds of research. Analyze what you want to accomplish. What results do you (your client, etc.) hope for? Are they realistic? Make a list and look at it often throughout the research process.

Finding the Law

Create a Word List

Most research tasks involve either too few potentially useful reference sources or too many. In neither case should you flounder through more and more books. The solution may be to *cartwheel.*

Cartwheel is a method of creating and expanding word lists to use your sources best and to lead you to new sources. (Cartwheel was developed by William Statsky, and can be seen in greater detail in _Legal Research and Writing: Some Starting Points,_ 5th edition (West Publishing, 1999)).

Cartwheel lets you turn your lists of facts (things, happenings, persons, places) and your list of objectives (see _Analyzing the Facts_) into words to "plug into" the indexes, tables of contents, references, and word lists within your sources. It helps if you phrase each word or idea _in as many different ways as possible_ to find more leads to useful information. You should take each word or phrase on your list and put it into the cartwheel, as seen in Figure 3.

Suppose that one important word from your fact lists is "bloody nose." Under _broader words,_ you might list "injury" and "trauma"; under _related procedural terms,_ possible types of lawsuits, such as for "battery" or "tort"; under _long shots,_ "fight" or "insult." Generate as many words as possible and plug them into as many indexes, tables of contents, computerized search programs, and other finding aids as possible.

You can use Cartwheel, use a system devised by another author or publisher, or use your own system. Some researchers prefer a system that includes a memory device such as TARP (Things, **Actions, Remedies,** and **Parties**) or TAPP (Things, Acts, Persons, Places). Generating new words (especially when you run out of ideas) is a key to unlocking "vaults" of information. This dictionary can help generate new words using any system if you look for related words in each definition.

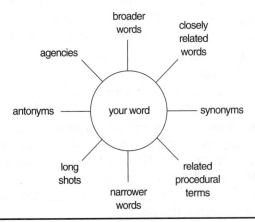

Figure 3 ■ Cartwheel

Do Your Search

Here are some guidelines to help you along:

- Keep *Sources of the Law* (especially Figure 4 on page 554–555) handy as you work.
- Start with *primary sources* (statutes, cases, regulations, etc.) if you know them.
- Use this dictionary to look up new words as you find them.
- *Be flexible.* Let the words on your lists, new Cartwheel words, and the references suggested by your sources tell you where to go next. Follow some side paths. You may not know exactly what you need until you find it.

Analyzing the Law

Reading Cases

Much law school training is based on the "case method." Students read, brief (summarize and analyze), and discuss the reported decisions **(opinions)** of **appellate** courts.

You will need to brief cases for many research problems. Once you have found a case that is potentially central to your research problem, read the **headnotes** printed before the **opinion.** (Figure 6 on page 561 is a collection of headnotes.) This will give you an orientation to the case.

Here is how to brief the case:

1. Write down all the **citation** information (names and numbers) that identifies the parties, the court, and the reporter volume.

2. Write down *who wrote the decision.* If it lacks a name, but says **"per curiam or memorandum decision,"** it is by all the judges.

3. Write down the *procedural history* of the case. From where did it come on appeal?

4. Write down the *result,* the judge's **holding.** This is a key part of your job, and often the hardest.

5. Write down the *reasoning justifying the holding* point-by-point. The judge may summarize for you, but be careful. Both here and elsewhere in the opinion, the words the judge used may be **dicta** (see that word).

6. Write down what the court did with the case. This might be to **affirm, reverse, remand,** etc.

7. Write down any important points made by judges who **concur** or **dissent**.

8. Write down the case's *later history,* if any, that you find. (See *Validate with* a **citator** below.)

9. Write down the important ways that the facts in this case are similar to (and different from) the facts in your research problem, and whether any **issues** *of fact* in the case or in your research problem cloud the comparison.

10. Write down the **issues** *of law* in the case that are relevant to your research problem and how they are (or are not) decided. Some researchers use the memory device IRAC (Issue, Rule, Application/Analysis, Conclusion).

Reading Statutes and Regulations

Reading statutes and regulations is as hard as reading cases. You must read them word-by-word because they are often very precise in places and very vague in others. Each comma may matter.

"*Briefing*" statutes is not as hard as briefing cases. The form of the brief doesn't matter as long as it contains the statute's **citation** and information on who is *included in* and *excluded from* the statute's reach, on *when* and *how* it operates, on whether it *commands* or only *permits* something, and on any details directly bearing on your problem. Quote the key parts directly unless they are too long.

If anything important about the statute is unclear after a careful reading, you must use the cases and historical data given in the statute's **annotations** to find the **legislative history.** You should always at least look at the annotations to see if you are interpreting something incorrectly.

Briefing **regulations** is generally similar to briefing statutes. You must also include information on the statutes that authorize the regulations.

Using the Research

Validate with a Citator

You have found what you want. Now what? First, make sure you have what you think you have. Are your cases, statutes, or regulations still good **authority?** The only way to find out is to trace them down through later cases and other sources to see if they have been criticized, overruled, changed, etc. Read the *Sources of the Law* section on Shepard's Citators and Key Cite (pages 566–568).

Cite It Right

A case or other authority is worthless if you (and those to whom you offer it as authority) cannot find it again. Always write down a correct citation. For example, *Ex parte Grossman* 267 U.S. 87, 88 (1925) gives the case name, volume, **reporter,** page, page of a **pinpoint citation,** and date. If you find the case in one reporter, but another reporter is its *official* place of publication, you should include *both* citations.

Copy down the citation *before* you take notes and make sure you copied it perfectly. (If you are not sure of the proper form, consult *The Bluebook: A Uniform System of Citation* or a computerized cite-checker such as *The Electronic Bluebook* or *Cite Rite.*)

Re-analyze, Including Both Sides' Positions

Once all your research is complete, reanalyze your arguments to see if there are any loose ends. Then analyze your arguments' strengths and the strengths of the other side's arguments. Upon what will *they* likely rely? Does that mean more research for you? It sometimes helps to work out how the other side is likely to analyze the issues using IRAC (Issue, Rule, Application/Analysis, Conclusion).

Write It Up

Order and label all your papers, make an informal index, and write a summary of what you *have,* what you *did,* and what you *concluded.* Keep it short, clear, and simple. Check your work against a book such as *Legal Writing: Sense and Nonsense* by David Mellinkoff (West Publishing) or *Modern Legal Usage* by Bryan Garner (Oxford University Press).

Sources of the Law

The rest of this appendix outlines answers to the following legal research questions:

> *What* are the materials used in legal research?
>
> *Where* are they?
>
> *When* do you use each of them?
>
> *How* do you use them?

Sources of the law are divided into two types: primary and secondary. (Both primary and secondary sources can be *official* or *unofficial.*) *Primary sources* include such things as **reporters** of court **opinions,** and collections of **statutes** and **regulations.** *Secondary sources* include materials _about_ the primary sources such as **digests,** encyclopedias, and **citators.** Both types of sources may be accessed through books and computer-assisted legal research.

Figure 4 on page 554 is a chart of various types of primary and secondary sources. It is adapted from William Statsky's _Legal Research and Writing: Some Starting Points,_ 5th edition (West Publishing, 1999). This appendix concentrates on finding and using opinions, statutes, and regulations, the first, second, and fourth items on the chart.

Primary Sources
Federal Statutes and Regulations

Where Do You Find Them?   The official source for recently passed federal statutes (called public laws in this form) is the _United States Statutes at Large._ The best unofficial source for recently passed federal statutes and information about bills going through Congress is the _United States Code Congressional and Administrative News (U.S.C.C.A.N.,_ West Group).

The official source for statutes once they have been sorted by subject into a permanent order is the _United States Code (U.S.C.)._ The two unofficial sources are the _United States Code Annotated (U.S.C.A.,_ West Group) and the _United States Code Service (U.S.C.S.,_ LEXIS Publishing). These unofficial sources are the main places to go for federal statutory research because they contain the law in the most useful form, come out sooner than the official U.S.C., and have **annotations** to **caselaw, legislative history, regulations,** etc.

The official source for proposed federal **administrative** rules and regulations is the _Federal Register._ It is published daily. (See the next paragraph for unofficial sources.)

The official source for most administrative regulations once they have been sorted by subject into a permanent order is the _Code of Federal Regulations (C.F.R.),_ although collections for many individual agencies also exist. There is no one unofficial source for administrative regulations, but WESTLAW, LEXIS, and various **looseleaf services** have major portions.

The four _official_ sources of federal statutes and regulations are available in paper (book and pamphlet) form and are available on-line from fee-based providers (WESTLAW and LEXIS). They are available free on-line on the World Wide Web, but sites, links to sites, and ease of searching the sites change regularly. The three unofficial sources are available in paper, WESTLAW, and LEXIS forms only. (See Computer-Assisted Legal Research for more information.)

TYPE OF LAW	FULL TEXT HERE	USE TO FIND IT	USE TO HELP EXPLAIN IT
Opinions Determine current validity with: Shepard's, Key-Cite, Auto-Cite, & Insta-Cite	Reports & reporters ALR, ALR 2d, 3d, 4th, 5th, & Fed. Legal newspapers Looseleaf services Slip opinions Advance sheets WESTLAW, LEXIS, CD-ROM, Internet	Digests ALR, ALR 2d, 3d, 4th, 5th, & Fed. Shepard's Legal encyclopedias, treatises, periodicals Looseleaf services Words and Phrases	Legal encyclopedias, treatises, periodicals, and newsletters ALR, ALR 2d, 3d, 4th, 5th, & Fed. Looseleaf services
Statutes Determine current validity with: Shepard's, Key-Cite, Auto-Cite, & Insta-Cite	Statutory Code Statutes at Large Session Laws Compilations Consolidated Laws Laws and Slip Laws Acts & Resolves Legislative Service WESTLAW, LEXIS, CD-ROM, Internet	Code index volumes Looseleaf services Footnotes in legal encyclopedias, treatises, periodicals	Legal encyclopedias, treatises, periodicals, and newsletters ALR, ALR 2d, 3d, 4th, 5th, & Fed. Looseleaf services
Constitutions Determine current validity with: Shepard's, Key-Cite, Auto-Cite, & Insta-Cite	Statutory Code or separate volumes WESTLAW, LEXIS, CD-ROM, Internet	Code index volumes Looseleaf services Footnotes in other materials	Legal encyclopedias, treatises, periodicals, and newsletters ALR, ALR 2d, 3d, 4th, 5th, & Fed. Looseleaf services
Administrative Regulations Determine current validity: Shepard's for some agencies, List of Sections Affected (LSA) for federal agencies	Administrative Code or separate volumes Register or Bulletin Looseleaf services WESTLAW, LEXIS, CD-ROM, Internet	Index volumes of the administrative code Looseleaf services Footnotes in other materials	Legal periodicals, treatises, newsletters ALR, ALR 2d, 3d, 4th, 5th, & Fed. Looseleaf services
Administrative Decisions Determine current validity: Shepard's and Key-Cite for some agencies	Separate decision volumes of some agencies Looseleaf services WESTLAW, LEXIS, CD-ROM, Internet	Looseleaf services Index to the decisions Digest volumes Footnotes in other materials	Legal periodicals, treatises, newsletters ALR, ALR 2d, 3d, 4th, 5th, & Fed. Looseleaf services

Figure 4 ■ Sources of the Law

TYPE OF LAW	FULL TEXT HERE	USE TO FIND IT	USE TO HELP EXPLAIN IT
Charters **Determine current validity:** Shepard's	Municipal Code or separate volumes Register or Bulletin State session laws Official journal or legal newspaper Internet	Charter or municipal code index volumes Footnote references in other materials	Legal periodicals and treatises ALR, ALR 2d, 3d, 4th, 5th, & Fed.
Ordinances **Determine current validity:** Shepard's	Municipal Code Official journal Legal newspaper Internet	Index volumes of municipal code Footnote references in other materials	Legal periodicals and treatises ALR, ALR 2d, 3d, 4th, 5th, & Fed.
Rules of Court **Determine current validity:** Shepard's	Statutory code or separate volumes Practice manuals Deskbooks WESTLAW, LEXIS, CD-ROM, Internet	Index to statutory code, rules volumes, practice manuals, or deskbook Footnote references in other materials	Practice manuals Legal encyclopedias and periodicals, newsletters, and looseleaf services Legal treatises ALR, ALR 2d, 3d, 4th, 5th, & Fed.
Executive Orders **Determine current validity:** Shepard's	Federal Register Code of Fed. Regs. USCCAN, USC, USCA, USCS WESTLAW, LEXIS, Internet	Index volumes to the sets of books listed in the column to the left Footnote references in other materials	Legal periodicals, newsletters, and looseleaf services Legal treatises ALR, ALR 2d, 3d, 4th, 5th, & Fed.
Treaties **Determine current validity:** Shepard's	Statutes at Large (until 1949) U.S. Treaties & Other Internat. Agreements State Dept. Bulletin International Legal Materials WESTLAW, LEXIS, Internet	Index volumes to the sets of books listed in the column to the left World Treaty Index Current Treaty Index Footnote references in other materials	Legal periodicals, newsletters, and looseleaf services Legal encyclopedias and treatises ALR, ALR 2d, 3d, 4th, 5th, & Fed.

Figure 4 ■ Sources of the Law (continued)

How Do You Use Federal Statutes and Regulations?   This section explains how to use the four most important sources (U.S.C.A., U.S.C.S., U.S.C.C.A.N., and C.F.R.). The explanations refer primarily to the paper versions of these sources because they are usually more difficult to use.

The *United States Code Annotated* (*U.S.C.A.*) reprints the fifty **titles** of the *U.S.C.* in over one hundred volumes.

There are three ways to find the section (subdivision of a title) you need. If you know the statute's popular name, go to the popular name tables in the end volumes. If you know the general area of law you need, read through the general index of the fifty titles. Once you choose a title, use that title's individual subject index. And, if you know only certain specific facts or legal catchwords, go to the general index in the end volumes first. (If nothing turns up, you may have to go through a word-list expansion exercise such as "Cartwheel" on page 549.)

Once you have the section you need, there is often a wealth of information on **legislative, executive,** and **judicial** handling of the subject, all in one place with references, with most of the executive and judicial information organized by West **Key Numbers.**

To update the *U.S.C.A.* volumes, you must use **pocket parts,** "Supplementary Pamphlets," and "Special Pamphlets." Also, make sure you are using the latest hardback volume because volumes are revised on separate publication schedules.

To update the U.S.C.A. and its pamphlets with the most recent news, you need the *United States Code Congressional and Administrative News* and its supplementary pamphlets. They contain easy-to-use tables that refer you to recent related legislation and regulation. And don't forget to determine each statute's current validity using a **citator.**

The *United States Code Service* works generally the same way as *U.S.C.A.* and covers the same statutes, etc. Its main references are to LEXIS materials rather than West's.

The *Code of Federal Regulations,* currently published entirely in colorcoded pamphlet form due to frequent revision, is an official source for most federal administrative law materials. Its fifty titles do *not* correspond to the *United States Code* titles that authorize them, but the titles do group generally by the federal agency that administers them. In the **citation** "2 CFR §7.1" the "title" is 2, the "part" or major subdivision is 7, and the "section" (everything after the "section symbol") is 7.1.

If you have a *United States Code* citation (for statutes in your area of law), the best way to find the right *CFR* section (for administrative regulations issued under the authority of these statutes) is to convert the United States Code citation directly through tables in the *CFR* pamphlet containing finding aids. Lacking that, you should use the general index in *CFR.* (If you find nothing and suspect that you are dealing with an entirely new area of law, check the various *Federal Register* indexes.)

To update your _CFR_ research, first make sure that you have the latest volume. (The titles are revised once each year in quarterly batches.) Then find the latest _CFR_ monthly update pamphlet called the List of Sections Affected. It tells which _CFR_ sections have been recently affected by new regulations, new proposed regulations, etc. Read the text of these changes in the _Federal Register_ (the page number is given). Finally, for last-minute updates, check the CFR Parts Affected tables in each subsequent issue of the _Federal Register_ and read the changes in the daily issues you are referred to.

State Statutes

Many researchers use state statutes more often than they use federal statutes, but not too much is said about them here because there are fifty different states. There are, however, some similarities among states that should be mentioned.

All states first print their new laws chronologically as **session laws,** sometimes modeled on the "public laws" of the _United States Statutes at Large_ (see the prior section). They are called by various names, such as _Acts and Resolves._ States then organize their statutes into **codes.** Most states have both official and unofficial versions of their codes, many modeled on the _United States Code Annotated_ (see the prior section), or containing many of its features, such as references to encyclopedias and other secondary sources.

Most state codes, in both annotated and nonannotated forms, and some session laws, are available on-line through WESTLAW and LEXIS. The World Wide Web has some of these materials, either through individual state sites or sites that collect material and links. Sites, links, and ease of searching the sites change regularly. (See Computer-Assisted Legal Research for more information.) The following information helps with both paper-based and on-line research.

To find state statutory law, you can start by looking up your subject in the Digest volumes of _Martindale-Hubbell._ Its use is explained on page 562. This may give you a quick, but _not_ authoritative, answer to your question and a reference to the state statute with the answer. Otherwise, go directly to the statutes and take a few minutes to read the explanatory material at the front of the first volume. This will alert you to anything unusual about the set's organization.

Next, check to see if there is a general index in the last volumes of the set. These vary in size and quality, so you may have to do some word-expansion exercises such as "Cartwheel" to expand your search possibilities. Once you find the right volume, check to see if _it_ has an index, and use that also. (Some code titles fill more than one volume, so check for an index in each volume that contains the code title.)

Finally, update your research with information from any **pocket parts,** supplements, or binders of **slip laws** available, and don't forget to determine each statute's current validity using a **citator.**

State Administrative Regulations and Local Ordinances

These lower-level sources of law are not always collected in one place. Their organization, style, and quality vary widely. Regulations and ordinances are often highly detailed, and at the same time vague, and they sometimes conflict with the state laws that authorized them. Persistence and care are needed to track them down and to understand them.

There are four general approaches to finding this material. First, you can check on-line, as WESTLAW and LEXIS regularly add more of this information, and some is available in bits and pieces on the World Wide Web. (See Computer-Assisted Legal Research for more information.) Second, you can check to see if your library collects it in one place. Third, you can e-mail, write, call, or visit the agency, department, or city government in question. And fourth, you can search the secondary sources (Shepard's state and ordinance law citators, A.L.R., digests, articles, looseleaf services, etc.). These are described starting on page 566–567.

Caselaw: The National Reporter System (NRS)

What Is in It?   Only about one percent of the cases decided by courts in the U.S. have been collected and printed, but there are well over a million cases now in books. Most of these cases are in the books of the *National Reporter System (NRS),* West Group. State **appellate** court cases considered important enough to publish are in one of the *regional reporters* and cases from federal courts are in one of the *federal court reporters* (such as the *Supreme Court Reporter*). For example, one of the regional reporters, the *Southern Reporter,* contains cases from Alabama, Florida, Louisiana, and Mississippi. Each individual book of a reporter is called a *volume,* and cases in each reporter are in rough chronological order. Figure 5 summarizes the NRS. The National Reporter System is on WESTLAW, which makes it far easier to use than the equivalent paper volumes. It is also on CD-ROM.

How Do You Use It?   The location of a case within the National Reporter System is given by an abbreviation known as a **citation** ("cite" for short). For example, the citation "121 N.W.2d 321" gives the location of a case in the 121st volume of the *North Western Reporter, Second Series* on page 321.

Cases are sometimes published in the NRS and in reporters put out by other publishers or by the states themselves. Only one of these publications is the official one; sometimes it is the NRS. When you have one

REGIONAL REPORTERS	BEGINNING	COVERAGE
Atlantic Reporter	1885	Connecticut, Delaware, Maine, Maryland, New Hampshire, New Jersey, Pennsylvania, Rhode Island, Vermont, and District of Columbia Court of Appeals
California Reporter	1960	All reported California opinions
Illinois Decisions	1990	All reported Illinois opinions
New York Supplement	1888	All reported New York opinions
North Eastern Reporter	1885	Illinois, Indiana, Massachusetts, New York (Court of Appeals only), and Ohio
North Western Reporter	1879	Iowa, Michigan, Minnesota, Nebraska, North Dakota, South Dakota and Wisconsin
Pacific Reporter	1883	Alaska, Arizona, California (Supreme Court only), Colorado, Hawaii, Idaho, Kansas, Montana, Nevada, New Mexico, Oklahoma, Oregon, Utah, Washington and Wyoming
South Eastern Reporter	1887	Georgia, North Carolina, South Carolina, Virginia and West Virginia
South Western Reporter	1886	Arkansas, Kentucky, Missouri, Tennessee and Texas
Southern Reporter	1887	Alabama, Florida, Louisiana and Mississippi

FEDERAL REPORTERS

Federal Reporter	1880	United States Circuit Court from 1880 to 1912; Commerce Court of the United States from 1911 to 1913; District Courts of the United States from 1880 to 1932; U.S. Court of Claims from 1929 to 1932 and 1960 to 1982; the U.S. Court of Appeals from its organization in 1891; the U.S. Court of Customs and Patent Appeals from 1929 to 1982; and the U.S. Emergency Court of Appeals from 1943 to 1961; Court of Appeals for the Federal Circuit from 1982; and Temporary Emergency Court of Appeals from 1972

Figure 5 ■ National Reporter System

FEDERAL REPORTERS	BEGINNING	COVERAGE
Federal Supplement	1932	United States Court of Claims from 1932 to 1960; United States District Courts since 1932; United States Customs Court from 1956 to 1980; Court of International Trade from 1980; Judicial Panel on Multidistrict Litigation from 1968; and the Special Court, Regional Railroad Reorganization Act from 1973
Federal Rules Decisions	1939	United States District Courts involving the Federal Rules of Civil Procedure since 1939 and the Federal Rules of Criminal Procedure since 1946
Supreme Court Reporter	1882	U.S. Supreme Court beginning with the October term of 1882
Bankruptcy Reporter	1980	Bankruptcy decisions of U.S. Bankruptcy Courts, U.S. District Courts, U.S. Courts of Appeals and the U.S. Supreme Court
Military Justice Reporter	1978	United States Court of Military Appeals and Courts of Military Review for the Army, Navy, Air Force and Coast Guard
United States Federal Claims Reporter	1982	United States Court of Federal Claims decisions beginning October 1982

Figure 5 ■ National Reporter System (continued)

citation to a case, you can find the other (if it exists) by using tables in the *National Reporter Blue Book* or by using the appropriate **citator.**

Each individual volume in the NRS has reference material about the cases in the volume. For example, each has a *Table of Cases Reported* (a list of cases by court system); a *Table of Statutes Construed* (a list of statutes discussed in the various cases in the volume); a *Table of Words and Phrases* (a list of important words and phrases defined in the cases);

and a small *Key Number Digest* (a list of the **key numbers** relevant to the cases). Each printed case is preceded by an "introductory section" that includes a synopsis of the case and other information as illustrated in Figure 6. Each reporter also has **advance sheets.** These are sometimes the quickest way to find out about new cases from state courts.

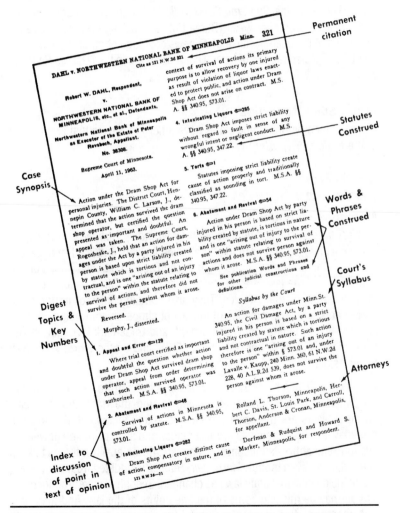

Figure 6 ■ Introduction to a Case in the National Reporter System

Caselaw: Other Sources

Non-NRS Federal Reporters.   The official **reporter** for decisions of the U.S. Supreme Court is called *United States Reports.* A frequently used annotated version is *United States Supreme Court Reports, Lawyer's Edition* (LEXIS Publishing). It is known simply as "Lawyer's Edition" (L.Ed.). Some volumes contain the **briefs** in the case. It is also available on-line from LEXIS.

Two **looseleaf services** print weekly copies of Supreme Court decisions. These are the *Supreme Court Bulletin* (Commerce Clearing House) and *United States Law Week* (Bureau of National Affairs). *Law Week* is more frequently used because of its news coverage of other legal matters. All other collected reports of federal court cases are in the *National Reporter System.*

Other State Reporters

As mentioned before, some states have official reporters that are not part of the *National Reporter System.*

Secondary Sources
Martindale-Hubbell

What Is in It?   The first volumes of the *Martindale-Hubbell Law Directory* contain a state-by-state listing of practicing lawyers and law firms. Unless you need this information, go right to the Digest volumes. They contain summaries of the law of each state by legal topic with examples of legal forms needed for many topics. They also contain copies of **uniform** and **model acts,** short summaries of the law of almost every foreign country, and reviews of federal copyright, patent, and trademark law. Martindale-Hubbell is available in book form, on LEXIS, and on the World Wide Web under its name.

How Do You Use It?   *Martindale-Hubbell* is not hard to use. It has a topical index with good cross-referencing to find the right subject areas. These subjects are the same for each state and include all the areas of everyday law. Each state has a smaller index and an explanation of what its citations and abbreviations mean. There are, however, a few things to keep in mind. First, even though *Martindale-Hubbell* is updated frequently, there is still the chance that state law has changed. Second, it is *very* condensed, so you may be missing some of the fine points of the law. And third, it is *not* an authoritative source. It is useful for quick, preliminary answers to many legal questions, but should not be cited.

Key Number Digests

What Is in Them?   *Key Number Digests* have been called one of the four pillars of legal research. (The other three are the *ALR Annotations, Shepard's Citators,* and computer-assisted research.) *Key Number Digests* are a comprehensive method of categorizing, indexing, and finding the legal subjects discussed in U.S. courtrooms.

A Key Number is a permanent number given by West Group to a specific legal subject as categorized by West. It is usually preceded by the Key Number symbol ☜ . West first subdivided all possible legal subjects into seven main headings, then broke these headings into thirty-two subdivisions and approximately four hundred "Key Number topics." Figure 7 on page 564 is a part of that breakdown. Finally, each of these Key Number topics is broken down into many Key Numbers *unique to each Key topic.* The Key Numbers in each Key Number topic do *not* correspond to those in other Key Number topics, so you must know both the topic and the Key Number. New Key Numbers are added to topics regularly, and old ones are further and further subdivided.

A West editor who reads a case that comes into the *National Reporter System* picks out *each legal point* and writes a brief summary of that point in a single paragraph. These paragraphs are given a topic and Key Number, are printed with decisions in case reporters (see Figure 6 on page 561), and are collected into *Key Number Digests* by topic and Key Number.

There are *Key Number Digests* for most individual state reporters, for most regional reporters, most United States court reporters, and for specific subjects (such as bankruptcy and education). The material in all these digests is then collected into the *American Digest,* a massive master index of caselaw summaries covering the whole country and most of its appeals courts since colonial days. The *American Digest* is divided into a *Century Digest* (1658–1896), a series of *Decennial Digests* (1897–1905, 1906–1915, etc.), *General Digests* (yearly between the last and the next Decennial), and updating pamphlets.

How Do You Use Them?   *Key Number Digests* are available in paper and CD-ROM form and on-line through WESTLAW. For computer-assisted use, first read the following general information, then go to page 573. All the *Key Number Digests* (except the *Century Digest,* which predates the Key System) work exactly the same way. If you want to know about "Theaters and Shows ☜ 6(18) athletic events" in Florida only, use the Florida Key Digest; for "Theaters and Shows ☜ 6(18) athletic events"; in the whole Southern region, use the *Southern Key Digest;* do the same for federal courts and the Supreme Court. For the whole country, use the American Digest.

1. **PERSONS**
2. **PROPERTY**
3. **CONTRACTS**
4. **TORTS**
5. **CRIMES**
6. **REMEDIES**
7. **GOVERNMENT**

1. PERSONS
RELATING TO NATURAL PERSONS IN GENERAL

Civil Rights
Dead Bodies
Death
Domicile
Drugs and Narcotics
Food
Health and Environment
Holidays
Intoxicating Liquors
Names
Poisons
Seals
Signatures
Sunday
Time
Weapons

PARTICULAR CLASSES OF NATURAL PERSONS

Absentees
Aliens
Chemical Dependents
Citizens
Convicts
Illegitimate children
Indians
Infants
Mental Health
Paupers
Slaves
Spendthrifts

PERSONAL RELATIONS

Adoption
Attorney and Client
Employers Liability
Executors and Administrators
Guardian and Ward
Labor Relations
Marriage
Master and Servant
Parent and child
Principal and Agent
Workers' Compensation

ASSOCIATED AND ARTIFICIAL PERSONS

Associations
Beneficial Associations
Building and Loan Associations
Clubs
Colleges and Universities
Corporations
Exchanges
Joint-Stock Companies and Business Trusts
Partnership
Religious Societies

PARTICULAR OCCUPATIONS

Accountants
Agriculture
Auctions and Auctioneers
Aviation
Banks and Banking
Bridges
Brokers
Canals
Carriers
Commerce
Consumer Credit
Consumer Protection
Credit Reporting Agencies
Detectives
Electricity
Explosives
Factors
Ferries
Gas
Hawkers and Peddlers
Innkeepers
Insurance
Licenses
Manufactures
Monopolies
Physicians and Surgeons
Pilots
Railroads
Seamen
Shipping
Steam
Telecommunications
Theaters and Shows
Towage
Turnpikes and Toll Roads
Urban Railroads
Warehousemen
Wharves

2. PROPERTY
NATURE, SUBJECTS, AND INCIDENTS OF OWNERSHIP IN GENERAL

Abandoned and Lost Property
Accession
Adjoining Landowners

Figure 7 ■ Example of Some Legal Subjects Subdivided

The most direct way into the Key Numbers is to start with a case that discusses the question that you want to answer. Few researchers are so lucky, but if you *do* have a printed case on point, you can go straight from the case's Key Number summary paragraphs to a digest. If all you have is a case *name,* you can look it up in the Table of Cases for the digest you want to use. This will give you, in addition to more information about the case, the Key Numbers that summarize its legal points.

A Descriptive Word Index is the best way into the digests. You start by categorizing your problem and generating an expanded list of *related* words using the "Cartwheel" method explained earlier or your own method of adding search words with the help of this dictionary. You then look up these new words alphabetically in each digest's Descriptive Word Index. Those that exist in the index will lead you to topics and Key Numbers. Once you find the Key Numbers you need, look them up in the digest.

It may take a long time to wade through the summary paragraphs. If you are working with the *American Digest* (rather than with one of the regional, state, or U.S. court digests), you may sometimes need to consult every digest in the system, plus the updates. (Be sure to see the Cumulative Table of Key Numbers to avoid having to look through every *General Digest.*) Only use the *American Digest* approach if you have no quicker alternative using a digest for a smaller geographical area or more limited range of subjects.

Finally, *do not rely completely* on the *Key Number Digest* paragraphs because they are overly condensed and sometimes misleading. Read the case referred to for what the judge really said. And never cite the summary as authority for a legal point. It isn't.

American Law Reports (A.L.R.)

The book version of *A.L.R.* is a complex law finder, but it is worth mastering because, if you find what you need, it comes in highly concentrated form. The on-line version is much easier to use. It operates the same way as, and is integrated with, the rest of the WESTLAW search system (National Reporter System, U.S.C.A., Key-Cite, etc.). See "How to Use" on page 575.

What Is in It? A.L.R. has hundreds of volumes, each containing several selected "lead" cases (some with summaries of the **briefs** and decision in addition to the full **opinion**). Each case is followed by a long **annotation.**

Each annotation refers to hundreds of other cases based on the same area of the law from various jurisdictions. The lead case is a way of pulling together the "core" of a legal subject area, such as "product liability: heating equipment." The other cases provide greater detail and take the subject into related fields. In this respect, *A.L.R.* (with its various indexes and digests) is a combination of case reporter, digest, and encyclopedia. It is cross-referenced with the *American Jurisprudence (Am. Jur.)* encyclopedia and many other West Group publications.

Recent A.L.R. volumes begin each annotation with sections called *scope* (what is covered generally), *related matters* (where to look for related topics not covered), *summary* (a brief review of the legal concepts), *practice pointers* (a list of information on pleading, evidence, and tactics), and an *index* of points covered. The bulk of the annotation is a detailed discussion of the caselaw with complete statutory and other references.

How Do You Use It?   American Law Reports includes the following series of books: *A.L.R.* (state and federal cases from 1919–1948), *A.L.R. 2d* (state and federal 1948–1965), *A.L.R. 3d* (state and federal 1965–1969, state only 1969–1980), *A.L.R. 4th* (state only, 1980–1990), *A.L.R. 5th* (state only 1990 on) and *A.L.R. Federal* (federal only, 1969 on). Volumes are updated on different schedules.

You will occasionally be referred directly from a **citator, treatise,** or encyclopedia to the one *A.L.R.* lead case that gives you everything you need. Otherwise, start by using the *Index to Annotations* (which cumulates individual indexes to *A.L.R. 2d, 3d, 4th, 5th,* and *Federal*). It classifies thousands of topics legally and factually.

The *Index* also has a table of statutes and regulations cited, a "history table" that shows how each annotation has been updated or replaced, and **pocket parts** that must be checked for the most recent entries in *A.L.R. 5th* and *Federal*. If the *Index* yields no results, you can try the *Digest,* which classifies annotations in *A.L.R. 3d, 4th, 5th,* and *Federal* into a few hundred legal topics.

Finally, once you have material you need, make sure to update it by checking separate volumes called Later Case Service for *A.L.R. 2d,* and by checking the pocket parts in each volume of *A.L.R. 3d, 4th, 5th,* and *Federal.* This can be crucial. Also, *A.L.R.* is still growing, with new indexes and services coming out all the time.

Citators: Shepard's, KeyCite, etc.

What Are They?   A *citator* is a set of books or a computerized database used to determine the current validity of a legal **authority** (such as a case, statute, regulation, or law review article) by listing the places that it has been cited (mentioned). Citators are a good way to find relevant authority and are the *only* way to validate your research. Citators confirm that the statutes you quote are still in force and unchanged, that the cases you rely on are still good **precedent** and the best available to prove your point, and that you have found the most relevant material. *You should never formally use a case, statute, or other authority without validating it with a citator.* On a complex, time-consuming project, you probably shouldn't even bother to take notes on a long case without cite-checking it first.

Until recently, all comprehensive legal citators came printed on paper from Shepard's, so all cite-checking was called Shepardizing. Shepardizing involves reading tiny symbols with exhausting care to follow long citation trails though countless books and supplementary pamphlets. Computerized cite-checking has lightened this burden greatly for those with access to use it. This appendix uses Shepardizing a case to illustrate paper-based cite-checking (Shepards is also available on CD-ROM and on-line through LEXIS), and uses KeyCite to describe computerized cite-checking (KeyCite is available on CD-ROM and through WESTLAW).

Shepardizing a Case through Books and Pamphlets. A typical listing under a case in a Shepard's citator will give *parallel citations* (other places the same case has been printed), the *history* of the case (has it been **appealed, overruled,** etc.?), the *treatment* of the case (other cases where it has been **followed, distinguished,** or otherwise mentioned), and a list of the **law journal** articles, **annotations,** etc. that have analyzed or mentioned the case.

A typical "simple" Shepardizing might go like this: You find Case A, which is very similar to your research problem and says exactly what you want to hear (good). You Shepardize that case and find that it was not *overruled* (good), was *followed* in two later cases (good), and was *distinguished* in three later cases (bad). You read and Shepardize the cases that followed Case A and find nothing useful (bad). You read and Shepardize the cases that distinguished Case A and find that two of them are very different from your original research problem and, besides, nobody else mentions them (good). But the third, Case B, is very similar (bad). You Shepardize Case B and find that it was overruled (good). You have a case worth citing.

Here is how to deal with the books: A set of Shepard's citators may cover more than one set of case **reporters,** so you may have to look around a bit. First, make sure that you have found a complete set of citator main volumes and supplements. You do this by getting the latest pamphlet (usually no more than a month old) and reading the box on the cover, which lists all volumes and supplements in current use. If your set is incomplete, your research is suspect and, perhaps, worthless.

Second, use all the volumes and check each one carefully for citations. Continue tracking down each chain of citations until you come to the end. Shepardizing is repetitive, so it's easy to accidently skip a crucial book, flip past a crucial page, or skim by a crucial cite. Be methodical. Also,

Shepard's citators use dozens of symbols and abbreviations of their own. Be sure to check the front of the volume for a table or explanation of any you don't know to avoid missing or misinterpreting key information.

Third, make sure you get all the information provided. For example, if one of the citations in the list is **j224NW2d**[11]**231,** you know that the case was mentioned on page 231 of volume 224 of the *Northwest Reporter, Second Series.* You also know from the "j" that the case was mentioned in a **dissent** (because you checked what "j" meant in the front of the book). And you know from the raised "11" that the judge in the later case discussed the specific legal point mentioned in the eleventh summarizing introductory **headnote** to the earlier case. And you are ready to beg for a computerized citator.

KeyCite, a Computerized Citator.   Computerized citators (such as KeyCite on WESTLAW or Shepard's on LEXIS) contain the same general types of information as Shepard's books, and you follow the same general citation trails, but the process couldn't be more different. With KeyCite, for example, you simply type in a case citation and the computer displays a list of citing materials, with most of the information in plain English rather than abbreviations and symbols. You can go directly from one citation to another. You can custom tailor the type of information displayed, choosing, for example, to see only those cases that have a strong negative impact on the cited case. Also, each citing case is given one to four stars to show how thoroughly it discusses the cited case.

KeyCite is also integrated with the rest of the WESTLAW system of case reporters, Key Number Digests, statute and regulation databases, law journals, ALR, etc. If, for example, one of the citing references given is an ALR annotation, you can go directly to that annotation if you are linked to it on-line. This allows you to "cruise" back and forth among various types of material very quickly. (See Computer-Assisted Legal Research for more information.)

Legal Encyclopedias

What Is in Them?   Legal encyclopedias, like general encyclopedias, are multivolume information sets arranged alphabetically by topic. They usually have extensive cross-referencing, so they are a good way to get a reasonably quick general handle on a legal topic, especially if you need background material or initial leads to major cases and statutes. They are not, however, good books to quote as authoritative sources of law.

The two large national legal encyclopedias are *Corpus Juris Secundum* (*CJS*) and *American Jurisprudence, Second* (*Am. Jur. 2d*). *CJS* is cross-referenced with *Key Number Digests* and the *National Reporter System.*

Am. Jur. 2d is cross-referenced with _American Law Reports_ and, increasingly, with the _Key Number Digests_ and the _National Reporter System._ Some states also have state legal encyclopedias.

How Do You Use Them? _CJS_ and _Am. Jur. 2d_ are available on WESTLAW, integrated with the bulk of WESTLAW's materials. (See Computer-Assisted Legal Research for more information.) The paper versions have huge general index volumes at the end of the series. Use these indexes fully. Be creative. Then, even if the general indexes lead you straight to a topic or section within a subject volume, do not bypass the subject and analysis outlines. They may lead you to additional material. (Once you reach the right topic sections, do not forget to check the **pocket part** for updates.)

Other Important Secondary Sources

Words and Phrases. _Words and Phrases_ (West Group) is a set of books plus supplements that list alphabetically thousands of legal, technical, and everyday words. Each word or phrase is followed by short summaries of how it was defined by judges in various cases. _Words and Phrases_ is large, but easy to use (see Appendix A of this dictionary for more information).

Looseleaf Services. A looseleaf service provides information on one specialized area of the law (such as tax law, family law, or even medical devices law), on one court, or on more general legal topics. Looseleaf services often send out supplements every week, which either add to or replace older sections. They usually include relevant **statutory** law, **regulations, caselaw,** practical advice, and news about major activities in the field. Four large looseleaf publishers are Commerce Clearing House (CCH), Bureau of National Affairs (BNA), Prentice-Hall (PH), and Matthew Bender (MB).

Treatises and Law Journal/Law Review Articles. Treatises are individual books or small sets written for lawyers and law students. (Treatises for students are sometimes called hornbooks.) They cover specialized areas of the law, such as contracts or federal practice. You can find treatises through your law library's catalog.

Law Review and Law Journal articles (plus shorter "notes" and "comments") analyze legal issues. They are usually written by law professors, practicing lawyers, or top law students. The footnotes can lead to important cases. You can find these articles through the _Index to Legal Periodicals,_ the _Current Law Index,_ or the on-line _Legal Resources Index._

Form Books, Practice Books, and Procedure Books. Form books are collections of sample forms that have been used in legal practice (rental agreements, wills, **pleadings,** etc.). They often have blanks to be filled in.

The larger form books annotate the forms with extensive information on the statutes they are based on, case decisions interpreting them, and practical advice. These forms, however, must always be tailored to the individual legal situation. Thousands of legal forms are available on-line and on CD-ROMs, ready to be custom-tailored and filled in on your computer.

Practice and procedure books (sometimes also called form books) contain the detailed technical rules by which each system of courts, and each individual court, operates. Many are annotated with case decisions and practical examples. Attempting to practice before a court without a knowledge of these rules is embarrassing at best.

Books by Advocacy Groups and General Publishers. Organizations such as the **ACLU, HALT,** and others publish paperbacks and pamphlets on areas of the law important to nonlawyers. These include such things as probate law, mental patients' rights, etc. Publications from trade associations, consumer groups, other advocacy organizations, and general publishers are often found in bookstores and general libraries. They should be relied on for general information only.

Books on Doing Legal Research

You may already know the basics of legal research, or you may want to start off with more detailed information. Here are some different types of books that may fit your knowledge level and learning style:

Books on a Specific Jurisdiction's Materials. These include books on finding and using the law of most of the major states and the federal government. If much of your work depends on the law of one jurisdiction, one of these books (such as West's Pennsylvania Law Finder) may be your fastest entry point.

Books and Materials for Paralegals and Other Nonlawyers. There are several "how to do legal research" books in this category (such as Statsky's *Legal Research and Writing: Some Starting Points*) as well as sections in more general works (such as the **N.A.L.A.** *Manual for Legal Assistants*). In addition, some commercial publishers (such as Nolo Press) and companies that teach individuals how to handle their own simple legal work tailor their legal materials for nonlawyer use. Many of these books and materials include information on computer-assisted legal research.

Books for Lawyers and Law Students. Nonlawyers can use many of these books effectively. They range from the handy (such as Cohen and Olson's *Legal Research in a Nutshell*) to the huge (such as Jacobson, Mersky, and Dunn's *Fundamentals of Legal Research*). If you can't "test drive" your choice in a law library, compare a few in a law school bookstore by checking how the books find and use something you've already found and used on a prior research project.

Books on Computer-Assisted Legal Research.   These range from free service-specific materials (such as those that accompany subscriptions to WEST-LAW and LEXIS) to books that include long lists of law-related Internet sites. Since specific research techniques and sites change rapidly, consider any book a short-term investment in getting up to speed quickly, and select a _very_ recent copyright date. (The section starting on page 572 concentrates on basic techniques and mental approaches to computer-assisted research.)

Law Libraries

If you are familiar with, and comfortable in, law libraries, you do not need this section. If, however, you imagine a law library as a huge, dark cave, filled with dangerous ambiguities lurking to embarrass you, read on.

How do you find a law library? Most small law firms have access to computer-assisted legal research and enough books to handle many specialized problems and simple problems of a broader nature. Large law libraries exist in large law offices, bar associations, courthouses, and administrative agencies. They can handle almost any research problem, but not always in the most convenient way. Extensive law libraries exist in most law schools, some government agencies and courthouses, and a few general libraries.

How do you get in? First, call around. Some are open to the public, especially some courthouse and law school libraries. All "depository libraries" must allow public access to materials (such as the Code of Federal Regulations) that they get free from the federal government. Some law librarians will bend policies, even ignore "no public entrance" signs, if you begin by asking a research question.

Before you go. Do the preliminary fact analysis and problem definition before you go, not in detail, but enough to know why you need the library (see _Know Your Facts, Know Your Objectives,_ and _Create a Word List_ sections). Read the _Concepts_ and _Sources of the Law_ sections of this appendix, but do not bother reading the _"How Do You Use It?"_ parts before you have the books in hand.

You're in. Now what? Take time to orient yourself, with a library map if needed. Ask for any free materials on library or source use. If necessary, ask the librarian for the location of the books you need and about computer and copier use. Don't hide what you don't know. Be effusive with thanks.

Then, before you start using the library's materials and computer resources, briefly review *why* you are there and what you hope to accomplish.

If you are using law books and other "paper-based" materials, think about some of the "rules for library use" from the **HALT** pamphlet *Using a Law Library* (HALT, Inc., Wash., D.C.): 1) Write down complete source information before you take notes, including date, volume, section, and page. 2) Read all prefaces and content descriptions. 3) Put a bookmark in abbreviation tables. 4) When you see a reference you *might* want, make a note about it. 5) Take breaks before you get tired. 6) Do not rush or take shortcuts. 7) Do not hoard books. Take only what you need; find out library policy on reshelving and follow it.

If you are using the library's computer, see the Computer-Assisted Legal Research section that follows here.

Computer-Assisted Legal Research

Much legal research is still done from books, but it is often done more quickly, easily, and accurately by accessing searchable **databases** for the materials discussed earlier in this appendix. The three main ways to access these databases are:

1. *Commercial legal database services such as WESTLAW and LEXIS.* A researcher typically connects to these services through a computer and either takes notes while searching the databases or transfers documents stored on a database to the researcher's computer or printer. These services are the most effective, but expensive, ways to do most legal research. (This Appendix uses WESTLAW as its primary example, but includes LEXIS's similarities and differences.)

2. *The Internet, especially the World Wide Web.* This is a vast and quickly changing storehouse of legal and nonlegal information that can be reached from any computer with Internet access. The Appendix gives you a general approach to using this confusing, but essential, resource.

3. *CD-ROMs and other storage media.* These are produced by commercial database services, government, and nonprofit organizations. They require no remote computer connection because they are used on-site. They contain the same type of information as in #1, and can be searched by the same techniques, so this Appendix does not discuss them. (See page 579 for a Website that lists available CD-ROMS.)

Commercial Legal Database Services: WESTLAW and LEXIS

What Is in Them?

WESTLAW contains the full text of many different types of documents: **cases** from the **National Reporter System,** federal and state **statutes** and administrative **regulations** and decisions, **Key Number** digests and encyclopedias, legal texts and periodicals, **ALR** and **KeyCite,** and a wide range of articles from **looseleaf services** and nonlegal newsletters and periodicals. LEXIS, while less comprehensive and integrated, contains many of the same materials and, where they differ, provides similar services that use their products (such as **Shepard's** Citators) rather than WESTLAW's. WESTLAW and LEXIS also provide direct access to other companies' information services. All of these documents and services can be searched using the same general techniques and can be "downloaded" to your computer or printer.

Once you learn how to use WESTLAW or LEXIS, the computer can search millions of words in seconds to find the documents you need. You can focus your research broadly or narrowly, and conduct searches by legal or nonlegal subject, by terms you choose (such as product names or persons) in the relationship you specify, and, in WESTLAW, by a specific West **Digest** Topic or **Key Number.**

The computer will then give you a list of documents that meet the criteria you've specified. You can display these documents in full text or by a specific part. You can then take a few notes from the screen, print or "download" text, or print a list to find the documents in the law library. Here is an example of how to use computer-assisted research to conduct your legal search:

■ Suppose you need to know whether a U.S. district court in the First Circuit is likely to overturn a decision by the Immigration and Naturalization Service regarding deportation. Courts will usually do this only when the agency's decision is not based on substantial evidence. But what is "substantial evidence"? A general definition does no good; you need to know how the U.S. Court of Appeals for the First Circuit defined this term in cases as similar to yours as possible. How do you find these cases?

■ Library research might require wading through so many books that you are tempted to rely on general definitions and quotes from cases "sort of" like yours. WESTLAW and LEXIS can, however, retrieve any case from the First Circuit using the words *substantial evidence.* Because a large number of cases contain these words, searching additional descriptive terms is better. You want the cases retrieved to also contain the word *deportation* (as well as *deport, deported* or *deporting*). A WESTLAW or LEXIS search can be refined further by searching for these terms only in synopsis and digest paragraphs (summaries of the main legal points and case disposition).

Computer-assisted research is sometimes the best way to do "creative" legal research, such as finding persuasive judicial statements not easily found by traditional methods. Here is an example of how a lawyer conducted a creative search:

- When a wily businessman discovered some proposed changes in a federal agency's regulations, he tried to rush through some purchases and sales before the new regulations took effect. The sales took longer than expected and he was stuck with a huge pile of goods. The federal agency refused to grant him an exception to the new regs, so the businessman sued.

- A lawyer who represented people who wanted to *prevent* the businessman from selling the goods needed a way to make a case against an exception based on what looked like either hard luck or mere stupidity.

- The law books are full of cases in which persons who used trickery were prevented from winning in court, but this businessman had not clearly done anything sneaky. There might not be any obvious legal phrases to lead the lawyer to the cases he needed, but he knew there were some good nonlegal ideas floating around that judges might have used in the past. So he searched WESTLAW for any cases in his jurisdiction in which the terms *chestnut, fire,* and *cats-paw* appeared. *Why?*

- To retrieve every judge's opinion that used phrases from the old story about the monkey who convinced a cat to pull hot chestnuts out of a fire. WESTLAW retrieved several cases in which a judge essentially said, "The Federal Courts are not in the business of being used as a cats-paw to pull a private businessman's chestnuts out of the fire."

- Not a person to rely on one precedent, the lawyer then searched for the combined terms *orphan, mercy, murder,* and *court.* Can you guess why?

- The computer quickly scanned millions of words and produced several cases in which a judge said, "This reminds me of a man who murders his parents and throws himself on the mercy of the court as an orphan." One of the cases was quite similar to the lawyer's. To find that case by traditional library research he might as well have thrown darts at a wall of books.

There are two other major advantages of commercial legal databases. First, they have many legal decisions that are not collected or distributed any other way. Database services also make it much easier to verify a case's current validity by tracing the course of litigation and how the case is mentioned in later cases and other authorities.

How to Use Them

Connect with the WESTLAW or LEXIS system, identify yourself by a user number and password, and identify your research. However, you should take your *first* research step *before* you use the computer. Before you begin, you should consider whether computer-assisted legal research is the most cost-effective method for your specific research issue. You should also define your issue and know what you want to find. (For more on this, review the *Concepts in the Law* and *Techniques of Research* sections at the start of this appendix.) For example, before you start paying for connect time you should consider the following: Is your research limited to a specific jurisdiction or type of court? What key terms, including synonyms, express your issue? Does your issue involve technical legal terms? In what relationship do you want your terms to appear in the documents retrieved? Should they be in the same sentence or the same paragraph? Once you know the answers to these questions, you can start your electronic research and maximize your efforts.

To start your research, select the information source you want to search. You might choose, for example, the database containing cases decided by the U.S. Supreme Court. This is abbreviated **sct** on WESTLAW. Now you are ready to enter a search request or query.

Suppose you want to know what the Supreme Court has said about attorney fees in bankruptcy cases. One way would be to request all Supreme Court cases where the words *attorney, fees,* and *bankruptcy* appear in the same sentence. To search WESTLAW or LEXIS for these three terms in the same sentence, you would type **attorney /s fee /s bankrupt!**. In this search the */s* connector specifies that these terms must appear in the same sentence. The exclamation point will retrieve any term that contains the root *bankrupt*. Searching the term **bankrupt!** retrieves all of the following: *bankrupt, bankruptcy,* and *bankrupting.*

But you may still miss relevant cases. Your search does not include synonyms, such as *lawyer, counsel,* or *costs,* that may be used in court opinions. Always include synonyms; computer-assisted legal research systems are very literal. They do not assume you want **lawyer** just because you searched for **attorney.** A better WESTLAW search is **attorney lawyer counsel /s fee cost /s bankrupt!.** (On LEXIS, you would need to say **attorney or lawyer or counsel /s fee or cost /s bankrupt!**) Plurals and possessives are retrieved automatically.

If your search is too narrow or too broad, you can modify it in several ways. To broaden your search, use a broader "connector" between your search terms. For example, use **/p** instead of **/s** to request that your terms be in the same paragraph instead of the same sentence or use a "but not" connector (%) to *exclude* a term. (On LEXIS, you would use the phrase **and not** instead of the % sign.) These are only a few of the connectors you can use to specify the relationship between the terms you search.

If your search is too narrow, check your database. Did you really want cases from all federal courts, not just the Supreme Court? If so, run your search again in the appropriate database. Also, make sure you are searching all important terms that could be used to describe your issue. If you are still stuck, try a "natural language" search, as described on page 577.

This is only one small example of how to do computer-assisted legal research. For example, in addition to the method described above, you can also search for specific phrases. (On WESTLAW, you must put the phrase in quotation marks, but on LEXIS you just type the phrase.) Use phrase searching when your terms *always* appear in the same order with no other intervening terms. Technical terms such as *habeas corpus* and *ex post facto* are good examples. You can also limit your search to a specific *field,* such as a case *synopsis.* You can even search for cases decided by a particular judge.

It is also possible to do a *Key Number Digest* search within the WESTLAW system. Key numbers categorize and index thousands of legal topics, with subtopics (then sub-subtopics) adding more numbers to the end of the identifying number. (See *Key Number Digests* on page 563 for basic information.) The computer-assisted version is faster, more flexible, and more thorough.

In the search request **48ak107(2), 48a** is the West digest topic, **k** replaces the key symbol, ☞ , and **107(2)** is the key number. A search within the topic 48a retrieves every case found within the topic; a search within 48ak102 retrieves every case found within the key number 102 under topic 48a; and a search within 48ak107(2) retrieves only cases found within the subclassified key number 107(2) under topic 48a. If you find too many irrelevant cases, search within a subcategorized key number. For too few relevant cases, search within a main key number or the whole key topic. You can also limit your search to a digest for your geographical region or, sometimes, for your specific legal subject. *Key Number Digests* can also be searched for specific words within a specific key topic or key number by using the techniques described earlier in this section.

Finally, both WESTLAW and LEXIS allow you to do an entirely different type of search within the same databases: a "natural language" or "plain English" search. You can ask a question such as "What is the statute of limitations in a personal injury action?" or make a request such as "Give me all the cases interpreting the statute of limitations in personal injury actions." This may not seem like "plain English" to most people, but the computer must first "translate" the request into the type of search discussed earlier. It decides which are the important words and looks for cases with the words near each other, looks for other forms of the words and for synonyms, and generally performs many of the "thinking" tasks you perform when doing a search with terms and connecting symbols.

A natural language search may find a general answer quickly, and it may help you to broaden your search thinking, but it is not a substitute for a more precise search. You may want to rephrase the question more clearly and concisely, restrict the question in ways supplied by the computer (such as to a specific range of dates), add related concepts from the computer's thesaurus, or switch to a terms and connectors search. As these search programs become more sophisticated, an interactive series of questions may make them even more useful.

Computer-assisted legal research systems such as WESTLAW and LEXIS provide extensive on-line and phone customer assistance and written support materials. Because services, databases, and commands change, you will need to consult these research systems directly for specific questions.

The Internet: Especially the World Wide Web

What Is In It?

The Internet can give you a huge amount of the world's collected information, assuming that you can find it, absorb it, and believe it. This information includes the text of many, but not all, cases, statutes, and administrative materials from federal, state, local, and foreign jurisdictions; legal periodicals, legal practice-area materials, legal forms, and law directories; massive amounts of information about government agencies, businesses, and nonprofit organizations; financial, scientific, medical, historical, geographical, and other information on almost every topic; plus news and opinions, both expert and far from expert.

Where Is It Located?

The Internet is a growing and changing network of computer networks. Information flows from computer to computer through millions of constantly different pathways. Some of this information sits in computers accessible to users through the Internet. These computers, called "servers," contain the computer-assisted legal research systems such as WESTLAW discussed in the prior section, plus the *document, linking, search,* and *listserv* sites discussed here. All of this is "on the Internet," as is your personal computer while it is connected to another computer outside its own locally wired group.

Much of the information on the Internet is available on a "system within the system" called the World Wide Web. The Web uses **hypertext** to directly link information in different documents stored at different sites. This means that you do not need to know where information is stored, merely how to get to it, and can often examine the information through the same sorts of word and phrase searches used on WESTLAW and LEXIS, but for free. The text of the U.S. Constitution, for example, is stored on many Web sites, and is accessible and "searchable" through many more.

How to Use It

- Start learning the Internet with the subjects you know best or the work you do most often.

  After an initial "surf" around the legal websites to see the range of things available, pick a familiar topic and dig in. You will learn and be productive faster, and develop a "built-in filter" that helps reject unreliable sites.

- Search narrowly if you know exactly what you want.

  Use as many descriptive words as possible. Use restrictive connectors (such as BUT NOT) to eliminate words and concepts. If permitted, use them to limit the search to words in the same phrase or sentence.

- Search broadly unless you know exactly what you want.

  Select a search engine from the list appearing on pages 579–580, use a search-word expansion technique from Finding the Law on page 549 to create many different searches, and don't use restrictive connectors. If available, try a "natural language search" that uses complete sentences.

- "Bookmark" all of your most useful sites.

  Add Internet addresses to your permanent collection (often called "Favorites") on the computer. You will otherwise forget many good ones or lose them when the link you used to get there disappears.

- Get help when stuck.

  Help comes in many forms. Search engines have "help" areas that explain their techniques. Someone on a *listserv* (a site where computer users answer each other's questions on specific topics) may have exactly what you need. Friends and co-workers may have faced the same problem.

Legal Resource Web Sites

NOTE: **_The web sites listed here are illustrative only_** because sites often come and go, improve and fall behind, change names and net addresses, and generally refuse to behave properly. Also, _one-subject sites are omitted to save space_ because hundreds of useful ones are available through many of the comprehensive sites listed below. Most of these sites have a master screen with "buttons" that let you first choose a type of information, then specific information within the type. Many have built-in "search engines" that let you type in a request for information. Even these sites were chosen from among many more good ones. A few hours "surfing" around the links of any of these will introduce you to the amazing variety of material that is easily available.

ABANet (http://www.abanet.org). The American Bar Association's many activities.

AccountingWEB (http://www.acountingweb.co.uk). Links to accounting information.

Chicago-Kent Law School (http://www.kentlaw.edu/legal_resources). Comprehensive links to legal information.

Cornell Law School (http://www.law.cornell.edu). Comprehensive links to legal information.

Dogpile (http://dogpile.com). A "metasearch" engine that searches other search engines for general information.

Findlaw (http://www.findlaw.com). Comprehensive links to legal information plus Lawcrawler, a good search engine.

Glen S. Bacal (http://www.azlink.com/lawyers/hotlist.html). A lawyer's selection of good sites.

Google (http://www.google.com) A good general search engine.

HotBot (http://www.hotbot.com) A good general search engine.

Information Publishing (http://www.inforsourcepub.com). A directory of available CD-ROMs.

Infoseek (http://www.infoseek.com) A good general search engine.

Internet Legal Resources (http://www.ilrg.com/gov.html). Comprehensive links to legal information plus Lawrunner, a good search engine.

Katsuey's Legal Links (http://www.katsui.com). A paralegal's selection of good sites.

LawGuru (http://www.lawguru.com). Links to state laws and more.

'Lectric Law Library (http://www.lectlaw.com/ref.html). Comprehensive, quirky links to legal information.

Legal News Network (http://www.legalnewsnetwork.com) A site with late-breaking legal news.

LEXIS Counsel Connect (http://www.counsel.com). The free part of LEXIS's legal information.

National Federation of Paralegal Associations (http://www.paralegals.org). Comprehensive links to legal information.

Newspapers On-line (http://www.newspapers.com) A site with links to thousands of newspapers.

Northern Light (http://www.northernlight.com) A good general search engine.

Ohio Northern University (http://eugene.onu.edu/internet/default.htm). Comprehensive links to legal information.

Tax Prophet (http://www.taxprophet.com). Information on taxes and links to tax-related sites.

Villanova Law School (http://www.law.vill.edu). Links to federal and state government sites.

West Legal Directory (http://www.lawoffice.com). The free part of WEST's legal information.

Yahoo (http://www.yahoo.com) A good general search engine.

A Final Note

While you're on the Internet, please let me know what you think about this dictionary. I'd especially like to know if anything is dead wrong or if you failed to find an important word. Nothing on the Internet remains constant, but the odds are that I am still at home at danoran@rcn.com, lurking virtually at danoran@aya.yale.edu, or in touch through the publisher at info@delmar.com.